ALSO BY PETER HEATHER

The Goths in the Fourth Century (with John Matthews)

Goths and Romans, 332–489

The Goths

The Fall of the Roman Empire

Empires and Barbarians

The Restoration of Rome

Rome Resurgent

Christendom

PETER HEATHER

Christendom

The Triumph of a Religion, AD 300–1300

ALFRED A. KNOPF
NEW YORK
2023

THIS IS A BORZOI BOOK PUBLISHED BY ALFRED A. KNOPF

www.aaknopf.com

Knopf, Borzoi Books, and the colophon are registered trademarks of Penguin Random House LLC.

Library of Congress Cataloging-in-Publication Data
Names: Heather, P. J. (Peter J.) author.
Title: Christendom : the triumph of a religion, AD 300–1300 / Peter Heather.
Description: New York : Alfred A. Knopf, 2023. |
Includes bibliographical references and index.
Identifiers: LCCN 2022030334 (print) | LCCN 2022030335 (ebook) |
ISBN 9780451494306 (hardcover) | ISBN 9780451494313 (ebook)
Subjects: LCSH: Church history.
Classification: LCC BR145.3 .H367 2023 (print) |
LCC BR145.3 (ebook) | DDC 270—dc23/eng/20220818
LC record available at https://lccn.loc.gov/2022030334
LC ebook record available at https://lccn.loc.gov/2022030335

Jacket image: World History Archive / Alamy
Jacket design by Jenny Carrow

Manufactured in the United States of America
First United States Edition

Contents

List of Illustrations and Photo Acknowledgements

List of Maps

Introduction

In AD 1250 or thereabouts, Grand Duke Mindaugas of Lithuania was baptized into Christianity. A representative of the last non-Christian ruling line of any substance within the entirety of the European landscape signed up to the religion with which the continent was now synonymous. He was duly rewarded: Pope Innocent IV promoted his duchy to the rank of kingdom. A few years later, in August 1253, the same pope officially recognized the legitimacy of a new Italian monastic order run by and for women: the Poor Clares, named after Clare of Assisi, friend, disciple and co-worker of the famous St Francis. In between, on 15 May 1252, he had also issued *Ad extirpanda*, an important legal order (papal 'bulls' are always named for their opening words) which legitimized torture in the interrogation of heretics right across the lands in which his holy authority held sway: the Latin Christendom which is the central subject matter of this book.

This small chronological cluster of events towards the end of the thousand-year period explored in this book highlights some of its most important themes. Any account of the origins and evolution of European Christianity is necessarily a story of conversion. When the narrative begins, with Emperor Constantine in AD 300, the first ruler of any part of the European landscape to accept Christianity, it remained a minority religion even within the Roman world, and the vast majority of the empire's Christians lived not in its European provinces, but in Asia Minor, the Middle East, Egypt and North Africa. By AD 1300, the entirety of the European landscape (barring the odd bit of Lithuania and the Arctic Circle) was Christian, while much of the original southern Mediterranean heartland of the Christian world had turned instead to Islam, establishing the inextricable link between Europe and Christianity that has prevailed ever since. But, as in the case of Duke Mindaugas and Lithuania, the intervening Christian conversions of an astonishingly large proportion of the European continent began with a change of religious allegiance on the part of a ruling dynasty. The particular nature of conversion processes that start with the very powerful will be a recurring theme in what follows.

In the close chronological juxtaposition of Pope Innocent's grant to the Poor Clares with his bull on torturing heretics can be found some of the book's other key themes. The Christ of the Gospels is famous for many things, but not least 'Love your enemies' and 'Turn the other cheek'. Thirteenth-century European Christianity sustained many of these recorded ideals because it retained, studied and venerated the New Testament account of Christ's teachings and actions. Both Saints Clare and Francis – along with many other charismatic Christian leaders in the early centuries of the second millennium – not only cherished these values in theory but sought to put them into practice. Both Clare and Francis really did renounce all their worldly goods; selling everything they had, they devoted their lives to the poor and sick and urged their followers to do the same.

But if some of their moral values were instantly recognizable as those of the New Testament, Clare and Francis were operating within a Christian religious structure whose institutional and doctrinal frameworks had changed out of all recognition since the first century AD. As late as 300, at the time of Constantine's conversion, Christianity possessed no central authority structure at all. It was composed of a series of mostly urban congregations, who elected their own leaders and – despite some commonalities in required beliefs, personal behaviour and institutional organization – for the most part ran their own affairs independently. Much remained in flux. Even such a fundamental Christian doctrine as that of the Holy Trinity only began to find a generally agreed formulation after Constantine's conversion, and many issues of theory and practice – in any religion these tend to be closely interconnected – remained unresolved for a long time.

Clare and Francis were cases in point. Despite their avowed New Testament values, they lived their religious lives within a specific understanding of what it meant to be a good Christian: an understanding which had been articulated by Paris theologians working within a century of their births. The preaching order which Francis founded was dedicated to spreading, Europe-wide, a view of Heaven, Hell and Purgatory. This encompassed both the effects of sin upon the post-mortem destinations of individual human souls, and how the behaviours of individuals, and of those who loved them in the here and now, could affect their souls' future and (in the case of the dead) current fate. This clear vision of the soul's three possible destinations after death, and of the precise effects of particular sins in deciding which would apply, emerged only in the twelfth and thirteenth centuries. The idea that good actions might make up for bad ones was an extremely old one within the Christian tradition, but no comprehensive or coherent set of tariffs and remedies had ever previously been worked out.

Nor, even if it had, would there have been the slightest possibility, before this era, of it winning widespread adoption. Despite what it liked to pretend (and some of its apologists still do), papal religious authority was an astonishingly late phenomenon within the developing European Christian tradition. Bishops of Rome, as the heirs of St Peter, had enormous prestige from an early date, and other Christian leaders periodically sought their opinion on important religious matters. They did not feel remotely bound to follow those opinions, however, if they disagreed with them. Correspondingly, as this book explores, emperors and kings exercised much greater actual religious authority than any pope for many centuries after Constantine, and not just in practice but also by right, since it was generally accepted that Christian rulers were directly appointed by the Almighty. Only in the eleventh century did long-standing papal prestige evolve into an initial formal claim that popes should exercise general religious authority, while it took most of the following century for this claim to become accepted in practice. The religious authority being exercised by Innocent IV in the early 1250s, in other words, was essentially brand-new. And, as the order *Ad extirpanda* makes all too clear, enforcing widespread acceptance of this new authority structure – and the doctrines and visions of good Christian piety it chose to support – was not just about the kind of persuasively consensual approach that the example and preaching of a Francis or Clare might generate. It also involved the application of considerable coercion, even if not all of it was as brutally direct as the physical torture that could now be legally applied to those deemed to be heretics.

This small cluster of events underlines a still broader point. 'Christianity' in an important sense is a misleadingly singular noun. The Christian religion to which Constantine gave his allegiance bore little resemblance to the articulated, monolithic religious–cultural structure that had emerged by the twelfth and thirteenth centuries, and that then dominated the vast majority of Europe's varied landscapes and populations until the Reformation took serious hold in the 1500s. It is precisely the emergence of this extraordinary structure in its full maturity which provides the central focus of this book. As such, its concern will eventually become the Latin Christianity dominated from Rome in the era of papal monarchy – medieval Christendom (literally 'the area where Christianity rules') par excellence. However, the separation from the Greek-based Orthodox communion was late and far from preordained, so that much of what follows, especially in the earlier chapters, has a broader geographical and cultural focus.

Around 1900, when the task was first undertaken by professional historians, and for much of the following century, accounts of the rise of Christendom used to be straightforward to write. From the first to the third centuries AD, the Christian faith spread gradually around the shores of the Mediterranean. In the fourth century, it then overwhelmed Graeco-Roman paganism after converting the emperor Constantine to take over the Roman world, before resoundingly defeating a host of other rivals to become the predominant religion of the entire European landmass. A thousand years after Constantine, all of Europe was controlled by Christian rulers. Christendom – that part of the world where official Christianity exercised a dominant hold on the totality of the population: lords and commons, rulers and ruled – had come into existence, and that was that. In this telling of the Christian story, the rest of European religious history – even the explosive period of the Reformation in the sixteenth century – figured as little more than a footnote: Christians making adjustments to precise beliefs and behavioural demands. A defining coincidence between the boundaries of Europe and the region of overwhelming Christian domination had been born in the Middle Ages, and from there the religion spread triumphantly over much of the rest of the planet in the great eras of European colonization and imperialism.

Such triumphalist outline visions of Christian history are no longer intellectually viable. In recent years, various European politicians have made a grab at Christianity when casting around for something distinctive that unites the peoples of the continent. A – rapidly declining – majority of Europe's population still describes itself as 'Christian' in national censuses but, in reality, that often only means 'as opposed to anything else'. Very few modern Europeans would pass muster as Christian in the minds of the medieval Churchmen who first won the battle for Europe's soul. Do the vast majority of today's self-proclaimed Christians baptize their children? Do they go to church? Do they attend confession and communion, and pay tithes? Do they learn the key doctrines of the Christian faith and organize their lives around the great Christian festivals, an annual cycle of commemoration that hardwires the key moments and messages of Christianity into the collective psyche? The answer is no – even if vast crowds do still congregate outside St Peter's on Easter Sunday.

This much is well known. We all recognize that Christianity has lost its hold on the consciences of many Europeans; the phenomenon of de-Christianization is commonly discussed; and many Christian denominations are struggling to survive. But the significance of modern de-Christianization for rethinking key elements of the story of how and why Europe first became Christendom has not yet been recognized.

Fundamentally, it is no longer possible to construct a narrative on the underlying assumption that its victory over all rivals in the dim and distant past is evidence of Christianity's essential superiority as a religion. Such a perspective was pretty much unavoidable when the first academically rigorous histories of Christianity were being written in the later nineteenth and even the early twentieth centuries. At that point, most Europeans were still regularly attending one Church or another, and European imperialism was spreading Christianity far and wide across the globe. My grandfather (whom I sadly never met) joined the British army in 1909 and on his first Sunday under the colours declared himself an agnostic. This avoided Church Parade, but he was detailed to clean the latrines instead. A quick conversion to the

Church of England followed, because he didn't like 'the agnostics' place of worship'. In that kind of context, it was hard to imagine that Christianity would not just carry on winning forever.[1] The de-Christianization of modern Europe since 1945, however, not only explodes triumphalist assumptions of continued Christian success, but must also transform the challenge of writing about the Christian past.

Today, any historian of Christianity must still reckon with a religion powerful enough to win out in a whole series of ancient and medieval contexts, and then to maintain this position of established cultural domination for centuries against a host of further challenges. But, by the same token, Christianity must also be seen as a religion that is not invulnerable in *all* contexts, and at *all* times. Rethinking the emergence of European Christendom from this vantage point, to my mind requires three so far largely ignored dimensions of the story to be given due and proper emphasis.

First: contingency. We now know – as scholars writing around 1900 did not – that, in the right circumstances, Christianity can lose – in the sense of failing to keep a tight hold on the consciences of the majority of Europe's population. This means that its original success must be subjected to much closer scrutiny. A century ago, it was difficult to take seriously any of the documented religious resistance to the official Christianity that triumphed across Europe. Whether we're talking challenges from the outside – such as Graeco-Roman and other paganisms – or from the inside – variant, so-called heretical forms of Christianity – the total triumph of official Christianity (as defined at a series of great Church councils, starting with Nicaea in 325) made it hard to suppose that any of these alternatives could ever have posed much of a threat. This perspective remains so deeply ingrained in the academic tradition that its influence has so far proved almost impossible to shift. Modern scholarship still tends to dismiss as utterly hopeless the anti-Christian efforts of the last pagan Roman emperor, Julian; while alternative, non-Nicene Christianities of the late Roman period generally rate no more than a few footnotes. But since we now know that official Christianity, in both its Catholic and Orthodox manifestations, wasn't destined to prevail forever, this raises the serious possibility that it really might have 'lost' at other points in the past. One central objective of this book, therefore, is to give – where appropriate – the religious opposition as much airtime as 'official' Christianity.

Second, much more emphasis needs to be given to how different Christianity actually was at different moments in time. Some of its beliefs, anchored in a canon of sacred texts, have been more or less constant, and in many other cases you can see continuous processes of refinement and clarification at work. This has strongly influenced existing traditions of writing about Christianity – particularly when undertaken by practising believers – which naturally focus on continuities and in beliefs and practices, and their gradual spread across space and time. But, while there are certainly important and real continuities, whose permanence is central to the whole existence of a Christian tradition, I would argue that, on close examination, they are neither as many nor as constant as official Christianity has liked to pretend. Equally important, when you cease to think about Christianity as a uniquely powerful cultural construct destined to win forever, the discontinuities can be recast as a vital dimension of the overall history of the developing religion, which again needs equal airtime. Examined closely, there are many ways in which early medieval Christianity was extremely unlike its late Roman predecessor, which itself profoundly differed from the early Church of the pre-Constantinian era; later medieval Christianity was substantially different again. Like all the major missionary religions, Christianity has the capacity – within a rhetorical self-presentation which consistently emphasized continuity – to reinvent itself pretty much from its bootstraps, according to context. In what follows, I will make the case that this chameleon-like capacity to adapt was as much crucial to Christianity's success as the religious continuities, allowing it to meet the very different religious needs of the widely varying bodies of religious consumers it encountered and encompassed at different points in its unfolding history.

Third, I want to examine much more closely the potential of Europe's populations through time to make alternative choices of religious allegiance. In this respect, legacy Christian triumphalism, it seems to me, still profoundly affects accounts of Christian conversion in the medieval period. Since Europe would eventually end up fully Christian, it is hard to avoid the assumption that once Christianity appeared, it would only be a question of time before people signed up to it. In the modern day, however, Europeans have chosen in large numbers not to adhere to Christianity in practice, whatever they might enter on census returns. This brute fact requires us to look for better answers than the old assumption that Christianity was just a superior religion. What exactly was it that made so much of Europe's medieval population originally adopt a Christian allegiance? Did everyone make this choice for the same reason? And can understanding those original choices help explain why a different choice has become an increasingly prominent feature of more recent European cultural history?

Christendom, then, is a response to what seems to me the pressing intellectual challenge of reassessing Christianity's rise to pre-eminence in the light of its modern eclipse, by re-examining the historical processes that first generated the defining coincidence between Europe and the cultural dominance of the Christian religion. It aims to give full weight to contingency, to Christianity's almost limitless capacity for self-reinvention, and to the potential of past populations to have made alternative choices. My aim here is not to produce another total history of Christianity, but to explore afresh exactly how Europe became Christendom: that part of the planet dominated by Christian rulers and overwhelmingly Christian populations. Its natural starting point, therefore, is the early fourth century AD and the conversion to Christianity of the Roman emperor Constantine, which produced the first Christian ruler of any state in history. It closes in the thirteenth century with the extinction of the last surviving non-Christian rulers within the European landscape.

Even this much, of course, amounts to a hugely ambitious project. I am extremely conscious of the limitations of my specialist expertise and the corresponding extent of my dependence on the work of a small army of other scholars (as the notes and bibliography make graphically clear). I am a late- and post-Roman historian, versed in the Greek and Latin primary materials of those eras and the diverse scholarly literatures those sources have generated. This project ranges far more widely, and its completion would have been impossible without immense assistance from corresponding scholarly literatures in the whole series of other fields with which it intersects at different points: New Testament studies, Early Christianity, Oriental studies, Islamic studies and, particularly, religious and legal studies of the central and high Middle Ages, to name but a few. But such a level of dependence is unavoidable in such a wide-ranging study, and, while it means that what follows is more by nature of an essay (if a long one!) rather than a detailed scholarly monograph, I'm firmly of the opinion that taking such a long-term view of the history of early and medieval Christianity offers major gains, which more than outweigh the potential problems that can follow from straying outside my particular areas of primary expertise.

There has been a strong tendency in the last generation of academic writing to avoid dealing with big historical topics over extended time frames. Much of this has been for very positive reasons: a desire to be truly expert in an era of ever-more sophisticated methodologies, in which the academic zeitgeist has tended to favour the intimate and fragmented. Partly, too, it reflects a negative reaction to the kinds of anachronistic values that characterized older so-called Grand Narratives produced by previous generations of western scholarship: an underlying Christian triumphalism in the field of religious history, for instance; or the closely related assumption that western civilization was an unproblematic 'Good Thing' in the many studies devoted to its rise. The overall effect of this very necessary intellectual reaction on many dimensions of the history of Christianity will again be obvious from my endnotes, whose dependence on a whole series of wonderful studies of aspects of the millennium with which this study is concerned also highlights the absence of any recent attempt to grapple with the overall phenomenon of European Christianization as a whole.[2]

But against this scholarly background, there are advantages to a longer time frame that go far beyond mere chronological completeness. In my view, the correct response to the deficiencies of value-laden Grand Narratives of the old school is not to avoid writing large-scale histories altogether, but to write better ones. Without a long-term perspective, important phenomena and recurring patterns will tend to be missed, in the same way that looking at a mosaic through a powerful magnifying glass will capture ever more detail but at the cost of vital dimensions of the whole picture.

This is particularly true of the history of Christianity, I would argue, because of one fundamental feature of the source base from which it has to be written. Because Christianity is par excellence a religion of the book, some Christians have always been literate, and historians of its development, even in the late Roman and early medieval eras, are blessed with an extraordinary range of sources, which often gives you much more to work with than for any other aspect of European history within the same time frames. The weight of material varies between different moments, but regularly yields not only densely documented situations, but even fully recognizable individuals. The vast majority of these sources, however, were written by true believers. And as a great deal of comparative sociological and anthropological study of religion has emphasized, and the recent trend towards de-Christianization among modern European populations confirms, true believers are only ever a minority of the total human population. This, too, needs to become hardwired into the story of emerging Christendom. While ideology and committed belief doubtless played their part, it is crucial to think very hard about the extent to which the documented motivations of devout Christians can be applied more generally to entire populations.

In general terms, this inherent bias in the sources has the overall tendency to reinforce broadly cultural explanations of Christianity's success, emphasizing the attraction and persuasiveness of its religious messages. If you step back from the surviving accounts of committed true believers, however, it rapidly becomes apparent that many kinds of coercion also underlay the emergence of European Christendom, and, consequently, that the operations of both public life and social and legal power are highly relevant to the story of its creation. This book argues, therefore, that we need to think again about the relationship between what would usually be considered separate fields of political, social and cultural history in a European past where state structures and dominant socio-political elites were often publicly committed to fostering and maintaining particular religious positions. All told, the capacity of medieval Christianity to generate a unity in religious culture among the vast majority of Europe's population is an extraordinary historical phenomenon, and one which clearly depended on a whole range of factors beyond the developing cultural specificities of the religion itself.

The study which follows is divided into three parts. Each one is devoted to an identifiable era of sustained revolutionary transformation, which helped turn a small sect of isolated, intensely committed, largely urban congregations into a mass religious movement, centrally directed from Rome, and capable of defining and delivering a range of required religious beliefs and practices tailored to all the constituent elements of the population of medieval Europe. Part One puts the spotlight on the late Roman world, where, following the conversion of Constantine, the Christian faith recruited classical philosophy and the culturally coercive mechanisms of the imperial state to turn itself into a theologically coherent, institutionally effective phenomenon capable of demolishing (sometimes literally) classical paganism; and, in the process, begin to win converts – for the first time – on a mass scale. Often discussed as the Christianization of the Roman Empire, this process can be more accurately cast as the Romanization of Christianity: one in which the religion turned itself into a branch of the Roman state in the fourth and fifth centuries. As Part Two explores, the disappearance of this Empire then necessarily plunged nascent Christianity into crisis. Not only did official imperial Nicene Christianity come much closer to being replaced in its former western provinces by an alternative definition of faith than is generally recognized, but the Church's institutional and educational frameworks had become dependent on the parallel structures of Empire: both crumbled as the latter disappeared. As a result, warrior values and broader cultural patterns, in which local congregations were relatively free to mix elements of intrusive Christian and their own existing belief, quickly became characteristic of early medieval Christianity, especially among the dispersed masses of Europe's peasantry. An important additional perspective on the developments unfolding in what was broadly the western half of the old Roman Empire is provided by events to the south and east. Here, it is important to look closely at the medium- to longer-term fate of Christian populations resident in those provinces of the eastern Empire which were being simultaneously swallowed up by the rise of the Islamic caliphates.

These new patterns of post-Roman European Christianity then began to change again, as explored in Part Three, when Carolingian and Holy Roman Ottonian emperors provided two initial centuries of more coherent religious leadership, between 800 and the end of the millennium. This second age of Christian Empire saw the religion spread for the first time, under imperial patronage, far beyond the borders of the old Roman Empire to capture much vaster tracts of the European landscape. Equally important, Charlemagne and his scholars laid down a new pattern for institutionalizing Christian learning, which quickly made western Europe – again for the first time – the intellectual powerhouse of a rapidly transforming Christendom. Then, from the mid-eleventh century onwards, an extraordinary set of further transformations helped generate medieval Christendom in its fully evolved form. Techniques borrowed from Roman law, allied with spectacular legal forgery, allowed the papacy to transform itself into an institution capable of exercising effective religious authority across virtually the whole of Europe. A sequence of popes then weaponized this authority to define and enforce new patterns of Christian piety among both the clergy and the different lay constituencies of European Christendom, finally bringing into being the basic outlines of pre-Reformation medieval Christianity, many of which have been preserved to the present in the Roman Catholic communion.

In endeavouring to do justice to this extraordinary historical process, I have been acutely conscious throughout of my many deficiencies. Perhaps the greatest, it might be argued, is the fact that I am not myself a Christian believer. I still love to go (occasionally) to church, and find deep inspiration in some Christian teachings, above all the Easter message that new hope can often be found even in the midst of deepest despair. All that said, I could not call myself anything more than a thoroughly lapsed Anglican (I avoid agnostic, having learned from my grandfather's experience). But the right answer to the old chestnut (beloved of old-style general history examiners) of whether the history of religion is best written by believers or non-believers has always been resoundingly 'both'. And, given that my aim here is to understand how the extraordinary religious structure that was medieval Christendom came to encompass vast swathes of the European population who were clearly not fully ideologically committed to the faith (as well as many who were), my lack of personal belief might actually be an advantage. On this matter, of course, as with the overall success or otherwise of this enterprise as a whole, the final judgement can only lie with the reader.

PART ONE

The Romanization of Christianity

I

'By This Conquer . . .'

Early in the second decade of the fourth century AD, the Roman emperor Constantine was deeply embroiled in his own game of thrones. In the previous political generation, imperial power had been shared between four generals, two in the western half of the Empire and two in the east. Diocletian had come to sole power in AD 285, but by 293 had made himself head of an imperial college: the Tetrarchy ('rule of four'), comprising two senior Augusti (himself and Maximian) and two Caesars (Constantius Chlorus and Galerius). In 305, the two Augusti retired, the existing Caesars were promoted in their place, and two new junior colleagues (Severus in the west, Maximinus Daia in the east) appointed. It was supposed to be a better mechanism for handing over imperial power than dynastic succession, but quickly broke down into multiple civil wars. Constantius Chlorus died the year after his promotion, at which point his son Constantine declared himself the western Augustus in his father's place. Maximian's son Maxentius threw his hat into the imperial ring as well, and, to add to the confusion, Maximian himself came out of retirement. By 312, Severus and Maximian had been eliminated, and the struggle for power in the west came down to a straight shoot-out between Constantine, who controlled Britain, Gaul and Spain, and Maxentius, ruler of Italy and North Africa. Vast as it was, the western Empire was never going to be big enough for both of them. Over the summer, Constantine gathered his armies and, Hannibal-style, forced his way over the Alps. Then God intervened. What happened next detonated the first of three massive revolutions which would, between them, turn a small, Near Eastern mystery cult into the dominant religious structure of the European landmass, from where it subsequently spread worldwide in the era of European imperialism.

The story was told, just after the emperor's death, by Constantine's biographer Eusebius, bishop of Caesarea, who heard it from the man himself:

> About the time of the midday sun, when day was just turning, he [Constantine] said he saw with his own eyes, up in the sky and resting over the sun, a cross-shaped trophy formed from light, and a text attached to it which said 'By this conquer'. Amazement at the spectacle seized both him and the whole company of soldiers which was then accompanying him on a campaign he was conducting somewhere, and witnessed the miracle. He was, he said, wondering to himself what the manifestation might mean; then, while he meditated and thought long and hard, night overtook him. Thereupon, as he slept, the Christ of God appeared to him with the sign which had appeared in the sky, and urged him to make himself a copy of the sign, and to use this as protection against the attacks of the enemy.

The sign was the Chi-Rho labarum, which the emperor employed on his military standards, and Constantine duly scored a stunning victory over Maxentius on 28 October 312 at the battle of the Milvian Bridge on the outskirts of Rome. A triumphant, thankful Constantine repaid his debt with rich gifts to the capital's Christian communities, and turned the barracks of Maxentius' elite cavalry corps into a huge church: St John's Lateran, the first headquarters of the medieval papacy.[1]

But this was only the beginning. Victory in the west was the precursor of still greater glory. By the end of 312, a parallel struggle for post-Tetrarchic imperial power in the eastern half of the Empire had produced its own winner: Licinius (initially an appointee of Galerius, one of the original Tetrarchs). The two reigning Augusti – Constantine in the west and Licinius in the east – immediately declared undying love, alliance and endless co-operation, but there was only ever going to be one outcome. It took over a decade but, after several separate rounds of conflict, Constantine finally eliminated his eastern rival in 324. Thanks to the vision that God had afforded him, the Christian Constantine remade the complexion of imperial politics, reuniting the entire Roman world under a single, unchallenged emperor for the first time since the mid-third century.[2]

Eusebius' account of the crucial visionary experience has been repeated and – exquisitely (Plate 1) – illustrated countless times, but it's deeply problematic. And I don't just mean the fact that Constantine saw a vision in the sky. I've never experienced one myself, but many people, across the entirety of human history, have, and at least the subjective 'reality' of supernatural religious experience – however you might wish to explain it – is not something to be discounted a priori. But Constantine's story also poses problems of a much more mundane kind, because the emperor appears to have had several different supernatural experiences, not all of which were Christian, at more or less the same time, and to have told different people different things about them. Apart from the combined vision/dream story told by Eusebius, three other variants survive. Writing about twenty years before Eusebius, the rhetor Lactantius – a distinguished university-level teacher of the Latin language and literature, in which elite children of the western half of the Empire were all customarily educated (their eastern counterparts received an identical training in Greek) – who knew the emperor, and was tutor to his eldest son, Crispus, in the early 310s, reports that Constantine had a dream on the eve of the Milvian Bridge, in which he was told to 'mark the heavenly sign of God' on his soldiers' shields.[3] The timing of the divine intervention is different in Lactantius' account, and there is no vision in the sky. Our second witness is another rhetor, this time from Gaul, who gave a formal speech on a ceremonial occasion to Constantine and his assembled court in 310, two years before Maxentius' defeat. In a passage, which must have had prior imperial approval, this speaker described another heavenly vision. Having turned off the main road to visit 'the most beautiful temple in the world . . . You saw, I believe, Constantine, your Apollo, accompanied by Victory, offering you laurel crowns, which brought an omen of thirty years [of life, or rule].'[4]

This time we have a vision, but of a different God (Apollo as the Sun God), and no dream. Last, but not least, in 321 a third rhetor, in another official – and hence imperially endorsed – oration, referred back to Constantine's victory over Maxentius. This speech mentions neither Divine visitation, nor any kind of cross in the sky. Instead, in the midst of battle, all of Constantine's troops are said to have been

1. The Rise of Constantine and the Christianization of Rome

Roman frontier
GALLIAE diocese names
Constantine's realm
306
added 316
added 312
added 324
0
300 miles
0
400 km
THRACIAE
Serdica
MOESIA
Constantinople
Chalcedon
Nicaea
PONTICA
Ancyra
Thessalonica
Troy
ASIANA
ORIENS
Ephesus
Antioch
Athens
Damascus
Mediterranean Sea
Jerusalem
Alexandria
AEGYPTUS

buoyed up by a vision of a heavenly army, led by the emperor's deified father, Constantius Chlorus, coming to his son's assistance.[5]

There have been many attempts to rationalize Constantine's multiple reported religious experiences. Most influential among recent efforts, Peter Weiss argued in 1993 that the visions of Apollo reported in 310 and Eusebius' cross in the sky referred to one and the same event, differently interpreted. Given that Apollo was, by this date, overwhelmingly represented as the Sun God, Weiss argued that what Constantine actually saw was a solar halo, which can take a kind of cross form, and that the emperor eventually came to understand this natural phenomenon as a message from the Christian God. This is obviously a possible way forward, and Lactantius' dream could then be reconciled with Eusebius' account – so long as you posit a delay of two years between initial vision and explanatory dream, whereas Eusebius clearly supposed that the dream occurred the following night. To my mind, however, all these reports need to be handled with a great deal more suspicion.

It was standard practice for ancient rulers, who claimed to be appointed by Divine Power (as all Roman emperors, and Constantine in particular, did), to report suitable omens as confirmation of their special destiny to rule. The future emperor Claudius reportedly had the – no doubt unnerving – experience of an eagle landing on his shoulder when he first entered the forum as consul, while some mysterious force ejected anyone else who tried to sleep in the nursery of the first Roman emperor, Augustus. No historian worth his or her salt (not even Constantine) would dream of taking these earlier stories literally, and both the convenience and variety of the stories the first Christian emperor told about his personal encounter with the God of the New Testament suggest that we're again some way from factual reportage.[6] The received image of a vision-powered Constantine – forced, like Paul on the road to Damascus, into a complete and sudden Christian conversion by a direct personal experience of the Almighty – becomes still more problematic when set alongside how the emperor presented his evolving religious allegiance to the Empire's population at large, over the course of his long and brutally successful reign.

The official religious self-presentation of Constantine's regime went through four distinct phases. In his first years, Constantine styled himself a loyal adherent of the religious ideologies of Diocletian's imperial college, the Tetrarchy, to which his father had belonged. While all Roman emperors claimed to be appointed and supported by Divine power, the specific divinity in question could change, or at least be presented in different forms. Many third-century emperors had portrayed their divine support as coming from the Sun God (Helios in Greek, Sol in Latin, or, more specifically, Apollo), understanding the pictorial image of the Sun as a manifestation of the supreme Divine principle which sustained the entire universe and all its intermediate spiritual powers. The Tetrarchs, however, reverted to a more traditionally Roman religious symbolism, presenting Jove (Jupiter) and Hercules as the divine supports of their – largely victorious – rule. Diocletian and Galerius added 'Jovius' – 'protected by Jove' – to their list of epithets, while Maximian and Constantius Chlorus adopted 'Herculius': 'protected by Hercules'. In his first years in power, Constantine issued coins which simply repeated his father's affiliation, styling himself 'Herculius'.[7] This changed suddenly in 310. Just as the Gallic rhetor announced Constantine's vision of Apollo, the emperor broke with Tetrarchic religious ideologies. 'Herculius' disappeared from his coinage, which was now emblazoned with *sol invictus*: 'the unconquered sun'.[8]

The third phase began in 312. It was in this period that Lactantius wrote about the emperor's dream of the Christian God. Constantine also showered favours on the Christian communities under his control, distributing cash and inaugurating some substantial church-building programmes. In surviving letters to North African Churchmen (in modern Tunisia, Libya and Algeria), he also stated that he and they shared the same religious affiliation, while a small number of early inscriptions and special coin medallions carried the Chi-Rho monogram.[9] The latter were very few, however, and were vastly outnumbered by coin types that continued to celebrate *sol invictus*. This studied avoidance of the obviously Christian in most public contexts is equally marked in the triumphal arch that Constantine erected in Rome to celebrate his victory over Maxentius (it still stands, next to the Colosseum). This is striking for its highly traditional portrayals of the emperor and of the divine power which had brought him victory, carrying not the slightest hint of any Christian affiliation whatsoever. The same ambiguity also jumps out from a new law passed by Constantine in this same phase, making Sunday a day of rest. This sounds like a Christian move, celebrating the day of the week on which Christ rose from the dead, but the law studiously refers to it only as 'the day of the Sun'. The first official spokesmen to celebrate the emperor's great victory over Maxentius in public, likewise, maintained the ambiguity, referring only to the support that Constantine had received from an unspecified 'highest divinity'. This term had gradually come into use in some non-Christian circles over the third century as another designation for the same underlying divine principle as *sol invictus*.[10]

Only from 324, in its fourth and final phase, did Constantine's regime declare itself unambiguously Christian. *Sol invictus* coins continued, but the Christian cross also became a common motif on his coinage, and, by this date, Christians had already themselves been making an iconographic equation between Christ and the Sun God, understanding the sun, like third-century pagan emperors, as the symbol of supreme, divine power: this time the God of the Old and New Testaments. In a whole series of public statements, likewise, Constantine now made his Christianity known to anyone who cared to listen. And to coincide with the twentieth-anniversary celebrations of his original accession to the purple, he called a summit meeting of representatives of every Christian community that then existed – both inside the Empire and beyond – which met at Nicaea (Iznik in modern Turkey) in 325, the year after his final victory over Licinius. There, Constantine publicly confirmed the strength of his Christian loyalties, not only by the care and attention he lavished upon the many bishops who came but by attending some of the sessions in person.[11] But if there can be not the slightest doubt of the former Tetrarch and solar monotheist's Christian allegiance by the mid-320s, how exactly should we understand the personal religious journey that had brought him to this point, given all the different things he had been saying about it in the intervening twenty years since he first came to power?

THE ROAD TO NICAEA

Many different psychological readings of the emperor's evolving religious loyalties have been offered over the years. They began in antiquity. A hostile pagan tradition claimed that Constantine turned to Christianity because it was the only religion which would forgive him for the execution of his eldest son, Crispus, and second wife Fausta. This satisfactorily vitriolic denigration of Constantine's motives also tied in with long-standing pagan critiques that Christianity's willingness to forgive sins removed necessary moral imperative from human action. But the timing is wrong. The emperor's Christianity had been aired unambiguously two years before Crispus' and Fausta's deaths in 326.[12] More modern attempts have ranged from the patronizing – Constantine was a 'rough soldier' who failed to grasp that it wasn't possible for him simultaneously to profess Christian and non-Christian solar monotheist affiliations – to the more sophisticated. Some have argued that he was really a non-Christian solar monotheist all the way through the 310s, although recent discoveries of early uses of the Chi-Rho symbol show this to be incorrect; others that, like some modern religious converts, what was at the time a slow process of conversion was later understood by the emperor as a sudden 'event'.[13] Any of these *might* be correct, but they all share the assumption that the emperor's personal religious beliefs ran in tandem with the evolving public religious stance of his regime. In my view, however, this assumption is methodologically unsustainable, because it ignores one key piece of the Constantinian jigsaw. The start of each new religious phase of Constantine's regime coincided with one of the emperor's major military successes. Once this fact, and its deeper significance, has been properly recognized, it requires us to rewrite all existing accounts of Constantine's personal religious history.

Constantine's switch to solar monotheism in 310 followed immediately after he defeated an attempt by the former Tetrarch emperor Maximian to reclaim power. Maximian, who had been forced into retirement by Diocletian five years previously, had already made two abortive attempts to regain his title. His remaining forces now routed by Constantine, Maximian was 'encouraged' to take his own life, which, realizing the futility of the situation, he duly did.

The second phase of Constantine's religious self-presentation – discarding Maximian's (and his father's) old epithet 'Herculius', in favour of a general non-Christian solar monotheism – began immediately after Maximian's death. The pattern then repeats itself twice more. The third phase – declaring his Christian allegiance to select fellow Christians, but otherwise affecting a non-specific solar monotheism – was inaugurated immediately after the triumph over Maxentius at the Milvian Bridge. And, likewise, the fourth and final phase: straight after the final destruction of Licinius in 324, Constantine began to declare his unambiguous Christianity to all-comers and in all contexts.

It is important to underscore the significance of this sustained correlation between Constantine's military victories and the different phases in his religious self-presentation. Both practically and ideologically, military victory played a central role in the functioning of the Roman Empire. Imperial politics did not operate by election. Would-be emperors were usually put forward by small groups of plotters among the senior ranks of the army and/or court bureaucracy. They then needed to win enough military backing, as well as broader consent among the politically significant landowning classes of the Empire – as the convoluted and periodically violent process that led from the unravelling of Diocletian's Tetrarchy in 305 to Constantine's reunification of the Empire in 324 underlines. Challenges to and dissent from an established emperor's rule, likewise, tended to take the form of attempted coups and usurpations, with the final outcome again usually settled on the field of battle. Defeating internal opponents – as Constantine did sequentially with Maximian, Maxentius and Licinius – was the Roman equivalent of winning a series of general election victories.

Except that, in the Roman world, the ideological stakes were much higher. Victory on the battlefield was the most important confirmation of a would-be emperor's right to rule – because Roman emperors did not regard themselves, and were not regarded by others, as mere secular rulers. Divinely chosen, divinely supported monarchs, they were understood to be ordained by the ruling forces of the universe to keep the Roman Empire safe, along with the civilization it protected.

This civilization saw itself as the ultimate exemplar of human order; a civilization, indeed, that played a unique role in the Divine Plan for humankind – and hence, so the closed loop of this logic went, the sustained Divine interest in those who ruled it. But there was a get-out clause. The ideology allowed for the possibility that, thanks to human error, the wrong man might end up on the throne. Therefore, the Divinity would only provide real support for the candidate who was *really* destined to rule. Beyond its straightforwardly practical connotations in so far as seizing and keeping power were concerned, military victory thus also played a critical ideological role: it was the unique attribute of a properly legitimate Roman ruler. What on earth could the support of the supreme, all-powerful Divinity mean in practice, if not the capacity to win on the battlefield?[14] Victory, the moment when immediate, direct divine support had been made fully manifest, was also – as a direct consequence – the moment of ultimate political and ideological strength in the Roman world. The fact that Constantine announced his major changes of religious affiliation only after each of his major victories – at moments when he was completely unchallengeable – means that he was doing it only when it was politically safe to do, and that these moments of change can therefore provide no reliable guide at all to the actual evolution of the emperor's internal religious beliefs.

Take, for example, the first phase of Constantine's reign: brought to power by his father's army, the new emperor styled himself Herculius. At this moment, precise religious allegiance was a highly sensitive political issue. Not only had the Tetrarchs reverted to older, non-Christian symbolism, rejecting the monotheistic *sol invictus* preferred by third-century emperors, but they had – eventually – also launched the so-called 'Great Persecution' against their Christian subjects. This began in February 303 with an initial edict confiscating Christian property. Subsequent edicts exiled Christian clergy (edict 2) and, eventually, demanded that Christians sacrifice to the traditional gods on pain of death, first the clergy in November 303 and then the population at large early the next year (edicts 3 and 4).[15] All these edicts were still in force when Constantine first came to the throne in 306, which – particularly given the unstable political context – gave him every reason to tread extremely carefully when expressing any religious views in public.

If you descend into the excavated underpinnings of York Minster, which was built more or less on top of the old Roman legionary headquarters – the Praetorium – you are standing close to where Constantine was first proclaimed emperor by his father's army in 306. At that moment, five other would-be emperors were claiming power across the Empire: three in the west, where, along with Constantine, Maximian, Maxentius and Severus – the official choice of western Caesar on Diocletian's retirement in 305 – all asserted their claims; the east, meanwhile, was divided between Galerius – the old Tetrarchic Caesar now promoted to Augustus – and his newly appointed subordinate Caesar, Maximinus Daia. In this context, it is completely unsurprising that, religiously, Constantine echoed existing Tetrarchic religious norms, styling himself Herculius for the next four years. To have done anything else would have been to stand out like a sore thumb among a crowd of rivals, at a point where links to Diocletian's Tetrarchy remained the hallmark of political legitimacy. The obvious risk was that some or all the others would unite against him as a convenient initial target in the winnowing-out process that was bound to follow.

In the event, Constantine showed adroit initial footwork in 306/7 to win immediate recognition as Caesar – i.e., he accepted a notional demotion from his original claim to his father's rank of Augustus – from the senior eastern Augustus Galerius, and then to ally himself with Maxentius to eliminate Severus. When he successfully eliminated Maximian in 310, Constantine could safely drop the Herculius tag, since there was no longer the same danger of a united opposition. His newfound allegiance to *sol invictus* – marked by both proclamation and the issuing of coinage – was part of a deliberate and broader move to establish his political legitimacy on a new foundation which minimized the importance of any ties to the preceding Tetrarchic era. The same oration which announced that Constantine had seen Apollo also declared, out of the blue, that he was in fact descended from a famous and highly successful third-century emperor, Claudius Gothicus. As far as we can tell, he wasn't – but asserting this fictitious lineage allowed Constantine to put forward an alternative, entirely non-Tetrarchic justification for his imperial title (the great Claudius had likewise identified his divine protector as the unconquered sun).[16]

Against this background, Constantine's original acceptance of the Tetrarchy's religious ideology via the Herculius tag looks – and has always looked – utterly expedient. There is no reason to think that either the first religious phase of his regime, or its later abandonment in 310 in favour of solar monotheism, reflected any serious upheaval in the emperor's personal and internal religious beliefs.

This point applies equally strongly to Constantine's two subsequent changes of public religious stance, in 312 and 324. Both were made in exactly the same circumstances, after the kind of thumping military success – over Maxentius and Licinius respectively – that was the perfect moment to announce something potentially problematic. Fundamentally, Constantine's announcement of changes of religious policy only when it was politically expedient to do so makes it highly unlikely that *any* of these public declarations provide a remotely reliable guide to the precise chronology of the emperor's internal religious journey (if indeed there was one), and any attempt to use them in such a way is methodologically flawed.

This sustained correlation between victory and religious declaration over the course of Constantine's reign underscores that the emperor's gradually emerging Christian religious affiliation is at least in part – if not completely – a story of his coming out as Christian, rather than of a Damascene religious 'conversion'. The favour he showed to Christians from 312 onwards, after the defeat of Maxentius, combined with letters in which he refers to North African Christians as co-religionists, strongly indicate that he was by this point already a firm Christian (as does Lactantius' dream story, which belongs to the same period).[17] Facing an impending showdown with Licinius, however, Constantine was carefully, neutrally monotheistic in most public contexts – presumably, for fear that a too-overt Christian affiliation might galvanize opposition in what was still largely a pagan Empire. There was, therefore, no real 'conversion' (in the sense of profound change of belief) behind the final, unambiguously Christian phase of his rule, which began in 324. Rather, this was the moment at which the emperor was finally secure enough to come out as Christian to the entire Empire.

That Constantine's entire religious journey might have been one of coming out, as opposed to conversion, is given further weight by some specific pieces of evidence, and by an important potential parallel in the next political generation – one which, as far as I'm aware, has never been brought into discussions of Constantine's religious evolution. It really needs to be.

By the mid-350s, imperial power was in the hands of Constantine's sole surviving son, the Augustus Constantius II (337–61). Having no children of his own, Constantius – who had significantly strengthened his father's pro-Christian policies – promoted his cousin Julian to the rank of Caesar: junior co-emperor. Though Julian had been brought up a Christian, he had secretly converted to paganism: a conversion he later dated to about 351. He kept the whole thing quiet for a decade, in the middle of which Constantius had made him Caesar (in 355). Once in post, Julian used a series of victories his armies won over barbarians in Gaul between 357 and 360 to establish his own independent ruling credentials. And in the winter of 360/61, he finally rebelled against Constantius' overlordship, making a bid for recognition as at least an equal Augustus. Even so, he continued to hide his paganism, attending church on the feast of Epiphany in 361. Only when the die was firmly cast, and all chance of a negotiated outcome had evaporated in the face of Constantius' intransigence, did Julian come clean about his paganism. He did so in a series of letters the following summer, which attempted both to justify his behaviour and to mobilize non-Christian support across the Empire.[18]

The parallel with Constantine's own carefully staged changes in religious allegiance – albeit in the opposite direction – is striking. In a charged political situation, a subversive religious allegiance was not something to reveal until either it was safe to do so – or when there was nothing to be lost.

When exactly Constantine became Christian – or, to put it another way, when exactly the story of coming out takes over from the story of conversion – is impossible to be certain, but there are a few clues. Constantine's mother, Empress Helena, quickly displayed a striking level of Christian devotion after Licinius' defeat, with her much-publicized visit to the Holy Land in 326 soon (if incorrectly) associated with the discovery of the True Cross. We don't know precisely when Helena became Christian, but her evident devotion in the 320s, as soon as it was politically safe to display it, makes it at least a possibility that she had long been one, and that Constantine might even, therefore, have received his Christianity at his mother's knee. Eusebius also reports that Constantine's revelatory dream came when, alone in prayer, he asked the Divinity to reveal to him the name of the God that his father, Constantius Chlorus, had always followed to victory – a comment that implies that Constantius himself was a Christian (albeit a closet one), providing a further indication that Constantine may have been brought up in a Christian context.[19]

Various pieces of circumstantial evidence back up Eusebius' implicit suggestion. First, Constantius Chlorus, though a reigning Tetrarchic Caesar, refused to implement the different edicts of Diocletian's Great Persecution in full. He did confiscate some Christian properties, as ordered in the first edict of February 303, but, tellingly, he failed to implement any of edicts two to four (exiling Christian clergy and then demanding clergy and laity sacrifice to pagan gods, on pain of death).[20] Second, Constantius' potentially latent Christianity – or at least Christian sympathies – might help make sense of why the Great Persecution was launched in the first place.

At this time, Christians were a pretty normal feature of the Roman world. No one thought, as they had in the first century, that Christians performed illicit, human sacrifices (the whole body and blood metaphor caused some initial confusion) and the Great Persecution is striking for its lack of popular enthusiasm. Unlike some earlier examples, it was in general a decidedly top-down process. According to Christian sources, it began when Christians in Diocletian's entourage were blamed for the failure of official sacrifices because they crossed themselves as the doomed animals were being slaughtered, thereby generating a series of ill-omens. But these same Christian courtiers must have been crossing themselves for many years before this; by 303, when the persecution began, Diocletian had been in power for the best part of two decades. To my mind, therefore, a much more specific motivation seems likely.

By 303, Tetrarchic politics were entirely focused upon succession. With the potential retirements of Diocletian and Maximian being planned (and perhaps already announced: they retired in 305, on the twentieth anniversary of Diocletian's accession), the pressing political question was succession; specifically, the identity of the two new

Caesars, who were to be appointed at the moment when the existing Caesars, Constantius and Galerius, would be promoted Augusti in place of the retirees. Lactantius blames the whole persecution policy on the lobbying of the eastern Caesar Galerius, reporting that he championed the policy to win influence over the pagan Diocletian. The last person Galerius would want to be picking the new Caesars was his current western peer, Constantius – not least because Constantius had an adult son (where Galerius did not). If it were known (or suspected) that Constantius had Christian sympathies, initiating a persecution was the perfect policy for causing him maximum political embarrassment, and for entrenching Galerius' own influence over the crucial choices of new Caesars. In my view, it's no great stretch to think that the whole policy of persecuting Christians was as much about undermining the influence of potential rivals for power within Tetrarchic ruling circles – Constantius Chlorus and his family – as it was about religion.[21]

This would also explain why there is so much confusion in the sources over what Constantine himself might have reported about his supposed conversion experience – or, rather, experiences. For even if Constantine had been a Christian since birth, he still needed a plausible conversion narrative by the time it was safe for him to reveal his allegiance. Any admission that he had always been a Christian would have immediately laid him open to charges that he had hidden his faith during the Great Persecution, to avoid personal danger. (This was in a sense true for entirely understandable political reasons – but that would not have helped.) How to deal with Christians who had lapsed in the face of the persecution, by renouncing or just hiding their Christianity, quickly became an extremely divisive issue within the Christian community in the 310s, after the so-called 'Edict of Milan' issued jointly by Constantine and Licinius in 313 officially rescinded the persecuting laws of 303/4. Any suggestion that Constantine also belonged among the lapsed would have immediately undermined his Christian credentials. To avoid such a toxic charge, the emperor had to be able to present himself as a post-persecution convert – as he duly did, even if the inconsistencies of his attempts reflect the ultimate artificiality of this narrative.[22]

All of which is to say that we can't believe a word of the emperor's public pronouncements about his evolving internal religious affiliations, and that his regime's changes in public policy offer no guide at all to the transformations, if any, which had occurred in Constantine's personal religious conscience since 306. My own suspicion is that he probably was always a Christian and revealed it only in stages, as it became politically safe to do so. However, it certainly also remains within the bounds of arguable possibility that he was originally some kind of solar monotheist who re-identified the Divinity in question as the Christian God somewhere between 310 and 312. That the story of Constantine's conversion was substantially fabricated to hide what was in essence a process of coming out as Christian is beyond doubt. But if we cannot be more precise about the emperor's internal spiritual life, can we do any better with his underlying motivations? Why did this son of a Tetrarch eventually break so dramatically with the centuries-old religious traditions of the Roman world? And what exactly was the nature of the Christian religious community by the early fourth century to which Constantine declared so public an allegiance after 324?

The nineteenth-century Swiss historian Jacob Burckhardt notoriously argued that Constantine converted to Christianity for opportunistic reasons. The emperor, Burckhardt wrote, saw in the spread, ideologies and organizational structures of the Christian religious movement a vehicle which he could harness to run his Empire more effectively.[23] But, if we look more closely at the nascent Christian Church that Constantine encountered at the council of Nicaea in 325, it quickly becomes apparent that Burckhardt's argument won't hold water. The early fourth-century Church had expanded and evolved from the 'Jesus Movement' of mid-first-century Palestine. Nonetheless, neither in number of adherents nor solidity of organizational structures, nor indeed in the uniformity of its ideological and behavioural demands, was the Christian Church of *c.* 300 large and coherent enough to make it an effective partner in the government of the largest Empire western Eurasia has ever known.

'MAKE DISCIPLES OF ALL NATIONS'?[24]

No one knows exactly what percentage of the Empire's population was Christian in 325. In the early second century AD, Christianity already numbered among its ranks some senators of Rome (admittedly only a few) and imperial functionaries, not just, as the contemporary Greek philosopher Celsus claimed, 'the foolish, dishonourable and stupid ... slaves, women and little children'. The movement clearly continued to attract new adherents, and – as the lack of popular enthusiasm for the Great Persecution shows so clearly – had by the early fourth century become a recognized part of the 'normal', if highly varied, population of the colossal Roman imperial structure. One well-established view has even concluded that, while Christians were still a minority in the Roman world when Constantine came to power, they were already a substantial one: some 10–20 per cent of the total population of the Empire, with numbers having increased rapidly in the final decades of the third century. Though based originally on the ancient evidence, as developed in an influential strand of explicitly Catholic French historiography, more widespread acceptance of such a view of Christian expansion has been significantly encouraged by the suggestion, based on the sociological study of modern religious movements, that early Christianity is likely to have gained new adherents at a steady rate of about 40 per cent per generation in the three-hundred-odd years between Jesus and Constantine. The statistical quirk inherent in constant expansion rates is that *total* numbers will increase only slowly for a lengthy period, but then suddenly explode. According to such a model, Christians would still have accounted only for about 10 per cent of the Empire's population by AD 300 – but a further 40 per cent per generation increase over the next two generations would mean that, by 350, about half of the Empire's total population was Christian. One generation after that, the model predicts, Christianity became utterly dominant.[25]

It's worth underlining what is at stake here. If you broadly accept this model, as have a number of influential studies,[26] two conclusions follow. First, Constantine's avowal of Christianity was one in a tsunami of contemporary conversions between 300 and 350. Second, it follows on from this, still more significantly, that his conversion played only a minor role in Christianity's overall success. Closer examination of this model of Christian expansion, however, reveals that neither the model, nor its overall implications, can possibly be correct.

To start with, the idea that half the Empire's population was Christian by 350, as the steady-state expansion model predicts, is just not credible. About 85–90 per cent of the Empire's population consisted of remote communities of widely dispersed peasants busy working the land, and it was only in the sixth century that Christian leaders even began to develop mechanisms for spreading their religion systematically into much of the countryside. (This process is examined more closely in Chapter 7.) Nothing like half the peasantry of the Empire can possibly have been Christian by the mid-fourth century, so the model's prediction for AD 350 is way off the mark. Equally unconvincing is the idea that 10 per cent of the Empire's total population was already Christian in 300. By this date, Christianity was – apart from some limited areas of North Africa, Egypt and Asia Minor – fundamentally an urban phenomenon. Given the overwhelming predominance of rural peasants in the Empire, for Christians to have comprised anything approaching 10 per cent of the total imperial population by 300, virtually the entirety of the Empire's urban population would have had to be Christian. This was manifestly not the case.

The Empire of the early fourth century was divided into 1,800 or so smaller and larger towns and cities (each responsible for administering substantial rural hinterlands). At the same date, the mark of an organized Christian community of any size was that it was run by a bishop. No simple listing of early fourth-century bishoprics has come down to us, but exhaustive historical investigation has concluded that, around AD 300, bishoprics existed in a maximum of about six hundred (or one third) of the towns and cities of the Empire. These identifiable Christian communities clustered especially in the south and east of the Empire and were thinner on the ground towards the west and north, in Spain, Gaul and Britain. This means that two-thirds of the Empire's cities had no organized Christian community at all; nor did Christians yet constitute a majority of the urban population in any of the other cities that did. Even where a Christian congregation had existed for several centuries (such as in Antioch, where the congregation's first-century foundation is recorded in the Acts of the Apostles), Christians still formed only a minority among the city's urban population in the mid-fourth century, a generation or two after Constantine.[27] Put these two facts together and they set some ball-park parameters for possible Christian numbers. If only a third of the urban populations of the towns of the Empire (representing about 10 per cent of the Empire's total population) had substantial, organized Christian communities, and if, even in these, Christians did not yet form a majority, Christian numbers in *c.* 300 cannot have been anywhere near the claimed 10 per cent; at most they will have been no more than about 1 or 2 per cent of the total imperial population.

Such a conclusion is strongly supported by the limited quantity of more specific information that has come down to us. The only actual pre-Constantinian Christian church known from archaeological excavation is that of Dura-Europos in what is now Syria. Dating to the mid-third century, the church was abandoned, along with the city itself, when captured by the Persians in 256/7. It was an adapted town house, comprising an open painted meeting hall, and a baptistery off to one side. But the hall could not have accommodated more than seventy people, which implies that Dura's Christian community was still very small. (The city's synagogue was much larger.) There were, it's true, larger Christian congregations elsewhere. Already in the mid-third century, more than 150 clergy were supported by the Christian community of Rome, which also took care of over 1,500 widows and orphans. Clearly, by this date the imperial capital's Christians comprised several thousand individuals and constituted probably the single largest Christian congregation anywhere in the Empire. But the capital's population in this era was between 750,000 and 1 million people, so that even a total Roman congregation of 20,000 Christians (which seems unlikely) would still only have represented about 2 per cent of the city's inhabitants.[28]

What, however, about those parts of the Empire where there was already a greater density of bishoprics by the early fourth century? By the time of the council of Nicaea in 325, Rome's North African provinces already had about 250 bishops, from which we can conclude that Christian communities existed in maybe half the small agro-towns of this region. Asia Minor, Syria/Palestine and Egypt each also mustered about a hundred bishops (where Italy, Gaul and Spain had no more than thirty each, and Britain half a dozen at best). Had Christianity made enough headway among the urban and rural populations of these regions to compensate for all the western areas of the Empire in which Christian believers were so few and far between?

Much of the available evidence is fragmentary or inconclusive. One small area of Asia Minor – Eumeneia, in a relatively isolated region of the province of Phrygia (in present-day western Anatolia) – has produced relatively large numbers of third-century Christian funerary inscriptions in rural contexts. From this, it has been suggested that in this area, at least, enough peasants had converted to make a majority Christian population overall. But inscriptions were relatively expensive, only put up by the kinds of more prosperous landowners who normally ran the Empire's city councils. This part of Phrygia didn't have city councils, so the rural distribution of these inscriptions is actually evidence, not for a Christian peasantry, but a Christian gentry, who would again have represented only a small percentage of the local population. They may, or may not, have been ruling over a Christian peasantry; there is simply no way to know. A life of the third-century bishop of Caesarea in Cappadocia, Gregory Thaumaturgus ('the wonder worker', *c.* 213–70), written over a hundred years after his death, claims that he converted the entirety of his city – but, again, such a claim is hard to assess. The life is not contemporary and the people it identifies as Gregory's fellow citizens uncertain: did it mean the core urban population, or the much more numerous peasantry of the city's wider territory?

A much better indication of the kind of congregation to be found in one of the more densely Christian areas of the Empire by *c.* 300 is provided by the cache of documents dating to the Great Tetrarchic Persecution recently unearthed in the Algerian city of Cirta, then a bustling agro-town of some 20,000–30,000 people. These texts reveal that the community's Christian clergy consisted of a bishop, three priests and twenty support staff. The community owned one house in the city and a few objects of gold and silver, while its storehouses contained (for baptismal or perhaps charitable purposes) 82 tunics for women and 35 for men, along with 47 pairs of women's and 13 pairs of men's shoes. All this looks like the infrastructure of a congregation of at most perhaps several hundred people, certainly not one comprising several thousands. So, even in North Africa – one of the most densely Christianized regions of the entire Empire – a Christian community of *c.* 300 comprised no more than about 5 per cent of the total population.[29] When you then factor in all the other parts of the Empire where the Gospel had made far less headway, this broadly confirms that overall Christian numbers at the time of Constantine's conversion could not have been greater than 1 or 2 per cent of the total imperial population.

A bit of further thought suggests where the problem lies in the sociology behind the more optimistic estimates that 10 per cent or more of the Empire's population was Christian by this point. The model which suggests that Christianity would have spread with a steady rate of increase of 40 per cent per generation is based on comparative data gathered primarily in the United States on two modern religious movements: the Unification Church ('Moonies') and the Church of Jesus Christ of Latter-day Saints (Mormons). After 1945, both movements gave up trying to proselytize through public meetings, concentrating instead on exploiting the private social networks of their existing members; the indications are that early Christianity did spread in broadly similar ways. But the expansion rate of 40 per cent per generation is derived from observations made over just two generations, or about fifty years of activity. It's a huge leap of faith to suppose that these religious movements will carry on expanding at the same rate for another two hundred and fifty years (ten more generations), which is what the model supposes. Do we really think that 50 per cent of America's population is likely to belong to either of these two churches in another two hundred years' time? This is what the steady-state expansion rate, played out over the long term, straightforwardly predicts. The answer is, surely not (although it is obviously safe for me to say this since I probably won't be around to be proved wrong). In reality, conversion rates to any new religious movement are likely to tail off over time, when more likely converts have already been swept up, and the movement comes into direct competition with other religious groups targeting the same potential audiences.[30]

A properly critical approach to likely Christian numbers, therefore, would suggest – contra Burckhardt – that Constantine's Christian affiliation was, indeed, utterly sincere. Becoming, or coming out as, a Christian in the hostile environment created by the Tetrarchy's signature policy of religious persecution was fraught with danger, and Christians represented only a very small constituency within the total imperial population. Many new adherents would convert in the course of the fourth century, but overall Christian numbers, in percentage terms at least, were still extremely limited in Constantine's time. What was more, as Constantine himself quickly discovered, early fourth-century Christianity was a movement whose internal functioning made it singularly ill-suited to any kind of partnership in Empire.

THE NICENE CREED

Apart from celebrating the happy coincidence between the emperor's twentieth anniversary, the defeat of Licinius, and his consequent ability to shout his Christian affiliations across the rooftops of the Empire, Constantine convened the council of Nicaea to address a serious theological quarrel currently blazing through Christian congregations of the eastern Mediterranean. It quickly became a commonplace among Christian reporters that, in that late spring of 325, 318 bishops – the same number that, according to the Old Testament, had served in the household of King Solomon – gathered in north-western Turkey. But if it was nice in retrospect to think of Constantine as the epitome of ancient wisdom reincarnate, the actual number of participants in the first ever world council of Christian bishops was in fact somewhere between 220 and 250. Despite the fact that the emperor was paying for transport, board and lodging, attendance was patchy. The vast majority came from no farther away than Egypt, with only perhaps half a dozen – including one valiant Brit – from the Latin west, although there was an additional leavening of visitors from outside the Empire. There was at least one bishop from Persia, and another from Christian communities under Gothic rule north of the Black Sea.

In later centuries, the complex apparatus of imperial bureaucratic practice would be deployed for Church councils of this magnitude, giving us full lists of participants, minuted records of daily proceedings (*acta*), and carefully drafted accounts of final decisions (canons). Much less, however, survives from Nicaea: a few unofficial and manifestly partial accounts from a handful of participants; twenty short canons; and a Creed or statement of belief (from the Latin *credo* 'I believe'). Of these, the single most important document is the Nicene Creed, framed as the solution to the doctrinal dispute that the council was called to resolve. Some practising Christians might think they are familiar with it, since a statement of belief called the Nicene Creed is used in many modern liturgies. They are not. What's now labelled the Nicene Creed in modern service books is a later statement of belief produced by the second great ecumenical council of the late Roman period: the council of Constantinople, held in 381.[31] The story behind this elision, and the nature of the doctrinal quarrel that, detonating through the Christian communities of the eastern Mediterranean in the later 310s, prompted Constantine to convene the Nicaean council in the first place, tell us something else of prime importance both about the early Christian Church and its further transition after Constantine's conversion.

The source of the quarrel lay in the Egyptian city of Alexandria, where, in 320, Bishop Alexander condemned one of his priests, Arius, for a line of teaching that, in the bishop's view, overemphasized the subordination of God the Son (i.e., Christ) to God the Father, and hence exaggerated the inherent distinctions between these two persons of the Trinitarian Godhead. In particular, Arius taught that the 'Son' had actually been created at some point by the Father, and that the two had not, therefore, been eternally co-existent. 'There was a time when He was not', apparently, was Arius' offensive catchphrase (though his philosophical system cannot be properly reconstructed, because Arius' writings were eventually condemned and largely destroyed). Arius refused to accept the bishop's condemnation, following which both sides quickly mobilized so many supporters among prominent bishops across the eastern Mediterranean – together with rival condemnations of each other's position – that Constantine decided that only a great council of the entire Church would have sufficient authority to resolve the dispute.[32]

Officially, both the modern Catholic and Orthodox communions still hold that true Christian belief has never changed: 'orthodoxy' being what has been believed – in a famous phrase of the fifth-century Gallic monk and theologian Vincent of Lerins – 'everywhere, always, by all'.[33] From this perspective, the protracted Arian dispute (named after Arius) is widely understood as a deviation from long-standing orthodoxy, but such a characterization does no justice to the evidence and hides the real significance of the quarrel. The extended argument at the council of Nicaea, and the lengthy process which eventually resolved the ongoing dispute, tell us two important things about early Christianity's development in the period up to 325. First, that considerable differences of opinion on even ostensibly central matters of Christian belief had previously been tolerated, at least in practice if not in principle, among the dispersed congregations of early Christianity. And second, that the council of Nicaea, under Constantine's auspices, inaugurated a new trajectory of development, which eventually saw tolerated diversity replaced by a much more rigid doctrinal definition.

The Arian dispute was not the first major theological controversy to rock the developing belief structures of early Christianity, and the same issue – the exact nature of Christ and His relationship to the Father – had been central to many of them. This is hardly surprising, given that the person and role in salvation of Jesus as Son of God – somehow both God and man – is a unique component of the Christian message, as well as being a far from straightforward theological concept. In the first and second centuries, these disputes were being played out in a Church consisting of small, widely dispersed congregations that were kept substantially separate from one another, not only by the periodically hostile attentions of the Roman state (of which the Tetrarchy's Great Persecution was merely the last), but also by the practicalities of travel. Transport was slow – no more than about 20–25 miles (30–40 km) a day on average, overland, in the ancient world – and highly expensive. This meant that contact between far-flung Christian communities – who, already by the early second century, stretched from northern Asia Minor, around the Fertile Crescent to Egypt, and then on westwards to North Africa and Rome, with a few outliers further north and west – tended to be far from continuous.

Up to about AD 200, there seem to have been few if any councils, even regional ones. Rather, these communities exchanged periodic letters and received occasional travellers – such as a famous bishop of Hierapolis, whose surviving funerary inscription records his journeys among Christians all the way from Ephesus to Rome – to maintain contact. This was a context that naturally generated small, self-directing congregations, spread out over the vast expanse of Empire.[34]

As what has been called the Jesus Movement began to gather converts after Christ's death, theological controversies periodically arose. In the early period, these often focused on exactly which texts transmitted legitimate traditions about who Jesus was, particularly in the sense of trying to understand the extraordinary combination of human and divine that Christians – at least from the earliest times for which we have records – believed him to contain, and how his life and death were destined to save humankind.

The earliest stage of what was, in fact, a slow process of doctrinal development is already visible in the oldest surviving Christian writings: the various letters (authentic and otherwise) of the Apostle Paul and some of his contemporaries, which form a central part of the New Testament corpus. Dating to the first generation after Jesus' crucifixion (*c.* 30–60), they document an intellectual process that involved situating memories of Christ's life and death, as these first Christians had come to understand them, against the many prophetic and messianic texts of the Old Testament. The process was worked out in full by the Christian apologists of the first three centuries AD, but the basic line of attack is already visible in Paul's letters. How was it that Jesus could be the Messiah, the triumphant culmination of so much Old Testament prophecy, when he had ended up dead, crucified? The answer lay in identifying in Jesus a different kind of triumph altogether: a man who was also God came not just to save Israel, but the entirety of humankind. But if everyone could agree from an early date that Christ was somehow Divine, there was extensive and lengthy disagreement over exactly what that meant.

Today, the New Testament features four Gospels. Each perhaps originated as a written memoir of Jesus' life and death, produced for one of the small congregations of late first- and early second-century

Christianity. At that point, the dispersal of the original Jerusalem community of Christians after the destruction of the city in AD 70, as well as the emergence of many new congregations dotted around the Mediterranean, seems to have given extra impetus to a necessary process of conscious memorialization, as first-hand witnesses died out. But as part of this process, other Gospel narratives – whose validity was eventually rejected – were also composed. Several of them came to light in a cache of thirteen leather-bound papyrus codices found at the end of the Second World War near Nag Hammadi in Upper Egypt, where they had been buried in a sealed jar. The manuscripts were written in the third and fourth centuries, but cross-references with extant papyrus fragments show that some of them, especially the famous *Gospel of Thomas*, were copies of much older texts, dating back to the late first and early second centuries: exactly the era when Matthew, Mark, Luke and John were being written. Some of these alternative Gospels transmitted an utterly different understanding of Christ's divinity and message of salvation to anything we're used to from the four Gospels of the now canonical New Testament. The Nag Hammadi finds are sometimes labelled 'Gnostic Gospels', since they describe a Christ who was not really a human being at all, suggesting a completely alternative view of what salvation might mean. In the most extreme versions, such as the teachings of the mid-second-century Marcion of Sinope, the God of the Old Testament was reduced to the status of a wrathful, second-order Divinity looking to trap human beings into mistaken beliefs, and Christ an entirely spiritual entity sent to earth in an outwardly human form to spread the true 'knowledge' (Greek *gnosis*: hence Gnosticism), which would allow human souls to escape from the deceiver's traps and reunite with their real Creator: God the Father of the New Testament. Marcion consequently rejected the religious validity of all the Old Testament and much of the New besides.[35]

These early disputes, which concentrated early Christian minds on the problem of defining a generally accepted canon of sacred Christian writings, had been largely resolved by the end of the second century. The editing process can't be recovered in detail but, in the intervening years – presumably via exchanges of sacred texts and occasional personal contacts – many of the dispersed early Christian communities came to recognize broadly the same New Testament canon, composed of our four Gospels, Acts and the Pauline letters (several of which are fakes, if very old ones). Some variation remained. In the east, a composite Gospel text called the *Diatessaron* – but assembled mostly from Matthew, Mark, Luke and John – was preferred to the individual accounts, while some Christians doubted the validity of the Revelation of St John; in Rome the Revelation of St Peter and *Dream of the Shepherd of Hermas* had close to canonical status, and the great third-century biblical scholar Origen of Alexandria (*c.* 184–253) showed by textual analysis that Hebrews could not have been written by Paul. It is also now clear that the texts even of the standard Gospels continued to be edited down to the third century, in part at least to weed out earlier readings that might support now unacceptable theological beliefs. But these are relative details. For the most part, the more extravagant texts and their radically alternative theologies were rejected by an emergent Christian mainstream before the year 200.[36]

Defining a canon, however, did not bring doctrinal disputes to an end. The third century saw continued disagreement about the nature of Christ, with a tendency for some theologies (often labelled Monarchian, from the Greek for 'single principle of authority') to stress the absolute divinity of Christ in such a way as to collapse most discernible differences between God the Father and God the Son. Both Sabellius in Rome (fl. *c.* 215) and Bishop Paul of Samosata (260–68) in the east were condemned for this. In 268, Paul was formally condemned and deposed by a gathering of seventy bishops in the Syrian city of Antioch. When he refused to accept the decision, it took a landmark appeal to the Roman emperor Aurelian to enforce the judgement (though this solar monotheist emperor had no interest whatsoever in Christian doctrinal niceties).[37]

In one sense, the Arian dispute at Nicaea in 325 can be seen as a beefed-up version of this earlier council of Antioch, with a now-Christian emperor present in person to help push through its decisions. When the council opened on 20 May, about twenty eastern bishops supported Arius' position. At the close of proceedings on 19 June, only two still did. Arius' teaching was condemned and he himself sent into exile, along with the two Libyan dissenters – a similar process to that of Paul of Samosata sixty years before. At the same time, however, Arius' condemnation at Nicaea opened a brand-new phase in the doctrinal evolution of the Christian religion.

Previous disputes over doctrine had essentially been resolved negatively; that is to say, by identifying extreme points of view that were judged incompatible with what most believers found acceptable. These had usually also involved local, not global, resolutions, worked out in the particular congregations where the problematic teaching had arisen. What happened at Nicaea differed from preceding disputes in two key respects. First, the fact that it could reasonably claim to be a council of the entire Church necessarily gave its findings much greater weight. Additionally, rather than merely condemning the particularities of Arius' teaching as incompatible with a relatively undefined Christian mainstream, it adopted the alternative, and much more ambitious, strategy of setting out a positive definition of the relationship of Father and Son, to which every Christian was now to subscribe. This definition was laid out in some crucial phrases of the original Nicene Creed:

> We believe . . . in one Lord Jesus Christ, the Son of God, begotten from the Father, only-begotten, that is, from the substance of the Father, God from God, light from light, true God from true God, begotten not made, of one substance with the Father, through Whom all things came into being . . .

While creeds had been in use, particularly in liturgies of baptism, among Christian communities since at least the second century, the Nicene Creed differed from all its documented predecessors. On the one hand, it was far more developed and far more precise than earlier known examples, which tended to be much simpler (e.g., 'I believe in God the Father almighty, and in His only-begotten Son our Lord Jesus Christ, and in the Holy Spirit'). It also went on explicitly to condemn a series of other specific alternative positions (closely associated with Arius and his supporters) in its final section (the so-called 'anathemas'):

> But as for those who say, There was when He was not, and, Before being born He was not, and that He came into existence out of nothing, or who assert that the Son of God is of a different hypostasis or substance, or is created, or is subject to alteration or change – these the Universal Church anathematizes.

This statement represented a revolutionary moment in the development of the Christian religion. For the first time, local variety in belief, implicitly tolerated by deliberately vague doctrinal formulation, had been suppressed in favour of much more exact, top-down prescription.

The key term chosen at Nicaea to define the relationship of Father to Son – 'of one substance', *homoousios* – was also a complete novelty. *Ousios*, with its meaning of 'essence' or 'substance', was a term with a long history in classical Greek philosophical discussions of the different manifestations that one overall Divine power might take. But it was a non-scriptural term, not appearing anywhere in the Old or New Testaments. According to Eusebius of Caesarea, the term was actually suggested by Emperor Constantine himself, as something to which Arius would be completely unable to subscribe, but there's no way to be sure this is true. Whatever the case, the extent of the revolution set in motion at Nicaea is visible in the extended and contested process which followed before the new definition of faith finally won widespread acceptance.[38]

In the hothouse atmosphere of the council, held under Constantine's presiding eye, all the participants (bar the two exiled Libyans) eventually signed up to the new Creed. But, on further reflection after the council had broken up, *homoousios* seemed to many a highly problematic term. Not only did it lack scriptural sanction, but for many Christians it also possessed resonances of the already condemned Monarchian teachings of Sabellius and Paul of Samosata. Put simply, if God the Father and God the Son shared the same essence, how were they different? In practice, therefore, Nicaea did not so much resolve the Arian dispute as kick-start an extended process of doctrinal definition. Such was the furore *homoousios* provoked that, for thirty-odd years under the emperors Constantius II (337–61) and Valentinian and Valens (364–78), the Nicene definition of faith was officially dropped and a new, much more vague definition – that the Son was 'like' (*omoios*) the Father – asserted in its place as the touchstone of Christian orthodoxy. Only when a second ecumenical council was held at Constantinople in 381, over fifty years after Nicaea, was the long-running dispute finally resolved in favour of the Nicene vision of the relationship between Father and Son. At this point, the essence of its teaching was restated in a new Creed (the one used in modern liturgies), which retained *homoousios*, but, among other changes, dropped the final anathemas.[39]

Modern commentators ideologically committed to Nicene orthodoxy as an ultimate statement of Christian Truth with a capital T, present this period between the councils of Nicaea and Constantinople – implicitly following Vincent of Lerins's characterization of Christian orthodoxy as 'what everyone had always believed' – as one where Christianity almost inexplicably veered off the correct path. But the real pattern of development is much more interesting. By the 340s, post-Nicene debate had slowly coalesced into four broad strands of opinion: those happy with *homoousios*; those who rejected any similarity of essence between Father and Son (anomians); and two compromise strands that felt the relationship was best expressed as 'similarity in essence' (*homoiousios*), or who opted for the simpler view that the Son was 'like' (*homoios*) the Father in some way. Constantine's son, Constantius II, eventually threw his weight behind the fourth, Homoean position, with the result that it replaced *homoousios* as official Roman Christian orthodoxy for a generation and more, perhaps because its vagueness allowed greater assent. Eastern and western councils at Seleucia (comprising 160 bishops) and Rimini (over 300) in 359 were followed by a final meeting in Constantinople the following year, which concluded with the bulk of eastern and western Churchmen signing up to Constantius' *homoios*, whose superiority over its rivals was stated in the accompanying claim that it was 'according to the scriptures'.

Responsibility for this break with Nicaea is usually placed by the council's apologists on a handful of misguided bishops who managed to get the ear of Constantius and his eventual successors, the – unrelated to himself – brothers Valentinian I and Valens. These bishops, it's said, constituted an influential 'court party' that was more sycophantic towards imperial power than the rest of their episcopal peers, who held to the True Faith. To my mind, this is an unconvincing response to the contemporary evidence for how many fourth-century Christians clearly found the Nicene definition of *homoousios* deeply problematic because of its potential Sabellian overtones. It also doesn't fully take into account the long, pre-Nicene history of fierce dispute (some might even say confusion) among the dispersed congregations of the early Christian world, over how to understand the conceptually difficult nature of Christ as both God and man.

Stepping back from the detail, the extended doctrinal furore after Nicaea makes best sense when viewed as part of a broader revolution working its way through post-Constantinian Christianity. The growing Church was transitioning from an older world of relatively isolated local communities, many of whom had their own traditions about how to understand the Christ portrayed in the Gospels (and their own baptismal creeds), to one in which increasingly unified doctrinal positions were being asserted on the basis of having been adopted by councils like Nicaea. By the 340s and 350s, local leaders, reflecting the different local traditions they represented, were now having to decide which of their peers believed the same as they did (even if they might be using different language to describe those beliefs), and which did not.

Seleucia, Rimini and the first council of Constantinople in 360 are not listed among the ecumenical councils of the late Roman period in official Church histories, because they adopted a theological solution that did not end up – post-381 – as received orthodoxy. But that is what they were understood to be when they met. All of these – just as much as Nicaea or II Constantinople – were full-scale meetings of representatives of the entire Christian Church, called by legitimate, sitting emperors. The Homoean definition of faith, with its own accompanying creed, was duly enshrined after Constantius' first council of Constantinople in 360 as official orthodoxy for the next twenty years in east and west, until the official imperial position reverted to Nicaea's definition of faith under the aegis of Emperor Theodosius I (379–95) after the second council of Constantinople in 381.

After this council, a slightly remastered Nicene orthodoxy quickly won broad acceptance in the east in the 380s, but the process was slower in the west, where the court of Valentinian II remained officially Homoean into the early 390s. Full acceptance of the Nicene definition of faith thus took the best part of sixty years to achieve. This was not because orthodoxy had been hijacked by a court party for two generations, but because the unfolding of the dispute was fundamentally changing the nature of Christianity.

NICAEA AND BEYOND

The Arian dispute is not (as it is often presented) a story of deviation from a well- and long-defined mainstream Christian belief-set, but of an intense struggle to establish one for the first time. In this respect, Vincent of Lerins's definition of orthodoxy is an anachronism as far as the pre-Constantinian Church is concerned, for Nicaea's definition of the Faith was not in fact a statement of what everyone had always believed. The emerging doctrines of Christianity in the centuries before Nicaea had left much room for variation of doctrinal opinion in how exactly one should understand Christ's distinctive combination of divine and human. The Nicene Creed, however, set the religion off along a new and much more ambitious doctrinal path altogether: the search for a single, precise and unified definition of faith.[40]

Resolutions passed at Nicaea also set in motion major new trajectories of development in both the structural functioning of authority within the nascent Church, and in definitions of the practical piety required of its adherents, whose numbers began to increase more rapidly as the fourth century progressed. Between them, these developments transformed Christianity out of all recognition by the year 400, turning it into a religious movement with a much greater sense of developed coherence.

A case in point is the council of Nicaea's landmark decision to harmonize the date of Easter, the most important of all the Christian festivals. The fact that, three hundred years into its existence, this decision still needed to be made shows quite how much local variation in practice continued to exist. And, in fact, Nicaea did little more than start the process of harmonization. While it declared that there should be one date for Easter, to be followed by all Christian congregations everywhere, it didn't say how that date should be calculated. Even a century later, several different methods were being followed, and it was only in the fifth century that all Christian congregations accepted the method originally worked out in third-century Alexandria that still prevails today. (Current differences between Catholic and Orthodox Easter datings result from the adoption or not of the Gregorian calendar in the sixteenth century, but all Christian communions follow the same Alexandrian method of calculating Easter.) As this underlines, the geographical dispersion of Christian congregations prior to the year 300 combined with the limited contact they had with one another to foster considerable local variation in even some of the most fundamental elements of belief and practice.

Some of this variation concerned minutiae: Nicaea's final canon reflected a discussion about whether it was better to stand or kneel at prayer on Sundays and during Pentecost (the eventual decision was in favour of standing). The long-standing discrepancies over the dating of Easter, on the other hand, reflect a deeper controversy concerning the movement's overall relationship with its ancestral Judaism, which stood at the heart of early Christianity. The solution adopted at Nicaea regularized a practice that developed first among the Christian communities of the west in the second century. This replaced an older norm, whereby, following indications in the Gospels that this was the time when Christ was crucified, Easter had been celebrated during the Jewish Passover (a practice retained by Christians in Asia Minor long into the third century, despite its formal condemnation by Bishop Victor of Rome in the 190s). The old norm, however, involved two basic problems for Christianity. First, the Jewish Passover can begin on any day of the week, meaning that Easter was not necessarily going to land on a Sunday, the day on which Christ's resurrection had been celebrated from the earliest days of the Jesus Movement. Second, it kept Christianity's greatest festival closely aligned with the rhythms of Judaism, which presented problems for Christianity's ongoing process of self-definition, growing away from the movement's originally strong Jewish roots.[41]

The council's mandate on Easter marked the culmination of this process. Jesus and His disciples, of course, were Jews, and for a long time the Gospel was understood by many of its adherents as marking the fulfilment of Jewish tradition. For these believers, it was necessary both to be circumcised and follow the Torah to be a fully fledged Christian, as well as to accept the Good News of the Risen Christ. Historians of Christianity used to argue that the so-called 'parting of the ways' between Christianity and Judaism occurred decisively in the first century, in the first generation of the movement (on the basis of the dream of the disciple Peter reported in Acts (10:9–16), in which God licensed him to eat everything and hence break Jewish dietary laws). It's now widely accepted, however, that Christianity continued to spread largely through the Jewish communities of the Mediterranean until well into the second century. The writing system of the earliest – second-century – Christian texts to survive on papyrus in the sands of Egypt, for instance, was directly derived from that of the Jewish community of Alexandria. Most early Christian communities, likewise, are found alongside a Jewish counterpart, the latter having themselves become much more widespread following the general dispersion of Jews from Judaea caused by the defeat of the two major Jewish revolts against Roman rule (in 66–74 and 132–6).

The destruction of the Temple of Jerusalem in the first of these revolts (in AD 70) also meant that, at the same moment as early Christianity was beginning to form, Judaism was itself faced with an equally profound process of self-definition. What did Judaism mean now that Temple sacrifice, its central religious rite, which could only be performed at Jerusalem, was no longer possible? A reboot, based on the intensification of cultic practices relocated to local synagogues, was the solution eventually worked out by rabbis living largely in the Jewish towns around the Sea of Galilee, but, in this evolving context, boundaries between Jews and Christians clearly remained fluid for much longer than used to be supposed. In the mid-second century, the early Christian leader Justin Martyr (*c.* 100–165) was worried that members of the congregation in Lyons were slipping off to synagogue. This remained a problem for Origen in third-century Alexandria, and for the council of Elvira and for John Chrysostom in fourth-century Spain and Antioch respectively. Which was where definitively resolving the date of Easter came in. The council of Nicaea's decision not only reduced the bewildering variety of practice that had evolved in the isolated, dispersed early Christian communities. It also drew a firm boundary between fourth-century Christianity and its own Jewish origins, which clearly had played a deeper and longer-lived role in the evolution of early Christianity than its assembled leadership might have been comfortable to recognize in summer 325.[42]

Nicaea also played a pivotal role in revolutionizing the religion's authority structures. As the council's invitation list makes clear, the recognized leader of local Christian congregations by the start of the fourth century was the bishop. This had not always been the case, although in some communities, episcopal authority emerged much earlier than in others: the surviving letters of Bishop Ignatius of Antioch, martyred at the end of the first decade of the second century, indicate that he already exercised firm control over his congregation. But as late as the third century, texts like *Didascalia Apostolorum* (a manual on Church discipline and practice) describe leadership functions within the Church as shared between bishops, itinerant apostles and prophets, confessors (those persecuted for their faith) and lay intellectuals. The second-century Church in Rome and Alexandria, likewise, consisted of several separate Christian congregations, each with their own leaders. In Alexandria, it was only with the episcopate of Demetrius (189–232) that the city's Christians recognized the authority of a single bishop, while in Rome, it perhaps happened later still: in the time of Bishop Dionysius (259–68). At the time of Constantine's conversion, such rural Christian congregations as there were often had their own bishops: so-called *chorepiscopi*. Such men clearly originally enjoyed much the same rights and duties as urban bishops, such as ordaining priests and deacons. However, these rights were progressively taken away from them in the fourth century, as the authority of the urban bishop was steadily reinforced. The council of Serdica in 343, for instance, removed their ordination rights, and rural *chorepiscopi* were steadily downgraded to the status of normal priests; but how soon these measures took real effect is unclear.

Even after all this structural reinforcement, bishops still shared decision-making and other leadership roles, such as teaching, with the other types of Christian leader mentioned in the *Didascalia*. It was, for instance, more than half-expected – in tune with its early roots, and the timbre of the New Testament texts – that Divine revelation would continue to validate alternative, less-institutionalized forms of religious authority. The late-second-century Church was mesmerized for a generation by the New Prophecy movement. This was based on Divine revelation to three prophets from rural Phrygia who had ecstatic visions that they claimed fellow devotees could share: Montanus, after whom the movement is sometimes named, and two women, Priscilla and Maximilla. The movement swept out of north-western Asia Minor to win converts as far away as Rome and North Africa. In the end, however, a majority of mainstream Christians decided against the legitimacy of its teachings, for reasons that are slightly unclear (since most of our information comes from hostile sources), and the movement subsided into a separate, schismatic branch of Christianity largely confined to more remote parts of Asia Minor. Even the eventual rejection of the New Prophecy movement, however, did not cement in place untrammelled episcopal authority among nascent Christianity's many local congregations.

Not only did more than half the Empire's cities not yet have a bishop at all by the early fourth century (p. 21), but even in those that did, episcopal leadership was still more consensual than authoritarian. This shows up clearly in the mechanisms by which new bishops were selected. Before Constantine, bishops were chosen by and from their local congregations, not imposed from outside or from above by other bishops or archbishops, although three existing bishops were normally required to participate in the ordination ceremony. This slow emergence of even limited episcopal authority provides a further reason – beyond the inherent theological complexities – why a recognizable Christian orthodoxy could not develop before the fourth century. Up to that point, the religion did not possess authority structures of sufficient strength through which a monolithic solution to the complexities of the Trinity could be identified and enforced.[43]

Nicaea set in motion a process that fundamentally reordered this older landscape of devolved, shared Christian authority, which had sustained such strong traditions of local autonomy. The very act of convening the council at all revolutionized decision-making at the top. While parts of the third-century Church had held councils with some regularity, as Eusebius' *History* and the letters of Cyprian of Carthage show, these had all been regional councils. Never before had anyone attempted to bring together representatives of the entire Christian Church. Nicaea's scale and ambition were utterly unprecedented and set a new standard for the future.[44] Henceforth, all the high-level problems encountered by late Roman Christianity would be addressed by similarly ecumenical councils, though it clearly took a while even for some of its more prominent Church communities to get the hang of the necessary record-keeping required to identify which rulings belonged to which council. In the early fifth century, a North African Church council enjoyed pointing out to the then Bishop of Rome that what he had cited as a canon of Nicaea was actually a ruling from the much less prestigious – and hence less authoritative – council of Serdica, held in 343.[45]

The council's decisions also affirmed the importance of hierarchy within the episcopal order, generalizing an idea – that some bishops had greater inherent authority than others – that had previously applied only in a few cases. The superiority of the bishop of Alexandria over all bishops of the different provinces of Egypt and Libya was confirmed; a similar regional primacy was acknowledged for the bishops of Rome and Antioch. These three were all ancient Christian communities, founded (according to tradition) by one or more of the apostles. Over the next fifty years, their special pre-eminence developed into a 'system' of five patriarchates, which became characteristic of Christianity in the late Roman period. The special recognition Nicaea granted to Antioch, Alexandria and Rome was extended first to Jerusalem, and eventually to Constantinople on the grounds that the latter – Constantine's new capital – was the 'New Rome' and should be accorded all the privileges of the old, even though there is no sign that the city had ever possessed an early Christian community. While the fourth and fifth centuries saw bouts of rivalry between different members of the five patriarchates, with accompanying assertions that one or another was more important, the generally held conception was that all five were equally important and should exercise similar influence over the development of Christianity as a whole, as well as regional dominance within their own domains.

Further down this emerging superstructure, the idea of metropolitan authority was ostensibly rolled out across the entire Empire, although the term 'archbishop' was not yet generally recognized. Following the established patterns of secular imperial administration, the capital city of each province became the seat of a metropolitan bishop (later, archbishop), who ranked higher than his peers (though below the patriarchs). Metropolitans were required not only to call regular meetings of the bishops of their provinces but could also exercise a veto over lesser episcopal appointments. At the local level, too, the authority of the bishops began to increase. By the end of the fourth century, control of new appointments had been taken out of the hands of the congregation, whose role was rapidly reduced to one of 'acclaiming' decisions that were now made by sitting bishops. The local standing of bishops was also extended by Constantinian legislation authorizing them to hold formally recognized court sessions, with jurisdiction over every kind of case, even the most serious. No appeals were allowed against their judgements, which notionally put them on a higher level than even the courts of provincial governors, the main workhorses of the late Roman legal system.

Nicaea began a process that, if fully realized, might have created the kind of internally coherent, hierarchically organized religion that would have made it the effective partner in Empire that Burckhardt supposed Constantine to have identified. But such centralizing reforms took time – and sometimes faced considerable resistance. Some Christian communities didn't appreciate the attempt to replace long-standing practice with newfangled bureaucratic neatness. In North Africa, the bishop of Carthage had long exercised an overall leadership over the bishops of the surrounding province of Proconsularis (broadly, modern Tunisia), but attempts to spread his metropolitan authority across the rest of North Africa were resisted, especially in Numidia (a province spanning much of present-day Algeria), where seniority had long been accorded to whichever bishop had been in office the longest, whatever his see. The new episcopal courts also ran into problems. According to Constantine's original design, either party – plaintiff or defendant – could request that a case be transferred to a bishop's court. But with Roman society being highly litigious, and bishops lacking formal legal training, this was a recipe for potential disaster, or, at least, for such a deluge of legal business as to leave bishops with little time for anything else. No details survive of the resulting chaos, but the original remit was quickly modified. By the year 400, the legal role of bishops had evolved into running a kind of small-claims court, dealing with less serious cases, and tending for the most part to arrive at consensually agreed solutions via mediation, rather than imposing resolutions according to the letter of the law. In the late fourth century, as illustrated in several surviving letters of the Latin theologian and bishop Augustine of Hippo (354–430), bishops themselves were using the Empire's other courts for more formal legal business.[46]

It was only when higher-status individuals, from the Roman gentry and above, started to become bishops (from the third quarter of the fourth century onwards), bringing with them their own inherent social status, wealth and prestige, that bishops in practice acquired anything like the aura of authority with which the decisions of Nicaea and Constantine's legislation had attempted to invest them. Ambrose of Milan (elected 374) in the west, and the Cappadocian Church Fathers in the east (Basil of Caesarea became bishop in 365), are early examples of bishops with this greater stature. In North Africa the regional episcopate took on new life in the 390s with the arrival of Augustine of Hippo and his friends: better-educated, well-connected individuals who started to fill its ranks. At this point, many of the most influential Christian intellectuals – such as the Latin theologians Jerome (*c.* 342–420) and Sulpicius Severus (*c.* 363–425) – still weren't priests, while some of the religion's most powerful patrons, such as the senatorial ladies who feature so prominently in Jerome's letters, remained much more formidable figures than the Churchmen who clustered around them.[47]

Again, we're looking here at a process, not an event. Just like local diversity in belief, the older patterns of authority within pre-Constantinian Christianity did not disappear overnight. Nonetheless, Nicaea initiated changes that transformed the practical operations of the Church as an institution just as profoundly as its ambitious theological agendas eventually changed patterns of required belief. Over the course of the fourth century, the local autonomy characteristic of the early Church was steadily eroded by substantially more top-down authority structures. Ecumenical councils were held periodically to take unchallengeable decisions on the most important issues. Regional patriarchates, supplemented on a more modest scale by emerging metropolitan archbishoprics, exercised a stronger supervisory function over ordinary bishops, and individual bishops themselves came to occupy a more authoritative position in relation to their own congregations. The result was a new type of much more centralized institutional structure, compared to its pre-Constantinian counterpart. Equally important, Nicaea also kick-started a revolution in basic religious practice in terms of required standards of devotion and behaviour within the Christian movement.

THE CHURCH OF THE MARTYRS?

The catalyst behind the key decision at Nicaea that fundamentally shaped the subsequent evolution of lay piety was the Melitian schism, named after the Upper Egyptian bishop Melitius of Lycopolis (d. *c.* 327). Histories of religions often tend to focus on developing systems of belief and authority, but patterns of lay piety – how members of the group were meant to live their lives and what rituals they were supposed to perform – are at least as important a variable when it comes to understanding the nature of any particular religious movement. Melitius was the leader of a group of Egyptian Christians who called themselves the 'Church of the Martyrs'. As the name suggests, this was a movement born of the horrors of the Great Persecution, which focused on the question of what to do about Christianity's 'lapsed' (Latin *lapsi*): those who had abandoned their faith in the face of threatened imprisonment, torture, or death during the persecution, whose edicts were officially in force for a full decade after 303, until Constantine and Licinius produced their joint declaration of religious toleration.

In the aftermath of the persecution, the question of readmitting the lapsed back into full communion was a toxic issue in many parts of the Church, particularly where there had been actual martyrdoms (which is why Constantine absolutely needed a plausible conversion story: p. 18). As with so many others we'll encounter in this book, this is a story told by the winners, so the full details of Melitius' position and actions are not certain. It seems, however, that having initially taken a relatively generous stance on readmitting repentant *lapsi* back into full communion, he eventually changed his mind and opted for the much tougher line that they should be permanently excluded from the company of the truly faithful 'Church of the Martyrs'. By the time of the council of Nicaea, he had gathered a party of twenty-eight Egyptian bishops (about a quarter of the total, although Melitius is accused of inflating their number by ordaining some himself) who refused communion with the rest of their peers, because they had readmitted the lapsed back into the Church too easily. An analogous dispute reared its head simultaneously in North Africa. This focused particularly on accusations that the new bishop of Carthage appointed after the Great Persecution (Caecilian, probably elected in 311) had been ordained by, among others, Bishop Felix of Aptungi, who had supposedly handed over religious texts to be burned during the Great Persecution, rather than facing up to potential martyrdom in protection of the holy books. Outraged, the hardliners elected their own short-lived alternative bishop of Carthage, and then, in 313, one Donatus, who proceeded to lead a dissident movement of North African conservatives for over forty years, until his death in Gallic exile in 355. Even afterwards, the dispute continued to rage among African Christians until, as we will explore in more detail later in the book, it was finally settled in the second decade of the fifth century.

In stark contrast to the ongoing conflict and division in North Africa, the delegates at Nicaea found effective mechanisms to draw a line under the Melitian dispute. Deemed too hard line, the Church of the Martyrs was ruled illicit, and Melitius banned from further ordinations. But those bishops he had already ordained were allowed to remain in office – in some cases alongside a non-Melitian counterpart – for life.[48] Of particular significance here is what the dispute tells us more generally about the intensity of devotional practice in early Christianity, and how its resolution at Nicaea initiated profound transformation in some of its key elements.

The Donatist and Melitian disputes occurred because, in the face of persecution, there had always been a significant body of early Christian believers who would not abandon their beliefs, and who were willing publicly to uphold the values of their faith even to the point of death. Here, the traditional image of the Roman Empire and early Christianity is the classic throw-them-to-the-lions trope. As Tertullian (*c.* 155–*c.* 220) famously put it,

> If the Tiber reaches the walls, if the Nile does not rise to the fields, if the sky doesn't move or the earth does, if there is famine, if there is plague, the cry is at once: 'The Christians to the lion!'[49]

Before the mid-third century, such persecutions tended only to affect particular localities. However, a new pattern of global persecution, initiated in AD 250 by the emperor Decius and culminating under the Tetrarchs, periodically required all inhabitants of the Empire (excluding Jews) to sacrifice to pagan gods. Many Christians refused, but it is impossible to know how many died. Numerous deaths went unrecorded, while some traditions record only names, which could easily become confused. Later, finding martyr relics became such a vogue activity that there was plenty of unconscious and more or less deliberate fabrication. But the fourth-century Church historian Eusebius of Caesarea gives an entirely believable, contemporary account of forty or so Christians of Palestine who were executed there in the time of the Great Tetrarchic Persecution, and there is equally good evidence that another forty-plus Christians had earlier perished in Gaul in the late second century. Altogether several hundred, therefore, and perhaps even a few thousand, Christians certainly died for their faith before Constantine brought the era of persecution to a close.

In some cases, contemporary eye-witness accounts of their suffering survive, and you don't have to be a True Believer to find the early Christians' devotion to their cause profoundly moving. The heartache of the imprisoned Carthaginian mother Perpetua remains utterly immediate, as her father tries to persuade her to abandon her faith by bringing her baby son into prison. Perpetua was still breast-feeding, and the emotional and physical distress that his cries generated in her jump out from what reads like a prison diary. But, aside from wanting to hold to her personal faith, she was also constrained by her love for an unbaptized younger brother, who had died of cancer some time before. She had experienced what she believed to be God-given visions (it's been suggested she might have been a Montanist), which showed her brother – his face now cleansed of the unsightly tumours that had killed him – now safely in Heaven, because she was sticking to her Christian faith. The intensity of her anxiety – caught between love for a child and a brother – is heartbreaking, whatever you think about her visions. When dealing with such accounts, however, it is important to be careful. Narratives of martyrdom were deliberately written to maintain the memory of the devout, often to establish a cult, and certainly to encourage fellow Christians to show the same level of devotion to the cause, so that a degree of conscious literary creation was inevitable. But that doesn't detract from the fundamental fact that hundreds of early Christians were ready to die for, rather than renounce, their beliefs.[50]

All of which emphasizes a key point about the intensity of early Christian spirituality. The earliest manuals of Christian spirituality – the second-century *Didache* and third-century *Didascalia* – reflect the rich local variations in practice of this era, in that they offer advice, not a set of rules to be followed to the letter. It was also possible to participate in the movement at different levels and to different degrees: novice, catechumen, where an individual had expressed an intention to be baptized, and full baptized member. But the regime governing the entry of fully baptized members into the Church was strikingly demanding. Several years of instruction were required, along with regular sessions with an exorcist in the run-up to actual baptism, which always took place at Easter. The daily round of expected Christian spirituality matched the rules of entry. Regular personal prayer at several different moments during the day was accompanied by a ritual lighting of lamps in the evening (reflecting again, perhaps, the Jewish origins of the Jesus Movement) and regular attendance at eucharistic meals of bread and wine, which often involved participants taking sacrament home with them to consume before other meals.

A whole series of ecstatic religious experiences were also considered a 'normal' part of Christian worship. Speaking in tongues – *glossolalia* (still widely evidenced in modern Pentecostal churches) – was common. The classic study of its modern examples defines the phenomenon as consisting

> of strings of syllables, made up of sounds taken from all those that the speaker knows, put together more or less haphazardly but emerging nevertheless as word-like and sentence-like units because of realistic, language-like rhythm and melody.[51]

Speaking in an actual foreign tongue, one previously unknown to the speaker, is also sometimes, if more rarely, reported. Dreams and other forms of revelation were likewise a widely accepted feature of early Christian spirituality. We've already met Perpetua's (unchallenged, notice) vision of her dead brother in Heaven, and she had other dreams besides. The validity of the *Dream of the Shepherd of Hermas* – a post-Apostolic prophetic revelation concerning good Christian practice – was widely accepted among the Christians of Rome, while the later-second-century Church was thrown into confusion by the New Prophecy movement (p. 39). The genuineness of these new revelations – and it's worth noting that two of the three key New Prophecy prophets were women, given the extent to which later Christianity was dominated by males – was accepted by many, including the author Tertullian, who was otherwise a strong supporter of episcopal authority.[52]

The evidence for a ferociously intense early Christian spirituality, then, needs to be taken seriously. Sustaining it all was the sense – as Jesus teaches in the Gospels – that the Second Coming might happen at any moment, and that it was necessary to have your soul in good order if you wanted to join the Lord in Paradise. It was also, emphatically, Bible-led. Apart from hunting through the Scriptures to help comprehend the nature and meaning of Christ, early Christians also searched them for instructions on how to live (*paranesis*), even when the sacred writings threw up apparent contradictions.[53] In his letters, Paul was already fielding questions from brethren surprised by the fact that the Second Coming was so long delayed. (What was bothering them was the fate of believers who – against original expectations – had died before Jesus' return.) The expectation of impending eschatological climax did not quickly disappear. It's deeply embedded in the one apocalyptic text that eventually – despite some dissenting voices – made it into the New Testament canon. The Revelation of St John, probably written in the final decades of the first century, anticipates the imminent end of the world. This expectation had been only partly eroded by the mid-third century, when the early Christian historian Sextus Julius Africanus produced his chronology of world history and human salvation, which concluded that the end of the world would follow in AD 500. In his view, world history was unfolding in six eras of one thousand years each, and the last of them would close in this year. Faced with this impending imperative of answering to the Lord, early Christianity made substantial behavioural demands upon its members. Not only were they not to attend all the normal pagan festivals and spectacles of the Mediterranean world, but they were often expected – not just when faced with the ultimate challenge of impending martyrdom – to reject all the ties and joys of normal life, including family.

Not all Christians lived up to these rigorous demands. The third-century persecutions had already generated *lapsi* aplenty, even before the Great Tetrarchic Persecution brought the matter to a head. Likewise, Tertullian felt the need to write a whole treatise to explain to his fellow North African Christians why they must not participate in the delights of the annual round of pagan city festivals (strongly suggesting that they normally did). But there were clearly many highly devout Christians, too, among whom there was extensive debate about whether really serious sins – sexual immorality, murder, apostasy – could be forgiven after baptism. In the minds of some, such forgiveness was impossible. Baptism was a one-off spiritual cleansing, after which no further remission of sin could be expected. Others, particularly in North Africa, thought that a second baptism – after proper penitence – might be necessary to cleanse the pollution. Still others thought that transgressive clergy, especially bishops, had so broken trust that they could never be restored to a position of authority.[54] It is against this backdrop that we can begin to grasp the full, transformative significance of the council of Nicaea's response to the Melitian schism.

There's a famous story in the Gospels where Christ is approached by a young man who asks what he needs to do to be saved. The answer comes back, 'If you want to be perfect, go, sell your possessions and give to the poor, and you will have treasure in heaven. Then come, follow me.' The young man goes away sad because he was rich, generating the further comment: 'It is easier for a camel to go through the eye of a needle than for someone who is rich to enter the kingdom of God.'[55]

On the face of it, this was an exchange that should have made Christianity an impossible religion for much of the Empire's population, and especially its elite; an exchange that should have confined Christianity to the status of a marginal, rigorist sect forever. But, after the young man had departed, Jesus offered a further thought to the disciples, who were wondering how, with such conditions, anyone could be saved. 'With man this is impossible, but with God all things are possible.'

The answer which the council of Nicaea provided to the Melitian schism, and indeed, that given by an earlier, much smaller council to the parallel Donatist schism, echoed this more optimistically inclusive view. It proposed a relatively generous solution to the problem of the lapsed, one that didn't react by putting up impenetrable barriers around a small community of the 'perfect', who could all claim to echo the devotional rigour of the martyrs. Repentant *lapsi* could be readmitted to full membership of the Church rather than being permanently condemned. Such an approach set the tone for an overall transformation in the nature of basic Christian spirituality in the post-Constantinian era, which refined some of the earlier intensity to provide a safe home for the less-than-perfect, who now began to flock to the Church in much greater numbers.

In the century or so after Nicaea, especially once Christianity had begun to spread to the point where new members were less often adults coming from completely outside the community, infant baptism became the norm, replacing the intense combination of extended instruction and ritual purification required for adult admissions to the early Church. Even in the case of adults, total preparation for baptism by the sixth century – including both instruction in the faith and rituals of exorcism – was limited to a maximum of twenty days, as opposed to the multi-year, multi-stage process common before Constantine. There was some instruction in the faith as baptized children grew older, but no more than adult entrants were receiving. In the post-Constantinian Church, the older patterns gave way relatively quickly to much more relaxed modes of entry to what was, simultaneously, becoming a very different type of religious movement.

This broader transformation shows up clearly in evolving Christian attitudes towards marriage, procreation and worldly wealth. A powerful strand within early Christianity regarded all the worldly ties concomitant with family life as a dangerous distraction from preparations for the Second Coming, even if marriage itself was just about acceptable. (As St Paul put it in I Corinthians 7:9, 'if they cannot control themselves ... it is better to marry than to burn with passion.') In the same spirit, just as some of the more extravagant Gnostic notions that all flesh and worldly matter had been created by some second-order evil divinity had also been ruled out of court, so early Christian rejections of the world were not absolutely total. But it is only in the fourth century that we start to find the first accounts of marriage as a positive Christian institution and, in the fifth and sixth centuries, the appearance of actual Christian liturgies of marriage as the act of marriage was redefined as something that might happen in Church, or at least according to a set format with explicitly Christian prayers and blessings. That Christ turned water into wine at the wedding in Cana was taken to suggest that marriage could be a positive Christian institution, and St Augustine (though only Augustine among early Christian scholarly commentators) was ready to argue that Adam and Eve had been made male and female in order to have sex in the Garden of Eden even before the Fall.

In much the same way, as a magisterial recent study has explored, Christian thinkers eventually made their peace with worldly wealth. There were some crashes along the way. Around the year 400, one fabulously wealthy Roman senatorial heiress, Melania the Younger, felt she had to liquidate her assets and give most of the proceeds to the poor to save her soul. But this was never going to be more than a minority response, and, if adopted more generally, would have created chaos. There was a market for real estate in the late Roman world, but not on the scale of Melania's holdings. Turning all her land into cash proved to be a serious problem and had unlooked-for effects, not least in depriving hosts of sitting tenant-farmers of the land which supported their families. Over time, therefore, Christian intellectuals responded more creatively to the issue of wealth by gradually evolving a series of justifications to allow the wealthy to keep most of their assets. So long as some of it was used for Christian purposes, then wealth could be regarded as a gift from God, offering the recipient opportunities to do good, rather than as the fundamental impediment to salvation that camels and needles might otherwise suggest.[56]

Disciplinary structures also slowly moved in similar directions. The norms of early Christian belief, whereby it was highly doubtful that major sins could ever be forgiven after baptism, carried on into the fourth century. Constantine delayed his own baptism until he was on his deathbed – a common practice, since people still feared the impact of subsequent sin upon the fate of their Christianized souls. Such penitential regimes as did exist were also punitive and public. Sinners had to make a public confession of their crimes before the entire congregation; they were then reduced to the order of penitents, excluded from communion, and committed to a severe course of prayer, fasting, sexual abstinence and almsgiving for a period that varied according to the seriousness of the transgression. You could also go through this entire process only once in your life, and certain prohibitions remained in force until death: a penitent might not marry, or, if already married, had to abstain from sex. It was also generally considered self-evident that penitential status made it impossible for the individual concerned to be a priest of any kind.

While perfectly appropriate for a small-scale, highly intense religious sect, this kind of disciplinary regime proved much too rigorous for a religion busy evolving into a mass movement. The evidence for penitential practice in the fourth and fifth centuries is particularly patchy, and strongly suggests that local variations continued. But there are clear signs of a general softening in tone. While generally excluded from taking communion, increasingly penitents were allowed to attend Church services, while death-bed communion was now also authorized. In Spain, penitents who had done their time could be admitted into the two lowest ranks of the clergy and, by the early sixth century in Gaul, an ecclesiastical council was not even willing to rule that a bishop who had confessed to sexual misconduct and the illegal appropriation of Church property ought to be permanently excluded from office. (The bishops agreed that he should undertake penance in a monastery but were undecided for how long.) Some monastic rules retained the full ferocity of the early Christian penitential regime, but there are strong hints that, already by the fifth century, the broader

Church was moving towards the private confession and less publicly humiliating modes of corrective punishment for at least some sins that would become the hallmark of early medieval piety.[57]

Following Constantine's conversion, the Christian religion transformed itself in a series of fundamental ways over the course of the fourth and fifth centuries. Although it was already very different from the Jesus Movement of first-century Palestine – a few tens of faithful followers, driven by intense personal experience but unsure yet as to what it all meant (were they fully realized Jews, or something else entirely?) – the pre-Constantinian Church of *c.* 300 still remained a relatively small movement of True Believers, whose rituals and required norms of behaviour were draconian, time-consuming and potentially even humiliating (in the case of serious lapses).

There were concomitant changes, too, in visions of how much of humanity was likely to end up being saved. Up to the third century, Paradise – a place in Heaven – was understood as a reward that would come only to a tiny minority of humankind: the faithful, essentially sinless believers who had stood fast to their religion through thick and thin right up until death – a mix of martyrs, virgins and maybe just a few others. Once again, the subsequent process of ideological adjustment was long drawn out, but, as membership of the Church expanded and disciplinary standards loosened, visions of the size and composition of Heaven's ultimate population steadily increased, with large numbers of the many less-than-perfect Christians who were now being baptized and attending services being included in the ranks of the saints. The same process also involved rethinking, simultaneously, the likely pathways to Heaven, since it quickly became clear that there had to be some way for the less than perfect at death to be purged of their sins post-mortem to be able – eventually – to enter the pearly gates. The intellectual complexities of these necessary ideological adjustments never reached their final resolution in the late Roman period, but already by *c.* 400 – not least (but not only) in some important reflections of St Augustine – Christians were understanding Heaven's gates as ever more welcoming, although this did nothing to dampen individual anxieties that Heaven might not be the final destination of their souls.[58]

As Christianity slowly but surely evolved into a mass religious movement in the fourth and fifth centuries, therefore, many of its older belief and disciplinary patterns had had to change. The early faith's eschatological promises were appealing to many, with hopes of life everlasting no small matter given the pressing reality of human mortality; for some, too, the ferocity of its original rules and of entry and behavioural demands were themselves an additional attraction. But the majority of the population, while impressed by Christian devotion, would never have been willing to show anything like the level of commitment these rules demanded. The subsequent 'fix', as it slowly emerged at Nicaea and afterwards, was to hold on to the eschatological excitement, but modify enough of the rest to make Christianity's everyday demands more manageable for the mass of humanity.

One of the best indications of this is a profound change in Christian architecture. Thanks to Constantine, who constructed the first ever purpose-built churches in Rome following his defeat of Maxentius, fourth-century Christianity started to acquire its own proper architecture, as opposed to the older house churches created, as at Dura-Europos, by modifying pre-existing buildings. These new churches generally took the form of basilicas, modelled on an old, standard public-building form of the Graeco-Roman world. Basilicas were rectangular in form, with shallow roofs, the larger ones subdivided internally by columns into several aisles, and usually equipped with an apse at one end. The apse was the natural position of authority to which the eye was immediately drawn upon entering the building and was traditionally occupied by the authority figure in charge of whatever proceedings were being held. Imperial audience chambers, such as that of Constantine himself (which still survives at Trier, precisely because it later became a church: Plate 4) took this form, with the emperor installed in the apse, as did town council buildings and the public rooms of governors' palaces. For Christianity, adopting such a building form switched the emphasis in Christian gatherings from a potentially dynamic meeting in a house church of more or less equal members of a community – where prophesying and speaking in tongues might be readily expected – to attendance at Church services where the focus was upon ritual performances taking place in the apse (where the altar was naturally placed), in front of an assembled congregation.[59] These services were now conducted by bishops and clergy who increasingly chose themselves, rather than being elected – as in the early Church – by their congregations. By nature of both the higher social standing of clerical recruits as the fourth century progressed and the evolving character of their office, these clergy expected to exercise much greater discipline and authority over their congregations. Fourth-century texts likewise put much less emphasis on the older regimes of deep personal piety played out at home, which the earlier pattern of small, local group meetings in converted house churches had acted to reinforce.

In all these dimensions, while maintaining some important links with the past, Christianity radically reinvented itself after Constantine's declaration of belief. Sect became potential mass religion, and, in the process, turned itself – in anthropologists' jargon – from the kind of religious movement that utterly rejected physical creation and concerns of this world, into one more accepting of the idea that there could be real spiritual virtue in a 'good' life lived according to at least some of the more generally accepted norms of human existence, such as acquiring family and wealth.[60]

There remained, of course, genuine and important continuities. Christians in *c.* 400 revered the same basic set of authoritative texts that their predecessors had identified as uniquely genuine by the end of the second century, and their theological beliefs were the product of an organic process of doctrinal evolution. But in many respects – size of congregations, hierarchies of authority, definition of belief structures, patterns of spirituality, wealth and architecture – a Christian of even the mid-third century would have been dumbfounded by how different the religion was becoming by the early fifth.

'IF YOU (STILL) WANT TO BE PERFECT . . .'

There was no overall design behind these changes, no master plan instituted at Nicaea either to conceive them or to work out how they might be implemented. Nor did things change overnight. Our best evidence for the lengthy and intense induction ritual of pre-Constantinian-type Christianity is preserved in a mid-fourth-century text. The catechetical lectures of Bishop Cyril of Jerusalem (*c.* 350–86) collect the bishop's instructional teaching for those about to be baptized. Twenty-five years after Nicaea, he was still placing huge emphasis on a full understanding of both the detailed belief structures and appropriately pious lifestyles required of baptized Christians, and there is not yet any sign of the simplified forms of admission to Church membership which came to the fore in the next two centuries.[61] But the changes in standards, demands and devotional practice were already underway, and they had an underlying logic. To function as a mass religious movement, Christianity not only required clearly established doctrines and stronger authority structures, but also some lightening of the demands it generally made upon the bulk of its members.

It is a clear sign of the reforms' gathering momentum, however, that in the later fourth century they began to generate a major crisis of conscience among some leading Christian intellectuals and their lay supporters. The surprising catalyst was an obscure Egyptian landholder by the name of Antony, who heard, as his *Life* tells us, Matthew's story of Jesus' encounter with the rich young man (of camel fame) through the window of a Church. Stung, this was enough to drive him into the desert fringes of the cultivated Nile delta, where, echoing Christ's defeat of Satan in the wilderness of Judea, he devoted his life to overcoming the temptations of this world (which revolved, as ever, around sex, money and power). Antony's fame spread round the Mediterranean after his death thanks to a biography, the Greek version of which carried the imprimatur of Patriarch Athanasius of Alexandria, but which was soon translated into Latin as well.

The intensity of Antony's response to the Gospel raised some awkward questions about the developing patterns of later fourth-century Christianity compared to the desperate devotion of past Christians, above all the willingness of the martyrs – whose cults were now being increasingly celebrated liturgically with great enthusiasm – to suffer and die for their faith. As another commentator, Jerome, put it disapprovingly in his *Life of Malchus*: 'After reaching the Christian Emperors, [the Church] increased in influence and wealth but decreased in Christian virtues.'

Where was the same kind of martyrial devotion to the Lord to be found now, in a world where Christianity was apparently flourishing but, simultaneously, transforming itself into a much less demanding religion? For some, Antony and his fellow desert ascetics provided the answer. They were living martyrs, their biographies often consciously describing them in terms such as 'athlete of God' – the language in which martyrs (so often executed in Roman sports stadiums) had customarily been celebrated – who pointed the way forward to what 'real' Christian devotion should now look like in a post-Constantinian world, where persecution had vanished. In the final quarter of the fourth century, a barrage of Christian commentators – some of them appalling self-publicists like Jerome – jumped on the ascetic bandwagon, recommending different types of asceticism, and instructing how to find your own metaphorical desert, even if you were living in Rome. Just as those who resisted persecution in the earlier Church had naturally acquired an alternative, non-institutional form of religious authority as confessors (p. 38), so now ascetics acquired a similar authority, which challenged the general direction in which Christianity as a whole had begun to travel. (Although, in fact, it was more often those who celebrated them to others in their writings rather than the ascetics per se who gained this authority; Jerome's personal 'desert' consisted of living with a large library of books and some copyists close to the main road between Constantinople and Antioch.)[62]

In principle, this ascetic challenge threatened to derail the whole process that was currently turning Christianity into a viable mass religion, but, again via a series of local initiatives, it was eventually tamed by the emergent Christian mainstream. Asceticism as a general phenomenon could not simply be rejected, since the Bible – the canon of authoritative texts on which the entire Christian religion rested – offered too many examples of indisputably holy individuals who lived lives of ascetic renunciation in the wilderness: not only Christ when overcoming Satan's temptations, but John the Baptist and Old Testament prophets too, like Elijah whom the ravens fed. But it was possible to challenge, or plausibly even shut down, more radical strands of the ascetic movement, if asceticism was being practised in what was perceived as the wrong manner, or for the wrong reasons.

What, for instance, did the ascetics themselves think they were doing? A group in Asia Minor, led by the charismatic ascetic bishop Eustathius of Sebaste, was condemned at the local council of Gangra in 342 for letting women cut their hair, wear men's clothes and act as Christian priests. The condemnation concentrated on the offence to God's established social order of male superiority on earth, but the practices of the group are fascinating. For most Christian commentators, contrary to Augustine's teaching, Adam and Eve had not had sex in the Garden of Eden. Human sexuality, and the customary Mediterranean social order of male domination, were viewed straightforwardly as products of the Fall. It is possible, therefore, that Eustathius' group thought that they had reversed the effects of the Fall and achieved humanity's destined heavenly state here on earth, returning to the prelapsarian (what a wonderful word that is) level of virtue that God had originally implanted in his creatures, perhaps with a famous passage from Galatians 3:28 in mind: 'There is no longer Jew or Gentile, slave or free, male or female. For you are all one in Christ Jesus.'

For the mainstream Church, however, Eustathius' practices were a step too far: hence the condemnation. A Romano-British lay intellectual, Pelagius, likewise won fame and a following in early fifth-century Rome by advocating that individuals could – indeed must – follow the patterns of renunciation of Christ's own life as a personal model. The only sure path to Heaven, Pelagius argued, lay in living a perfect life following the example of Jesus and the disciples. This provoked a furious response from Augustine, who found this both far too optimistic an account of human nature – for him it was not possible for any individual to perfect themselves – and one that wrongly diminished the roles of divine grace and Christ's crucifixion in the salvation of humankind.

By moving robustly against some more radical ascetic groups – Priscillian, a fourth-century charismatic ascetic leader from Spain, was condemned and burnt alive for what were described as 'magical practices' (almost certainly he had engaged in nothing of the sort) – as well as by some carefully formulated general argumentation, asceticism was manoeuvred into less threatening forms.[63] By the early fifth century, mainstream Christian thinkers had come up with new arguments that robbed asceticism of much of its original power. Sheer asceticism for its own sake, they proposed, was not the point: it had to be a personal response to the overwhelming love of God, or it was all a wasted effort. Ammonius of Nitria, according to the collected sayings of the fourth- and early fifth-century Egyptian Desert Fathers, once asked Antony,

> 'Since my rule is stricter than yours, how is it that your name is better known amongst men than mine is?' Abba Antony answered, 'It is because I love God more than you.'[64]

Ascetics could be – and were – also accused of the besetting sin of pride in their own feats of religious endurance. If the point of all human life was to respond to the love of God, then looking after your own soul – which was the most obvious focus of solitary asceticism – offered little inherent opportunity for displaying what both Christ and Paul, in one of the most famous passages of the New Testament, identified as the greatest of all virtues (I Corinthians 13:4–7, 13):

> Love is patient, love is kind. It does not envy, it does not boast, it is not proud. It does not dishonour others, it is not self-seeking, it is not easily angered, it keeps no record of wrongs. Love does not delight in evil but rejoices with the truth. It always protects, always trusts, always hopes, always perseveres . . . these three remain: faith, hope and love. But the greatest of these is love.

Athanasius' biography had Antony covered on this important point by presenting him as the 'doctor of Egypt', a man whose virtues won so much favour from God that his prayers brought down a host of heavenly favours for others. This was a fair enough defence in its own way, but the criticisms of ascetic practice had real bite. By the early sixth century, the officially preferred form of asceticism in the eyes of leading Churchmen, as expressed in a whole series of statements issued at a wide range of Church councils, had become disciplined communal monasticism, not solitary asceticism. Monasticism had the virtue of putting a seasoned, authoritative abbot in charge of ascetic communities, to make sure that no dodgy beliefs or practices were being followed. Being a solitary hermit was still allowed under the new monastic regimes, but only after a long period of 'training' – i.e., conditioning alongside your fellow brethren in a small, potentially claustrophobic community for years, perhaps decades.[65]

Communal monasticism, in a number of different forms, will play an important role at many points in this narrative. In its initial fourth- and fifth-century manifestations, however, it played a crucial role in tempering the explosive impact of solitary asceticism upon the consciences of an influential strand of upper-class Christians. Equally important, it allowed influential thinkers like Augustine to put the whole ascetic enterprise into proper perspective. Wanting to respond to God's love for humankind with a life of total abstinence was no problem at all. But this couldn't be allowed to drift into criticism of other Christians who lacked the same kind of strength, and whose recent inclusion in the ranks of the Church had necessarily turned the religion away from the older, more intense patterns by which it had functioned when it was the preserve of a small sect of True Believers.[66]

By the end of the fourth century, the first of the three great phases of religious revolution which eventually created medieval European Christendom was gathering momentum. Constantine's public adoption of the Christian religion, and the removal of any further threat of continued persecution from the previously largely autonomous local congregations of earlier Christianity, had allowed new patterns of religious practice to come to the fore, ushered in by decisions taken at Nicaea and the longer-term processes they initiated. Greater communication between regional congregations, and alliance with the Roman state, pushed the evolving movement towards sharper, more unified doctrinal formation, and more effectively centralized institutional structures. At the same time, Christianity's expanding membership inevitably generated an overall easing of the terms of membership and led to greater intellectual détente with some of the more worldly concerns of everyday life. Fully to understand the late Roman revolution in Christianity, however, and to grasp why its legacy has played such a major role in Christian history, we need to ask who exactly were all these new recruits who signed up to Christianity in the fourth century, and why did they convert?

2

Conversion in a Christian Empire

Christian conversion is usually envisaged as a profound transformation of an individual's world-view generated by personal experiences of great intensity. The Gospels give us Jesus calling the disciples; the Acts of the Apostles Paul's vision on the road to Damascus. A general understanding of what a proper conversion ought to look like was thus fully formed by the start of the second century, and was further reinforced as the Christian Roman Empire came into being. Emperor Constantine witnessed a Cross in the sky (or sometimes said he did); the Egyptian Desert Father Antony heard the Gospel's call through the window of a church. The later fourth century saw the composition of the most sustained account ever written of an individual journey from intense doubt, through many sidetracks, to ultimate faith in the Christian God: the *Confessions* of St Augustine (b. 13 November 354), bishop of Hippo Regis (modern Bone in Algeria) from 396 to 430.

The *Confessions*, Augustine's autobiography, tells the story of a well-educated, serious-minded young Roman of lesser gentry stock from Thagaste, a small town in North Africa. His mother was Christian, but, in tune with practice at the time, he wasn't baptized as a child. Growing up, his developing love of the classical Latin language and literature – in which, like all his peers, he was intensively educated – made the Bible, then available only in inferior Latin translation, an unattractive and unconvincing source of spiritual truth (Augustine's Greek was not so hot, but the Greek Bible, too, was composed in everyday rather than educated language). Interested in philosophy, the young Augustine developed into a brilliant teacher of rhetoric, first in the regional capital of Carthage (from 375) and then in Rome (383) and Milan (384), cultural and political centres respectively of the western Empire. Rhetoric was the characteristic higher education of the imperial upper class (in Latin or Greek, depending on which half of the Empire you lived in). Though based on the advanced study of language and literature, it was understood in Graeco-Roman ideological terms – because of its focus on reasoned argument – as a necessary attribute of the fully rational, therefore civilized, individual. Working in a discipline with so much cultural cachet, a renowned teacher of rhetoric could hope to attract fame and fortune by being appointed to a lucrative endowed post in one of the Empire's great metropoles. He – and it was always a he – might even consequently attract enough imperial attention to win appointment to still more lucrative posts in the imperial bureaucracy.

On arriving in Milan, with his eyes still firmly set on winning the kind of attention from court grandees that this kind of career required, Augustine continued to delight, too, in the company of his long-term (but entirely anonymous) mistress, by whom he had a much-loved son, Adeodatus, the 'gift of God' (b. 372). A combination of these worldly preoccupations and dissatisfaction with his mother's Christianity – not least the wrathful God of the Old Testament – had also led him into flirtations both with Neo-Platonist philosophy, which looked for spiritual enlightenment in more traditional Graeco-Roman cults, and a dualist religion with vaguely Christian overtones: Manichaeism. Mani (*c.* 216–*c.* 274) was an Iranian prophet whose teachings bore some resemblance to those of the second-century Christian Gnostics, who understood the material world to have been created by a second, evil (though less powerful) God, and hence to be fundamentally flawed in its entire essence. For the young Augustine, this seemed to offer a more convincing explanation of the existence of evil than more orthodox Christianity. It also had the great advantage, like earlier Gnostic analogues (p. 29), of authorizing him to ditch the Old Testament as a text of religious authority. (The sometimes vengeful, often wrathful deity portrayed in many of its books was, according to Manichaeism, the lesser, evil God, seeking to trap human beings into the wrong course of action, not their true spiritual Father.) In his *Confessions*, Augustine exhaustively catalogues all these different stages in his spiritual evolution, the whole story mediated by a pervasive, intense introspection and punctuated by moments of deep anxiety and distress.[1]

Augustine's spiritual struggles eventually came to a head in August 386, in a house in Milan, where he was then living with a childhood friend, Alypius, and seeking favour at the court of the emperor Valentinian II. As he recalls in *Confessions*, a visitor told the young men about the effect that reading a Latin translation of the *Life of St Antony* had recently had on a small group of imperial civil servants. The men in question immediately abandoned promising careers to devote themselves to God's service. The story prompted a moment of particularly intense self-loathing in Augustine, who had previously been inspired by other stories of individuals giving up everything for Christ but had been unable, so far, to take the plunge himself. As he put it: 'You [i.e., God] set me before my face, so that I should see how vile I was, and how twisted and filthy, covered in sores and ulcers. And I looked and was appalled, but there was no way of escaping from myself' (*Confessions* 8.7.16).

Eventually, the two friends dragged themselves out into the garden, but Augustine eventually left Alypius, wanting to weep on his own as he contemplated his own inability to leave the world behind.

> I threw myself down somehow under a certain fig-tree, and let my tears flow freely. Rivers streamed from my eyes, a sacrifice acceptable to you [Psalm 51:17] . . . I felt my past to have a grip on me. It uttered wretched cries: 'How long, how long is it to be?' 'Tomorrow, tomorrow.' 'Why not now? Why not an end to my impure life in this very hour?' (8.12.28)

In the depths of this despair,

> Suddenly I heard a voice from the nearby house chanting as it might be of a boy or a girl (I do not know which), saying and repeating over and over again, 'Pick up and read; pick up and read.'

Taking this strange children's song as a message to himself, Augustine went back into the house and picked up his copy of Paul's New Testament Epistles,

> I seized it, opened it and in silence read the first passage on which my eyes lit. 'Not in riots and drunken parties, not in eroticisms and indecencies, not in strife and rivalry; but put on the Lord Jesus Christ, and make no provision for the flesh and its lusts.' (8.12.29)

He had opened the book at Romans (13:13–14), whose message could not have been clearer. With God's help, Augustine found the courage to take the final, decisive steps on his spiritual journey. He parted from his mistress (after over a decade together) but kept his teenage son with him. The following Easter, father and son were baptized, along with a small group of friends, in the cathedral of Milan. (Adeodatus died the following year, aged sixteen.)

Augustine was one of the most sophisticated intellects of his age. Given that *Confessions* was composed much later than the actual moment of his conversion, it is no surprise that the story shows signs of self-conscious, artful construction. Shortly after his garden experience, so *Confessions* goes, Augustine retreated to a rural villa at Cassiacum (just outside Milan) with a small group of family and friends: an enterprise modelled, to judge by the philosophical dialogues it generated, far more on a Platonizing philosophical community than anything we might now recognize as a Christian monastery. His continuing spiritual journey, from philosophical contemplation to the Christian bishop that he later became, gets no coverage in his story, which stops at this point. For *Confessions* was written with a specific purpose in mind. When Augustine returned to North Africa in the early 390s, he came to occupy a prominent position as spokesman for the official Nicene Church in a series of high-profile religious disputes. But he had left Carthage decades before as a known Manichaean heretic: *Confessions* was written not least to do all the necessary explaining for his intervening conversion, and more. It is a carefully crafted text, into which Augustine poured all his skills as a trained teacher of rhetoric, as well as drawing on strong pre-existing models – the Bible, the *Life of Antony* – of what a 'good' Christian conversion *ought* to look like. Nonetheless, for all this craft, the basic garden story rings true. There was far too much at stake for Augustine to engage in outright fabrication, and nor is there any doubting the overall intensity of the spiritual journey and of the fundamental changes of lifestyle and direction that eventually brought him back to Africa as a Christian bishop.[2]

Nonetheless, *Confessions* is also singular in the extreme, and we need to be wary of taking it as any kind of model for how and why the majority of the new Roman Christians of the post-Constantinian era came to the faith. An alternative, potentially much more revealing late Roman conversion story concerns one of my favourite characters from the vast acreages of literature that have come down to us from the period: a certain Pegasios, bishop of Ilios (ancient Troy) in the 350s and early 360s.

Pegasios is known only from his cameo appearance in a single letter written by Emperor Julian, son of Constantine's half-brother, whose own carefully concealed conversion to paganism in the early 350s sheds so much light on the political calculation behind Constantine's revelation of his Christian allegiance between 306 and 324 (p. 16). Sometime in 362/3 Pegasios, the Christian bishop of his home city, applied for a job in the new-style pagan priesthood that Julian, now entirely open about his non-Christian religious allegiance, had just begun to establish. The emperor wrote the letter to assure his officials in Constantinople that Pegasios was an appropriate candidate for the position of pagan priest. Pegasios had a reputation as a Christian bishop who had been destroying pagan temples, which made the officials want to reject his application; the emperor was writing to banish their doubts.

Julian and Pegasios had first met almost a decade previously. In 354, Julian had been summoned to the imperial court at Milan by his cousin, the then emperor Constantius II. At that point, he was studying Greek philosophy with various teachers in Asia Minor, and the journey to Italy took him so close to the legendary city of Troy that he decided to visit its monuments. He did not go just as a tourist. The *Iliad* and *Odyssey* are full of divine manifestations and interference in the affairs of humankind; allegorically interpreted, the poems had become key religious texts for educated pagans of the late Roman period.[3]

Julian was at that point under the impression that all the city's pagan sanctuaries were in ruins. But, on arrival, he was greeted by Bishop Pegasios – completely unknown to him previously – who conducted Julian to a temple dedicated to the Trojan hero Hector. Far from being destroyed, Julian wrote, 'I found that the altars were still alight, I might almost say blazing, and that the statue of Hector had been anointed till it shone.' The same turned out to be true of a second temple, dedicated to Athena, where Julian noticed that – unlike most Christians, who regarded pagan gods as demons – Bishop Pegasios did not cross himself or hiss to ward off evil spirits. Then, on the final stop of the tour:

> Pegasios went with me to the temple of Achilles as well and showed me the tomb in good repair; yet I had been informed that this also had been pulled to pieces by him. But he approached it with great reverence . . . and I have heard . . . that he also used to offer prayers to Helios [in Julian's theology, the supreme sun god] and worship him in secret.

What religious label should we apply to Pegasios, and how should we understand his religious journey from Christian bishop to pagan priest that emerges from the letter? Not only did it take Pegasios in the opposite direction to Augustine – away from Christianity – but there is no sign of the same kind of spiritual angst which attended the latter's every move. As bishop of Ilios, Pegasios had happily tended the city's pagan shrines and, when a new job opportunity appeared in the early 360s in the form of Julian's pagan priesthood, the Christian bishop happily seized it. Based on the letter – and this is the sum total of our knowledge – a whole range of scenarios are more or less equally possible. The most common has been to suppose that Pegasios was a closet pagan. Alternatively, Pegasios may not really have cared about religion in the slightest and was simply interested in holding any position that added to his prestige within his hometown of Ilios. After all, Constantine had tried to turn bishops into major figures in local society (p. 41) and Julian was looking to do the same with his new pagan priesthood.

A third possibility, however, is that Pegasios' own belief structures allowed him, without a major issue of conscience, to serve either as Christian bishop or as pagan priest. As Christianity began to spread through the imperial upper classes, their many surviving writings show that it was far from uncommon for traditionally educated Romans of the fourth century to generate their own amalgams of Christianity and classical culture. This was more or less what Augustine did during the several months he and his friends spent at Cassiacum, his initial conversion leading to a classicizing philosophical take on what Christian conversion might mean in practice: reading, thinking and writing philosophical dialogues with a select group of companions in the attractive seclusion of an *agriturismo*. Augustine eventually decided that this wasn't proper Christianity and went on to hold a bishopric back in North Africa. Other upper-class Roman Christians, however, found that adopting Christianity didn't mean having to disrupt their customary lifestyles. An older contemporary of Augustine's was a fellow teacher of rhetoric by the name of Ausonius. He moved from the university of Bordeaux to become tutor to the son of Emperor Valentinian I at the imperial court at Trier, and then eventually to hold high office in the imperial bureaucracy in the 370s. In this, he exemplified the kind of career path Augustine had in mind when he first journeyed to Milan. Throughout, Ausonius remained Christian, but his surviving literary output shows him writing in all the traditional genres of classical literature, with lots of reference to gods, goddesses and all the core texts of the classical (as opposed to the Christian) literary canon. Less New Testament; more Virgil, Cicero, Livy and Ovid. Looking at Ausonius' literary output, and general lifestyle, there's not much sign that, for him, being Christian demanded any real change at all. In much the same way, a generation later, an educated east Roman called Synesius became bishop of his hometown of Cyrene in the province of Libya – this, despite having substantial doubts about standard Christian teachings on such fundamental matters as how souls were created, whether the Resurrection was literally true, and the ending of the world on the Day of Judgement. Not only was Bishop Synesius able to square these scruples with the duties of episcopal office (although he did promise not to air them in his sermons), but those who elected him knew all about his reservations yet were happy for him to become bishop.

Many different answers to these fundamental questions were clearly floating about. Ausonius had a younger protégé, Paulinus of Nola, who eventually decided that being Christian meant breaking decisively with the normal rhythms of upper-class life. He became a bishop, lived in celibacy with his wife and devoted himself to the cult of the martyr saint Victor, as well as (much to Ausonius' chagrin) ceasing to write in the established classical genres. The fourth century was clearly full of upper-class, recently converted Romans putting together personalized combinations of their new religion with inherited cultural forms and belief.[4]

Putting Pegasios in the context of these other fourth-century

Christian conversions introduces a major cultural phenomenon that will play a recurring role of profound importance in the story of emerging European Christendom. At first sight, conversion sounds like a one-way street: an individual rejecting one set of beliefs and embracing another. But in every case we've just encountered – even that of Augustine, in the Cassiacum period at least – change was not absolute. Greater or lesser amounts of existing cultural baggage were imported – sometimes accidentally, sometimes quite deliberately – from previous religious or cultural allegiances into the new one, so that, in practice, most conversions turn out to be fascinating mixtures of the new and the old. This sometimes attracts the umbrella term 'syncretism', from the Greek for 'mixing together'. In some Christian writing, syncretism has utterly pejorative connotations, signifying an incomplete or imperfect conversion that allows non-Christian cultural elements to survive where they should not. It also tends to lump together a range of similar but not identical phenomena: from the unconscious persistence of old cultural habits, which may or may not be shorn of their original significance, to the conscious intellectual choices of a Synesius of Cyrene and everything in between.[5]

Conversion, in other words, is a deceptively simple word. For every Augustine, there is potentially a Pegasios, and also a Synesius. Conversion to Christianity clearly meant a wide range of things to different fourth-century Romans. To arrive at a fuller understanding of what was going on in the decades after Constantine, we need to take a closer look at both the nature and the underlying causes of the processes by which Constantine's new religion began to win more converts.

PATTERNS OF CONVERSION

It's impossible to generate a detailed, blow-by-blow account of Christian conversion in the years after 324, but some outlines of what unfolded are clear enough. Most importantly, the two political generations after Constantine saw no systematic extension of Christian religious structures – churches, and the priests to animate them – into the Roman countryside. Across much of the vast rural acreage of the Roman west, the fourth and fifth centuries saw few or no churches built. The only archaeological signs of rural Christianity are chapels (many of which have been found in Spain, Piedmont and even as far afield as Lullingstone in Kent) and burial complexes attached to rural villas, of which one astounding example has emerged recently at Carranque in Spain. Such buildings were built by and for members of the Roman landowning elite; there is not the slightest sign of any calculated attempt to spread Christianity to the Roman peasantry in the fourth century, most of whom can only have remained resolutely pagan. The often-cited *Life* of Bishop Vigilius of Trent (modern Trento) even records the nasty fate of three Christian missionaries sent by Bishop Vigilius (353–405) into the city's rural alpine hinterland in the early fifth century: attempting to preach the Gospel, they were burnt alive. Much of the west Roman countryside, if not so brutally hostile, simply had no opportunity to become Christian at all.[6]

There was clearly some – though not actually measurable – increase in Christian numbers both in the towns, where many communities acquired bishops for the first time (only about a third of the Empire's cities had a bishop at the time of the council of Nicaea), and in those limited rural areas – such as Egypt, North Africa and Asia Minor – where Christianity had already made some headway. But, before the last quarter of the fourth century, there is no sign – even in cities with ancient Christian communities such as Antioch – that Christianity became the dominant religion, while surviving evidence indicates that here too syncretic religious patterns remained common. A fourth-century curse tablet, discovered in the hot water spring at Bath, hexes a thief 'whether he be Christian or pagan', in what had clearly become a formulaic expression. (The tablet was found in the entirely pagan context of a temple dedicated to Sulis Minerva.) In later fourth-century Antioch, likewise, much of the population was still enjoying the full range of available religious festivals – Christian, Jewish and pagan – much to the annoyance of its Christian clergy; while fourth-century religious amulets from Egypt, catering for all religious persuasions, were produced with Christian symbols on one side, and their pagan counterparts on the other (Plate 6).[7]

The impression these historical oddments convey is sustained by a more detailed look at everything we know about fourth-century Roman Egypt, whose hot, dry sand preserves a much wider range of evidence, particularly unofficial evidence, for religious practice than anything to have survived from other parts of the Empire. Egyptian religion had already been pushed in new directions in the third century AD, as the financial consequences of a major military crisis began to bite. From the 230s onwards, the rise of a new dynasty in the neighbouring Persian Empire had massively increased the level of threat faced by Rome on its main eastern frontiers in Mesopotamia and Armenia. The resulting struggles over the next few decades saw the destruction of three major Roman expeditionary armies, forced the abandonment of not insubstantial territories, and led to the deaths on campaign of two emperors and the capture of a third, Valerian, who was led round in ceremonial chains behind his Persian master. By the end of the century, Rome had finally restored stability to its eastern frontier, but only at the cost of a major military expansion: in the decades after 230, the size of its army grew by somewhere between 50 and 100 per cent. Given that the Empire had always had to spend around 75 per cent of its tax revenues on the military, such an enormous expansion in troop numbers could not but generate a matching fiscal crisis, which set the imperial authorities scrabbling round for every source of revenue they could find.

One readily available pot of cash consisted of the remaining public endowments of the ancient Egyptian temples, which dated back to the age of the Pharaohs. These had been 'nationalized' as early as the reign of Augustus in the first years of the first century AD, and their coffers raided sporadically ever since. What monies remained were finally confiscated in the mid-third century, with the result that major elements of existing pagan practice collapsed: funded festivals dried up, and traditional Egyptian priestly families found new ways to make a living. The first study to examine this material systematically concluded that, as a result, non-Christian religion as a whole had already collapsed in Egypt by the early fourth century, which allowed Constantine's new imperial faith to expand into a religious vacuum. Closer examination, however, has prompted a different conclusion. The total picture of religious life in fourth-century Egypt can be more accurately characterized as one of 'active' syncretism.

There are signs of a significantly expanding Christian religiosity – more bishops, churches, monasteries and baptisms too. Likewise, naming patterns in certain Egyptian regions also show a switch towards Christian rhythms, with names of apostles and martyrs growing in popularity. But all these signs of growing Christianity coexisted in the Egyptian countryside with deeply entrenched traditional understandings of harmful and beneficial divine power, and of the most effective forms of ritual behaviour and communication to mobilize or ward them off. Taken as a whole, the evidence suggests that Christian conversion at most bolted some elements of a new religious piety onto an established world-view, rather than generating any more profound reconstruction of relations between humanity and the divine.

The broader evidence base demonstrates, likewise, great continuity in local temple and traditional religious rites throughout the fourth century, despite the confiscated endowments and an increasingly visible Christian establishment. In sum, the general population continued to practise many of the old, existing patterns of religious behaviour, with only the mildest of Christian glosses. Abbot Shenoute, of the great White Monastery in Upper Egypt, complained about monks who were producing magical amulets for the general population. Practical guidebooks to magic also survive, which combine traditional forms of divination with new Christian alternatives under the one cover: according to the consumer's taste, Christian or non-Christian practices – or both – could be employed to achieve the desired effect. And while the range of evidence may be fullest from Egypt, there is every reason to suppose that similarly syncretic religious patterns prevailed more generally. In Asia Minor for instance, another region with some more established Christian communities, mid-fourth-century regional councils at Gangra and Laodicea (in particular) felt it necessary to condemn a range of syncretic behaviours. The assembled leaders anathematized everybody from Judaizing Christians, who rested on the Jewish Sabbath and ate unleavened bread on Jewish feast days, to Christian priests who, like some of their Egyptian peers, practised fortune-telling and made magical amulets. As at Antioch in the same era, it was common practice for congregations to attend all the major festivals alike: Christian, Jewish, even pagan. All of which complicates the concept of conversion still further. Not only might there be different levels of intensity of conversion – as demonstrated by the range of documented individual examples from Augustine to Pegasios – but conversion as a whole was often a surprisingly two-way process.[8]

Syncretic, two-way patterns of religious change clearly operated among the elites of the Roman Empire; in this, Augustine, Pegasios and their peers were the rule rather than the exceptions. A Codex Calendar from the year 354, produced in Rome for a member of the city's senatorial class, combines pagan astrological markers and festivals with commemorations both of saints and the relics of martyrs. Pagan visual imagery likewise turns up in Christian contexts in the Church of St Constanza at Rome and in Christian catacombs on the Via Latina. The mid-fourth century also saw attempts to render the Bible into a Latin verse form that was less painful to elite ears than existing translations.[9] Much more important than any of these particular examples, however, is the systematically syncretic outcome that emerged in response to the single greatest issue facing potential elite Roman converts in these years. How much of the classical culture and its justificatory ideologies, which played such a central role in their lives and outlooks, could legitimately be retained following conversion? The eventual answer to this question not only smoothed the path to widespread elite conversion; it also had a profound impact upon the further development of Christianity itself.

As we've already seen with Augustine, members of the Roman landowning elite were customarily educated in either Greek or Latin language and literature, depending on the half of the Empire into which they were born. Trained slaves taught basic reading and writing, but the core of a well-established elite curriculum was delivered in the schoolrooms of grammarians (from whom the more ambitious or more talented might move on to study under a rhetor like Augustine), who used intense study of a small body of set texts over several years to train their students in carefully defined forms of 'correct' Latin or Greek (the ancient grammarians' definitions of 'correct' Latin or Greek endings are still taught in modern schoolrooms). Richer students then customarily moved on to higher-level studies, traditionally in rhetoric and philosophy (taking courses with several different teachers, who were mostly self-employed) but, increasingly, in Roman law as well (with just a few students pursuing other high-level subjects such as medicine and astronomy). Such higher-level studies were available in a limited number of bigger cities of the Empire: usually where substantial public libraries were available and sometimes also publicly funded teaching posts. The cost of books (usually papyrus scrolls) was so prohibitive that teachers could never afford large personal libraries, instead gathering where public book collections were available for themselves and their students to use. In the western Empire, these cities included Rome, Milan and, eventually, Ravenna in Italy, along with Bordeaux, Lyons and Trier in Gaul. In the east, Athens, Alexandria and Antioch were long-standing centres of academic excellence, while Constantinople too was soon equipped with libraries and its own public teaching chairs. Beirut quickly emerged as a centre of legal studies, and many of the other old Greek cities of the eastern Mediterranean also boasted long-standing academic traditions.

In functional terms, this meant that the late Roman elite spoke and wrote artificial, literary forms of both languages. Everyday language had already moved on, in the west towards Romance/vulgate Latin and in the east to a simpler Greek vernacular, largely because evolving pronunciation patterns meant that the differences between many of the grammatically 'correct' endings could no longer be heard. Mastering these artificial languages, and the narrow literary canons through which they were learned, took five or more years of expensive, private education. But in the Romans' own understanding, this education, which allowed members of the landowning elite to recognize one another as soon as they opened their mouths and provided students with a wealth of shared allusions and in-jokes, was far more than just an elite caste marker. Grammarians – and the rhetors and philosophers at the centres for higher-level studies – not only taught language and literature but used their texts to transmit shared moral values and a common understanding of how their educational wares created undeniably superior human beings. Language and grammar were used to teach an introduction to formal logic – and therefore, so the justificatory ideology went, only the grammarians could create fully rational human beings, who had achieved a level of civilization that was simply unavailable to fellow humans excluded from its benefits. The Latin model closely followed its Greek antecedent, so that members of the late Roman elite were inculcated with the same value system, whatever the language of their education.

In the full articulation of this ideological system, it was precisely because Rome protected this uniquely superior way of life that the Divinity took such a direct interest in the fate of the Empire as to guarantee victory for its legitimate ruler (see p. 13). It was also a direct reflection of the power of this cultural self-understanding that emperors in particular, but also other grandees, wanted to fund the public libraries that made the centres of higher-level studies possible. Far more than functioning libraries in the modern sense, these institutions were usually housed in grand, spacious edifices, where the books didn't take up too much room, and were set alongside famous works of art, including statues of their founders. To establish a library was not only to show off your own wealth. It also demonstrated that you were a person who understood the importance of the rationalizing culture that book collections did so much to sustain.[10]

Because this shared elite culture was so central to the Roman elite's understanding of what made them superior, the question of how much value could continue to be placed on it after Christian conversion rapidly became complicated. On the face of it, Christianity celebrated an alternative wisdom that was accessible to, and might even be more effectively received by, the completely uneducated (as were so many of Jesus' disciples), direct from God. But the late Roman grammarians' position was based on nearly a thousand years of an elite's self-understanding of its own superiority, which was not easily jettisoned. As the fourth century unfolded, elite Christian converts initially came up with a variety of different answers on the extent to which their inherited value system was compatible with their new religion. For some more intellectual individuals, like the Augustine of the Cassiacum period, or his older contemporary Marius Victorinus, it seemed that classical philosophy could be understood as offering an attractive path towards the Christian God, operating in parallel with the teachings of the Church, and Ausonius, as we have seen, found his new religion entirely compatible with old cultural forms. But for others, the lines between the two discourses hardened. Soon after 350, Bishop Basil of Caesarea wrote a manual on an education in Greek literature that greatly downplayed the old emphasis placed on it as the unique path to a superior, civilized life; so too, in his own way, did Augustine in his post-Cassiacum years. (Ausonius, by contrast, was deeply offended by Paulinus of Nola's decision to abandon the old norms of upper-class literary activity.) But, through all this, the long-established structures of upper-class education carried on uninterrupted, because of the central role it continued to play in distinguishing the elite from everyone else – and, where there was any incompatibility, for many people its tenets continued to take priority over the alternative offerings of Christianity.[11]

Despite some moments of hostility, therefore, Roman elite conversion was ultimately characterized by an important degree of syncretism, which saw its existing cultural patterns carried over into the new religious era in two key ways. First, in terms of religious practice, most pre-Christian religious devotion in the Roman world was private rather than public. Only the Capitoline and imperial cults, deemed essential to the safety of the state, ranked as public and received state financial support. Every other cultic act belonged to the private realm and was governed by private choice. This same basic pattern continued to prevail as the Roman elite switched its allegiance to Christianity. In the countryside, as we've seen, this manifested itself in the construction of private chapels within villa complexes, served by privately recruited priests. The fourth century saw no developing parish church network, just a dotting of private Christian chapels paid for by Christian Roman landowners who, as the new religion spread, gradually replaced their old, equally private pagan household shrines (sometimes literally: the fourth-century Christian chapel at Lullingstone villa was built directly on top of its old pagan nymphaeum).

In the cities, too, newly Christian members of the Roman elite often avoided the institutional Church. In Rome itself one elite convert, the philosopher Marius Victorinus, even asked whether it was necessary to go to church at all to be a Christian. He eventually decided that it was – but his bishop was willing to baptize him privately, to avoid embarrassing such a great man by forcing him to mix with the plebs. Others solved the problem in a different way. Aside from the great basilicas with which Constantine endowed the city, most church building in fourth- and fifth-century Rome came in the form of its famous *tituli*: district-level foundations that later became the basis of a network of parish churches across the city. Contrary to older interpretations, however, this was not a centrally directed expansion of church provision, organized by the bishop of Rome for the general good of his flock, but a set of private chapels constructed by individual members of the Roman elite for their own use, endowed with their own privately commissioned church plate (sometimes on an extraordinarily lavish scale), and employing their own priests. This makes perfect sense, both of the geographically random spread of the early *tituli* across the city – there being no attempt to provide any general or uniform coverage – and of the literary evidence we have for the hothouse nature of Christian religiosity in later fourth-century Rome. This saw competing intellectuals and holy men, like Jerome and Pelagius, orbiting around upper-class patrons of great wealth and power, in ways which made them essentially independent of the regular Church authorities. Many of these patrons were female, leading the theologian Jerome to refer disparagingly to the *senatus matronum* – the senate of matrons – who effectively ran Christianity in the city of Rome. (Jerome, who eventually lost out in the struggle for these patrons' favour, had to retreat to the Holy Land to create an alternative career for himself after the death – possibly from bulimia – of one young lady to whom he'd been giving dietary advice on ascetic practice.)[12]

Upper-class Christianity in Constantinople followed similar patterns. The bishop of Constantinople – who, along with the bishop of Rome, was one of the five patriarchs of late Roman Christianity – only gained full control of the churches of his city in the sixth century. Up to that point, many were independent, elite foundations, constructed for private use. And while emperors were responsible for bringing some important martyr relics to the city, many others ended up in private chapels. The lady Eusebia, born and married into senatorial rank, brought the bodies of the Forty Martyrs of Sebaste – imperial troopers supposedly martyred by Constantine's final enemy, Licinius – to Constantinople; and Caesarius, the Praetorian prefect who had at one point acted as regent for the entire Empire, those of St Thysias. Although we don't have the same kind of literary evidence as for Rome – nothing similar to the density of letters provided by Augustine and Jerome – the city's Christian life seems likewise to have functioned on the basis of competing imperial and upper-class religious salons, looking to attract and patronize the most important Christian leaders of the day. In this environment, even the patriarch remained a relatively marginal figure, not at the centre of the most important Christian developments in the city, and he could easily find himself in trouble if he annoyed the wrong patrons. This was the case even for such an important individual as the famous preacher John Chrysostom (now an untouchable bastion of orthodoxy in the modern Greek Church). After a distinguished career as bishop of Antioch, Chrysostom became patriarch of Constantinople in 397, but then managed to alienate Empress Eudoxia, wife of the emperor Arcadius, to such an extent that he found himself sent into exile not once but twice: first briefly in 403, and then permanently from 405 until his death two years later.[13]

While the Roman landowning class was steadily converting to Christianity in the decades after Constantine's conversion, it did so firmly on its own terms, with apparently only limited engagement with the existing institutional Church. However, a second, even more significant syncretic dimension was added to the overall process of its conversion, because the educational culture of the Roman upper class quickly became fundamental to the further development of the new religion it was adopting in increasing numbers.

The first wave of elite fourth-century converts could be scathing in their denunciations of the grammarians' educational wares. Augustine, Paulinus of Nola, Jerome and Basil of Caesarea all rejected the grandiose claim that grammarians alone could produce perfected, divinely rational humans. For Augustine, the veils hung at the entrances of schools of literature 'do not signify the prestige of elite teaching so much as the covering up of error' (*Confessions* 1.15.22). (Veils were customarily used in the Roman world to emphasize the sacred nature of what was contained behind them: hence the force of Augustine's inversion.) He developed his point, focusing on the shocking behaviour of various classical gods and goddesses recorded in the texts that grammarians studied so earnestly: 'If [the grammarians] described [the gods'] lusts in a rich vocabulary of well-constructed prose with a copious and ornate style, they received praise and congratulated themselves' (*Confessions* 1.18.28).

Such condemnations belong to the era when Christianity was still establishing itself among the Roman elite, when the grammarians' value systems seemed to represent an obstacle to proper Christian reverence for the potential wisdom of the unlearned. By the fifth century, however, Christian commentators had not only ceased to complain about the grammarians but had begun to see their schoolrooms as a necessary source of those well-educated young men who increasingly dominated the leadership of the Church as bishops and other higher clergy. As a standard trope of the time put it, the point was not to do away with grammarians, but to attract their pupils subsequently to 'more serious' Christian studies; a turn to the Bible after Cicero and Virgil rather than an outright rejection of the initial training offered in classical letters.[14] Over time the classical schoolroom even became central to the further development of Christianity itself, because the manner in which late Roman Christian commentators approached the Bible increasingly drew inspiration from the ways in which grammarians edited and interpreted their own canons of Greek and Latin texts.

The grammarians' standard mode of study, honed over the centuries, is set out in late Roman discussions of their art – *artes grammaticae* – and in some of the surviving commentaries on key texts. First, the student carefully prepared the chosen text for reading aloud (a discipline known as *lectio*, which was no small feat because Roman manuscripts did not contain punctuation or word breaks). The text in question was then explored for interesting linguistic and rhetorical features and important historical, cultural, moral and religious content (*enarratio*), before being emended, if necessary, to bring it into line with 'correct' Latin or to correct any errors of fact (*emendatio*). The student was then in a position to bring out the full importance of the text within the culturally canonical corpus (*iudicium*). All of which proved a perfect tool for tackling a major intellectual problem at the heart of developing Christianity.

Early Christianity, as we've seen, had successfully defined a recognized canon of sacred texts by the end of the second century: affirming both its claim to be the realization of the Jewish tradition by retaining the Old Testament, while excluding some of the wilder accounts of who Jesus was and how his existence would bring humanity to eternal life. That was only the first stage. The various books of the Old and New Testament had been written at different moments, in wildly different contexts, and with very different authorial agendas, over the best part of a thousand years. The oldest books of the Old Testament date back (probably) to the sixth or seventh century BC, while some of the New Testament belongs to the early second century AD. And the Old Testament, crucially, had not originally been written with its subsequent role in Christianity in mind. All of which meant that trying to work out how key Old Testament passages could be understood as foretelling the appearance of a crucified Messiah – as was already being done in the first century (p. 28) – was only a first move in turning this inchoate mass of material into a structured, coherent body of teachings in which you could find definitive guidance concerning not only correct Christian belief, but also the proper forms of a good Christian life. The need to distil a vision of correct Christian behaviour out of Holy Scripture (*paranaesis*, as the process was known) was as great a stimulus to biblical study as the need to forge a unified set of theological doctrines. However, there was also the additional problem that various Christian communities had made their own translations of the Jewish scriptures (from Hebrew into Greek and Latin) and the New Testament (from Greek into Latin) at different moments, meaning that there was not even a recognized received text of the Holy Scriptures with which to work.

In tackling such intellectual problems, Christian thinkers adapted the grammarians' techniques of textual criticism. Such borrowings of technique had already begun before Constantine with Hippolytus (*c.* 170–235) in the third-century Latin west, and his much more famous contemporary Origen (*c.* 184–253) in the Greek east. Origen focused on trying to establish authoritative texts, and on exploring and reconciling the various component books of the newly defined Christian canon of the Old and New Testaments to identify and bring out a unified underlying message.[15] The techniques of the grammarians materially assisted both endeavours because what they specialized in, having once established a corrected text, was a whole series of possible ways of reading any passage – literally, figuratively, allegorically, prophetically, via innumerable exhaustively defined figures of speech – to bring out its fundamental meaning – or, to be precise, what any particular interpreter might want to identify as its fundamental meaning – from a series of potential alternative readings. The grammarians had been doing this for centuries with the texts of Homer and Plato, making particular use of allegory to generate a series of religious and moral teachings. Through these mechanisms, they identified the underlying unity of the divine wisdom they were passing on to their pupils. (In reality, however, this unity had been created out of disparate and often contradictory materials by a highly creative, drawn-out process of competitive interpretation, in which all the different possible ways of reading the key texts were slowly winnowed down to extract the oneness of meaning sought.)

Origen, the greatest, most prolific biblical scholar of the third century, wanted to establish a uniquely Christian education system, in which the borrowed techniques of the classical grammarians would be taught solely through Scripture and a developing Christian commentary tradition, of which Origen himself was a pioneer. But grammarians already existed in large numbers – one per substantial market town within the Empire, more or less – and, especially as upper-class conversion to Christianity proceeded, soon ceased to look like promoters of a dangerous alternative value system. There was no reason to reinvent the wheel. The great labour of scriptural commentary, of reconciling the differences between and bringing out the various dimensions of Truth that God had hidden within the Old and New Testaments, was increasingly taken up by the products of the classical schoolroom as the fourth century progressed. This new breed of Christian intellectuals (which included Augustine and Jerome, despite their overt rejection of their classical education) struggled not only technically to establish authoritative texts (Jerome is famous for going back to the Hebrew originals to try to establish better Latin translations of the Old Testament), but also creatively. How, for instance, was the vengeful, occasionally violent God portrayed in the Old Testament to be reconciled with Jesus' teachings about love and forgiveness in the Gospels? Biblical commentary, the creative reconciliation of the parts into a greater, unified whole, was likewise at the heart of all the great controversies that unfolded as Christianity first became a mass religion in the aftermath of Constantine's conversion. A convincing non-literal exposition of texts such as 'if thine eye offend thee, pluck it out' had to be offered if the ascetic impulse within the religion was to be prevented from turning into a condemnation of the mass of ordinary Christians.[16]

For instance, the great fourth-century 'Arian' dispute over Trinitarian doctrine proceeded fundamentally by biblical commentary, because the whole dispute revolved around rival readings of major biblical texts. Three of the Gospels – the synoptics: Matthew, Mark and Luke – present a Jesus who is Christ but who, at the same time, is deeply human. These Gospels of course support his divinity, but it is their Jesus who prays to God the Father in the Garden of Gethsemane: 'Not my will be done, but Thy will.' If we just had these three Gospels, you could still end up with a Trinity, but it would never have been an equal one. The Nicene position, by contrast, depended on privileging Jesus' portrayal in the Gospel of John, which throughout, not least in its magnificent opening – 'In the Beginning was the Word, and the Word was with God, and the Word was God' – presents the reader (or hearer) with a much more equal relationship between Father and Son. Either way, the intellectual problem is the same. To generate a fully coherent picture of the relationship between God the Father and God the Son, the apparently different Jesus of the synoptics has to be reinterpreted in the light of the Gospel of John, or vice versa. In the Arian dispute, both sides went to war with the same weapons: assembling lists of proof texts from elsewhere in the Bible, which apparently supported their preferred position, and deploying allegorical, figurative and metaphorical readings of those passages that, read literally, didn't seem to square with their position.

For present purposes, which side eventually won out is much less important than how the process unfolded. Fundamentally, the literary-analytical techniques of the grammarian were deployed in the middle and later years of the fourth century to resolve a deep inconsistency – when the texts were read literally – in the biblical presentation of the relationship between Father and Son. The argument was eventually resolved in favour of John, but the length of the post-Nicene debate – it was a good fifty years, as we saw in the previous chapter, before its definition of the Faith won full acceptance – makes clear that neither side, both of whom were deploying the same techniques of reading, had arguments of immediately overwhelming power.[17]

Even if we can't say anything very precise in terms of actual numbers of converts, therefore, a range of sources brings the broad character of the unfolding conversion processes of the mid-fourth century firmly into view. As yet, much of the peasantry – the vast majority of the Empire's population – remained outside the loop, and even where Christianity was making some rural headway (Egypt, North Africa and parts of Asia Minor), it did so in highly syncretic forms that directly echoed local pre-Christian spiritualities, and often co-existed with still-functioning traditional religious institutions and practices. The basic character of the elite conversion process was similar in principle. Much of it unfolded outside, and partly in competition with, the increasingly episcopal-dominated structures of the official Church, as the elite maintained long-standing traditions of private worship. Over time, too, the weight of elite value systems proved impossible to reject. As a result, just as pre-Christian peasant pieties influenced the new religious forms that helped turn Christianity from a small religious sect into a functional mass religion, so the textual editing and analytical techniques of the grammarian greatly accelerated and standardized ongoing processes of finding in Scripture both theological truth and necessary guidance on proper Christian behaviour.

The highly syncretic nature of the fourth-century conversion process is a major historical phenomenon in itself. But it also prompts another, equally important question. Why did Christian conversion gather pace, especially among the Roman imperial elite, in the decades after Constantine's declaration of a Christian allegiance?

In the nineteenth century, when the first scholarly histories of Christianity were being written, there was barely any need to ask this question. At that point, the Christian religion – even if divided into several post-Reformation variants – remained completely dominant across the European landmass and was spreading rapidly worldwide on a rising tide of European imperialism. In such a context, the reason why Christianity had spread in the late Roman era seemed obvious: because it was the 'true' – or at the very least a 'better' – religion compared to its competitors. This kind of reflex answer is no longer possible, and not just for the culturally relativist reason that asserting the overwhelming virtues of one's own cultural constructs, with the associated disrespect for everyone else's, is a highly colonial, profoundly patronizing exercise. There is also another reason why the initial spread of Christianity in the Roman world must rank as a far more pressing intellectual problem in the early twenty-first century than it did around the year 1900. Over the last hundred years, the Christian religion has lost its hold on the consciences of much of the population of Europe – which must necessarily make us ask more searching questions about its initial success.

As we've already seen, the idea that Christianity was already on course for religious domination of the Roman world by AD 300 is not convincing, since it's impossible to place the overall numbers of Christians above 1 or 2 per cent of the population at the moment of Constantine's conversion (see p. 22). But by the mid-sixth century, two hundred years or so after Constantine's conversion, the vast majority of the Empire's population was at least being baptized. It is a straightforward chronological observation, therefore, that widespread Christian conversion within the Roman world followed Constantine's declaration of a Christian allegiance. But chronology is not necessarily the same thing as causation, and the dominant strand in recent writing about the spread of Christianity in late antiquity contains little or no discussion of the possibility that the structures and mechanisms of the Roman imperial system might have played any significant role in the process. This isn't an accidental omission but is firmly tied to the idea that the structures of the imperial state were much too feeble to have bent a thousand years of organic Graeco-Roman cultural development out of its long-established, non-Christian trajectories of development. In my view, both the nature and the chronology of Roman conversion in the decades immediately after Constantine strongly indicate that the structures of the imperial system, and, in particular, the precise ways in which they shaped competition between members of the landowning elite, played a critical role in the process. The governmental structures of the Roman state were weak, but in ways that required local elites to engage with the system, and this – in my view – provided an extremely powerful mechanism that dramatically accelerated the overall process of elite conversion.

The current unwillingness to assign any substantial role to the Empire in advancing the process of Christian conversion is grounded in part in a specific, evidence-based view of the capacities of the limited governmental systems of the Roman state. However, this view is powerfully reinforced by a more general conviction – common to several influential lines of modern historical interpretation (above all, the French *Annales* school and some other strands of the so-called 'Cultural Turn') – that has come to regard the core subject matters of more traditional historical analyses, such as 'events' and 'states', as having much weaker explanatory potential, when it comes to really important transformations, than less easily discernible, long-term processes of evolutionary change.[18]

The influence of such perspectives on treatments of late Roman Christian conversion among the last scholarly generation has been profound. Responding to the fact that elite Roman Christianization did not move forward via the preaching of bishops, the process has been largely portrayed as a product of the interactions and choices of members of small-scale elite networks, often based on marriage and personal interconnection: the indiscernible choices of many individuals eventually combining to turn the wheels of history.[19] But while I would agree both that elite interconnections played a fundamental role in the process, and that the imperial governmental structure suffered from profound limitations in its political and administrative effectiveness, nonetheless there are compelling reasons for thinking that elite Christian conversion is best understood, in overall terms, as a direct product of the internal workings of the late Roman state.

'THERE IS NO ONE ROAD . . .'

Constantine's open letter to the populations of the eastern provinces he had acquired by defeating his great imperial rival Licinius in 324 not only announced his Christianity, but culminated in a general declaration of apparent religious tolerance:

> My own desire is, for the general advantage of the world and all mankind, that my people should enjoy a life of peace and undisturbed concord. Let those, therefore, who are still blinded by error, be made welcome to the same degree of peace and tranquillity which they have who believe.[20]

In the remaining thirteen years of his reign there is plenty of evidence that Constantine substantially practised what he preached, continuing to offer patronage to individuals and institutions who did not share his own faith. Licinius' chief administrator, the non-Christian Praetorian prefect Julius Julianus, was retained in office by Constantine after his former boss's defeat, and was even awarded the consulship (the highest honorific dignity the Empire had to offer). Earlier, Constantine had kept on one of Maxentius' leading men, Rufius Volusianus, another non-Christian, as Praetorian and urban prefect, after the battle of the Milvian Bridge. Non-Christians also figure reasonably strongly at court throughout the remainder of Constantine's reign. A run of inscriptions from the sacred Greek site of Delphi show that Count Flavius Felicianus, one of Constantine's military commanders in the 330s, played a major role in revamping the shrine of Apollo's great oracle during these years. (It can hardly be a coincidence that, in one official pronouncement, Constantine intimated that he considered these oracles an authentic source of divine advice.) A pagan Neo-Platonic philosopher by the name of Sopater likewise flourished at Constantine's court as an imperial advisor, while the emperor continued to hand out many of the imperial favours that traditional cults and cult centres had come to expect. Athens, the greatest centre of traditional pagan philosophical teaching, received a generous grain allowance at imperial command, while random surviving inscriptions show that in the cities of Termessos and Sagalassos in Asia Minor (modern Turkey), the emperor's name was added to the list of his predecessors in standard expressions of the imperial cult.[21] There was no Great Persecution of pagans, which was only common sense, as such a policy would have been completely insane. The Great Tetrarchic Persecution of the early fourth century had shown how difficult it was for the pagan majority population of the Empire effectively to persecute a small minority of Christians. Any attempt at the reverse could only have failed miserably.

But toleration is neither a full nor a sufficient characterization of the religious climate prevailing in the Roman Empire in the fifty years after 324. In all this time, only one imperial regime, that of Emperor Jovian (363–4), operated with the proverbial playing field level in matters of religion. From it, there survives an officially authorized celebration of Jovian's first consulship on 1 January 364, which sets out its major policies. These included the licensing of religious plurality:

> You [i.e., Jovian] realize that, while there exists only one Judge, mighty and true [God], there is no one road leading to Him, but one is more difficult to travel, another more direct, one more steep and another level. All, however, tend alike towards that one goal and our competition and our zealousness arise from no other reason than that we do not all travel by the same route.[22]

Jovian was a Christian emperor, but in this striking passage his regime accepted that everyone was finding different paths to the same God, and emphasized that all strands of religious opinion could operate freely. This contrasts markedly with Constantine's patronizing dismissal of traditional paganism, even while allowing it to continue. Jovian's regime, however, only lasted a few months. Within a few weeks of the speech, he died from carbon monoxide asphyxiation in mysterious circumstances, when a charcoal brazier was placed too close to his bed. Some blamed it on pagan plotting against the Christian Jovian but, given his hyper-tolerant policies, it seems much more likely that he was eliminated by Christian hardliners (unless, of course, it was just an accident). With the exception of Jovian, and the almost equally brief sole reign of his predecessor, the apostate emperor Julian – who strongly favoured traditional pagan cults over Christianity – the post-Constantinian religious climate at the imperial centre was consistently and firmly slanted in a Christian direction, from 324 to the end of the century.[23]

This had some immediate impacts. At a point in Constantine's reign, a handful of pagan temples that were associated with particularly offensive cultic practices, such as ritual prostitution, were forcibly closed. Bishop Eusebius of Caesarea (who provides the most famous version of Constantine's vision of the Cross) mentions three in particular (Aphaca, Aegae and Heleopolis) in his *Life of Constantine*. That's probably a complete list, since Eusebius was desperately looking to cast the emperor in as strong a Christian light as possible.[24] Constantine also banned blood sacrifice, that element of pagan practice which Christians had always found most offensive. Early Christian commentators refer with disgust to the stench of blood and burning flesh that pervaded the great pagan festivals. It's not what immediately comes to mind as you wander around shining white marble ruins under a blue Mediterranean sky, but these were fundamentally places of death, sometimes on an industrial scale. The Altar of Hieron II, tyrant of Syracuse in the third century BC, can still be seen there: some 650 feet (200m) long, it was built to sacrifice hundreds of animals at once. Our main source for Constantine's ban on blood sacrifice is again Eusebius. Unusually for him, however, he doesn't quote an actual legal text. Given that such a law is not to be found in the mid-fifth-century collection of late imperial legislation, the Theodosian Code, some have doubted that the ban – at least as a general order – ever really existed. But imperial legislation was not yet being collected systematically in Constantine's day, nor was it to be until the 430s, and there were good reasons why the text of this order might not have survived to that point, given that it was rescinded in the reign of the pagan emperor Julian. The ban is also referred to in passing in a law of Constantine's son, the western emperor Constans, which added extra teeth to his father's measure by citing continued blood sacrifice as a reason for forcibly closing down more pagan temples than the three that Constantine had shut.

How effective the original ban had been, given the further twist added in the time of his sons that continued blood sacrifice was a reason for shutting more pagan temples, is difficult to judge. The basic problem attending all imperial legislation, especially on contentious matters like religious practice, is that there was no automatic enforcement mechanism. One of the key limitations facing Roman central government (and one of the main reasons why the Empire's potential role in the Christianization of its elites has been largely dismissed) is that its bureaucratic machinery was too small and too underdeveloped to exercise close control over day-to-day affairs in the 1,800-plus city communities into which the local populations of the Empire had, by the start of the fourth century, come to be organized in administrative terms.

Faced with the beauty, efficiency and durability of some of its products – roads and aqueducts, sewers and walls – and the ruthless brutality of some of its military operations, it is hard always to keep these limitations properly in perspective. But Roman emperors ran a truly enormous body of territory – the largest state western Eurasia has ever known, stretching all the way from Scotland to Iraq – encompassing a staggering variety of socio-economic and climatic conditions from the temperate climes and wet hillsides of northern Britain to the semi-arid desert fringes of the southern Mediterranean. All this space was governed with the assistance of only a small number of state functionaries at a time when most things – certainly men and supplies – moved at a maximum speed of about 25 miles (40 km) a day. Most information was communicated in physical writing on non-searchable pieces of papyrus, which, when received, were simply deposited in a large room with a huge stack of similar documents, from which it might – or might not – be possible to retrieve them subsequently.

In practice, therefore, as Roman emperors were not able to exercise close control over most aspects of life in the local communities of the Empire, considerable autonomy had to be devolved to groups of local landowners, organized largely into town councils. The most important job of these councillors, as far as emperors were concerned, was the vital business of extracting tax revenues from the Empire's largely agricultural economy, without which neither their armies nor the whole imperial edifice itself could continue to exist. As long as the taxes came in relatively smoothly, the local grandees were often left to operate with substantial autonomy. Taxation aside, the main intrusion by the imperial centre into these localities came when regional grandees sought central assistance (directly from emperors if they were influential enough, or from imperial functionaries if they were less important) to win or protect some kind of advantage over their local rivals. Such lobbying did generate a lot of business. Thanks again to the preservative qualities of hot sand, we know that one Egyptian governor received a staggering 1,804 petitions in just three days; while, during a brief stay in Alexandria in the 190s, Emperor Septimius Severus produced five formal legal rulings a day in response to incoming queries. And these, of course, were only the ones that made it to his desk.[25] But all this governmental activity should not be confused with close control. If taxes were paid promptly, local communities would otherwise be left to their own devices. This clearly included deciding whether, or not, to enforce imperial decrees on other, more contentious – or less pressing – matters.

Grasping this situation perfectly well, emperors sometimes enacted dramatic-sounding laws to get demanding pressure groups (like pushy

Christian bishops) off their backs, knowing that the new rules would be enforced only in instances where there was already a majority on any particular town council in favour of them. The clear signs of this kind of non-systematic enforcement structure in action can be found by the mid-350s, when, thanks substantially to the survival of an extensive letter collection from the Antiochene rhetor Libanius, we get a fuller picture of the medium-term effects of Constantine's ban on blood sacrifice and its partial extension under his sons. By this time, some more temples were certainly being shut, presumably because blood sacrifice had been reported as taking place within them by elite supporters of Christianity in the communities concerned. But the majority of pagan temples still remained open for licensed religious devotions of other kinds. Wine and olive oil could be thrown around to your heart's content (perhaps one reason why Hector's statue at Ilios looked so greasy during Julian's visit) and candles could be lit. Blood sacrifice, however, could only be practised safely in secret; or in a community that remained so resolutely pagan that no report of it was ever going to make its way back to the centre.[26]

By this point, however, the patchy enforcement of laws such as the ban on blood sacrifice was not the only, or even the most important, way in which the emperors' Christian allegiance was affecting the developing religious culture of the Empire. Even if non-Christian belief and much non-Christian practice was still legally tolerated, this did not mean that all strands of religious opinion within the Empire were treated with absolute equality. Constantine and his sons created a political climate which emphasized that Christianity was now the religion of imperial choice. This was done not just by set piece public statements, such as Constantine's open letter to the eastern provincials in 324, and by drafting a few new laws, but via a raft of more specific measures that massively reinforced the overall tone.

One traditional mechanism for displaying imperial favour was to advance the status of chosen local communities. A legal grant of city status, for instance, gave a local landowning community autonomy over much of its own business, with the right to control how certain sums of money could be spent. (Communities – however large – had to hand over any locally generated funds to the dominant city council, with no say over how they would be distributed.) Constantine used this device to favour the small town of Orcistus in Phrygia, deep in the heart of Asia Minor. In this settlement, the local landowning elites who ran its council were already substantially Christian before Constantine's conversion. The pagan Tetrarchs had punished Orcistus for its Christian allegiance by removing its autonomous status, which clearly made the town a cause célèbre. Once in control of the east, Constantine prompted its citizens to petition him to reverse the policy and, when they did so, graciously restored their independence. The same process can also be detected at work in the half dozen or so known cities that petitioned for, and received, the right to add the name of the emperor, or another member of his family, to their official nomenclature.[27]

All this activity sent a clear message that Rome was now a Christian Empire. If they wanted imperial favours, even non-Christians had to adapt to the new religious climate. Late in Constantine's reign, in around 333, the councillors of Hispellum (Spello, near Perugia in modern Umbria) petitioned the emperor for the right to hold a biennial festival for the imperial cult at their own temple precinct, instead of always having to help pay for a joint event at the town of Volsinii – an awkward, roundabout journey of 60-odd miles (100 km) along difficult mountain roads. This, however, was a traditional pagan cult, and though Constantine granted their wish – a cost-free way for him to win popularity – he used the exchange to make a point. As the large, publicly displayed commemorative inscriptions that record the emperor's favour put it, the celebrations at Hispellum were henceforth to be conducted free from 'the deceits of any contagious superstition' (*contagios ae superstitionis fraudibus*). In the official rhetoric of Constantine's reign, this can only mean that there was to be no more blood sacrifice. The petitioners were thus forced to refer to their own traditional non-Christian practices – blood sacrifice – in highly disparaging tones in the most public of contexts as the price for the concession they wanted.[28]

The same willingness to adapt was equally important for individuals who wanted to maximize their chances of flourishing in the new religious climate. The philosopher and rhetorician Themistius was an avowed pagan who nonetheless won great favour in the 350s at the Christian court of Constantine's son, Constantius II, when he was appointed to a lucrative official professorship at the new university of

Constantinople. Even more important were the less formal benefits that came Themistius' way, such as the right to sit at the dinner table of the emperor himself. Such intimacy allowed him to put in good words for his friends – 'anyone you mention is immediately better off', as Libanius put it – especially as Constantius' 'pleasure in granting such favours exceeds yours in receiving them'.[29] Themistius' influence became so great that, in the late 350s, he was commissioned to help recruit new members for the imperial Senate of Constantinople, which had just been revamped explicitly to match – in size, status and importance – the much older Senate of Rome.

On the surface, Themistius' career shows that pagans could still make it big in the Christian Empire of the 350s, but there is more to the story. Constantius recruited Themistius because he served an extremely useful function. At a time when more pagan temples were being shut down – or at least were being reported as such (remember that Pegasios was thought to have destroyed the temples of Ilios when he had not) – much of the landowning elite of the Empire, who effectively ran the Empire, nonetheless remained pagan. Having Themistius as a spokesman for, and general conduit of imperial favour to, this class was a reassuring statement that religious change was going neither too far nor too fast. But to win the emperor's favour, Themistius had to construct a carefully crafted public persona, which stripped away anything culturally challenging to the emperor's Christianity. As philosopher and imperial servant, Themistius combined knowledge of the past, rational thought and rhetorical effectiveness in such a way as to make him politically useful. He also explicitly damned his philosophical rivals, the Neo-Platonists, some of whom (as we'll see in the next chapter) led the pagan opposition to Christianity.[30] Themistius was living evidence that it remained possible for pagan members of the landowning elite to protect or advance their interests in the Christian Empire of the Constantines – but only if they adapted, at least in public, to the new ideological climate of overt Christian superiority.

This new climate gives us an explanatory context for what Emperor Julian's letter tells us about Pegasios of Ilios. The bishop was known at the imperial centre as a Christian enthusiast who had been destroying the pagan temples of his home city. The only possible source of these stories of temple destruction could have been Pegasios himself, in some kind of report written to the court of Constantius II by the early 350s that he had been pulling down the pagan temples of his city. As Julian found, on arriving in Ilios in 354, Pegasios hadn't done anything of the sort – the temples were still intact – but he wanted people to think so. All of which is resounding testimony, both to the limitations of the Empire's bureaucratic machinery – clearly, no one had bothered or was able to check the report – but also to the extent to which it already seemed desirable to erect at least a façade of conformity to the emperors' religion of choice to secure imperial favour.

It is in this more informal aspect of elite public life in the Empire – the need to conform to prevailing imperial ideologies to secure necessary or desirable favours – rather than in formal acts of imperial legislation, that we find the real capacity of imperial regimes to influence the religious life of the Empire's elite. This dimension of exchange between local elites and central government, so far missing from discussions of the Christianization of the Roman upper class, needs to be understood as central to the entire process.

THE EMPEROR'S NEW CULT

The fourth century was not the first time that thorough-going religious–cultural change had ripped its way through the landowning elites of the Roman world. In the century or so after the conquests which brought the Empire proper into existence – broadly, the hundred years after 50 BC – the lives of newly conquered provincial elites were utterly transformed by an initial bout of cultural revolution. In the western regions of the Empire, this took the form of learning Latin, wearing togas, eating grain as bread rather than porridge, and turning old rural residences into Mediterranean-style villas. Self-governing cities, modelled on the ancient Greek city state (the *polis*), spread like wildfire, each run by a council of local elite landowners according to a standard constitution which was adopted, with only minor changes, right across the Empire. The religious component of this cultural sea-change came in the form of the imperial cult, provincial branches of which quickly appeared in every major city of the Empire – complete, in many cases, with their own huge temple complexes staffed with the cult's characteristic officers, the *sacerdotae provinciae* and *flamines perpetua*. Surviving inscriptions – many of them funerary monuments – document the apparent enthusiasm of provincial elites to build and maintain these temples from their own funds, to hold its priesthoods, and to continue to pay for the subsequent development of the cult (providing for different elements of its expensive cycle of festivals, such as sacrifices, games and horse races). Such uniform commitment to the imperial cult is remarkable, given that there's hardly a province of the Empire that didn't violently resist its original incorporation into the Empire, and revolt at least once subsequently: Gaul, Hungary, Britain and Judea (twice) to name but a few. Yet the same cultural–religious revolution, with only minor local variants, was quickly established and persisted, all the way from Hadrian's Wall to the Euphrates.[31]

This extraordinary phenomenon used to be understood as 'Romanization': a cunning plan imposed from the imperial centre to convert newly conquered peoples into good Romans. This isn't what happened. Apparently driven by local agency, the establishment of the imperial cult was a bottom-up, not top-down transformation, with individual initiatives playing the starring role: not so much Romanization, but the much more interesting phenomenon of self-Romanization.

To qualify for an invitation to join the imperial cult, provincial elites had to demonstrate that they were properly Roman in character, which meant investing in a proper Roman infrastructure for their towns; and, personally, in proper classical educations. Several years of learning correct Latin at the hands of a self-employed grammarian was expensive, classical-style buildings did not come cheap, and it sometimes cost so much money to erect temples to the imperial cult that individuals found themselves in debt (a reported reason why Boudicca was able to muster so much support for her revolt in Britain).[32] Given all the outlays involved, why did provincial elites buy (literally) into this expensive cultural revolution?

If you asked anyone at the time why they were putting so much effort and cash into becoming Roman, they would probably have given you an answer that was substantially ideological. As we've seen, education in Latin (or Greek) underpinned the self-image of unique rationality that defined the Graeco-Roman elite's vision of its own superiority. City councils, too, played an important role in the model. In the Graeco-Roman world-view, institutions of local self-government were considered a rationalizing force in themselves, leading educated individuals to arrive at the best possible solution to their community's problems through a process of reasoned debate. According to this model, it was, by definition, impossible to be fully rational without participating in civic debate. There was a term for someone living by themselves: 'idiot' (from *idiotes*: Greek for 'private', with strongly pejorative connotations).[33]

But neither the presence of a coherent ideological justification for all the expenditure involved in the process of self-Romanization, nor the seeming exercise of choice on the part of members of provincial local elites must be allowed to conceal the fact that this process was fundamentally not a voluntary one. Each individual member of a newly conquered provincial elite could decide whether or not to participate in the process – but all faced a powerful cocktail of incentive and constraint which made it overwhelmingly likely that the majority would do so.

A Roman 'city' (*civitas*) consisted both of its core urban area and a dependent rural territory, which was administered from that core. The city council (*curia*) characteristically comprised local landowners (*curiales*) with enough property to qualify for membership (the amount of property varied according to the size and wealth of the city in question). Obtaining a formal, legal grant of city status represented a huge overall gain for ambitious provincial elites, as such a grant brought with it a number of specific advantages. First, the standard city constitution granted certain rights of local taxation, which the newly incorporated city council could impose (and spend). Still more important, the senior executive officers of the council, who took turns in holding office for limited periods, received Roman citizenship, something which brought its recipients considerable benefits, including certain legal protections. The same was true of the imperial cult, local branch membership of which included not only ambitious provincial figures but local representatives of the imperial centre, such as the governor and his officers. For an upwardly mobile provincial landowner it was, quite simply, the best place to make the right friends and influence them. Not to participate (and participate with enthusiasm) carried with it the dangerous risk that your local rivals would be able to whisper their side of the story into the gubernatorial ear unchallenged.

On the back of the Empire's crushing military superiority, therefore, imperial rule exported an utterly dominant cultural model into the provinces, which provincial elites had to be able to navigate effectively to succeed in the brave new Roman world created by legionary might. If you didn't acquire the necessary culture, if you failed to get your community recognized as a self-governing town, and if you weren't allowed to join the ranks of your local imperial cult, you were firmly excluded from what was now the only game in that town.[34]

So, while it might have the appearance of free choice – one justified in highly positive ideological terms as the triumph of rational civilization – self-Romanization was no choice at all. The only way to live long and prosper was to buy a Roman entry ticket, whatever the cost. For all the apparent agency being exercised at the local level, we're actually looking at a process where the pressures to conform were so strong that most local agents were only ever going to make one choice.

Because the imperial cult did not develop into a dominant world religion, the scholarly consensus has no difficulty in identifying the process for what it was: an entirely necessary socio-political move on the part of local elites seeking to maximize their position. It is surprising that the same kind of analysis has not also been applied to elite conversion in the late imperial period, because, looked at closely, this second Roman cultural revolution of the fourth and fifth centuries, which saw provincial landowning elites adopt Christianity in large numbers, bears close comparison with the mechanisms of its predecessor, which had, so effectively, transformed its barbarian ancestors into good Romans.

By the late Roman period, the internal structures of Empire had been transformed by the rough and tumble of four hundred years of history, and the incentives at play behind active provincial elite participation in the structures of Empire in the era of Constantine and his Christian heirs had changed. Every free inhabitant of the Empire had long since been a Roman citizen (formalized by the *Constitutio Antoniniana* back in AD 212), and local city revenues had also been confiscated by the imperial centre: another of the sources of ready revenue (like the incomes of ancient Egyptian temples) that desperate third-century emperors raided when trying to fund the military expansion required to fight Persia.[35] By the fourth century, local elites still had the bother of raising monies, but could no longer spend the vast majority of the proceeds; they were required instead to hand them over to central government. As a class, however, the landed fortunes of the provincial elites did not perish alongside the financial autonomy of the cities they ran. For the most part, private provincial landowning fortunes survived the third-century crisis more or less intact.[36] What we see working itself out from the late third century onwards, therefore, is a renegotiation of the relationship between provincial landowners and the structures of Empire. This generated three major new types of incentive for provincial elites to embed themselves within a restructured Roman imperial system.

The first of these incentives was a consequence of the now overwhelming importance to elite life of the Empire's legal system. The basis of elite wealth, like most pre-modern elites, was landowning, to such an extent that even new wealth acquired by other means (such as through trade or military service) was quickly invested in agricultural property. Particular individuals might fall anywhere in a spectrum from gentry to aristocracy – the former tending to possess just a single block of land in one locality, the latter identifiable by their larger and more dispersed portfolios of estates. However great or small, their landed holdings were defined and protected by the complex, written Roman legal system, which, from the *Constitutio Antoniniana* onwards, governed the entirety of the Empire's landowning population. The vast majority of surviving Roman jurisprudence concerns civil, property law. This defined who owned what, and set down the procedures by which that land could be both safely exploited (various forms of lease agreement, share cropping, and so on) and securely handed on to the next generation (via such procedures as marriage settlements, wills, sales). The importance of this legal system to upper-class life cannot be overstated, since to make any arrangement concerning landed wealth that had not been sorted out in accordance with proper legal procedures was to risk a legal challenge from other interested parties – usually a relative of some kind – in the courts. Grander Roman landowners certainly employed gangs of thugs to protect their local interests, but they did not have substantial bands of armed men at their disposal to protect the basic source of their wealth. Such protection was the preserve of Roman law, whose successful navigation required elite landowners to engage with the imperial system at numerous levels.[37]

By the time of Constantine, all new law was being made by emperors, in consultation with appointed legal officials. Up to the third century, much of the necessary innovation in the Roman legal system derived from a body of case law built up in the writings of independent legal experts (so-called jurisconsults). But from the mid-third century onwards, the emperor had become the legislator of choice, and through a variety of instruments composed in his name – everything from responses to petitions and queries to general edicts – provided the main vehicle by which the law developed to deal with new problems. At each stage, landowning elites needed to navigate imperial legal structures effectively to safeguard their wealth.

To any Roman citizen involved in any kind of legal dispute, strong connections within the Empire's bureaucratic structures were the key to a successful outcome. Big landowners might take their problems directly to the emperor, hoping to secure some kind of letter from him to assist their case (which is why Septimius Severus found himself answering five petitions a day). Lesser landowners sought assistance further down the pecking order, seeking out lower-level patrons who had the right kind of leverage to ensure the outcome they were looking for. This process – finding the right patron to fix your legal case – is documented in a wide variety of fourth-century sources, including the letter collections of various Christian bishops who, like the philosopher Themistius, showed not the slightest embarrassment about attempting to secure desirable outcomes in court for their friends. There was often much at stake. The official correspondence of the Roman senator Symmachus, urban prefect of the city of Rome in 384, for example, details a case between two persons of senatorial rank in which every dirty trick in the book was being used to chisel the less connected of the two litigants out of their estate. Legal contests of this kind would always be messy, of course, since both parties would be playing the hunt-the-patron game: not for nothing did emperors customarily close their letters with the

Greek *eutyche*: 'Good luck'! But this only emphasizes the point. Securing and advancing your wealth necessarily required elite landowners at every level to establish an effective range of friends and connections within the imperial system.[38]

The second force attracting provincial landowners into the orbit of the late imperial universe was the pull of the new tax systems, developed in the later third and early fourth centuries to fund the military expansion which eventually stabilized Rome's eastern, Persian front. These systems still operated on a city-by-city basis, in the sense that city councils were responsible for raising the required cash. But central imperial officials now interfered much more directly in what happened locally, instituting a cycle of fifteen-year surveys (called indictions) to assess the total sum that each city territory would be required to pay. Each city territory was then subdivided into a number of units of value – *iugera* (singular *iugum*): from the Latin for the amount of land that could be ploughed in one day – each of which was required to pay the same sum per annum. Larger landowners might possess estates amounting to multiple *iugera*; several smaller landowners might collectively constitute just one. The whole system was by far the largest and most complicated act of government ever attempted by the Roman state, requiring everything from analyses of the productive capacities of each local economy within the Empire, to ongoing records of tax payments and arrears. It also oversaw the largest and most valuable flow of wealth ever created in the ancient world, with all these tax proceeds (a mixture of payments in cash and kind) redistributed from each of the localities to the imperial centre, and then out again towards the frontier regions where much of the army was still stationed. Controlling this elaborate fiscal machinery not only consumed most of the energies of the numerically limited imperial bureaucracy, but its practical operation again incentivized the Empire's landowners to involve themselves with the imperial system of governance in several key ways.

Getting a favourable initial assessment to minimize your basic tax liability at the start of each fifteen-year cycle was a priority. This should not be thought of as a straightforwardly scientific valuation process; rather, it involved much special pleading and mobilizing connections to achieve the best possible outcome. As Bishop Basil of

Caesarea put it to a friend who had just been appointed to the job, being in charge of tax assessment gave you the opportunity to benefit your friends, harm your enemies, and generally to make a lot of money (fourth-century Christian ecclesiastics like Basil happily wrote letters in search of advantageous assessments for their friends). But the need for effective connections within imperial officialdom didn't stop there. With tax payments being made at three points in the year, the actual amounts paid were to some extent negotiable: bad weather and poor harvests might lead to temporary reductions. In practice, therefore, tax payments could be further minimized for anyone with influential friends. Whatever the weather, the best plan was clearly to pay as little as possible up front, even if the remainder was still considered 'arrears' to be paid off later. When in search of political support at moments of stress, emperors periodically granted tax amnesties: in order to maximize the opportunities provided by such amnesties, taxpayers needed to be as much in arrears as possible.[39]

The picture I'm building up here might initially seem to contradict the broader argument that the later Roman Empire possessed only a relatively feeble state structure. In fact, it doesn't. Employing comparatively few officials, the Empire lacked the administrative capacity to undertake properly scientific acts of government, like systematic assessments of the landed economies at its disposal, while the workings of government in every dimension were profoundly affected by the amount of influence that individual citizens could exert on the process through mobilized chains of connection within the system. My point is that the practical workings of this rickety state structure required elite landowners to involve themselves intensely in its operations, in terms of maximizing their connections to influential powerbrokers within the system, at whatever level was appropriate to their own wealth and standing. To put it another way, the prevailing weakness of the overall state structure *demanded* that Roman landowners engage with it, since the potential benefits of doing so were enormous, and the possible costs of failing to do so catastrophic. In this sense, the later Roman Empire cannot be understood as a simple unified entity which enacted the policies imposed by emperors and their senior officials. We should rather see the late Roman imperial state as a defined political space or institutional context in which dominant social groups came together to negotiate their interrelations and safeguard their interests.[40] In this sense, the rickety state structures of the later Roman Empire exerted a huge and, in fact, gradually increasing gravitational pull on its constituent provincial landowners in the fourth century, as the logic of how to maximize their interests in the face of its new fiscal and legal structures became clear. Then, just as Constantine finally declared his Christian allegiance, an equally revolutionary restructuring of imperial governance was gathering momentum. This restructuring provided local landowning elites with a third powerful incentive to involve themselves in the operations of Empire.

In the early Empire, local *curiae* made all the key decisions at city level in conjunction with provincial governors, who often had to adjudicate in disputes between competing councillors. The confiscation of most of the remaining city revenues in the fiscal reorganization of the third century effectively killed off the locally competitive political processes associated with this earlier system. Following this reorganization there was no point in disbursing your own funds to win power in your home city, since there was no longer a city budget to spend at the end of it all. At the same time, the fiscal and legal restructuring of the Empire necessitated a larger imperial bureaucracy, whose status and benefits grew with its numbers. In 249, there were only about two hundred and fifty senior imperial administrators for the entire Empire. A century and a half later, there were three thousand in each half of the Empire, most of whom now held their positions for only a decade (where previously it had been twenty-five years), so that, in practice, more than one individual held each post per political generation. These men (they were all men) retired with top senatorial status (as *illustres*: there were now three grades of senator, and only imperial officials could acquire this top status). In addition, there were over twenty thousand medium- and lower-level posts: still a small bureaucratic machine in comparative historical terms, but a huge expansion for the Roman Empire.[41]

Older scholarship – influenced by what the interwar generation of historians saw going on around them in contemporary Russia, Italy and Germany – saw this governmental restructuring as representing the rise of a suffocating, authoritarian state structure that just about kept the Empire in being for a few more generations after the crisis of the third century. On closer inspection, however, a different picture has emerged. The majority of the new Roman bureaucrats were recruited from the provincial, curial landowning classes, who used to dominate their city councils. Men from these classes wanted such jobs both because the confiscation of city funds had emasculated city politics, and because becoming a member of the imperial bureaucracy was now the most effective path to success – and not just at the centre. This is where the fact that lengths of service in the bureaucracy reduced over the fourth century becomes significant. Not only did this reduction in tenure allow more individuals to hold jobs, but retired bureaucrats (who had served increasingly foreshortened periods in office at the centre) – *honorati* – went on to acquire all the profitable and influential jobs in local politics: conducting the fifteen-year tax assessments, and sitting with the governor when he heard lawsuits. 'Judge' (*iudex*) becomes the standard term for a provincial governor in the later Empire, but the governor was not so much judge, in the modern sense of the word, as court president. After hearing the evidence, he pronounced verdict and sentence in consultation with the *honorati* sitting alongside him. Not only did becoming an imperial bureaucrat bring lots of attractive privileges, but it also – in structural terms – rapidly became the best way to maximize your position in local landowning society.[42]

At the very moment when the Constantinian dynasty declared its new religious allegiance, therefore, the landowning classes of the Empire were queuing up for jobs in a rapidly expanding imperial bureaucracy. The twentyfold increase in senior positions in just the century and a half after 250 seriously understates the full range of the offer. Not only could more than one individual per generation hold each top job once service lengths reduced to ten years, but there were also both official and unofficial waiting lists for all these positions. And these were all extremely senior positions. Jobs lower down the system were still very attractive to lesser landowners, and another characteristic feature of the later imperial bureaucracy further increased the numbers of elite individuals with a stake in the system. For those who wanted the benefits of the position, but not an actual job, grants of honorary bureaucratic status were available. Such grants still had to be actively obtained by mobilizing a chain of patronage connections reaching into the imperial court, whence a codicil of honorary appointment would eventually be forthcoming. We don't know how many honorary grants were made in total: that they were numerous is suggested by the fact that this obscure corner of the system became ever more elaborate over time. The original honorary grants of office were eventually superseded by a second (superior) type of honorary grant, which conferred upon the grantee the same status as an actual ex-officeholder. All appeared over the course of the fourth century.[43] Far from being a distant authoritarian body, the growing imperial bureaucracy of the late Roman period was a highly attractive career destination – actual or honorary according to taste and circumstance – for provincial landowning elites, whose old patterns of local political competition had been destroyed by the confiscation of city funds.

Just like the original emergence of city councils under the early Empire, all this worked itself out as a bottom-up process, though its nature was decisively shaped by the new incentives that had been put in place at the top. Emperors in search of ready cash may have begun to recruit more bureaucrats, but the process of expansion was quickly taken over by local elites who wanted a piece of the action. Even in the time of Constantine, emperors were already trying to limit the flow of *curiales* into the bureaucracy, with little success – although in the end, no emperor actually tried that hard. All the extant laws attempting to expel provincial landowners from the bureaucracy to make them serve instead on their home city councils (and there are several) contain extensive amnesties, because such recruitment was a cheap and effective means for emperors to win friends and influence people among those by and for whom the Empire was run. In the end, the most attractive features of bureaucratic positions were the rights and status that accompanied them; the actual salaries didn't cost the state that much. The overall result, nonetheless, was a complete revolution in modes of interaction between local landowning elites and the imperial state. A few of the old councillors stayed at home, either because they lacked ambition or because, as a number of sources hint, there remained a handful of attractive roles to be filled at the local level. But for the majority, the status and privileges of bureaucratic service were unmissably attractive. By the early fifth century, the *honorati*, as a group, were becoming so prosperous that they were increasingly buying up landed estates in their home provinces, cementing their local political dominance in the form of landed property.[44]

The new imperial bureaucracy that emerged in the fourth century was a phenomenon created by elite consumer demand, which utterly and rapidly transformed patterns of elite life within the Empire. It also provides a crucial context for the non-episcopal, privatized process of Christian elite conversion that was unfolding simultaneously.

'THE MAN WHOM GOD LOVES . . .'

As both waves of Roman cultural revolution demonstrate so unequivocally – that of the first century AD as well as its successor in the fourth – major cultural change at the top could never be a politically neutral phenomenon in the Roman world. The imperial elite defined itself by a shared ethos dictated by the prevailing ideologies of the imperial system, and cultural proficiency was an absolute necessity for success within it. Despite the changes transforming the empire, a full education in the Latin and Greek of the imperial upper class remained as much a prerequisite for success in the fourth century as it had been in the first. The Empire's developing legal and fiscal structures provided enormous incentives, despite, or rather *because of*, the overall limitations of central government, for local elites to plug themselves profitably into the system. This process eventually generated a profound restructuring in relations between the imperial centre and the provinces. By and large, emperors acquiesced in a process that took bureaucratic expansion out of their control, and allowed many members of the old provincial ruling classes to rebrand themselves as real or honorary imperial bureaucrats. But each individual act of curial rebranding required positive engagement with the system, if only to extract a crucial letter with the emperor's name upon it. As in the first century, this was an extremely competitive process.

In the midst of this restructuring, Constantine declared his Christian allegiance, which almost all of his fourth-century successors maintained with enthusiasm. Christian emperors were willing to grant some favours to non-Christians, but were uncompromising in their personal religious preferences, to which they required non-Christians to accommodate themselves. Communities like Hispellum's had to accept the disappearance of blood sacrifice; and the likes of Themistius had to self-fashion philosophical personas that were explicitly critical of their more partisan pagan co-religionists. Such accommodations originally reflected the ideological and practical strength of Constantine's position by 324, as the last man standing in the civil wars that had marked the unwinding of the Tetrarchy's legacy in imperial politics. The Divinity had shown its hand: it was impossible to argue with the reality of multiple God-given victories over pagan opponents, as one contemporary pagan poet, Palladas, was forced to admit. Palladas wept for the fate of traditional religion: 'We Hellenes [i.e., pagans] are men reduced to ashes, holding to our buried hopes in the dead; for everything has now been turned on its head.' But, at the same time, he had not the slightest doubt that God had spoken, given the utter decisiveness of Constantine's victories, and was quick to condemn Constantine's defeated pagan rival Licinius: 'When a certain person [Licinius] hates the man whom God loves, he exhibits the height of folly. For he clearly girds himself for battle against God himself, incurring supreme wrath for his envy; for one must love the man whom God loves.'

Despite Palladas's personal religious convictions, the totality of Constantine's victory showed the unmistakable hand of God. The only reasonable response, Palladas ruefully acknowledged, was to accept the Divine will.[45] Many Romans shared his sentiments.

Because Constantine and his sons – if less directly – were able to pass on their imperial power to Christian successors, Christian emperors subsequently controlled the distribution of favours for the bulk of the fourth century. And as we have seen, bureaucratic expansion meant that there were even more favours than usual at stake in the form of actual and honorary positions in the imperial administration. These clearly did go disproportionately to candidates sharing the emperors' new faith, so that a majority of senior officials in many court positions were Christians already by the mid-350s, in the reign of Constantius II.[46]

Some of these elite Christians surely were highly devout, like Augustine, Jerome, Paulinus of Nola, and Melania the Younger. But our existing source base is heavily skewed in favour of *enthusiastic* Christian converts. All our written texts from the late Roman period survive because they were eventually copied by medieval monks. Monks copied many things for many reasons (including plenty of erotic Latin poetry), but this transmission mechanism of course means that we are going to hear most about the vigorously Christian among the converting Roman elite, whose activities won great religious renown in their own lifetimes and continued to be celebrated subsequently, not least in the form of saints' *Lives*. At the same time, it's also clear that the majority of elite converts neither sold off lands like Melania, nor dropped out of normal public life like Augustine, Jerome or Paulinus of Nola.

Most of the known early Christian office-holders, by contrast, are just names to us. That's to say, we don't know what *kind* of Christian convert they were, and the word 'conversion', as we have seen, covers a multitude of sins in the mid-fourth century, including allowing a man of Pegasios' ambiguous religious persuasions presumably to appoint himself a Christian bishop. Mid-fourth-century commentators report that ambitious individuals responded to emperors' embrace of Christianity very much as you would expect, by declaring the religious allegiance that they thought would best serve their interests: a phenomenon on which fourth-century pagan commentators like Themistius and Symmachus both pour occasional scorn.[47]

There is no way to know exactly how many of the rapidly Christianizing Roman elite of the fourth century were truly devout, and how many converted largely for economic and political reasons (or, like Pegasios, perhaps, merely pretended to). But before we get too carried away with the idea that some kind of irresistible Christian revivalist spirit was rushing through the Roman landowning elite in the fourth century, it is important to remember that many descendants of the same elite families would, just a few centuries later, find conversion to Islam equally attractive, for very similar reasons.[48] Throughout history, elites – who have the most to lose and gain – have been particularly vulnerable when major cultural change transforms the political processes governing the distribution of favour. Even if elements of the Roman elite were entirely genuine in their adoption of Christianity, the real point, as a combination of Pegasios' practical behaviour and Palladas's ideological response underlines, is that – genuine or not – the vast majority felt that they had no choice but to come into line in some way with the new imperial cult sweeping through the fourth-century Empire. The emperor was willing to tolerate some carefully tempered dissent, but even this much ran the risk that a well-connected converted competitor might use the operations of public life to undermine you. Unless you were willing to oppose outright, as a minority certainly were, then – real, fake, or something in between – an accommodation had to be made. The alacrity with which many converted is a strong indication in itself that, for many, deep religious convictions were not in play.

Other historical examples of this kind of phenomenon are easy enough to find. A classic instance would be the willingness of the great majority of the Tudor landowning elite to accommodate itself to the changing religious preferences of Henry VIII and his children in the sixteenth century.[49] But a broader modern analogy for this adaptive behavioural pattern, I would argue, is the kind of one-party state model that operated in the old Soviet bloc. A few brave individuals always resisted systemic pressures to conform, but the vast majority – if lucky enough to have any choice at all – would always choose to join the party, because it was the only available path to the best possible everyday life for the less ambitious, and especially for those targeting fame and fortune. Which prompts an important methodological observation. If, in such contexts, you examine the actions of single individuals, the process of coming into line with the new ideology will look at first sight like one of free choice, since any individual could always choose not to accommodate themselves to the Soviet system, or not become a Christian in the fourth century. But this is misleading. So powerful are the systemic pressures working in favour of ideological accommodation that the majority will always move in that direction. The choice is always there to be made, but such are the pressures in play that it is far from a free one.

In the case of the Roman Empire, this prompts one overall conclusion. When set against the internal workings of Empire, and the partisan nature of imperial religious policy under the Constantinian dynasty, the self-Christianization of large numbers of the Roman elite after 324 has to be considered a direct consequence of Constantine's religious choices – at least, in the sense that they were maintained by the overwhelming majority of his fourth-century successors. Hence, in subsequent decades, the imperial landowning elite were operating in a context where public life was consistently skewed in favour of Christian participants, and the bulk of the imperial elite responded accordingly. This much of the Christianization of the Roman world really has to be understood, therefore, as a political process: one dependent upon and generated by the imperial state; or, more precisely, by the granular functioning of public life at the elite level. If we are fully to understand the relationship of Empire and Christianization, however, we need to expand the chronological range further, and move on from the processes of elite conversion that unfolded in the middle of the fourth century to explore what happened from the 380s onwards, after a critical mass of the landowning elite had already come into line with the emperor's new cult.

3
The Altar of Victory

The culturally coercive capacity of the Roman imperial state has always figured somewhere in accounts of Christianity's rise. The Theodosian Code, assembled in the 430s as a definitive guide to laws currently applying in both halves of the Empire, preserves a run of legislation from the previous half-century whose explicit purpose was to shut down traditional pagan cultic practice. The legislation came in stages. In 381, and again in 385, the eastern Emperor Theodosius I banned all sacrifice for purposes of telling the future. A decade later, this developed into a complete ban on all forms of sacrifice, which in 392 was extended to the use of incense and other forms of more private devotion. In 408, the western Emperor Honorius decreed that non-Christians could no longer serve in the imperial administrative bureaucracy; eight years later, the eastern Emperor Theodosius II, grandson of Theodosius I, followed suit. These laws were matched by others – first permitting and then commanding – that pagan temples were to be destroyed, even in that traditional Christian no-go area: the deep countryside. Destruction began with temples on imperial estates in 407/8; then, in 435, private landowners were ordered to do the same.[1]

Despite all this, the Roman state has been accorded no more than a walk-on role in most modern historical accounts of this half-century of Christian iconoclasm. Instead, its prime agents have traditionally been identified as a series of tough, independent-minded Churchmen who browbeat emperors into action and forced the imperial state to serve the interests of an independent institutional Christian Church. As with the process of elite conversion which preceded it chronologically, however, a closer look at the totality of the evidence for the dissolution of the pagan temples suggests that the overall role of the Roman imperial system requires substantial upward revision. The initiatives of bishops and other Christian leaders did play a significant part in the details of what unfolded in particular localities, but their capacity to act depended on a political–cultural context which was set firmly at the centre. This argument stands in such contrast to some of the prevailing literature and suggests such a different overall view of the relationship between Roman state and Christian Church around the year 400 – with the latter being far more dependent on the Empire than is generally recognized – that it is important first to explore the roots of the opposite point of view.

Star billing has often been given to Ambrose, the forceful bishop of Milan for much of the last quarter of the fourth century (374–97). His bones are still on display in an embossed silver urn in the Milanese cathedral that bears his name, set alongside those of two martyrs who, as we shall see, made a crucial intervention at an awkward moment in the bishop's career. Iconographically, one of Ambrose's saintly attributes is a whip, appropriately enough given that he's chiefly remembered for a sequence of confrontations with two reigning Roman emperors – Valentinian II and Theodosius I – from which, so the available primary sources tell us, the bishop emerged completely victorious, thanks to his own unshakeable faith in the power of the Christian God.

In 384, an influential faction at court was attempting to persuade Valentinian II to allow the pagan Altar of Victory to be restored to its traditional position in the Roman Senate. The altar had originally been erected by Augustus, along with a statue of the goddess Victoria, after his victory over Mark Antony and Cleopatra in 30 BC and had played an important role in senatorial ceremonial ever since. Incense was burnt on it, and libations poured before it; the altar was also the place where oaths – not least those of loyalty to a new emperor – were traditionally made. In 382, however, Valentinian's older brother, the emperor Gratian, had disestablished all the traditional public cults of the city of Rome, and ordered the altar removed. When Gratian was murdered in a coup in the summer of 383, a faction within the Roman Senate, reinforced by strong connections to Valentinian's Milan-based regime, tried to have the altar restored. The request was formally presented to the Christian emperor on behalf of the Senate in an official letter drawn up by Rome's then urban prefect, the senator Symmachus. Cast in graceful, moderate language, its plea for religious toleration has often drawn approving nods from modern commentators.

The petitioners, the letter stated, 'seek to have restored the religious institutions that have served the state well for so long'. It pointed out that many previous emperors had participated in the rites, even some of Valentinian's Christian predecessors. The whole point of the altar and its associated cult was to guarantee imperial success, and 'who', the letter asked,

> is such a good friend of the barbarians that he does not want the altar of Victory back? We are cautious with regard to the future and avoid omens of change. If she [Victory] cannot be honoured as a god, at least let her name be honoured. Your Eternities owe a great debt to Victory and will owe more still. Let those who have gained nothing from her turn their backs on her power, but do not yourselves forsake her friendship and patronage with the triumphs it brings.

Bishop Ambrose's blunt retort – written before he'd seen the senatorial missive – stands in marked contrast to Symmachus' graceful cadences. Emperor Valentinian, he wrote, should not restore the pagan altar. 'How will you', he demanded of Valentinian,

> reply to the bishop who says to you: 'the Church does not ask you for gifts, for you adorn the pagans' temples with your offerings? The altar of Christ spits at your presents, as you have set up an altar to idols. The voice is yours, yours is the hand, the subscription is yours and yours the deed. Our Lord Jesus refuses and spurns your obedience, because you obey idols, for he said to you, "No man can serve two masters."'

Duly browbeaten, Valentinian came down on Ambrose's side. The bishop followed up with a second salvo for good measure, which went through Symmachus' letter point by point, refuting it with a ruthlessness which cannot but command respect, even if not affection. At one point, Symmachus argued that removing the altar of Victory had caused the previous year's famine. On the whole, Ambrose thought otherwise. His reply, heavy with sarcasm and exaggeration, noted that harvests had failed throughout human history, 'when the earth seethed with pagan superstition', and that pagan temples had been abolished decades previously: 'has it only just occurred to the pagans' gods to avenge their wrongs?' Besides, he pointed out, the pagan gods can't have been that angry, given how good this year's harvest was turning out to be: 'The people of the countryside ... rejoice in their prosperity, the harvests exceed all expectation and satisfy hunger in full, giving an abundant answer to their prayers.'[2]

Having seen off the pagans, and established his dominance over the imperial court, so the traditional account has it, Ambrose redoubled his success in a further confrontation with Valentinian's regime in 386, when he seized control of a church, the Portian Basilica in Milan, which the imperial court wished to use to celebrate Easter. At this point, the dispute over the nature of Christ 'settled' at Nicaea was still going strong. Valentinian's regime supported a non-Nicene position, and the Nicene-supporting Ambrose picked a fight to assert the superiority of his own views. After a brief confrontation when the bishop's Nicene congregation physically occupied the church, the emperor again backed down. Shortly afterwards, the martyrs Gervasius and Protasius (executed perhaps in the second century) supposedly confirmed that Ambrose's actions had divine approval, by revealing their physical whereabouts to the bishop in a dream. Ambrose unearthed their remains, which were formally translated from a suburban cemetery to the same basilica, whereupon the martyrs duly performed a series of miracles – in particular, making a blind man see – which 'proved' (to Ambrose at least, if not necessarily to everyone else) that everything had unfolded according to God's will.

A few years later, Ambrose was equally forthright in a series of confrontations with the eastern emperor Theodosius, who was briefly in Milan after coming to Valentinian's aid when his rule was menaced by a usurper, Maximus. First, the bishop – who wanted to assert the separateness of the priestly office – refused to allow Theodosius to take communion with the priests at the altar, sending him packing to join the rest of the congregation in the nave. He then forced Theodosius to rescind an order stating that the local bishop needed to pay for the restoration of a synagogue in the eastern city of Callinicum (now Raqqa, Syria) that had been burnt down by Christian rioters. The *pièce de résistance* came in 390, after the citizens of Thessalonica had rioted and killed one of Theodosius' leading generals. In retribution, the emperor had allowed detachments of soldiers to plunder the city, killing as many as five thousand people in the process. Outraged, Ambrose forced the emperor to do formal penance the following winter before he would readmit him to communion. This was followed, in spring 391, by the newly penitent Theodosius' general ban on sacrifice, and some historians have been quick to see two and two here making four. Not only had Ambrose browbeaten Theodosius into personal submission, but he had then used that leverage to institute broader religious change by persuading the emperor to take wider action against residual pagan cult practices, which quickly escalated into the full-scale closure and destruction of pagan temples over the next thirty years.[3] On closer inspection, however, this magnificently heroic vision of Ambrose's career, with its associated image of Church dominating empire in matters of religion, fades to grey.

For a start, this account of a courageous Ambrose is based overwhelmingly on the bishop's own accounts of his supposed triumphs – and these, it turns out, are both self-serving and deceptive. No bishop of Milan, before or after him, achieved anything like the same prominence, and, looked at carefully, it becomes clear that the bishop's career was the product of very particular circumstances, and not of any seismic structural shift that had empowered bishops in general, and a more independent corporate institutional Church, in dealings with the emperor and his court.

Ambrose's two initial triumphs – the Altar of Victory and the Portian Basilica – came at the expense of what was probably the weakest imperial regime of the entire fourth century. In 375, on the sudden death of his father, the western emperor Valentinian I, Valentinian II was acclaimed emperor, aged four, by a small cabal of officers and court aristocrats. His acclamation was in direct challenge to his older half-brother, Gratian, who had already been named emperor before their father's death. Gratian quickly suppressed this putsch on behalf of his young half-brother, but in 383 Gratian was assassinated in a *coup d'état* which saw the Rhine Army commander, Magnus Maximus, take power over much of the west. Valentinian, now twelve, was again named emperor by a small group of Italian military officers and court officials. At the time of the Altar of Victory controversy in 384, Valentinian was barely a teenager and his regime controlled only a fraction of the western Empire (Italy and North Africa), with Maximus ruling Britain, Gaul and Spain. Valentinian's regime continued to exist, in fact, only because Maximus was trying to persuade the eastern emperor Theodosius I – who broadly supported Valentinian – to recognize him as a legitimate colleague, and hence head off the possibility of civil war. As soon as it became clear that Theodosius was not going to play ball, Valentinian lost his usefulness, and Maximus simply marched into Italy in 387. Valentinian and his mother fled east.[4]

Neither the Altar of Victory nor the Portian Basilica were triumphs over a Roman emperor enjoying the fullness of power; and in both cases Ambrose's success required help from inside the imperial court. Although Ambrose states – and I'm guessing that he wouldn't lie about this outright – that, when he wrote his first letter to the emperor, he had not yet read Symmachus' petition, he clearly already knew precisely what it contained. In other words, informants at court had briefed him extensively, and we know that they fed him information on other occasions too. The entire episode, in fact, illustrates some of the murkier workings of power and influence at the imperial court. When Gratian had ordered the Altar of Victory removed in 382, Symmachus immediately led a senatorial delegation north to try to get the emperor to change his mind, but they had been denied access to him – the easiest way for Gratian to avoid possible embarrassment. Valentinian's regime was much weaker than Gratian's, however, and it included Symmachus' father-in-law, Praetextatus, as the Praetorian prefect of Italy. Symmachus was himself the urban prefect of Rome and sent his letter as a formal missive – a *relatio* – from prefect to emperor, which could not be barred – as his earlier embassy had been – from the imperial presence. Unable to deny Symmachus any access to the emperor, the Christian opposition to the altar at court turned to other methods, briefing Ambrose to deliver a pre-emptive broadside that would make it all but impossible for the emperor to grant his prefect's request, even though the ground had been carefully prepared. What we're really seeing here is not so much a bishop berating the emperor, therefore, as one faction at a divided and structurally feeble imperial court mobilizing Ambrose to block off a move on the part of its rival.[5]

If Valentinian was a cipher at the head of a feeble, barely tolerated western imperial coalition, the same was not true of Theodosius. But Theodosius, primarily and fundamentally the emperor of the east, was never in Milan for long. All of Ambrose's stunts were pulled against an imperial court that was trying to make the west governable for the young Valentinian, after restoring him to the throne. This, again, was not a regime in full, long-term control of the western reins of power. When dealing with the massacre at Thessalonica, moreover, Ambrose's exchanges with the eastern emperor were more complex than simply forcing him to do penance. The massacre had put Theodosius in a difficult position. He was a self-proclaimed Christian emperor whose self-presentation had always stressed his merciful qualities, both at the beginning of his reign in 380/81 in his dealings with the aristocracy of the eastern Empire, and later on in 387, when a tax riot in Antioch led to treasonable vandalism to the imperial images, and generated fears that there might be a general massacre there. Ordering the massacre at Thessalonica therefore contradicted the regime's ideological self-presentation and the emperor needed to restore normal service to calm potential political unrest. Looked at closely, Ambrose's own writings indicate that it was less of an imposition of penance than a carefully orchestrated double act. Ambrose offered the emperor the option of penance as a way out of his current embarrassment; the emperor took it. The penance also lasted for a lot less than the eight months claimed by one of our main sources, the Church historian Theodoret. Shortly after this public relations exercise, Theodosius headed off to Constantinople, and that was the end of the matter. Ambrose exercised no lasting influence on Theodosius' regime, and rapidly declined to marginality even in the west, since, after the defeat of Maximus, Valentinian's regime relocated north of the Alps, leaving the bishop firmly isolated from court.[6]

Ambrose's magnificent exercise in self-promotion has exerted an almost hypnotic fascination over the years, but accepting it at face value both generates a misleading understanding of the bishop's own prominence and has deeply distorting knock-on effects for our overall view of Church-state relations in the late fourth century.[7] As the broader run of evidence makes clear, Roman emperors exercised far more general authority in religious affairs than any individual bishop, as a more detailed examination of the destruction of pagan temples makes clear.

SERAPEUM

Theodosius' ban on sacrifice was quickly followed by the destruction of one of the greatest pagan temple precincts of the ancient Mediterranean, an event whose aftershocks rippled right across the Roman Mediterranean. Built in Alexandria in the third century BC by Pharaoh Ptolemy III Euergetes, the Serapeum was dedicated to the god Serapis. Serapis was a syncretic hybrid god, combining elements from the cults of two older deities: Osiris and Apis. Although his worship pre-dated the Ptolemies – the dynasty descending from the general of Alexander the Great, who inherited Egypt and its environs in the post-mortem carve-up of his empire – they deliberately fostered the cult, adding new attributes to his divinity to unite both their Greek and Egyptian subjects. Aspects of the Greek gods Hades and Demeter were folded in, giving the revamped Serapis great powers over the underworld; and a dash of Dionysus, to provide a little extra benevolence. Not much now survives above ground of Serapis's great temple, placed as it was in the most prominent spot in Alexandria, on top of its (not very high) acropolis, but we do have an appreciation from the fourth-century historian Ammianus Marcellinus:

> The Serapeum, splendid to a point that words would only diminish its beauty, has such spacious rooms flanked by columns, filled with such life-like statues and a multitude of other works of art, that nothing, except the Capitoleum [in Rome], which attests to Rome's venerable eternity, can be considered as ambitious in the entire world.

The temple's design was based on the great Serapeum of Memphis, in Lower Egypt: temple buildings elevated on a huge platform, which you had to climb a hundred steps to reach. Gleaming marble on the outside, it was painted and gilded inside, the main room dominated by a statue of the god himself that was so huge his hands appeared to touch the side walls. Serapis was portrayed here as Hades, with robe, Greek hairstyle and beard, but with a basket of grain on his head, symbolizing fertility and his ancient connection to Osiris; Hades' three-headed dog Cerberus was at his feet. According to the theologian and philosopher Clement of Alexandria, the statue was dark blue, constructed from a variety of precious materials. Of all the other works of art within the precinct, only one survives: an Apis bull statue that you can still see in Alexandria's Graeco-Roman museum. Other rooms within the complex, some of whose underground chambers can still be visited, contained the remnants of the city's fabled library, rescued from the great fire which consumed most of it during Caesar's conquest of the city in 48 BC.[8]

What happened to the Serapeum in the early 390s is not completely clear: we have competing pagan and Christian accounts, but none from an eyewitness. The most widely accepted narrative is that the then patriarch of Alexandria, Theophilus, took possession of a disused pagan temple, perhaps a Mithraeum (but definitely not the Serapeum itself), with the intention of turning it into a church. It's possible that Theophilus was taking advantage of Theodosius' recent law banning sacrifices and worship at the shrines of temples, formally excluding all persons 'from profane entrance into temples by the opposition of Our law'.[9] Theophilus had possibly set his sights on a pagan cult site that had recently shut its doors in response to this measure.

On exploring the temple, the patriarch found either some sacred cult objects (the pagan tradition) or evidence of pagan human sacrifice (the Christian), which he triumphantly paraded through the city to discredit the pagan opposition. This prompted a huge riot among the city's still significant non-Christian population, which ended with some of the rioters barricading themselves inside the Serapeum. At this point, Emperor Theodosius became involved, and a compromise was negotiated. Supposedly at the request of Theophilus, the rioters were allowed safe passage out of the temple complex. Imperial troopers then dismantled the Serapeum stone by stone, removing its treasures. But not Serapis himself. According to one story, a crowd gathered round Serapis and gazed at the statue in wonder. But one brave iconoclast eventually found the courage to swing an axe (as with most colossal statues of the ancient world, much of its internal structure was wooden). This was enough to convince everyone that Serapis possessed no magical powers, and the statue was smashed to pieces.[10]

While significant in itself, the destruction of the Serapeum also stands in the middle chronologically of a renewed bout of temple destruction in the eastern Mediterranean, after something of a lull following the limited closures that had occurred in the reign of Constantius II in the 350s (p. 88). As at Alexandria, bishops played a major role in this second round of temple trashing, often mobilizing monks to act as hit men in chief. The process seems to have begun in Syria in the 380s, the role of monks being underscored by a local, hostile commentator, the pagan rhetorician Libanius:

> [They] hasten to attack the temples with sticks and stones and bars of iron . . . Then utter desolation follows, with the stripping of roofs, demolition of walls, the tearing down of statues and the overthrow of altars, and priests must either keep quiet or die. After demolishing one, they scurry to another and to a third, and trophy is piled on trophy. Such outrages occur even in the cities, but they are most common in the countryside.

Libanius was piling on the rhetorical fireworks – his stock in trade – to try to persuade the emperor to intervene. But he also gives some specific examples, and his account finds general corroboration in other sources. The *Life* of Bishop Marcellus of Apamea confirms that its eponymous protagonist was dedicated to the art of temple demolition in 380s Syria, from where the process quickly spread right around the Mediterranean.

The destruction of the Serapeum, at the start of the next decade, acted as a catalyst for further violence in Egypt. During the late fourth and, particularly, the early fifth centuries, a cluster of Egyptian monastic leaders, including Shenoute of the famous White Monastery in Upper Egypt, Makarios of Tkộw, and Moses of Abydos, mobilized their brethren to smash up pagan sanctuaries, kill pagan priests, and even to break into people's houses to destroy private shrines. Further west along the Mediterranean coast, all the temples were closed in Carthage (which occupied a site on the eastern edge of present-day Tunis) in March 399. According to one much-cited account, the *Life* composed by one Mark the Deacon, this is also the era when Bishop

Porphyry of Gaza (395–420) took on and defeated the most enthusiastically pagan council of all the eastern cities. The bishop converted Gaza's population and destroyed its temples, above all the famous Marneion, a temple of Zeus Marnas, the local Hellenistic incarnation of Dagon, patron of agriculture. This famous landmark was set on fire, we are told, using a potent combination of pitch, sulphur and fat. Once burned out, its stones were triumphantly used to pave the city's streets. While the *Life* is problematic (the work of a later fifth-century forger, rather than the straightforwardly contemporary account that it pretends to be), there is no doubting the general level of violence deployed in the two generations after *c.* 380 against many pagan sanctuaries and their precious cult objects.[11]

The ferocity of this revolutionary moment in the cultural history of the ancient Mediterranean, ending well over a thousand years of continuous pagan religious evolution, remains vividly on display today in the damage done to many of the cult statues that grace the museums both of the Mediterranean region itself, and of the European colonial powers which so determinedly appropriated its antiquities from the eighteenth century onwards. Many of these statues are carved with crosses to neutralize the power of any demons they were thought to have contained; others bear clear marks of disfigurement, with noses struck off and other facial features obliterated. The statuary of ancient Egypt's great temples, beloved of the tourist trade, all bear the marks of Christian iconoclastic attention. At sites such as Karnak, Philae and Dendara, gods' faces have all been carefully chiselled off, the legs of human and animal figures attacked. Alongside these disfigured statues were added new icons of saints, or even whole churches (five, in the case of the great Amun temple of Luxor), to destroy the demonic powers that previously controlled these spaces. As perhaps the greatest of all these Christian iconoclasts, Abbot Shenoute of the White Monastery, put it:

> At the site of a shrine to an unclean spirit, it will henceforth be a shrine to the Holy Spirit. And at the site of sacrificing to Satan and worshipping and fearing him, Christ will henceforth be served there, and He will be worshipped, bowed down to and feared. And where there are blasphemings, it is blessings and hymns that will henceforth be there.

As has been observed in modern colonial contexts (Hawaii in the nineteenth century; the Pacific cargo cults of the twentieth), the overturning of a long-held set of beliefs often prompts a wave of frantic apotropaic violence towards the symbols and places associated with the discredited system: a fierce physical expression of ideological revolution.[12]

All of which puts into perspective some of the grander claims made for Bishop Ambrose's role as the catalyst for this second great bout of temple destruction. It was already gathering momentum in the eastern Mediterranean in the decade prior to the bishop's imposition of penance on Theodosius, and any claim that the bishop of Milan was somehow responsible for the Serapeum's destruction is misplaced. Theodosius actually issued his famous decree closing temples at Thessalonica on his way back to Constantinople, not in Milan (in the presence of the bishop), which weakens the case for Ambrose having had any serious input into its creation at all.[13] More generally, despite the leading role played by representatives of the Church in many of the local acts of violence, the precise chronology and unfolding political process behind the renewed destruction of pagan temples from the 380s onwards indicate something else: that the real order of relations between Churchmen and the imperial state, at least when it came to temple destruction, was very different from what has often been claimed. Local church leaders on the ground were not acting independently of the imperial will but were responding to a new climate of possibility that had been set at the centre.

All Christian moves against pagan cult sites in the time of Constantine and his sons up to the 350s were made on imperial orders, rather than being initiatives of individual Churchmen. This does not mean that influential Christians at court had no input into the policy – they surely did – but that the limited numbers of temples shut down under Constantine and his sons were all direct or indirect victims of the state, and the legislation it passed. This pattern did not change in any fundamental way in the 380s. The pagan commentator Libanius firmly blames the renewal of temple destruction in Syria firmly on the then chief administrative officer of the eastern provinces, the Praetorian prefect Maternus Cynegius. According to Libanius, Cynegius interpreted the law of 381 forbidding sacrifice for divinatory purposes so broadly that it had become a licence for the widespread temple destruction about which Libanius was now complaining. Libanius also says that the emperor didn't know what was happening. While this might have been true, given the inherent limitations of imperial control in the localities (p. 87), Libanius was appealing directly to the emperor, and so trying to give him a means to change the policy which would not cause any loss of imperial face. This, together with other factors (such as Libanius' inflated rhetoric), makes it extremely difficult to know both precisely how many temples were destroyed in Syria in the 380s, and the extent to which this was direct imperial policy. But one thing is clear: imperial legislation, and its interpretation and enactment by official representatives of the state, stood at the heart of the process.

This is confirmed by the few specific accounts that survive. Bishop Marcellus of Apamea, for instance, was called in to deal with the local temple of Zeus by an unnamed 'official' who wasn't able, for some reason, to complete the job by himself. Our source is the bishop's *Life*, which maintains that Marcellus' Christian virtue was required to overcome the power of the evil spirits inhabiting the sanctuary, but it may just have been a question of Marcellus being able to provide the manpower. Similarly, Theophilus, even though, as bishop of Alexandria, he was one of the five patriarchs of the late Roman Church, didn't try to take on the Serapeum himself. His own ambitions ran only as far as annexing a disused pagan site. The destruction of Serapis's shrine was carried out by Emperor Theodosius' local officials and their troops on the emperor's orders. According to the *Life* of Bishop Porphyry, likewise, a series of explicit imperial orders were required from the imperial court of Theodosius' son Arcadius for the final extinction of pagan cults in Gaza. And even if some of the particular details recorded in the *Life* cannot be trusted, it is striking that a reasonably contemporary forger – working sometime in the fifth century – imagined that an imperial decree was the best way to proceed when tackling a nest of obstinate pagans.[14]

What the overall shape of the evidence tells us, in other words, is that the kinds of vicious acts of local iconoclasm celebrated in the life and writings of monks like Shenoute – and manifest in all the defacing and graffiti still visible today – have to be seen as part of a broader process that originated with, and was dependent upon, the authority of the imperial Roman state and its officials. By the fifth century, the state-sponsored shutting down of pagan religion, in all its manifestations, was so well established that bishops and monks were pretty much free to do as they pleased. But this is not where things began. While the final phase of temple destruction may have been largely enacted by local initiative, it was authorized and made possible by imperial legislation passed in the final two decades of the fourth century. And even this final phase required – in its early stages, and perhaps a bit longer, too, if we can believe anything in the *Life of Porphyry* – the active support of imperial officials such as Cynegius in 380s Syria, and even (on occasion) the participation of imperial troopers, as in the dismantling of the Serapeum.

This reinterpretation of late fourth- and early fifth-century Christian iconoclasm squares with the broader process of religious change we have been exploring. Fourth-century Christian bishops were not – initially at least – figures of overwhelming authority, either within the burgeoning Christian community or more generally in Roman society at large. Even the most influential among them struggled to shape the faith of the wealthy lay aristocracy and gentry, whose conversion played such a key role in the overall Christianization of the Empire, and which proceeded in the middle decades of the fourth century for reasons and by mechanisms which were largely outside episcopal control.[15] The grand role Constantine originally envisaged for bishops as figures of great local legal authority was also dialled back. Only when substantial numbers of the Empire's local and regional elites started to become bishops did the office begin to acquire greater clout.

Against this background, it is easy to see why bishops alone would not generally have been able to take on the kinds of vested local interests that protected pagan cult sites. Sometimes, this took the form of angry mobs, highly resistant to unwanted processes of religious change. Marcellus of Apamea eventually came to a sticky end when he was consumed by a fire he himself had set to a rural pagan shrine within his diocese. For the most part, however, the public religious allegiance of any particular city community tended to be dictated by the attitudes of local grandees, acting collectively through their town councils.[16] As we have seen, both the pagan Tetrarchs and the Christian Constantinian dynasties rewarded and punished city councils on the basis of their public declarations of religious affiliation, emphasizing that it was collective local elite opinion which dictated any particular city's stance.

The socially undistinguished Christian bishops of the earlier fourth century struggled to act effectively against so much formal and informal local power, but what was happening at and through the imperial court steadily transformed the situation as the century unfolded, in two vital respects. First, official imperial support could increasingly be obtained to face down local pagan resistance, even in the powerful form of a united, pagan town council: the general kind of process envisaged in the *Life* of Porphyry of Gaza. Second, more fundamentally, the structural revolution we have examined in the inner workings of local Roman elites and their connections to the imperial centre reduced the likelihood of such resistance so profoundly over the course of the fourth century that the kind of direct intervention described in the *Life of Porphyry* became increasingly unnecessary. By around 400, the dominant voice in local affairs belonged to the *honorati*, acting and retired imperial officials; such men, by virtue of having found preferment within the imperial system, were ever more likely to have adopted Christianity as the fourth century progressed. By one and the same process, therefore, not only did the kind of official assistance described in the *Life of Porphyry* become easier to solicit from an increasingly Christian officialdom, but the likelihood of meeting local pagan resistance within communities was increasingly reduced, thanks to local grandees leaving for imperial service and then returning to their home societies afterwards as participants in the system.

When, from the 370s onwards, these same men started to become bishops as well, the loop tightened: everything was pushing in the same direction. As with elite Christianization, however, this process began at the imperial court and was pushed forward by the kinds of ways in which local elites interacted with the imperial system. Seen this way, it would be surprising had the final phase of suppressing paganism *not* begun with imperial laws and officials, rather than with individual bishops and monks.

Looking back on the momentous events of the fourth century from the calmer waters of the mid-fifth, a series of Church historians – Socrates, Sozomen, Theodoret and Philostorgius – had many different stories to tell, and differed significantly among themselves, not least on doctrinal allegiance. But they all painted a similar picture of Christianity's triumphant destruction of pagan religion in the era of Theodosius I and afterwards, and the violent expression of Christian energy which revealed that pagan cult sites, previously believed to have been sources of benign divine assistance, were actually the haunts of malevolent demons who were decisively expelled. The violence of this final phase in the dissolution of the temples contrasts markedly with the apparent calm of the preceding half century separating Constantine's declaration in favour of Christianity and Theodosius' accession. During this time, as we've seen, much of the key progress – among the movers and shakers of the Roman world, anyway – was actually made through much quieter processes of individual choice.[17]

If we look at these apparently contrasting phases more closely, however, two things become clear. First, the two phases – one relatively calm, the second increasingly violent – were for all their differences in character precisely that: two phases of one overall process. The licensed violence of the bishops and monks from the 380s onwards could not have happened without the slower, much less dramatic antecedent conversion of the imperial system, which passed the laws and provided the formal and informal support that made it possible to smash up temples either side of the year 400. Second, the imperial system was itself central to both phases. Elite conversion was powered by the perception that declaring yourself Christian offered an advantage in the struggle to maximize your position where patronage and connection increasingly mattered, and elite conversion then made it possible to accelerate the Christianizing agenda that shut down pagan cults, forcibly where necessary, from the 380s onwards. In other words, imperial Roman state structures were not an obstacle to the unfolding triumph of the Christian Church – something to be browbeaten into submission, Ambrose-style – so much as its central player. All of which raises fundamental questions about the precise nature of Church-state relations within a Christian Empire.

CITY OF GOD

The most sustained theoretical treatment of the relationship between the Christian Church and the Roman state produced in the late imperial era is Augustine of Hippo's *City of God*. Written in instalments between 413 and 426, it accords the Roman Empire and its rulers only a strictly limited role in the overall Divine Plan for human salvation.

According to Augustine's definition, the City of God is the heavenly body of all believing Christians due to be saved in the Final Judgement at the end of time, and to dwell thereafter in the New Jerusalem of Heaven. The City's privileged membership is absolutely not confined to inhabitants of the Roman Empire, but – already in Augustine's time, and even more so in the future – was bound to contain individuals from elsewhere: not least barbarians of various kinds. As Augustine puts it: 'The heavenly city, while on its earthly pilgrimage, calls forth its citizens from every nation ... not caring about any diversity in the customs, laws and institutions whereby they severally make provision for the achievement and maintenance of earthly peace ... '[18]

There is, as far as Augustine is concerned, no essential coincidence between the boundaries of the Roman Empire and the boundaries of the City of God. While the Empire does have some role to play in the unfolding history of human salvation, and certainly exists by the Will of God, that role, for Augustine, was contingent and time limited. God supported the Empire not because its founding fathers were uniquely virtuous, but because their lust for glory at least meant that they didn't fall prey to worse vices: 'This unbounded passion for glory checked their other appetites. They felt it would be shameful for their country to be enslaved, but glorious for her to have dominion and empire; and so they set their hearts first on making her free, then on making her sovereign.'[19]

In Augustine's view, the Romans' desire for domination acted as a brake on corruption and venality and gave their society a – relative – moral superiority, which made God choose the Empire as His vehicle: for a time. The effective implementation of this desire for domination – i.e., the geographical extent of its power – also meant that it was able to institute conditions of peace for much of humanity, which was both a good in itself and created advantageous circumstances for the spread of Christian belief. (The limitations of geographic knowledge in late antiquity made it easier for Augustine to suppose that the *Pax Romana* extended over a larger portion of the planet's population than was actually the case.) But, by the same token, in Augustine's view, Divine support was highly contingent, and likely to be time limited as it had been for preceding world Empires (such as those of the Egyptians, Alexander the Great and the Persians). When a 'better' vehicle came along, God would once again switch His backing, because there was no absolute superiority to the quality of life the Empire supported.[20] As Augustine saw it, there was nothing unique about the Empire's overall role in God's plans for the salvation of humankind.

Two events, occurring some three decades apart, probably helped concentrate Augustine's mind on the likely time-limited nature of Roman dominion and the Divine support which had brought the Empire into being. These were the military disaster at Hadrianople (modern-day Edirne, in Turkey), where the Goths had defeated and killed the eastern emperor Valens and two-thirds of his elite field army on one day in 378; and, in August 410, when the city of Rome was sacked for the first time in eight hundred years, also by the Goths. Coming to adulthood in such a context, it's possible to understand why Augustine was ready to contemplate the idea that *Roma* was not going to be that *Aeterna*. Be that as it may, in the *City of God* he constructed a view of the growing Christian Church as an institution that was fundamentally independent of the Roman state. Where the Empire could count on only contingent, time-limited assistance, the Church was God's eternal vehicle for human salvation.[21]

As such, Augustine's magnum opus provided the essential theoretical underpinning for a vision of the Christian Church as a corporate entity which was, and should be, completely independent of the authority not only of the Roman Empire, but of any other worldly authority whatsoever. This ensured the text's enduring popularity in the high Middle Ages and after, when actual practice began to mirror Augustine's vision of a truly independent Church. But, if certainly prophetic, Augustine's vision was actually way ahead of its time. In the late Roman period, neither practical reality, nor indeed the prevailing ideological superstructure remotely matched the ideal type of Church-state relations set out in the *City of God*.

It is worth stepping back from the detail of events for a moment to think about the key components of Christian religious authority, because seeing who was exercising this authority in the late Roman period – and why – will help us better understand the precise relationship between Church and Empire in the aftermath of Constantine's conversion. One obvious element – of particular importance in an era when, as we have seen, many basic theological doctrines were first being fully defined (p. 35) – involved the ultimate regulation of what constituted 'orthodox' or generally accepted belief. Many different individuals, operating in various contexts, will always contribute intellectually to the theological groundwork, but a key indicator of where religious authority really lies is who has ultimate responsibility for making sure that Christianity holds to 'correct' doctrine. Religious authority likewise entails responsibility for defining and enforcing correct standards of Christian behaviour for both clergy and laity, and for making Church law (which, among other things, codifies many of those standards in legal form). Control of senior appointments within the Church hierarchy provides the third key marker. If you analyse the functioning of the Christian Church in the late Roman period against such a checklist, a clear pattern emerges. Contrary to the ideal vision of ecclesiastical independence set out in Augustine's *City of God*, it quickly becomes apparent that ultimate Christian religious authority resided firmly in the office of the emperor.

The two centuries after Constantine's 'conversion' were a decisive period in the making of Christian doctrine, when many Christian teachings, particularly as regards its distinctive Trinitarian Godhead – Father, Son and Holy Ghost – reached full definition. Christian intellectuals – initially both lay and ecclesiastical, though the latter gradually came to dominate as the authority patterns of early Christianity were slowly eclipsed – did most of the thinking and writing that powered the debate. But the final choice between the different intellectual positions, defining and validating 'orthodoxy', was the responsibility of a series of ecumenical councils. The initial meeting of representatives of the entire Christian world at Nicaea in 325 was followed at irregular intervals by further ecumenical councils at Serdica (342), Constantinople (381), Chalcedon (451), and then a second council at Constantinople in 553. Strikingly, all these gatherings were held in the east (even Serdica, modern Sofia, was in the Greek-speaking half of the Balkans). Correspondingly, most of the intellectual running in the big theological debates was being made in the eastern half of the Empire too, by rival Christian intellectuals working primarily in Greek. Apart from the council of Chalcedon, at which Pope Leo I contributed a major document known as the *Tome of Leo*, Latinate westerners, even bishops of Rome, tended just to send observers and let eastern Churchmen get on with it.

Many of the assumptions of Greek philosophy and science, not to mention the literary analytical techniques of the Greek grammarians (who specialized in providing reading strategies for resolving contradictions within the texts of the classical canon, not least between Plato and Aristotle) also provided the basic methodological tools and intellectual building blocks out of which orthodox late Roman Christian doctrine was gradually constructed.[22] North Africa apart – although here we're largely talking about Augustine, whose work had little Empire-wide influence in his own lifetime – the beating heart of late Roman Christianity lay in the Greek east, reflecting both its own origins and the fact that classical philosophy had always been primarily conducted in Greek rather than Latin.

Even more important was the central role in the conciliar process played by Roman emperors. On the logistical front, the precedent established by Constantine at Nicaea continued. Emperors underwrote the mechanics of developing doctrine by providing transport, and board and lodging, sometimes to hundreds of bishops at a time (much to the annoyance of the pagan historian Ammianus Marcellinus, who was scathing about the frequency and cost of Church councils under Constantine's son Constantius II). Apart from the recognized ecumenical councils, there were some other equally large meetings which arrived at what were eventually identified as 'wrong' doctrinal answers. As a result, these meetings don't figure in standard lists of ecumenical councils, although that is what they were understood to be when they were convened. Seleucia and Rimini (359), held in each half of the Empire at the behest of Constantius II to license his preferred vision of non-Nicene orthodoxy (p. 33), Constantinople in 360, and the so-called 'robber council' of Ephesus in 449 (which briefly championed a vision of how human and divine were mixed in the person of Christ, only to be rejected at the council of Chalcedon two years later) all fall into this category.

The emperor's role in unfolding Trinitarian doctrine was not limited to logistical support. It was always an imperial decision whether and when to call an ecumenical council. No one else had the authority to do so, and this principle was never challenged. Obviously, when they thought such a meeting necessary or imminent, Churchmen would lobby vigorously at court; but without the imperial say so, ecumenical councils simply couldn't happen. Moreover, emperors usually also set at least part of the agenda for discussion – which was only natural since there was often much at stake.

Individual emperors varied greatly in the intensity of their interest in precise matters of doctrine. Not all were like Constantius II or, in the sixth century, Justinian I, both of whom were known for their love of theological niceties, and fierce advocacy of particular strands of opinion. But all emperors were interested in peace and unity within the Church, another major theme of late Roman doctrinal debate, since their legitimacy as self-declared, God-chosen rulers was always called into question by Christian religious divisions. All emperors were ready to involve themselves in matters of doctrine at least to that extent, in the – often forlorn – hope of generating overall Christian harmony. In practice, too, the imperial will proved more important than conciliar debate to the doctrinal outcomes that eventually emerged.

This was evident in the unfolding debate on the correct way to describe the relationship between God the Father and God the Son. In 325, the council at Nicaea came up with the term *homoousios* ('of the same substance': suggesting that these two persons of the Trinity shared an identical essence) to describe it, but it took two generations for the term to win final acceptance because of suspicions it might not make it possible to maintain any real distinction between the Father and the Son (see p. 32). Debate on the matter only finally came to an end in the 380s, when supporters of rival, non-Nicene definitions – which had been 'orthodoxy' for the decades in between – lost imperial support, and a majority of eastern Churchmen argued that *homoousios* could be glossed in ways which safeguarded the necessary separation between Father and Son. All this found its full expression at the ecumenical council of Constantinople, convened and run by Emperor Theodosius I in 381. While rival Churchmen may have been doing most, or even all, of the thinking, their presentations of alternative ways of reading the biblical texts were not by themselves sufficient to resolve the argument. For one thing, as we have seen, it was not intellectually obvious which of the rival lines of interpretation – privileging the Gospel of John's presentation of Christ over the more human figure to be found in the synoptic Gospels, or the synoptics over John – was correct; both sides employed the same kinds of literary techniques to get round apparently contradictory biblical passages. More importantly, neither side had political or legal leverage to make their view stick without outside assistance. As a result, the imperial court became the key battleground, with proponents of the different theological positions struggling to win imperial backing for their cause, in preparation for obtaining the ultimate validation that came with approval at a full-scale ecumenical council.[23]

Throughout the late Roman period, because the emperor controlled the calling of ecumenical councils, all the major theological debates simply had to come to court. The relationship between God the Father and God the Son (discussion of which was responsible for the calling of the councils of Nicaea and Serdica and the first council of Constantinople) was closely followed by intense discussion of the exact relationship of the Holy Spirit to the other two persons of the Trinity; and further debates on how to understand the admixture of human and divine elements in the Incarnate Christ (the latter responsible for two further ecumenical councils: Chalcedon and Constantinople II, as well as the council of Ephesus, whose findings were subsequently quashed). In all of this, it is worth emphasizing just how deeply emperors were involved in the ecumenical conciliar process. They didn't just call an ecumenical council and let Churchmen get on with it. Each council was the product of intense lobbying, and emperors usually knew what answer they wanted to achieve before the meetings began. Even Constantine, praised for listening to his bishops with deference at Nicaea, and for not presuming to dictate to them on matters of doctrine, nonetheless jumped in to bang heads together and make the majority of bishops (even many who afterwards showed great distaste for it) come into line with the concept of *homoousios*, when it started to look like the best available option. At subsequent councils, where our records become much fuller, it was entirely normal for trusted regime officials, who were not themselves clergy, to chair the key sessions.[24]

Throughout the fourth and fifth centuries, individual Churchmen were periodically critical of imperial involvement in matters of doctrine. It is even possible to string these moments of criticism together to generate a picture of a Church structure that was determined to be independent of imperial interference. To do so, however, is anachronistic. Churchmen generally criticized emperors for interfering in matters of religion only when they were currently supporting a position to which the cleric in question was hostile – and in such cases, the Churchmen never stopped agitating for a change in the imperial position. When they produced the 'right' answer, however, imperially run, imperially fixed councils were absolutely fine.[25] In reality, the late Roman world offered no viable alternative. Because emperors controlled both the calling and the conduct of doctrine-defining, ecumenical councils, the imperial court could not but be central to the formation of Christian doctrine.

Imperial authority was equally central to any effective enforcement of agreed doctrinal settlements, for theological debate in itself never really ceased. Proponents of all the different major theological positions of the late Roman period never completely disappeared. There were still Arians around long into the fifth century in the east and even beyond in the west. But when a critical mass of ecclesiastical opinion had found a way to gather behind a particular position, and there was no longer any prospect of an alternative finding sufficient traction at court to overturn an emerging consensus, emperors again assumed centre stage. Even if by mobilizing the range of measures available to them, emperors could not make a 'heresy' disappear entirely, the available levers of legal power and carefully crafted incentivization via the distribution of patronage and punishment were effective enough to make it impossible for unofficial Christianities to flourish as large-scale movements in control of numerous Church buildings.

Some of the enforcement options available to emperors were relatively informal. By weight of his prestige alone, Constantine was able to bring most eastern Churchmen into line with *homoousios* as defined at Nicaea; in the end, all he had to do was exile Arius himself and two dissenting Libyan bishops. By the 380s, stronger measures were required, because the vigorous intellectual debates of the intervening period had created sharply defined factions, sometimes with their own separate Church hierarchies and buildings. The first council of Constantinople in 381 was followed by a series of anti-heresy laws, in which Theodosius I did to the opponents of his newly defined Christian orthodoxy what he would soon do to paganism. Heretics' churches and other properties were confiscated and their clerical leaders sent into exile, while rich lay supporters were fined large sums of gold and banned from careers in the imperial service.[26] None of this was enough to eradicate the alternative points of view completely, but support tended to fall away so substantially that heretical groups were quickly reduced to little more than sects, insufficient in size to present themselves any longer as alternative orthodox Churches. And at that point, emperors ceased to care very much about them.

Broadly speaking, this pattern held true for all the major disciplinary disputes, too, the biggest of the fourth century being Donatism, which took root in North Africa. This dispute had its origins in the Tetrarchic Great Persecution, with Christian believers who had held true in the times of trial facing the problem of what to do about their weaker brethren who had lapsed in various ways (*lapsi*). In the Donatist view, the ordination of Caecilian, the new bishop of Carthage in 311, was invalid because one of the presiding bishops was said to have handed over copies of the Scriptures to be burned during the persecution. The Donatists therefore ordained their own bishop (the eponymous Donatus), and the North African Church split down the middle. After Constantine's victory over Maxentius at the Milvian Bridge in 312, both sides petitioned him, and Constantine called a small council of the western bishops to decide which party represented the 'true' Church. It decided against the Donatists. Several appeals, further councils, and an imperial ruling later, Constantine upheld this original decision and deployed military force (or so it seems: we hear about this mainly from Donatists) to end the schism. The intervention proved a complete failure. As many historians have commented, Donatists, with a long track record of enthusiastically embracing persecution by the Roman authorities in pagan days, were, by definition, predisposed to resist imperial force. By the early 320s, Constantine gave up, allowing the Donatists de facto toleration, which they exploited to expand the number of Christian communities adhering to their communion.[27] In these early days of the dispute, the Donatists attempted to win recognition from the rest of the Empire's senior Churchmen that they represented the Universal (Catholic) Church in North Africa, but emperors chose instead to recognize Caecilian and his successors, no matter that the North African Church itself seems to have been split equally between the two. But while emperors vacillated, which they did through much of the fourth century, the dispute rumbled on as schism – a quarrel over authority rather than theology – with many North African towns having both Donatist and non-Donatist churches and clergy.[28]

This situation only began to change in the 390s with the emergence of a new generation of energetic leaders among the anti-Donatist, 'Catholic' Church of North Africa. These included Augustine as bishop of Hippo (Annaba in modern Algeria) and his close collaborator, Bishop Aurelius of Carthage (391–430). Over the next twenty years, this reinvigorated Catholic leadership managed to undermine the Donatist movement and effectively end the schism. Overwhelmingly, this new unity was achieved, not through the supremacy of the Catholics' intellectual arguments, but by their ability to mobilize the power of the imperial state at key moments. These included Augustine's crucial argument that the dispute was not just a disciplinary matter, since Donatism also encompassed theological error, so that the Empire's powerful anti-heresy laws – so effective in shutting down Arianism in the eastern half of the Empire under Theodosius I in the 380s – should also be extended to Donatists.

The Donatists had always insisted that only a baptism conducted by one of their own clerics – untainted by association with a Church of *lapsi* – had spiritual validity, meaning that they regularly rebaptized Catholic converts. This went against mainstream Church teachings that it was the virtue of God Almighty, not that of the presiding priest, which made baptism effective. In the early 400s, Augustine's strategy was to persuade the western imperial court, which controlled North Africa, that the Donatists' preference for rebaptism effectively made them not just schismatics but heretics, and that imperial officials should therefore enforce the powerful heresy laws against them. Augustine and Aurelius put together a highly effective campaign, preparing extensive dossiers detailing violent Donatist outrages. (Itinerant Donatist monks, so-called *circumcelliones*, periodically intimidated and sometimes actually beat up prominent Catholic supporters and clergy, including even some bishops, in the North African countryside.) This evidence was enough to convince the regime of the young emperor Honorius (son of the recently deceased Theodosius I) of the correctness of their case. As a result, imperial pressure began to build on the Donatists, prompting both a sequence of conversions to Catholicism and a great deal of further violence against Catholic clergy, which only added further grist to the anti-Donatist mill. In 405, Honorius' regime – effectively under the control of his leading general Stilicho – passed a formal act of union between Catholics and Donatists in North Africa, abolishing any recognition of the latter's separate status, a move facilitated by the appearance at the imperial court in Milan of the Catholic bishop Maximian of Bagai, who showed everyone wounds received at the hands of Donatist tormentors. The new implacability of the imperial will was confirmed by a council held in Carthage in 411 (from which full minutes survive), attended by both Catholics and Donatists, and presided over by an imperial representative: one Marcellinus, a senior bureaucrat sent from Italy for the event. The council, however, was anything but impartial. As with most of the more significant late Roman Church councils, its outcome was predetermined. The council duly found in favour of Augustine and Aurelius, and the full panoply of anti-heresy legislation was deployed against the Donatist Church. Like the Arians, Donatists did not completely disappear, but, thanks to the imperial legislation, they did lose all their churches and were abandoned by their richer supporters. Over the next two decades, the Donatist movement subsided as an institutionally separate Church.[29]

In this way, during the late Roman period all the main doctrinal and disciplinary struggles of the evolving Christian Church were fought out at court, through lobbying imperially summoned – and imperially fixed – councils. The full weight of both informal imperial authority and more formal legal power was required to resolve these disputes. The emperor's role in setting and enforcing general standards of practice for clergy and laity, and in making senior ecclesiastical appointments, was equally substantial. As the fourth century progressed, a significant body of imperial legislation increasingly underscored the customary rules – or, better, norms – for clergy and laity, which were derived from a variety of practices and written material: inherited ways of doing things; conciliar decisions at various levels (local and regional, as well as ecumenical); and an assorted range of other written materials.

As the Church evolved from a small sect of true believers into a mass religious movement, so it generated new ways of organizing itself. Some of this reorganization, in the western Roman Empire, came in the form of formal written rulings – decretals – solicited by local congregations from the bishop of Rome, who as heir to the see of St Peter, the first among Jesus' disciples or apostles, enjoyed higher prestige than any other bishop of the Latin-speaking world.[30] While some of these letters circulated widely in the west, they didn't do so very often – simply because, at this stage in the development of the Church, the heirs of St Peter were rarely asked for their opinion on Church practices. When Dionysius Exiguus – Dennis the Little (*c.* 470–544), a monk who invented the Before Christ/Anno Domini system for reckoning time, but also did important work in the field of Church law – put together the first formal collection of papal decretals in the early sixth century, it contained only forty-one rulings, generated over about one hundred and fifty years: an average of about one ruling every four years.

The contrast with imperial legislation on Church matters in both quantity and tone is striking. Book Sixteen of the Theodosian Code from the 430s, consists entirely of imperial legislation on religious matters made between the time of Constantine – around 320 – and its own creation, and Justinian's Code collected a great deal more subsequent legislation in the early 530s. Between them, these two lawbooks show

Roman emperors making several hundred different regulations on matters pertaining to the Christian Church between the fourth and the sixth centuries (where popes made forty-one). And imperial rules carried the full force of law; they were not guidance to be followed or not according to whether the guidance suited the recipient's purposes. Authority to regulate Church matters was shared very widely in the late Roman period, but, again, once a law had been solicited and passed, the emperor's authority was paramount.[31]

When it came to ecclesiastical appointments, emperors weren't much concerned about who was bishop of the kind of tiny diocese you might find in and around the Pyrenees, or the more obscure parts of Upper Egypt. But they cared very much about who controlled the great churches of the Empire's central and regional capitals. This often did not mean Rome itself, even though it was one of the five patriarchates. By the fourth century, the western half of the Empire was being run from Milan or Trier, and later Ravenna; the key cities of the east were Constantinople, Antioch and Alexandria. Rome remained a cultural capital for both pagans and Christians, but was rarely visited by emperors: indeed, it received only four such visits – for about a month at a time – in the entire fourth century. (Papal elections, therefore, did not attract too much direct imperial interference, although when they led to violence – as in the election of Pope Damasus in 366 – that was another matter.) In the case of sees they cared about, emperors exercised the right to control appointments. And any sitting bishop, whatever his status, who fell foul of the regime could expect to receive his marching orders – as happened, spectacularly, in the case of John Chrysostom, deposed as patriarch of Constantinople in the early fifth century (p. 76).[32]

So, whatever the likes of Augustine wanted to believe, the emperor was to all intents and purposes the practical, functioning head of the Christian Church in the late Roman period. Churchmen of many different persuasions played key roles in formulating policies, doctrines and disciplinary standards, and in lobbying hard for them. But imperial officials presided over the key meetings, and the decisive lobbying happened at court. When push came to shove, the imperial role in the formulation of correct doctrine, in defining and enforcing expected standards of practice, and in selecting key personnel was paramount.

Nor was this domination purely based on the practicalities of imperial legal and political power. Late Roman political theory claimed that the emperor was directly appointed by God, and carefully selected by Him to rule as His vicegerent on earth. These ideas had very old roots in non-Christian, Hellenistic ideologies of kingship, created to develop the images of power surrounding the dynasties that emerged to rule different parts of the empire of Alexander the Great – but the conversion of the Empire to Christianity generated remarkably little change in the nature of the claims being made about the emperor's spiritual status. The Divinity in question was simply relabelled the Christian God, and the Divine purpose recast as one of bringing the totality of humankind to Christianity, rather than creating perfect, rational *civilitas* for the few.

As a result, the change in identified deity brought no reduction at all in official claims about the closeness of the emperor's relationship to the Divine. Every aspect of the emperor's existence, from his treasuries to his bedchamber, remained sacred; every imperial ritual, from the greatest public ceremonial to the smallest, most intimate moments (such as the act of *proskynesis*, prostrating yourself even during a private audience in the imperial presence to show due respect), were orchestrated to ram home the point. The emperor was no ordinary mortal and, in public at least, was expected to maintain a superhuman impassivity as the ceremonies of Empire unfolded around him. Constantine perhaps got just a bit carried away with this idea. His original burial arrangements set his remains in a great mausoleum (the Church of the Holy Apostles) in Constantinople, surrounded by altars to the twelve apostles. It is usually said that he thought of himself as the thirteenth apostle. But the thirteenth individual in the middle of the twelve apostles is usually Christ – which does raise questions about who exactly Constantine thought himself to be. His son Constantius II quietly rearranged things to make a slightly more modest statement. But only slightly: Constantius and his successors, east and west, all the way down to Justinian in the sixth century and beyond, were entirely consistent in their claim to have been hand-picked by God to rule with Him and for Him on earth.[33]

Augustine in the *City of God*, individual Church leaders on the wrong side of 'official' Christianity (and hence critical of the specific way in which the current emperor was 'interfering' in Church affairs), even ascetics dropping out of Rome's self-proclaimed divinely ordained society – all provided alternative, contesting discourses to the official ideologies of the Roman imperial state. But when it comes to aggregate behaviour – how the majority of people (including leading Churchmen) actually acted – the only possible conclusion is that the claims of the Roman state to exercise ultimate religious authority proved overwhelmingly dominant. We cannot say, of course, how many Churchmen quietly objected in principle to the amount of practical power that the emperor and his officials exercised over Church affairs, and therefore courted imperial favour with their fingers crossed behind their backs. But everyone, even Augustine, ostensibly respected the emperor's right to interfere, energetically lobbying for the weight of state support to be thrown behind their particular position, rather than constructing structures entirely independent of the imperial system (although building up strong bases of local support was certainly important for winning the argument at court).

Overall, the evidence suggests that far more clerics accepted the emperor's basic ideological claim – that he was much more than a secular ruler – than ever disputed it. In a session of the fourth ecumenical council, at Chalcedon on 25 October 451, 370 assembled bishops (or their representatives) hailed Emperor Marcian as 'king and priest'. Again, at the fifth ecumenical council in Constantinople a century later, 152 bishops were happy to declare that nothing should happen in Church matters without the emperor's explicit approval.

Christianity's actual relationship with the late Roman state in the fourth and fifth centuries was, then, precisely the opposite of what Augustine claimed that it should be in the *City of God*. This explains the determination and length with which Augustine felt it necessary to argue his case, but it must not distort late Roman religious reality. The Christian Church of *c.* 400 was not an institution separate from the other structures of Empire but had, in practice, been created by its intersection with the imperial system. It was precisely this intersection that had transformed it from a minority sect into a mass religious movement. The Empire's patronage mechanisms, binding together centre and locality, played a key role in prompting large sections of its local and regional landowning elites to come into line with the religious preferences of a sequence of Christian emperors, at a time when a major expansion of the imperial bureaucracy meant that the imperial court had an extraordinary quantity of patronage to distribute. This in turn created the right conditions, once a critical mass of movers and shakers at local level had changed allegiance (however nominally), for the physical dissolution of most of the old pagan temples in the few decades either side of the year 400, first by imperial-backed action, reinforced later by more local initiatives once the overall political climate (and a raft of imperial legislation) meant that it was safe for local agents to act. All the time, engagement with Empire was bringing wealth, new authority structures, and even a greater doctrinal and internal cohesion to a rapidly developing Christian religion.

Augustine's *City of God* shows the analytical qualities of its author's penetrative mind: as Augustine predicted, the Christian Church and the Roman imperial state were separable entities, and their coincidence in time and space *was* destined only to be temporary. But what emerged in the fourth and fifth centuries is an early version of what historians of other eras have come to label the Confessional State: a political entity whose formal and informal structures upheld a particular set of religious behaviours as 'true religion', and which based its own ideological legitimacy on the claim that this was its primary function.[34] The imperial state and its inner workings, in other words, played a decisive role in the Christian takeover of the Roman world. Without them, the victory of Christianity is inconceivable.

'THE HIGHEST GOD'

This central conclusion to Part One also provides a vital perspective without which it is impossible, I think, to reckon the real historical significance of one final late Roman religious phenomenon: the career of Constantine's apostate nephew, the emperor Julian. Julian was brought up a Christian but rejected the faith in the early 350s, in part (as his own writings attest) because of his growing intellectual fascination with classical culture. He also saw, however, the deepest moral hypocrisy in the fact that his imperial

Christian cousins – Constantine's sons: Constans, Constantine II and Constantius II – had happily secured imperial power for themselves on their father's death in 337, by organizing a pre-emptive massacre of large numbers of their relatives, including Julian's own father.[35] Julian didn't reveal his new religious allegiance, however, until 361, by which time he had been Caesar for half a decade and was in open rebellion against his enthusiastically Christian and now only surviving cousin and senior colleague, the Augustus Constantius II. Julian's sole rule over the entire Empire began in November 361 when Constantius died of disease marching towards an impending showdown with his younger colleague, naming Julian as his successor. It ended just 18 months later with Julian's death on campaign in Persia, in a cavalry skirmish. In that year and a half, Julian mounted a high-level challenge to the unfolding Christian takeover of the imperial system.

Turning to Julian at this point is obviously to go back in time from the Confessional Christian Empire of the 420s, which had already shut down most pagan temples. It is only when armed with a solid understanding of the key mechanisms which had created this Christian Empire, however, that it becomes possible to arrive at a more balanced judgement on the central question of Julian's career: was there any chance that he could have stopped the rise of Christianity in its tracks? Without first exploring how the imperial system actually became Christian, it would be much too easy to let hindsight conclude for us – because we know that Christianity subsequently developed (for a period) into an unstoppable world religion – that Julian's policies stood no chance at all. In fact, when his policies are reconsidered against the processes which actually made the Empire Christian, it quickly becomes clear that they stood a very real chance of success. As both the de-Christianization of modern Europe and the Islamicization of the Near East underline, it is important to recognize that accepting a Christian religious allegiance is no irrevocable historical process, and the reign of Julian the Apostate represents a moment when the rising tide of Christianity might really have been turned.

Athanasius, the highly combative patriarch of Alexandria, dismissed Julian's attempt to restore traditional religious observance as a 'small cloud', and there are many aspects of his character and reign that have made it all too easy for modern historians to do much the same. Julian liked to style himself a philosopher, but what he really liked was theurgy: the art of using ritual magic to make direct contact with the gods. Julian's preferred philosophical teacher was one Maximus of Ephesus, whose favourite party tricks included making candles light spontaneously, and statues speak. Clearly gullible, Julian was also dangerously impulsive, something that eventually resulted in his death. While on campaign in Persia, he was killed in that cavalry skirmish because he'd rushed into battle without his armour. His death had strategic consequences: it left a large Roman army trapped on Persian soil with little prospect of getting safely back across the frontier before its supplies ran out, forcing his successor, Jovian, to negotiate a humiliating peace deal, ceding substantial territories to the Persian Shah in Shah ('King of Kings').[36] Looked at more carefully, however, the evidence suggests that Julian's mission to restore the worship of the old gods was not so utterly hopeless as Athanasius' oft-quoted putdown suggests.

Julian's opening salvo against Christianity was a carefully crafted decree of religious toleration issued on 4 February 362, shortly after Constantius' death. This gave every religious group who had suffered from any kind of legal impediment under his Christian predecessor full freedom of religion: Jews and pagans, but also all those different strands of Christianity excluded from the unified Church that Constantius' councils had constructed in the later 350s. Julian's plan, explicitly aired in his letters, was to allow these different strands of Christianity free rein to attack one other, so that any continued attempt to spread the religion at the expense of traditional paganism would collapse into incoherence. The financial and legal privileges enjoyed by the official branch of Christianity – freedom of priests from curial burdens, monetary support, and the right of bishops to preside over courts – were also removed.[37] Julian may have been impulsive and gullible, but he was also smart.

At the same time, Julian took the organizational structures of traditional paganism by the scruff of the neck. Unlike the full-time professional Christian priests who existed in most parts of the Empire, pagan priests were, by and large, 'ordinary' members of the local social elite who took responsibility for key religious functions, such as performing sacrifice – as much freemasons as counterparts to the Christian clergy (which was one reason why the imperial cult had been such a powerful stimulus to self-Romanization among provincial elites; you didn't have to give up the day job). Securely in power, Julian instituted major structural changes to these traditional patterns of pagan worship. He appointed a single priest for each of the cities of the Empire, to supervise the overall provision of pagan cults within its boundaries (the position that Pegasios of Ilios had wanted to swap his bishopric for: p. 64). He also put in place a new hierarchical structure, installing provincial high priests to supervise those at city level; and laid down moral guidelines for how priests were to behave. They needed to be beyond criticism and to conduct themselves modestly; in particular, they were not to attend theatres, chariot racing or wild beast hunts, nor associate with disreputable classes of people such as actors and charioteers. Julian also provided central funding for this restructuring. The high priest of the province of Galatia received 30,000 measures of wheat and 60,000 of wine, four-fifths of which were to be spent on charitable purposes.[38]

All of which sounds pretty familiar. A coherent organizational hierarchy of full-time priests, an emphasis on holiness, and the devotion of significant funds to charitable purposes all strongly recall distinctive features of contemporary Graeco-Roman Christianity. What Julian did, in other words, was to take some characteristic structures of emergent Christianity and use them as the basis for reorganizing traditional pagan religion. The resemblances are much too close to be coincidental, and make perfect sense given the central intellectual problem the emperor was having to confront.

As far as Julian was concerned, Christianity was a uniquely false religion, singularly devoid of even the tiniest grain of spiritual truth: a point repeatedly reiterated in his surviving writings, in which he often refers to Christians as 'atheists'.[39] Under Constantine and his sons, however, this religion had made astonishing progress among the Empire's ruling elites, in just a few decades. Julian's problem, therefore, was how to explain – not least to himself – how such a false religion was nonetheless managing to 'win', in terms of entrenching itself ever more effectively in imperial society. The explanation – for Julian – had to lie in Christianity's non-religious features (since, by definition, he could not allow it any spiritual virtue). Julian's attempted reorganization of pagan cultic practice was his answer to this disturbing conundrum. Christianity was winning, he clearly believed – in fact he *had* to believe – because of its structural cohesion, the apparently impressive holiness of its priests and its generous charitable provisions. If he could retool paganism to meet these practical challenges head on, then the overwhelming religious truth contained within traditional cultic practice would undoubtedly prevail.

How viable was his approach to reviving traditional religion? Julian believed that every other existing cult (including Judaism) had at least some spiritual validity, and he tried to generate unity among them to fight the Christian menace, not least by appointing a single priest for each city. Here, however, he faced an immediate problem. The traditional cults had never been understood as a unity in theoretical terms, nor operated like that in practice. Apart from participating in the public cults that, it was believed, guaranteed the protection of the Empire, people had otherwise been free to engage with whatever other cults they chose – and many of these cults had essentially been competitors with one another in what was effectively a religious free market. Out in the countryside in particular, the range of traditional cults was vast and often extremely localized. Roman Anatolia alone, for instance, throws up a weird and wonderful variety, from Papis to Mén to Sabizios, and many others known to us only as names from stray inscriptions. How, and why, they were worshipped are lost to history.[40]

As has often been remarked, then, 'paganism' was a Christian intellectual construct, something for Christianity to define itself against, but which did not really exist. While Christians lumped the entirety of the religious opposition together as one whole, adherents of the different cults would not have seen it that way. That being so, you might think, Julian's innovations were bound to fail.[41] But peasant smallholders in the back of the imperial beyond, where the greatest religious variety prevailed, were not Julian's target. For him, the key group comprised those same provincial landowning elites whose individual changes of allegiance were already starting to Christianize the imperial system.

For this demographic, the idea that there was a fundamental and underlying unity to the multiplicity of existing pagan cults was not new at all. In the second and third centuries, some of the oracular answers being generated by the major shrines of the eastern Mediterranean had taken a novel turn. Many were collected together by the philosopher Porphyry of Tyre, whose late third-century work *Against the Christians* was so influential that Constantine banned it. What's striking about these oracles is their increasing reference to one 'Highest God', standing at the apex of all the other spiritual powers in the non-Christian universe, including daemons (not necessarily evil powers outside Christian thinking, where they were regarded as Lucifer's fallen angels) and the traditional pagan gods. The frequency of these mentions reflects an increasing trend among the Empire's elite to perceive a fundamental spiritual unity behind the multiplicity of cults they observed around themselves, based on an underlying belief that all the various gods were emanations of the one fundamental Divine principle. This included those worshipped in the old Pharaonic temples of the Nile delta, several of which have thrown up appreciative Greek graffiti left by pagan pilgrims of the late Roman period.

The theology behind such views derived from teachings of Plato, whose work had long formed part of the standard elite education in the eastern, Greek-speaking half of the Empire, and which had subsequently been brought west in Latin translation. (As far as we know Augustine, born a generation after Julian, never read a word of Plato, but he was certainly familiar with the basic idea-set.) Late Romans adhering to such views would have understood themselves as Platonists, but modern scholarship uses the term Neo-Platonist to reflect the fact that many centuries of further thought separated these believers from anything that the great man had originally taught (not least an utterly bogus reconciliation of the rival teachings of Plato and Aristotle). A key figure in the development of Neo-Platonist thought was a third-century philosopher by the name of Plotinus, originally from Lycopolis in Egypt, who eventually settled in Campania in southern Italy. His vision of the purpose of life was, to use a highly approximate analogy, quasi-Buddhist. ('Our aim is not to be sinless, but to be God' is one of his striking aphorisms.) For Plotinus, humans were rational because their souls contained a fragment of the same original divine essence (the 'One'), from which everything else had come into being: it was the central purpose of life for the individual soul to regain its lost unity with the One. Study and contemplation – not least of ancient literature, with allegorical interpretations of Homer (full of divine interventions of various kinds, and many a journey) playing a starring role – were his chosen routes back to the One, and his biographer – Porphyry, also a Neo-Platonist – claims that Plotinus experienced the ecstasy of achieved reunion three times in his life.[42]

This overall vision of the universe enjoyed considerable traction among the elites that Julian was trying to attract to his cause. Not that all philosophers, nor even all of Plotinus' pupils, were united in their approach. Porphyry, who journeyed far from his native Tyre to live and teach in Rome, adhered to Plotinus' emphasis on the importance of study and contemplation as the central paths to spiritual growth. Others, particularly the philosophers who most interested Julian, thought that reunion could be properly achieved only by carefully crafted ritual, which would facilitate contact between this world and the higher realm from which the rational human soul derived. Each of these thinkers had their own inner circles of devotees, who would themselves go on to become practising philosophers. But most also earned their livings by teaching introductory courses on Greek philosophy to much wider groups of fee-paying students, many of whom then went on to the public careers that formed the customary stock in trade of the late Roman elite, taking with them a shared understanding of at least the outlines of Neo-Platonist thought. (When speaking to the Senate of Constantinople, which he did on behalf of a sequence of Christian emperors on many different occasions in the middle decades of the fourth century, the philosopher Themistius regularly drew on these ideas and clearly expected them to be understood by the entirety of his audience, Christian as well as pagan.) Their wide distribution among the Roman elite also shows in the increasing number of third-century Greek inscriptions dedicated to the *Theos Upsistos*, the same 'Highest God' referred to in the oracular material collected by Porphyry. Julian himself had his own particular theological preferences, strongly influenced by his favourite teachers, which not all would have shared. But that there was one Highest God, and that all the traditional cults of the Empire represented different paths to the same end, was common currency among the elite of the Empire by the time Julian came to the throne.[43]

Julian's basic approach, therefore, was in line with the existing thought patterns of his target audience. Landowning elites generally were open to the idea that there were many paths – including Neo-Platonist ones – to the One True God. In some ways, the more difficult element in Julian's religious agenda was to persuade even his fellow non-Christians to accept the more radical claim that Christianity could never provide a valid path to this Divine Essence and that its adherents were completely beyond the pale of religious acceptability.

Implementing this dimension of his agenda proved far from plain sailing. On 17 June 362, shortly after leaving Constantinople to begin preparations for his Persian campaign, Julian issued an edict that only individuals of the correct moral standing should be allowed to operate as teachers of language and literature: the bedrock of elite cultural education. Though the edict itself says nothing about religion, Julian also sent out with it an official covering letter, which made it clear that Christian teachers, by definition, failed the test. In Julian's view, the classics were pagan religious texts that a Christian could never teach 'properly'. His position, while intellectually coherent, did not win universal consent, even among the emperor's pagan supporters. When one highly respected, reputedly Christian teacher, Prohaeresius, was driven out of the profession because of the edict, it was greeted with dismay even by non-Christians, and he had to be readmitted by special dispensation. Otherwise the emperor's greatest fan, the pagan historian Ammianus Marcellinus considered the edict 'worthy of eternal silence'.[44]

After two generations of official Christianity, the traditional structures of public pagan sacrifice had also broken down. Julian noted in his own letters that in the whole of Cappadocia he struggled to find one real pagan ('Hellene' in his language) who knew how to conduct a proper sacrifice. Some historians have argued that pagan sensibilities on the matter had changed so substantially, in the three and a half decades since Constantine's ban, that large-scale public sacrifice was no longer an attractive prospect to an audience that had bought into the Christian condemnation of all that blood and death. One of his own theurgic masters, Chrysanthius, likewise turned down Julian's invitation to come to court (although he did later take a job within the emperor's new pagan priestly hierarchy, as high priest of Lydia).[45] Not all pagans, even some of those of the same basic persuasion as Julian himself, were enthusiastic about his clarion call for pagan revival.

Not only did Julian have plenty of work to do to convince a critical mass of non-Christians to buy into his religious project, but he also faced plenty of Christian hostility besides. He responded to this resistance with the same kind of manoeuvres that Constantine and his sons had employed in favour of their more enthusiastic religious supporters, albeit in the opposite direction. The Christian port city of Maiuma (which had been renamed Constantia) lost its independent city status, and again came under the control of the nearby pagan stronghold of Gaza; Caesarea in Cappadocia was punished by demotion and loss of legal independence because its inhabitants had destroyed the city's temples to Apollo and Jupiter.[46] An acid test of the viability of Julian's religious policies for many modern commentators, however, was the emperor's lengthy stay in the city of Antioch, from July 362 to April 363. The headquarters for his upcoming Persian campaign, Antioch also had one of the oldest Christian communities in the Empire, and Julian's plans for pagan revival brought him into direct conflict with it.

Just outside the city lay a famous shrine to Apollo, long a source of oracular guidance. But, in 351 a church had been built there to contain the remains of a former bishop of Antioch, Babylas, martyred in the Empire-wide persecution of Christians instituted by the emperor Decius in the 250s. Its specific purpose was to neutralize the oracular powers of Apollo's shrine and silence the god. Taking exception to this, Julian ordered the martyr's remains to be exhumed and returned to Antioch – but, shortly afterwards, and much to Julian's fury, a fire broke out at the shrine, destroying its temple. This was only one in a sequence of disputes between the emperor and the citizens of Antioch, prompting Julian to write a satirical tract – the *Misopogon* or *Beard Hater* (the title refers to Julian's preference for a beard, which was a traditional attribute of a classical philosopher) – which he had posted up in the city. Not surprisingly, historians have tended to see Julian's experiences in Antioch as clear evidence that his religious experiment was doomed to failure, with or without his early demise in Persia.

This is too hasty a conclusion. Many cities of the Empire did not have anything like such well-established Christian communities as Antioch; two-thirds of them (1,200) had not even had a bishop just a generation before Julian came to the throne. There were also other issues at play in Antioch besides religion. The concentration of Julian's huge expeditionary army of well over fifty thousand men in and around the city caused price rises and food shortages: it was these, as much as his religious policies, that provoked hostility towards the emperor, particularly among the city's ruling council. There's also the problem that Antioch is, if anything, so well-documented that Julian's travails there tend to swamp the broader run of evidence for how the Empire as a whole responded to his religious initiatives.[47]

Overall, the response to Julian's religious initiatives was decidedly mixed, in the proper sense of the word. Surviving inscriptions, for instance in the Greek city of Pergamum, show that a number of local communities responded positively, while major repairs were also undertaken of the temple to Hadrian, part of the old imperial cult, at Ephesus. We know, too, that a number of individuals – such as a widely ridiculed teacher of rhetoric in Constantinople called Hecebolius – changed their religious allegiance back again to fall in line with Julian's preferences, perhaps prompted by the Emperor's edict against Christian teachers. Such 're-conversions' shouldn't cause too much surprise. Not every Christian conversion was powered by the same kind of intense reflection as that of Augustine, and the same kind of moderate, 'belief in the Highest God' religious sensibilities which made it possible for Bishop Gregory Nazianzen's father to switch painlessly from Neo-Platonic pagan monotheism to Constantine's Christianity could easily work in the opposite direction. Taken as a whole, the responses to Julian's letters show the full range of possible reactions. Christian-dominated city councils like Antioch's refused to do anything; pagan councils – Gaza of course, but also Batnae and Emesa – responded with huge enthusiasm; others still, like that of the Thracian city of Beroe, made enthusiastic noises in their official statements without actually doing anything specific – much the most sensible response to a sudden policy change at the centre in a one-party state.[48]

All of which suggests that Antioch is in fact misleading as a case study in the amount of hostility Julian's initiatives generally provoked. The emperor clearly faced substantial difficulties in trying to unite the many different pagan cults of his Empire, but there were nonetheless plenty of positive pagan responses to Julian's policies, and plenty of signs, too, that many others were happy enough to identify the 'Highest God' in whichever way the incumbent emperor saw fit: central protagonist of the Judaeo-Christian biblical canon, or Neo-Platonic 'One'. And Julian, of course, had the same range of mechanisms of cultural constraint available to him as his immediate Christian predecessors. The promotion and demotion of city communities and particular individuals remained powerful tools of patronage. Had Julian been able to exercise them over a longer timescale, particularly if he'd managed to pass on power to a non-Christian successor, at a time when the imperial bureaucratic expansion was still gathering pace, there's no obvious reason why these tools would have been any less effective when employed in a paganizing direction than they had been in generating Christian compliance. After all, very similar mechanisms of patronage and constraint would later turn Christian elites into Muslim ones across most of the former eastern Roman Empire – and that was a much greater leap of faith altogether.

Overall, Julian was offering his own amalgam of elite-level pagan theology, combined with an institutional reorganization of cultic practice inspired by the functioning of Christianity and its greater emphasis on priestly piety. In a very real sense, this was no more than a variant on what contemporary Christianity was itself offering. In the fourth century, as we have seen, a developing relationship with classical culture and the structures of Roman imperialism turned the faith along some new paths. Its new authority structures mimicked, and were reinforced by, those of the Empire, and its belief systems were being transformed by its intellectual encounter with classical philosophy and the grammarians' techniques of literary analysis. In effect, both post-Nicene Christianity and Julian's revamped paganism were new combinations of Christian and non-Christian cultural forms and the defining structures of the Roman imperial system. That being so, it is not immediately clear that Julian's version of the mix was so inherently inferior that it was bound, by definition, to lose out to its Christian rival – or not, at least, in the mid-fourth century. At this point, the new Christianity of the late Roman world remained only half-formed; its congregations were still riven with fierce disputes over doctrine and discipline, while almost all of the Empire's peasantry remained pagan, the bulk of the temples firmly open.[49]

Once the full extent of the role played by the structures of Empire in turning Christianity into an effective mass religion has been recognized, then, by the same token, it becomes more possible to think that those structures could have been mobilized to spread a different kind of religion in the form of Julian's alternative amalgam of traditional and Christian institutions and beliefs – just as, in earlier centuries, the same mechanisms had so effectively spread elite adherence to the imperial cult.

In Julian's case, however, one vital ingredient was still missing: the incontestable Divine validation provided by overwhelming military victory. Constantine had earned his freedom of religious manoeuvre by emerging as the last man standing from the multiple civil wars engendered by the collapse of Diocletian's political compromise of the Tetrarchy; a brute fact that not even convinced pagans could ignore. Julian, despite earlier victories over the barbarians of Gaul (considered an inferior kind of enemy compared to the Persians), had not. It was Julian's quest for Divine validation through victory in battle that led him to launch his otherwise inexplicably mammoth strike into the heart of the Persian Empire.

Relations between Rome and Persia had become increasingly tense in Constantius II's later years. In 359, war re-erupted on the Empire's easternmost border and Persians sacked the Roman fortress of Amida (modern Diyarbakir in eastern Turkey). It was a military calamity, and some kind of response was clearly called for. Julian's strategy, though, was highly risky: a massive assault aimed directly at the Persian capital of Ctesiphon, far down the River Tigris. What he needed was a big enough victory to show that he had Divine backing. He got close. His armies captured a string of fortified towns down the Euphrates, devastated the area around Ctesiphon, and, after forcing a river crossing, even won a respectable victory over the Persian field army at Pirisabora. If Julian had managed to get himself and his army home after these successes, more or less in one piece, then he would have probably done enough to claim victory – and the future could have been totally different. Julian's restoration of the old gods would then have received the necessary Divine imprimatur. If this had also allowed him to hand on power to a pagan successor, there is no obvious reason to suppose that recently – and syncretically – converted Roman landowning elites would not have largely swung back into line with the imperially sponsored worship of Julian's alternative vision of the non-Christian 'Highest God'.[50]

The central conclusion that emerges from this exploration of the first of the three great revolutions which underlie the emergence of medieval Christendom – the triumph of Christianity over traditional Graeco-Roman paganism in the fourth and fifth centuries – is how fundamentally dependent it was upon the structures and mechanisms of the Roman imperial state: a conclusion that is only reinforced when the career of Emperor Julian is brought into the equation. More traditionally pious Christian histories, of the kind it was reasonable to write when Christianity still predominated over western culture, have tended to downplay the role of the Empire and its systems in this revolutionary religious transformation.[51] But large-scale conversion to the new religion from what was a tiny numerical base followed Constantine's declaration of his Christian allegiance, rather than preceded it: Christianity's trajectory towards religious domination of the Mediterranean world was not clearly set by the year 300. It then unfolded in two perceptible stages: the self-Christianization of much of the Roman landowning elite in the second and third quarters of the fourth century, which generated only a limited amount of overt religious conflict; followed, around the year 400, by a second and much more violent phase of temple destruction and cult suppression. Both these phases, in their different ways, were equally dependent on the operating structures of the imperial state.

By the mid-fourth century, the idea was firmly entrenched among provincial landowners that they stood a greater chance of success in the rapidly evolving patronage, fiscal and legal systems of the later Empire if they declared themselves Christian. Many no doubt genuinely converted. However, the overall degree of syncretism is striking, and for every Augustine who turned to orthodox Roman Christianity after enormous soul-searching there were probably several like Pegasios, happy to be either his city's bishop or its chief pagan priest, according to current imperial preference. At this stage, everything was still up for grabs, which makes Julian's desire to restore the old gods potentially far more significant than a mad romantic gesture. The same webs of patronage that were beginning to turn local elites towards Christianity could still have been manipulated to take them in a different direction. This is not to say that Christianity would have been extinguished if Julian's religious project had gathered momentum, but it would have been decoupled from the imperial system. It would probably have reverted to the rhythms of pre-Constantinian Christianity: a world less hierarchically structured, doctrinally more diverse, more ascetically world-rejecting, and of distinctly smaller congregations.

But once the machinery of state was dominated by Christian office-holders, as it seems to have been in the east at least by the mid-380s, the ground had been prepared for phase two. Christian pressure groups were able to influence ever more oppressive anti-pagan legislation at court; Christian officials such as Maternus Cynegius, responsible for unleashing renewed destruction of the temples in Syria (p. 118), were happy to encourage local anti-pagan initiatives – and even, occasionally, to mobilize state functionaries to demolish the odd temple. This in turn paved the way for much more vigorous direct action, which the state both licensed in its laws and, through the attitudes of its officials, encouraged in practice. This phase saw the closure and destruction of the majority of the remaining pagan temples, after which there was no longer any relatively easy way – as there still had been in Julian's time – to restore a non-Christian religious order.

At the same time, Christianity itself was being rapidly transformed, both by its engagement with the Roman state and by the day-to-day experience of having to cater for the expanding congregations being brought to the Church by state-inspired conversion processes. Christian communities now existed throughout the cities of the Empire; greater institutional coherence slowly emerged, as did rules of piety and practice that better suited a mass religion than a small sect of devout believers; and fierce argument eventually generated a more defined, positively framed set of doctrinal teachings. In all this, the power of the imperial state was again central. The new Church hierarchy of metropolitan archbishops and patriarchs was explicitly modelled on the administrative hierarchies of the Empire; imperial legislation did everything from suppressing heresy to defining the institutional and legal roles of bishops; and the growing presence of members of the Roman landowning elite in the ranks of the clergy transformed the nature and function of clerical office still further, enhancing episcopal authority at the expense of the other figures with whom the clergy had shared religious authority in pre-Constantinian Christianity. In both theory and practice, the emperor was the unchallenged and unchallengeable head of the post-Constantinian Church.

However prescient Augustine might have been about Christianity's longer-term development, the practical realities of late Roman Christianity are inescapable: the emperor hired and fired senior Churchmen pretty much at will; made laws regulating Church affairs; and alone possessed the right to call together councils of the entire Church, the highest decision-making body of Roman Christendom. This right, never challenged, gave him more or less infinite informal powers to set agendas and twist arms to generate desired outcomes on really key matters.

In his *History of the Decline and Fall of the Roman Empire*, the eighteenth-century historian Edward Gibbon began a tradition of lamenting the extent to which men of talent were sucked into the Church in the later Roman Empire, to the detriment of its public life. His critique, much echoed since, is based on a fundamental misapprehension. In the late Roman period, the Christian Church was not the separate corporate entity that it became in the central Middle Ages. It was in effect a department of the imperial state, and joining its ranks was another way to serve the emperor.[52]

A proper understanding of the role of the emperor as the (largely) undisputed head of the Christian Church offers one final important, but often unacknowledged, perspective on the whole process of doctrine formation so central to the revolution unleashed within Christianity by Constantine's conversion. Given the centrality of imperial authority to both the formulation and enforcement of 'orthodoxy', the reality is that any strand of Christian theological opinion that wanted to establish its predominance – including the Arians and Donatists who eventually lost out in the process – had no choice but to operate as a 'court party'. This is how orthodoxy was in fact defined and enforced in the late Roman period: through councils that emperors called and dominated, and through the punitive, discriminatory legislation they passed and enforced against alternative Christian believers whom these councils identified as heretics. Not to operate effectively at court was to resign yourself to permanent minority status.

At least as important, then, as the Christianization of the Roman Empire – a traditional topic of historical analysis – was the Romanization of Christianity. In the fourth and fifth centuries, pre-Constantinian Christianity was as much bent out of its existing trajectories of development by the Empire, as the Empire was by its new religion. The centrality of the Empire to the first of these revolutionary moments in the development of medieval Christianity also provides the key to understanding why it was so quickly followed by a second. Since late Roman Christianity was dependent on the structures of Roman imperialism, which now explicitly defined itself as a Confessional State whose stated purpose was to uphold true religion in the form of Nicene Christianity, it was inevitable that the subsequent unravelling of the Roman imperial system, in both west and east in turn, should have unleashed a further religious revolution of its own.

PART TWO

The Fall of Roman Christianity

4
Nicaea and the Fall of the West

The Roman imperial system, which by AD 400 had dominated western Eurasia and the Mediterranean for almost half a millennium, fell apart in two distinct phases. In the course of the fifth century, central Roman control of the western Mediterranean and its northern hinterland was replaced by regionally based successor states, all the way from North Africa to the British Isles. The vast majority of these (but not all) were effectively run by some kind of alliance between existing provincial Roman landowning elites and the emergent dynastic leaders of military forces that were relatively recent migrants onto Roman soil. This political revolution took some time to work itself out, but by the final decade of the fifth century almost none of the old Latin-speaking portion of the Empire remained under the direct control of Roman emperors.

Further east, the Greek-speaking half of the Empire survived the process of western collapse essentially intact, its emperors continuing to control all of Constantinople's traditional holdings in the eastern and southern Mediterranean throughout the sixth century. But in the first half of the seventh century, much of the eastern Roman Empire's territory in the European Balkans was taken over by intrusive Slavs and Avars, coming respectively from the north-eastern reaches of the Carpathian mountain system and the Central Asian Steppe. More challenging still was the rise of Islamic Arab power, which, by the end of the same century, had seized control of many of Constantinople's richest revenue-producing provinces – Syria, Palestine and Egypt – and reduced most of the others, particularly coastal Asia Minor, to a devastated war zone. The imperial capital did not fall, however, and continued to operate as the political centre for a rump Empire whose rulers continued

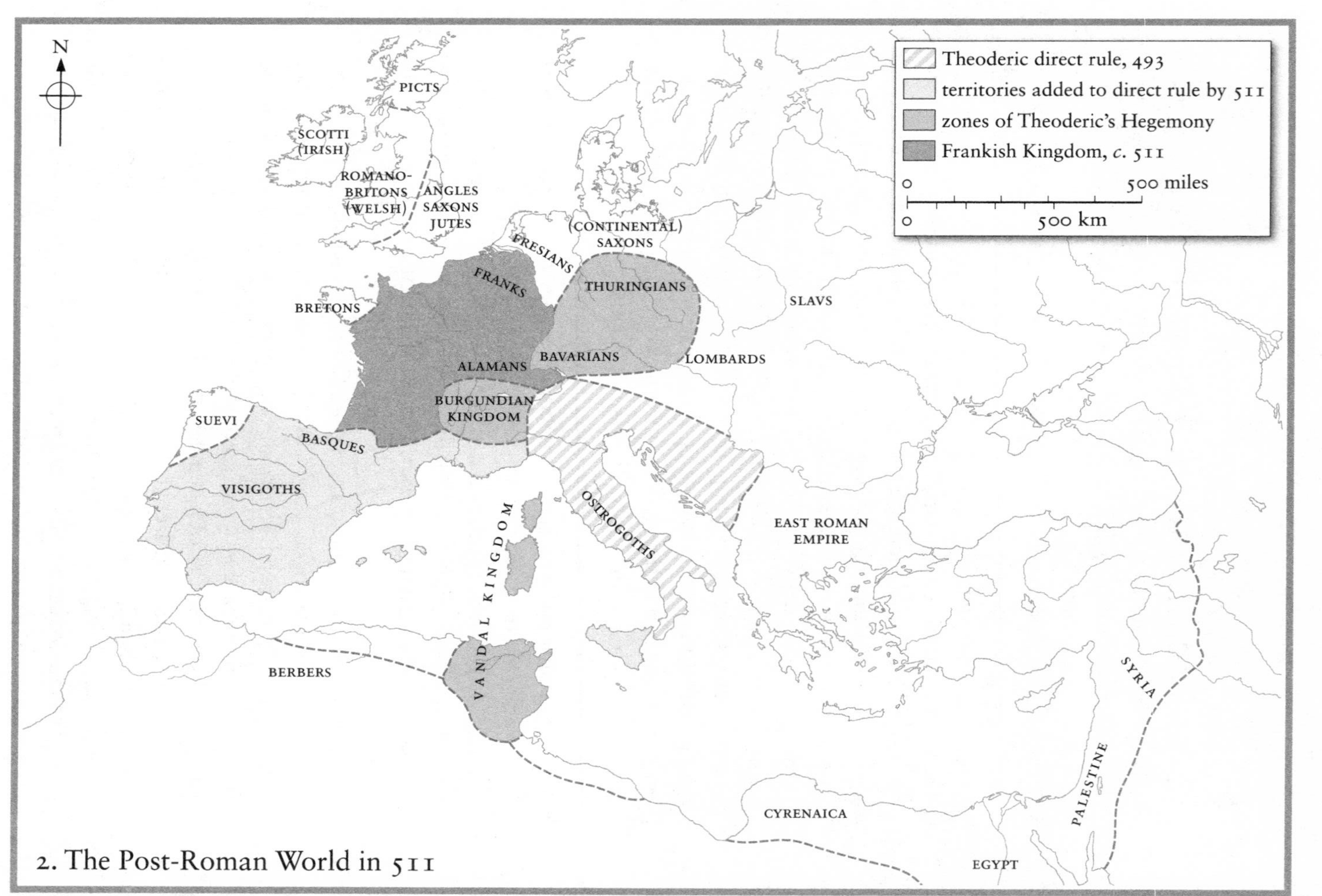

2. The Post-Roman World in 511

doggedly to style themselves 'Roman'. But over the seventh century they lost between two-thirds and three-quarters of their annual revenues. As a result, the state they ran from the early eighth century onwards had changed in some fundamental ways, reduced from dominant global power to a second-class regional power at the eastern end of the Mediterranean. The scale of this diminution marks the effective end of any real continuity with the old Roman imperial system.

At first sight, these sequential phases of imperial unravelling – while certainly dramatic – might seem little more than a footnote in the rise of medieval Christendom. The opposite could not be more true. Christianity was hard-wired so fundamentally into the Roman imperial system by the early decades of the fifth century that – as is the case with any Confessional State – subsequent bouts of existential political crises were bound to generate major ideological and practical challenges for the 'true religion' whose protection provided the self-declared justification for the state's existence. These challenges took different forms and generated different overall outcomes in the fifth- and sixth-century west and in the seventh- and eighth-century east, but the two periods of religious crises are mutually illuminating, and between them they fundamentally destabilized the established patterns of late Roman Christianity. The place to begin an exploration of what amounted to a second revolutionary phase in the development of the medieval Christian religion is North Africa, in the late fifth century.

HUNERIC AND CLOVIS

On 1 February 484, King Huneric of the Vandals and Alans, who had crossed the Rhine together in 406 and eventually seized control of much of old Roman North Africa and its capital city of Carthage in 439, presided over the opening of a full council of all the Christian bishops of his kingdom, which had convened in one of the largest churches of the city – the Basilica Fausti – at his command. Carthage had seen five previous councils of the North African Church, but this was by far the most momentous. At stake was the future of Nicene Christianity – Roman imperial orthodoxy – within his kingdom. Huneric called the council as an occasion for debate between Nicene

Church leaders, the dominant voice of orthodox imperial Roman Christianity since the second ecumenical council of Constantinople in 381, and their doctrinal rivals, the Homoeans. Nicenes commonly called Homoeans 'Arians', but this was a deliberate strategy of damning by association: the epithet was designed to lump their theological rivals inexorably together with the arch-Christian heretic condemned at the first ecumenical council. In fact, there is no evidence that Homoean Christianity had any direct connection with Arius' teachings at all. It is, as we've seen, much better understood as an alliance of conservative Christian opinion which found it difficult to accept that the non-biblical term *homoousios* ('of the same essence') – enshrined at Nicaea – adequately accounted for the biblical evidence for the roles and relationships of the Father and the Son within the Christian Trinitarian Godhead (see p. 34). Homoean Christianity had itself even been official Roman orthodoxy in the middle decades of the fourth century, originally enshrined as such by twin councils in the eastern and western halves of the Empire, at Seleucia and Rimini respectively, called by Emperor Constantius II in 359, and confirmed by a further council of Constantinople the following year.

We have one detailed account of the events surrounding Huneric's council and its aftermath. It comes with the snappy title of *History of the Persecution in Africa in the Times of Geiseric and Huneric*, composed by one Victor, certainly a Nicene clergyman and probably the bishop of Vita, a small town in the province of Byzacena (modern Tunisia). Huneric's own brand of Christianity was Homoean, a faith he shared with many of the new rulers of the states that had come to replace Roman imperial rule across the western Empire over the fifth century: the Suevi in western Spain, Visigoths in Spain and Gaul, Burgundians in south-west Gaul, and soon, too, Ostrogoths in Italy. Huneric took an uncompromising view of the Nicene faith. Earlier in his reign, he had exiled nearly five thousand Nicene clergy from the various churches in and around Carthage to the fringes of the desert, so when the summons to attend the council had arrived back in May 483 the Nicenes must have suspected the worst. Their fears were duly realized. The council saw no serious exchange of views; the result of the 'debate' was a foregone conclusion. What Huneric sought, and obtained, was a triumphant confirmation of the theological correctness of the Homoean position. He followed this up with fierce edicts of persecution that required the whole population of his realm (encompassing modern Tunisia with parts of Algeria and Libya, a toehold in western Sicily and the island of Sardinia; Map 2) to come into line with Homoean Christianity: now 'official' Christian orthodoxy for the population of the entire Vandal-Alan kingdom.[1] Dissenting Nicene bishops were sent to the mines or into exile in Corsica, and a series of brutal attacks on specific high-status supporters of Nicaea within the Vandal kingdom was carried out. Victor, who documented all this, concluded that it was just par for the course for a barbarian ruler:

> Those of you, who love barbarians and sometimes praise them, in a way worthy of condemnation, give thought to their name and understand their ways. Surely there is no name by which they could be appropriately called other than 'barbarian', a fitting word connoting savageness, cruelty and terror? However many may be the gifts with which you befriend them, and however many the acts of compliance with which you placate them, they can think of nothing other than looking on Romans with envy ... They desire not a single one of the Romans to live. And in cases where ... they have spared their subjects until now, they spare them to use as slaves: for they have never loved a single Roman.[2]

On the whole, modern historians have been happy to follow Victor's lead, dismissing Huneric's religious initiative as no more than a brief and ill-conceived aberration within an overall story of Nicene theological orthodoxy that managed to transfer its domination from the Roman to the post-Roman west without serious disruption.

Huneric's persecution died with the king himself in November 484, just a few months after it began. It was followed into the dustbin of history a few decades later by the entire Vandal-Alan kingdom, which was extinguished in just a few months of efficient warfare by the armies of the east Roman Emperor Justinian in 532/3. And while many of the first-generation rulers of the post-Roman west were also Homoean Christians like Huneric, none of the others ever attempted to bring their Nicene subjects into line with their personal religious beliefs by brute force. In reality, all the initial royal support for Homoean Christianity had to all intents and purposes disappeared by the end of the sixth century. After dealing with the Vandals, Justinian's armies also destroyed the Ostrogothic kingdom (and its Homoean allegiance) in about twenty years of campaigning from 535, while the independent Burgundian kingdom, along with its support for the councils of Seleucia and Rimini, was extinguished by the Franks in the early 530s. The Homoean Visigothic kingdom in Spain remained unconquered, but officially converted to the *homoousios* of Nicaea at the third council of Toledo in 587. At this point, the dominance of Nicene Christianity over the post-Roman west was more or less complete – as a result of which, historians have been much less interested in Huneric's religious policies than in those of his much more famous peer: Clovis, king of the Franks.

The Franks, divided in the imperial era into a number of separate subgroups, originally occupied territories east of Rome's northern Rhine frontier. Clovis inherited control of his father's particular group of warriors in the early 480s, which, at that point, made him no more than one among half a dozen or more small-scale warband leaders in just one of these subgroups: the generally pagan Salian Franks, who were now established on both sides of the former imperial frontier along the Lower Rhine. Clovis proved an ambitious and decisive leader. First, he eliminated all of his Frankish rivals, adding their warriors to his own ranks, to make his own Merovingian dynasty (so-named after Clovis's grandfather, Merovech) a ruling line of indisputably royal status. Then, he massively expanded an originally limited powerbase, centred on part of modern Belgium, scoring major victories over a series of sub-Roman, Alamannic and Burgundian rivals, and, most famously, defeating and killing the Visigoth King Alaric II at the battle of Vouillé in 507 (Map 2). By the time of his death in 511, Clovis had taken over nearly all of what is now France (except the very south), and parts of western Germany as well. Third, and unlike Huneric and the rest of his peers at the head of the first-generation successor kingdoms to emerge in the post-Roman west, Clovis converted to Nicene, Catholic Christianity. And for the nascent Frankish kingdom, Clovis's career was only the beginning: his sons and grandsons, in particular, continued to expand its boundaries. The kingdom eventually rose to such a level of domination over the bulk of west European Latin Christendom that under Charlemagne, the most celebrated Frankish ruler of all, the imperial title was revived for the first time since the disappearance of Roman emperors. On Christmas Day 800, Charlemagne was crowned emperor in a famous ceremony conducted in the city of Rome.

The total eclipse of the Homoean successor states, especially when compared to the grand historical destiny of Clovis's Catholic Frankish kingdom, has had the effect of relegating Homoean Christianity to a minor footnote in the broader history of the Christian religion in the post-Roman period. It has never been viewed as a major branch of the Christian evolutionary tree, posing a serious threat to the continued dominance of orthodox Nicene Christianity. Which is one basic reason why, more generally, the fall of the Roman Empire – or, more precisely, the unravelling of the west Roman imperial system – has not generally been seen as marking a revolutionary moment in the history of Christianity. Rather, the picture generally painted has been one of generally serene continuity. Older accounts had the figure of the pope – his powerbase conveniently located in the old imperial capital – stepping smoothly into the power vacuum left by the disappearance of imperial authority. More recently, it has been argued that the next great step change in Christianity, following its Constantinian revolution, generally came in the seventh century rather than the fifth. The disappearance of the west Roman imperial state, in this view, posed no great challenge to Christianity except where social structures, too, collapsed alongside those of the state, and that only happened north of the English Channel. There, the emergence of Anglo-Saxon kingdoms was accompanied by the destruction of much of late Romano-British Christianity in the areas which fell under their control, but this process affected too small a fraction of the old Roman world to be worth any great emphasis.[3]

Such perspectives, however, do not in my opinion do full justice to the evidence. The disappearance of the Empire's political structures in the fifth century posed serious challenges to a still-nascent Nicene Christian establishment on a whole series of levels, right across the Roman west. Over the following centuries, the collapse of religious authority structures and the educational infrastructure directly associated with the workings of the Christian religion in the Roman era unleashed a further set of structural transformations within Christianity, which were just as profound as those that had followed Constantine's 'conversion'.[4] More immediately, Huneric called his council within a few years of the final collapse of the central authority structure of the western Empire. It's traditional to date the Empire's death knell to 476, with the deposition of Romulus Augustulus, though you could equally pick the moment, four years later, when assassination took the life of Julius Nepos, the last western emperor recognized in Constantinople. Whatever your preference, it is no chronological coincidence that Huneric's council should have followed on so closely. Once misleading hindsight – the fact that Nicene Christianity eventually became accepted orthodoxy across the entire European landmass – is stripped away, it becomes clear that the political collapse of the imperial Confessional State, with which that particular ideology had become so deeply entwined, posed such a direct challenge to its continued prominence that it came within a whisker of not surviving at all. To understand why, we need to take a much closer look at both the religious history of the Vandal kingdom, and the precise circumstances of Clovis's conversion to Nicene Christianity, against the backdrop of the new world order that emerged in the immediate aftermath of western Roman imperial collapse.

THE POST-ROMAN WEST

From his capital in Carthage, Huneric ruled the old North African Roman provinces of Proconsularis, Byzacena, Numidia, Mauretania Caesarensis and Tripolitania, together with the island of Sardinia (see Map 2). The kingdom had been created in the 430s by his father, Geiseric, who had moved his extremely disparate group of followers – largely composed of a mixture of agriculturalist Germanic-speaking Vandals from modern Slovakia or thereabouts and Iranian-speaking Alan nomads, who had been roaming north of the Black Sea until the final decade of the fourth century – from Spain to North Africa early in the decade, and then captured Carthage by storm in 439. Geiseric's conquest of Roman North Africa was reasonably characteristic of what was happening elsewhere in the mid-fifth century across the Roman west, which was falling under the control of a series of kings who had similarly come to power at the head of what were originally intrusive bodies of outside, non-Roman soldiery – 'barbarians' in traditional terminology – even if they had often been living on Roman soil for more than a generation by the time they finally established independent kingdoms across the broken landscape of an extinct Empire. By the final quarter of the fifth century, the former provinces of Roman Britain were largely controlled by small-scale Anglo-Saxon dynasts, who arrived with armed retinues from across the North Sea. Frankish kings, under Clovis and his successors, were expanding their control over northern and central Gaul. Visigothic kings ruled over south-western Gaul and much of the Iberian peninsula; their Burgundian and Suevic counterparts south-eastern Gaul and north-western Spain respectively. Italy in its entirety was ruled by Odovacar, who had deposed Romulus Augustulus and, in a highly symbolic move, despatched the western imperial regalia to Constantinople in the autumn of 476 with an explicit message that there was no longer any western emperor to wear them. Son of a king of the Sciri, then established on the Great Hungarian Plain, Odovacar had moved into west Roman military service in the 460s and then come to power at the head of a *coup d'état*. But his reign was short-lived. At the end of the 480s, Theoderic the Amal led his powerful Ostrogothic confederation into Italy to complete the line-up of 'barbarian'-dominated first-generation successor states.[5]

The causes of this political revolution have been long and intensely debated. In recent years, some historians have played down the role of these external forces in the fifth-century collapse of imperial Rome, as well as the amount of violent disruption involved: an approach which has reinforced long-standing tendencies to see the fall of the Roman west as an event that largely bypassed the nascent Christian Church, which remained more or less untouched as the Empire collapsed around it. This account argues that the collapse was substantially engineered by some important interest groups of local provincial landowners within the Roman world who wanted to withdraw from the structures of Empire to lower their tax bills: they allied themselves instead with semi-outsiders (such as the Vandals and Visigoths) – who were already part of a broader Roman commonwealth – to help negotiate a path to local autonomy. Arguments of this kind downplay the barbarians' importance as historical actors, in terms of both numbers and coherence, envisaging not the settlement of 'peoples' – entities comprising tens of thousands of human beings, mixed in age and gender, as groups like the

Vandals and Visigoths used to be understood – but rather 'warbands'. This concept denotes much smaller warrior – hence overwhelmingly male – communities, of hundreds or perhaps a thousand or two fighters on the move, with only limited numbers of dependants, capable of making only a correspondingly limited impact on the territories they moved through.[6]

A second, related, line of historical reinterpretation draws on new understandings about group identity that have emerged over the last half-century. Previously, groups like the Vandals or Visigoths were understood as well-established population aggregates with their own distinctive material and non-material cultural profiles, as befitted ancient 'peoples': a view dovetailing with early twentieth-century nationalist assumptions that it was 'normal' for individuals to possess singular, unchanging identities into which they had usually been born. More recent research has focused on the fact that identity can be both multiple and mutable. Seen through this lens, the archaeological remains that were hitherto thought to provide groups like Goths and Vandals with their distinctive material cultural signatures do nothing of the sort. Looked at more closely, likewise, the historical sources turn out to be full not of unchanging 'peoples', but of barbarian groupings in flux, constantly being broken and remade. Taken together, this downgrading of both numbers and cultural distinctiveness has made it possible for historians to emphasize the evidence for co-operation, as opposed to conflict, between provincial Romans in search of autonomy from the imperial system, and non-Roman neighbours, paving the way for alternative narrative reconstructions in which the choices of dissident Roman landowners play a much larger role than barbarian intruders in the collapse of the western Empire.

Like prevailing visions of the Christianization of the Empire, this recent historical approach privileges long-term change over mere 'events' in explaining imperial collapse. In this view, outside invasion (envisaged always as small in scale) becomes much less important than evolving attitudes among Roman elites: both their increasing dissatisfaction with the workings of the Roman imperial system, and their increasing willingness to view outsiders less as 'barbarian others' and more as potential collaborators in strategies for advancing shared interests. Just like that famous moment when Mrs Thatcher declared that

President Gorbachev was no longer an existential threat to the free west, but 'someone we can do business with', west Roman elites came to see barbarian warband leaders as useful tools through which they could negotiate their way out of an overdemanding imperial system.[7]

All the key pillars of these revisionist historical arguments find some support in fifth-century sources, in which you do find western provincial Roman elites engaged in intense negotiations with recently immigrant warlords. Nor were the military powerbases at the heart of the successor kingdoms, such as Huneric's Vandals and Alans, or the Visigoths, comprised of ancient 'peoples' with distinct, long-standing identities. The force Huneric inherited from his father and grandfather was a new coalition, constructed in the 410s and 420s from what had been two entirely separate groups of Germanic-speaking Vandals (the Silings and Hasdings: Huneric's family was originally the Hasding ruling line) and an originally much larger body of Iranian-speaking Alans, led by several separate kings of their own. These discrete groupings crossed the Rhine together in a loose coalition on the last day of 406. Then, over the next decade, they came gradually together into tighter alliance under unitary Hasding leadership as they moved through southern Gaul and over the Pyrenees into Spain. The Visigoths, likewise, were a new coalition, comprising three main contingents who arrived independently on Roman soil between the mid-370s and *c.* 410 (the Tervingi and Greuthungi, who crossed the Danube separately in 376, and the survivors of a third force led into Italy in 405/6 by a king called Radagaisus). Franks and Ostrogoths, similarly, were brand-new coalitions created on Roman soil. The same is even true of the Anglo-Saxon political units that carved out new kingdoms in various parts of old Roman Britain.[8]

Neither were these groups implacably opposed to Roman civilization. Rich villas and town houses continued to be built during the Vandals' hundred-year occupation of Rome's North African provinces, while the imagery, ceremonies and even the dress styles of the Vandal court directly imitated luxurious late Roman norms. Latin was still being taught in Roman-style schoolrooms across the kingdom, and its rulers liked to be celebrated in classical verse: the Vandal court may have persecuted Nicene Christians, but it continued to patronize classical literature, supporting the work of no fewer than fifteen known Latin poets writing in and around Carthage. The Vandal elite also heartily enjoyed the decidedly Roman pleasures of bath, theatre and horse-racing, not to mention the all-important but less culturally specific joys of the hunt. A range of similar evidence allows the same overarching point to be made about most of the other first-generation successor states.[9] But while all this is true enough, there are strong reasons, nonetheless, why the revisionist picture of local Roman elites using non-Roman warlords to negotiate voluntary exits from the Roman imperial system remains an insufficient description of western Roman imperial collapse.

First of all, the deals negotiated between local Roman elites and the incoming dynasts were not equal agreements; indeed, some even less fortunate provincial Romans didn't succeed in brokering any kind of deal at all. The villa-owning elites of Roman Britain, visibly prosperous in the archaeology of the fourth century, completely failed to survive the transition to Anglo-Saxon rule. When the historical record picks up again from *c.* 600, there is not the slightest sign of any of their descendants in the English lowlands, the beating agricultural heart of Roman Britain.[10] And even where deals were done, as they were across most of Rome's former continental provinces, they involved substantial losses for many Roman landowners. One line of argument suggests that the incoming warriors were supported by reallocating existing tax revenues, which would not have involved any losses at all. But this is not what the sources report. Nor is it plausible that the incoming Vandal-Alan, Frankish, or Gothic military elites at the heart of the successor kingdoms would have settled for anything less than capital shares in the landed wealth of the new political entities which their military muscle had carved out of the Roman body politic. In Vandal Africa, Huneric's father Geiseric confined confiscations in favour of his followers to the province of Proconsularis in the immediate vicinity of Carthage, a province full of ancient estates belonging to absentee Roman senators like our old friend Symmachus. In other kingdoms, sitting Roman landowners lost a portion of their lands and labour force. This doesn't look much like the outcome of a voluntary process of disengagement from Empire.

As we have also already seen, the ties which bound local landowners into the Roman imperial system, for all the limitations of its governmental systems, were powerful: powerful enough to have played a major role in setting the same landowners decisively along the path of self-Christianization in the fourth century. Rather, as these ties were ruptured during the fifth century, provincial Roman elites were usually left with only one option: to make what deal they could with whatever barbarian coalition was most powerful in their neighbourhood, which is not at all the same thing as suggesting that they had positively sought such deals from the outset.[11] Why they found themselves caught up in this difficult situation brings us back to the outsiders with whom they were eventually forced to negotiate.

The new military coalitions at the heart of the successor states may not have been the ancient peoples envisaged in the earlier twentieth century, but they were more imposing than the more extreme revisionist positions tend to allow. On a handful of occasions, immigrant groups encompassing tens of thousands of human beings – far beyond anything that might reasonably be described as a 'warband' – crossed the Empire's frontier. The sources for the original Rhine crossing on 31 December 406, which eventually generated the Vandal-Alan coalition, are not strong on detail, but they are obviously describing large-scale demographic phenomena: even most revisionist historians accept that several tens of thousands of individuals were on the move in this case. As to the size of the consolidated force – distilled from this originally loose alliance – which Huneric's father led to North Africa, the one number worth serious consideration is provided by Victor of Vita. He reports that when the coalition crossed from Spain, Geiseric mustered it into seventy groups of, notionally, one thousand individuals each: men, women and children. Victor was writing primarily for North African Catholics under Vandal rule: his account of what were, for his target audience, recent events of great significance would have had to be plausible. There's every chance, therefore, that he is giving us a reasonable order of magnitude here: several tens of thousands of people, but probably less than Geiseric's notional 70,000.[12]

Some of the other groups of outsiders were clearly just as large. In 378, the combined Tervingi and Greuthungi were numerous enough (with assistance from a warband of Huns and Alans) to kill at least ten thousand professional Roman soldiers on a single day at the battle of Hadrianople. Few battles of this era were anything like so decisive, so there must have been a strong element of luck involved, but all the same, such a victory could never have been achieved by a few warbands. Radagaisus' expedition into Italy in 405/6, likewise, was so large that it was only brought to heel by a Roman army of thirty regiments (again, well over ten thousand men) reinforced by numerous Hunnic and Alanic auxiliaries, and its defeat saw twelve thousand of Radagaisus' former followers drafted into the Roman army, with their dependants placed as hostages in various Italian cities. Contemporary sources also suggest a similar order of magnitude for the Ostrogothic coalition that Theoderic the Amal led to Italy over the autumn and winter of 488/9.[13] While some fifth-century incursions into the empire probably did involve intruders that can reasonably be described as warbands – Anglo-Saxons, and Franks prior to the reign of Clovis – it's clear that more substantial migrant groupings were at the heart of Vandal, Visigothic and Ostrogothic kingdoms.

Equally important to note is that few – if in fact any – of these migrants were actually invited onto Roman soil. The majority invited themselves. This is true for the loose coalition that crossed the Rhine in 406, Radagaisus' force that marched into Italy the previous year, and Theoderic's Ostrogothic alliance. Before entering Italy in 488/9, Theoderic's alliance had forced its way into Constantinople's Balkan territories, in search of larger diplomatic subsidies from the eastern Empire. Its subsequent departure for Italy was the agreed solution to a developing political impasse in the eastern Empire between Theoderic's ambitions and those of the eastern emperor Zeno. Even in the case of the two separate Gothic groups, of Tervingi and Greuthungi, who separately asked Emperor Valens for asylum from Hunnic attack in 376, the element of invitation is more apparent than real. Valens was already engaged in a full-scale conflict with Persia, close to 2,000 miles from the Danube, to which all of his field forces were committed, which meant that he had insufficient troops available in the Balkans to deny all the Goths entry into imperial territory. With his armies in action elsewhere, the emperor had no choice but to go for the least-worst option: admitting one group of Goths – the Tervingi – while attempting to exclude the other. It was much more an exercise in damage limitation than an invitation in the real sense of the word.[14]

Large and uninvited, these migrant coalitions posed a direct threat to the Roman imperial system. At heart, the Empire taxed an overwhelmingly agricultural economy to support the military forces which kept it in being. As with most pre-modern states running large 'professional' armies, the best estimates indicate that around 70 per cent of all its tax revenues were spent on the military. Large, politically independent immigrant coalitions undermined this structure in both the shorter and longer terms, whether they planned to or (far more likely) not. Most immediately, they inflicted serious losses on the Empire's expensive military machine: the Goths involuntarily admitted in 376 by Valens destroyed two-thirds of the eastern Empire's field army on that day at Hadrianople two years later. These losses remained visible in an east Roman military listing of *c.* 395, from which sixteen units of elite heavy line infantry are missing: shattered at Hadrianople, these regiments were never reconstituted.[15] Still worse was the effect on the western Empire's armies of a long series of conflicts with three separate large groups of outsiders from the first decade of the fifth century onward: Radagaisus' followers, in Italy in 405/6, the Rhine invaders of 406, and the combined descendants of the Tervingi and Greuthungi who, under the leadership of Alaric, moved their centre of operations definitively onto western imperial soil from 408. Alaric's forces were responsible, among other things, for the sack of Rome in 410 – an event which encouraged Augustine's ruminations on the Empire's less than central position in the Divine Plan for humankind (p. 124).

The besieged Empire's resulting decade and a half of military grind against these outsiders was not completely unsuccessful. By 415 the Goths had been starved into compliance, engaging from 416 in joint campaigns with Roman forces against new invaders from across the Rhine, the Vandals and Alans who had moved into Spain in 409. A contemporary local chronicler, Hydatius, bishop of Aquae Flaviae (modern Chaves in Portugal), recorded the initially encouraging results, with both the Siling Vandals and Alans – originally the most numerous element in the coalition – destroyed as independent entities. The survivors went on to accept the rule of the Hasding Vandal monarch Gunderic (Huneric's grandfather).[16] These losses changed the balance of power within the Rhine invaders as a whole, destroying the Alans' original dominance, and bound its surviving personnel together into a closer-knit political confederation. The consequences became dramatically apparent when, after a brief hiatus, Romano-Gothic forces renewed their attacks in 420. In 422 the Vandal-Alan coalition won a stunning victory outside the walls of Córdoba, having persuaded the Goths to switch sides at a crucial juncture in the battle, which reportedly left twenty thousand Romans dead. Again, a west Roman military listing drawn up shortly afterwards graphically illustrates the impact of all this warfare on Roman military capacity: about two-thirds of the west Roman field army units that had existed in 395, at the end of the last major bout of internal Roman civil war, had been ground to dust.[17]

Major defeats not only undercut the immediate military power of the imperial system; they also undermined its longer-term viability. Each defeat at the hands of intrusive outsiders forced the imperial authorities to negotiate with the group in question, a process that always involved ceding blocks of imperial territory. In this way, the Visigothic coalition eventually received licensed settlement areas in south-western Gaul, while Geiseric's victories allowed the consolidated Vandal-Alan force to seize Carthage and the most valuable of Rome's North African provinces. These settlements, and the violence which preceded them, both reduced imperial tax revenues. Ceded territories obviously ceased to pay taxes to the Roman centre, and it was also normal for the imperial administration to give a 6/7ths tax reduction for several years to any area that had been fought over, even if imperial sovereignty was eventually restored. All these losses of revenue in turn made it difficult to maintain or repair the imperial army – a point dramatically visible in that same military listing of the 420s. By this date, south-western Gaul was under Visigoth control, Britain had fallen out of the system altogether, and Spain had been paying significantly reduced taxes for a decade. As a result of this cut in annual tax revenues, dead soldiers could only be replaced by stopgap measures: not by the proper recruiting of new units, but – in the case of over half the field army replacements – by promoting second-rate garrison forces to field army status. And this was even before the Vandal-Alan coalition took control of the western Empire's richest North African provinces in 439.[18]

The effects of these large uninvited immigrant groups and associated bouts of substantial violence on the imperial system were, in sum, powerful and direct.[19] As well as downgrading the empire's military capacity and eroding central control over a growing proportion of the western Empire's tax base, they also created a new political context in which local provincial Roman landowning elites became highly vulnerable. These elites were creatures of the Empire. As their enthusiastic response in the fourth and early fifth centuries to the emperors' new Christian cult emphasizes, it was the imperial system that defined and protected the landed wealth which made them who they were (as discussed in Chapter 2). When, as its armies and revenues declined over the course of the fifth century, the Empire began to lose the capacity to protect these landowners' interests, they quickly found themselves in a precarious position. Because their wealth was based on landowning, they could not easily abandon the home regions in which their estates were situated (apart, that was, from the small group of super-elite, who had estates to fall back on in other parts of the Empire[20]).

All of which gives us a fuller perspective from which to view the negotiations between Roman landowners and emergent successor-state kings during the final generation of the western Empire, between *c.* 450 and 475. If a Gothic, Vandal, or Frankish king started to dominate your neighbourhood, as a local Roman landowner you actually had no choice but to do a deal – no matter, as we have seen, that such a deal tended to cost you part of your capital wealth. It was either that or lose everything. Any account that describes as 'peaceful' and 'voluntary' the process that, by the 480s, had put Huneric and his dynastic peers among the Goths, Franks and others in charge of different portions of the old Roman west is, in the end, ignoring important preceding phases of what was one overall story. None of these immigrant groups was implacably hostile to Roman civilization; none of the emergent dynasts headed ancient 'peoples' with long-standing cultural identities. They were also generally open to doing deals with provincial Roman landowning elites. In anything but the short term, however, the interests of these dynasts were fundamentally opposed to those of the central Roman state. While we can ditch the idea of 'savage barbarians' from our narrative reconstructions, we must acknowledge the role of these large external coalitions with their own political agendas; and a fifth-century political process shaped by periodic, large-scale violent confrontation between those migrants and a central Roman authority whose financial and military power they directly challenged. Huneric's core support was provided by a newly built coalition, not an ancient people, but his rule in Carthage was the result of a process of violent self-assertion on the part of that coalition against the interests of the west Roman imperial centre.

The immigrant coalitions had no concerted plan to bring the Empire down in the fifth century, but, as it progressed, enough of them were acting in similar ways to rob the imperial centre of a critical mass of its tax revenues. As a direct result, the Roman state lost its capacity to maintain sufficient armed forces to protect the interests of its local provincial elites.[21] To understand why this process should also have ended up with a new king in Carthage who vigorously promoted non-Nicene, Homoean Christianity, we first need to explore one further dimension of fourth-century Roman Christian history in a little more detail.

LITTLE WOLF

Central to what unfolded around Carthage in the early 480s is the life and career of a figure who lived 150 years earlier: Ulfilas, 'Little Wolf', 'the Apostle of the Goths'. His story has its origins in the already vigorous rural Christianity found in certain parts of Asia Minor even before the reign of Constantine. Ulfilas was born sometime early in the fourth century in the domains of the pagan Gothic Tervingi, who, by the 330s, ran a moderately powerful, semi-subdued Roman client state adjacent to the Empire's Lower Danube frontier, in what is now Moldova and Romania. Descended from Christian Roman prisoners captured by the Goths raiding across the Black Sea in the last quarter of the third century, Ulfilas was clearly aware of his family history, to the extent that he even knew where his parents or grandparents had lived: the village of Sadgolthina, near the city of Parnassus in Cappadocia (about 50 miles (80 km) from the modern Anatolian city of Aksaray). Ulfilas grew up fluent in Latin and Greek, as well as Gothic, in a Christian community that was established enough to send a bishop to the council of Nicaea.

He was already a lesser cleric (a reader) in this Christian congregation when, probably about the age of thirty, he came to Constantinople in 340/1 as part of an embassy to Emperor Constantius II. The Constantinian dynasty liked to show its care for fellow believers in neighbouring states, and in the course of the mission Ulfilas was ordained as the new bishop of the community of Gothic Christians by one of the emperor's leading ecclesiastical advisors, Bishop Eusebius of Nicomedia. Ulfilas's ordination was perhaps one of the main reasons for the embassy, since religion was – and consistently remained – an issue in relations between the Empire and the pagan leadership of the Tervingi. When in the late 340s the Goths managed to reassert greater diplomatic independence, Ulfilas and many of his fellow Christians were expelled: a sign that the Gothic leadership regarded them as a potential imperial fifth column. The bishop led so many of them across the Danube into Roman territory in 347/8 that Constantius II labelled him 'the Moses of our time'. Nonetheless, Ulfilas's subsequent career remained closely intertwined with the Gothic world north of the Danube, and two aspects of its central features helped shape the religious policies of King Huneric a century and a half later.[22]

Ulfilas's landmark achievement was to make the first translation of the Bible into the Gothic language. (Supposedly, he left out parts of the Old Testament that were too bloodthirsty, on the grounds that the Goths were warlike enough without any extra divine validation.) A few fragments of a Gothic Old Testament have survived on papyrus, but what has mainly come down to us, in a handful of manuscripts deriving from the Ostrogothic Italian kingdom of the sixth century, is the bulk of the translated Gothic New Testament. The Gospel translation – preserved, most luxuriously, in the *Codex Argenteus* of Uppsala University library, a production written in gold and silver ink on dyed purple parchment of exquisite fineness – is a simple word-for-word rendering of a standard Greek New Testament text of the fourth century. It can't have sounded much like spoken Gothic, since it slavishly follows Greek grammar and word order, which likely enough reflects Ulfilas's original translation methods. The Gothic translation of the Epistles, by contrast, shows signs of considerable reworking – if, that is, the word-for-word approach of the Gospel text reflects Ulfilas's original technique – perhaps because the Epistles were the prime battleground of subsequent theological debate. Where and when Ulfilas, and presumably a team of helpers, did the work is unclear: north of Danube before 348, south of the Danube afterwards, or – likely as not – both. Not much else survives, but there are scattered fragments of other translated works: a liturgical calendar in Gothic, along with a palimpsest of a biblical commentary on the Gospel of John. This is enough to confirm what other sources tell us: alongside his translation of the Bible, Ulfilas produced a full range of Gothic liturgical materials.[23]

Ulfilas also became a partisan in the fierce doctrinal debates over the nature of the relationship between Father and Son which raged across the eastern half of Roman Christendom in the aftermath of Nicaea's adoption of *homoousios* in 325. Quite what Ulfilas himself originally believed is not certain; in all probability, his beliefs reflected the understanding of the Trinity current among the Christian communities of third-century Asia Minor from whom the Goths took their prisoners. Either way, he signed up to the alternative Homoean imperial religious orthodoxy at Constantius II's council of Constantinople in 360, and held to it subsequently.[24]

Ulfilas is key to the religious policies of Huneric's reign because of his role – direct and indirect – in the long sequence of events that, starting with Hunnic attacks north of the Danube in the mid-370s, eventually brought the western Empire to its knees. When Rome's near Gothic neighbours sought refuge from the Huns on Roman territory in 376, the ageing Ulfilas was involved in the lengthy diplomatic process that saw Emperor Valens eventually decide to give shelter to the Tervingi, with whom the Empire had a long history of close relations. One condition of the Tervingi's admission was that their new leadership formally adopt Christianity. Christianity had been an issue in Gotho-Roman relations for decades, and, after Ulfilas's expulsion across the Danube, the Tervingi had periodically persecuted the remaining Gothic Christians north of the Danube, creating numerous martyrs in a particularly nasty outbreak of religious violence in the early 370s. Against this backdrop, it is hardly surprising that accepting Christianity became a condition attached to the brand-new phase of unprecedented intimacy initiated by the Goths' admission onto imperial soil.[25]

Traditionally, historians felt it necessary to come up with some kind of ethnic explanation for the Goths' attachment to Homoean Christianity, suggesting that its more hierarchical Trinity, in which the Son was 'like' the Father (*homoios*) rather than 'of the same essence' (*homoousios*), was somehow easier to explain to Germanic barbarians. But such ethnic explanations ignore the reality that Homoean Christianity was as impeccably Roman in origin as its Nicene competitor, and could be equally effectively supported with a barrage of New Testament texts. (That Jesus is reported as having prayed to the Father in the Garden of Gethsemane, 'Not my will but Thy will be done,' did not, on the face of it, suggest a fully equal relationship between these two persons of the Trinity.) Such explanations are also completely unnecessary because the Gothic Tervingi, the first major Germanic-speaking group to convert to Christianity, became Homoean Christians in 376 at a point when this was still official Roman Christian orthodoxy – and had been for the best part of two decades. After the brief pagan interlude provided by Julian the Apostate, his successors – the brothers Valentinian I and Valens – continued to uphold Constantius' doctrinal settlement. 'Like' – *homoios* – was perhaps easier to translate into Gothic than *homoousios*, whose full explanation required a grounding in Greek philosophy, but the Goths' original Christian allegiance was simply to 'official imperial Christianity' as it stood at the moment they crossed the Danube in 376. It helped, of course, that Ulfilas was of the same persuasion, and could supply the converts with a full range of religious texts in their own language – texts that he himself had translated.[26]

But if their original reception of Homoean Christianity can be straightforwardly explained as the Goths coming into line with the official religion of the Empire, what happened next cannot. Whereas in 381 the vast majority of the Empire's Christian congregations quickly accepted Emperor Theodosius' modified version of the Nicene definition of faith after the second ecumenical council of Constantinople, enforced by imperial legislation, the Goths did not. By this time, not only the Tervingi but also the Greuthungi (who had moved onto Roman soil illegally later in the autumn of 376) were established on east Roman territory. Their joint defeat of Valens at Hadrianople in 378 eventually forced the Roman state to offer them both a compromise peace settlement in 382, which specifically protected their cultural autonomy as well as resettling them in the Empire's Balkan provinces. This agreement was unprecedented. Though the Empire had accepted immigrants throughout its history, sometimes even allowing them to keep their weapons, it usually accepted only smaller groups, and always on its own terms. Tolerating the continued autonomy of a large block of militarily powerful immigrants had never been done – for the very good reason, as we have seen, that it directly threatened the fiscal-military structure on which the entire imperial edifice rested. Unsurprisingly, the Roman state remained far from fully reconciled to this new relationship in the 380s and 390s; the Goths, for their part, were naturally (and justifiably) suspicious of their hosts.

Many of the Goths who settled in imperial territories under the treaty of 382 ended up fighting for Theodosius in two civil wars against western usurpers in the late 380s and early 390s. They incurred substantial losses in the process. On the second campaign, they suffered so many casualties at the battle of the Frigidus river (in present-day Slovenia) in September 394 that one Roman commentator concluded that Theodosius had won two victories: one over the usurper Eugenius, a second over the Goths. As this comment underlines, losses of military manpower directly threatened the Goths' continued autonomy. If they lost too many fighters, the imperial authorities would be presented with an opportunity to reset the relationship that had been forced on them by Hadrianople – and there was every reason to suppose they would take it. The Goths knew this perfectly well. Hence a minority of them refused to fight in both of Theodosius' civil wars, and when the emperor died unexpectedly in January 395, most rose in revolt.

In the end, it took another twenty years to establish a new Romano-Gothic diplomatic order: a period punctuated by occasional military conflict and many diplomatic fluctuations, until, in the mid-410s, the outlines of a new deal acceptable to both sides had begun to emerge. By this point, the originally separate Tervingi and Greuthungi of 376 had coalesced into a new – Visigothic – confederation (which also included many additional recruits, particularly from Radagaisus' defeated expedition into Italy, p. 168), and switched their centre of operations westwards to exploit the greater turmoil generated in the western Empire by the major invasions of 405 and 406 (the latter of course including the Vandals). Over the next decade, the bare bones of a new agreement between the consolidated Visigothic confederation and the western Empire began to emerge, based on two main pillars with the Goths established in south-western Gaul. On the one hand, the Empire gave legal recognition to the Goths' settlement in what is now the Garonne valley in Aquitaine – just distant enough from the western Empire's seat of power in Italy not to pose an immediate threat. In return, the Goths promised military assistance – most immediately against the Vandals and Alans who were by this date occupying most of the Iberian peninsula.[27]

All this is crucial to a proper understanding of Huneric's North African religious policies because, throughout the military and diplomatic twists and turns that brought the new Visigothic coalition into being, its constituent Goths remained Homoean Christians. While Roman sources are all but silent on this point, that this was no accident but, rather, a conscious choice on the part of the Goths' leadership is confirmed by two events. First, in 409/10, the Visigothic king Alaric raised the Roman senator Attalus as his own puppet emperor, to ramp up diplomatic pressure on the legitimate rulers of the Roman west; in the process, Alaric made Attalus accept baptism into Homoean Christianity. Second, over time, the Gothic leadership spread its version of Christianity to every receptive audience that came within its diplomatic orbit. Only one instance of this is explicitly documented. Having previously adopted Nicene Christianity, the Suevi (a smaller grouping that had crossed the Rhine in 406, and with whom the Goths now shared the Iberian peninsula) came under Visigothic hegemony in the 460s, when their ruler, Remismund, married a Visigothic princess. As part of the process, the Suevi adopted Homoean Christianity. In the other cases, we have no details, but Burgundians, Gepids, Heruli and Ostrogoths all ended up as Homoean, rather than Nicene Christians. The same was true of the Vandals and Alans who crossed the Rhine in 406.[28]

The precise date at which the Vandals converted to Christianity is unclear. Reportedly, they used a verse of Scripture as a rallying call in their great victory over the western Roman Empire in 422, while a separate source comments that God allowed them to invade the Empire so that they might be converted. These references indicate a conversion date of somewhere between 406 and 421. We're also told that Geiseric originally converted to Nicene Christianity before switching to a Homoean allegiance – a process that echoes the conversion of the Suevi. Everything points to the Visigoths being the crucial catalyst in the Vandals' final doctrinal choice. Not only were the Visigoths generally the source of the Homoean Christianity that spread so widely among the fifth-century intruders onto western imperial territory, but they played a crucial role in the Vandals' thumping victory over the Empire in 422 outside Córdoba, deserting their Roman allies at a crucial moment in the battle. Geiseric's son and successor Huneric was also first married to a Visigothic princess – an alliance probably forged in Spain in the 420s before the Vandals moved on to North Africa, and which emphasizes the closeness of relations between the ruling dynasties of the Visigoths and Vandals at this point.[29] But if the Homoean Christianity of the Vandals and Alans, destined to become such a major factor in North Africa sixty years later, can be traced back to their close connections to the Visigoths in the 420s, this only prompts more questions. Why did the Goths not change to Theodosius' restored Nicene Christianity along with the rest of the Empire's population after 381, and why was Homoean Christianity attractive to so many outsiders to the Roman system? While there remains no internal Visigothic source material to help us answer these questions, the ways in which the Vandal leadership used Homoean Christianity, once its followers were settled in North Africa, provides convincing answers to both.

RENDER UNTO CAESAR

Although the prime focus of Victor of Vita's *History of the Persecution in Africa* is the persecution of Nicene Christians in 483/4, it is also our main source of information for what happened in and around Carthage after its seizure by Geiseric in 439. Right from the outset, Victor asserts, the Vandals were unrelenting persecutors of the True, Nicene Christian Faith. Looked at more closely, however, Victor's detailed record of Geiseric's actions reveals a more complex picture.

The Vandals' initial conquests in North Africa, from their arrival there in 428/9 to the negotiation of a first peace treaty with the Empire in 435, were marked by periodic bouts of the kinds of looting and violence you would probably expect. Victor claimed that 'innumerable'

Nicene bishops and priests were tortured and put to death by Vandals as they sacked and pillaged Nicene churches for their treasures. Yet he mentions only two by name: Pampinianus of Vita and Mansuetus of Urusi. While events of this kind surely did occur, and clearly generated panic – Possidius of Calama, Augustine's biographer, fled to the Algerian city of Hippo, while Augustine had to pen circular letters encouraging pastors to stay with their flocks – whether this amounted to a conscious policy of religious anti-Nicene persecution at this stage looks doubtful. It was only after Geiseric captured Carthage in 439 and a more comprehensive peace with the Empire was eventually negotiated in the mid-440s, following the failure of a projected joint attempt by the eastern and western Empires to reconquer Carthage in 442 (when Hunnic attacks across the Danube forced the eastern contingent to return to Constantinople), that the Vandal king had real freedom to put more considered religious policies into operation.[30]

In Carthage, now the capital city of the new Vandal kingdom, Geiseric's Homoean clergy took possession of the city's cathedral, the Basilica Maiora, and seized three further churches: the Basilica Restituta and two funerary churches dedicated to the important North African martyr St Cyprian. All four were inside the city walls; a number of churches in the suburbs remained in the hands of the Nicene Church hierarchy.[31] More churches were also confiscated across the province of Proconsularis, one of the three North African provinces (along with Byzacena and Numidia) that Geiseric now controlled, and the one in which he primarily allocated landed estates to his followers, since it both surrounded his capital in Carthage and faced outwards towards the main sea routes from southern Italy and Sicily, from where any future Roman counter-attack might be expected. This settlement process also rapidly acquired a religious dimension, because in any locality that now housed Vandal or Alan settlers, local Nicene churches and their supporting property endowments were confiscated for Homoean use. The king also imposed a ban on the celebration of services by Nicene clergy in the same settlements.[32]

A number of Nicene bishops were not compliant. Geiseric exiled six from Numidia and Byzacena for reportedly preaching sermons hostile to the Vandal regime. (Quodvultdeus of Carthage, the leading clergyman in North Africa, had suffered a similar fate immediately after his city fell, together with many of his clergy.) In all these cases, the king refused to allow replacement ordinations, even after the exiles' deaths, so that the total number of Nicene bishops within the Vandal kingdom started to decline. But one inheritance of the fourth-century Donatist dispute about how to treat Christians who had lapsed in the Great Tetrarchic Persecution was that North Africa enjoyed a great density of bishops. Trying to present themselves as the 'true' Church, both Donatists and Catholics had created new sees with abandon, so that there were over six hundred North African bishops by the 420s. (In comparison, Gaul and Egypt had about a hundred each.)[33] There remained plenty of Nicene bishops to go round, then – even when, in 457, a new west Roman regime abrogated the peace treaty, following which Geiseric took further religious reprisals. He enforced the ban on Nicene services in Proconsularis more harshly, refusing to allow any deceased prelates to be replaced.[34]

Geiseric's conquest of Carthage set in motion a major revolution in the religious landscape of North Africa. A large portfolio of buildings and property was transferred to the Homoean Church at the king's command, while Nicene clergy suffered selective curtailment of their freedom of operations. But all of this stopped far short of the full-scale persecution the kingdom witnessed in the time of Huneric. Throughout Geiseric's reign, the Nicenes retained several churches in the suburbs of Carthage, while bishops and leading laymen (*honorati*) of Proconsularis eventually petitioned successfully for permission to hold Nicene services in buildings close to their lost churches.[35] Similarly, while the king's refusal to allow any new ordinations in Proconsularis after 457 in principle posed a long-term threat to Nicene Christianity in the province, its immediate effects were again relatively minor. As late as 484, the province still boasted fifty-four Nicene bishops (half as many, after all, as were available for the whole of Gaul). Even more importantly, none of Geiseric's measures (apart from the odd episcopal exile) applied at all to the other two provinces of the kingdom, Byzacena and Numidia. In other words, throughout Geiseric's reign the Nicene Church operated with complete freedom in two-thirds of the Vandal kingdom, and was far from shut down in the remainder.

One basic distortion in Victor's religious history of the Vandal kingdom, therefore, is very clear. He used its first book to present Geiseric and Huneric as equal persecutors of Nicene Christianity, but the two kings pursued entirely different kinds of religious policy. Geiseric never launched a general persecution of North Africa's Nicene Church, and showed not the slightest desire to convert all of his realm – Byzacena and Numidia as well as Proconsularis – to Homoean Christianity. When Geiseric's comparatively soft religious policies are added to what we know more generally about the nature of the Vandal-Alan coalition he led to North Africa, it's probable that the undoubted damage the king visited on the Nicene Church of North Africa – even in Proconsularis – was not the direct result of targeted persecution. Rather, it was collateral damage in a policy of religious conversion and consolidation that was aimed at another audience entirely: his own warriors.

Christianity of any kind was a brand-new phenomenon among the Vandal army that fought its way into Carthage on 19 October 439. Its leaders had only become Christian in the 420s, and the rest comprised a highly diverse mixture of peoples: Germanic-speaking Vandal farmers mingled with groups of Iranian-speaking Alan nomads, some Goths, some Romans, and many others besides. Even if the pre-Christian belief structures of the Siling and Hasding Vandals (of which we know nothing) were probably reasonably closely aligned, those of the Alans, recent inhabitants of the totally different cultural context of the Eurasian steppes, must have been completely alien to their Vandal allies. The group's Homoean clerical establishment, likewise, can only have been in its infancy. It surely possessed some Holy Books (presumably in Ulfilas's translation), liturgical vessels and vestments copied or inherited from the Visigoths. But before the conquest of Carthage, it possessed no property or annual income from which to support itself, while its numbers would have been limited both by this lack of finance and by a shortage of recruits from among an as yet only partially converted population.[36] In 439, the Homoean Christianity of Geiseric's followers amounted to a thin veneer atop huge cultic diversity.

In this context, Geiseric's policies can be seen as an attempt to put down strong Homoean Christian roots among the body of diverse warrior manpower which had propelled him into power. His reallocation of churches and their endowments in Carthage and Proconsularis to his supporters established fertile conditions for the emergence of a stronger Homoean clerical establishment wherever Vandals and Alans were settled in large numbers. And while this appropriation of wealth could not in itself overcome the immediate shortage of trained priests, it did put in place the necessary resources for a major institutional expansion; moreover, some clerical recruits may have been available straightaway among North Africa's Roman population. Homoean Christianity had been imperial orthodoxy in the Roman west down to the 380s, at which point its clerical and other supporters had been numerous. Not all of this support was immediately extinguished when Emperor Theodosius I made his U-turn back to Nicaea, even if most western Churchmen clearly were as happy to sign up to this new religious settlement as they had been to the old. Maximinus, a Homoean priest of Italian origin with whom Augustine was debating theological niceties as late as 427/8, cannot have been the sole survivor; the burgeoning Vandal Church may well have been able to recruit some clergy from among surviving Roman Homoeans.[37] At the same time, Geiseric's ban on Nicene Church services in the relevant parts of Proconsularis ensured that Homoean clergy enjoyed a religious monopoly as they set about inculcating their version of Christianity among the king's followers settled in that province, but the Nicene establishment in the unoccupied provinces of Byzacena and Numidia was left completely untouched. Rather than an outright attack on the Nicene Church, as Victor of Vita had it, Geiseric's policies were designed for one purpose only: to make his own warriors Homoean.

Such a targeted policy made sense for two reasons. The force Geiseric led to Africa was large, culturally diverse and, mostly, owed no long-standing allegiance to his Hasding dynasty. Building greater loyalty within the group via a shared profession of faith made perfect sense. Second, in the period up to 439, this force had been unified by its opposition to the generally hostile Roman environment in which it was operating. Once the immediate Roman threat was lifted with the conquest of Carthage, however – and particularly as Geiseric's followers began to disperse across Proconsularis in the 440s – the situation changed.

In this new context, Homoean Christianity offered some spectacular advantages as a unifying force. Not least, Romanized Christianity had long argued that no power could exist unless the omnipotent and providential God so willed it (p. 13). In adopting Christianity, in any form, a highly successful monarch like Geiseric – the triumphant conqueror of Carthage no less – could add ideological lustre to his ruling credentials. For the new Hasding regime, moreover, Christianity also represented a neutral religious force, standing outside the wide range of different cults his disparate following had previously observed. Where it would probably have been impossible to sell the Hasding or Siling Vandals' Germanic paganism to Iranian-speaking Alans, all were equally open to the force of missionary Christianity. Choosing Homoean over Nicene Christianity added two further specific benefits. First, its Gothic adherents (most prominently Ulfilas) had already translated key Christian texts and service books into a Germanic language, which the Vandals at least (and maybe now the Alans, after thirty years of coexistence) were able to understand. Second, and just as attractive to Geiseric, Homoean Christianity was *not* official Roman imperial orthodoxy. The Vandal kingdom of North Africa had been created by violence, not peaceful imperial acquiescence, and a possible Roman counterstrike remained a real threat to its continued existence down to the late 460s. So, where the Roman Empire offered Geiseric both a functioning model of entwined religious and political loyalties, Homoean Christianity offered an alternative brand of the religion with which to recast the model for his own purposes: he could embrace a version of Rome's religion and, at the same time, define himself against official imperial orthodoxy.[38]

As far as we can tell, Geiseric's policy was reasonably successful. As in the other successor kingdoms such as Ostrogothic Italy or Visigothic Spain, there may well have been some Nicene believers among his Vandal and Alan followers, but the group as a whole broadly held to the alternative Homoean brand of Christianity, as officially espoused by its ruling dynasty, throughout its history. Geiseric's policies likewise eventually bred a self-confident Homoean Church establishment, which from the late 450s began to push its own agendas, the first of which was that all those serving in the households of the king and other members of the royal family should become Homoean.[39]

While the obvious potential utility of Homoean Christianity for generating unity among Geiseric's warriors is undeniable, it is important not to become reductive about the king's motives: to oversimplify both the complexities of his world-view and the context in which he was operating. Born when the Hasding Vandals still occupied their old territories in the Middle Danube, he was a boy of six when they crossed the Rhine and not yet a teenager when they took their share of Spain in 412. As a young man of about twenty he had fought in the great victory over the Romans in 421, and later used his son Huneric to cement the crucial Visigothic alliance that had made the victory possible. Conviction may therefore have played as substantial a role in his developing religious policies as it had done for Constantine back in the early fourth century, especially if he did – as reported – convert from Nicene to Homoean Christianity. At the very least, the Vandals' astonishing survival act, and the extraordinary success of his own political career, must have fuelled an overpowering sense of having been chosen by God. By 439, against all the odds, the surviving members of the Vandal–Alan coalition had covered vast distances from Central Europe, come through brutal conflicts with Roman armies (in which many of their peers had been killed), and crossed a large body of water to take possession of Carthage and its famously rich hinterland, in a total journey spanning several decades. North Africa in general, and Carthage in particular, were always personified as a goddess holding rich ears of wheat: jewels in the western imperial crown.[40]

If you think about the extraordinary story of the Vandals' migration as lived human experience (and not simply as yet another oddity from long ago), the Judaeo-Christian Bible offers one obvious analogue: the Children of Israel fighting their way out of Egypt to take possession of the Promised Land. Alongside more straightforwardly rational calculations of the costs and benefits of Homoean Christianity, there's every reason to suppose that the Vandals' own 2,500-mile (4,000-km) exodus, which culminated in the seizure of the richest provinces of the entire western Empire, led Geiseric and his followers to think of themselves as a new Chosen People, who had fought their way through countless tribulations – above all the losses inflicted upon them by the Roman state between 416 and 418 – to achieve their ultimate, and extraordinary, prosperity. In this context, it was only natural for them to regard their own version of Christianity as superior to that of the Empire, for what could have generated such an outcome if not God's Will?

Perhaps the most significant point that follows from seeing through Victor of Vita's fabrications is that Geiseric's religious policies – unlike those of his son – were much closer to the norm among the emerging fifth-century successor states of the former Roman west. The majority of these new ruling dynasties likewise chose Homoean rather than Nicene Christianity, presumably for a similar range of reasons: the availability of key Christian devotional and liturgical texts in a readily understandable Gothic translation, and, especially, that Homoean Christianity offered an ideology that was distinct from official Roman Orthodoxy, whose spiritual head was the emperor himself. In terms of building or maintaining group identities among newly constructed coalitions in a context of at least periodic conflict with the central Roman state, seizing on this alternative brand of Christianity made perfect sense.

Such a choice necessarily generated conflict with the pro-Roman Nicene Churchmen within the different successor groupings' growing areas of influence. This was most intense in North Africa, because Geiseric's relations with the western Empire were marked by a significantly greater degree of violence than was normal elsewhere. In 439 Geiseric seized the richest lands of the western Empire by force, at a point when, although already weakened, the imperial system hadn't yet fully unravelled. The Empire subsequently made three major attempts to recover these lands by military force. (This attempt at reconquest was, incidentally, also the one policy that actually stood any real chance of reinvigorating western imperial power, by simultaneously eliminating one of the new centrifugal forces unleashed on the Roman west, and restoring an important chunk of its lost tax base.[41]) As a natural result, Geiseric remained long suspicious about the imperial contacts of some of his Nicene Churchmen (especially, but not solely, successive bishops of Carthage), and sensitive to hostile sermons.

But similar tensions can be seen in the Visigothic and Burgundian kingdoms. In the early 470s, when he was expanding the borders of his kingdom from the banks of the Loire to the Straits of Gibraltar, the Visigoth King Euric also exiled several Nicene bishops – including Sidonius Apollinaris, bishop of Clermont Ferrand – who had resisted his annexation of their cities, and refused to allow new ordinations when some of these sees fell vacant. Both Euric and his son and successor, Alaric II, remained sensitive about the metropolitan archbishoprics of two key frontier cities: Arles, in what is now Provence and, much further north, the city of Tours in the Loire valley. In both cases, evolving fifth-century political geography departed from the map of ecclesiastical authority inherited from Rome, for both were metropolitan sees with subordinate suffragan bishops who now found themselves divided between different kingdoms (of the Burgundians and Franks respectively).[42]

Most of the time, however (and this, Victor of Vita's protestations to the contrary notwithstanding, was clearly also true of the Vandal kingdom), Nicene Churchmen enjoyed reasonable working relationships with their Homoean rulers – though they did, of course, lose the legal support of the imperial state, once their territories had passed out of imperial control. When the Visigothic king Alaric II reissued a version of an existing imperial law code to reassure his Roman subjects that the established order was (generally) going to be maintained – the Breviary of Alaric, promulgated on 2 February 506 and largely based on the Theodosian Code of 438 – he omitted all the Theodosian legislation against heretics that had effectively destroyed the coherence of the original Roman Homoean Church of the 380s and 390s.[43] But since the religious preferences of the successor-state kings were primarily directed towards maintaining unity among the militarized followings that had put them in power, rather than the totality of their newly acquired Roman subjects, this usually left plenty of room for co-operation. As in Geiseric's North Africa, where the Nicene Church of two-thirds of the kingdom functioned essentially without hindrance, similar patterns held good across most of the former Roman west.

A notable case in point was the episcopal career of Caesarius of Arles (502–42). The first decade of the sixth century was one of great upheaval in southern Gaul. Frankish power threatened to eclipse Visigothic dominion, before Theoderic the Ostrogoth restored stability by adding much of Provence and Aquitaine, together with the bulk of Spain, to his Italian kingdom. At the time, Arles was a frontier city between the Gothic kingdoms and their northern Frankish neighbour, which was looking to expand towards the Mediterranean. Caesarius' early career saw him being hauled up to answer separate accusations of treason (by collusion with the Franks) before both the Visigoth Alaric II and the great Theoderic himself. Acquitted in both instances, Caesarius proved such a hit with the Homoean Ostrogothic king (who, according to the saint's *Life*, was immediately struck by the bishop's holiness) that he obtained Theoderic's direct personal support for all his subsequent activities. In the early 520s Ostrogothic expansion northwards brought about the effective reunification of all the dioceses of Caesarius' metropolitan province within one kingdom for the first time since the end of the western Empire (previously they had been under Burgundian control) – allowing the archbishop to hold the series of reforming synods for which he is chiefly famous with his full complement of episcopal subordinates present, and to whose broader significance we will return in Chapter 7. Relations between this Nicene bishop and his Homoean king, despite initial suspicions, could in fact hardly have been closer.

The *Life of Caesarius* even echoes the bishop's rationale for co-operating so closely across this religious divide. In Matthew's Gospel (Matthew 22:15–22), some followers of the Pharisees attempt to trap Jesus by asking him whether it was right or not to pay tribute to the Romans. He asked them in turn whose face was on the coinage. When it turned out to be the emperor's, Jesus responded: 'Render therefore unto Caesar the things which are Caesar's; and unto God the things that are God's.' The opposition retreated in confusion. The *Life* reports that Caesarius drew on this text to authorize the establishment of good working relationships with the Homoean ruling dynasties who had replaced Nicene Roman emperors across large parts of the Roman west in the fifth century.[44]

That these relations were generally amicable has led modern scholars to treat the Homoean allegiance of most of the first-generation successor-state dynasts as a minor sideshow in the development of Christian history: a small epilogue to an old doctrinal battle won once and for all in the fourth century. That is much too hasty a conclusion.

HUNERIC AND THE BAPTISM OF CLOVIS

Properly understood, then, Geiseric's religious policies open an important window into how and why Homoean Christianity took hold among so many of the fifth-century intruders into Roman imperial territory. It offered kings a powerful, unifying ideology with which to bring together their newly formed, often culturally disparate followings, and it possessed the added advantage of being in direct competition with that brand of Christianity adopted by the Roman emperors against whom these kings were often struggling to establish their realms (a process that recurs so often through human history that there is even a specific term for it: schismogenesis). But these observations do not explain the much more aggressive religious policies of Geiseric's son and immediate successor. Huneric attempted to impose Homoean Christianity by force, not only on his immediate military followers but on the entire Roman population of his nascent kingdom. What impelled him to such a dramatic departure from his father's approach and the broader norms of Homoean–Nicene co-operation that characterize the wider religious history of the former Roman west?

In the eyes of most scholars, Huneric's persecution of Nicene Christianity was a desperate measure that stood no chance of success. Roman North Africa, after all, was good Catholic country. It produced St Augustine, one of the most important intellectuals of the entire Latin Christian tradition, and boasted a proud history of resisting persecution in the pre-Constantinian period and beyond: the Donatists, for instance, had fought on there for the best part of a century, after Constantine originally decided in favour of their opponents. Huneric's policy was also quickly dropped by his successor, Gunthamund, who recalled the leader of the North African Nicenes, Bishop Eugenius of Carthage, from exile before the end of 487.[45] Viewed from this perspective, Huneric's actions can easily be absorbed into the standard narratives of post-Roman religious continuity, his Homoean Christianity no more than a marginal, misguided, doomed side branch of the Christian evolutionary tree.

Sharp new light has recently been shed on what actually happened in North Africa between February and November 484, when Huneric's persecution was in full swing. It is the product of much closer examination of a ninth-century manuscript from the library of Laon Cathedral in northern France – *Codex Laudunensis 113*. This codex contains long extracts from Victor of Vita's *History*, together with a second text, one unique to this manuscript: the *Notitia Provinciarum et Civitatum Africae*. This lists the provinces and cities of the North African kingdom, together with the names of the cities' Nicene bishops, early in the reign of Huneric. By the early 480s, parts of two Mauretanian provinces in the west, Tripolitania in the east, and the island of Sardinia had been added to Geiseric's original kingdom. The list was probably compiled as Nicene leaders took stock of the current religious situation in the Vandal kingdom during the months prior to Huneric's council of Carthage in February 484. What gives the *Notitia* such historical importance, however, is the fact that the list was then updated again shortly after, with notes added next to 139 of the 461 names, recording what had become of the bishops in question. Thirteen had been exiled to Corsica (something corroborated by Victor of Vita); another was sent to the mines. By far the most common annotation, next to 90 of the 139 names, is the abbreviation *prbi*. This is helpfully glossed by a summary at the end of the text which divides the Nicene episcopate into two categories: *qui perierunt* ('those who have perished', from which the abbreviation *prbi* derives) and 'those who have endured' (*qui permanserunt*).[46]

What exactly does 'perished' mean? It used to be interpreted as 'dead' in the straightforwardly physical sense of the word – but that doesn't make any sense. Given that the original list was produced in 483, and the annotations added before the end of 487 (when Eugenius of Carthage, listed here as exiled, was recalled), the idea that about 20 per cent of North Africa's Nicene bishops had died in the intervening four years is implausible – even taking into account Huneric's persecutions. In many Christian contexts, moreover, the verb *pereo* – 'I perish' – also tends to carry the force of spiritual rather than physical death. The updates to the *Notitia*, then, indicate something else. They are telling us that, during Huneric's persecution of 484, ninety Nicene bishops had swapped sides to Huneric's preferred Homoean brand of Christianity, and – in the view of the update's author, a Nicene – had hence 'died' to the faith. This is both an inescapable conclusion, and an extraordinary one. Huneric's persecution only lasted a few months: from February 484 to the king's death the following November. But in that brief period fully 20 per cent of the Nicene episcopate of North Africa changed doctrinal allegiance.[47]

What this text conjures up, in other words, is a picture of religious turmoil in the North African Nicene Church, with a large-scale swapping of allegiance at its highest echelons. It's a picture that doesn't remotely tally with traditional, triumphalist visions of Orthodox Christian religious history, in which the Homoean alternative never really threatened anybody but was merely an absurdly simplified view of the Trinity that only suited a bunch of barbarians until they learned to know better. Throughout this chapter we've been exploring some of the many problems inherent in such views, and the extraordinary success of Huneric's persecution brings these problems fully into focus. The king's religious policy was brutal and divisive, certainly, but not remotely hopeless if one-fifth of the Nicene Catholic bishops of his kingdom were willing to shift their allegiance to Homoean Christianity in just a few months. While Nicene Christianity had finally emerged as the preferred definition of official imperial orthodoxy, it had done so only about a century before Huneric's council, and, moreover, it was pushed through by force where necessary; this in an empire where the mass of the population was not yet even Christian. Against this backdrop, it is hardly surprising to find that Nicene religious allegiances were not yet so firm as they would later become, and especially so in an era where the western half of the Roman confessional imperial state that supported Nicaea had been so peremptorily dismantled – at spearpoint – by representatives of the non-Nicene opposition. In a world where political structures were commonly held to be directly sustained (and overthrown: delete as appropriate) by the Will of God, then the political replacement of Nicene emperors by Homoean kings could very reasonably be taken to suggest that the councils of Seleucia and Rimini in fact offered a more correct definition of the relationship between Father and Son than had Nicaea.

Church leaders swapping sides also makes much better sense of the impassioned appeal for Nicene unity with which Victor of Vita closed his account of the persecution.[48] If even its bishops were busy going over to the opposition, sounding such a rallying cry to an audience of Nicene North African Christians was both urgently necessary in its own specific context, and warns us more generally not to take the post-Roman victory of Nicene Christianity so much for granted. Huneric's persecution was successful enough to demonstrate that there was still serious potential in the later fifth century for Homoean Christianity to reassert the status it had enjoyed in previous decades as official Christian orthodoxy. The point is only reinforced by taking a closer look at the precise circumstances surrounding the baptism of the Frankish Clovis half a generation or so later.

Traditional accounts of Clovis's conversion and subsequent baptism – so often illustrated because it was taken to symbolize an indissoluble link between the French monarchy and Catholic orthodoxy (Plate 14) – derive from the *Histories* of Bishop Gregory of Tours. This wonderful ten-book work was composed in stages between the 570s and Gregory's death in office on 17 November 594. As the bishop portrays it, Clovis was baptized into the Nicene faith before winning any of the great victories that established his kingdom, over the Germanic Alemanni in the mid-490s, the Burgundians around 500 and, above all, over the Visigoths at the battle of Vouillé near Poitiers in 507. After those victories, Clovis – again according to Gregory – then eliminated a series of Frankish rivals to cement his control of the new entity he had created. Gregory understood all these victories to be God's reward for the king's religious wisdom, making his career into a kind of Nicene crusade against all those dreadful Homoeans (labelled 'Arians') who were, in Gregory's view, polluting the ex-Roman west.[49] But Gregory was writing three generations after the baptism, by which point it had already passed into myth; in particular, his chronology for Clovis's reign is completely askew. On closer inspection, Gregory has slotted Clovis's campaigns into his narrative at neat five-year intervals, whereas, in reality, these campaigns were probably interspersed with, not followed by, the king's elimination of multiple rival Frankish warband leaders – all of which Gregory places after the battle of Vouillé. Of much greater importance for the religious history of the post-Roman west, however, is that Gregory's account also fundamentally misdates and obscures the real circumstances of Clovis's baptism into Nicene Christianity, hiding how close the former Roman west came to an entirely non-Nicene, Homoean Christian future.

The baptism is also mentioned in one, much more contemporary source: a letter of Avitus of Vienne, the leading Nicene bishop (*c*. 490–518) of the neighbouring Burgundian kingdom, which was at this point under Frankish hegemony. Two key points emerge from Avitus' letter, which was written in response to an invitation to attend the baptism. First, the date: Avitus' letter shows that Clovis was not baptized before his great victories, but after them, probably on Christmas Day 507. Then comes the really explosive part. According to Avitus, the king didn't just jump from Frankish paganism into Nicene Christianity. Rather, he had been vacillating between which version of Christianity to choose: the faith of Nicaea or its Homoean rival. Or, as Avitus puts it, with just a touch of Nicene bias:

> The chasers after various schisms, by their opinions, different in nature, many in number, but all empty of truth, tried to conceal, under the cover of the name 'Christian', the lies that have been uncovered by the keen intelligence of Your Subtlety . . . A ray of truth has shone through. Divine foresight has found a certain judge for our age. In making a choice for yourself, you judge on behalf of everyone. Your faith is our victory.[50]

In other words, Clovis had been considering different – or, for Avitus, 'schismatic' options before finally settling on the doctrine of Nicaea. That an alternative, Homoean choice on Clovis's part was a real possibility is confirmed by the fact that two of his sisters had previously been baptized at some point into Ulfilas's faith. One, Lantechildis, had perhaps been baptized a Homoean within Gaul itself, for she is recorded as being rebaptized into the faith of Nicaea alongside Clovis himself. Audefleda, Clovis's other Homoean sister, had married Theoderic, the Homoean Ostrogothic king of Italy, as part of an alliance Clovis had forged, probably in the 490s, with Theoderic; Audefleda (and perhaps also Lantechildis) may have accepted Homoean Christianity at that point. Around the year 500 Theoderic was the dominant figure in the western Mediterranean; Clovis still a secondary one. This marriage, and the diplomatic alliance it brought, came at a relatively early stage in the establishment of the Frank's power, providing a convincing context in which the king too might have given, as Avitus suggests, serious thought to converting to Homoean Christianity himself.

The king's great victories of the mid-500s, and his eventual acceptance of Nicene Christianity, moreover, were linked with an alternative and competing diplomatic alliance he subsequently forged with the eastern Roman Empire. His victory over the Visigoths at Vouillé in 507 was the culmination of a series of aggressive moves by which Clovis explicitly separated himself from his earlier alliance with the Ostrogoths, and directly challenged Theoderic's hegemony over the former Roman west in the middle of the first decade of the sixth century. In doing so, Clovis had backing from Constantinople, which was highly suspicious of Theoderic's growing power. In 507, an east Roman raiding fleet off Italy's Adriatic coast kept Theoderic's army busy: too busy, indeed, to come to the help of the Visigoth King Alaric in his impending showdown with Clovis. The new Frankish king of Gaul's opting for the Christianity of the council of Nicaea over its rival councils of Seleucia and Rimini, therefore, must be understood in a broader diplomatic context: Clovis's decision to seek east Roman assistance as he challenged Theoderic in the west.[51]

All of which opens up a tantalizing alternative history. Had Clovis not chosen the faith of Nicaea, as – like his sisters – he so clearly might have done, every ruling line of the former Roman west (south of the Channel: at this point the Anglo-Saxon kings remained resolutely pagan) would then have owed allegiance to Homoean Christianity. The potential of this situation to have generated a completely different historical outcome, one which could easily have seen Homoean Christianity replace its Nicene rival as the dominant religious strand across the post-Roman west, has never been recognized. However, when the developing situation in the west is reconsidered in the light of the religious consequences of the second phase of the imperial political crisis, which led to the dismantling of the eastern half of the Roman system in the seventh century, it quickly becomes apparent that, around the year 500, the long-term western dominance of Nicene Christianity was hanging delicately in the balance.

5
Islam and the Fall of the East

Clovis's baptism into Nicene Christianity in 507 was only a first step towards the eclipse of Homoean Christianity in the post-Roman west. Much of Gaul was now ruled by a Nicene monarch, and when he died four years later, his sons inherited his religious allegiance along with his Frankish kingdom. But the greater part of the western Empire's former territories still remained under the control of dynasts with loyalties to Homoean Christianity: Burgundians in south-eastern Gaul, Visigoths in south-western Gaul and the Iberian peninsula, Vandals in North Africa, and Ostrogoths in Italy and Dalmatia (Map 2).[1] Still more, by the time of Clovis's death, it was Theoderic the Ostrogoth, Homoean king of Italy and much else besides, who had emerged as the dominant political figure of the former Roman west. Though Clovis gained much territory from his defeat of the Visigoths at Vouillé in 507, Theoderic gained still more. Once Constantinople's raiding ships had ceased to occupy his forces' attention, Theoderic moved them from Italy into Gaul in 508/9, defeating Clovis and pushing the Franks decisively back from the Mediterranean coast. Then, in 511, Theoderic added the rest of the still substantial Visigoth kingdom to his expanding portfolio of territories, ruling it directly from the former imperial capital at Ravenna.

In the decades that followed, Clovis's sons and grandsons played their part in swinging the balance of post-Roman royal allegiance back towards the Nicene faith, destroying the independence of the Burgundian kingdom and its residual Homoean loyalties in the early 530s. But it was east Rome – already strongly implicated, as we have seen, in Clovis's rejection of Theoderic's Homoean Christianity – that under Emperor Justinian I (527–65) made the more decisive contribution. In the mid-sixth century, his armies destroyed the Homoean monarchies of both the Vandal and Ostrogothic kingdoms in a series of wars that took east Roman armies into the heart of the west. As sequences of historical events go, Justinian's wars of conquest were dramatic stuff, and their consequences for the longer-term development of western Christianity were much greater than is usually recognized.

'BY THE AUTHORITY OF GOD . . .'

Justinian is famous for many things. His greatest architectural monument, the Cathedral Church of Hagia Sophia (Holy Wisdom), still stands in modern Istanbul. With a nave measuring 260 feet (80 m) long and a dome that soars 180 feet (55 m) towards heaven, it was at the time of construction the largest vaulted interior in the world – and remained so throughout the medieval period. The whole edifice rests on four massive masonry piers, which allowed the exterior walls, arches, even the dome itself to be breathtakingly slender in construction, and is pierced by so many windows compared to the traditional basilica church form that its overall impression was (and is) of a vast interior flooded with light.[2] Justinian's thorough-going reform of Roman law, meanwhile, was not only important in itself, but would play a defining role in the creation of medieval Latin Christendom. (He also married a blonde actress called Theodora, whose supposed sexual voracity is immortalized in the gossipy scholar Procopius' *Secret History*: arguably the most effective piece of character assassination ever written.[3]) The most significant religious intervention of Justinian's regime, however, came with his decisive overturning of the prevailing political balance of power in the former Roman west.

Justinian's invasion of the North African Vandal kingdom in September 533 has often been seen as the first instalment of a strategic plan to reconquer all the lost territories of the Roman west. In reality it was a last-ditch gamble, the product of the emperor's desperate need for some kind of success to restore his shattered political credibility after only six years on the imperial throne. Justinian was an outsider in Constantinople. A soldier with a Balkan peasant background, he had risen, improbably and stratospherically, through the ranks of the imperial army to become emperor. Having elbowed aside – sometimes by assassination – a series of plausible rivals, Justinian implemented a set of sweeping legal reforms, which, he claimed, could only have succeeded 'By the Authority of God'. He also picked a fight with Persia, east Rome's traditional enemy. But when calamitous defeat followed in summer 531, the political vultures started to circle.

The following January saw what looked at first like a fairly routine outbreak of factional violence in Constantinople. The main form of mass entertainment in the imperial capital was chariot racing, supported and partly organized by four factions who each supported their own team: Greens, Blues, Whites and Reds (Blues and Greens being by far the most powerful). These factions were far more than fan clubs, operating as mafia-style organizations that effectively ran their own neighbourhoods within the city. Sometimes, their rivalries got out of hand, triggering riots which the city authorities had to put down by brute force. In January 532, a particular savage outbreak – the so-called Nika riot (named for the slogan – 'Victory' – shouted by the rioters) – was quickly exploited by the emperor's rivals to agitate against Justinian's rule, and then eventually to mount a coup. The emperor responded by sacking some unpopular ministers, but it wasn't enough.

At the end of a week of rioting, one Hypatius, nephew of a previous ruler (Anastasius I, 491–518), was eventually declared emperor by the rioters. Justinian, hunkered down in his palace, held on to his throne, but only by ordering his troops to massacre Hypatius' supporters gathered in the Hippodrome. Altogether, a staggering thirty thousand people died in the city (out of a total population of around half a million), while raging fires started by the rioters destroyed the original church of Hagia Sophia (which Justinian's cathedral was built to replace), the Senate House, many of the palace's outer buildings, and a whole series of ceremonial arcades at the heart of the city. As he sat among the corpses amid the smoking ruins of his imperial capital, Justinian could not have looked less like a divinely appointed ruler in spring 532 had he tried.[4]

Against this backdrop, Justinian's campaign against the Vandals is best understood as that old historical archetype – the last desperate gamble of a bankrupt regime, searching for success abroad to make up for failure at home. In the event, the campaign proved brutally and spectacularly effective – and, for Justinian's reign and historical reputation, utterly transformative. In September 533, Justinian's most trusted senior commander, General Belisarius (who had led the slaughter in the Hippodrome), landed about fifteen thousand men on the east coast of Tunisia. On the battlefield, Belisarius found that a recent reorganization of the east Roman army – which put greater emphasis on the integrated use of heavy and light arrow-firing cavalry alongside its traditional infantry mainstay – gave it a massive and decisive advantage over the kinds of armies deployed by the western successor states, including the Vandals. Two major battlefield defeats followed for the successor state (in September and December 533), and six months after Belisarius' landing the last Vandal monarch, Gelimer, surrendered. The Vandal kingdom of North Africa had ceased to exist.

Electrified by the speed and scale of this first victory, Justinian looked for other targets. Next in line was Ostrogothic Italy. Crossing the Mediterranean in 535, Belisarius' army seized Sicily, then, a year later, mounted a full-scale invasion of the Italian mainland. Once again, the general's forces (once the cavalry arrived in Italy in late 537) employed their battlefield advantage to the full, apparently achieving another astonishing success in the summer of 540 when the Ostrogothic king Wittigis and his capital city, the almost impregnable Ravenna, surrendered. This time, however, success was more apparent than real, and it took another decade and a half of hard fighting to wear down Ostrogothic resistance in Italy. But western expansion had by this point become a defining policy of Justinian's regime, and, as the fighting continued, the emperor took the opportunity presented by internal discord in the Visigothic kingdom (now confined largely to the Iberian peninsula) to send a much smaller, third military expedition there in the early 550s. This force quickly, and without much resistance, brought several southern coastal cities, including Cartagena, Malaga, Sagunto and Assidonia and their agricultural hinterlands, under east Roman control.

The invasions of North Africa and Italy looked initially like brilliant victories, but both generated lengthy, costly insurgencies that took the best part of fifteen years to subdue. Worse, the Persians took advantage of the diversion of so many resources to the west to launch a series of brutally effective raids on Rome's eastern front. These saw, among other disasters, the sack and capture of Antioch, the second city of the Empire, in the summer of 540. Many historians have wondered, therefore, whether the western conquests undermined the Empire's overall strategic position in the longer term, even if their immediate success allowed the emperor to go to his grave as the much-celebrated, self-styled 'Conqueror of Many Nations'.[5] What matters to us here, however, are the largely unintended religious consequences of Justinian's western adventures.

At the start of the sixth century, the ruling dynasties of four of the five major western successor states owed their allegiance to Homoean Christianity. Only the Nicene Franks stood apart from the pattern. Justinian's expansionary campaigns directly destroyed two of these Homoean dynastic states – those of the Vandals in North Africa and Ostrogothic Italy – and the Homoean Church establishments they supported, with profound consequences for the history of Christianity in the post-Roman west.

In North Africa, the emperor was initially cautious. His first post-victory edict prohibited any confiscations of Homoean Church property and ordered that Homoean priests could be rebaptized into the Nicene clergy, where they could retain their existing roles. North African Nicenes were not happy. Early in 535, under the presidency of Bishop Reparatus of Carthage, a council – convened symbolically in the Basilica Fausti, where Huneric had launched his persecution against the Nicenes – demanded the immediate return of all confiscated Nicene properties, refused to absorb Homoean clergy into their ranks, and demanded a total ban on all Homoean Church services. The following summer, Justinian gave in to these demands and, in the months that followed, Belisarius enacted a policy of effective genocide, quickly shipping out any captured Vandal and Alan warriors to the east, where they were conscripted into forces facing up to the Persian menace, and confiscating the entirety of the landed properties that Geiseric had originally granted his followers in Proconsularis. This effectively destroyed the local communities which the Homoean Church had served – and, in consequence, the Homoean Church of North Africa itself quickly and completely dissolved. It is never mentioned again in any surviving sources.[6]

In Italy, probably because the Goths were more numerous and east Roman forces never managed so total a victory, Justinian's peace offers always allowed surrendering Goths to return home (with the exception of a few particularly troublesome warrior groups, who, like the Vandal contingents, were shipped off to serve on Constantinople's eastern front against Persia). Most Gothic communities in Italy were clustered in the north-east and north-west of the Italian peninsula, and along the Via Flaminia between Rome and Ravenna. Since some local Gothic communities survived in a way that their Vandal counterparts did not, so, in all likelihood, did at least elements of the Homoean Church establishment that served their needs. One remarkable papyrus of 551 lists the staff, eleven years after its capture, of the Homoean church of St Anastasia in Ravenna (the building still stands): two priests, two deacons, a financial officer, a seven-man writing office (whose products probably included the beautiful *Codex Argenteus* of Ulfilas's Gothic Bible: p. 173), and five porters. Several members of staff signed their names in Gothic. St Anastasia's was a cathedral church, so, before the city's capture in 540, there would have been a Homoean Gothic bishop as well. There was no sign of him in 551.[7]

What happened to the Homoean Church of Italy in the longer term, after the final defeat of the Goths in the mid-550s, is not clear. Justinian's formal legal settlement for his newly conquered Italian territories – the Pragmatic Sanction of 13 August 554 – says nothing explicit about his intentions for the Church, the implications for which are ambiguous. On the one hand, the Pragmatic Sanction declared valid all acts of the Gothic rulers of Italy down to Theodahad (an ineffectual king, who was murdered by his successor Wittigis at the start of the war proper in 536). This potentially included royal gifts of land and buildings to the Homoean Church. But the decree also stated that all existing east Roman law would now come into force – and this included legislation of Theodosius I which, way back in the 390s, had mandated the closure of the east Roman Homoean Church by confiscating its churches and properties. What actually happened on the ground in the remaining Gothic communities of north-eastern and north-western Italy is not explicitly documented in any surviving source material.

In the late 560s and early 570s, however, much of northern Italy, where many Goths were settled, quickly fell under the control of a new invader: the Germanic-speaking Lombards. Intrusive groups of Lombards had established a powerful realm in the Middle Danube region in the last decades of the fifth century as Attila's Hunnic Empire collapsed. They then moved on to Italy en masse when a new power – the Avars – emerged from the Great Eurasian Steppe to establish their own nomadic Empire in central and eastern Europe in the middle of the sixth century, a decision given further impetus by Constantinople's failure to establish secure control of Italy north of the Po. Although the evidence for their broader religious allegiances is ambiguous, the Lombards' leadership, at least, again favoured Homoean Christianity, so there may have been a considerable element of religious continuity at the local level in northern Italy, with Gothic communities and their Homoean clergy being absorbed into the Lombard confederation. But in areas further south, which remained under east Roman rule, there is no further mention anywhere of an organized Homoean Church after the mid-550s. Significantly, the extensive letter collection of Pope Gregory I (590–604) documented many features of the contemporary religious situation of east Roman Italy but made no mention of any continuing Homoean presence. Whether the Homoean Church's disappearance south of the Po was the result of deliberate dismantling, as happened in North Africa, or the inevitable consequence of all the losses the Goths had suffered in twenty years of warfare is uncertain. What is clear is that, by the start of the seventh century, Homoean Christianity had vanished as a religious force across much of post-Roman Italy.[8]

Justinian's wars were also indirectly responsible for the final eclipse of a third western Homoean Church community: that of the Burgundian kingdom. This had grown up in the mid- to late fifth century, its domains spanning what is now the Rhône valley and south-western Switzerland. Burgundy had always been a medium-rank power. It lost out to the Visigoths in the competition for some of the best bits of southern Gaul in the third quarter of the fifth century, and then subsequently had to play its more powerful neighbours – the Frankish and Ostrogothic kingdoms – off against one another to preserve its independence. In 534, however, confronted with a likely east Roman invasion of Italy, the Ostrogoth King Wittigis was forced to abandon Gothic interests in south-eastern Gaul. The Ostrogoths ceded their residual claims over the Burgundian kingdom to the Franks, who promptly invaded Burgundy and eliminated its king, Godomar. In 536, moreover, with Belisarius now ashore in southern Italy, Wittigis negotiated the peaceful transfer to the Franks of his kingdom's last remaining territories around Arles, in order that its established Gothic garrisons could return to Italy to fight. As a result, Burgundy fell decisively under Frankish control, following which Homoean Christianity quickly disappeared there, too.[9]

After Justinian's final defeat of the Ostrogoths in the early 550s, therefore, only one Homoean successor state remained: the Visigothic kingdom. Now largely confined to the Iberian peninsula, it too was in crisis. Justinian's last western military adventure had annexed a portion of its Mediterranean coastline, in 551, the ease with which he did so being symptomatic of some deeper problems. The kingdom had never fully recovered its internal stability following the rise of Frankish power under Clovis in the late fifth century. Many of its warriors relocated from Aquitaine to Spain in the 490s, the precursor to massive defeat at the hands of Clovis in 507. At which point many of its former territories in central Gaul were lost to the Franks, while the rest of the kingdom, as we've seen, quickly fell under Ostrogothic rule for the best part of two decades. Though the kingdom reasserted its independence in 526, its internal operations were weakened by dynastic discontinuity and continued Frankish military pressure in the following decades, leading some regions to assert local independence. This fragmentation was arrested by King Liuvigild (568–86), who crushed these local independence movements in a process of reunification.[10]

To mark the end of this reunification process, in 580 Liuvigild called a council of the Visigothic Homoean Church at Toledo. Here, the council modified its traditional Christian doctrines by acknowledging the full and equal Divinity of the Son with the Father. (The Holy Spirit continued to be allocated a lesser position, aligning the kingdom with a view of Trinitarian relationships that had been aired previously under the label of 'Macedonianism', after Macedonius, a mid-fourth-century bishop of Constantinople.) The council also ruled that it was no longer necessary to rebaptize Nicenes who wanted to swap allegiance. The underlying purpose of both these changes was clearly to bolster the kingdom's restored political cohesion with a matching dose of religious unification. Liuvigild presumably hoped that his compromise doctrinal position, combined with the concession on baptism, would make it easier for his Nicene subjects to come into line.[11]

What's striking here is that the king and his advisors had clearly decided that traditional Homoean doctrines would no longer serve. We have no direct access to their thinking but, as we have seen with Constantine and beyond, this was a world where political success – usually measured in terms of military victory – was held to come directly from God, giving massive ideological legitimacy as well as practical power to the victor in competitive political processes. By Liuvigild's time, the self-confidence of Homoean Christianity – which, from its adoption at the councils of Rimini and Seleucia in 359 under Constantius II, had always claimed to be universal Christian orthodoxy, temporarily displaced by the mistaken *homoousios* championed by the councils of Nicaea and Constantinople II – had been eroded. Thanks to the military triumphs of the Franks and, above all, of Justinian, most of the post-Roman west was now controlled by rulers whose religious allegiance lay with Nicaea; the only exceptions were the still-pagan Anglo-Saxons in Britain and Liuvigild's now resurgent Visigothic kingdom. Even the small kingdom of the Suevi in north-western Iberia had converted to Nicaea just before Liuvigild conquered it. God's Will always showed itself most clearly on the battlefield, as Christian monarchs from Constantine onwards had proclaimed loudly and clearly – and, from the perspective of the late sixth century, it had clearly not backed the Homoeans.

Faced with a broader context that can only have emboldened the Nicene Church establishment within his own kingdom, Liuvigild responded with a partial change in religious policy. His attempted compromise, though, proved unsuccessful. While one prominent Nicene bishop, Vincent of Zaragoza, pledged allegiance to Liuvigild's reformed Homoean Church, the sources preserve no hints of any kind of mass conversion to the 'Macedonian' option proposed by Liuvigild's council: certainly nothing on the scale of the Nicene episcopal defection to Huneric's position in the Vandal kingdom of the mid-480s. Worse, one of Liuvigild's own sons, Hermenigild, rebelled against him, declaring for Nicaea. Though the rebellion was eventually defeated and Hermenigild executed in April 586, it endured for five long years, suggesting considerable opposition to the king's religious policies. When Liuvigild himself died a few days after his rebellious elder son, it was left to his second son and heir, Reccared (586–601), to draw the logical conclusion. In 587, only a year after gaining the crown, Reccared declared his personal change of allegiance to Nicaea. Two years later, he called the third council of Toledo, a meeting of Homoean and Nicene clergy and the leading men of his kingdom. Assembled in May 589, the council's Acts officially confirmed the conversion of the Visigoths and their entire kingdom to the Nicene faith. Eight Homoean bishops and their subordinates, five distinguished Gothic nobles and all the leading men of the Goths (*omnes seniores Gothorum*) signed up to the Nicene Creed. Following Liuvigild's line in 580, rebaptism was again declared anathema, removing any ritual barriers to an easy transition.[12]

Toledo III marks the final extinction of the Homoean challenge to Nicene orthodoxy. Religious historians, ancient and modern, have tended to dismiss it as an odd religious aberration, the preserve of brief-lived, largely Germanic dynasties at the head of the first-generation successor states to what had been the western Roman Empire. From everything we have seen, it was far more than that. Not only was it official Roman imperial Christian orthodoxy for the best part of a generation in the east – longer in the west – after the councils of Rimini and Seleucia in 359, but it then enjoyed an afterlife of two hundred years before that fateful meeting at Toledo in 589, remaining powerful enough to prompt a fifth of the Nicene bishops of North Africa to shift their allegiance to it in Huneric's persecution during the spring and summer of 484. Even a century later, it kept a strong hold on some of its adherents. Toledo III was followed by no fewer than four separate revolts against Reccared, which – even if they surely had political aims besides – attempted to rally support under the Homoean flag.[13] Without Constantinople's continued interest in western affairs in the first half of the sixth century – Emperor Anastasius' alliance with Clovis, prompting the Frankish king to choose Nicaea over Seleucia and Rimini, and the eastern Empire over Ostrogothic Italy; then, above all, Justinian's unpredictable and extraordinary episodes of western expansion – there is no reason to assume the new ruling dynasties of the Gothic, Burgundian and Vandal successor states would have voluntarily surrendered their Homoean religious allegiance. And just how existential a threat such a situation would have posed to Nicene Christianity is vividly illustrated by the next religious upheaval – one both dramatic and profound – to convulse the Mediterranean world in the aftermath of Justinian's extraordinary conquests in North Africa, Italy and southern Spain.

FIVE PILLARS OF WISDOM

In the mid-seventh century, the political and cultural orientation of the Mediterranean's eastern and southern shores, and the adjacent territories in the Near East, were changed forever. For over seven hundred years, two great powers had dominated the rainfall-defined, revenue-producing centres of the eastern Mediterranean and its hinterland. The Roman Empire controlled Egypt, Asia Minor and the western reaches of the Fertile Crescent in ancient Palestine. Its great Persian rival controlled Mesopotamian Iraq and the Iranian Plateau further east, while the two powers divided between them (in different ways at different moments) Syria, Armenia and Transcaucasia. From the third century AD onwards, a new Persian dynasty, the Sasanian, tightened its control of its Iraqi and Iranian heartlands, and extended its power further up the Tigris and Euphrates (causing, among other Roman setbacks, the abandonment of Dura-Europos and its ancient church, p. 22). But from around AD 300 onwards, despite many outbreaks of conflict, major boundary changes were few and far between. Even when the western Roman Empire fell, the status quo in the east remained.[14]

All this was overturned in the seventh century by an explosion of Arab power, united and driven forward by the rise of Islam. To the east, it utterly crushed the Persian Empire. Muslim victory at the battle of al-Qadisiyyah in 636 brought the whole of Iraq under Arab domination, while the battle of Nahavand, east of the Zagros Mountains six years later, sounded the death knell for Sasanian control of Iran. The last Sasanian king of kings, Yazdegerd III, was assassinated in 651, after which it simply remained to the advancing Muslim forces to mop up resistance. Further west, Constantinople's losses were almost as catastrophic. A first great Arab victory came at the battle of the River Yarmouk in 636, south-east of the Sea of Galilee, after which the great cities of the Roman Near East toppled like dominoes over the next five years. Armenia and Egypt followed in the 640s and 650s, and over the following half century Arab armies pushed steadily westwards, conquering Libya and Justinian's new North African prefecture, whose capital at Carthage fell in 697. By this date, most of the great revenue-producing centres of the ancient Near East had fallen under Muslim control. There was more to come. In the early eighth century, campaigns on the Iberian side of the Straits of Gibraltar brought all the Visigothic kingdom, apart from a small Christian enclave around Pamplona in the north-west, under Muslim control. For all Justinian's pretensions, the real conqueror of many nations in the middle of the first millennium was undoubtedly Muhammad – or, rather, the religious movement he had initiated.[15]

The detailed historical processes behind this extraordinary political revolution remain mysterious and controversial in equal measure, largely because of the nature of the early Islamic historical tradition. No narratives of the life of the Prophet survive that were composed before the ninth century. By this time, Islam had been through two major revolutions of its own: a first civil war or *fitna* (656–61), which generated the original divide between the Sunni and Shia branches of Islam and the rise of the Umayyad Caliphate centred on Damascus in Syria; and the Abbasid revolution, which overthrew Umayyad rule in the mid-eighth century, shifting the Caliphate's capital to Baghdad in Iraq. The first surviving lives of Muhammad thus naturally give an account of the Prophet that legitimized Islam as it was evolving under Abbasid control in the aftermath of these revolutions. What relationship these ninth-century narratives bear to the realities of the early seventh century is uncertain – precisely in the same way that the importance of later understandings of Jesus' nature and significance colour the text of the surviving Gospels, making it impossible to recover 'the historical Jesus' from their accounts (p. 29). What is clear is that clans which had emerged as important by the ninth century wanted to demonstrate the closeness of their seventh-century ancestors to the Prophet himself, and from as early in his life as possible. Signs of divine support also form a powerful strand within these narratives, with accounts of Muslim forces winning overwhelming victories against unlikely odds.

The broad outline of events that can be gleaned from these much

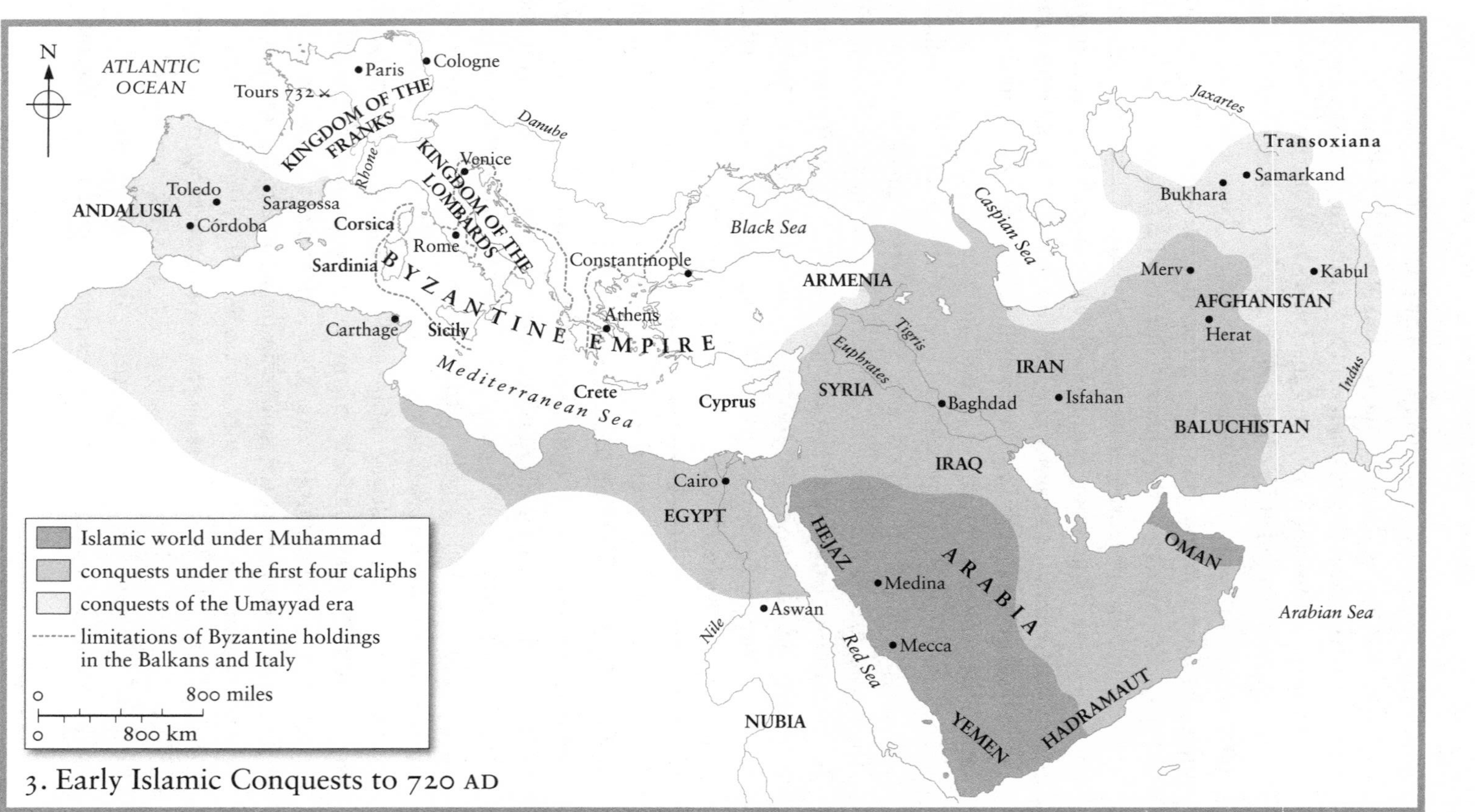

3. Early Islamic Conquests to 720 AD

later accounts, both of the Prophet's life and of the early Muslim conquests, is likely to be accurate enough. A decisive moment came in 622 with the *hejira*, when Muhammad moved from Mecca to Medina to establish the first Islamic political community. This is the event from which the Islamic era is dated, and the system was already in use by 651. In their details, though, these earliest surviving accounts vary considerably, often contradicting one another even regarding the details of celebrated episodes. There is also a marked tendency within the developing Islamic historiographical tradition for the amount of detailed information to increase over time, with later ninth- and tenth-century versions containing much more than the first life of the Prophet, written just after the year 800. The likeliest explanation is that a creative process of inventive retelling played a powerful role in what has come down to us. Nor is there much help to be had from non-Islamic sources. Any Sasanian historical tradition of substance was destroyed with the fall of the last shah, while the east Roman court in Constantinople took no pleasure in cataloguing the disastrous defeats that denuded it of many of its east Mediterranean territories. Contemporary seventh-century eastern Christian texts from areas now outside east Roman control – Egypt, Syria, the Caucasus – provide partial exceptions, but yield no contemporary account either of Muhammad's life or of the early Muslim conquests.[16]

The one major exception to the lack of early Islamic source material is the Qur'an itself. Islamic tradition holds that its 114 *surahs*, or chapters, were directly dictated to the Prophet from God via the angel Gabriel, but provides competing reports as to when these oral messages were edited into the standardized written form that eventually prevailed. Nonetheless, this process certainly occurred somewhere in the seventh century, and quite possibly within a few decades of Muhammad's death, making the Qur'an more than a century older than any of the other surviving sources for the life and teaching of the Prophet. And while the *surahs* provide little in the way of connected narrative information (they are analogous in some ways to 'Q', a common supposed collection of Jesus' sayings thought by some to underlie the many similarities between the three so-called synoptic Gospels – Matthew, Mark and Luke – for those more familiar with early Christian materials), they do make clear the basic tone and content of Muhammad's teaching.

For the purposes of this book, what is really striking about the text (apart from the so-called 'satanic verse' – *Surah* 53:19–20, which refers to three presumably native pre-Islamic Arabian deities: *al-Lāt*, *al-'Uzzá*, and *Manāt*) is the extent to which it draws upon and modifies existing Judaeo-Christian tradition. The Qur'an presents Muhammad himself as the seal – the culmination – of all the prophets of the Old and New Testaments, including both John the Baptist and Jesus (who is called the son of Mary, rather than the Son of God). Jerusalem, specifically the rock on Temple Mount where Abraham nearly sacrificed Isaac, was the point from which Muhammad ascended temporarily to Heaven, and provided the first focus for Muslim prayer before devotions were redirected towards Mecca. And these are only a few highlights. Many of the *surahs* refer to Old and New Testament characters, though the stories they tell about them are then modified and welded together into an entirely original religious synthesis.[17]

But if the Qur'an shows that Muhammad's message originated in a Judaeo-Christian religious context, it doesn't tell us much about its initial reception among the Prophet's Arabian audience: which groups adopted it and when; and who had become involved in the movement (and for what reasons) by the time the conquests began, shortly after the Prophet's death on 8 June 632. As a result, any detailed reconstruction of the events will probably never be possible, but two better-documented factors help explain the astonishing success of Muhammad's religious movement.

First, even before Muhammad's lifetime, political revolution was underway in parts at least of the Arab world. Arab groups occupying the desert fringes of the Fertile Crescent (Map 3) were significant protagonists in the southern, desert conflict zone between the Roman and Persian Empires from the third century onwards. Although the challenging conditions made it impossible for conventional armies to operate there, the fringes of the desert offered many opportunities for profitable raiding, and for distracting your imperial rival's attention from the heavily contested Armenian and Syrian fronts to the north. Hence both sides recruited, paid and armed Arab allies to protect their own provinces from desert raiders, and to cause as much trouble as possible for the opposition. Piecing together the available information in contemporary Roman sources for the fourth to the sixth centuries, one central point becomes clear. Thanks at least in part to the wealth and weaponry with which both sides supported them, the political and military networks of their Arab allies increased substantially in size and power over the period. In the fourth and fifth centuries, the Romans maintained a series of separate allied Arab chiefdoms on the fringes of the Palestinian and Syrian deserts. By the sixth century, both Rome and Persia supported single, unified networks, fronted by the Ghassanid and Lakhmid dynasties respectively. The increased power of these groups is clearly visible in the fact that they had their own seats at the negotiating table during Roman-Persian peace talks, and regularly pursued their own agendas independently of their imperial patrons.[18]

Second, a titanic meltdown in Romano-Persian relations in the early seventh century presented their Arab neighbours with a once-in-many-lifetimes opportunity to overturn long-standing patterns of imperial domination. Although the two empires had long been each other's favourite enemy, each generally recognized that total victory over the other was impossible. For the most part, therefore, conflict between the fourth and sixth centuries was limited to the odd siege on the central Mesopotamian front, subverting allegiances of one another's client kings in the Caucasus, and stirring up isolated Arab raids. Any of these offered the opportunity for an immediate propaganda coup – something that would play well with domestic political audiences – without risking too much in the way of expensive, large-scale warfare. In the fifth century, when both empires faced other dangerous enemies from the Central Asian Steppe (Attila's Hunnic Empire for east Rome; the White Huns or Hephthalites for the Persians), even run-of-the-mill squabbling was deliberately minimized. Peace reigned and, for a period, an alternative ideology of mutual support was in vogue between the empires, which, in more peaceable moments, were even referred to as the 'twin stars of the firmament'.[19]

In the decades either side of the year 600, however, the long-standing patterns of limited conflict spun viciously out of control. In part, this was due to the toxic ideological inheritance of Justinian's reign, which saw expansionary warfare return to favour as a means of generating internal political harmony within Constantinople, and also to unprecedented levels of Roman success in the latest round of campaigning. This culminated in 591 when the eastern emperor Maurice gained control of many of the strategic passes through the eastern Taurus Mountains from the compliant Persian king of kings Chosroes II, whom Maurice had helped regain his throne following an internal Persian rebellion.

The scale of this Roman victory, however, only served to throw superpower relations entirely out of balance. Chaos followed. A decade later, in November 602, Maurice was deposed and executed by one of his leading generals, Phocas, who came to Constantinople at the head of a mutinous army. East Roman politics degenerated into a prolonged civil war that finally ended when Heraclius, a general with a powerbase in North Africa, stormed into the imperial capital from the Bosporus in October 610. While all this was unfolding, the same Chosroes II quickly turned to independent operations for his own gain. With the east Roman military-political establishment bitterly divided among itself, the way into Roman territory was clear. By the time Heraclius entered Constantinople, all Armenia had been lost and Persian forces had systematically reduced the Roman fortresses guarding Mesopotamia. In 611, Chosroes' armies struck deep into Roman Syria, and pushed north onto the Anatolian plateau to seize Caesarea. Damascus fell to the Persians, leading to the loss in 614 of all Palestine, including Jerusalem and, along with it, what was – as far as the Romans were concerned – the most precious of holy relics: the True Cross.

The eastern Empire was on the point of collapse. Chosroes refused all peace offers from an increasingly desperate Constantinopolitan political establishment, including an extraordinarily abject embassy in 616 that was willing to recognize Chosroes as 'supreme Emperor' and styled the Romans his 'slaves'. A successful Persian invasion of Egypt was complete by 621, with sea raids simultaneously hitting Cyprus and the Aegean islands. The nadir came in late July 626, with Constantinople itself menaced by the Persians on the south side of the Bosporus, and a huge allied Avar army immediately outside the city walls to the north. By this date, the nomadic Avars, whose initial appearance in central Europe led the Lombards to shift their centre of operations to Italy, had constructed a powerful multi-ethnic Empire, and Chosroes recruited it as a natural ally against Constantinople.

In the end, however, the Persian shah's projected conquest of

Constantinople foundered on a combination of the city's impregnable land fortifications, on which the Avar attacks came to grief, and the Roman navy's control of the Bosporus, which prevented the Persian army on the other side of the straits from making any worthwhile contribution to the assault. Heraclius himself, moreover, was in Armenia, retraining his field forces and negotiating a critical new alliance with the powerful steppe empire of the western Turks. The following year, the alliance bore fruit. In 627, a huge Turkish army stormed through the Caucasus to conquer the Persian client kingdom of Iberia (present-day eastern Georgia), in the process providing Heraclius with forty thousand men for further operations. This combined army marched south into Iraq, defeating a Persian force just outside Nineveh in December, and employing scorched-earth tactics to batter the Sasanian economy. In early 628 Chosroes was deposed in a coup. A sequence of short-lived Persian regimes followed, until Heraclius was able to extract the deal he wanted. The Persians withdrew from all the conquered Roman provinces, most of whose administrative structures they had left untouched, and Heraclius returned in triumph: the True Cross safely back in Roman hands.

But what at first sight looks like a great Roman victory was really a draw caused by mutual exhaustion following a full twenty-five years of enervating warfare. Heraclius handed back Maurice's gains, so boundaries reverted to pre-591 lines, emphasizing that Heraclius' overall position was in fact much less dominant, not least because his Empire was bankrupt. In the depths of the crisis, Heraclius had halved military pay, ended free bread distributions in the capital, and had stripped the capital's churches of precious metals to pay for his Turkish alliance.[20] Nor was Persia's position any stronger. Huge amounts of political and economic capital had been expended in a generation's worth of total war that had ended with the devastation of the Persian Empire's Mesopotamian economic heartland. It was precisely at this moment, with the two battered empires at their weakest point, that Islamic Arab expansion began.

Typically, both Rome and Persia kept a close eye on their Arab clients, and intervened in their internal affairs if political developments took a dangerous turn; in the 580s, Emperor Maurice dismantled the Ghassanid allied network when it showed too much independence.

Chosroes, likewise, had eliminated the then head of the Lakhmid confederation at the outbreak of his war against Phocas. But the fixation of both empires on total mutual war between 603 and 628 meant they had neither time nor resources to devote to the Arabian peninsula. Muhammad's movement started in the Hejaz region, and gathered political and military momentum in 621 with the move from Mecca to Medina (Map 3). This area lay outside the frontier regions dominated by the Ghassanid and Lakhmid networks, but, although the unreliability of the details reported in Islamic historical sources makes it impossible to know exactly which Arab groups were brought into his expanding alliance system and when, Muhammad quickly extended his control right across the Arabian peninsula in the 620s, free from the prospect of any pre-emptive imperial intervention. Subsequently, when the newly united forces of Arabian Islam went onto the offensive outside the peninsula, they were fighting two bankrupt empires.[21] Muhammad's Islamic movement exploded into and exploited this power vacuum to devastating effect.

Chosroes' Persian Empire was utterly extirpated by the middle of the seventh century, and, although Constantinople survived as the capital of an independent state, its power and reach were drastically reduced. In the hundred years following Heraclius' pyrrhic victory over the Persians, the rise of Islam saw east Rome diminish in nature from the dominant imperial power of the entire Mediterranean to a medium-sized regional force at its eastern end. By 640, the key Roman economic heartlands of Egypt, Syria and Palestine had all fallen to Arab conquest, while western Asia Minor, the other region of maximum agricultural productivity for the sixth-century east Roman Empire, had been turned into a battleground – something well evidenced in the archaeological remains of two of its great, ancient metropolises, Sardis and Ephesus. Faced with subsequent, periodic Arab raiding, neither of these cities recovered from Persian sack. Sardis was reduced to a fort with a nearby village. Ephesus – one of the greatest cities of the ancient world – became a fortress with a small fortified civilian settlement around what had been the extramural Church of St John: most of the ancient city site was simply abandoned. The archaeological picture from the other old Roman cities of western Asia Minor is similar. Even Constantinople didn't escape the demographic and economic cull. Its population declined drastically in the seventh century, probably by as much as 90 per cent from a fifth-century maximum of half a million people.[22]

Using comparative figures from the sixteenth-century Ottoman Empire, which had much the same geographical shape as Justinian's eastern Roman Empire and a similar predominantly agrarian economy, we can calculate that Islamic conquest, combined with evident economic collapse in western Asia Minor, must have cost the seventh-century rulers of Constantinople somewhere between two-thirds and three-quarters of their previous tax revenues. This overwhelming structural diminution forced Heraclius and his successors into wholesale changes just to survive.

The main job of imperial government remained war-making – and the post-Islamic conquest Empire still needed substantial armies, because the Arab threat remained. But only a fraction of the previous revenues were still available. Limited monetary taxes continued, and soldiers received some cash payments, but the basic remuneration of the military increasingly took the form of land grants, with the entire administrative structure of the Empire adapting to a new fiscal-military model. The result – appropriate to the scale of its losses – was a much simpler, 'small state' structure for the sad remnants of Justinian's once great Empire.[23]

Such a crisis of Empire could not but have a powerful religious component. Since the time of Constantine, emperors had claimed to be divinely appointed rulers, mandated by the Almighty God of the Old and New Testaments to bring Christian civilization to the entire globe. So, when two-thirds of that Empire was suddenly swallowed up by the standard-bearers of a new religion, it naturally engendered an intense bout of soul searching. If you believed, as was officially proclaimed, that Divine Providence shaped events on earth, God was clearly unhappy with his east Roman subjects. The Old Testament offered much relevant food for thought, with the Children of Israel facing regular punishment for outbreaks of lack of faith and/or deviant beliefs. Such analogies suggested that some kind of heresy must be the root cause of the Empire's problems. From Heraclius' perspective, the obvious ecclesiastical issue was the continued furore over the council of Chalcedon, and its contested account of how to understand the mix of human and divine in the nature of Christ. Despite a string of different imperial initiatives, particularly under Justinian who devoted a second ecumenical council to the issue (the second council of Constantinople in 553), this dispute had remained unresolved into the late sixth century, and even generated separate local anti-Chalcedonian Churches in certain parts of the eastern Empire (particularly Egypt and Syria).[24] There are signs that a united imperial approach was finally bringing the matter towards a resolution around the year 600, but then the lengthy Persian occupations of Syria and Egypt allowed the strong anti-Chalcedonian congregations of these provinces to operate without threat of persecution, and to broaden, once again, their base of support. Prompted by his patriarch of Constantinople, Sergius, Heraclius' response, after recapturing the lost provinces in the late 620s, was to champion a new compromise position, which banned further discussion of the much-disputed nature of Christ and posited instead that He had one unified will. (The adherents of this position were called Monothelites, from the Greek *mono*, one, and *thelos*, will.)

Unfortunately for Heraclius, the new emphasis on Christ's will failed to staunch the military disasters, which kept on coming, now at the hands of the Islamic Arabs. Moreover, the Monothelite formula, despite an initially promising take-up in the east, stirred up great opposition in the Latin west, particularly in Rome, where a sequence of popes was united in opposition to it. By the 660s, when most of the strongly anti-Chalcedonian congregations – in Syria and Egypt – were firmly in Arab hands anyway, Heraclius' successors rowed back from the Monothelite position. His grandson Constantine IV had it formally condemned at the third council of Constantinople in 680/1. At this point, it looked plausible to argue that the Arab conquests should be understood as God's wrath being visited upon the anti-Chalcedonians – especially because Constantine IV had managed to fend off a four-year-long Arab siege of Constantinople (between 674 and 678), and then extract a favourable peace treaty from the Umayyad Caliphate.[25]

By the end of the century, however, a further ideological response to renewed defeat became necessary. Constantine's successes encouraged his son, Justinian II (685–95, 705–711), to widen his imperial ambitions. Justinian II put the face of Christ on his silver coinage – the first ruler of Constantinople ever to do so – and launched an optimistic attempt to reconquer the lost eastern provinces from the Umayyads. His army was substantially composed of recently subdued allied Slavic soldiers that he had transplanted from the Balkans to Asia Minor. However, when it came to the decisive battle at Sebastopolis (probably Elauissa Sebaste in south-western Turkey) in 692, most of the Slavs swapped sides. Justinian was defeated and deposed, following which seven different imperial regimes rose and fell in twenty-two years (including the brief and vengeful return of Justinian, complete with a gold nose – the original had been cut off by his opponents with the idea that this disfigurement would stop him from reclaiming the throne). But Arab victory inexorably followed Arab victory, Divine indignation with the east Romans also manifesting itself in a major earthquake that caused a huge amount of damage in Constantinople and its surrounding regions, until in 717 a large Arab army stood for a second time outside the walls of the imperial capital.[26]

This was eventually beaten off, after a year-long siege, by a new Roman hero, Emperor Leo III (717–41), who followed up his military victory with new religious policies to win back Divine favour. When a Confessional State suffers relentless defeat, especially at the hands of an alternative religion, a suitable ideological explanation must necessarily be found. Leo found one in the shape of the Empire's Jewish population, who, he decreed in the early 720s, were to undergo forced baptism. This initial attempt to assuage Divine wrath was followed by a series of edicts between 726 and 729, in which the emperor declared long-standing forms of Christian imagery – particularly any representations of Christ – to be in breach of the Second Commandment: 'thou shalt not make unto thyself any graven images.' This initiative, perhaps inspired by the condemnation of figural art championed within the Islamic world, inaugurated two distinct and prolonged periods of east Roman iconoclasm, between 726 and 787, and 815 and 842. While Leo's ideological sea-change caused uproar in some quarters of the imperial Byzantine Church (thus called after Byzantium, the pre-Constantinian name for Constantinople), at first iconoclasm appeared to have the desired effect. Both Leo and his son and successor Constantine V (741–75) saw a sustained diminution in the level of Arab threat. In fact, this had far less to do with changing religious orthodoxy in Constantinople and much more to do with events in the Umayyad Caliphate, whose ambitions of conquest collapsed into the recurring patterns of internal conflict that led eventually to its replacement by Abbasid rule in the mid-eighth century. From a Byzantine perspective, however, it seemed reasonable to conclude that God had shown Himself in favour of a hard line on religious imagery.

Many aspects of the iconoclast dispute remain controversial, not least because – as so often in Christian history – most of the writings of its supporters were condemned and destroyed when the Empire definitively rejected the policy in 842. One central point, however, needs emphasizing. During both periods of iconoclasm, the Empire's religious and political establishment adopted and rejected competing ideological positions on images with remarkably little disruption or protest. The first period was formally ended in 787 by a second council of Nicaea, attended by around three hundred bishops. Many of the same bishops, however, had also been at an earlier council of the robustly iconoclast Emperor Constantine V in 754. This gathering, attended by 338 bishops, had also understood itself as an ecumenical council and equally formally voted in favour of a declaration – in complete contradiction to what was later asserted in 787 – that icons were graven images and should therefore be destroyed. Despite this previous vote, the great majority of the assembled bishops in 787 simply signified their assent to the new and contradictory policy with no further comment. Only ten of the more strongly dissident archbishops were singled out for punitive treatment (they had organized a demonstration which had prevented the holding of a council to end iconoclasm the year before), and even they were reinstated to their old positions after formal recantations. The pattern repeated itself at the opening and closing of the second iconoclasm. Each major change of policy involved sacking the sitting patriarch of Constantinople – the eastern Church's senior cleric – but that was about it. There was little sign of large-scale popular unrest. Certain monks protested against iconoclasm; many icons were, of course, pictures of deceased holy men and women, so that destroying their images could be construed as a challenge to the ascetics' claims to religious authority. But the absence of substantial, sustained popular protest during the periods of iconoclasm suggests that mass popular piety within east Roman

Christianity had not yet developed the strong focus on icon veneration that would later become one of its characteristic features: at this point, religious devotion based around icons was probably still largely restricted to monastic circles. The sequence of moves in and out of iconoclasm look like 'macro-level' religious decisions, ideological positions adopted or rejected for political reasons, which impacted primarily on the ruling elites, both secular and ecclesiastical, of the Constantinopolitan court: a means of defining 'them' and 'us', 'loyalists' and 'traitors' in times of intense political stress.[27]

As far as this court world was concerned, the immediate existential crisis generated by the initial rise of Islam had passed by the later eighth century. The replacement of the Umayyad Caliphate by the Abbasids involved, among many significant shifts, a relocation of the centre of gravity within the Islamic world. The Abbasid capital moved from Damascus to Baghdad, some 500 miles (800 km) east and a far less effective strategic base for further inroads into what remained of the east Roman Empire. Even so, it was now pretty much impossible to maintain the fiction that God had ordained Roman rulers to bring the world to Christianity, when so much of that world had come crashing down around them.

Fortunately, Judaeo-Christian tradition offered a different kind of justificatory ideological model, one to which the rulers of Constantinople could now resort to justify their continued claim to Christian imperial status as they came to terms with the longer-term consequences of so much defeat. With Islam consuming most of the east Roman Empire, Constantinople's rulers increasingly drew on the Old Testament to style themselves the leaders of a new Chosen People, sailing a Byzantine Ark of salvation through desperate adversity towards final Triumph at the end of time.[28]

The rise of Islam also had a huge impact on what remained of the broader structures of Roman Christendom as a whole. Three-hundred-year-old trajectories of Christian religious development, which had gathered momentum since the early fourth century and, in the process, so dramatically transformed the patterns of pre-Constantinian Christianity, were themselves now bent decisively out of shape. In the medium to longer term, therefore, Muhammad's new religion played a decisive role in the second of the three great revolutions that eventually created the monolithic cultural construct that was medieval Latin European Christendom.

THERE IS NO GOD BUT GOD . . .

If the Muslim conquest of most of the east Roman imperial system's southern and eastern Mediterranean provinces sent what remained spiralling into crisis, it generated even greater problems for the enormous number of its Christian former subjects who suddenly found themselves under non-Christian rule. Add in the further Islamic conquest of most of the Visigoth kingdom in the Iberian peninsula in the 710s, and by the early eighth century more than half of the former Christian Roman Empire of Constantine and his successors – east and west – was now ruled by Muslim caliphs. And though most of this territory lay beyond the physical geographical boundaries of what would become the heartlands of medieval European Christendom, these conquests nonetheless marked a formative moment in the development of the Latin Christian world from which it sprang.

Christianity had been born in Palestine, and most of its important early congregations had grown up around the southern and eastern shores of the Mediterranean. Rome was something of an outlier, next to the other great Christian centres located in Carthage, Alexandria, Antioch and in many of the towns and cities of Syria, Palestine and Asia Minor. In the late Roman period, although Christianity certainly had spread north of the Alps and the Pyrenees, most of the religious innovation in doctrinal dispute and the revolution in Christian piety and practice that followed Constantine's conversion was initiated by Church leaders, Christian intellectuals and holy men from Asia Minor, Syria, Egypt and North Africa. The territories swallowed up by the advance of Islam contained what had, up to this point, been the beating heart of Roman imperial Christendom: all the religion's most ancient congregations (bar Rome), and most of its established centres of intellectual and spiritual creativity (p. 126).

The Christian populations of the conquered provinces were now forced along new paths of cultural, and eventually religious, development. In the long term, interaction with their Muslim conquerors generated large-scale Islamic conversion, which eventually reduced the remaining Christian communities of the conquered regions to small minorities.[29] As this profound cultural revolution started to unfold in the decades after the Islamic conquests, Christianity's centre of gravity began to shift accordingly. This process transformed the western half of the former Roman Christendom, if by default rather than design, into a new Christian heartland. As we shall see in the chapters which follow, most of the key developments in the subsequent history of post-Roman Christianity would have their origins not in the south-eastern Mediterranean, whose thinkers had dominated the religion's development up to the Arab conquests of the seventh century, but further west and north, fuelled by many new generations of Christian intellectuals and leaders from Latin western Europe. It is difficult, actually impossible, to envisage such a sea-change in the development of medieval Christianity occurring without the Islamic conquests.

Before we explore these later patterns of religious development in the west, however, we need first to take a closer look at what happened to the Christian populations of its old heartland under Muslim rule. Not only does this defining moment in the history of Christianity deserve close attention for its own sake, but the processes of Islamic conversion which followed offer an important final perspective on the potential of Homoean Christianity to threaten Nicene predominance in the former Roman west.

Conversion to Islam presents its own fascinating puzzles. Muhammad's religious movement never developed anything along the lines of the Christian genre of conversion literature: the self-conscious exploration of a slow, sometimes tortured evolution of internal personal belief underlying a final religious epiphany, canonized within the Christian tradition by the *Confessions* of Augustine. Conversion within the Islamic tradition, at least its final act – which is all that is ever recorded – appears to be a much simpler affair. To become Muslim, all the individual had (and has) to do is to recite the *Shahada* ('Testimony') in front of witnesses: 'There is no god but God. Muhammad is the messenger of God.'

The two statements appear frequently in the Qur'an, the first about thirty times in various forms – but never together in the same *surah*.

Very quickly, however, they were combined to define the fundamental belief-set required of practising Muslims. By the last decade of the seventh century, inscriptions on the Dome of the Rock in Jerusalem, the first major public monument of triumphant Islam, proclaimed: 'There is no God but God alone; He has no partner with him; Muhammad is the messenger of God.'[30] As a result, historians have had to approach the phenomenon of Islamic conversion in the first few centuries after the conquest much more from the 'outside' than is apparently the case for its Christian counterpart, whose surviving literature offers a series of detailed personal case studies in spiritual transformation.

The first modern textbook accounts of Islamic conversion among the Christian populations of the former Roman east were based on brief references to conversion in some early Islamic historical narratives. These suggested that conversion happened astonishingly quickly, two sources claiming, for instance, that the population of Egypt was already Muslim before the end of the seventh century. And since most of the modern commentators who first discussed the subject in the nineteenth and early twentieth centuries were western, European and at least culturally Christian intellectuals, they also tended to look for practical explanations for the new religion's success. Operating in a period of unchallenged western global domination, western scholarship of the same period was generally happy to ascribe Christian conversion in the late Roman period to the fact that victorious Christianity was just, in some way, a 'better' religion than the paganism it replaced. For obvious reasons, however, such scholarship found similar lines of thought inherently unattractive as an explanation for Islam's success, since in its view there was no link between the Islamic religion and 'advanced' (and thoroughly self-satisfied) European culture. Explanation turned, therefore, to much more convenient, non-religious lines of explanation: the practical and material reasons why so many people might have converted so quickly to Islam. In particular, the fact that Christians under Muslim rule had to pay an additional poll tax – the *jizya* – figured prominently among suggested motivations for mass conversion: if you converted to Islam, you avoided the tax. However, more thorough consideration of the full range of surviving materials from the early Islamic period has since revised these initial attempts at historical reconstruction in some profoundly important ways.[31]

For one thing, as we've seen, none of the early Islamic historical sources are really that early. No properly contemporary full-scale Islamic history dates from before the Abbasid takeover of the mid-ninth century, and their accounts of the preceding Umayyad era often lack conviction, since they tend to be coloured by Abbasid self-justification which condemned the Umayyads as worldly, and improperly Islamic. But some genuine Umayyad-era materials of a more fragmentary kind (such as inscriptions and administrative or legal papyri) do survive. These sources indicate that the poll tax was not in fact a significant prompt to early conversion. Indeed, wholesale conversion – at least of non-Arabs – was often discouraged in the Umayyad period. Islam at that point was seen by at least some of its adherents more as the perfected religion of a new Chosen (Arab) People than as an evangelical enterprise to which all of humankind was destined or even invited to belong. By the last decade of the twentieth century, a more convincing overall picture began to emerge, thanks in particular to the work of Richard Bulliet. He returned to the issue of conversion from a new methodological direction, focusing on the extensive genealogical dictionaries that form a large percentage of the surviving corpus of Abbasid-era Islamic writings. His fundamental argument was that the point in family lineages where ancestral names changed from regional native languages to Arabic marks the moment of familial conversion. The dates generated have to be approximate – not least because cultural Arabization, as we shall see in a moment, could in practice precede religious conversion – but, when multiple lineages are quantified into an overall picture by hundred-year blocks, the method does provide a reasonably reliable overview.

As a result, a very different, more uneven picture emerges. In Egypt, it took until the ninth century – not the seventh, as the Abbasid-era narrative sources suggest – for Islam to win over anything like a majority of the native population, while a substantial Coptic Christian minority remained a powerful social force there for centuries. Further north, in Syria, Muslims did not number half the population until the mid-tenth century, a hundred years later than Egypt. The pace of initial conversion was similarly slow in Iraq, the old heartland of the Sasanian Empire, where Muslims numbered less than 20 per cent of the total population in AD 800 – though by the 880s, half the Iraqi population had converted to Islam. This later pace of change was mirrored in Iran, whose Muslim population reached 50 per cent of the total in just the century after 750. Taken as a whole, the evidence suggests that large-scale Islamic conversion was more a phenomenon of the second century of Islam and Abbasid rule than it was of the preceding Umayyad era.[32] All of which just prompts a further question. Why did people convert in such numbers?

As we saw in the case of conversion to Christianity in the late Roman period, both extremely self-interested and strongly devout examples of conversion, together with every possible admixture of the two, are either explicitly or implicitly documented in our surviving sources (p. 67). Much more productive than adopting a blanket approach to motivation, in my view, is to concentrate, therefore, on the actual mechanics of conversion – precisely who converted and when – as it emerges from more detailed sources: not least, in the case of early Islam, the surviving papyri from post-conquest Egypt. As ever, the hot dry sands of the desert preserve there the kinds of sources that elsewhere have long since crumbled to dust.

These papyri confirm the broad picture constructed from more impressionistic sources: that, while individual shifts of religious allegiance were not unknown, large-scale conversion was not a major phenomenon of the first, Umayyad-dominated century of Islamic history. In this era, a largely Arab conquering elite tended to be quartered in self-contained, purpose-built garrison towns in the new provinces of the emerging Caliphate. Fustat (Old Cairo) in Egypt, and Kufa and Basra in Iraq, all had their origins in what was a typical process of settlement. This kept the incoming Muslim conquerors generally segregated from native populations, supported economically by the taxes which the latter continued to pay largely as before the conquest. (This was an entirely different settlement process to what had unfolded in the west in the fifth century, where Vandals and others received substantial individual grants of real estate: p. 166.) As a result, much of the existing east Roman and – further east – Sasanian administrative machinery was initially left in place under Umayyad rule, not least because there was nothing to replace it.

This mode of settlement naturally tended to limit conversion. The conquering Muslim elite did not generally mix with their native Christian (or Zoroastrian) subjects. Retaining existing administrative systems also meant retaining most of the people who ran them – because pre-modern governmental systems, as we saw in the case of the Roman Empire, could not be separated from the prevailing social structures through which they operated. Consonant with this, the few apparently authentic initial surrender treaties (notably those for Alexandria and Damascus), which survived by becoming embedded in later narratives, formally conceded that existing socio-political and, indeed, religious structures would be left intact. This was the basic deal Islamic conquerors offered their new subjects, in return for financial payments.

Documentary papyri from Egypt, together with a range of less specific materials from across the early Islamic world, indicate that such arrangements lasted for about half a century, down to the last decade of the seventh century. These arrangements also gave the first phase of Umayyad rule some specific characteristics. Following east Roman patterns, areas conquered from Constantinople had a gold currency, with coinage designs echoing traditional Roman types; areas further east continued with the silver coinage and basic iconographic patterns of the old Sasanian Empire. The language of administration remained whatever it had been – Greek or Persian as appropriate – and many senior administrators kept their jobs. The father and grandfather of St John of Damascus, both Christians from a prominent local family, occupied senior positions under Umayyad rule into the early eighth century, even as their native city began to function as the caliphal capital.

Egyptian papyri give us more insight into what was happening further down the social and administrative scale, where, again, there was little change before 700, with one important exception. The huge, landed estates of top-level east Roman aristocrats seem to have been broken up. At least, the Apions, the one such family we know a lot about in the fifth and sixth centuries, fail to resurface under Muslim rule. They had owned substantial estates in the Oxyrhynchite *nome* (the Fayum region of Middle Egypt, about 100 miles (160 km) south of Cairo) and enjoyed strong political connections to the imperial court in Constantinople. You can easily see why the Arab conquerors might not have wanted to leave this kind of Roman aristocrat in place. However, the local Christian landowning gentry, who had run the lower reaches of the Roman system at the sub-provincial level as pagarchs (a controller of a defined rural district: a *pagus*), not only remained in place but continued to exercise considerable independence. Though answering now to the new Muslim rulers of Egypt, who set the overall tax bills, they continued to decide how taxes were to be allocated locally, a level of autonomy which sustained their existing social prominence (p. 100).[33]

The next fifty years, however, saw much more fundamental change. Most dramatically, the language of administration switched from Greek to Arabic. This development was not confined to Egypt. In the 690s, under the reforming Umayyad ruler Abd al-Malik, a new standard coinage was adopted right across the Caliphate, in both its former Persian and Roman territories; the new, aniconic coins replaced representations of rulers with verses from the Qur'an (perhaps one stimulus for Byzantine iconoclasm). In Egypt, Muslim pagarchs started to replace Christians from around AD 700, completely eclipsing them by the middle of the eighth century. A Christian landowning lesser gentry continued to exist, but its administrative remit was now confined to village-level tax collection. At the same time, the new Muslim pagarchy began to exercise greater independence in the organization of tax affairs, issuing bills to individual taxpayers and developing local business interests in the process. By the mid-eighth century, around the time of the Abbasid revolution, prominent Muslim landowners start to appear for the first time in the Egyptian countryside, completing the process whereby non-Muslims started to disappear from the upper echelons of society and administration begun half a century before. The same process, with variations, was working itself out simultaneously elsewhere in former east Roman lands. After several decades of service to the Umayyad caliphs, for instance, the family of John of Damascus was finally dismissed in the reign of al-Walid (705–15).[34]

In cultural terms, the first century of Islamic rule has recently also come into focus as an intensely creative period of interaction between a new Muslim elite and their Christian subjects. In the post-Crusade period of the high Middle Ages, the surviving Christians of the Near

East tended to retreat into cultural/linguistic ghettos, a process which has long hidden exactly how much interchange there had been between Muslims and Christians in earlier centuries. The rediscovery of this earlier phase has been one of the great leaps forward in modern oriental studies, from which two particularly striking lines of development have emerged. On the one hand, this interaction generated the first known Christian literature in Arabic, as Christian administrators and intellectuals learned Arabic to continue to serve their new masters, and to express their religious concerns in a new language. Our understanding of the late Umayyad and early Abbasid periods has been enriched by the rediscovery of the first Christian Arabic theologians, and an appreciation of how many new Christian literary genres, again often in Arabic, emerged in this period, as eastern Christians responded to the fact of Muslim conquest.

This underscores the significance of another, better-known dimension of cultural exchange from the period: the enthusiastic reception of Greek science, philosophy and mathematics by Abbasid court scholars, which played a central role in the transmission and survival of these ancient works to the present day. The Islamic movement of so-called 'reasoned discourse' – the first flowering of a Muslim tradition of logical disputation, again at the Abbasid court – likewise, had powerful roots in classical Graeco-Roman dialectic. But, if cultural exchange was certainly much more intense in the first Islamic centuries than used to be thought, there is also not the slightest doubt about who was setting the rules. Christian theologians working in Arabic had to respect some basic red lines of Islamic teaching. In Arabic Christian texts, Jesus is consistently referred to as 'the son of Mary' – i.e., not the 'Son of God' – while explicit discussion of Trinitarian theology was carefully avoided: both would have offended Muslim sensibilities concerning the untouchable Oneness of God. Some Christian Arabic liturgies of the period even adopted the first half of the *Shahada* – 'There is no god but God'.[35]

Which brings us to the second major cultural development of the period. At the same time as cultural interaction between conquerors and conquered was gathering momentum, so was a parallel process which eventually culminated in the formalization of second-class, *dhimmi* status for the Christian subjects of Muslim rulers. As set out in the caliphal decree *Shurūt Umar*, Christians were not to be forcibly converted and were protected from violent persecution. They were, however, required to pay an additional *jizya* poll tax, to wear distinctive clothing that marked them out as non-Muslim, and to show public deference to Muslims (by giving way on the street, for instance). They were also forbidden to make any public displays of their own, alternative religious affiliations: church bells could not be rung, processions were not allowed on major religious festivals, and no attempt to convert practising Muslims would be tolerated.

Following Abbasid-era Islamic historical tradition, the 'Umar' in the decree used to be identified as Umar I (634–44), Muhammad's successor-but-one after Abu Bakr. More detailed study has demonstrated, however, that the *Shurūt* was actually the work of the Umayyad Caliph Umar II (717–20). This redating is significant, because it suggests that the first half century of Islam saw no clear definition of what it meant to be a Christian under Muslim rule (as evidenced, too, by the continued prominence of Christian pagarchs in the administration of Egypt). When originally issued, moreover, Umar's decree was only one of several competing attempts to define Christian status in the lands of Islam. Some were more generous, allowing religious processions and the public celebration of Christian feast days, some less so, but all involved an element of legal subordination. It was only in the mid-ninth century, in fact, from the reign of the Abbasid caliph al-Mutawakkil (847–61), that the *Shurūt* came to be generally enforced. Its detailed provisions are a mixture of the kind of legal disabilities that the Christian Roman state had enforced upon Jews and heretics (p. 130), together with a version of the sumptuary dress codes that had formalized higher and lower status in the old Sasanian Empire.[36]

These twin processes – of cultural interaction and legal subordination – set the context for what would become a still more powerful third development of the early Islamic centuries: actual conversion from Christianity to Islam. Intuitively, it is pretty obvious that individuals and groups who were not absolutely committed to an existing Christian allegiance (and, as we have seen, processes of Christian conversion in the late Roman Empire were slower, more partial, and much less profound than often supposed) might well wish to convert to escape an increasingly well-defined second-class status – even if conversion was being discouraged to some extent under the Umayyads. Exactly how such conversion processes worked in practice can be followed in one unusually well-documented case study from a corner of the new Islamic world: the Córdoban martyr movement of mid-ninth-century Spain.

ISAAC TABANOS

In the first half of the eighth century, Córdoba quickly emerged as the capital of a new Islamic province comprising virtually the whole Iberian peninsula except for a small Christian enclave in the far north-west (Map 3). By the mid-ninth century, this province was still an emirate, or principality, notionally subordinate to the Abbasid Caliphate in far Baghdad. But soon after the Abbasid revolution – which involved the actual and ritual vilification of their Umayyad predecessors, including the desecration of all the caliphal tombs in the old Umayyad capital of Damascus – a branch of the old Umayyad ruling house fled to Spain, establishing itself there as the province's emirs. In practice, they ruled independently of Baghdad (and, in 929 under Abd-ar Rahman III, would even claim the title of caliph in an unambiguous assertion of their independent religious and political sovereignty). Three political generations before this, however, Córdoba was rocked by a sharp bout of religious unrest. Between 851 and 859, forty-eight Christians were convicted and executed on two charges: either of denigrating Islam (forbidden under the *Shurūt*), the offence of the majority; or, in twelve cases, for religious apostasy.

According to the two contemporary sources that survive – one by the priest Eulogius, the other a letter of his companion the scholar Paulus Alvarus – the martyr movement proper was triggered by two specific incidents: the execution of a priest called Perfectus, who was eventually put to death after making some unguarded comments about the Prophet; and a Christian merchant publicly flogged for pretending to be Muslim (by failing either to wear the prescribed clothing or to show the public deference required by his *dhimmi* status), probably in order that he could sell his wares more freely. Their examples inspired a succession of imitators, who voluntarily sought out the kinds of confrontation with Muslim authorities that could only end in their own deaths.[37]

Isaac Tabanos was the first of these voluntary martyrs. An Arabic-speaking, former senior tax official of the Umayyad regime in Córdoba, he gave up his career to retire to a family monastery at nearby Tabanos and devote himself to a fiercely ascetic Christian monastic regime: a sign, perhaps, that Isaac was already suffering severe anxieties about whether or not his soul was destined for Heaven. Hearing about the martyred priest and flogged merchant, Isaac left his monastery and sought out an imam teaching in one of Córdoba's public squares. Initially pretending to be interested in converting to Islam himself, Isaac then declared in a loud voice that Muhammad was 'an adulterer, a magician, and a criminal'. The Córdoban authorities promptly arrested him. But they hesitated to execute him (a year had elapsed since the death of Perfectus); at his trial, the judge even suggested that he had either been drunk or had lost his mind. But Isaac insisted on repeating his claims in court, and was eventually put to death.[38]

Those executed for apostasy included a certain Leocritia. She was formally a Muslim, born to Muslim parents. But another of her relatives was a nun, from whom the young Leocritia picked up Christian beliefs. Both their Latin personal names and familial circumstances suggest that her parents had only recently converted to Islam, since they still had Christian relatives; the other eleven martyrs executed for apostasy all seem to have come from similarly complex religious backgrounds. They were apostates in the sense of belonging to families that were semi-Muslim but still had Christian relatives, rather than themselves having gone through any very formal process of switching from Islam to Christianity.[39]

Because Iberia was conquered in the early eighth century, intense Christian-Muslim interaction began about half a century later there than in the Near East. This meant that a more developed model of interfaith relations could be imported into the peninsula. By the 850s (employing Bulliet's methodology again), conversion to Islam had reached something like 20–30 per cent of the Christian Iberian population, although there was very likely a clustering effect, with many Muslims concentrated in a restricted number of settlement hubs such as Córdoba. Arabization also spread quickly among the Christian servants of Muslim rulers, since there was no need for any lengthy period in Iberia when Latin had to remain the language of Islamic government while Arabic evolved linguistically into an effective administrative tool. Paulus Alvarus complained bitterly about high-status Christians who, driven by worldly ambition, had entered the service of the Muslim rulers of the peninsula, and of their neglect of Latin in favour of perfecting the Arabic they needed for administrative careers. (Similar concerns had earlier driven the priest Eulogius north from Córdoba to the surviving Christian enclave of Pamplona, where he obtained copies of texts by Augustine and by authors of the classical canon through which educated Latin had always been taught: Virgil, Juvenal and Horace.[40]) But the middle of the ninth century was also the period when the *Shurūt Umar* was finding more general acceptance across the Islamic world as a standard model of appropriate interfaith relations. The existing Christian administrators of the Umayyad emirs of Spain thus found themselves in a complicated cultural context, where a deeper knowledge of Arabic was the key to success, and where, at the same time, the substantial penalties for remaining Christian were being more generally enforced. After the death of the Córdoban emir Abd ar-Rahman II on 22 September 852, his successor, Muhammad I (852–86), enacted the *Shurūt* in stricter form, banning Christians as *dhimmis* from exercising any authority over Muslims and taking an aggressive line towards the building of churches.[41] As a result, the Christian servants of Muslim rulers in Spain found themselves facing the same kind of unpalatable choice that had earlier confronted the family of John of Damascus in the east. As the winds of cultural change blew through the courts of their Islamic conquerors, they could give up their inherited Christianity and become Muslim, as did one – anonymous – fellow tax official of Isaac Tabanos. If, alternatively, they remained Christian, they could either accept demotion and second-class status – like the family of John of Damascus – or, like Isaac Tabanos, take the path of overt resistance that might lead to martyrdom.[42]

While partisan Christian sources memorialize those who refused to conform, such individuals were again clearly the exceptions. Since a trend towards conversion inexorably gathered momentum, we can only conclude that most of the elite families affected by these processes made the first choice and did indeed become Muslim. Not only that, but the path of overt resistance created so many difficulties, including for those who wanted to remain Christian, that the Christian authorities themselves acted to discourage it. As the martyr movement gathered steam, Abd ar-Rahman II deployed the compliant Bishop Reccafredus (probably by this point the archbishop of Seville) to pressure the clergy of Córdoba publicly – perhaps even at a council in 852/3, though the evidence on this is not absolutely clear – to condemn the protests and try to bring the martyrdoms to an end. In doing so, Reccafredus and his allies drew on an old Christian discourse that had developed under the old pagan Roman emperors. Where no active persecution was underway – as was the case in Córdoba – it was not spiritually valid to seek out martyrdom by provoking the authorities to kill you. This was not martyrdom but suicide. Some Christians – like Paulus or Eulogius, or, unsurprisingly, the martyrs themselves – didn't share this view. Most, however, did. Over time, the effective choice for elite Christian families effectively narrowed to one of either retiring quietly from public life or accepting the path of Arabization, which usually also led to Islam, the faith of the new rulers of over half of the old Christian Roman world.[43]

This process is analogous to that which unfolded among the landowning administrative classes of the Roman Empire in the fourth century, once the imperial centre was set on an irrevocable path towards Christianity. Then, as we've seen, the perception that there was a potential advantage in accepting the emperor's religion was enough to generate an initial tendency towards conversion among those in search of imperial favour. Soon, it became a hindrance not to be Christian; then, from the 390s onwards, non-conformity became a positive bar to patronage and promotion (p. 104). Change the names and add in a stronger dose of cultural shift – not, this time, from classical culture to a classical–Christian hybrid, but from Latin and Greek to Arabic, and from Christianity to Islam – and the two processes look extremely similar.[44]

In both instances, despite some resistance, much larger numbers, clearly, eventually came into line with the cultic practices of their new rulers: Christianity – specifically Nicene Christianity in the late fourth century – and Islam in the eighth and ninth. In both cases, some individuals were presumably motivated by genuine religious conviction. Even if there is no literary genre in which an Islamic Augustine could give voice to her or his preceding inner turmoil, Islam's decisively swift overthrow of the established political order of centuries across the Near East and the Mediterranean bore the validating imprint of Divine support. At the same time, there were presumably other Muslim converts – just like Pegasios and Synesius, who brought an extraordinary amount of non-Christian baggage with them into their new roles as bishops in the fourth and early fifth centuries – who did not suffer from many pangs of Christian conscience when compromising with the new religion, even to the point of eventual conversion to Islam. In between those groups who converted either through complete expedience or deepest conviction, there must also have been the usual, considerable middle ground. Contingency, too, presumably played its part in multiple individual life stories to which we have no access: if Leocritia, for instance, hadn't spent so much time with her Christian relative, would she have become involved in the martyr movement?

Overall, however, aggregate behaviour demonstrates that the vast majority of the landowning and administrative elite of the southern and eastern Mediterranean was willing to convert first to Christianity in the fourth and fifth centuries, and then to Islam in the eighth and ninth, as the ruling ideologies which governed the rules of participation in public life changed around it. This tells its own story. Put enough pressure on people with a great deal to lose, not least because much of their everyday functioning involved them in ongoing competition with one another, especially if that pressure can be applied incrementally over several generations, and the tide of aggregate choice will inevitably flow with increasing vigour towards conversion. The point is very simple. Where the choice is between poverty and prosperity, not just for a particular individual but for all their loved ones and putative descendants as well, then pressures to conform will be difficult to resist and the majority will always tend to come into line. This is especially the case when the old belief patterns were bound up in the workings of a Confessional State that had so evidently and resoundingly failed.

THE BAPTISM OF CLOVIS (REVISITED)

Looking at the impact of Islam's arrival on how political pressures worked within elite social circles in contexts where ideological, and especially religious, preferences play a major role in the competitive processes of public life, reinforces what we've encountered in the conversion of the late Roman elite from paganism to Christianity. It also casts fresh light on a moment of the greatest significance for Christendom's development in the west: the Frankish king Clovis's decision, in 507, to be baptized into Nicene Christianity.

As we've seen, Nicaea's competitor, Homoean Christianity, was an altogether more substantial phenomenon than is generally recognized. So far, we have encountered it as a major threat to imperial Roman Nicene orthodoxy in the post-Roman west, but the Islamic – and indeed late Roman – analogies suggest that it was potentially even an existential one. If Clovis had chosen Homoean Christianity in the first decade of the fifth century, the court cultures of *all* the continental western successor states – Frankish, Gothic, Vandal and Burgundian – would then have been set in favour of Ulfilas's brand of Christianity. And if Justinian had not launched his military campaigns into North Africa and then Italy – campaigns which directly destroyed two of the major Homoean successor states (the Ostrogoths and Vandals) and allowed the Franks to swallow up a third (the Burgundians) – the political-religious domination of Homoean Christianity across the post-Roman west is likely to have prevailed, unchallenged pretty much indefinitely. What's more, neither of these counterfactual changes is that hard to envisage. We know that Clovis was hovering between Nicene and Homoean Christianity. We know, too, that Justinian's conquest policy was no deeply held, long-standing aspiration to restore Rome's old borders, but a desperate response to his military defeats at the hands of Persia, and the internal political crisis which resulted. If Justinian's Persian wars had gone better, and there had been no Nika riot, he would not have gambled on sending a fleet to North Africa and the Homoean monarchies of the west would have been left in peace, at least for several decades.

In other words, two highly contingent choices were responsible first for generating the only Nicene successor state of the former Roman west, and then for the destruction of three of its major Homoean rivals. Reverse these two choices, and, from the year 500 onwards, the former Roman west would have been completely dominated by Homoean monarchs for the foreseeable future. The resulting situation would have directly paralleled conditions in Rome's former eastern provinces after the Islamic conquests (and indeed those of the Roman Empire in the mid-fourth century), where the sustained alternative religious preferences of a sequence of Muslim (and Christian) rulers was quite enough, over the long term, to prompt landowning elite subjects to change their inherited religious allegiances, slowly but surely, to match.

Even the few decades of incomplete Homoean domination that actually transpired in the post-Roman west were enough to generate some known elite Nicene Roman converts: from one Mocianus in the Vandal kingdom (to go alongside all those Nicene bishops who changed sides in 484, of course); to the brothers Opilio and Cyprianus, who learned Gothic at the court of Theoderic in Italy; to a certain Syagrius, who immersed himself in the Burgundian language of his new masters.[45] We can also add in the Nicene bishop Vincent of Zaragoza, who came into line with Liuvigild's Macedonianism in the 580s (p. 202). In themselves, these look like isolated examples. But they are enough to demonstrate that the same kind of pressures were at work in Homoean-dominated court circles of the later fifth- and sixth-century west as eventually proved so effective in Islamic-dominated eastern circles of the seventh and eighth centuries (or indeed the Christian Roman imperial court of the fourth). If we take hindsight out of the equation – as properly we must since we now know that Nicene Christianity was not destined to maintain its hold forever, and in all circumstances, on the population of Europe – there is more than enough here to allow us to glimpse a dramatically different religious outcome for European Christendom.

The perception that well-entrenched Homoean ruling dynasties were showing even the slightest preference towards fellow believers – Huneric's initial policy position, for instance, before he launched his persecution[46] – would have been enough to kick-start a trickle of conversions among landowners less committed to Nicaea. From here, it is perfectly plausible that momentum would slowly have built until a

Homoean allegiance – like Islamic faith in eighth-century Egypt and Syria, or a Christian faith in the fourth-century Roman Empire as a whole – became a prerequisite for social and political success. At the very least, such a process would have been enough, eventually, to reduce Nicene Christianity to a minority, second-class status in the same way that, once Islamic conversion had reached a critical mass, the remaining Christians of Rome's former eastern provinces were forced to accept the *dhimmi* laws of the *Shurūt Umar*.

Events turned out otherwise, of course. The choices of Clovis and Justinian fell in alternative directions, and, as a result, imperial Nicene orthodoxy was able to survive the Homoean challenge after the fall of the Roman west, whereas Islam triumphed over it after the fall of the Roman east. While certainly important, however, that contrast is only telling part of the story.

The unravelling of the Roman imperial system in both east and west initiated a second period of revolutionary development within the Christian religion, which was not limited to the dramatic crises of allegiance that the failure of any Confessional State, its defining ideologies stripped away, will always engender. Equally important, in terms of its practical internal functioning, late Roman Christianity had also developed a deeply symbiotic set of relationships with the administrative, legal and cultural structures of the Roman imperial system. In the post-Roman west, many of these structures quickly crumbled, unleashing a further set of profound transformations in the inner workings of Latin Christianity. The best place to begin an exploration of how and why post-Roman western Christianity was so different to its late Roman predecessor is the far north-west of the old Roman world, where further processes of conversion created entirely new trajectories of religious transformation.

6

'Not Angels': Conversion in North-western Europe

In the early years of the fifth century, faced with Visigoths and Vandals much closer to its heartlands, the west Roman state left the British provinces that it had ruled for almost four centuries, abandoning them to their fate. The only remotely contemporary native account to survive was written in the sixth century by the British cleric Gildas, who graphically portrayed the dire situation in which the Christian Romano-British elites now found themselves, confronted by raiders from both Ireland (known to Gildas as the 'Scots') and Scotland ('Picts'). The British responded by recruiting warbands of Germanic-speaking mercenaries from across the North Sea: groups of non-Christian Angles, Saxons and Jutes, who were near neighbours of Rome and had occasionally served in its armies. In the next generation, probably sometime around AD 440, the mercenaries decided that Britain was ripe for the taking. They rebelled against their Romano-British employers, calling in reinforcements from home – a series of warband-sized units, who began to take piecemeal control of the most productive farmlands of former Roman Britain, now central and southern England. There was serious periodic resistance but, by the end of the sixth century, an incremental flow of Germanic-speaking warrior groups had established its dominance over most of former Roman Britain, generating, in the first instance, a number of relatively small, non-Christian Anglo-Saxon kingdoms. A mysterious early document known as the *Tribal Hidage* lists no fewer than thirty-five named Anglo-Saxon entities, but it is not clear that all of these had originally been independent kingdoms – nor even, if they had been, that this would represent an exhaustive list. Either way, by the year 600, the settlement-era pattern of small, locally independent principalities

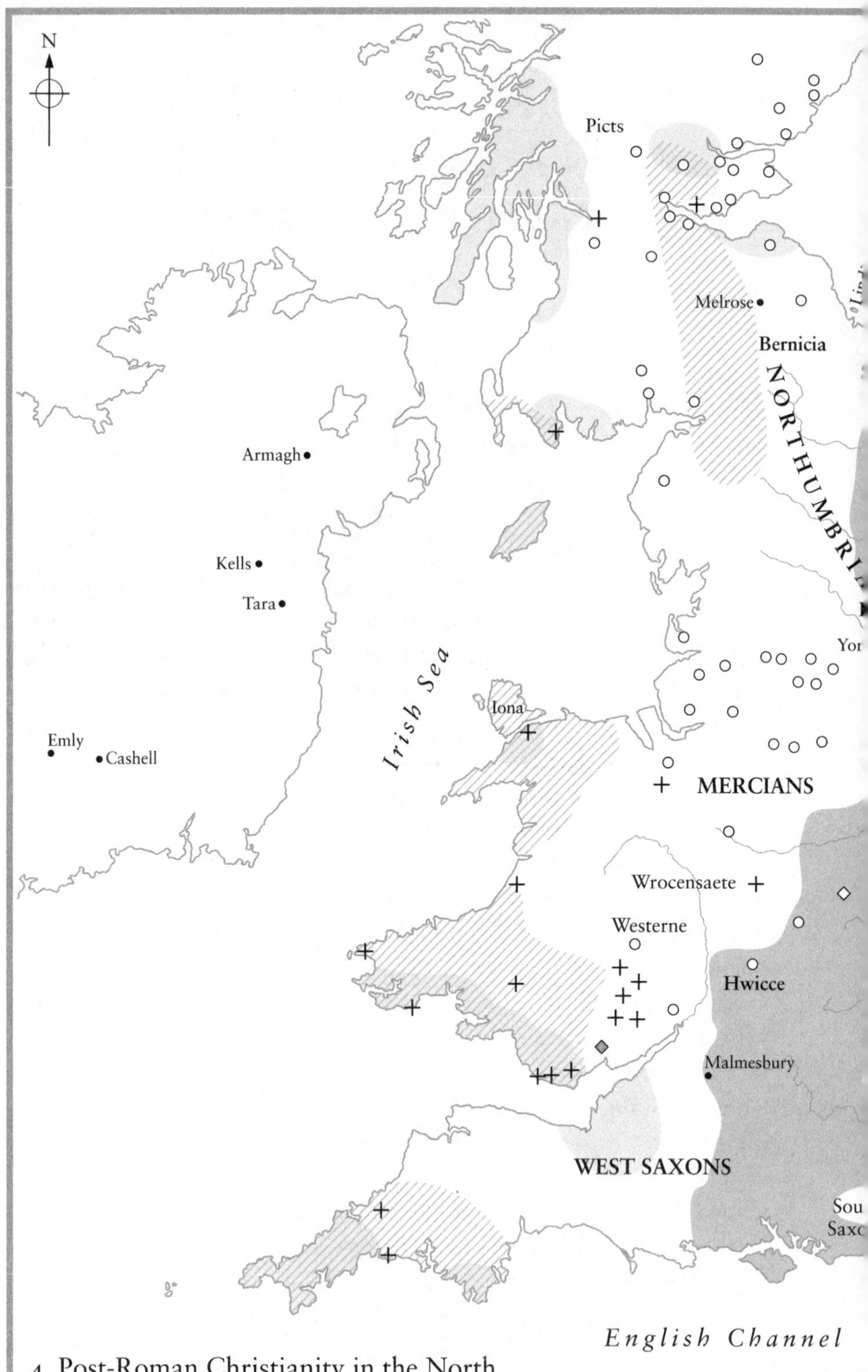

4. Post-Roman Christianity in the North

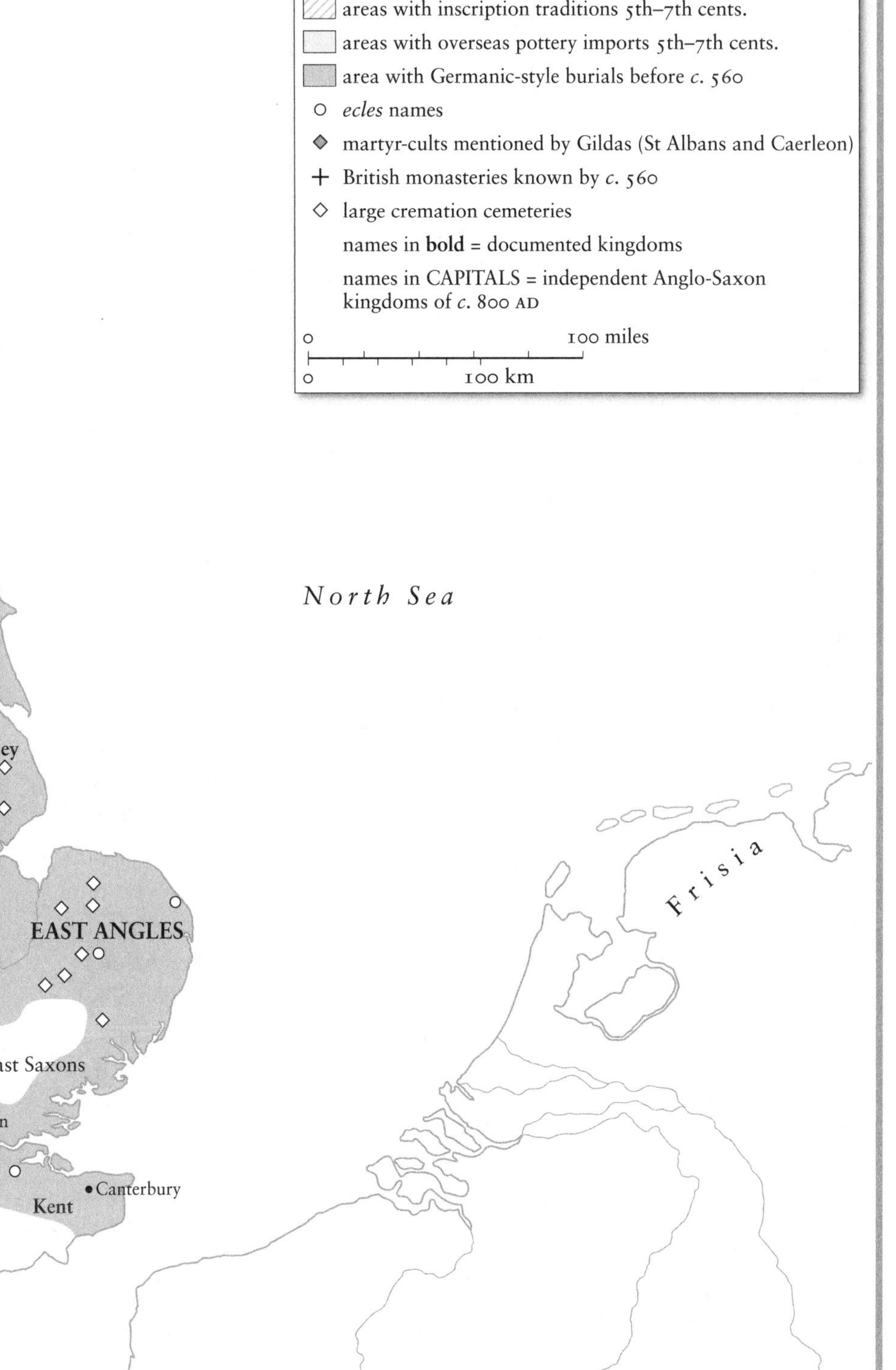
areas with inscription traditions 5th–7th cents.
areas with overseas pottery imports 5th–7th cents.
area with Germanic-style burials before c. 560
ecles names
martyr-cults mentioned by Gildas (St Albans and Caerleon)
British monasteries known by c. 560
large cremation cemeteries
names in bold = documented kingdoms
names in CAPITALS = independent Anglo-Saxon kingdoms of c. 800 AD
0
100 miles
0
100 km
North Sea
Frisia
EAST ANGLES
East Saxons
Canterbury
Kent

was giving way to larger, consolidated monarchies, and individual rulers of these bigger kingdoms sometimes became powerful enough to exercise a recognized form of hegemony over some of their peers (Map 4).[1]

The monk-historian Bede (673–735) traces the Christianization of this developing Anglo-Saxon world to a slave market in the city of Rome, where – so the story goes – Pope Gregory I ('the Great': 590–604) saw some beautiful, blond children for sale and wondered who they were. On being told that they were Angles from Britain, he replied, according to Bede, *non angli sed angeli*: 'not Angles but angels'. Gregory promptly despatched a band of forty monks led by one Augustine, the future first archbishop of Canterbury. They reached the south-east coast of England in 597, their arrival kick-starting the gradual conversion of all the Anglo-Saxon kingdoms. Kent, Augustine's original destination, was converted by 601 at the latest; the final bastion of Anglo-Saxon pagan resistance was the Isle of Wight, which turned to Christianity in 681. By far the fullest telling of what unfolded in between is charted in loving detail in Bede's *Ecclesiastical History of the English People*, which he completed in 731, not long before his death, working in the great double monastery of Monkwearmouth–Jarrow.[2] The work is a magnificent tour de force – but it is not remotely the whole story.

For a start, Christianity had already reached England before Augustine and his band of monks came ashore. By 597, the Christian wife of King Æthelberht of Kent, the Frankish princess Bertha, had been in Kent for some fifteen years, together with her personal chaplain, Bishop Liudgard. While Bede mentions this, he does so in passing, and his history fails to explore what is clearly an important backstory to Augustine's mission. The religious loyalties of Æthelberht's royal Frankish wife surely explains why Augustine's mission landed in Kent in particular, rather than anywhere else in the Anglo-Saxon world. His marriage to Bertha reflected growing Frankish influence north of the Channel, and Augustine's arrival was surely smoothed by careful prior negotiation in which the Christian king of the Franks played an important role. Indeed, Frankish interpreters (mentioned briefly by Bede) facilitated the initial conversations between the missionaries and the king.[3]

Further north, the pagan princely houses of Anglo-Saxon Northumbria had also already been in contact with some of the Christian

Irish dynasties, who had established a presence, along with the important monastery of Iona, along the west coast of Scotland in the fifth and sixth centuries. Bede's conversion narrative gives an important, if secondary, role to the influence of these Irish monks – but this is another strand of the broader Anglo-Saxon conversion story that had again begun well before Augustine's arrival in Kent.

Last but not least, the Irish had originally acquired their Christianity in the fifth and early sixth centuries, from Romanized Britons who, at the moment of Augustine's arrival, still maintained a series of small, independent kingdoms in those parts of western and northern Britain that had not so far fallen under Anglo-Saxon control (Map 4). While the Angles, Saxons and Jutes were busy carving out principalities in eastern Britain, British missionaries – of whom St Patrick (the Latin-educated offspring of probably Cumbrian minor Roman gentry, most likely born around the year 400) is by far the best documented – were spreading Christianity west into Ireland. The subsequent arrival of Irish missionaries in western Scotland and northern England represented a kind of reimportation of Christianity back to the British mainland.

By the late sixth century, Christianity was a defining cultural characteristic of the remaining independent British kingdoms of the north and west; moreover, among the mass indigenous population of the territories that had already fallen under Anglo-Saxon control, some British Christians clearly remained. The cult site of the early fourth-century Romano-British Christian martyr St Alban, just north of London, continued to function throughout the fifth and sixth centuries, while a few early Anglo-Saxon placenames that include *eccles* (from the Latin for 'church') suggest the presence of surviving church buildings in some parts of the conquered territories.[4] While Bede made a hero of Gregory the Great, Augustine's message took root in fertile ground: prepared, in different ways, by Christian Franks, Irish monks and Britons.

Set in this broader context, moreover, the conversion of the Anglo-Saxons – starting with Augustine's arrival in Kent in 597 and finishing with the baptism of the last pagan rulers of the Isle of Wight in 681 – is no isolated event. Rather, it comes in the middle of a highly productive missionary era in north-western Europe, between the fifth and early eighth centuries. This period saw the Christianization (or re-Christianization) not only of Anglo-Saxon England, Ireland and parts of Scotland, but of Frisia (the modern Netherlands) and some other parts of what now is western Germany, as newly converted Irish and Anglo-Saxon missionaries took the faith across the English Channel and the North Sea.

All these missionary endeavours need to be explored as part of a single, larger enterprise, representing a distinct cluster of related missionary moments largely carried forward by a set of British, Irish and Anglo-Saxon missionaries, who influenced each other's work in both positive and negative ways. Despite its overtly evangelical message, the Christianity of the first millennium AD showed only a patchy commitment to missionary work. For centuries after the fall of the western Empire in particular, most of the post-Roman Christian world showed little interest in spreading the word into new territories beyond the old imperial frontiers – perhaps because lingering Roman ideas of civilization and barbarism meant that their populations were regarded as a subhuman 'other': a world where the Gospel couldn't possibly flourish.[5] By contrast, having themselves just been converted from this 'other', enthusiastic Irish and Anglo-Saxon Christians shared a much more obvious commitment to Christ's command to spread the Gospel to 'all the nations'. Indeed, some Anglo-Saxon missionaries expressed an explicit desire to re-export the Faith back to what they still understood as their ancestral continental homelands. Hence a broader conversion period in north-western Europe – lasting from Patrick in fifth-century Ireland to the work of Anglo-Saxon and Irish missionaries (such as Willibrord, Boniface and Clemens) south of the Channel in the later seventh and early eighth centuries – can be understood as a discernible grouping of interrelated evangelical enterprise.

Analytically, too, grouping these missionary moments together is the most effective way to utilize the surviving source materials. Bede's *Ecclesiastical History* provides far and away the most detailed narrative of any of the individual conversion processes that unfolded in these centuries, but even this is far from complete, and other Anglo-Saxon materials of the seventh and earlier eighth centuries only go some way to filling in the gaps. The work of the other missions is reflected in much more disparate and fragmentary materials: a range of saints' *Lives*, letters, legal materials and Church council decisions, supplemented by some important archaeological evidence. All of this gives us nothing like a complete picture of any one of the individual missions. However, when taken together, it does offer greater insight into at least some of the key characteristics of what were clearly a broadly similar set of conversion processes.

MISSIONARIES AND KINGS

Common to all these evangelical missions is the strikingly small number of missionaries initially involved in carrying the Gospel into each of these new territories. Augustine's original task force numbered just forty. A few reinforcements followed, but the emphasis is on 'few': not all Gregory's papal successors were equally (or at all) committed to the Anglo-Saxon mission. The Irish contribution to Anglo-Saxon Christianization likewise came in the form of a handful of influential individuals, mostly from Iona and its related houses in southern Scotland and the Borders, and matters were no different in Ireland and Frisia. Irish Christianization began with a handful of British missionaries in the fifth century, while Willibrord, Boniface and their few Irish peers were also operating south of the Channel in the later seventh and early eighth centuries with only limited numbers of assistants.[6]

In the case of England, it has sometimes been wondered if Bede's determination to focus on a handful of great Roman and Irish missionary heroes has perhaps distorted our picture of the actual scale of the missionary effort, by suppressing a broader native British contribution to the spread of Christianity in Anglo-Saxon England. British Christians do get a bad press in the *Ecclesiastical History*, Bede implying that their Christianity was antiquated, not fit for purpose. For one thing, he emphasizes, they were wedded to the 'wrong' method for calculating Easter. At the time the British provinces dropped out of the Roman imperial system around the year 400, the council of Nicaea's decision to harmonize the date of Easter had yet to take full effect. The British Church was not yet following the Alexandrian system, based on a nineteen-year cycle, but an alternative one (also followed by some Gallic churches at the time), based on a cycle of eighty-four years.

Naturally enough, the Irish, whom the British proceeded to evangelize, adopted the same method – but by the time Augustine arrived in 597 the rest of the western Church (including all the churches of Gaul) had come to adopt the Alexandrian method. Consequently, British and Irish churchmen seemed distinctly deviant in this important matter.[7] Bede's considerable dislike of the British Church is also clear in the emphasis he places on the refusal of its leaders to accept the authority of Augustine as Pope Gregory's appointed archiepiscopal primate for the British Isles, and on what he sees as their failure to preach the Gospel to the Anglo-Saxons before the arrival of Augustine's mission.

Some of Bede's determined downplaying of any indigenous role in the Christianization of the Anglo-Saxons surely does represent deception by omission. For instance, two early Anglo-Saxon kingdoms of the west Midlands – Hwicce and Magonsæte (roughly the areas of modern Gloucestershire, Worcestershire, Warwickshire and Herefordshire: Map 4) – had been converted to Christianity by the 660s, but Bede doesn't tell us how this happened. Here, there is every reason to think that native British Christians were responsible, since the earliest documented form of Church organization in these areas resembles adjacent British rather than emergent Anglo-Saxon patterns. Significantly, Hwicce and Magonsæte were the westernmost Anglo-Saxon kingdoms of the seventh century, largely surrounded by Christian British principalities.[8]

That said, the significance of the overall native British role in the Christianization of the rest of Anglo-Saxon England should not be overestimated. When, in the first decades of the fifth century, the British provinces dropped out of the imperial system, Roman Christianity was still essentially an elite and urban phenomenon. The consequent Anglo-Saxon takeover of south-eastern Britain both quickly eliminated the Latinate, villa-owning, Christian landowning class of lowland Roman Britain and prompted the disappearance of Britain's Roman towns as properly urban centres. The available archaeological evidence indicates that both villas and towns had effectively ceased to exist in these regions by the middle of the fifth century at the latest. Their elimination thus destroyed the principal sources of organized Christianity in southern and eastern Britain – and, hence, any immediate capacity on the part of native Christian British to spread the Word of God to incoming Anglo-Saxons.

The evidence also suggests that we need to make a general distinction between the eastern regions of Roman Britain, which came under Anglo-Saxon control in the mid-fifth century, and more western territories, like Hwicce and Magonsæte, which were conquered only rather later. In the east of the country, Romano-British Christianity survived only in isolated pockets. Apart from the cult of St Alban, Augustine also came across some Kentish – presumably native British – Christians who maintained a cult of a certain St Sixtus, without the slightest knowledge of who this Sixtus may have been. Pope Gregory advised that Augustine was to suppress the local Sixtus and replace him with a festival for a Roman martyr by the same name. Further west, in a more central zone running north–south from the Scottish Borders to the Channel, where native Romano-British control had endured perhaps even until the mid- to late sixth century, indigenous Churchmen had had almost a hundred and fifty years since the departure of the Romans to develop stronger Christian institutions. By the time the Anglo-Saxons spread into this north–south belt, therefore, Christianity had managed to spread beyond the restricted elite and urban Christian congregations of *c.* 400. All the early *eccles* placenames belong to this zone, as do the kingdoms of Hwicce and Magonsæte, which were carved out in the late sixth century at the earliest. In these areas, therefore, incoming Anglo-Saxon overlords were confronted with a substantial native British Church, which may well have played a major role in their eventual conversion. The same had not been true of those eastern areas – from Sussex and Kent in the south, to the coastal regions of Northumbria – annexed by Anglo-Saxons in the fifth century. So, while Bede's narrative deliberately minimized the British contribution, his *Ecclesiastical History* is probably not fundamentally misleading in its overall portrayal of the initial conversion of the bulk of Anglo-Saxon England – like the related evangelization of Ireland and Frisia – as essentially the work of a handful of influential foreign missionaries.[9]

The basic strategy adopted by all these missionaries, as it emerges from our varied source materials from all three regions, was substantially dictated by the overall shortage of manpower. In all three, contacts of various kinds had already spread some knowledge of Christianity before the actual missionaries got to work. These contacts included trade, especially in slaves; diplomatic dealings, including sometimes even marriage alliances (as in Bertha and Æthelberht); and cross-border raiding, to name just a few. And once the missions were underway, the distinctive lifestyles of the dedicated clerics who were willing to undertake these extraordinary journeys into what were for them unknown lands must also have made an impact upon the broader populations they encountered. All the missionaries were monks of some kind, living under vows of poverty and celibacy: they must have presented striking images of worldly renunciation, particularly in societies with no established traditions of Christian monasticism. But, initially at least, early medieval missionaries did not have the general population in their sights. Missionary work in the post-Roman west was fundamentally a top-down process, heavily reliant in the first instance on winning over local rulers to the cause.[10]

Patrick made a first visit to Ireland courtesy of some slave traders, who captured and shipped him there from his native Cumbria in the early decades of the fifth century. He did eventually escape back to Britain, but didn't stay for long, returning to Ireland again now as a missionary. He went directly to the country's many kings, working, first and foremost, to convince them of the value of his religion. The same pattern held true in Anglo-Saxon England. Augustine's main target on arriving in Kent was King Æthelberht himself. The two met initially in the open air on the Isle of Thanet – to make it more difficult for Augustine, Bede tells us, to ensnare the king by magic. The Roman mission then targeted the kings of the East Saxons and East Anglians, and, eventually, King Edwin of Northumbria. The picture was the same across the North Sea, where various kings of Frisia, particularly a certain Radbod, feature heavily in the details that survive about the activities there of missionaries such as Willibrord and Boniface.

It wasn't just the prevailing shortage of missionary manpower that dictated this approach. Kings were targeted for specific reasons. First and foremost, royal protection made it possible for missionaries to work in safety. In Kent, the main outcome of the Thanet conversations was that Augustine and his fellow monks were allowed to move into the heart of Æthelberht's kingdom, the royal centre at Canterbury. There, Æthelberht publicly adopted Christianity: by 601, Pope Gregory specifically addressed him as a Christian king. The missionaries were then able to exploit his royal authority for religious ends, acquiring a formal, legally protected status for themselves within the kingdom of Kent. Bede tells us that soon after his conversion, Æthelberht issued a law code 'after the Roman manner'. Astonishingly, its contents have survived, by the thinnest of margins, in a single post-Norman Conquest manuscript: the *Textus Roffensis* from Rochester Cathedral. One of the central concerns of Æthelberht's rulings – which may have been committed to writing only at some point after the king's death, though probably still at an early, seventh-century date – was to define and protect the status of Augustine and his fellow clergy. The initial clauses detail the compensations that were to be paid for stealing Church property from clergy of different ranks. The scale ran from an elevenfold compensation for thefts from bishops, to threefold from ordinary clerics.[11]

This royal protection was highly necessary, and without it missionaries could easily come to grief. Two English brothers named Hewald (known only from a brief mention by Bede) were killed trying to convert the continental Saxons (southern neighbours of the Frisians) in *c*. 700. Boniface, likewise, was eventually murdered in Frisia in 754: one of his surviving books may still betray the marks of the sword cuts it received as he tried to ward off the hostile attentions of the robbers who ambushed his band of brothers. A few decades earlier, another prominent Anglo-Saxon continental missionary, Willibrord – sometimes labelled 'the Apostle of the Frisians' – narrowly survived a tricky moment on the island of Fositesland (perhaps modern Heligoland). According to a group among the local population, he had slaughtered some sacred cattle and violated a sacred spring (even missionaries get hungry and thirsty). The local ruler wanted to satisfy the offended gods by sacrificing some human victims, who were to be chosen by lot (that's to say, the gods would pick them). Doubtless to Willibrord's and his companions' relief, the lots fell on some unlucky others – but the threat to them was real enough.[12] Royal support wasn't enough to protect you completely, but operating without it was hazardous.

Once they had converted, newly Christian kings could be co-opted to use their influence in favour of the faith. As Bede describes it, Æthelberht didn't exactly force his subjects to become Christian. 'He had learned from his instructors and guides to salvation that the service of Christ must be accepted freely and not under compulsion. Nevertheless, he showed greater favour to believers, because they were fellow citizens of the kingdom of heaven.' We have met this phenomenon of royal patronage being deployed preferentially for fellow believers several times before, in late Roman, Vandal and early Islamic contexts. It was just as effective among the Anglo-Saxons, even if the inducements on offer were different.

Anglo-Saxon society was hierarchical, with a restricted warrior elite of freemen and nobles sitting above a much larger peasant class, many of whom – presumably of Romano-British descent – were slaves or semi-free. To these elites the king was a source of wealth, both moveable (in the form of treasure and highly valued craft items such as top-quality weaponry) and landed. Heroic poetry – from *Beowulf* to the more historic events in *The Battle of Malden* – includes many references to lords giving faithful warriors gold, horses, fine clothing and expensive weaponry. Enough of the gold at least has been recovered from Anglo-Saxon treasure hoards – most famously at Sutton Hoo, but at other sites too, such as the astonishing 11 lbs (5 kilos, much of it fittings ripped off weaponry and clothing) in the recently discovered Staffordshire hoard – to confirm that these descriptions were not poetic licence. Likewise, as they reached an appropriate age to marry, elite warriors often wanted land to supplement what they might inherit from their families, in order to establish viable independent households.[13] As a prime source of both moveable and landed wealth, Anglo-Saxon kings exercised extensive powers of patronage over their leading warriors; the warriors in turn, once established as estate holders with their own dependent peasants, were then well placed to pass the favour on down the social scale. As far as the spread of Christianity was concerned, the overall effect of the lordly persuasion played out at every level could be dramatic. A letter of Pope Gregory to his fellow patriarch of Alexandria tells us that the combined efforts of Augustine and his monks brought ten thousand individuals to baptism on Christmas Day 597. Bede reports other mass baptisms in Northumbria in the River Glen, close to the Northumbrian king Edwin's royal palace of Yeavering, following the despatch there of Augustine's companion Paulinus.[14]

The power of greater kings could extend well beyond their own borders, an additional dimension of royalty that missionaries were quick to exploit for religious effect. When Augustine arrived in Kent, Æthelberht was then the most powerful king in southern England, and diplomatic relations between the various kings of later sixth- and seventh-century Anglo-Saxon England operated within reasonably well-defined protocols of over- and under-kingship. The process that established these royal pecking orders was often violent and messy, but, once his hegemony had been established, an overking could expect to draw on certain kinds of service such as military and economic support, and a certain deference in matters of religion, even if under-kings continued to rule their own territories. For Christian missionaries, this could sometimes be a stumbling block. Bede mentions Anglo-Saxon under-kings who declared themselves unable to accept Christianity until their pagan overlords had died (Edwin of Northumbria being a case in point: no missionaries were invited into his kingdom until after the death of his non-Christian overlord, Rædwald of East Anglia). More frequent, however, are examples of Christian overkings using their influence to persuade under-kings to convert, or at least to allow missionaries into their kingdoms.

While Frankish influence certainly played a role in Æthelberht's original decision to accept Augustine's mission, it is striking that the king eventually sought his Christianity from Rome rather than directly from Francia. Bede doesn't explore the complexities of the king's decision-making in any detail, but this probably wasn't an accident. Given that, in the Anglo-Saxon context, accepting a fellow-ruler's cult was an acknowledgement of subordination, Æthelberht may have been keen to find an alternative source of Christianity. Once converted, however, Æthelberht used his status as overking in southern England to allow Augustine's mission to spread its wings to the neighbouring kingdoms of the East Saxons (Essex), which controlled what remained of old Roman London and was ruled by his nephew Sæberht, and the East Angles. Æthelberht's son and successor Eadbald, however, lacked the same authority: after Æthelberht's death, the rulers of Essex quickly departed the Christian fold. One of Edwin's successors, Oswald of Northumbria, likewise sponsored the baptism of his under-king, Cynegils of the West Saxons (Wessex), and similar patterns can also be observed in the spin-off missions to the Continent.

The later work of Anglo-Saxon missionaries in Frisia, particularly Willibrord and Boniface, was facilitated by a similar set of relationships. Between 695 and 714, King Radbod of Frisia stood in a dependent relationship to the Frankish prince Pippin of Herstal, the effective ruler of the north-eastern Frankish territory of Austrasia (comprising parts of modern France and Belgium: Map 5), and it was Pippin's influence over Radbod which allowed the Anglo-Saxon missionaries to preach. After Pippin's death, Radbod forced the missionaries out. Some were killed and various churches burnt, while Willibrord was forced to return to Frankish territory until Pippin's son, Charles Martel, re-established a sufficient degree of hegemony for him to return in 719. While other contacts – not least trade and marriage alliances – helped prepare the ground for formal missionary work, the cluster of fifth- to eighth-century conversions in north-western Europe was fundamentally about kings, courts and mass baptisms.[15] The fact that the missionary effort had such a royal focus in turn dictated the *kind* of Christianity that was taught.

ONWARD CHRISTIAN SOLDIERS

To make this fundamentally top-down process work, the missionaries had to preach a Christianity that would find traction among Anglo-Saxon kings and their chief retainers, and their equivalents in Ireland and Frisia. In the case of England, both archaeological materials and much of the surviving Anglo-Saxon poetry offer us striking images of an elite warrior society focused around feasting and drinking in royal mead halls, and, in a wonderful scene, which you can only wish might be true, Bede recalls the moment when religious reflection in one of Edwin of Northumbria's halls was lit up by an existential contribution from one of the king's warriors:

> When we compare the present life of man on earth with that time of which we have no knowledge, it seems to me like the swift flight of a single sparrow through the banqueting-hall where you are sitting at dinner on a winter's day with your thegns and counsellors. In the midst, there is a comforting fire to warm the hall; outside, the storms of winter

> rain or snow are raging. This sparrow flies swiftly in through one door of the hall, and out through another. While he is inside, he is safe from the winter storms; but after a few moments of comfort, he vanishes from sight into the wintry world from which he came. Even so, man appears on earth for a little while; but of what went before this life or of what follows, we know nothing.[16]

Several examples of such halls have been excavated at the Northumbrian hilltop site of Yeavering – probably the royal centre of *Ad Gefrin* named by Bede and the scene of the imagined discussion. Built around AD 600, this commanding royal site consisted of a sequence of massively built wooden structures with floor areas of up to 3,300 square feet (300sq m): the archetypical mead hall. (At Yeavering – perhaps not so surprising given that these wooden structures were centres dedicated to feasting and alcohol consumption – several of the buildings were destroyed by fire.)[17]

Violence was central to the lives of the kings and the great men who periodically gathered to feast in these halls, shaping their entire existence in a personal and direct way. While a greater degree of political cohesion was slowly emerging in the era of Christianization as the larger kingdoms of the heptarchy – the seven consolidated Anglo-Saxon kingdoms – began to emerge, this did not alter the prevailing nature of Anglo-Saxon elite life. In essence, Anglo-Saxon England was a productive agricultural landscape shared between a number of actual and would-be ruling families, whose resources they exploited to support the warriors through whom they competed against one another. As a result, the prevailing character of Anglo-Saxon elite life was shaped by a perennial and highly militarized competitive political process, which saw kings and their armed retainers work out their rivalries – over the generations – through rounds of small-scale, often repetitive combat: no more, usually, than a few thousand on each side at the most, sometimes only hundreds. These were close-order encounters between individuals who could see, hear and smell the adversaries they were attempting to kill. Enough skeletal damage has been recorded in recovered human remains to confirm that this was not poetic myth but reality. Missionaries to Anglo-Saxon England, therefore, had to work out how Christianity might appeal to the priorities of elite men and women who spent their lives trying to maximize personal advantage in a political context that periodically exposed them to extreme violence. Working in Ireland in the fifth and sixth centuries, and in Frisia in the early eighth, posed the same basic intellectual problem: what could a highly militarized audience of kings and warrior retainers find attractive in the Gospel of Christ?

For some, the attraction lay precisely in a religiously authorized escape from an all-pervasive violence whose only likely end was a potentially agonizing early demise. (Medieval medicine brought little solace. One of the most chilling things I have ever read is an off-hand reference in the *Anglo-Saxon Chronicle* to a king dying of his wounds three months after the battle in which they'd been inflicted.) In the late seventh century, one high-status Mercian warrior called Guthlac left the service of his king for the abbey of Repton, before moving on to solitary asceticism on the marshy island of Croyland, where he had to fend off the attentions of British-speaking demons. A trickle of Anglo-Saxon kings, likewise, sought to 'retire' to monasteries when they had had enough of alcohol-fuelled bloodshed, sometimes to no avail. Ex-king Sigebert of East Anglia was dragged out of retirement in the early 640s by his old warriors who wanted their former commander to lead them against Penda, the all-conquering pagan king of Mercia. They still lost, and Sigebert was killed.[18] The *Chronicle of Ireland*, likewise, records six 'repentant' kings who retired to monasteries before the tenth century. There's more than enough here to give the lie to the picture of untroubled heroism painted by much of the poetry. Warfare in early Anglo-Saxon England – as in Ireland and Frisia too – was nasty, brutal and personal. There must have been many more undiagnosed cases of post-traumatic stress syndrome in the post-Roman early medieval west than the reported instance of a Frankish warrior-turned-monk who suffered from recurring nightmares of the blood oozing from the wounds of his dead opponents. For the many other traumatized individuals who pass unmentioned in our sources, Christianity offered ideological justification and institutional support for abandoning the life of the warrior – or, at least, for limiting its worst excesses. Hence Adomnán, the ninth abbot of the monastery of Iona, was able to persuade many of the warrior elites of southern Scotland, the Borders and northern Ireland (a total of ninety-one chieftains and clerics) that fell within his pastoral sway to sign up to a Law of Innocents (the *Cáin Adomnáin*) at the great synod of Birr in 697. This agreement extended the same legal protections to women and children that monks had already enjoyed in Irish-dominated contexts, supposedly since the time of St Patrick. The penalties were ferocious for any who broke the rules.[19]

For the most part, however, missionaries were working with warrior elites who remained precisely that. Only a tiny minority of the warriors of Britain and Ireland ever turned to religion for escape. So, what was Christianity's attraction for everyone else? We have no first-hand information. No warrior of the early medieval British Isles wrote his own version of the other Augustine's *Confessions*. Nor do we know much about the religious competition. Neither the Irish nor the Anglo-Saxons were completely illiterate before the missionaries arrived; they wrote, respectively, with the Ogham and runic scripts, both of which had been in part developed – as the letter forms show – from the Latin literacy of the Roman Empire. But both these scripts were designed for carving short inscriptions in stone, wood and other durable materials (all the letter forms comprise straight lines), and there is no sign that they were ever used to produce full-length texts on papyrus or parchment.[20] Among the Anglo-Saxons and Irish, and in Frisia too, the full-scale literacy associated with book production (whether in Latin, or in written forms of native languages) arrived only with Christian missionaries. All the longer written texts to survive from these contexts therefore necessarily date from after the acceptance of Christianity – by which point there was little reason to record a full account of older, inferior and now rejected systems of religious belief. This in turn frustrates attempts to reconstruct the nature of pre-Christian cults and belief structures among the Anglo-Saxons, Irish and Frisians.

In the Anglo-Saxon case, different kinds of surviving texts, from Bede's *History* and other writings to king-lists and poems, preserve the names of various actual or potential pre-Christian deities, but some of these are so obscure that it's unclear whether they were really gods at all. Others – like Thunor (Thor), Woden, or Tiw – are well known from later Norse material, but that material is so late (the earliest, Icelandic, stories about these gods date from *c.* 1200) that there's every chance that their attributes, roles and characteristics had altered in some fundamental ways in the intervening half-millennium.[21] Similarly, only a handful of pre-Christian Anglo-Saxon cult sites have been identified on or in the ground. But even some of these are potential rather than actual, and none offers much indication of the nature of pre-Christian Anglo-Saxon religious practice. These aside, all we have to go on are a few stray hints in the written evidence.

Anglo-Saxon medical texts – produced in monastic contexts as late as the tenth and eleventh centuries – still included some charms with clear echoes of non-Christian thought worlds. The same is true of earlier texts, such as the late seventh-century *Penitential* of Archbishop Theodore of Canterbury (668–90). This is a very early example of a class of Christian text that grew in importance in the ninth and tenth centuries, whose purpose was to lay down appropriate penances for different types of sin. What has come down to us as Theodore's *Penitential* is probably a composite text, not all of it written by the archbishop himself, which reflects early, substantially seventh-century Anglo-Saxon practice. The penitential list includes penalties for a few behaviours that seem distinctly pre- or non-Christian. A relatively heavy forty-day penance is laid down, for instance, for a woman who tasted her husband's blood, and even more severe penalties for 'whoever causes grain to be burnt where there is a dead man for the wellbeing of the living and the house'. The severity of both penances indicates that pre- or non-Christian beliefs (rather than strangely random behaviours) were being singled out, but there is no way of knowing exactly how they worked. There is likewise a hint of a non-Christian belief system – again, given the heavy penalties attached to it – in the tendency of women to place a 'daughter on the roof or in an oven to cure a fever'.[22]

Quite what non-Christian thought-world – or worlds – underlay these individual behaviours, however, is forever lost to us. We are largely trapped in an idealized vision of early medieval conversion as retold after the event by Bede and other Christian commentators, and many important dimensions of the actual process will always elude detailed reconstruction. But when the kinds of arguments that missionaries are reported to have used are set alongside both the stark realities of the warrior lifestyle and a few reported moments when the mask of the official story slips just a little, we can make some progress in understanding the appeal of the particular form of Christianity that was presented to different early medieval warrior constituencies between the fifth and early eighth centuries – even if the full workings of the process itself and the religious system(s) it superseded will always be substantially hidden behind Christianity's unsurpassed capacity to control the narrative.

One standard missionary tactic, which shows up in a range of sources, was to concentrate on the incoherence of rival religious teachings – something recorded in Christian texts, of course, with an in-built tendency to assume that Christianity was an inherently superior religion. For all that it is highly probable that major inconsistencies did exist in the pre-Christian religious thought of the Irish, Anglo-Saxons and Frisians – inconsistencies that Christianity, its doctrine honed over hundreds of years of written exegesis with a healthy dose of Graeco-Roman philosophy thrown in, was well placed to exploit. None of the myths and religious traditions of the Irish, Frisians, or Anglo-Saxons had been committed to writing by the time that Christian missionaries arrived, so there had been no scope for even beginning the lengthy process of turning these disparate stories into something more like systematic theology. (Just for illustrative comparison, surviving texts of the Norse myths date from the thirteenth century, after more than two hundred years of dialogue with developed Christian theologies, and they still preserve multiple strata of sometimes inconsistent belief systems.[23])

With entry-level dialectics – logical disputation – part of early medieval Christian curricula, it was entirely plausible that a trained monk could out-argue the teller of an incoherent selection of local traditions about various gods. As Bishop Daniel of Winchester advised his protégé Boniface in the early eighth century:

> Accept their statement that [their gods] were begotten by other gods through the intercourse of male and female and then you will be able to prove that, as these gods and goddesses did not exist before, and were born like men, they must be men and not gods . . . If they maintain that the universe had no beginning, try to refute their arguments and bring forward convincing proofs; and if they persist in arguing, ask them, Who ruled it? How did the gods bring under their sway a universe that existed before them? Whence or by whom or when was the

> first god or goddess begotten? Do they believe that gods and goddesses still beget other gods and goddesses? If they do not, when did they cease and why? If they do, the number of gods must be infinite. In such a case, who is the most powerful among these different gods?

The ability of the missionaries to present Christianity as a superior religious system with a much more coherent account of life, death, the universe and everything, surely gave them a powerful advantage over the competition.[24]

This was reinforced by the textual armoury with which Christian missionaries came equipped. In the modern world, anthropologists have observed the awe that writing itself can inspire among the non-literate, not least as a new technology for communicating with the divine powers at the heart of the universe. Something of the same effect can be seen in the conversion processes of the early Middle Ages. Both the Irish Ogham and Germanic runic scripts were sometimes used for religious purposes as effective mechanisms for transmitting vital messages to superhuman powers. But then Christian missionaries arrived with a religion that was fundamentally shaped and transmitted by the libraries of books they brought with them – and that was altogether more impressive. Sometimes the physical appearance of the books themselves was astounding. Writing from Frisia to sponsors back in England, Boniface asked for a copy of the Epistle of Peter written in gold letters: a cultural shock-and-awe strategy that carried the inherent extra authority of being swathed in technological superiority.[25]

More generally, Christianity – like 'democracy' and 'freedom' in the heyday of American world hegemony – could plausibly be presented as the key cultural attribute of the obviously more developed, richer and superior portion of humankind (at least, to a north European audience). As Bishop Daniel again put it to Boniface in the same letter, if the pagan gods 'are omnipotent, beneficent and just, they must reward their devotees and punish those who despise them'. Just witness, he added, how Christians were 'allowed to possess the countries that are rich in oil and wine and other commodities', while the heathens are left with 'the frozen lands of the north'. In a north European context, this message carried real force. As Boniface urged his fellow missionaries: 'heathens are frequently to be reminded of the supremacy of the Christian world and of the fact that they who still cling to outworn beliefs are in a very small minority.'[26]

Beyond its self-association with perceived and systematically projected cultural superiority, Christianity had additional attractions for kings and their elite warrior henchmen, to whom the faith was consistently sold on the basis of the power of its omnipotent God to bring victory on the battlefield. As Bishop Daniel pointed out, it was a clear sign of the unique efficacy of their God that Christians, divinely empowered to conquer rich lands, had all the best stuff, while pagans had to make do with the freezing, desolate north. (It helped, of course, that neither Boniface nor his target Frisians had the slightest knowledge of the wealth and other wonders of the contemporary, rapidly Islamicizing Near East.) Writing to King Æthelberht in a similar vein, Pope Gregory assured him that the support of the Christian God would bring him renown superior to anything that his pagan peers could possibly achieve. In selling this argument, the Old Testament was extremely helpful, featuring a God of battles who regularly smote the unrighteous. The same line was plugged in Irish contexts. The *Life* of St Columba (521–97), founder of Iona, records that the prayers of the saint, supercharged by his ascetic virtue and all-pervasive holiness, were a regular source of victory for the righteous: 'Some kings were conquered in the terrifying crash of battles and others emerged victorious according to what Columba asked of God through the power of prayer.' Drawing on older traditions, the *Life* was penned by Iona's ninth abbot Adomnán. He was famous, as we have seen, for a law attempting to limit the collateral damage of warfare, but even he had not the slightest embarrassment in supposing that the saint would have involved himself in the details of contemporary conflicts.[27]

The persuasive potential of such arguments might not have seemed immediately evident to the pagan Anglo-Saxons, who had come to dominate south-eastern Britain by defeating their Christian British neighbours. By around AD 600, however, Æthelberht's personal frame of reference in Kent, at least, was not so much the subdued, defeated Christian British to his west, as the infinitely more impressive Christian Frankish Merovingian royal dynasty across the Channel, into which he had married. Even if the king deliberately avoided getting his Christianity directly from the Franks to circumvent any obvious expression of political subordination, his wealthy southern neighbours were, nonetheless, an important frame of economic – and hence cultural – reference in the Kentish kingdom. Compared to those in other Anglo-Saxon kingdoms, Kentish cemeteries are remarkable for the prodigious quantity of gold jewellery found particularly in sixth-century burials. Kent's precocious wealth probably reflects Frankish payments for goods received (much of it, probably, in return for exported slaves). Towards the end of the century, Kentish jewellery started to follow Frankish designs, because its social elites were aping contemporary Merovingian norms. Control of cross-Channel trade routes was not only hugely important to Kent's powerful position within Anglo-Saxon England as a whole (something readily exploited by the missionaries); it exposed the kingdom directly to Frankish influence, of which Æthelberht's marriage to Bertha was only one expression.[28]

Yet, even reinforced by the additional French connection, the success-in-battle angle doesn't fully explain the attraction of Christianity for Anglo-Saxon (or indeed Irish and Frisian) kings – not least because they continued – regularly – to be killed in battle, irrespective of whether or not they had embraced the Gospel. One of Bede's greatest heroes is King Oswald of Northumbria. Born about 604, he was a member of the ruling dynasty of Bernicia, one of two originally separate kingdoms (the other being Deira) which were in the process of uniting into the kingdom of Northumbria when Augustine's missionaries arrived. In the defining moment of his royal career, in 633 or 634, as Bede recounts it, Oswald confronted an intimidating alliance of the Christian British King Cadwallon of Gwynedd and the pagan King Penda of Mercia, which had already killed two previous Northumbrian kings, just north of Hadrian's Wall, at Heavenfield near Hexham.[29] Oswald's army was small, his prospects poor. Before the battle, Oswald erected a wooden cross, holding it upright himself while the post-hole was backfilled, and praying with his army. Oswald won, of course, against the odds, and Bede lauds his piety. But a few years later, at the battle of Maserfield (possibly the site of the Shropshire town of Oswestry, though other locations have been suggested), God's help ran out: Oswald was killed by the avenging Penda of Mercia, who had re-emerged as a dominant figure in the Midlands after his defeat at Heavenfield. Not only that, but Oswald's corpse was brutally dismembered, his arms and head nailed to a board as a grisly victory trophy. (There is still an extra head in the tomb of St Cuthbert in Durham Cathedral, which may once have belonged to Oswald.) Not an ideal case study, you might be thinking, in the power of the Christian God.

Except that for Oswald, because of his religion, death was not the end of the story. Penda thought he'd won, but, as Bede presents it, striking Oswald down had just made him more powerful than the pagan king of Mercia could possibly imagine. In Book 3 of the *Ecclesiastical History*, Bede follows Oswald's death with five chapters detailing the many and varied miracles performed by the pieces of his dismembered corpse, which rapidly acquired relic status. On the spot where he had been cut down, sick animals and paralysed children were cured, the infusion of his blood making the soil so holy that it could both heal the sick and put out fires. Once identified and reassembled by his brother Oswiu in the year after his death (a potentially approximate process you might think), the king's remains gave off a heavenly glow which cured both demonic possession and mortal illness. Oswald was quickly recognized as a saint – though, reflecting the bitterness of political rivalries in Anglo-Saxon England, the monks of Bardney in Lindsey (another previously independent kingdom falling under Northumbrian control, largely covering what is now Lincolnshire) resisted accepting his remains because, although he was certainly holy, Oswald had been for them a foreign ruler.[30]

All of which suggests that the attractions of Christian belief had another, more visceral dimension for the warrior elites of north-western Europe, which went far beyond licensing escape from the violence, or anodyne (not to say undeliverable) promises of victory in battle. The story of Oswald demonstrated that a properly Christian death could be repackaged as the greatest victory of all, allowing the hero to carry on showing his glory from beyond the grave.

Christianity's teachings on death had much to recommend them. Violent death was a basic fact of life experience, which equally applied to elite women as mothers, wives, sisters and daughters of professional warriors. The priority was not in trying either to avoid death or to delay it for as long as possible (the overall futility of which is shown beautifully by the fate of Sigebert of East Anglia, dragged from his monastery to die at the hands of the pagan Penda), but to die gloriously, or at least with honour. The need to maintain honour in the face of imminent, painful extinction was fundamental to Anglo-Saxon value systems and runs through its heroic poetry. *The Battle of Maldon*, a poem written to memorialize an Anglo-Saxon defeat at the hands of some Viking raiders near the Essex town of the same name in 991, is a pretty lousy account of the actual engagement; it gives no detail on numbers, movements, or the battle's tactical/strategic significance. But we still know by name which warriors ran away from the Vikings, because the poet lovingly demonized them – named individual by named individual – for doing so. The temptation for any sane person, faced with the same fate as Oswald (and so many others), was to flee imminent extinction; the point of warrior culture was to bind fighters together in the shield wall at moments of acute stress. Knowing that your reputation might be ruined for all eternity by some wretched poet was one powerful, if negative, motivation. There were positive ones too: all the bonding over alcohol and food in the mead hall, and the ritual, cultural celebration of honour in death, was aimed at creating a band of brothers on the battlefield.[31]

As long as you forgot, or downplayed, Jesus' commands to turn the other cheek and love your enemies – or creatively redefined them, as the victorious king of Wessex did when allowing two defeated princes of the Isle of Wight to be baptized in 681 before executing them – Christianity could fit neatly enough into this highly charged emotional and cultural context. Christianity offered greater confidence to every potentially doomed warrior that dying in a state of grace – analogous to dying with honour – would lead straight to heaven. It offered a theology of salvation that had been battered into coherence through centuries of informed reflection that no pre-literate religious system could possibly match, and its overall authority was reinforced both by its books and its status as the defining creed of the more advanced, more prosperous parts of the known world. Whether you happened to win on any particular day or not was of much less importance, in other words, than the greater confidence that came with Christian conviction that dying correctly would lead to celebrated memory and the rewards of Heaven. As the thegn in Bede's sparrow scene concludes, 'If this new teaching has brought any more certain knowledge, it seems only right that we should follow it.' In this powerful sense, the new religion did not in the least undermine the prevailing values of early medieval warrior culture. Rather, it reinforced them, adding the extra promise of Christian salvation for those who faithfully held to its teachings.

The more advanced forms of literacy that came with Christianity, more capable than runes or Ogham of transforming much longer pieces of poetry and prose into permanent written form, were also soon harnessed to strengthen the memorialization of heroes, both in Ireland and England. Genealogy and heroic poetry – the bedrock of celebrated heroic memory – quickly took written form in the early Christian era on both sides of the Irish Sea, making it much more possible for the glorious memory of a Christian king or hero – as Pope Gregory promised Æthelberht – to live forever. And then there were all the new, imported genres of composition, such as Bede's *Ecclesiastical History* itself. Bede wrote self-consciously in a tradition of historical composition that stretched back to Eusebius of Caesarea's account of the pre-Constantinian Church. But his work celebrated the memory of Christian kings (not least Oswald), as well as heroic clerics, and he dedicated the *Ecclesiastical History* to Ceolwulf, the then king of Northumbria. Literate Christianity's overwhelming capacity to control the narrative in perpetuity by the production of written texts was quickly harnessed for secular as well as religious purposes in the conversion period, therefore, allowing some key warrior priorities, such as the preservation of an eternal reputation, to be pursued in new and exciting ways.[32]

For some of its new warrior constituencies, Christianity also possessed a more straightforwardly practical utility. The archaeological evidence for unprecedentedly rich barrow burials (like Sutton Hoo) and the creation of more-developed monumental centres of power (like Yeavering) adds another dimension to what Bede has to tell us about the overlordship of Æthelberht over southern England, or the emergence of a united Northumbria out of the dynastic wrangling of Bernicia and Deira.

Centralized, royal authority in Anglo-Saxon England was undergoing a general step change in the generation or so either side of the year 600, as the power of overkings began to solidify, and the number of independent local dynasties declined. This process was in no way interrupted by the arrival of Christianity. In around AD 600, Æthelberht of Kent was the most powerful of all the Anglo-Saxon kings and, in the early seventh century, overlordship seems generally to have been the preserve of kings who, like him, had immediate continental connections. Rædwald of East Anglia is said by Bede to have inherited Æthelberht's overking status. But from around the mid-seventh century, the baton of political dominance passed to the kings of more distant northern and western territories: Northumbria and Mercia initially, then eventually Wessex. By around AD 800, these 'big three' English kingdoms had subsumed within themselves all the previously politically independent kingdoms (starting with the smaller, fringe entities that barely figure in Bede's narrative, such as Hwicce and Magonsæte to the west of the Mercian heartland, but eventually including larger heptarchic kingdoms such as Sussex and Kent), with the exception of East Anglia. In addition to Bede's narrative, the charter evidence from Hwicce, preserved at Worcester, is particularly informative of the processes at work. The fundamental reason behind the success of the three greater kingdoms seems to have been that, with open borders into what were previously British territories, they were able significantly to expand their frontiers westwards and northwards in the seventh and eighth centuries. This gave their kings much more land to grant to warriors, and hence an ability to attract them in larger numbers than more restricted rivals. An ability to expand its borders, in other words, was central to a kingdom's long-term status and power. The Hwicce charters also show how this expansion impacted upon previously independent under-kings, who were forced, over time, to cede ever-greater control over their territories' internal affairs – particularly the crucial process of granting land to warriors – until their independence effectively disappeared.[33]

Christianity thus arrived in Anglo-Saxon England at a key moment in its development. A brutal and relentlessly competitive Anglo-Saxon political process, the natural extension of waves of aggressive invasion and settlement carried forward by multiple mutually competitive warbands, was limping towards new patterns of greater stability, with some of the originally numerous independent local dynasts beginning to elbow themselves more permanently above their rivals. The arrival of Christianity intersected with this developing situation on a number of levels, adding further layers to the faith's attraction for kings and their supporting cast of warrior retainers.

For Æthelberht of Kent, embracing Christianity had a straightforwardly practical advantage. Since the kingdom's precocious wealth was the result of cross-Channel connections, it made excellent sense to secure them by coming into line with the religion of its powerful southern Frankish neighbours, even if overt subordination was avoided by securing missionaries from Rome. More generally, Christianity offered a heightened form of ideological support for kingship, based on well-tried Roman models, in its proposition that successful kings were made so by the one Omnipotent Divinity, Creator of the Universe, for His own purposes. Aggrandizing in itself, this idea could also be taken to a higher level. Each of the newly converted Anglo-Saxon ruling lines of the seventh century quickly acquired its own royal saint. The cult of Oswald was carefully fostered by his brother and eventual successor, Oswiu, to cast a comforting glow of divine approbation over the entire ruling line of the newly united Northumbria, as this king's highly successful reign (*c.* 642–70) saw the definitive submergence of their former dynastic rivals from Deira. Although there are strong hints that pre-Christian Germanic ideologies of rulership also regarded successful warriors as particularly favoured by the gods, the Christian version offered a much more grandiose version of the idea. This emphasis on divinely sanctioned kingship strongly favoured more stable government through its biblically sanctioned models of how a good king should act, and even offered some practical assistance in generating heightened authority.[34]

In drawing up a law code 'after the fashion of the Romans', the newly converted Æthelberht was breaking new ground. There is nothing to suggest that pre-Christian Anglo-Saxon kings (or, indeed, pre-Christian kings in the Germanic-speaking world full stop) had ever previously issued this kind of general legal decree, although they must, of necessity, have involved themselves in resolving the disputes of their greater followers. Besides the fact that they probably didn't have the advanced forms of literacy required to produce written law codes before the missionaries arrived, law codes represented something even more significant than the impact of new writing technologies. Issuing general rulings for your subjects amounted to a major expansion in the prevailing royal job description, asserting an elevated vision of royal authority that conveniently coincided with the increase in power of at least some Anglo-Saxon ruling lines which seems already to have been underway.

Following the examples of the greatest Roman emperors and kings of the Old Testament, Christian kings were meant to spread justice across the land, not just fight successful wars. Bede records of Edwin of Northumbria that the righteousness of his rule could be measured in the fact that a woman could travel the length of his kingdom unmolested. In the long run, the combination of the missionaries' new ideologies and advanced literary technologies would be deployed in a vast array of governmental functions that helped stabilize and regularize royal power: raising revenues, administering armies, building forts and bridges, and settling legal disputes.[35] But all this took time and the fundamental character of Anglo-Saxon kingship changed only gradually. So it is not surprising to find that kings had some more immediate gains in mind when they embraced the new religion, for politics – whatever its accidental, longer-term outcomes – was, as it remains, a process fundamentally focused on short-term priorities.

Viewed from this perspective, one attraction of the new religion was that it licensed decisive action against two important local targets in this world of developing royal power. First, it directed Christian rulers to suppress non-Christian Anglo-Saxon religious cults. This was significant given the religious dimension that clearly existed to political allegiance, since different dynasts had their own favourite cults and overkings were expected to promote allegiance to their own chosen deities. Christianity, however, didn't just add the additional favoured cult of a current overking on top of everything else – a process that allowed the reassertion of older religious allegiances once any particular overking had been overthrown. On the contrary, the new faith demanded the total suppression of alternative cults forever, which, in political terms, meant suppressing one of the forces working in favour of persistent local independence over longer-term consolidation.

Something similar may also have been true of a second aspect of the developing Anglo-Saxon political process: the expansion into British territories of the west and north, which underlay the eventual dominance of the kingdoms of Northumbria, Mercia and Wessex. Though the British were Christian, they rejected – or were presented by Bede

1. An early portrayal of Constantine's vision of the cross and victory based on Eusebius of Caesarea's famous but highly misleading account of the emperor's conversion.

2. Constantine presides at Nicaea. The council inaugurated a new order of overarching imperial authority over the emerging Christian Church.

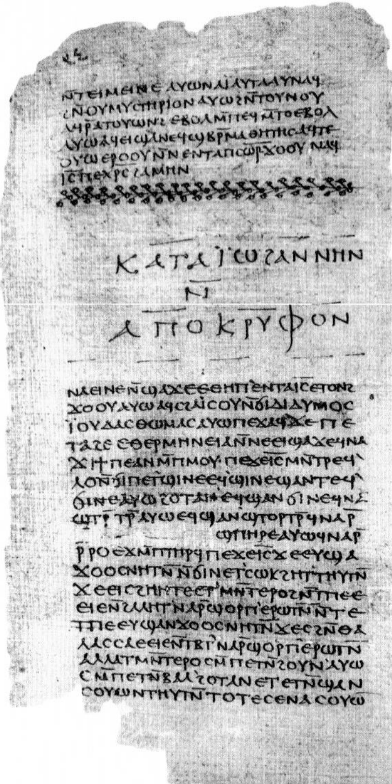

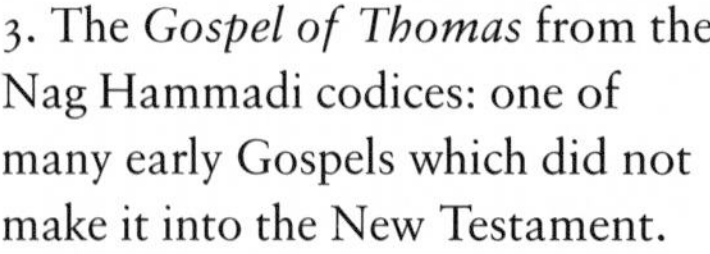

3. The *Gospel of Thomas* from the Nag Hammadi codices: one of many early Gospels which did not make it into the New Testament.

4. The imperial audience chamber from Constantine's palace at Trier; the first custom-built churches of the fourth century adopted the same basilica form.

5. Augustine's moment of desolation before his final conversion; many other contemporary converts suffered nothing like the same degree of angst.

A syncretic Egyptian magical gem of the fifth century with the traditional Ankh on one side d the sacrifice of Isaac on the other.

The Altar of Hieron II at Syracuse allowed the simultaneous sacrifice of hundreds of oxen, the nd of religious practice most abhorred by early Christians.

8. The Temple of Trajan at Pergamon – constructed by 'voluntary' subscriptions – vividly demonstrates the culturally coercive power of the Roman imperial system.

9. A cross carved into a frieze at the Egyptian temple at Philae, typical of the desecration accompanying the final suppression of traditional religion across the Mediterranean

10. Julian the Apostate's attempts to stop the rise of Christianity, utilising many of the mechanisms underpinning its success, was far from hopeless.

11. The destruction of the Serapeum in Alexandria was made possible by the previous conversion of a critical mass of the Roman provincial landowning elite.

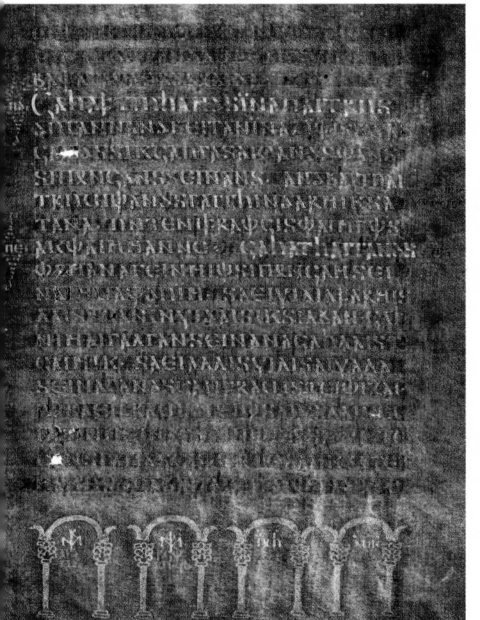

. The *Codex Argenteus* of Ulfila's Gothic ew Testament: a stunning monument to the ›werful Homoean opposition to Nicene ıristianity.

13. Theoderic's palace in Ravenna; the king and his court were originally portrayed between the pillars but 'cancelled' after Justinian's conquest of Italy.

.. The baptism of Clovis; the king adopted Nicene (rather than Homoean) Christianity as part an alliance with Constantinople late in his reign.

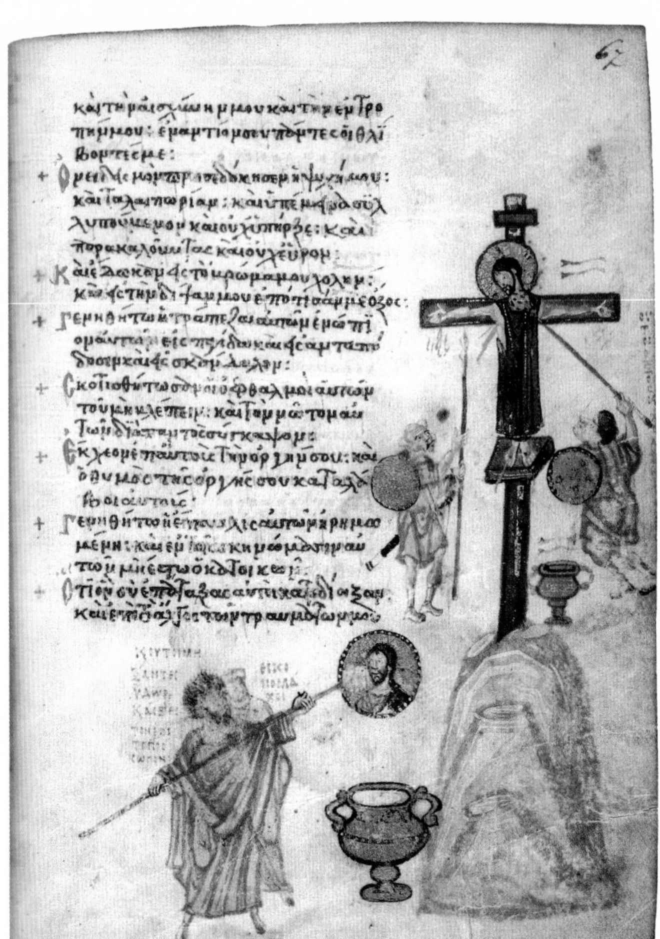

15. Iconoclasts whitewash an image of Christ; iconoclasm was one possible ideological explanation for east Rome's loss of divine favour as manifest in the Muslim conquests.

16. The front panel of the Franks Casket pairs Weland the Smith with the Magi, its inscribed texts alternating between Latin and Old English.

7. The perfect late Roman capitals of the *Codex Amiatinus*, produced in Bede's monastery, show that Anglo-Saxon scribes could follow the continental scriptorial traditions.

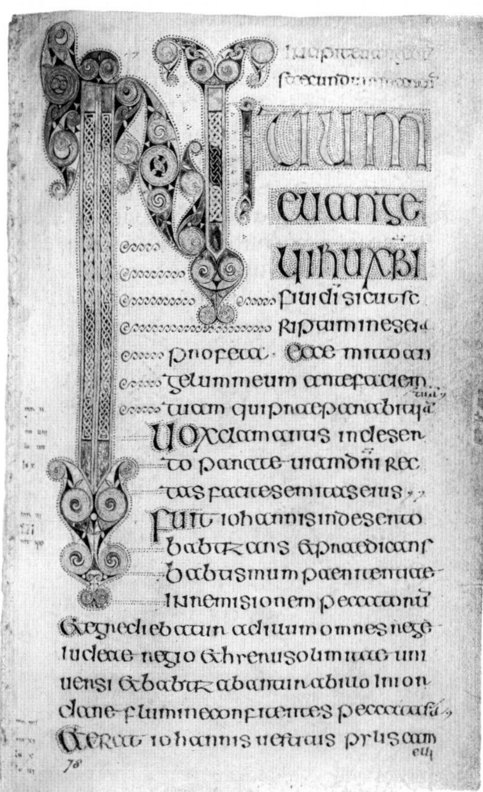

18. Overwhelmingly, however, Anglo-Saxon scribes preferred a smaller cursive script – illustrated from the Book of Durrow (*c.* AD 700) – inherited from British and Irish neighbours.

19. Originally founded in 544, Clonmacnoise was one of the great royal monastic houses of ear Christian Ireland, associated with the kings of Connacht and Meath.

20. A pilgrim presents his leg to be cured. Unknown in early Christianity, this type of religious exchange became central to Christian practice from the sixth century.

1. Ezra's book cupboard from the *Codex Amiatinus* illustrates the standard early medieval method of storing books.

22. Isidore of Seville and Braulio of Saragossa maintaine classically inspired traditions of compositional literacy but faced criticism for doing s

23. The papal spin on Christmas Day, 800: Charlemagne and Leo kneel as equals beneath St Peter; the emperor alternatively understood his crown as God's direct gift.

24. Good King Wenceslas (*d.* 935) receiving hi martyr's crown. Christianity spread largely by royal decision in this era; Wenceslas was kille for taking some of its teachings too literally.

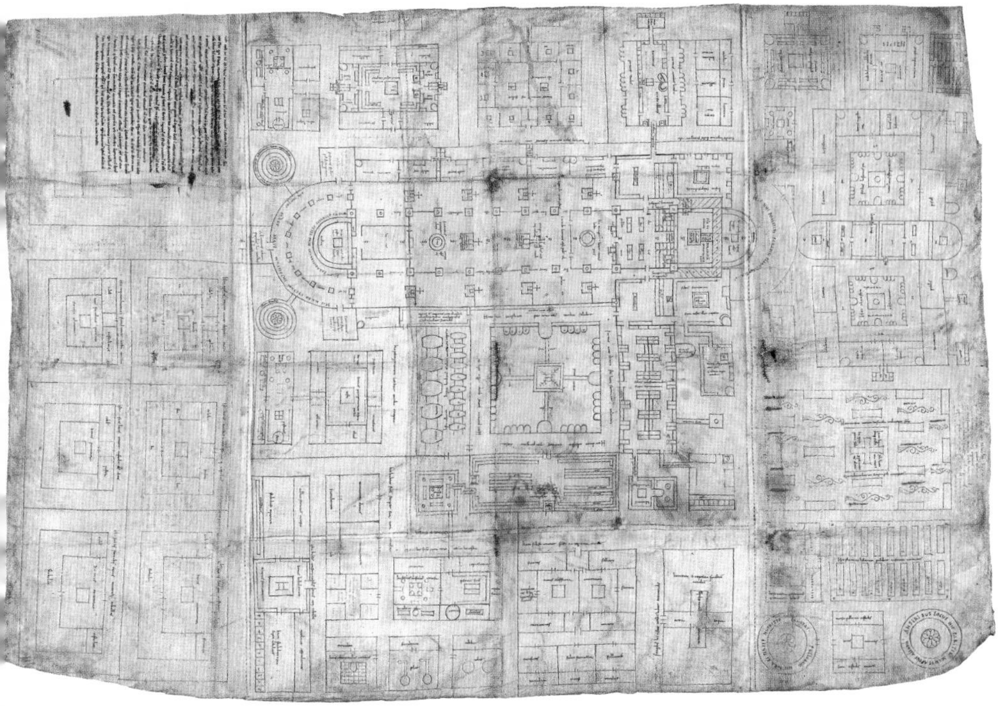

25. The *Plan of St Gall* illustrates an ideal architectural setting for the enclosed monastic life of prayer canonized in the revised *Rule of St Benedict*; it also put renewed stress on education and learning.

26. Pope Gregory VII being given refuge at Canossa, where he extracted penance from the Holy Roman Emperor Henry IV.

27. The missionaries Cyril and Methodius created the first written Slavic but became entangled in the complex international diplomacy by which Christianity spread in the ninth century.

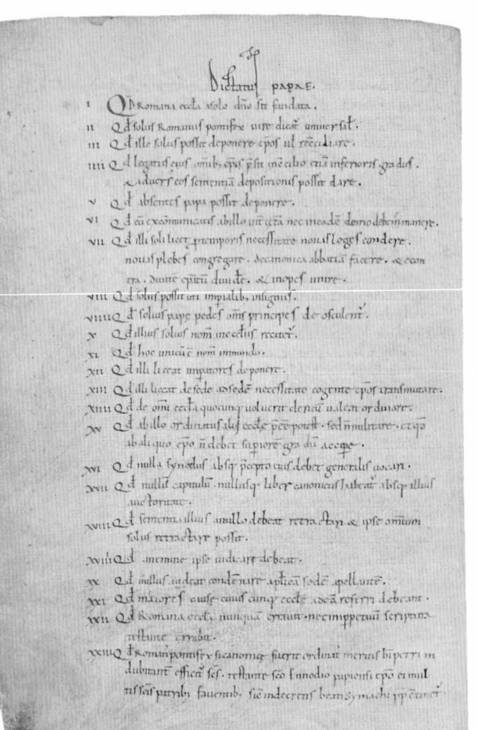

Dictatus papae.

28. The *Dictatus Papae* claimed that popes should exercise the rights which had given emperors and kings overarching religious authority since the time of Constantine.

29. Adhemar of Le Puy, with mitre and armour, outside the walls of Antioch: the crux moment when the First Crusade stood on the brink of failure.

30. Albert of Buxhoeveden – first bishop of Livonia – helped extend the crusading movement to the southern shores of the north-eastern Baltic.

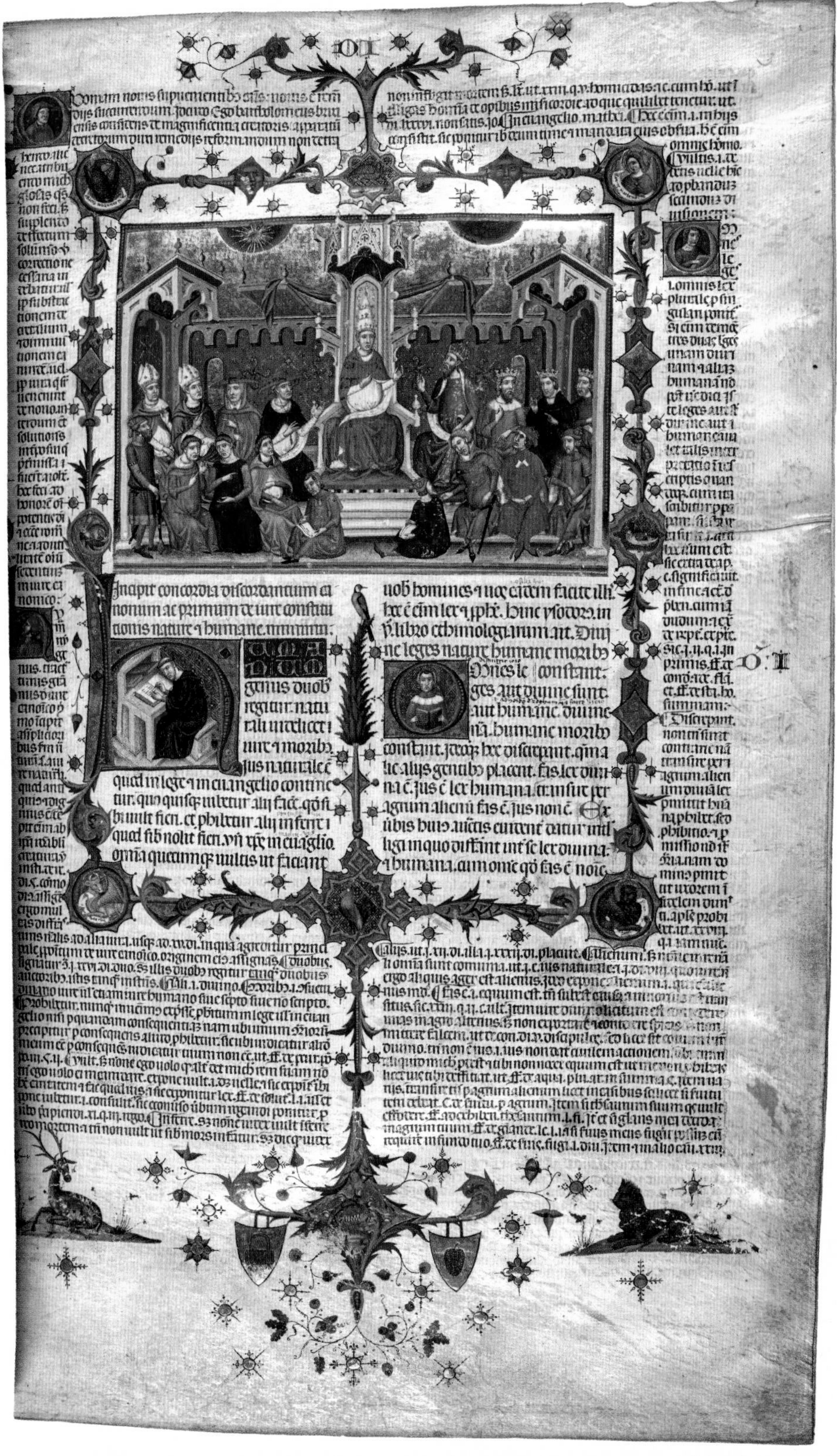

31. This fourteenth-century manuscript of Gratian's *Decretum* illustrates the text's characteristic arrangement of legal ruling at the centre and justificatory glosses around the edge.

32. The Eucharist, one of seven sacraments defined by the Parisian theologians; they combined them with Purgatory and systematized penance to revolutionize practical parish piety.

33. Peter Lombard drives a cart pulled by the seven Liberal Arts, whose study was central to the shared curriculum of Latin Europe's emerging university structure.

34. The Beguines – particularly associated with female cloth-workers in Flanders – were one of a series of new religious orders licensed in the central Middle Ages.

;. Pope Innocent III approves the *Rule* of Francis, whose innovative calling, like that : St Dominic, was to produce hundreds of ghly trained preachers.

36. Templars being burnt at the stake; Lateran IV's vision of piety was enforced not just by imaginative religious innovation but by periodic applications of extreme force.

. Montségur in the Pyrenees, last refuge of many supposed Cathar heretics; inventing and rsecuting imaginary enemies was another key component in the enforcement of Lateran IV.

38. A parish church in Romney Marsh, where surviving visitation documents illustrate how pervasive low-level informing combined with humiliating public punishment to enforce Lateran IV at parish level.

39. By the thirteenth century, marriage was one of the seven sacraments, in total contrast to ear Christianity's complete rejection of the ties and institutions of 'normal' life.

as having rejected – the legitimate archiepiscopal authority of Augustine. Their deviant form of Christianity, as Bede saw it, allowed the British to be viewed as less than 'proper' Christians – and hence legitimate targets for Anglo-Saxon expansion.

Christianity thus fitted neatly into the developing Anglo-Saxon world of the seventh century, not only at the level of the individual warrior, where death was a daily event, but by providing ideological justifications both for supressing local separatism and for continued expansion at the expense of the British.

Whether, or to what extent, Christian conversion contributed to the developing political process in Ireland is harder to say, essentially because the available narrative evidence is scant and the charter evidence non-existent. Fifth-century Ireland was a land of very small kingdoms (*tuatha*: sing. *tuath*): perhaps as many as a hundred and fifty. As in Anglo-Saxon England, these units coincided with established systems of overkingship, which, over time, generated some decline in the overall number of *tuatha* (though there were still many tens of them in the twelfth century when the Normans arrived), and some increase in the power of overkings from at least the eighth century onwards, with the emergence of four powerful regional overkingships centred on Tara (in the north), Cashel (the south), Connacht (in the north-west) and Leinster (in the south-east). That the ideologies and institutions of Christianity played some part in advancing this political consolidation, as they did in Anglo-Saxon England, is likely enough, and is suggested by some isolated examples. In particular, the ninth-century Munster overkingship of the Eóganachta dynasty at Cashel was often held by individuals who were king and, at the same time, bishop and/or abbot of the important ecclesiastical centre of Emly: a simultaneous (and entirely unique) combination of sacred and secular lordship. More generally, it is quite clear that particular monastic foundations were associated with particular royal dynasties, and participated actively (to the point of engaging in actual fighting) in processes of political competition. Unfortunately, however, the narrative material – preserved by the Annals and embedded in saints' *Lives* – is too fragmentary to support more detailed arguments.[36]

It is important, therefore, to keep a strong sense of perspective. The arrival of missionaries did not revolutionize the political process on either side of the Irish Sea. Christian kings were still killed; their law codes were routinely ignored. Mercia's dominant position in central and southern England in the eighth century was in large part due to the activities of the thoroughly pagan seventh-century Penda – nemesis of several Christian competitors until cut down by Oswald's brother Oswiu – whose career clearly owed nothing to the new religion; and very small-scale local kingships flourished in Ireland for centuries. Even without Christianity, Anglo-Saxon England would probably have come to be dominated by a smaller number of larger, more consolidated kingdoms, notwithstanding the fact that Augustine's religion offered a range of institutions and ideologies that helped push the process forward. In this important sense, therefore, the greatest significance of these related missionary drives in Britain, Ireland and Frisia was certainly religious rather than political. They successfully brought large chunks of north-western Europe to the Christian faith, and, in the process, materially changed the nature of the Christian religion itself. Once again, we come face-to-face with Christianity's astonishing capacity to remain recognizably itself while championing a transformed set of ideas and behaviours; to reinvent itself over time for a whole series of utterly alien contexts, far beyond the boundaries of first-century Palestine in which it was born.

MISSIONARY POSITIONINGS

The foundations for Christianity's transformation into a religion suitable for Irish, Anglo-Saxon and Frisian warriors were laid during its earlier transformation into the official religion of imperial Rome. Emphasis on selected passages from the Old Testament focusing on the God of Battles were used to justify claims that legitimate, divinely appointed Christian Roman emperors were bound to triumph in warfare. This political perspective was easily transferable to post-Roman kings – especially with the added proviso that, as Bede emphasized in his presentation of Oswald, God's triumph could take different forms. This was all part and parcel of the more general transformation of Christianity, away from its 'world-rejecting' roots and into a mass religion that could function in the here and now for the not-quite-so totally devout, while still retaining much of its original focus on the prime importance of the world to come.

Other adjustments made this potentially alien religious system more accessible to its new audience of north European warrior elites. Pope Gregory's original advice to Augustine and his band of brothers had apparently been to destroy all pagan shrines and temples. However, in a subsequent letter to Abbot Mellitus, a member of Augustine's original team who was following on behind the main group, the pope changed his mind. Perhaps with the violent resistance that heavy-handed Christianization had recently provoked in rural Sicily in mind, Gregory now favoured adaptation over destruction. Pagan temples in England, he advised, 'should on no account be destroyed'. They were to be rid of their idols, then cleansed with holy water, 'altars set up in them, and relics deposited there'. Pagan feast days, likewise, should be replaced with an appropriate Christian counterpart, 'such as a day of Dedication or the Festivals of the holy martyrs whose relics are enshrined there'. On such occasions, he advised, celebrants could adapt their existing rites to the new religion: 'they might well construct shelters of boughs for themselves around the churches that were once temples, and celebrate the solemnities with devout feasting.'[37] By the seventh century, there were enough saints and martyrs available to suit any occasion.

Gregory here was drawing on long-standing Christian traditions. The self-Christianization of Roman landowning elites in the fourth century had also involved a large dose of syncretism, allowing these groups to import many of their existing religious ideas and practices into a rapidly evolving Christian faith. These included some elements that stood at odds with key features of the religion's development up to that point, such as a much greater tolerance of wealth and sex, increased dependence on the classical grammarians' techniques of literary analysis, and much more authoritarian hierarchical structures. The missionary strategy now advocated for southern Britain in Gregory's letter authorized a further round of syncretic adjustment, for which the other, North African Augustine had offered a characteristically subtle justification. Since the Holy Spirit has been at work in all human societies from the beginning of time, he wrote, there will be some elements of customary religious practice everywhere that must be understood as divinely inspired, and could hence be legitimately retained in any missionary process.[38]

As an overall approach to Christian conversion, however, such syncretic strategies had one serious drawback. Repurposing old temples may have helped ease religious transition, but it also involved a potential for licensed ambiguity. Followed to the letter, Gregory's advice meant that congregations would still be gathering at the same sacred location, on the same day, and still having a religiously related party. Some participants would presumably get the point that, ideologically, the world had nevertheless changed; others would have their fingers firmly crossed behind their backs in favour of surreptitious continued worship of the old gods; and others were probably still there, as they always had been, primarily for the beer. There's actually serious doubt about whether, or to what extent, pre-Christian Anglo-Saxon religion involved recognizable temples in the old classical Mediterranean sense of the word, which Pope Gregory clearly had in mind.[39] Leaving aside the contentious issue of religious buildings, however, Christian conversion in the early medieval north-west proceeded substantially in line with the spirit of accommodation outlined in the letter to Mellitus. Similarly syncretic patterns are equally visible (in this case, without Gregory's official licence) in Ireland as in Anglo-Saxon England and can be observed in the vast majority of conversion contexts, including those in which Irish and Anglo-Saxon missionaries were operating on the European continent. In practice, there was little choice but to follow this kind of strategy whenever a handful of missionaries was tasked with converting an entire society. As a direct consequence, however, emergent, post-Roman north-west European Christianity developed its own highly specific characteristics.

Enough textual and artefactual fragments survive to demonstrate that a creative cultural dialogue lay at the heart of the north-western conversion process. It is immediately visible in some Anglo-Saxon poetic retellings of the Gospel. Part of the *Dream of the Rood*, a conversion-era Christian poem, is inscribed on the magnificent eighth-century Ruthwell Cross, which once adorned the Northumbrian village of the same name. The poem tells the story of the Crucifixion from the anthropomorphic viewpoint of the Cross itself. In it, Christ's ending, far from the abandoned, dismal demise of the ultimate scapegoat for human sin portrayed in the synoptic Gospel narratives, becomes the glorious, blood-soaked death of a heroic warrior king:

> Then the young hero made ready – that was God almighty – strong and resolute; he ascended on the high gallows, brave in the sight of many, when he wanted to ransom mankind. I trembled when he embraced me, but I dared not bow to the ground, or fall to the earth's corners – I had to stand fast. I was reared as a cross: I raised up the mighty King, the Lord of heaven; I dared not lie down. They drove dark nails through me; the scars are still visible, open wounds of hate; I dared not harm any of them. They mocked us both together; I was all drenched with blood flowing from that man's side after he had sent forth his spirit.

Another Anglo-Saxon poet refers to the Apostles as those 'Twelve mighty heroes', with St Peter becoming 'that great swordsman'. It was not until the tenth century that Anglo-Saxons stopped illustrating Christ as an armoured warrior.[40] Such images also spilled over into the Anglo-Saxon version of the Harrowing of Hell. This was an old Roman-era Christian tradition that, in the three days between Crucifixion and Resurrection, Christ had descended into Hell to release the souls of the righteous from pre-Christian times, whom the Devil had had in his grasp until that moment. It had its roots in a handful of biblical passages, but, in a ninth-century English manuscript, we find the tradition reworked as a liturgical play to be performed in a monastic context – and here again, even among monks, Christ is portrayed as a triumphant warrior king, breaking open the gates of the Devil's fortress to free righteous souls imprisoned there since the beginning of time.[41]

Beyond transforming Christ into the kind of hero that a target audience of warrior elites could readily admire, more intimate cultural parallels were also employed to make Christian messages stick: processes illustrated by the extraordinary Franks Casket, perhaps originally a reliquary, made from carved whalebone. Carefully inscribed for the most part in Old English runes, the language shifts at one point to Latin in the Roman alphabet, before – with striking virtuosity – finishing with more Latin, but now written in runic letters. Pictorially, the juxtaposition of Christian and pre-Christian is equally marked. The front panel of the casket pairs the adoration of the Magi – portrayed fairly straightforwardly, except for the addition of a bird (maybe a raven?) alongside the wise men – with a scene from the story of Weland the Smith from pre-Christian Anglo-Saxon tradition (Plate 16). What did this juxtaposition mean? As told in the Anglo-Saxon poem *Deor*, Weland was the smith of the gods, who was deliberately lamed by a mortal king who wanted to keep him captive for his skills. On the casket, Weland is portrayed with his broken leg. Beside him is a dead boy, probably the king's son, because in *Deor* the smith enacts a terrible revenge. He kills the king's son and then gets the boy's sister drunk so that he can rape her. The daughter is apparently on the panel, too, being offered a drink from her brother's skull. But why and how exactly were Weland and the Magi put together conceptually? There are competing interpretations, but the fundamental point – even if we will never be able to fathom every aspect of this pagan-Christian connection – is that the casket offers us a tantalizing glimpse of a missionary era, one in which all kinds of conceptual parallels and analogies were being exploited to make Christian teachings accessible to a new audience.[42]

The capacity to make such parallels and exploit them for religious ends must have grown over time, as the original missionaries learned the native languages and deepened their understanding of Anglo-Saxon and Irish cultures – and, especially, once native convert recruits were added to their ranks. In the case of the Anglo-Saxons, very little extra Christian manpower came from Rome after the initial group of clergy accompanying Augustine. The process of conversion was quickly taken over by local converts, who were better placed to make the kind of analogies and equations between the new religion and older belief structures that we see illustrated on the Franks Casket, and which turned Christ and the Apostles, more generally, into a heroic warband. Not only were such recruits capable of making syncretic equations themselves, but they were clearly also being trained primarily by Irish (and perhaps some British) clergy, who had presumably already been making their own syncretic connections. This doesn't show up so clearly in Bede's narrative, which focuses primarily on Augustine and the contribution of the Roman mission. But the literary culture of early Christian England tells a clear story. Some early Anglo-Saxon Christian scribes were perfectly capable, when they wanted to, of producing texts that directly followed the scriptorial norms of Mediterranean Latin

Christianity. A classic case in point is the *Codex Amiatinus*, a complete manuscript of the Bible from Bede's monastery of Monkwearmouth–Jarrow, produced in his own lifetime. It is written in perfect late Roman capitals (Plate 17) and closely followed an Italian model. In the majority of cases, however, Anglo-Saxon Christian scribes used a smaller, cursive script that they inherited directly from Irish and – perhaps less directly – British Christianity (see Plate 18). Palaeographically, therefore, Anglo-Saxon England formed part of a distinct insular world, which operated with entirely different norms to its continental Christian peers, something which did not begin to change until the tenth century. All of which emphasizes how, after the first generation at least, direct Roman influence on developing Anglo-Saxon Christianity was much less important than that of the Irish (and perhaps the British).[43]

The creative evangelism of these predominantly native north European missionaries affected not just the presentation of the Christian message, but also its form and content. In Ireland, Christianity's long-standing ascetic traditions were reinvented in a highly idiosyncratic form. Monasteries of a more familiar type existed there (on which more in a moment), but Irish Christianity also threw up the particular ascetic tradition of eternal pilgrimage for the love of Christ (*peregrinatio pro amore Christo*), in which individuals committed themselves to a life not only of asceticism – harsh disciplinary regimes were also part of the package – but to constant (or at least regular) movement, refusing to allow themselves to become comfortable in any particular environment. Early Irish society was constructed around powerful local kinship structures, which provided the individual with status and protection. To lose them was to put yourself utterly at risk, as a kind of outlaw. Hence, being forcibly evicted from your kin group was among the most severe penalties that an offending individual might face. In this context, voluntarily giving up protection and status for the love of God was a sign of the greatest devotion. Contemporary sources record a string of self-exiling Irish ascetics appearing among the Anglo-Saxons and Franks from the late sixth century onwards. They sometimes generated considerable consternation, since the contemporary norms of western monasticism at this time more often stressed the importance of a geographically stable life within the single monastery (see p. 58). The particularities of Irish Christianity, moreover, also extended into matters of belief, one of which concerned a flexible reading of the Harrowing of Hell.

Whereas the Anglo-Saxon monastic version of the Harrowing of Hell stayed firmly within the bounds of Christian orthodoxy in imposing strict limits on the number of souls that Christ released from the Devil's embrace – mainstream Christian tradition usually thought in terms of just a few famous biblical patriarchs and prophets, along with a handful of other especially righteous individuals – the same tradition was sometimes mobilized in a less authorized form to calm a key concern of many converts. The missionaries' target audience of warrior elites based much of its concept of status on lineage and ancestry: the idea that, in embracing Christianity and ensuring their own passage to Heaven they might be separating themselves for eternity from their non-Christian ancestors, was clearly an issue for them. (On being told that his unbaptized ancestors were confined to Hell forever, the Frisian king Radbod supposedly told his missionaries to forget baptism, since he preferred the company of his ancestors in Hell to that of the Heavenly Host.) But we know of at least one Irish missionary – a certain Clemens, encountered on the continent by the Anglo-Saxon missionary Boniface – who reworked the Harrowing of Hell to assure potential converts that Christ had freed all 'good men' – much more broadly defined – from Hell, baptized or not.[44] Boniface eventually had Clemens condemned as a heretic, but we don't know how many he had already successfully converted on the basis of his alternative teachings. In any case, the Irishman was surely not alone in resolving some of the inherent issues of conversion by bending older Christian traditions in a more flexible direction.

Such moments – whether found in texts, reported personal encounters, or material objects – when the mask of the official conversion story slips, offer glimpses of the real story of the dynamic mutual interaction between Christianity and indigenous cultural tradition that unfolded as the faith took hold either side of the Irish Sea and the Channel between the fifth and seventh centuries. People weren't just converted to a fixed form of Christianity: the religion itself was transformed in important ways to make it more accessible to its new target audience. All we have from this early medieval process of adjustment is a series of isolated incidents, which have survived

Christianity's otherwise overwhelming capacity for narrative control. Better documented, more modern case studies of the kind of mutual transformation that is so often such a central feature of actual religious conversion on the ground offer serious food for thought about what was really going on in the post-Roman north-west.

An excellent example is provided by the so-called 'African Initiated Churches', religious movements in modern South Africa that began with foreign, largely European missionaries in the colonial era, but which from the 1920s onwards (like developing Anglo-Saxon Christianity after the early decades of the seventh century) were taken over by indigenous converts. By 1991, the membership of such churches amounted to 9.2 million people, or 47 per cent of all baptized Christians in South Africa. All these churches share much in common with each other, and, of course, draw heavily on the ancestral colonial Christian roots from which they sprang. But according to their own pre-existing, culturally specific understandings of human spirituality and the nature of divine power, and of how these different lines of force might interact, individual Church communions have simultaneously spun off along their own particular trajectories. 'Lady bishops', for instance, have long been a feature of some of those local Christianities in which women had long played a central role in negotiating human interactions with the divine, such as the Zionist Apostolic Churches. Cultural heritage has also had significant effects upon the creative reception of even what would seem the most basic of Christian tenets. The AmaNazaretha Church, which operates in Zulu territories, not only continues to allow polygamy, but also – responding to the norms of a Zulu culture which accords sons no autonomous importance while their fathers are still alive – has evolved over time to downplay the religious significance of the figure of Jesus, even adjusting its basic creed to exclude any reference to the Son:

> I believe in the Father
> And in the Holy Spirit
> And in the Communion
> Of Saints of the Nazarites.[45]

Applying this kind of broader perspective to early medieval north-western Europe, it's unsurprising that the missionaries' syncretic approach initiated an extended, creative dialogue – as it had earlier in Roman contexts – about precisely which pre-Christian religious values and practices might legitimately be retained, and to what extent, and at what points the Gospel could be adapted to suit local audiences.

While different specific answers were clearly offered at different moments in different localities by different missionaries, some general patterns emerge. The missionaries, of course, had their official doctrinal red lines – though 'converts' did not always or immediately recognize them. King Rædwald of East Anglia wanted to add Christ to his existing pantheon of gods, while the two sons of King Sæberht of Essex didn't see why they couldn't receive communion while continuing to sacrifice to the old gods. Such unreconstructed syncretism is straightforwardly condemned by Bede, but it's highly likely that Christianity, especially early on, was often viewed as an add-on in cultures used to multiple divine powers. In Kent, it wasn't until the mid-seventh century, under King Earconberht (*c.* 640–64), that idol worship was formally banned, two generations after Augustine's arrival, while Kentish and Wessex law codes of the 690s still felt it necessary, a century after the missionaries appeared, to punish 'sacrificing to devils'. That many people held multiple, apparently contradictory religious allegiances for much of the seventh century is also suggested by some of the surviving material evidence, such as the Franks Casket, which would have been meaningless had not the Weland stories still been circulating when it was created in the early eighth century; or the helmet found in a seventh-century Anglo-Saxon burial site at Benty Grange, Derbyshire. The helmet combines a boar crest – long associated with pre-Christian gods of war (such as Freyr and Freya in later Norse tradition) – with a series of cross-engraved plates. For warriors facing violent death, hedging your bets – or perhaps better: maximizing sources of potential divine assistance – was a self-evidently sensible move.[46]

More generally, despite a documented trickle of outliers like the Mercian Guthlac or King Sigebert of East Anglia, who rejected the life of the warrior for Christian monasticism, adopting Christianity involved surprisingly little direct challenge – in overall terms – to the basic value systems of the warrior elites of north-western Europe. At a macro level, as we've seen, God and His saints were regularly co-opted via prayer into the struggle for victory, while, at the level of the individual, the new religion made no attempt to challenge traditional, feud-defined concepts of honour. As is often the case in more or less stateless societies, prevailing honour codes among the Anglo-Saxons required all members of a kin group (defined by blood, marriage and association) to support one another in the face of harm inflicted by, or dispute with, a member of a different group, even to the point of being willing to inflict violence and death. The written law codes of early Christian Ireland and of Anglo-Saxon kings (the latter certainly penned by Churchmen, whose leaders were prominent in the attendance lists at the meetings which generated them) sometimes attempted to regulate the extent of feud-based dispute, but they never challenged its basic premise that kin collectives were honour-bound to resort to violence, if necessary, to support any of their fellow members. This relatively lenient approach to violence in practice coexisted with a developed strand within Christian Irish ecclesiastical writing that condemned all kinds of violence outright: its vehemence perhaps a reflection of the extent to which Irish Churchmen were having to live with this warrior culture as an unavoidable feature of their everyday lives.[47]

On the other side of the Irish Sea, simultaneously, emergent Anglo-Saxon literary culture – genealogies, myths, heroic poetry, probably all of which were written by educated Christian clergy – actually reinforced warrior values. As we have seen, literacy was used to build up a corpus of written versions of traditional and more recent tales – everything from *Beowulf* to *The Battle of Maldon* was still circulating in tenth-century Anglo-Saxon England – which memorialized and transmitted warrior values in more permanent forms than any of the oral versions that presumably preceded them. These cultural products didn't just passively reflect the values of the Anglo-Saxon military elite; they played a positive role in moulding behaviour. You wanted to be as much like Beowulf as possible, the great slayer of demonic monsters, so that some wretched armchair poet couldn't damn your reputation forever by recording that you had run away at the crunch moment of battle, like Odda's son Godric at Maldon against the Vikings in 991.[48]

Warrior values even began to insinuate themselves into the lifestyles of local Christian clergy and the emergent Church's institutional structures. The seventh-century Anglo-Saxon Bishop Wilfrid of Northumbria travelled the country with his own retinue of 120 warriors ready and willing to fight for him – as they did on one occasion in Sussex, remembered in his *Life*, when Wilfrid was praying piously for their success behind the shield wall. The bishop also fiercely resisted the subdivision of his huge see, which originally covered the entire kingdom of Northumbria (at that point stretching far north and west into the Scottish Borders), even though it would have made for more effective pastoral care to have several bishops at work over such a large area. This wasn't just vainglory. Wilfrid required extensive revenues to maintain his retinue and the other trappings of elite status – like his famous treasure hoard of gold, silver and precious gems held in his church at Ripon – which allowed him effectively to project himself as a formidable man of power in Anglo-Saxon society. And who's to say that, at this stage, Wilfrid's public persona did not represent a more effective display of the authority of the new Christian religion in the eyes of most people than Guthlac's self-imposed, impoverished isolation among the British-speaking demons of Croyland.[49] In many ways, Wilfrid is but a step away from the Eóganachta kings of Munster who were simultaneously abbots and/or bishops – another striking illustration of the very particular forms that Christianity could adopt as part of an extended missionary process.

Another aspect of warrior culture profoundly shaped the nature of Christian spirituality as it evolved in the aftermath of conversion. Christ commanded His followers to love their enemies, an injunction that took on complex resonances within feud-based honour systems in which violence was endemic. The act of killing within such systems – at least, killing anyone of equal status to yourself – was never without consequences, and usually had to be compensated for in some way. This normally took the form of paying off injured parties, usually relatives of the dead person, for damages they had suffered – often conceptualized as remedying likely losses of potential future income from the deceased family member, rather than as suffering punishment for what we would now consider the crime of murder. Indeed, in general terms, theft tended to be subject to much greater penalties, since killing – at least if done openly – was a basically honourable act (a 'fair fight' in Hollywood Western terms), whereas theft involved taking someone else's possessions in an underhand manner.[50] Because it was impossible for Christianity to condemn violence outright in such cultural contexts, a whole new mechanism evolved for defining and dealing with some of the inescapable elements of religious transgression inherent in the lives of Christianity's warrior converts.

The process began in Ireland. In Irish law codes of the early Christian era, the traditional compensation payment that had long been offered after a killing acquired a second component: compensating the Church for the offence given to God.[51] This was a workable compromise; existing value systems were stretched to accommodate some element of sin without any outright condemnation of the killer, or their total expulsion from the ranks of the faithful. Nor were the recommended compensations for killing generally that fierce. Irish texts recommended the strikingly low penance of one week's fasting on bread and water for a layman who admitted plotting to kill another, and not much more for one who actually committed the act. Across the Irish Sea, Archbishop Theodore of Canterbury took a tougher line, recommending seven to ten years' penance for various types of killing – but this was again reduced to just a forty-day exclusion from the Church for a layman who had been ordered to kill by his lord, and was hence acting according to the demands of prevailing honour codes. As late as the turn of the ninth century, the monk-scholar Alcuin of York (in other contexts, as we shall see, a noted ecclesiastical reformer) wrote in defence of a murderer, absolving him of crime because the killing avenged the death of the man's former king.[52] Against this backdrop, it is perhaps not so surprising that, as Bede reports it, a key reason for the murder of King Sigebert of Essex in the mid-seventh century is that he was far too ready to forgive his enemies (and one of his two assassins was himself a baptized Christian).[53]

A surprisingly lenient attitude to killing is only one feature of the new form of Christian spirituality which developed to serve the needs of north European warriors. More generally, the conversion process applied the idea of appropriate compensation – central to the operation of feud – to a wide range of potential transgressions of God's law. It found written expression in a brand-new Christian genre: the penitential. First created in sixth-century Ireland, it quickly spread to the Anglo-Saxon world, which produced one seventh-century manual of its own, ascribed to Archbishop Theodore.

The idea of penance was not a new one, but penance in pre-Constantinian Christianity had been public and humiliating, and not necessarily available for purging every kind of sin (see p. 48). In the late Roman period, penance seems to have become both more private and less ferocious, but no Churchman of that era ever produced lists of sins with appropriate compensatory acts. This new Christian genre was a counterpart of the kind of written law code that tended to be generated in warrior societies post-conversion (like that of Æthelberht), which again concentrated on compensation for damage, rather than crime and punishment. The penitential consisted of long lists of spiritual remedies, downgraded punishment for the kinds of violent transgression to which warriors were prone, and introduced a new range of appropriate punishments. Different authors within the developing genre prescribed a wide (and contradictory) variety of penitential acts, with plenty of bread and water and Church exclusion thrown in, some even allowing monetary payments or the acts of a substitute to work off the spiritual consequences of transgressive acts. This new penitential approach to the problem of sin was destined to play a central role in the broader spiritual rhythms of later medieval Christendom, but its origins lay in the intrusion of the cultural values of north European warriors into Christianity.

Alongside these processes of ideological accommodation, kings and their henchmen also found ways to mobilize imported Christian institutions to advance their interests, in the process transforming those institutions. In his lengthy *Letter to Egbert*, bishop of York, of 734, Bede complained about Northumbrian aristocrats who had been buying land from the crown over the previous few decades to set up what he calls 'false' monasteries. They had been doing so because monasteries represented a lucrative, stable investment opportunity for the aristocrats' considerable moveable wealth. Not only was any 'monastic' land subject to fewer royal dues than the nobles' other estates, but it also represented an entirely new form of completely private property in late seventh-century Anglo-Saxon aristocratic society. Up to this point, elite land seems to have been owned collectively by kin groups, its transmission between the generations governed by customary tradition. In legal terms, any current holder of an estate only possessed a life interest in it and could not dictate what would happen after their death, meaning – among other things – that if you fell out with your children, you could not disinherit them. But monasteries (and Church institutions in general) operated within Roman laws of property. These were based on a much stronger concept of absolute private ownership, giving the beneficiary not only a life interest in, but the right to dispose of an asset in any way they chose (sale, inheritance, whatever). In this context, founding monasteries opened up an attractive investment opportunity for Anglo-Saxon elites, which they proceeded to exploit with gusto, even to the point, sometimes, of disinheriting their children; one eighth-century Church council had to deal with the case of little Bucge, whose grandmother had made her the heir and abbess to the monastery she had founded, much to the annoyance of an intervening daughter.[54]

Such had been the aristocratic rush into monastic foundation throughout Northumbria over the preceding thirty years, Bede's letter complains, that its king was now running short of the landed resources that had previously been distributed as life leases to reward younger warriors. In fact, it seems that 'unsatisfactory' would be a fairer label than 'false' for these monastic foundations. Bede went on to admit that the new institutions weren't entirely bogus: some kind of religious life was pursued within them. His main gripe was that the founder-purchasers, while styling themselves abbots, continued to be married – something that horrified the ascetic Bede. All the same, the overall process clearly shows us Anglo-Saxon warrior elites repurposing Christian monasticism, surely in part to save their souls, but also because it provided them with an attractive way to manage their worldly wealth. All of which underscores that conversion was in practice about so much more than importing new views of sin, life and death. (The letter also shows, more generally, that even such a devoted Christian monk as Bede had no problem with the basic idea that kings should be granting land to deserving warriors.)[55]

At a higher social level, moreover, Anglo-Saxon royal dynasties had been founding private monasteries for their own purposes for even longer. From about the 670s onwards – a generation or so before the aristocratic foundations which so annoyed Bede – there is charter evidence, particularly from the kingdom of Hwicce, which shows a local, currently still independent royal line establishing its own, grander monastic foundation. At the level of royal dynasties, monastic foundation seems to have operated as a type of insurance policy. By this date, the projection of Mercian hegemony outwards from its original core territories in the Midlands was already threatening to demote the lesser rulers of some surrounding territories – such as the Hwicce – from princely independence to the status of subordinate regional aristocrats within a greater Mercia. In the case of the Hwicce, the process took about a century to unfold fully, its stages marked by the ruling dynasty having to hand over more and more control of a series of important rights over different categories of land, until the former kingdom's independence was completely eroded. In such a context, 'banking' a portion of your dynastic endowment under a new Roman legal umbrella, by acquiring private hereditary rights over new monastic foundations, which were much harder for the increasingly dominant Mercian overkings to touch – made excellent sense. But, like the aristocratic monasteries of Northumbria, these new foundations were straying a considerable distance from established mainstream monastic tradition, which was supposed to focus, via a life of poverty and sexual renunciation, on individual spiritual responses to the love of God (p. 58).[56]

In early medieval Ireland, too, monasticism involved far more than an ascetic response to the love of God. Large-scale monastic foundation is recorded from the sixth century onwards, and, by the time more detailed evidence survives, important houses were often headed and controlled by important dynastic networks. No other abbots, apart from those of the Eóganachta-controlled monastery of Emly, are simultaneously recorded exercising royal functions, but many known Irish abbots were of royal lineage – not least St Columba, the founder of Iona, who had close connections to the UíNéill overkings of the north of Ireland. Scholarship, sanctity and pastoral care were part of the Irish monastic job description, but well-connected abbots of important monasteries often feature in the surviving sources as major political players, and Irish monasticism as a whole clearly followed an overall trajectory of development that took it far from the norms of the eastern Mediterranean where Christian monasticism was born.[57]

None of this should be taken to mean that Christianization was a one-way street of exciting new opportunities for elite north-west European converts. Many elements of established Christian practice were adapted to accommodate immovable features of their lives, but conversion to Christianity nonetheless demanded major changes. The old gods had – eventually – to go; new dimensions of transgression and compensation entered their lives. There were major consequences, too, for another key dimension of elite life: marriage. Marriage at the elite level was always about much more than true love; exchanging and combining parcels of land to create political alliance and sufficient income to sustain a viable new elite household with its likely offspring was always central to matrimonial calculation. By AD 600, Christianity – with its deeply rooted sensitivities on the subjects of sex and marriage – had long since evolved monogamous marriage norms, which not only banned multiple simultaneous liaisons, but disapproved of remarriage after the death of a partner, and defined incest much more broadly than anything required to minimize the dangers of genetic disaster. But in many northern Germanic societies – to judge by queries sent to different popes by both Augustine from Kent, and Boniface from east of the Rhine a century later – so complicated was the problem of putting together such parcels of land that it was normal to maximize the lifespan of existing marriage settlements (and of any associated political alliance) by agreeing to supply (presumably as part of the original agreement) an appropriate replacement should one of the original partners die prematurely. Hence both Augustine and Boniface encountered what is sometimes labelled levirate marriage (the term being a derivative of the Latin *levir*: 'husband's brother'): a younger brother marrying a widowed sister-in-law, or a stepson marrying his father's second, third, or even fourth wife. And although no written sources report that pre-Christian Anglo-Saxons were polygamous, they may well have been. Several continental Germanic-speaking societies of this era recognized various forms of legitimate sexual partnership, broadly categorized by whether and how much property had changed hands, and also accepted that some of these different forms of partnership might be pursued simultaneously.[58]

In this context, Christianity's prescriptive marriage laws presented something of an inconvenience to the newly converted elites of north-western Europe, although Anglo-Saxon and Irish society responded in different ways. In England, there were early teething troubles: Æthelberht's son Eadbald apostatized briefly to marry his father's widow (not the Frankish princess Bertha, his birthmother, who had predeceased her husband, but her successor). Maintaining the alliances created by that later marriage clearly seemed more important to him at the moment of succession (when a king was always at his most vulnerable) than remaining Christian. And the otherwise reportedly good Christian King Sigebert of Essex was cursed by the Irish-trained Northumbrian monk-bishop Cedd for feasting with one of his retainers who had been excommunicated for a forbidden marriage.

By the end of the seventh century, however, the Anglo-Saxon elite had come broadly into line, a transition that may have been helped by the founding of the new monastic tax havens. A perennial problem for all elite families with a finite stock of land was that over-division of its assets over time among too many heirs might reduce holdings to blocks of land that were economically incapable of supporting the family's continued elite status (status distinctions among free Anglo-Saxons – and the Irish too – were universally defined by the size of an appropriate landed holding). Another use of monastic foundations, therefore, was to provide an alternative and potentially more permanent method of creating appropriately sized blocks of landed assets than older habits of marriage-partner replacement. Monasteries also provided a series of suitable homes for offspring, male and female, who were currently surplus to family breeding requirements. Such individuals could now be supported economically, perhaps given the interesting job of abbot or abbess, roles which (in theory at least) also had the useful effect of prohibiting them from producing offspring to make additional claims on a family's landed assets. Christian monasticism and Christian marriage laws might even be mobilized in tandem, therefore, to manage familial assets in the new cultural context. This did not, however, resolve all the potential issues. Accidents of mortality meant that some of those placed in monasteries when deemed surplus to familial requirement had later to be recalled to dynastic duty from their devotions to God. Christian tradition, however, viewed monastic vows as irrevocable, and extracting heiresses from monasteries remained a documented complaint of Churchmen well into the eighth century.[59]

The Irish, by contrast, generally took a more straightforward approach, which makes Cedd's cursing of otherwise good King Sigebert seem all the more brutal. The same Clemens who took such a creative approach to the Harrowing of Hell also saw no problem with levirate marriage, which figures regularly in the Old Testament: a text which might be considered an entirely legitimate source of advice for believing Christians. Boniface condemned Clemens for this as well, but it is likely that levirate marriage persisted for lengthy periods in continental conversion contexts. In Ireland itself, things could be simpler still. Polygamy remained effectively legitimate, especially for kings, albeit sometimes morphing into a pattern of serial monogamy licensed by divorce laws, thereby contradicting the increasing emphasis in the marriage doctrines of more mainstream Christianity upon sanctity and indissolubility. Here again the Old Testament could be trundled out in justification – after all, Solomon had seven hundred wives and three hundred concubines – and Christian Irish kings continued to marry multiple wives down to the twelfth century.[60]

CHURCH AND PEOPLE

Most of the surviving source material from this related cluster of conversions reflects Christianity's interaction with the warrior elites of north-western Europe. But if these were the missionaries' initial target audience – without their support, any larger-scale success would have been impossible – they were also looking to spread the Gospel throughout the population, and to create a broader Church structure to service its religious needs. What kind of organization had emerged by the early eighth century – the end of the original conversion period – and to what extent had it taken root among the people?

At the top end of the new Anglo-Saxon Church structure, an expanded network of bishoprics eventually emerged. Pope Gregory's original design, based on the defunct administrative patterns of old Roman Britain, was for two archbishoprics – Canterbury and York – each with twelve dependent dioceses. Anglo-Saxon England never achieved that level of episcopal density, but by around 700, a century after Augustine's arrival, a dozen bishops were in post across the different Anglo-Saxon kingdoms. Their establishment was substantially the work of one remarkable individual: Archbishop Theodore of Canterbury. A native of Tarsus in what is now Turkey, he fled seventh-century Islamic expansion, journeying west to Rome; from there he eventually moved on to Kent, arriving in 669 at the grand old age of sixty-six. Over the next twenty-one years, he worked tirelessly to revolutionize the upper echelons of an Anglo-Saxon ecclesiastical network that had grown up haphazardly over the previous seventy years. On Theodore's arrival, Wilfrid was the sole bishop of an undivided see of Northumbria, and only three other bishops were in post across the whole of Anglo-Saxon England (one of whom – Wine of London – had to be more or less immediately deposed because of irregularities surrounding his election). After four years of information gathering, Theodore was ready to act. Calling a Church council at Hertford in 673, Theodore and his by then four fellow bishops enacted a series of measures to regularize and strengthen ecclesiastical hierarchies. This included subdividing the vast bishopric of Northumbria – hitherto resisted by the stubbornly aristocratic Wilfrid – and recasting York as a metropolitan archbishopric in charge of three other north English sees.

While it took another decade of wrangling for the resulting dispute with Wilfrid to be settled (in 686/7), Hertford was a decisive step towards generating a more pastorally effective ecclesiastical structure. While the dozen or so bishoprics of the mid-eighth century were divided between politically separate kingdoms, they had continued to adhere to Theodore's broader vision (minuted in the proceedings of Hertford) of maintaining some sense of corporate identity via periodic meetings over the subsequent decades. While just four sets of actual canons – episcopal conciliar rulings – have come down to us from Anglo-Saxon England between the later seventh and early ninth centuries (at which point, Viking raiding began seriously to disrupt normal business), we know there were more. Additional meetings are referred to incidentally in charters – the title deeds of monastic and cathedral communities – because one of the regular concerns of such councils was to settle property disputes involving ecclesiastical institutions. Other more generally important business was also covered: a synod held at the unidentifiable Clofesho in 747, for instance, laid down much stricter standards of expected behaviour for priests. Moreover, as councils became more regular in the late eighth century, they evolved into major ecclesiastical events. Accompanying the twelve bishops who gathered at the synod of Chelsea, in 803, for instance, were seventy-eight abbots, priests and deacons.[61]

The main job of a bishop was not to provide primary religious care in person, but to supervise the work of ordinary priests working with the mass of peasant producers who made up the bulk of the population. Over the seventh century, a structure of local pastoral care began to emerge across Anglo-Saxon England to bring the new faith to the mass of the population. In the documents of the era, these new religious institutions are referred to in Latin as *monasteria* – 'monasteries' – but for the most part they were not monasteries in the generally understood medieval sense of that term.

Some 'normal' monasteries had come into existence by the start of the eighth century. Bede lived in one: the double monastery of Monkwearmouth–Jarrow, established by Benedict Biscop (*c.* 628–90). Biscop was a Northumbrian noble who abandoned the secular life for the cloister. Making five separate visits to Rome, he established his own monastic foundation after the pattern of those he had observed on his journeys. By the early 700s, as close study of the literary resources Bede drew upon in his many writings has made clear, Monkwearmouth–Jarrow was home to six hundred brethren and the largest library of Anglo-Saxon England. (This weighed in at over two hundred books, substantially based on the many texts which its founder had brought back with him from his travels.) The reported number of brethren might have included dependent peasant tenants, but, even if so, the economic demands of such an establishment were still formidable. Assuming that it housed six hundred monks, exclusive of peasant tenantry, creating a monastery of this size was a bit like stationing a large Roman military unit on some undeveloped part of the frontier. An entire local economy would have to be restructured to provide for its needs. Monastic diets required unusual foods, including a great deal of fish to satisfy fasting requirements (in particular the avoidance of meat). Besides which, there were all the raw materials needed for copyists and authors – not least the formidable Bede himself, who, in thirty years of active composition, produced over sixty works in a wide variety of genres.[62] By this date, the Wiltshire settlement of Malmesbury, in southern England, had emerged as a second major monastic centre of Christian learning in the Anglo-Saxon world. Named after its founder, the Irish scholar-saint Máeldub, it quickly established a significant reputation and produced Aldhelm (*c.* 639–709), early Anglo-Saxon England's only serious rival to Bede as a Christian intellectual. The major archiepiscopal cathedral complexes of Canterbury and York were likewise home to monastic communities which developed into centres of Christian intellectual excellence, due in no small measure to their Roman connections. Both Augustine at the beginning and Theodore of Tarsus came to Canterbury fully armed with key religious books, which were copied and passed on to York and Northumbria as the mission spread its wings. Best estimates suggest nevertheless that the York, Canterbury and Malmesbury collections were probably only about half the size of the library which Bede so enjoyed.[63]

The vast majority of the new *monasteria*, however, were rather different, much more modest establishments: centres for small teams of itinerant priests. These men lived a collegial, and semi-monastic, existence. Though they had some time for study and prayer, the bulk of their lives was devoted to travelling around the districts under their care to provide pastoral guidance for the new Christian flocks of Anglo-Saxon England. Hence, in the scholarly literature, these institutions have come to be known as minster (from *monasterium*) churches. Perhaps surprisingly, apart from an early initiative in Kent which seems to have led nowhere, this growing network of local churches does not seem to have been established primarily by the bishops who were certainly responsible for some oversight of the priests' work. Many of these early minsters were royal foundations. King Oswiu of Northumbria founded twelve of them across his kingdom in thanks for his final victory over the resolutely pagan King Penda of Mercia in 655. Oswiu's predecessor and older brother, Oswald, and Oswald's godson Cynegils, king of Wessex, had earlier jointly granted Dorchester to Bishop Birinus in 634/5. Other foundations were the work of aristocratic benefactors, with at least some of Bede's 'false' monasteries probably playing some kind of pastoral role.

We don't know how many of these centres had been established by the eighth century; given that all were rebuilt several times over subsequent centuries, their architecture provides few clues. But it's possible sometimes to identify them via more extensive documentary evidence that survives from the tenth century onwards. At that point, the original ecclesiastical geography of early Anglo-Saxon England was beginning to break up into a new pattern of one parish church per human settlement, with many new churches being built. As this process began to unfold, earlier foundations – now sometimes labelled 'mother churches' – are identifiable from the exclusive rights they continued to exercise over baptism and burial, while responsibility for other religious duties (including regular church services) was passed on to numbers of daughter churches. In this later era, the dependent territories of identifiable original minsters often broke up into a dozen or more replacements, giving some sense of how many had originally existed. Overall, it has been estimated that some hundreds of minsters of various kinds were in existence before the new parish system of the tenth century and beyond revolutionized church provision (but not all these minsters, of course, need have been built in the seventh and eighth centuries).[64]

The provision of pastoral care in conversion-era Ireland, in so far as it can be reconstructed, operated along different lines. Although continental, especially Roman ecclesiastical influence was strong enough to dictate a pattern of relatively few bishops in Anglo-Saxon England, overseen by a pair of archbishops, Irish Christianity seems to have been strongly influenced by the norms of British Christianity, largely responsible for the original missionary work across the Irish Sea. Fifth- and sixth-century British Christianity operated with many more bishops than the one bishop per city-territory unit model set out in the canons of the council of Nicaea. If this model had applied among the British, there would have been no more than a handful in post at any one time, but in fact several tens are known. And this British model, charging bishops with responsibility for smaller territorial units than was generally the norm in continental Christianity, could easily be adapted to the Irish political landscape, which was divided into a large number of small *tuatha* or kingdoms. A *tuath* was notionally defined as a piece of territory that might be walked across in a single day, and the generally supposed model of one bishop per kingdom would have generated many tens of bishops – perhaps even a hundred or more – across the totality of the Irish landscape, as opposed to the dozen or so in eighth-century Anglo-Saxon England.[65]

The overall pattern of ecclesiastical hierarchy that operated in

Ireland at this point – and which continued to operate among the British from whom the Irish inherited it – was also different. There were no archbishops in Ireland, and no sign, either, of regular Church councils. In both western – non-Anglo-Saxon – Britain and across the Irish Sea, abbots of major monastic houses, which were often much richer than ordinary bishoprics, and lay Christian intellectuals (Latin *sapientes*: 'the wise') attended the few Church councils we know of, such as that which instituted the *Cáin Adomnáin* (p. 251). This council was not called by an archbishop or even a bishop, but by the abbot of Iona, and to judge by who signed its witness list and in what order, some of the abbots and lay intellectuals ranked higher in authority than many of the attendant bishops. The heightened authority of Irish abbots appears to have been the result of Christianity's intersection with pre-existing Irish cultural conditions, producing broad monastic alliances of mother and daughter houses whose chief abbot was a figure of much greater significance than the bishop of any individual *tuath*.[66]

This sharing of religious authority between slightly less important bishops, abbots and lay intellectuals, with no sign of formalized metropolitan authority structures, also strongly recalls the authority patterns of earlier Christianity in the Roman world. Up to the time of Constantine, early Christianity had also operated with rural bishops (*chorepiscopi*) alongside an urban-based bishop, ministering to any rural Christian congregations within a city's dependent territory. The hierarchical oddities of British and Irish Christianity have often been attributed to some kind of peculiar process of local development, but it is also possible that the more bishop-centred authority structures characteristic of mainland Europe in the fifth and sixth centuries, along with its attendant metropolitan archiepiscopal structures (all of which were eventually transported to Anglo-Saxon England), had not yet reached full development at the point that British Christianity dropped out of the Roman imperial system around AD 400. Nicaea started a process of change, downgrading *chorepiscopi* into mere priests, but this change did not happen immediately. If the operations of the British Church had never felt the full force of the post-Constantinian revolution in metropolitan authority, this would certainly help explain why British bishops so strongly resisted Augustine of Canterbury's archiepiscopal claims to outrank them (p. 242). In that case, the institutional hierarchical oddities of the British and Irish churches had the same origin as their deviant approach to the dating of Easter: at the time the British Church fell out of the Roman imperial system, uniformity had not yet been fully established.

Ireland and the west of Britain, then, present us with contrasting religious structures to the more centralized hierarchy that eventually evolved – after continental norms – in Anglo-Saxon England. Both systems, however, could generate substantial changes to the prevailing patterns of religious belief and behaviour among the mass of their respective populations. In the absence of other forms of material culture – and with written evidence only surviving for the activities of the political elite – we can gain some insight into prevailing attitudes to death and any afterlife from excavated cemetery evidence. Most of the cemeteries in existence when the missionaries arrived in *c.* 600 – many of them already long-established – continued in use for at least the next 150 years (see Map 4), before giving way to a new burial pattern centred on extensive graveyards around the emerging network of minster churches. This has sometimes been taken to mean that it took until the mid-eighth century for Christianity to have any substantial impact on broader popular understandings of death and the afterlife, but this is much too hasty a conclusion.

At the time the missionaries arrived, the Anglo-Saxon kingdoms were marked by one striking difference in funerary practice. In East Anglia, and up much of the east coast, large urnfield cremation cemeteries – closely echoing funerary practices previously found across the North Sea in present-day Schleswig-Holstein – were common. (Later Norse texts ascribe a particular meaning to cremation; the rising smoke carried the dead person's soul up to the next life and the higher it rose, the better the outcome – and it's possible pre-Christian Anglo-Saxons saw the practice in much the same way.) Further west, in central and southern England, smaller inhumation cemeteries prevailed. One more or less immediate impact of the arrival of Christian beliefs among the Anglo-Saxons was to terminate the decidedly pagan practice of cremation burial in eastern England.

Although we lack detailed information about pre-Christian Anglo-Saxon understandings of death, careful archaeological analysis of how physical remains were treated, especially considered against possible anthropological parallels, suggest that the arrival of Christianity also affected prevailing practices of inhumation, too, long before the eighth-century shift to churchyard burial. As in many cultures, pre-Christian Anglo-Saxon burial practice in both the east and more western areas – cremation as well as inhumation – involved the disposal of bodies in a two-stage process. Before burial or eventual cremation, dead bodies were exposed to the elements for a period, perhaps, to judge by the postholes found in cemeteries, on raised wooden cradles. This had some practical purposes. Because the human body is over 50 per cent water, a desiccated corpse requires about a quarter the amount of fuel than it would otherwise for its effective cremation. But anthropological parallels suggest that delaying burial until physical decomposition had set in was also about making sure that the corpse harboured no angry dead spirit which had failed to move on, remaining in this world to haunt the living. Small children and newborns also seem not to have been buried in the same cemeteries as adults, but instead were disposed of separately, and comparative anthropology again suggests that this might have been at least in part because they were viewed as a particularly potent source of angry spirits. Much of this can only be inference, but there is more than enough here to warn us not to underestimate the sophistication of pre-Christian Anglo-Saxon world-views.

That said, the fact that the same inhumation cemeteries remained in use throughout the seventh century does not mean that the missionaries had failed to have an impact. Indeed, some changes in actual practice can be detected, including a marked reduction in the quantity of grave goods being buried with the dead as the seventh century progressed. In the fifth and sixth centuries, around half of burials were adorned with a rich array of various items, reflecting gender and probably also status as well. By the end of the seventh century, by contrast, the vast majority of burials consisted of unadorned bodies, which are impossible to date precisely. As with the end of cremation practices, this would suggest that the arrival of Christianity was having an effect on prevailing understandings of the afterlife. At the very least, it clearly became much less important for individual Anglo-Saxons to enter the next world adorned and armed with the accoutrements of their current existence.[67]

A century after their arrival, the impact of the missionaries was also visible in some substantial changes to religious belief and practice in the here and now. By the early eighth century, the mass of the English population, peasant and elite, probably was being baptized – although not necessarily voluntarily. Two law codes of the 690s, one from Kent, the other from Wessex, had made non-baptism an offence punishable by fines. The same codes also agree that the other defining aspects of Christian piety in Anglo-Saxon England by *c.* 700 were not working on Sunday, making Christian marriages, and not sacrificing to devils (i.e., the old gods).[68] It is striking that three out of these four religious behaviours – not sacrificing to devils apart – were simple and external, making non-compliance easy to detect and punish. They were also either singular, once-in-a-lifetime events (baptism and marriage) or relatively undemanding. Strikingly, the injunction to keep the Sabbath was a negative one: not to work, rather than actually to attend a Christian religious service. While there can be a considerable gap between theory and reality when it comes to early medieval law-making, these legal religious requirements look credibly practical, given the amount and overall quality of the available religious provision.

Altogether, a few hundred minster churches came into existence across Anglo-Saxon England in the seventh and early eighth centuries. This was far more than the handful of post-Roman survivals Augustine's missionaries found on their arrival in 597 – but fell a long way short of the fifteen thousand parish churches that had emerged by the thirteenth century to create a fully developed one-church-per-rural-settlement pattern. In the seventh and eighth centuries, in other words, there was nothing close to a full-time Christian priest available for every community in England, and no certainty that all the minster priests had enjoyed anything like a full training in the faith they taught (there were no seminaries for training them). Nor could they even – had they been able to read – draw upon well-stocked collections of Christian service books and instructional manuals.[69]

It is also true to say that the pre-Viking Anglo-Saxon Church as an institution was not always purely focused on a religious mission.

Throughout the seventh and eighth centuries, the influence of kings remained strong over its developing structures, and indeed in all matters of religion. Shortly before Archbishop Theodore's arrival in 669, it was King Oswiu of Northumbria's intervention at a crucial moment that ensured that the kingdom of Northumbria would follow the Roman (i.e., the now widely accepted Alexandrian) rather than the customary British/Irish method for calculating the date of Easter.[70] And, as Theodore attempted to break up Wilfrid's massive Northumbrian see, he well understood that he needed royal backing. As Bede documents in his *Ecclesiastical History*, seventh-century Anglo-Saxon kings generally appointed – or at least exercised a veto over the appointment of – the bishops of their kingdoms, and the situation remained broadly the same in the following century. Kings and their chief non-clerical advisors regularly attended the larger Church councils, while the councils' increasing regularity in the second half of the eighth century – at least for the Church south of the River Humber – was a by-product of the growing Mercian hegemony over this part of England, which – conveniently – broadly coincided with the ecclesiastic province subject to the archbishopric of Canterbury. At the 673 synod of Hertford, Theodore had looked forward to regular Church councils, but it was only when all of England south of the Humber was subordinate – if to differing degrees – to Offa of Mercia from the 780s onwards that such meetings seem to have become a regular occurrence. In this era, too, the formidable Offa was able to persuade the pope to create a new – albeit short-lived – archbishopric at Lichfield in the heart of Mercia, because the then-dominant hegemon of the southern Anglo-Saxon world did not want his senior Church leader – the archbishop of Canterbury – to have his headquarters in what had recently been an independent alien kingdom far from the centre of his own powerbase (this, even though Kent was then subordinate to his rule).[71] The seventh-century expectation (so evident in Bede's narrative) that there should be one bishop per Anglo-Saxon kingdom, personally chosen by and subordinate to the king, was still alive and well in the eighth century. It never really went away, it seems, and was instrumental in closely tying the Church to some immediately political agendas.

Royal authority also represented a mechanism by which non-Christian aristocratic values embedded themselves within the English

Church. As their supporting landed endowments built up, bishoprics became attractive positions for members of the elite to occupy. At worst, this could lead to outright simony: the sin of buying high ecclesiastical office. It was for this failing that Theodore deposed Wine, bishop of London, on his arrival in 669. As far as we can tell, Wine's was an unusually conspicuous case of corruption but, like most of early medieval Europe, Anglo-Saxon England was a gift-giving culture, with participants in any kind of relationship expecting to give and receive appropriate gifts. This meant, in practice, that there was a huge grey area between showing due respect and thanks – by presenting your benefactor with an appropriate gift upon receipt of a favour – and undiluted corruption: buying high office outright. With kings always looking to reward trusted henchmen, the potential for elision between the upper levels of the Church and secular aristocratic hierarchies was evident. We do not have enough biographical information from the eighth century to get a sense of what percentage of Anglo-Saxon bishops might have had non-ecclesiastical careers first, but in 747 the council of Clofesho felt it necessary to remind leading Churchmen that they should neither carry arms nor hunt – two other classic expressions of aristocratic status, which sit happily (or unhappily) alongside gift-giving. All of which strongly suggests that the value systems of secular and ecclesiastical leaders – perhaps, too, the actual personnel – were not so distinct from one another. In a similar vein, kings' regular presence at councils dealing with ecclesiastical property disputes indicates that decision-making was as much influenced by immediate political agendas as long-term ecclesiastical interests.[72]

In reality, therefore, the Church that emerged from the missionary era in Anglo-Saxon England was a religiously limited operation. It comprised a relatively small number of delivery points (churches) given the total area and population that needed to be covered, with a limited number of clergy to spread the religious message through the broader populace. Many of these clergy, moreover, were not very intensively trained, while others at the top of the hierarchy were intimately involved with the more worldly concerns and value systems of elite society. It is entirely consonant with these limitations that, alongside the simple demands on exterior behaviour recorded in the law codes, the most intense form of personal Christian piety that Bede could envisage for the bulk of the laity – a standard echoed by the council of Clofesho in the mid-eighth century – is that they should simply know by heart the Lord's Prayer, the Apostles' Creed, and have some understanding of the Trinity.[73] The so-called Apostles' Creed is a shorter, simplified version of the Nicene Creed that seems to have been developed for liturgical use in fifth-century Gaul.[74] This is Christianity 101 at best, consisting basically of a few incantations with no requirement for any kind of more intense spiritual life or regular ritual participation. And if this restricted expression of Christianity was Bede's ideal, for much of the population the reality was probably even more limited.

Across the Irish Sea, the general level of Christian knowledge and participation closely resembled that of Anglo-Saxon England, despite the different overall shape of the prevailing ecclesiastical structures. In Ireland, baptism, alongside occasional attendance at services and a required knowledge of the Creed and the Lord's Prayer (which the Irish customarily recited in Latin rather than the vernacular) was the most that could usually be expected of the mass of the population. Ireland also generated some flourishing centres of book production and Christian learning, based initially on importing texts from the Continent and western Britain. Like their Anglo-Saxon counterparts, these institutions created not only magnificent, illuminated products, like the famous *Book of Kells* (created around the year 800), but much larger numbers of unilluminated, partial biblical texts (much more suitable for travelling missionaries), biblical commentaries, grammars and works in the new genre of tariffed penitential literature (p. 276), which were more characteristic of the developing Irish tradition. Indeed, as well as playing a key role in emerging Anglo-Saxon centres of high-end ecclesiastical education, Irish clerical scholars also made a particularly important contribution to the development of linguistic studies in Latin.

It quickly became apparent to these non-native speakers of Latin that the grammatical primers imported from the Continent for teaching the language that was so essential for Christian knowledge – particularly the widely used *Ars Minor* and *Ars Maior* of the famous mid-fourth-century teacher Donatus – needed extensive supplementing, because Donatus' grammatical discussions and exercises assumed an extensive pre-existing knowledge of the language among his students. Irish scholars consequently developed an extensive range of more introductory materials for their students which filled these gaps, and, once again, passed all this material on to their Anglo-Saxon pupils, who in turn continued to develop the tradition. Because books were so expensive, intellectual centres for intensive study could exist only where there were resources to pay for parchment and ink, which, in the Irish context, generally meant a handful of larger monastic foundations with great landed endowments, such as Kells, Armagh and Iona.[75]

The one potential exception to this pattern of rudimentary and superficial Christian observance among the mass of the peasantry – on both sides of the Irish Sea – were tenants living on Church lands, especially those owned by larger monastic properties. In the overwhelmingly agricultural economies of the early Middle Ages, the only way to ensure a regular income for permanent Christian institutions such as monastic and cathedral communities was to provide them with landed endowments whose surplus production would feed the monks and cover their other expenses. But landed endowments were worth nothing without a labour force. In both Ireland and England, as the landed endowments of larger monasteries built up, so the servile peasant tenants working those lands were customarily freed (it being a recognized expression of Christian virtue to free slaves) and came to be regarded as quasi-members of the community. The workforce remained separate in some ways. They were not required to be celibate – it would obviously be self-defeating for the workforce not to reproduce itself – and were perhaps buried in separate cemeteries. (At least two burial grounds were in simultaneous use at Bede's stamping ground of Monkwearmouth–Jarrow: one for monks proper, perhaps; the other for the workforce.) But monastic penitential texts of the early medieval period imply that the communities' peasantry participated – or were supposed to participate – in substantially more intense forms of Christian piety than the rest of the population. This involved not just baptism and a handful of prayers learned by rote, but regimes of fasting and sexual abstinence at designated times of year, and much more regular attendance at church services: something rather closer to early Church practice compared to the minimal, superficial Christianity required of the wider population.[76]

This relatively small-scale exception aside, the partly realized systems of pastoral care that emerged from the missionary era could provide only a very limited form of Christianity in both Ireland and England (and the point would also hold true later in Frisia). It is hardly surprising, therefore, that the theme of deficient pastoral care runs through several of Bede's writings. In one scene from his *Life of St Cuthbert*, a group of Geordie peasants laugh at some monks being swept out into the North Sea in their small boat, because 'They have abolished people's old devotions and nobody knows how the new ones should be observed.' Bede addressed the problem more directly in his letter to Bishop Egbert of York, complaining both that, even after the subdivision of Wilfrid's greater see, the various bishops of Northumbria's were unable to check up regularly on the quality of church services, and that more remote peasant communities in their still-vast dioceses were being left entirely untended. So, while enough minsters of different kinds had come into existence by the 730s to provide limited quantities of pastoral care for many communities, an overall rebooting of religious belief and behaviour towards any more intense form of Christianity was quite impossible. Once-in-a-lifetime rituals like baptism were possible for pretty much everyone; the same did not apply to more regular religious devotion, since the shortage of priests and the distances involved meant that more regular – daily, weekly, or perhaps even monthly – church services were often unavailable.[77]

What this meant in practice is that the kind of syncretic religious outcome we have observed in elite warrior circles must also have prevailed further down the social scale, with a barebones form of Christian faith forming a thin additional layer on top of, and alongside, many traditional peasant beliefs and practices. In this context, the early law codes' demand that the population not sacrifice to devils seems significant. Syncretic multiplication of cults, common early on among kings, was probably equally prevalent among the peasantry, and generally creative processes of syncretic conversion opened up many a grey area between sacrificing to devils and legitimate practice. These older practices are likely to have varied enormously, since significant numbers of the unfree peasantry of the Anglo-Saxon kingdoms will have been of indigenous Celto-Roman origins; others still would have come from the very different cultural context of the Germanic-speaking Continent. It's likely enough that these older practices focused, as all documented peasant analogues tend to do, on fertility and crops, but the exact nature of beliefs, and religious behaviours required in response, are even less knowable to us than the details of northern warrior traditions.[78]

Despite these many limitations, bringing the warrior elites of north-western Europe to the Christian faith was a major triumph for the small groups of committed missionaries who began the process. Convincing Anglo-Saxon warriors, who'd achieved their present prosperity in south-eastern Britain by overcoming Christian British opponents, to take on the religion of their defeated opponents has to be reckoned a substantial achievement. To make this happen, the missionaries had not only to learn new languages, but to develop a new form of Christianity. This new iteration of the faith had to differ in key respects from anything that had gone before, since its main target audiences not only had to kill each other regularly in battle, but were tied to honour systems that charged them periodically to kill in defence of the interests of their kin groups. None of this should have sat easily alongside Gospel teachings to love and forgive your enemies and turn the other cheek, but a few light penances and some modified teachings squared the circle.

This capacity to reinvent itself in new contexts is a key component of Christianity's capacity to spread so widely, and no particular form of the religion can or should – at least in analytical terms – be considered more 'true' than any other. But it did mean that the Christianity that took hold in north-western Europe in the early Middle Ages was extremely different – in terms of overall demands and practices – to either its pre-Constantinian or late Roman predecessors. This is perhaps not so surprising given that, in these centuries, a cultural construct fashioned in a Roman imperial context was struggling to reinvent itself for the decidedly non-Roman societies of Ireland and Anglo-Saxon England. What is perhaps more surprising is that a raft of structural changes, substantially (but not totally) consequent on the unravelling of the Roman imperial system, meant that the mainstream Latin Church of continental post-Roman Europe underwent an analogous set of changes in the same era.

7
Latin Christianity Restructured

The unravelling of the Roman imperial system in the Latin west posed an immediate ideological challenge to the domination of the Nicene Orthodox Church, which that system had established and supported. If the faith of Nicaea represented divine truth, then why, by the year 500, had God allowed most of the former western Empire's provinces to fall under the control of Homoean successor kings? That challenge, as we saw in Chapter 5, had eventually been overcome. But even as Clovis converted to Catholicism in 507, and Justinian destroyed the Vandal and Ostrogothic kingdoms a generation later, the continued unravelling of the old structures of the imperial system were setting in motion a profound restructuring in the practical workings of Latin Christianity.

EMPIRE TO COMMONWEALTH

Most obviously, the destruction of the whole western imperial system by the middle years of the seventh century took with it the established, central decision-making body of Roman Christianity. Despite occasionally discordant voices, high-level religious decision-making after Constantine's conversion had been built, both in practice and in principle, on recognition of the emperor's fundamental right to act as head of the Church, with the power to make and enforce binding decisions for all Roman Christians. This was done, as we've seen, through the emperor's own law-making and, periodically, by calling ecumenical councils: representative gatherings of the bishops of the entire Christian world, usually working to agendas that had been pre-agreed and pre-prepared at the imperial court, with the emperor also responsible subsequently for enforcing the councils' decisions.

It has sometimes been argued, on the basis of another burst of Christian theological dispute – the so-called Three Chapters controversy – that the underpinning ideology of imperial religious authority was already facing serious erosion by the late fifth century, especially in the Roman west where Churchmen were developing a stronger sense of independent corporate identity. In one influential older variant of this position, the Roman papacy – bishops of Rome being the self-proclaimed heirs of St Peter, the 'Prince of the Apostles' – has sometimes been seen as stepping directly into the power vacuum left by the disappearance of western emperors, to exercise an overarching religious authority in the post-Roman west. Looked at more closely, however, the surviving evidence demonstrates that this era did not see the rise of an independent corporate Church (with or without papal leadership). Emperors continued to exercise unchallengeable religious authority over their domains, but, as their geographical reach declined, new structures began to emerge at regional level, based on the religious authority of successor-state kings. A closer look at the Three Chapters controversy – the last great theological dispute of the late Roman period – will allow us to explore both the evolution of these new patterns of authority and some of their longer-term consequences.

In the century either side of the final disappearance of western emperors, broadly *c.* 425–525, the imperial Church as a whole – east and west – was ripped apart by a bitter theological dispute over how exactly the divine and the human were combined in the person of Christ. The biblical evidence asserts that Jesus was both human and divine – but offers no further details. Probing the matter further might sound today like an exercise in theological technicality, but in the fifth century it quickly came to be seen as a fundamental problem, with profound implications for Christian understandings of salvation. Did Christ as God die on the Cross? And was this what had saved humankind? But could an immortal, eternal Divinity actually die?

By 431, these questions were provoking fractures at the highest level. Nestorius, then patriarch of Constantinople and the most senior figure in the east Roman Church, was deposed that year at the third ecumenical council, held at Ephesus, for arguing that only the human element of Christ had died on the Cross, which implied that the human and divine aspects of Jesus had remained separable after the Incarnation, and that Christ as God had not actually suffered death. Nestorius' chief opponent, ultimately responsible for his downfall at Ephesus, was Patriarch Cyril of Alexandria, who asserted (in direct opposition to Nestorius) the indivisibility of the 'one incarnate nature of God the Word'. For Cyril, it was absolutely necessary for Christ as God to die on the Cross, otherwise humanity could not be rescued from the consequences of the Fall. The dramatic collision of views at Ephesus set some basic parameters for the subsequent argument. Nestorius' views were condemned as heretical (though he had many followers, and a Nestorian Church community subsequently continued to flourish within the Persian Empire), and Cyril's understanding of salvation – that Christ as God had to die on the Cross to ensure human salvation – was duly enshrined as orthodoxy, with the Ephesus council's rulings fully accepted in both east and west.

That was not, however, the end of the debate. For many Churchmen, Cyril's formulation – 'one incarnate nature of God the Word' – left too little room for Christ's humanity as it is described in the Gospels. No one was going to return to Nestorius' teachings, but bitter dispute continued, and a fourth ecumenical council, at Chalcedon in 451, was called by the eastern emperor Marcian to try to draw a line under the argument, in the same way that the second council of Constantinople had managed to end the Arian dispute seventy years before: by finding a compromise position to which a critical mass of Churchmen could subscribe and which would allow the remaining dissenting minority to be persecuted into insignificance.[1] Marcian came to the council with a compromise in mind, which the council's discussions duly affirmed. After the Incarnation, its proceedings declared, Christ continued to exist 'in two natures' – human and divine – while at the same time the participants confirmed the condemnation of Nestorius. Pope Leo I – probably the best known of all late Roman popes thanks to the survival of an extensive collection of his letters – contributed a formal theological treatise to the council, the so-called *Tome of Leo*. This text restated a standard western understanding of the matter – 'one person in Christ but two natures' – and was also incorporated into the official proceedings of the council.[2]

Still, the dispute had not remotely run its course. As usual, when gathered in a single room under the watchful eye of an emperor and his officials, the assembled bishops signed up to the council's mandates. Once away from direct imperial oversight, however, the bickering began again; for many the phrase 'in two natures' was too reminiscent of Nestorius' teachings, even though the council had confirmed his condemnation. By 482, thirty years after Chalcedon, eastern Churchmen had become so bitterly divided on the matter that Emperor Zeno (474–91) published his 'Act of Union' (the *Henotikon*). This stated that the Faith had been satisfactorily defined at the first two ecumenical councils of Nicaea (325) and Constantinople (382). Chalcedon was not condemned, but its status was downgraded; no longer an ecumenical council, its decisions were no longer binding, Zeno's edict aiming to sideline it as a source of further dispute. Initially, the *Henotikon* just about restored peace to the eastern Church, since all four sitting eastern patriarchs (of Alexandria, Antioch, Constantinople and Jerusalem) endorsed it. But there remained many supporters of Chalcedon at lower levels of the Greek Church, and, because the *Tome of Leo* had been formally incorporated into its proceedings, the papal see had a strong stake in upholding Chalcedon's full ecumenical legitimacy. In Rome, feelings ran high. Two years later, Pope Felix III held a synod which denounced the *Henotikon*, and formally excommunicated and anathematized Acacius, the then patriarch of Constantinople. Rome and Constantinople were now in schism (labelled the Acacian schism, after the excommunicated patriarch).[3] Rather than unity, then, the *Henotikon* unleashed a three-way split, between pro- and anti-Chalcedonian opinion in the east, and a papal see, now operating in a world without sitting western emperors, irrevocably committed to upholding Chalcedon's full ecumenical status.

The first sustained attempt to restore unity to the entire Church, east and west, came under the emperor Justinian, whose conquest of Italy brought the papal see effectively back under imperial rule from the late 530s onwards.[4] Like his predecessors faced with the seemingly intractable Arian and Donatist disputes in the fourth and early fifth centuries, the emperor and his advisors sought first to find some kind of compromise that a critical mass of ecclesiastical leaders could sign up to, and then to deploy a full range of positive and negative 'persuasions' to force enough of the rest into line. The outlines of a theological compromise were worked out in discussions between a new generation of eastern Churchmen in the 530s. Because Cyril had himself once conceded that it was not illegitimate to talk about Christ having 'two natures' (in an attempted compromise statement of faith issued after the council of Ephesus in 433), it was just about possible to defend Chalcedon's definition of the person of Christ – 'in two natures' – to anti-Chalcedonians, so long as this did not exclude the valid use, in other contexts, of their own preferred 'one nature' formula, and that there was no doubt that Christ as God had died on the Cross. Once this was agreed, as it quickly was in the early 530s, the sticking point became the council of Chalcedon's written endorsements of the orthodoxy of three fifth-century bishops – Theodore of Mopsuestia, Theodoret of Cyrrhus and Ibas of Edessa – whom the anti-Chalcedonians considered irredeemably tainted with Nestorian heresy. After lengthy negotiations with all the interested parties in the east, Justinian issued a first religious edict in 543/4, which condemned those sections of Chalcedon's written proceedings (the so-called 'Three Chapters') that declared the three orthodox. In 551, after much lobbying of eastern Churchmen as the outlines of the emperor's proposed religious settlement firmed up, Justinian issued a second edict: *On the True Faith*. This re-affirmed Chalcedon's ecumenical status, but also asserted, after the teachings of Cyril of Alexandria, that Christ as God 'suffered in the flesh' and that, after the Incarnation, the one fundamentally unified Christ was composed of two natures. The edict's substantive points were all supported by extracts from the writings of Cyril of Alexandria, and it closed with thirteen anathemas: ten supporting its positive points, and three individually condemning each of the Three Chapters.[5] Justinian had found a compromise that would work for a critical mass of eastern Church opinion: ditch the unacceptable bits of Chalcedon but uphold the rest, while deliberately framing it in terms of Cyril's teachings. Important in itself, the edict was also designed as the foundation document for a new ecumenical council, number five, to be held in Constantinople in 553. Its purpose was formally to ratify Justinian's compromise solution, and finally draw a line under the savage dispute that had been dividing eastern Churchmen, and western Churchmen from their eastern brethren, for over a century.

But Justinian's compromise strategy – which worked well enough in the east – generated howls of protest in the west because of the condemnation of part of Chalcedon's text, the Three Chapters. One initially vocal protester was Pope Vigilius, who had come to office in March 537 shortly after Justinian's forces took possession of the city of Rome. North African bishops – another branch of the Latin western Church and now also again under imperial control after Justinian's conquest of the Vandal kingdom in the early 530s – were still more adamant, refusing point-blank to sign up to a letter of consent to the emperor's proposals that had accompanied Justinian's first edict. A deacon of the Carthaginian church, Facundus, wrote a fiercely worded condemnation of the emperor's policy; later, the head of the North African Church, Bishop Reparatus of Carthage, called a council that even excommunicated Pope Vigilius for eventually acquiescing in Justinian's designs. As a group, these North African Churchmen rejected the emperor's attempts to interfere in matters of faith in the way that Justinian's fourth- and fifth-century predecessors had done to resolve earlier disputes, and, up to this point, it is possible to read the Three Chapters controversy as a sign that, in parts of the west at least, a corporate Church identity had emerged that was capable of resisting late Roman patterns of imperial religious authority.

What happened next, however, offers a much clearer insight into how top-level patterns of religious authority were evolving in a Latin west now lacking its own imperial court. Hauled off to Constantinople on imperial orders late in 545, Pope Vigilius at first refused to attend Justinian's council in the late spring of 553. Instead, he issued a formal refutation of Justinian's initiative in the middle of the council's deliberations, upholding the ecumenical authority of the entirety of the text of Chalcedon (Vigilius' *First Constitutum*, 24 May 553). But imperial pressure was unyielding and Vigilius was given an ultimatum: unless he endorsed the new council's ecumenical status and its condemnation of the Three Chapters, he would never be allowed to return to Italy. Finally, he gave in, issuing a formal written acceptance of both points on 26 February 554, and was duly released. Although he died en route, his papal successors followed Vigilius' U-turn, continuing to support the eastern imperial position, fully endorsing the decisions of Justinian's council and condemning the Three Chapters. Pope Pelagius I (556–61) maintained – lying through his teeth – that the condemnation represented no change in papal policy at all. Even Gregory the Great (590–604), who eventually acknowledged the volte-face, continued to justify it on the grounds that new information, not available to Leo I back in the day, had since come to light.

Thanks to Justinian's wars of conquest, Constantinople's control of the city of Rome was firmly established by the mid-sixth century. In these circumstances, neither Vigilius nor his successors had sufficient independent religious authority to maintain an alternative position to that championed unequivocally by a sequence of eastern imperial regimes. Papal acquiescence quickly became the springboard for the more general enforcement of the council's doctrinal rulings in those parts of the Latin west now under the aegis of Constantinople. This combined the usual mix of blandishment and oppression. Bishop Reparatus of Carthage was deposed (never to be heard of again), and new Church councils in Numidia and Proconsularis soon endorsed Justinian's fifth ecumenical council and its condemnation of the Three Chapters. By the late sixth century, only two Italian ecclesiastical provinces – the archbishoprics of Milan and Aquileia – continued to oppose the Constantinople council's rulings. Unlike the city of Rome, both were by this point outside imperial control, in territory recently conquered by the Lombards.[6] As this extended sequence of events makes crystal clear, even in the later sixth century, the main obstacle to the emperor's religious authority and practical control of the Church was provided by the limits of his political reach, not by any alternative ideology or functioning ecclesiastical independence.

Nor was the bishop of Rome remotely capable of filling the general vacuum in high-level religious decision-making left by the unravelling of the western Empire in those other parts of the Latin world where an emperor's remit no longer ran – the majority of the Spanish peninsula and the entirety of the old Gallic provinces. An older strand of the scholarly literature sometimes argued the opposite: that the bishop of Rome was already beginning to acquire some of the pre-eminent authority that, by the high Middle Ages, would make the papacy function more or less as we understand it now, as the effective head of western, largely Latinate Christendom. But a closer look at the evidence cited in support of such visions of enhanced papal importance serves both to put such claims properly in perspective and to underline what was really happening to Christian religious authority structures at the highest level in the post-Roman west.

Bishops of Rome based – and still base – their claims to a unique level of religious authority on two key points about St Peter, Jesus' right-hand man in the Gospels. He was, they maintained, the city's first bishop; second, he passed on the authority that attached to him as the so-called 'Prince of the Apostles' to all subsequent bishops of Rome. You can still see the biblical cornerstone of papal authority, taken from Matthew's Gospel, inscribed on the facing pillar as you enter St Peter's in the Vatican: 'You are Peter, and on this rock I will build my Church, and to you I give the keys of the Kingdom of Heaven.' By itself, however, this verse does not substantiate anything, making no mention of either Rome or its bishopric; neither are the papacy's two claims about St Peter explicitly confirmed in any of the earliest Christian texts, such as the Gospels or the Acts of the Apostles.

In the late Roman period, this gap in the biblical documentation was recognized, and somebody made an attempt to fill it. Around AD 400, a forgery known as the *Clementine Recognitions*, composed in Greek and translated into Latin, started to circulate. Purporting to be a letter of Pope Clement I (bishop of Rome from around 88 to 99) to James the brother of Jesus, then leader of the Church in Jerusalem, it tells how Clement had been converted and trained by St Peter, and how Peter had passed on to him his own unique religious authority as Jesus' most important disciple. As such, the *Recognitions* 'proved' both of the bishops of Rome's key claims. Though it probably only formalized assertions that had long circulated orally, the forgery clearly demonstrates an ideological ambition for the bishop of Rome to be recognized as superior in some way to the four other patriarchs of the later Roman Empire – the bishops of Alexandria, Antioch, Jerusalem and Constantinople – who all claimed to be either apostolic foundations (like Rome), or in the case of Constantinople, to be the 'New Rome' and hence worthy of all the honours and recognitions due to the old (p. 40).[7]

This forgery coincided, too, with equally clear signs of a greater practical ambition. In the early Church, the antiquity and prestige of the Christian community of the city of Rome (it was one of the oldest and, quickly, one of the largest: p. 22) made its leader an occasional source of advice to other co-religionists, but literally on only a handful of known occasions between the first and the fourth centuries.[8] After Constantine's conversion and the formalization of Christian hierarchical structures at Nicaea and after, the context in which the established prestige of the see of Rome was operating changed substantially. For one thing, as new Christian communities proliferated in central and southern Italy, bishops of Rome acquired and exercised archiepiscopal, metropolitan powers across the region, with the right to hold (as did other archbishops) local disciplinary councils of their dependent bishops and to have some say in their appointment. More significantly, Rome was the only one of the five patriarchates situated within the territory of the western Empire. As such, it sought new ways to express this unique status across those parts of Latin Christendom which lay beyond the reach of its immediate metropolitan archiepiscopal authority.

In the fourth and fifth centuries, requests for legal and theological advice from other western bishops to Rome did increase in frequency, and the nature of papal replies evolved. The simple letter-form employed in the small handful of known earlier replies gave way under Innocent I (401–17) to the characteristic papal decretal. This was modelled on the imperial rescript, used for centuries by emperors to give authoritative rulings on the bottom half of a letter, in reply to legal queries set out on top. Mimicking imperial rescripts was a significant move, revealing a papacy that wanted its rulings to be understood as legally binding. In the first decades of the fifth century, popes Innocent I, Zosimus, Boniface I and Celestine I (covering the years 401–32) provided this more formal type of ruling to Christian congregations as far away as Spain, Gaul and North Africa.[9] In the same era, Pope Leo I and some of his peers likewise attempted to give an air of greater institutional functionality to Rome's status, claiming the right to operate as a court of appeal in difficult cases involving western bishops, and periodically awarding a badge of office – the pallium, a long woollen scarf – to senior regional archbishops of the western Empire (especially those of Arles and Thessalonica) who fell within Rome's claimed patriarchal jurisdiction. In 445, the emperor Valentinian III even issued a formal legal declaration that: 'If the authority of the Apostolic

[Roman] See has sanctioned or should sanction anything, such regulation shall be as law . . . for all men.'[10]

This pattern of determined self-assertion continued after the formal dissolution of the western Empire. In 494, at the height of the Acacian schism, Pope Gelasius I wrote a dismissive letter to the eastern emperor Anastasius, who had been trying to persuade him to accept the terms of the *Henotikon*:

> There are two powers which for the most part control this world, the sacred authority of priests and the might of kings. Of these two the office of the priests is the greater in as much as they must give account even for kings to the Lord at the divine judgment . . . You must know therefore that you are dependent upon their decisions and they will not submit to your will.

This was a revolutionary claim. Gelasius' letter set out a doctrine that was utterly at odds with Roman imperial ideology, which held that emperors were personally chosen by the divinity and for that reason should exercise overarching religious authority. In complete contrast, Pope Gelasius asserted that God not only wills that sacred power and secular powers operate in separate spheres, and should not interfere in the other's areas of competence, but underlined the inherent superiority of the sacred.

In this era, greater ideological self-assertion was again matched with moves towards the more regular exercise of practical authority. Working in Rome in the first decade of the sixth century, the learned monk Dionysius Exiguus, from Scythia in the eastern Empire, completed two compilations of Church law that sought to emphasize the prominence of the papacy in Church law-making. The first compilation retranslated into better Latin (in two separate editions) the canons of the ecumenical councils and some other regional-level meetings from their original Greek (among many other distinctions, Dionysius was fluent in Latin and Greek, an increasingly rare phenomenon in the post-Roman west). The second text (the *Collectio decretorum Pontificum Romanorum*) collected papal decretals from popes Siricius to Anastasius II (384–498), making available a decent-sized collection of papal decisions. Pairing this second text with the new council canon translations explicitly asserted the principle that papal decretals ranked as high in inherent legal authority as the rulings of imperially called ecumenical councils.[11]

Considered in isolation, these phenomena – the ideological assertion of the principle of papal supremacy; Gelasius' assertion of the concept of 'secular' to strip emperors of their religious authority; and the evolution of the decretal letter-form, combined with the issuing of an official collection of such rulings deliberately equated in status with those of ecumenical councils – might seem to amount to something close to the overarching religious authority claimed and enjoyed by the Roman papacy in the high Middle Ages. Set in their detailed late and post-Roman contexts, however, the picture looks rather different. By the mid-first millennium, the papal see came nowhere close to asserting either its effective superiority over supposedly secular rulers, or to persuading most of the leaders of the western Church that its uncontested prestige should translate into actual religious authority over the Latin Church.

Gelasius' letter had an enormously influential future ahead of it, but that future lay far in the distance in the high Middle Ages, by which point it appeared in every serious collection of canon law. In its own time it quickly disappeared without trace and was not quoted again for centuries. The reason is straightforward. The letter was written while Italy was under Ostrogothic rule, meaning that the pope could assert his independence – writing in a manner that he knew the emperor Anastasius would find insulting while safe from any direct imperial response. All this changed with Justinian's conquest of Italy in the 530s, which renewed direct imperial authority – albeit exercised, this time, from Constantinople – over the Roman see. For the next hundred and fifty years or so, the principal focus of papal activity, and source of papal power, became Constantinople: at one point, three successive Greek-speaking popes served as bishops of Rome. Whatever independent religious authority popes may have tried to assert in the brief interval between western imperial collapse and Justinian's conquest of Italy all but disappeared.

A closer look at the decretal evidence only emphasizes the limits of actual papal authority in the post-Roman west. For one thing, very few decretal rulings were actually given in this period. Dionysius Exiguus found only forty-one for the entire hundred-and-twenty-year period separating popes Siricius and Gelasius: roughly one per three years. At the height of the decretal-driven revolution in canon law of the twelfth century, they were coming at a rate of thirty a year, ninety times more frequently. In other words, popes were not being asked for their opinion at all regularly in the late and post-Roman periods. Second, they had to wait to be asked. Popes of this era lacked any agents in other parts of the west who might have allowed them to move proactively; that being so, popes had no choice but to be generally passive and reactive. Third, the papal approach to decision-making within these late antique decretals remained highly consensual. Rather than directly asserting their own authority in answering questions, popes consistently grounded their responses in such uncontroversial sources of Christian tradition as the Bible and the writings of the Church Fathers. Finally, and perhaps most importantly, there was no enforcement mechanism. Recipients were often asked – in the text of the decretal response – to publicize the ruling widely, but popes possessed no means or sanctions whatsoever to force other western Churchmen to do anything that they didn't want to.[12]

All of which both emphasizes the limits of papal authority in this era and directs our gaze towards the real location of high-level religious authority in the post-Roman west. Attention has sometimes been drawn to more aggressively written letters (not in decretal form) from popes such as Innocent I or Gregory the Great, in which they laid down the law in a much more authoritative tone. But these were directed to recipients within Rome's recognized metropolitan jurisdiction in central and southern Italy, and Sicily, where papal authority was strong and direct. Here, bishops could be appointed or fired, and difficult questions settled by written order. But for northern Italy and all points beyond, when exercising patriarchal rather than metropolitan archiepiscopal authority, popes had to tread more carefully, and might still be ignored. To win a long-running jurisdictional dispute with Bishop Hilary of Arles in the 430s, for instance, Leo I had to petition the emperor for assistance. It is no accident that the strongest statement of papal religious authority from the late Roman period – that anything sanctioned by the papacy 'shall be as law . . . for all men' – is to be found in a piece of imperial legislation, which Leo had secured to help prop up his own position.[13]

Not only does this structural dependence on imperial authority reveal a basic weakness in the papal position in the late Roman period; it also meant that popes, lacking any other enforcement mechanism, generally had to fall back on persuasion in their dealings with western Churchmen outside their own defined region of metropolitan authority. Even this did not often work. Both before and after the end of the western Empire, popes found that Churchmen tended to call on the religious authority of the bishop of Rome only as and when it suited them, and for their own purposes, while otherwise completely ignoring it. At the start of the sixth century another bishop of Arles, Caesarius, established a nunnery and wanted to allocate some of his see's property to support it financially. This ran contrary to established Church law, so he petitioned consecutive popes for permission. Three turned him down flat, but Caesarius transferred the lands anyway: he finally got a fourth to grant him a special exemption. It was of course the exemption that Caesarius chose to 'obey'. At the century's end, likewise, Pope Gregory I was worried about corruption in the Frankish Church and wanted a reform council to tackle the issue. The reigning queen, Brunhild, agreed to call one if Gregory granted the pallium to her current episcopal favourite, Syagrius of Autun. The pallium was duly granted, but no council followed – and there was nothing Gregory could do about it.[14]

After the disappearance of western imperial authority, in other words, post-Roman Latin Christendom no longer possessed any central high-level authority structure at all. In the absence of imperial authority, it fragmented into a series of Christian 'microcosms': local Churches aware of each other's existence but tending to function in practice as independent religious units. This phenomenon can be partly explained in terms of the breakdown of the cultural and economic ties that had held the Mediterranean region together in the Roman period, keeping Christian Churchmen in broad contact with one another, but which fractured in the middle centuries of the first millennium. The pattern of Christendom increasingly fragmenting into a series of locally autonomous religious entities was reinforced as the faith spread to much more distant congregations in Ireland and Scotland, who had never been part of the Mediterranean networks at all.

But the emergence of some of these western Christian microcosms can also be directly ascribed to the fall of the western Empire. Contemporary source materials from the post-Roman period demonstrate unequivocally that successor-state kings quickly inherited within their own realms the overarching religious authority which had previously belonged to Roman emperors. Each of these rulers, after practical Roman example and Roman ideologies, claimed to be appointed by God, and to rule by virtue of their special relationship with the Almighty. As with their imperial predecessors, this made them far more than secular rulers, empowering them to act as effective heads of their own regional churches. This defined the nature of high-level Christian decision-making in the post-Roman west and set clear parameters within which broader relationships between the Churchmen of any individual realm and both the papacy and Churchmen of other realms might continue to operate.[15]

Key decisions over doctrine in the post-Roman west therefore came to be focused on the different royal courts of its various kingdoms. In sixth-century Visigothic Spain, King Liuvigild's attempt to forge a compromise position between Homoean and Nicene Churchmen, and his son Reccared's subsequent conversion to Nicaea in the 580s, took the form of royal initiatives, in the sense that the key decisions were taken by the monarch (though the ecclesiastical input was doubtless substantial). It was when Visigoth kings were persuaded of the case for doing so that Homoean Christianity was finally abandoned in the Hispanic kingdom, and royal power was mobilized by both Liuvigild and Reccared in support of their religious decisions (see p. 202). The similarity between this process and Oswiu of Northumbria's choice of the Roman Easter date at the synod of Whitby in 664 is striking; while leading Churchmen brought forward their arguments over the different possible datings of Easter, it was the king of Northumbria who made the key decision between the competing positions.

In senior Church appointments, too, the royal writ was paramount. The writings of Gregory, bishop of Tours for over twenty years from August 573, form one of the most compelling bodies of source material for the functioning of the Christian Church and its relations with royal power to have come down to us from the immediate post-Roman period. Gregory's *oeuvre* consists of a ten-book history focusing on Gaul from the late Roman period down to his own day (it massively increases in detail as it hits the mid-sixth century) and a series of separate collections of miracle stories, recording numerous wonders worked by St Martin (Tours' patron saint), various Christian martyrs and confessors, and a number of Christian saints.[16] These different writings document many incidental instances of royal influence over episcopal appointments within the Frankish domains; they show that, while there were many factors in play, the appointment of bishops was ultimately in the king's gift, and a candidate who failed to secure royal approval stood no chance of success. (While Gregory sometimes complains about undue royal influence, he also boasted that his own appointment had come by royal order.) No equivalent narrative source survives from the Visigoth kingdom, but a handful of surviving letters from King Sisebut (612–21) similarly show him both dictating episcopal appointments (the recipient of one peremptory royal letter was 'immediately' to appoint its bearer bishop of Barcelona) and upbraiding bishops for their various misdemeanours. Here, then, the overall level of royal authority over ecclesiastical appointments south of the Pyrenees looks very similar to the Frankish kingdom to the north, and the Anglo-Saxon kingdoms north of the Channel.[17]

Kings also played a key role in setting and enforcing appropriate standards of Christian behaviour for both clergy and laity. In the late Roman period, such matters had been one of the main tasks for Church councils at every level – from the local up to the ecumenical – and this remained the case after the western Empire disappeared. But with the disappearance of Roman emperors, high-level Christian conciliar structures came to operate not across the Latin west as a whole, but on a kingdom-by-kingdom basis. After the Visigoths' conversion to Nicene Christianity, for example, the great and the good of the kingdom – both its secular and its ecclesiastical leaderships (although it was the Churchmen who ruled on ecclesiastical matters) – met at Toledo in 633, and thereafter on a further sixteen occasions up to 694. Royal authority was required to call these councils, and their agendas confirm that the Visigothic kings, like late Roman emperors, also helped decide the order of business. Apart from a wide range of rulings on religious matters, these councils also enacted measures on such key royal issues as treason and succession.

The same pattern broadly holds true for the Christian Church of

Frankish Gaul. In 511 Clovis, the first of Gaul's Merovingian Frankish kings, called a council of the Nicene Churchmen of his new kingdom at Orleans. Subsequent conciliar activity remained sporadic until the early 580s, when Clovis's grandson Guntram initiated a much more intense sequence of kingdom-wide reforming councils. This rapidly evolved into a self-conscious tradition, focused on raising standards both of Church discipline and lay piety across the realm. A rare late sixth-century manuscript containing the canons (rulings) of Church councils allows us to follow the growth in momentum. This manuscript originated in Lyons in Burgundy (which had been absorbed into the Frankish Gallic kingdom in the early 530s) and is now physically divided between libraries in St Petersburg and Berlin. In the twenty years or so after Guntram's first council at Mâcon in 581/2, Frankish bishops collected in this manuscript all the earlier Church rulings they could find (largely in chronological order). They then added to it – council by council – all the new rulings, again in chronological order, that they were making themselves. That they were consciously and deliberately informing themselves about older rulings and using them to inform their own discussions is shown by their increasing care to cross-reference precedents. In the end, the manuscript contained so many chronologically arranged councils that finding appropriate rulings became cumbersome. In the early seventh century, therefore, this Frankish ecclesiastical reform movement culminated in the production of the so-called *Vetus Gallica*, a new, thematically arranged code of canon law for the Frankish kingdom. This new text presented chosen rulings from the chronologically ordered manuscript under explicit, thematic headings, making it much more convenient to find the current state of the law on any particular topic, rather than having to go through all the known councils one by one, looking for relevant rulings. But *Vetus Gallica* was Church law solely for the Frankish kingdom: the product of a vibrant post-Roman Frankish Church community taking determined responsibility for the progress of Christianity within its own jurisdiction.[18]

Fully to understand the functioning of religious authority in the post-Roman west, a few additional points need to be emphasized. First, the legal community of the Frankish Church – or, indeed, its counterpart in the Visigothic kingdom – did not operate in isolation. The bishops had a strong sense of belonging to a wider Christian world: one of the older texts copied into the chronologically arranged Lyons manuscript and drawn upon heavily for the later *Vetus Gallica* was Dionysius Exiguus' Latin translations of the Greek ecumenical and other councils. The late sixth-century Frankish bishops clearly understood themselves as moving forward on the basis of existing Christian tradition, and wanted to make their new decisions in the light of authoritative earlier rulings. Second, papal authority did not figure at all strongly in the minds of Frankish Churchmen. Dionysius' collection of papal decretals was known in the kingdom, but only one papal letter is cited in *Vetus Gallica*. Francia's bishops clearly did not accept the claim that papal rulings, however formally expressed, ranked as high in authority as ecumenical councils. When tackling new problems, likewise, the Frankish bishops were happy to depend upon their own intellectual resources and saw not the slightest need to refer matters to Rome. Not only were the decretals not drawn upon to any serious degree in the bishops' decision-making, but there is no indication that any papal observers were ever present at any of these councils – or that anyone thought they should be. Third, the Frankish Church community depended on the support of its king to function. Only with Guntram's backing did a kingdom-wide reforming tradition get off the ground in the 580s. And although we lack explicit information to this effect, it's likely enough that, as with his Roman imperial predecessors, Guntram not only called councils but helped with their expenses. In effect, the bishops of Francia had turned their own meetings into quasi-ecumenical councils, claiming for their decisions the level of authority that had previously been imputed to Nicaea, Constantinople and Chalcedon.[19]

Similar patterns of religious authority operated in the Visigoth kingdom. The seventh-century, kingdom-wide councils of Toledo were called by kings, while the developing, collected body of ecclesiastical legislation that they generated (the *Hispana*, initially compiled by Isidore of Seville) again included copies of older councils and the Latin translations of Dionysius Exiguus. The Visigoth bishops also drew on the collected rulings of many of the sixth-century Frankish Church councils. But, while evidently conscious of being part of a bigger Christian world, like their Frankish peers they set about dealing with any further issues entirely from the resources of their own intellects and faith. No outside experts were called in; no difficult matters referred to Rome. Any attempt at outside interference was resented. In early 638 Bishop Braulio of Zaragoza wrote to Pope Honorius on behalf of all his fellow Visigothic bishops who had just gathered for the sixth council of Toledo (which began on 9 January 638). A letter from the pope (not itself extant) had arrived on the eve of the council, in which Honorius criticized the Visigoth bishops for previous failures to remedy a series of ecclesiastical abuses. Remaining utterly – if icily – polite, Braulio rejected the criticism. Honorius' arguments were, he wrote, 'unjust' – and he provided chapter and verse to show that the pope didn't know what he was talking about:

> when it was opportune, we did censure transgressors, and we did not keep silent when it was our duty to preach. Lest your apostolic highness think that we are producing this to excuse ourselves and not for the sake of truth, we have deemed it necessary to send you the previous decrees along with the present canons.

Braulio's letter closes with the further comment that the pope's recommended punishment for a certain category of sinner was inappropriate: 'We have never seen this done anywhere by the decrees of our forefathers, nor is it to be found in the divine words in the pages of the New Testament.' While studiously decorous in its language, Braulio's letter leaves not the slightest doubt that the pope should get on with sorting out his Isaiah from his Ezekiel (alongside his other errors, Honorius had muddled the two biblical prophets in an attempted quotation) and let the Visigoth bishops do their jobs. Everything suggests that Braulio's attitude would have been shared by the vast majority of Churchmen right across the post-Roman west.[20] Bishops of Rome, as heirs of St Peter, and guardians of his relics along with those of the Apostle Paul, had enormous prestige – but no one (except, perhaps, the odd pope) thought this should translate into any kind of general authority over the western Church.

At the highest levels, therefore, western Christianity was quickly restructured in the post-Roman period. Across what remained of Latin-speaking Roman Christendom (much of Britain having been taken over, of course, by Anglo-Saxon pagans), a kind of Christian commonwealth – *oikumene* in the Greek – replaced the Christian western Empire. Late

Roman Christianity had operated with a recognized centralized structure for high-level decision-making, based on the religious authority of the imperial office and its prime role in calling for and enforcing the decisions of ecumenical councils. High-level decisions in post-Roman Latin Christianity, by contrast, were taken at the level of new regional units, largely structured by the political boundaries of the new kingdoms which emerged from the wreck of the western Empire. Periodic contacts continued between these units, and they took some conscious notice of one another's decisions, but each considered itself fully competent to respond to the issues with which it was faced, with no acknowledgement of any papal authority. This high-level restructuring was matched by the evolution of new organizational structures at lower levels within this Christian commonwealth, as western Christian leaders struggled to meet two defining challenges that now confronted them.

ON THE CORRECTION OF RUSTICS

In the early 570s, Bishop Martin of Braga, in north-western Portugal, replied to a request from a fellow bishop of the same region, Polemius of Asturga, for advice on converting peasants to Christianity. Bishop Martin belonged to a final generation of late Roman Churchmen who travelled freely about the Mediterranean. Born in Pannonia (modern Hungary) around 520, Martin journeyed to the Holy Land where he became a monk, before ending up in this relatively obscure corner of the Iberian peninsula, where he was ordained bishop in 550 or thereabouts. His letter to Polemius, *On the Correction of Rustics* – 'rustics' designating the peasantry ('yokels' might best capture the Latin) – takes us straight to the heart of the first of two great challenges facing the newly fragmented religious authority structures of the post-Roman west. How, Polemius had asked Bishop Martin, was the Word of God to be spread effectively among the mass of its widely dispersed rural populations? Given that about 90 per cent of the total population – in both the Roman and post-Roman eras – consisted of peasants, this was a challenge that the emergent Christian faith was always going to have to face at some point in its development, irrespective of the Roman imperial system's collapse. And bringing peasantry to the faith posed particular problems in more northerly, non-Mediterranean landscapes.

In the Mediterranean littoral, good agricultural land tends to be found in relatively concentrated pockets surrounded by arid wilderness or mountain (or both). Such geography naturally produced a world of agro-towns, with most of the peasantry tending to live close to a larger settlement centre within each cluster of fertility. This underlay the emergence of the characteristic Graeco-Roman form of local political organization: the *polis* (Greek) or *civitas* (Latin), a 'city' comprising both urban core and adjacent (and administratively dependent) rural hinterland. Growing to initial maturity in this environment, it was only natural that Christianity had evolved a ground-level authority structure based on one local leader for each city-based concentration of population. As a result, local Roman Christianity came to be structured on the basis of one bishop per city territory, with the bishop holding monopoly rights over baptism and preaching within his diocese to ensure minimal deviations from accepted orthodoxy – crucial safeguards in a world where so much of Christian belief and practice remained hotly contested for so long.

This all worked perfectly well in coastal Asia Minor, the Near East, Egypt and North Africa, where one bishop per major agro-town generated a relatively effective network of episcopal provision. The bishop's typical community in these areas was neither too large nor too dispersed to prevent him from providing a reasonable degree of pastoral care (even if, as we've seen, patterns of developing Christianity in rural areas – the countryside of Roman Egypt, for instance – tended to be highly syncretic; see p. 70). But major difficulties surfaced when the same structure was transferred to non-Mediterranean landscapes with a much greater spread of fertile land, particularly in Rome's European provinces. In this world, the standard Graeco-Roman order of local government – urban core, dependent rural territory – had been made to fit in civil administrative terms, but the result was much larger territories around each individual city. When episcopal dioceses were then superimposed on this pre-existing pattern of imperial *civitas* administration, the result was a relatively small number of much larger dioceses. Where North Africa had over six hundred bishoprics from AD 400 (a figure admittedly inflated by competitive ordination during the Donatist dispute; p. 131), the whole of Gaul contained only 118, many of which were concentrated in and around the Alps and Pyrenees. This created real problems when Churchmen finally attempted to spread salvation systematically into the countryside. In an institutional structure that empowered only one individual to preach and baptize, how were the dispersed peasantry inhabiting the wide stretches of non-Mediterranean Europe to be brought to the faith?

As far as we can tell, the process had not got far before the deposition of the last western Roman emperor, Romulus Augustulus. By the late fifth century, Christianity was strongly established in some northern towns – Le Mans, in northern Gaul, already possessed eighteen churches, Paris thirty-five – but all the evidence for a concerted approach to the process of spreading Christianity into the countryside dates to the post-Roman sixth century and beyond.[21]

In this era, bishops as dispersed in space and time as Caesarius of Arles (502/3–542) in south-eastern Gaul, Gregory of Tours (573–94) further north, and Iberia's Martin of Braga (*c.* 550–80) all faced up to the problem of how to generate effective Christian piety among the rural populations of their dioceses. All three of these bishops made a basic and striking equation between peasants and religious deficiency. The same equation also turns up in many of the regional Church councils of the sixth and seventh centuries. It was during this era that the abstract noun *rusticitas* (from the Latin adjective *rusticus*, 'rural') became synonymous with inappropriate, or even straightforwardly non-Christian, religious attitudes and behaviour, even among town dwellers: hence the title of Martin of Braga's response to Bishop Polemius.

Martin's letter introduces us to a methodological crux at the heart of any attempt to understand the nature of religious devotion in the countryside of the post-Roman west. On close inspection, there turns out to be no obvious correspondence between the list of failings catalogued by the bishop, and what we know of traditional pre-Christian cultic practice within his diocesan stomping ground in north-western Portugal. The latter, having largely survived the cosmopolitan religious impact of Romanization, is pretty well documented in inscriptions up to the time of Constantine. Over four hundred pre-Roman gods and goddesses are named in the epigraphy of the region, and some of these cults were apparently still flourishing in the post-Roman period. But

Martin doesn't refer to any of these divinities. Much of the religiously deviant behaviour he complains about consists of what is clearly a stock list of commonplaces, with much the same kind of things turning up in the works of Caesarius and Gregory (not to mention contemporary Church council canons): consulting soothsayers, performing propitiatory rites to safeguard health, happiness, or make the crops grow; the making of love potions; observing old Roman festivals like the Kalends of January (the start of the new year) rather than Christmas; the proliferation of healing amulets, divination, and the leaving of offerings at a host of supposed sources of divine power, such as springs and crossroads.

So how exactly should we envisage the general religious flavour of the countryside of the post-Roman west? In just a few cases, texts report deviant religious behaviour that is specific enough to suggest some genuine continuity of local pagan cults from the pre-Christian past down to the sixth century. A would-be Gallic stylite saint of the later sixth century called Vulfoliac, eventually lured down from his pillar by Gregory of Tours, had a documented backstory which involved persuading a group of peasants to demolish their still-functioning temple to the goddess Diana. Vulfoliac's monastic mentor, Aredius, was likewise famous for specifically anti-pagan religious iconoclasm. But, a handful of such moments aside, much of what our sixth-century bishops seem to be complaining about is not continuity of ancient pagan practice but what looks much more like deviant forms of Christianity: various forms of superstition and religious backsliding sitting alongside some kind of simultaneous Christian allegiance. Caesarius of Arles, for instance, condemns those who make the sign of the cross before consuming sacrificial banquets (whatever those might be), or who chant the names of saints and angels alongside those of stray divinities from the pagan past. Baptized Christians who wouldn't work on Thursday because it was Jupiter's day (or perhaps because they just wanted the day off) also come in for criticism. When these kinds of reported behaviours are set in the context of the institutional and other limitations which affected sixth-century Churchmen looking to reach such a widely dispersed peasant population, they become not only explicable but bring the underlying nature of contemporary transformations in rural religiosity much more sharply into focus.[22]

Some sixth-century Churchmen worked tirelessly to overcome the range of practical challenges that stood in the way of generating an effective form of rural Christianity. Unlike their counterparts in the British Isles, bishops in the post-Roman Gaul, Italy and Spain were more directly involved in building new rural churches to meet the needs of peasant populations. The surviving evidence is anecdotal rather than comprehensive, but over the sixth century many 'proto-parish' churches, under the direct control of local bishops, were constructed in various corners of the relatively huge dioceses of the Christian north-west to make it more possible for peasants to get to church. By the time of Bishop Gregory, twenty-four such churches existed in the Touraine (the French diocese centred on the city of Tours). Similar networks existed in parts at least of north-western Spain (where, thanks to Bishop Martin, we have specific information for Braga and the neighbouring dioceses of Porto and Tuy), and in areas closer to the Alps. One of the main concerns of the council of Carpentras – which Caesarius, as metropolitan archbishop of Arles, called in 527 – was to strengthen such networks and individual churches by protecting the property endowments which provided them with an annual income. Diocesan bishops had ultimate control of these revenues, but Carpentras banned them from siphoning off so much for other purposes that not enough was left to provide for parish priests, or for adequate supplies of liturgical vessels, vestments and books.[23]

Some senior bishops also tried to provide more, and better-trained, priests: an issue addressed by another of Caesarius' regional synods at Arles in 524. This upheld long-standing bans on twice-married men, or men married to women who'd had two or more husbands, from serving as priests. Being married more than once was taken as a sign of an unbridled love of physical pleasure, which did not resonate well with Christianity's long-standing suspicions of sexuality. At the same time, however, the synod reduced the training period for new priests, who were supposed to live a more religious lifestyle during this period, to a single year. (Caesarius had originally envisaged such training as a much more open-ended 'lengthy period', *multo tempore*.) The synod did not go into detail on what form this training should take, but Hispanic materials can probably fill the gap. The third council of Toledo in 589 ordered 'schools' to be established for the training of priests across the entirety of the Visigoth kingdom. Young men were to live as quasi-monks in cathedral precincts under a properly qualified master, even if, later, they went on to marry (marrying once did not yet disqualify you from the priesthood – or indeed from being a bishop, although you were expected to stop sleeping with your wife when promoted to the higher rank).[24]

Alongside these improvements in rural religious infrastructure went a much stronger emphasis both on the importance of religious teaching, and on the development of forms of Christian worship designed to work for peasants. Caesarius was notorious for locking his church doors after congregations had been admitted, ensuring that they stayed for his sermons (which in the sixth century came at the end of services). He also pioneered another key change in Church practice. As we have seen, in both early and Roman imperial Christianity, only bishops were allowed to preach. This rule worked well enough for small, largely urban-based Mediterranean congregations; for sixth-century, non-Mediterranean Christianity, however, this had the serious drawback of limiting Christian instruction to the one congregation where the bishop currently happened to be taking a service. Caesarius responded to the issue with characteristic intelligence. First, he urged all bishops within his metropolitan jurisdiction to preach every Sunday – a ruling strongly implying that even this was not yet standard practice. Then, in a revolutionary move, at the council of Vaison in 529 he persuaded his fellow bishops to agree to allow priests to preach. This had the potential dramatically to increase the amount of Christian teaching that could be delivered to rural congregations in the metropolitan province of Arles on any given Sunday. It is a clear sign of the new rule's utility that, over the next century, it won general acceptance. Already by the 560s, one Spanish provincial council endorsed it, and it was officially adopted for the entire Visigothic kingdom at the fourth council of Toledo in 633.[25]

The impact of Caesarius' move was reinforced by further initiatives to provide newly empowered priests with better preaching materials. The sixth and seventh centuries saw the emergence, in both Gaul and Spain, of a new range of dedicated sermon collections, as well as collections of other materials which could form the basis of sermons. It was again Caesarius who spearheaded this initiative, and he was responsible for one highly influential collection, comprising both his own preaching, and recycling – often in adapted form – the sermons of St Augustine of Hippo. Other known early medieval collections include the so-called *Eusebius Gallicanus* from Gaul (an anonymous collection of seventy-six fifth- and sixth-century sermons collected around 550) and the seventh-century Toledan *Homiliary* from the Visigothic kingdom. In all these sermon collections, again drawing inspiration from Augustine, the emphasis was placed on simple, clear language – the so-called *sermo humilis* – rather than on the kind of rhetorical tours de force that Bishop Ambrose was famous for back in fourth-century Milan and which had played an important role in convincing the young Augustine to convert to Christianity.

A similar emphasis on the importance of plain language is also a striking feature of the Prefaces to the numerous miracle collections put together by Gregory of Tours in the last quarter of the sixth century. For Gregory, pastoral effectiveness overrode grammatical accuracy. Gregory was doing God's will in collecting all these stories of manifest Christian virtue and, even if he did sometimes get his Latin endings confused, his mother reassured him (he tells us) that the simplicity of his language meant that they could be understood by ordinary people. While Gregory's miracle collections were certainly meant to be read, the format of the many individual stories of Christian virtue that each of them contains is highly suggestive. They largely consist of anecdotes covering recognizably everyday situations, which would have taken no more than a few minutes to read aloud, and all of which culminated in a straightforward moralizing conclusion about what it meant to be a good Christian: each story, in other words, a potential sermon in the making.[26]

Gregory's miracle stories, together with the other sermon collections, manifest a pressing concern among sixth-century Church leaders to generate a coherent vision of what Christian piety should mean for relatively uneducated rural congregations. This saw some of the more complicated doctrines of Christianity being recast in readily digestible form. The main dispute that had rumbled on among Nicene Church leaders in the fifth-century west (when they weren't busy confronting Homoean rivals) was a postscript to the quarrel, earlier in the century, between Augustine of Hippo and the British ascetic leader Pelagius over the extent to which humans had free will to effect their own salvation, or required God's grace even to make a first move. Where Pelagius argued that individuals had to exert their will to give up the world in order to be saved, Augustine considered fallen human beings so weak that God's grace was of overwhelming importance to their salvation. However, if taken to the extreme, Augustine's views might imply (and certainly did to his critics) that it was God's will which decided whether any individual was saved or not, removing any need for good deeds on the part of the individual, and raising the potential problem of predestination: that God had decided your eternal fate whatever you did or did not do. Caesarius and the assembled bishops of his archdiocese tackled this problem at the council of Orange in 529, coming up with a cheerfully simple response. To be saved, every individual needed both to live a good Christian life and be blessed with Divine grace. This is a fair-enough answer in its way but striking for the extent to which the assembled bishops stayed away from the dangerous and theologically complex territory of potential predestination, opting for a compromise formula that could be easily presented to their congregations.

Different western Churchmen of the period glossed the meaning of this 'good Christian life' in different ways, but the message was always a simple one, containing a few consistent themes. Most importantly, people needed to be baptized. But to make this central ritual of the Christian faith accessible to as many – and as easy to perform – as possible, the required preparation was substantially downgraded from the pre-Constantinian era. Twenty days was now the maximum recommended period for both formal instruction and any accompanying rituals of exorcism, as compared to the multi-year, multi-stage regime characteristic of early Christianity. Instruction focused on being able to recite, and presumably have at least some basic understanding of, the so-called Apostles' Creed – the most succinct of the traditional statements of Christian belief.

The general theological and moral message now being transmitted by clerics – to judge by all the sermon collections and Martin of Braga's treatise – was straightforward. Christ's Incarnation and Resurrection had freed Christian believers from enslavement to the Devil and opened the prospect of eternal life. In this world, meanwhile, the good Christian should attend church regularly, as well as avoiding theft, fornication, adultery and murder. There were also some efforts to regulate sexual intercourse between married couples. Sex was to be avoided during menstruation and the major Church feasts and fasts of the year, Martin and others teaching that any transgression here would produce handicapped children. No attempt was made, however, to instil any more intense form of individual spirituality. The collection of sermons from Toledo, for instance, contains little reflection on the suffering and death of Christ, and the responsibility of individual human sin for causing it – themes that would lie at the heart of later medieval lay piety (see Chapter 13). The vast majority of the *Homiliary*'s sermons, even those for Easter which naturally focus upon Christ's death on the Cross, stress instead the good news of resurrection and promise of eternal life. In the same way, Gregory of Tours' miracle collections – not to mention his *Histories* – present a simple, moral and highly rational universe. Pious Christian behaviour generates good outcomes: *rusticitas* exactly the opposite. Compared to the kind of more intense pious sensibility characteristic of later medieval Christianity, this was a simple and attractively upbeat message.[27]

But if there's no doubting the effort some sixth-century leaders put into the task of restructuring Church organization in their dioceses and providing the necessary materials better to spread the faith into the countryside – constructing churches, training priests, devising new practices and statements of the faith that were appropriate for this new audience – there is real uncertainty about how much actual rural piety was generated by this raft of initiatives. Even in the Touraine, which boasted twenty-four parish churches in the time of Gregory of Tours, parishioners still had, on average, a 6-mile (10 km) walk to their nearest church. In reality, therefore, most people were not attending services on the vast majority of Sundays; it is inconceivable that, on their day off, peasants were regularly walking 12 miles to church and back. A council held at the Gallic town of Agde in 506 probably gets us rather closer to reality in its stipulation that good Christians must attend their bishop's cathedral or one of his parish churches at least at Christmas, Easter and on other major festivals. But even this much was probably a best-case scenario. A four-hour hike for the fit would not have been an attractive prospect, particularly in midwinter, let alone for the young, the old and the sick.

It is also extremely unlikely that, despite all the new initiatives, much preaching went on outside urban contexts in the post-Roman west. We lack detailed information from this period, so the better-documented patterns of the high Middle Ages offer an important comparative perspective. In the eleventh and twelfth centuries, after the establishing of more intensive clerical education regimes than anything which existed in the early medieval west, and in a world with many more service books and Bibles, it was still only cathedral clergy, from a bishop's household entourage, who actually preached sermons. Nothing suggests that there would have been more extensive provision in the sixth century, when, to judge by Caesarius' urgings on the subject, even bishops did not necessarily preach every Sunday. For the most part, therefore, Christian services consisted of the laity occasionally observing some very simple religious rituals being performed in front of them, rather than any kind of participatory experience mediated by intense exploration – through teaching and preaching – of a deeper Christian spirituality.[28]

It is also far from clear exactly of what most Christian services consisted. As the sixth and seventh centuries progressed, there grew up other Christian centres in the countryside that fell outside the bishop's jurisdiction. The seventh century saw the appearance, both in Gaul and Spain, of a new wave of monastic foundations based now in the countryside (whereas previous monasteries had generally been established in or close to towns). Gaul in particular saw the establishment of over a hundred new monastic houses, many inspired by the appearance on the Continent of wandering Irish monks. Irish monastic spirituality, as we have seen, put a high premium on exchanging the all-important ties of kinship – essential to prosperity and even personal safety in its native Ireland – for a life of eternal pilgrimage (Latin *peregrinatio*) and hardship, which was seen as the most effective way of displaying your love of God. Gallic sources reflect the arrival of Irish ascetics inspired by these ideologies in the last quarter of the sixth century (prominent among whom was the monk-missionary Columbanus), who both established their own new foundations and encouraged a generation of Frankish elite converts to follow their lead.[29] In the same period, too, many less ascetically inspired landowners were, with the encouragement of Church councils, establishing new churches on their estates.

Both phenomena had the benefit of increasing the number of rural centres at which some kind of Christian experience was available. But a few hundred new foundations were not enough to solve the fundamental problems of distance. In later medieval England, over ten thousand parish churches and priests would eventually be required to provide a centre of Christian worship for every rural community. Nothing on remotely this scale was happening anywhere in the sixth and seventh centuries. Equally important, the main job of the new monasteries was not pastoral care (although surrounding populations sometimes attended services in monastic chapels), while some, particularly the influential new foundations inspired by Columbanus, fell explicitly outside the bishops' jurisdiction, and hence could not be integrated into any systematic religious provision for the peasantry. The same was true of the landowners' new churches, which posed particular problems of their own. These were established for a whole series of reasons, some of which had less to do with the performance of Christian piety on the part of the landlord class, and more with securing its worldly interests. Tax breaks, social control, and generating new revenue sources in the forms of offerings and other renders (which were now demanded notionally to support the new church, but of which the landlords often seem to have claimed a percentage) were as much on their menu as pastoral care, and often complained about in contemporary clerical literature. It was also up to landowners, rather than any bishop, to nominate the priest who would be in charge of the new church. This would usually be one of their own peasants, answerable of course to the lord who appointed them, and who received little or no training for their new role.[30]

Despite numerous innovations, then, there remained a systemic under-provision of Christian pastoral care for rural populations during the sixth and seventh centuries, while the quality of what was on offer looks decidedly mixed. By AD 600, most peasants probably were being baptized – or at least had the opportunity to be so at some point in their lives – but the further you travelled from the cathedrals at the heart of large northern European dioceses, the more questionable the extent and quality of the religious experience available. Episcopal-controlled baptismal churches still being few and far between, the Christian message was being delivered to most by less-regulated institutions established by landlords, haphazardly supplemented by the occasional new monastic foundation.

The inherent problems of this under-provision were exacerbated by some of the other strategies adopted by Christian leaders to spread the faith among rural populations. Some were straightforwardly coercive. The writings of bishops such as Caesarius of Arles and Isidore of Seville, living at either end of the sixth century and either side of the Pyrenees, put much emphasis on persuasion and the positive side of the Christian message. But both were equally of the view that, if all else failed, Christianity could and should be beaten into particularly recalcitrant peasants. The third council of Toledo went further, ruling in 589 that any physical coercion short of death was a legitimate means to bring rustics to the faith.[31] Financial coercion was also employed. By the end of the sixth century, many Christian institutions – particularly the larger bishoprics but also some of the more important monasteries – were major landowners: the best guess being that something like a third of all land in the continental successor states belonged in some way to different Church institutions at this point, and great Christian landlords had no compunction in exploiting their control. This was justified, naturally, as concern for the salvation of their tenants' souls. In the post-Roman period, substantial numbers of peasants were either slaves or tied to the land as semi-free labourers, the course of their lives dictated by a strong element of landlord power. And while it became part of early medieval aristocratic piety in the sixth and, particularly, the seventh centuries to free your slaves, this was usually only by half a step into the tied, permanently dependent legal category of the semi-free. With such men and women lacking the right to take their labour elsewhere, landlords continued to exercise significant power over a substantial portion of the peasantry of the post-Roman west. In the view of both Gregory the Great and Caesarius, there was every reason to jack up rents for peasants who wouldn't convert. It's obviously impossible to know how many peasants were intimidated or blackmailed into Christian compliance in the sixth and seventh centuries, but there's no reason to think it a tiny minority. The attachment of anyone converted to Christianity by means of a sound thrashing or potential bankruptcy is likely to have been half-hearted at best.[32]

Strange as it may seem, coercion was probably not the most religiously problematic strategy employed to win over peasants to the faith in this era. Persuasion was not only a morally preferable way to bring people to Christianity, but, in cases where force wasn't an option, it was also necessary. Alongside the slaves and serfs of the early medieval west there existed substantial populations of free peasants who weren't under close seigneurial control (although it is impossible to reckon the relative percentages). This meant, in the same way that missionaries working in the British Isles had had to recast Christianity as a religion for warriors, sixth- and seventh-century continental Churchmen were faced with the problem of making it positively work for those peasants who had a choice about whether or not to accept it. Apart from providing explanations for, and comfort against, all the heartaches of everyday life – ill-health, poverty, death – this meant a further reorientating of Christianity towards the enormous range of issues involved in making crops grow. The challenges confronting the peasant in this most essential of tasks were many: the technologies available for maintaining basic soil fertility were rudimentary, while the weather, insects and all kinds of disease – human, vegetable, animal, or combinations of all three – presented constant and unpredictable problems. Localized crop failures were regular. When, in the eighth and ninth centuries, Frankish chronicles become fuller, local famines are recorded, on average, in every fourth year, supplemented, occasionally, by much more widespread crop failures. Our knowledge of the religious traditions Christianity replaced in the post-Roman countryside is rudimentary, but they were firmly anchored around the agricultural year, centring on cycles of festival and sacrifice designed to obtain divine assistance for the crops, and to show due thankfulness after a successful harvest, interspersed with propitiatory rites to ward off any number of potential intervening disasters.[33] It is hardly surprising, therefore, that in the post-Roman countryside rurally focused Churchmen initiated a progressive reinvention of Christianity to meet the urgent needs of their new rural parishioners.

Around the Provençal city of Arles, for instance, it was long-established practice to offer New Year libations to ensure the fertility of the fields for the coming season. Caesarius' solution was to replace this festival with a sprinkling of holy water on the same fields, altering the day slightly to coincide with the supposed anniversary of Christ's baptism in the Jordan (the first Sunday after Epiphany). This worked well and had clearly been done before: peasants around the Mediterranean now bathed in rivers, springs or even the sea in late June to celebrate the Day of John the Baptist, where they had previously done it to ensure the success of the wheat harvest. Some of Caesarius' other innovations faced greater resistance, particularly his attempts to replace the traditional New Year festivities of Kalends with the feast of Christmas.[34]

Caesarius' efforts need to be understood as part of a longer process, stretching back to the fourth century and Christianity's transformation into a full-scale mass religion, whereby it gradually developed a much fuller liturgical year to match the well-established festival cycles of the pre-Christian Mediterranean world. Easter and Epiphany were already being celebrated long before Constantine's conversion, but the fourth century saw the development of a full-scale Lenten season, and the separation of Advent from Pentecost. That this was part of a strategy – built out of local individual responses rather than centrally directed – to arm Christianity with counterparts to well-established pre-Christian celebrations is suggested by the emergence of celebrating Christmas on 25 December. This initiative began in Rome to provide a Christian alternative to the pagan Saturnalia, and slowly spread from there to the rest of the Christian world. The origins of Advent are mysterious, but early/mid-December was regarded as the end of the agricultural year and had its associated pre-Christian rites. The plethora of Christian martyrs could also be mobilized as appropriate to provide Christian alternatives to pagan festivals: John Chrysostom deliberately promoted the cult of Julian of Anazarbus (Julian of Antioch) because the date of his martyrdom coincided with an established pagan festival in the city of Antioch, and this kind of initiative must have been repeated on many occasions in different locations.[35] But while Caesarius and his many forebears between them effectively Christianized the established pre-Christian festal cycles of the urban and agricultural years between the fourth and sixth centuries, in one other key respect he tried – and failed – to resist the transfer of older religious sensibilities and habits into the dawning Christian era.

Although much of the detail cannot be recovered, the religious sensibility central to traditional belief patterns clearly took the form of an underlying expectation that appropriate religious behaviour could shape future events by persuading the relevant supernatural force(s) to act in one way rather than another. Bad events could be fended off, and good outcomes guaranteed by mobilizing divine power in an appropriate way, which involved a full and diverse range of ritual, incantation and sacrifice. Drawing as he often did on influential lines of thought that can be traced back to Augustine of Hippo, and further back into pre-Constantinian Christian thought, the early sixth-century Caesarius considered it utterly impossible – and in fact inappropriate – to think that the will of an eternal, omnipotent Christian God could be so influenced by mere human behaviour. His vision of the interaction between human and divine was therefore utterly at odds with the quid pro quos at the heart of traditional pre-Christian religious sensibilities. In this line of Christian thought, the Divine will had no care at all for the things of this world, but was focused solely on saving the soul for Paradise hereafter – and this, Caesarius believed, should also be the overwhelming and only concern of any believing Christian. He therefore roundly condemned, and tried to suppress, all the traditional mechanisms still employed by his parishioners to try to bend supernatural forces to their immediate worldly ends – prayers, libations, animal sacrifices and dedications of food, clothing, or tools at a vast range of holy sites, not to mention 'magical' amulets worn to fend off ill-health.[36]

Skipping forward a generation to the writings of Gregory of Tours in the last quarter of the sixth century, it quickly becomes apparent that Caesarius' attempts to keep believing Christians focused on the hereafter had fallen on resoundingly deaf ears. Gregory tells us that he cured his father's gout by using a recipe derived from the Book of Tobias (from the Apocrypha), and that he himself wore a healing amulet round his neck to fend off the debilitating migraines to which he had been prone as a youth. This amulet contained biblical verses, not old Graeco-Roman magical incantations, but the practice was fundamentally the same. From the briefest reading of Gregory's miracle collections, it becomes evident that, half a century later, the view which Caesarius had considered essentially pre-Christian – that bad outcomes could be fended off and good ones secured by appropriate religious behaviour – had become absorbed into mainstream early medieval Christian piety. Such syncretism was manifest in many Christian texts of the period, and would remain a dominant strand within Latin Christianity for the rest of the Middle Ages and beyond.

Not only does this absorption of pre-Christian sensibilities into Christian practice provide us with another example of syncretism at work, there is, I think, a further point to be made. Gregory's miracle collections and the stories they told were designed to advance the process of Christianizing rural populations. Read carefully, they take the form of an argument, carefully constructed to demonstrate what to Gregory was an irrefutable truth: that the new Christian saints' cults were more powerful than the old magical practices so detested by Caesarius. In other words, as Gregory saw it, Christian saints could now serve exactly the same range of function as the old pagan cults had done before – only far more effectively.

What Gregory presents us with in all his stories of saints and their miracles – somewhat counter-intuitively to modern eyes, which often associate such phenomena with ignorance and superstition – is a fundamentally rational universe. The power of the Christian God is at work everywhere and underlies everything. True virtue is always rewarded, so that the sarcophagi of the holy dead will move miraculously to ensure that saints can be properly venerated, or to keep a married couple together in death, their overwhelming virtue manifest in the chastity they maintained throughout their lives. The stories also stack up an exhaustive catalogue of miraculous cures, including bringing a toddler back to life (a moving reflection of the overwhelming precariousness of everyday life in a world in which half the population would die by the age of fifteen), with the aim of encouraging people of faith to bring their ills to the saints' shrines, sure conduits of Divine power. Throughout Gregory's stories, appropriate religious behaviour – *reverentia* – brings success; impiety – *rusticitas* – brings disaster. Swear a false oath on a holy relic and the offended saint will catapult you up to the ceiling in a striking act of rejection, whereas faithful religious processions will fend off the plague, and make ferocious storms subside. Gregory's lesson is clear. Trust in God, and look to Him and His saints for all the comfort that you need in the face of the troubles and woes of human existence, both in the here and now as well as the hereafter. Proper Christian piety, directed towards the network of holy shrines that had spread across the landscape, will meet people's needs much more effectively than the pagan shrines they were increasingly replacing.[37] The actual form of the stories indicates that their expressed world-view – the superiority of Christian magic over all its rivals – had not yet been fully internalized by their target audiences when they were composed: Gregory's catalogue of Christian miracles was intended to persuade that Christian magic was more powerful than any possible rival. Christian magic would certainly win out in the longer term, but Gregory's repetitive vehemence suggests that the battle was not yet won in Gaul in the last quarter of the sixth century.

Our picture of this first phase of targeted rural evangelism is far from complete. For the first time in Christianity's history, however, the surviving source material does at least show us Church leaders making committed efforts to solve both the institutional and spiritual problems posed by the first of the two key challenges they faced in the post-Roman period: bringing the dispersed peasant populations of non-Mediterranean Europe to the faith. The limitations of the Christianity which evolved in the post-Roman countryside also reinforces the point that conversion was a profoundly two-way street, the incorporation of early medieval peasants into the Christian faith involving as many important modifications to prevailing patterns of Christian piety as it did significant changes to the existing belief-systems and religious practices of the converts. This is a recurrent theme; we've already seen something similar in the degree to which Roman elite cultural values became part of developing Christianity in the fourth century, and in the *modus vivendi* the faith established with prevailing warrior values in Ireland and Britain between the fifth and seventh centuries. The changes required to make the faith work both for early medieval peasants and warriors were greatly facilitated by the ways in which, simultaneously, Church leaders were responding to the second great challenge they faced in these years: this one a direct result of the unravelling of the old Roman imperial system.

8

Culture and Society in the Post-Roman West

In the mid-seventh century, Bishop Braulio of Zaragoza – one of the most distinguished scholars of the age and pupil of the even greater Isidore of Seville – was set a knotty biblical problem by one of his students, a certain Fructuosus. It concerned Mathusale, grandfather of Noah (of Ark fame). According to the Book of Genesis, Mathusale lived to the grand old age of 969, and begot his son Lamech (Noah's father) at the age of 167. Lamech was 188 when Noah was born, and the Flood came in Noah's six hundredth year. If you do the maths, Mathusale was 955 at the time of the Flood and hence outlived it by fourteen years. But he wasn't on the Ark. Genesis clearly specifies its eight human occupants: Noah, his three sons, and their four – typically anonymous – wives. So where was Mathusale during the Flood?

Various images come to mind – a nonacentenarian clinging to a log for forty days and nights – but Braulio's answer was simple. Fructuosus' Bible, he wrote, contained textual errors. The issue, Braulio went on, had been resolved back in the fourth century by the great late Roman biblical scholar Jerome in his *Hebrew Questions on Genesis*. Mathusale was actually 187 at the birth of Lamech, who was himself 182 when Noah was born. Do those sums, and Mathusale's death at 969 coincides with the year of the Flood. Braulio didn't say whether he thought Noah let his grandfather drown, or whether he had died of natural causes beforehand, but, either way, Mathusale did not outlive the flood.[1] This exchange is utterly characteristic of the ecclesiastical culture of the post-Roman west: one devoted to and focusing on ultra-precise readings of a Bible text which was prone to textual variations. Recondite and entirely academic though they might appear, the training and intellectual preoccupations of this great Spanish triumvirate – Isidore, Braulio and Fructuosus – bring the second great challenge faced by post-Roman Latin Christianity strongly into focus.

BEYOND THE DARK AGES

In traditional historiographical stereotypes, largely constructed by outraged classicists, the third quarter of the first millennium (*c.* 500–750) marks Europe's Dark Ages: a time when reason and classical philosophy gave way to ignorance and superstition. Churchmen continued to read their Bibles, but these were written in terrible Latin, riddled with grammatical errors. And the handful of ecclesiastics who did even this much were exceptional; no one else was literate at all. But this stereotype isn't the whole story – or even half of it.

In the later eighth century, western copyists came up with a new script and new modes of copying texts, which, to their minds, rendered earlier manuscript copies in older scripts totally out of date. As a result, they developed a strong tendency to discard older manuscripts once they had copied them – meaning that very few examples have survived dating from earlier than the second half of the eighth century. This massively complicates the process of reconstructing the intellectual culture of Latin Europe in the post-Roman third quarter of the first millennium. With a vanishingly small number of manuscripts surviving from the period, it is extremely difficult to employ contemporary texts from the sixth to the mid-eighth centuries as evidence for reading and copying in any straightforward way. The lack of original manuscripts dating from this period was, of course, a major contributory factor to the 'Dark Age' label; but at least some of this absence of evidence is illusory, caused by the destruction attendant on the alternative scriptorial predilections of later monks. As a result, argument has often to rest on the more indirect evidence of what their compositions suggest about what the known authors of the period had been reading, and – as has become apparent in recent decades – much of the traditional characterization of education and learning in these centuries (and certainly the stubbornly persistent 'Dark Age' label) is both inaccurate and misleading.

One important intellectual advance has been the realization that 'literacy', though a singular noun, is actually a composite term. Today, we tend to lump together reading and writing. In many pre-modern contexts, however, reading and composition – the art of creating written texts in different genres involving varying degrees of complexity – were separate skills, acquired by different people for different purposes. The physical act of writing – messing about with pens, parchment and ink (the latter requiring some unpleasant human-derived ingredients) – was yet a third skill: one often given a lower status than those of reading and composition. In the Roman world, composition was characteristically an oral process of dictation to compliant scribes, and even reading was usually done out loud. In one letter, the Roman statesman and philosopher Cicero complained that a sore throat had made it impossible for him even to read (although it didn't seem to stop him dictating the letter), while one of Bishop Ambrose's party tricks in fourth-century Milan was to allow people to watch him read silently to himself in public – so rare a skill that his biographer singled it out for comment.[2]

Reconsidered against this broader intellectual framework, and paying much closer attention to the evidence that has survived, the educational and literary cultures both of post-Roman Churchmen and the societies that produced them have proved more dynamic than the Dark Age label would suggest. The intellectual achievements of some leading individual Churchmen, such as Braulio – and, perhaps above all, his teacher Isidore of Seville – were prodigious. Born in about the year 560 to a family from southern Spain, Isidore received a classical education in Latin language and literature under his brother Leander, architect of the third council of Toledo which brought the Visigoths to Nicene Christianity in 589, and whom Isidore succeeded as bishop of Seville around the year 600. After Isidore's death in 636, Braulio compiled a list of his compositions. It makes impressive reading: twenty works on *grammatica* (educational works tied into the classically derived study of language and literature), and a host of others devoted to Church discipline, biblical exegesis and history. Isidore's most famous work, the *Etymologies*, is often described as an encyclopaedia (which is broadly how it was used in the Middle Ages), but was actually a philosophical grammar, constructed on the axiom that a word's etymological origin provides insight into the cause (and thus the essence) of the thing it signifies, as exemplified in the distinction between an Art and a Discipline, which opens the entire work:

> A discipline (*disciplina*) takes its name from 'learning' (*discere*) . . . And an art (*ars*, gen. *artis*) is so called because it consists of strict (*artus*) precepts and rules . . . Plato and Aristotle would speak of this distinction: an art consists of matters than can turn out in different ways, while a discipline is concerned with things that have only one outcome. Thus, when something is expounded with true arguments, it will be a discipline; when something merely resembling the truth and based on opinion is treated, it will have the name of an art.[3]

Compiling the *Etymologies* required careful exploration of each term included, with multiple illustrations drawn from a wide body of classical literature (which is why the work could later be used as an encyclopaedia). After Isidore's death, Braulio finalized the work's arrangement into twenty books, though it naturally falls into two halves. Books 1–8 make their way through the classical educational curriculum based on the first-century BC Roman scholar Varro's classification of the liberal arts (grammar, rhetoric, dialectic, mathematical sciences, medicine and law) before demonstrating that each subject found its fulfilment in Christian doctrines and worship. Books 9 and 10 investigate languages, peoples and social groups, forming a bridge to the survey of natural history that comprises the second half. Based partly on Pliny the Elder's *Natural History*, Isidore's own survey was wider and included extra topics ranging from building to warfare to tool-making. Its author's sustained erudition, on display throughout the text, was based on a personal library of over four hundred books, which also shaped the intellectual formation of his pupils. As well as completing the work of his master, Braulio generated his own impressive list of publications: a letter collection combining Christian wisdom with classical learning, further revisions of the *Hispana* (the collected rulings of Visigoth Church councils), various devotional works, and probably also a major revision of the civil laws of the Visigoth kingdom.[4]

Nobody in the early medieval west wrote quite so much as Isidore, but he had many learned peers in the other Christian microcosms of the post-Roman west, individuals busy producing sermons, canon law, liturgies, saints' *Lives* and devotional works aplenty during the supposed Dark Ages. On closer and more sympathetic inspection, the secular elites of the western successor states also turn out to be more literate than previously suspected, if clearly with varying degrees of intensity. The great majority were passively literate: trained, if not to compose, then at least to read their Bibles. They were usually also functionally literate, since they needed to cope both with written legal documents (albeit perhaps with the help of specialists) and their own list-based administrative tools, which allowed them to manage the landed estates on which their wealth was based, not to mention transmit those estates efficiently on to the next generation via written marriage and inheritance settlements. In the last decades of the twentieth century, a treasure trove of documents written on slate and dating from the later sixth to the mid-eighth centuries has come to light in central-northern Spain: many of them fall into this administrative-legal category. In this case, an unusually durable medium has preserved types of texts that must have been written in vast quantities across much of the post-Roman west on flimsier scraps of papyrus or parchment, or sometimes even wooden tablets (like the famous *Tablettes Albertini* from Vandal North Africa).[5]

Significant numbers of the post-Roman secular landowning elite went far beyond this kind of functional literacy. They were literate at a higher level, trained to appreciate and sometimes even to compose works written in complex Latin literary genres. In the spring of 566, a classically educated poet called Venantius Fortunatus arrived at the Gallic courts of King Clovis's Merovingian grandsons (the Frankish kingdom was at that point divided between three of them). Born in northern Italy between 530 and 540, growing up in the period of Justinian's reconquest of the region, Venantius received an intense classical education in Latin language and literature, culminating in high-level studies at the old imperial capital of Ravenna. Travelling to Frankish Gaul, he moved smoothly between its different courts, acquiring a wide range of secular and ecclesiastical patrons (Gregory of Tours among them) and finding an enthusiastic audience for his verse, composed in a wide variety of genres and metres. Some were purely for entertainment: Frankish aristocrats enjoyed inviting Venantius for the weekend and having him sing for his supper. But he also produced more substantial works – everything from political commentaries on major state occasions, to eulogies for prominent individuals, to moving verses of consolation. Particularly striking are the verses he wrote for one Frankish aristocrat who had just lost both his wife and newborn son in childbirth:

> Noble Vilithuta, dear wife of Dagaulf, lies torn from her husband's embrace . . . Born of noble blood in the city of Paris, she was Roman by upbringing, barbarian by race. She brought a gentle spirit from a fierce race; the greater glory was to conquer nature . . . The father and husband in his grief felt all the more intensely, for in one death he grieved burying two . . . Nevertheless the husband has this consolation for his spouse, that her labour is not without reward. For anything which could be seen as female adornment she gave readily to the churches and to the poor. She left nothing here of those matters which will come to nothing, so now she has rich treasures laid up in advance.

Translation doesn't do any justice to Venantius' skill as a poet, but it does bring out one point of the greatest importance. Many of his patrons – like Gregory of Tours – were of Roman descent, but, as these verses make clear, at least some of those of Frankish descent likewise wanted Venantius to commemorate their lives (and losses). After three generations of coexistence and intermarriage, beginning with Clovis's late fifth-century foundation of the Merovingian kingdom, people still more or less knew which courtiers were of Roman or Frankish descent, but kings and their aristocrats – whatever their ethnic roots – now shared a common Latin literary culture, showing a marked appreciation for the complex classical verse Venantius had to offer. Enough patronage came Venantius' way, not least from the Frankish Queen Radegund (famous, among other things, for establishing the monastery of the Holy Cross in Poitiers to which we'll return at the end of this chapter), to allow him to thrive as a self-employed poet living off patronage and commissions in Gaul for over three decades, until he secured the bishopric of Poitiers around the year 600. Doubting historians have sometimes questioned whether Merovingian courtiers could really understand Venantius' verse, but this again is classicists' prejudice. A collection of letters survives from the same court circles in which Venantius flourished and these confirm the classicizing literary competence of several of the individuals – again of both Roman and Frankish descent – who turn up both as patrons of Venantius and in the writings of Gregory of Tours. Even Gregory, for all his advocacy of plain language that his mother could understand, liked to swap Latin texts with Venantius, to emphasize that he knew Virgil even if he chose not to quote him, and to make out (even if it wasn't quite true) that his deviations from classical Latin grammatical norms were a deliberate choice.[6] Venantius' career allows us to see that a lively, Latinate literate culture was flourishing in the elite circles of Frankish Gaul in the later sixth century.

The same taste for classical literary culture survived more generally across the courts of the post-Roman west, not least at that of Isidore of Seville's favourite Visigothic king, Sisebut (612–21). A few of this king's own letters have been preserved, along with a saint's life he wrote and a verse treatise on the phases of the moon (the latter dedicated to Isidore). While not so learned as the bishop, Sisebut was culturally at home in his company, having received a less intense version of the same classical education. In the middle of the seventh century, likewise, Braulio counted a wide range of Visigoth aristocrats among his epistolary network. His surviving letters are decidedly Christian-biblical (rather than classical Roman) in their frame of cultural reference – perhaps not surprising, given that so many of them are consolations on the death of loved ones – but their tone, style and language again all echo classical Latin norms, emphasizing that the same kind of Latin culture could be found in elite Visigothic as well as Frankish circles.[7]

But if there was plenty of Latin literacy about in Dark Age Europe, much of it profoundly shaped by a classical and late Roman Christian heritage, it now sat upon an entirely new educational infrastructure. Late Roman landowning elites – gentry and aristocracy – had been educated both to read and write by professional, self-employed teachers of language and literature – grammarians, who could be found in most of the Empire's market towns. This curriculum was reinforced, for those who could afford it, by the rhetors and philosophers who taught at the centres of higher-level studies (see Chapter 2). The children of the elite generally spent several – expensive – years exploring a small canon of set texts with these teachers, learning 'correct' Latin and acquiring the common cultural framework that prepared them for public life in the Roman world. In the post-Roman west, however, not only did the old centres of higher-level studies quickly cease to function, but the entire class of professional grammarians disappeared. In Britain, St Patrick is the last individual known to have been educated by a professional grammarian, around AD 400; in Gaul and Spain, grammarians had disappeared by the late fifth century. They persisted a little longer in Italy: in the first half of the sixth century, grammarians and rhetors could still be found at least in Rome, Ravenna and Milan (this was the tradition in which Venantius was educated). But then the Italian tradition, too, broke down.[8] Why these forms of study should have died out right across the western Empire, alongside the demise of the Roman imperial system, is no great mystery. The entire educational system fed directly into the intense competition for public office, wealth and influence that – as we have seen – consumed so much of the energies of Roman elite life, and in which, without classical cultural proficiency, you stood little chance of success. But, while the old Graeco-Roman ideological association of classical culture with human superiority was far from broken in the post-Roman west – witness Venantius' warm reception in the courts of Gaul, and the enthusiastic adoption of classical culture by aristocrats of Frankish descent – elite career structures had changed beyond recognition.

Unlike the Roman imperial system, the western successor states were not built around large-scale taxation to fund professional armies, which had in turn required the state to maintain the extensive bureaucratic and legal structures that provided the focus of elite careers in the later Empire. Latin Christendom's new rulers, in stark contrast, depended instead upon military service performed in person by members of their secular landowning elites, at the head of their own bodies of armed retainers. This sea-change in the fundamental nature of elite life happened extremely quickly. As early as the first decade of the sixth century, many of the Roman landowners of southern Gaul were fighting (on the losing side) for the Visigothic king Alaric II against Clovis at the battle of Vouillé in 507. By the second half of the century, organized contingents of landowners, drawn from the different city territories of the Frankish kingdom, and serving with an appropriate number of their dependents, formed the backbone of the kingdom's larger armies. The same was true in Visigothic Spain, where all landowners – whatever their increasingly distant and probably now also mixed ethnic origins – were legally liable to provide personal military service when summoned, and could be fined if they failed to appear.[9]

What successor-state kings now needed from the mass of their elite landowners – and what they consequently rewarded – was no longer the complex literacy appropriate for high-ranking administrators, but effective military service. Because most of our surviving sources from the period were originally written by Churchmen, or preserved by medieval monks, there is a marked tendency for these texts to document those descendants of old Roman landowning families who ended up serving at high levels in the Church: men like Gregory of Tours, scion of an important landowning family from Clermont Ferrand, or his many peers who appear in his writings or contemporary saints' *Lives*. And, echoing these sources, there has been a tendency among historians to suppose that most surviving landowners of Roman descent turned towards ecclesiastical careers in the post-Roman period. But if you focus less on surviving individual biographies and look for more general indications of scale, a different picture emerges.

There were only about 350 episcopal positions across the whole of the former Roman west – Gaul, Spain and Italy. And, once appointed, these were all jobs for life. Just the western half of the Roman imperial system, by contrast, had offered a minimum of three thousand top-level jobs in any ten-year period to its educated landowners at the height of imperial bureaucratic development around the year 400, and there were many other attractive jobs at lower levels within the system for those of less exalted status (p. 99). Some of these landowning families didn't survive the collapse of the imperial system but, of the many who did, only a small minority took up ecclesiastical careers. Even allowing that some subordinate clerical positions were also attractive, the Church was not remotely large enough a structure to absorb all the leftover landowners of Roman descent in the post-Roman period. Most of them quickly turned to serve their new rulers as warrior landowners. This in turn explains why the grammarians went out of business and the centres of higher learning disappeared. With the dismantling of the structures of Empire that had employed its graduates, a highly expensive education in classical language and literature – not to mention higher-level expertise in philosophy and law – lost its practical applications. Even though Latin and classical studies in general retained much of their cultural cachet as elite caste markers, intensive classical training rapidly became a marginal luxury in a world where battlefields, not bishoprics, replaced bureaucracies as the defining milieux of elite life.[10] Elite families no longer saw any need to pay out large sums of money for an education which had ceased to be fundamental to their children's chances of life success, and the grammarians consequently went out of business.

So, while classical culture, and even some types of complex composition, did not disappear in the post-Roman period, the educational structures underpinning elite literacy were fundamentally transformed. With the disappearance of the grammarians, basic education became centred instead on the familial household, with elite women – mothers – playing a major role in the initial education of their children. One incidental consequence of this was that differences in levels of literacy between men and women in the Roman period now tended to erode, and, if anything, elite women became better educated than their menfolk in the early medieval west. Hence substantial numbers of educated women appear in the literary networks of early medieval bishops: half a dozen or so, for instance, in Braulio's surviving correspondence. In one case, at the (otherwise unknown) Lady Apicella's explicit request, Braulio's consolations were accompanied by copies of the books of Tobit and Judith (from the Apocrypha).[11]

This change from professional to home education had powerful knock-on effects upon prevailing patterns of elite literacy. In the longer term it hastened a linguistic shift, even in elite circles, from Latin to the various forms of old Romance, which would eventually become modern French, Spanish and Italian. A handful of anecdotes make clear, however, that the spoken language of the elite remained a form of Latin (rather than old French or Spanish) until as late as the tenth century, when elites could still generally understand one another all the way from southern Spain to north-central France.[12] But without the grammarians and their rule books, it became increasingly difficult to maintain the fixed, universal form of written Latin characteristic of the late Roman elite. Because people were no longer being intensively schooled in the differences between the different 'correct' word endings as set down in the grammarians' rule books, the inflections of classical Latin began to be lost in everyday usage, and the spoken Latin characteristic of post-Roman elites quickly veered away from the classical norms of their Roman predecessors into much simpler patterns. This simplification, unavoidable in a world where the educators were not strictly enforcing the grammarians' rules, also made texts written in more complex, classicizing Latin increasingly difficult to understand. Hence, although elites continued to speak a type of Latin among themselves, more learned linguistic forms soon became incomprehensible to the untrained reader. In 721 a young Frankish noble called Gregory was invited to read a Latin Bible in front of a distinguished guest, the Anglo-Saxon missionary Boniface. The youth read well – but, when pressed, was unable to explain what any of it meant. In the grammarians' terms, he could manage stage one of dealing with a text (*lectio*, reading it aloud) but nothing more. According to his biographer, this encounter had a happy ending: Gregory – the future Bishop Gregory of Utrecht – went off determined to learn Latin properly. By the eighth century, home schooling was clearly not enough to prepare you for written Latin.

This underlying shift was already underway two centuries before.[13] By the sixth century, non-professional teaching had begun to undercut competence in the more complex forms of Latin composition. While the courtiers of Merovingian Gaul appreciated Venantius' mastery of classical Latin metre, few if any of them were able to compose verse themselves. Writing Latin poetry – based on metre (not rhyme) and hence requiring a secure grasp of the correct emphasis traditionally allotted to each syllable of every word – had always been regarded as the ultimate test of skilled composition, and there is little evidence of it being much attempted in sixth-century Gaul. The courtiers did write prose letters, a more straightforward genre, and did so with a clear idea of the kind of elevated style set down for epistolography in the classical rhetorical handbooks, but, even so, their letters were consistently non-classical in details of spelling and grammar.[14] It's important not to fall into the trap of thinking – as Latin masters have (just occasionally) been prone to over the centuries – that 'correct' Latin automatically equates with higher intelligence. The grammarians' version of 'correct' Latin, preserved and transmitted in their rule books, had artificially frozen a particular moment of linguistic development, which both restricted further change and automatically labelled any deviation as 'decline'. But, artificial or not, getting your word endings wrong in the late Roman period would have immediately identified you as a social inferior, whereas in mid-sixth-century Gaul it was already ceasing to matter. The death of the professional teaching classes – above all the grammarians, but also the purveyors of higher-level studies – therefore represented a major cultural shift, generating an increase in merely passive literacy among post-Roman elites, an increasing prevalence of diversity in elite Latinity, and an accompanying decline in its capacity to compose in the more demanding of the traditional literary genres. It also posed a profound challenge for the post-Roman Latin Church because, in the late Roman period, the structures of classical education had come to play an increasingly important role in training its leadership, and in the construction of greater coherence within the developing Christian tradition.

CHURCH AND EDUCATION

Some Christian intellectuals of the late Roman period – notably St Augustine – initially rejected the grammarians' educational wares as a pernicious source of continued paganism. But since a classical education in language and literature was hard-wired into both the intellectual formation and the career opportunities of elite Roman society, it had proved much easier to accept as an unmoveable given of the late Roman world – especially given the speed with which the cultural coercive capacity of the Roman imperial system had brought these elites to some form of Christianity. And, as members of the Roman elite came to hold senior positions in the Church in increasing numbers, the kind of education offered by the grammarian came rather to be seen not as any kind of problem, but rather as an excellent initial preparation for the 'more serious' biblical studies that would follow.

As we've seen in Chapter 2, the skills of the grammarian were extremely well suited to the great ongoing project of Christian religious development, ironing out the many textual problems and internal contradictions that presented themselves in a jumble of Old and New Testament texts, composed in different contexts over the best part of a thousand years. Both the more precisely defined theological doctrines of the imperial Roman Church, and the new patterns of recommended practical piety central to Christianity's initial evolution into a properly mass religion, rested upon a bedrock of grammarian-inspired, creative readings of highly disparate biblical texts. These many and varied resolutions of individual biblical problems, employing all kinds of allegorical, metaphorical, prophetic, oracular and other figurative readings to get round the many inconsistencies thrown up by a straightforwardly literal approach to the Old and New Testament texts, had made it possible to create an increasingly coherent religious structure from unpromisingly contradictory raw materials. The results, often written up in biblical commentaries, could then be transmitted to the broader faithful, whether literate or non-literate, in the form of sermons. Not only did these endeavours resolve many specific issues, like the chronology of Noah's grandfather, but they played a fundamental role in generating the overall intellectual coherence that proved such a powerful tool in the hands of missionaries faced with more inchoate oral pagan theologies and cosmologies (Chapter 6). Given all this, the disappearance of the grammarians and higher-level classical studies not only threatened the Church's supply line of ready-made, well-trained potential leaders, but also disrupted the broader educational tradition upon which the necessary and still ongoing project of biblical commentary had come to depend.

When it became clear that the educational structures of the imperial era were fast disappearing, attempts were made to fill the gap. In the early sixth century, one of the leading administrators of the Ostrogothic kingdom, which dominated Italy and surrounding territories at that time, Cassiodorus, in alliance with Pope Agapetus (535–6), advanced ambitious plans to establish a school of higher-level Christian studies in the city of Rome. This would have been a kind of Christian equivalent to the level of training provided by rhetors, philosophers, lawyers and others in the Roman period – and, thanks to its wonderful libraries, Rome had long been a centre of such higher-level studies. In the event, Justinian's conquest of Italy put an end to this initiative, and by the later sixth century, not only were the old centres of high-level study ceasing to function, but the old pattern of secondary-level schooling with the grammarian had been broken. Recognizing this in later life, Cassiodorus' response was to establish a monastic study centre, the Vivarium (named after the mass of live fish which inhabited its ponds) near the Calabrian city of Squillace in southern Italy, set 'among orchards, beside a happy stream'. There he gathered a library of essential texts – the most famous of its manuscripts still extant being a complete manuscript of the Bible, the *Codex Grandior*, which eventually found its way to Rome and then on to Bede at Monkwearmouth–Jarrow[15] – and set about training a new generation of Christian scholars. Cassiodorus laid out his vision of an essential Christian curriculum in his *Institutiones*, divided into two parts: the first, a programme of Christian reading (starting with the Psalms) which would eventually produce a fully trained biblical scholar; the second, exploring the classical liberal arts, which in his view still provided the necessary preparation for both the philological and interpretative dimensions of biblical study.[16] Cassiodorus' celebrated initiative was only one of several in the same era looking to fill the educational gap left by the disappearance of the grammarian. All focused on the closely related enterprises of identifying an appropriate Christian curriculum, assembling or producing the necessary texts (Cassiodorus' older contemporary Boethius produced a number of Latin translations of Greek philosophical primers to fill the gap left by the declining knowledge of Greek in the west), and creating institutions – such as the Vivarium – where study could be pursued.[17]

With bishops generally living near their main church, among small communities of fellow clerics, cathedral complexes and monasteries were in practice the only possible locations for such training schemes to take permanent root. Gregory of Tours received his education in the households of two bishops: first in his home city of Clermont Ferrand (under the supervision of Archdeacon Avitus, who later became bishop himself) before moving on to further study at Lyons, one of the west's old centres of higher-level studies, where his great-uncle

Nicetius was bishop. Braulio was trained initially in the monastery of the Eighteen Martyrs near his home city of Braga, under the direction of his brother John, before moving on to Seville and the household of Bishop Isidore.[18] Set against the prevailing, fragmented patterns of religious authority of the post-Roman west, however, neither cathedral schools nor monasteries represented secure mechanisms for delivering a sustained, high-quality Christian education in the early medieval west, and could not hope to replace in full both the grammarian-based and higher-level educational structures of the preceding Roman period.

One major problem facing any centre of Christian learning and teaching in the period, as it had been for their Roman imperial predecessors, was the prohibitive cost of books. The Lindisfarne Gospels famously required the skins of 150 calves to produce just the one volume; in addition, many of the colours for its illuminations were made from highly expensive pigments imported from the distant Caucasus. While few books were produced on so lavish a scale, a single, more modestly framed copy of Bede's *Ecclesiastical History* nonetheless weighed in at thirty calf skins. In the ninth century, a book of that size cost sixty silver coins – a sum that might otherwise buy you four sheep or fifteen piglets.[19] With any kind of worthwhile teaching collection requiring in excess of a hundred volumes (as set out by Cassiodorus in the *Institutiones*), the start-up costs were colossal.

By the sixth century, some cathedrals had already amassed considerable wealth. Initially Roman law had tended to regard any property given to a Christian institution as belonging to its individual head, but, by the fifth century, the idea that Church institutions were corporate bodies, capable of owning property indefinitely, had taken hold. As a result, permanent institutions like cathedral churches could build up extensive landed endowments, accumulating large portfolios of agricultural land and other valuable assets from gifts and wills – if not often on the enormous scale of Bishop Bertram, who left his own see of Le Mans almost 1.5 million acres (over 600,000 hectares) in landed estates. Gregory's see at Tours acquired its extra wealth from extensive pilgrim traffic to the shrine of St Martin, which was his pride and joy, the subject of one of his miracle collections, and perhaps also the prime source of funds for the new cathedral he constructed.[20]

Not all sees were so rich, however, and they all had to meet other regular expenses. By the sixth century, it was customary in Gaul and Italy to divide a cathedral's income four ways: a quarter each for the bishop, the clergy, lights and buildings, and the poor (in Spain, it was split three ways, with the poor reliant on the generosity of bishop and clergy). There were no funds in this division explicitly dedicated to acquiring and copying texts, or for education: the size of any funds devoted to these activities was dependent on the interest of individual bishops, which could vary widely. In their different ways, a Caesarius, a Gregory of Tours, an Isidore, or a Braulio must have spent considerable sums on advancing Christian learning. None of Isidore's own books survived the cultural after-effects of Arab conquest and Islamicization in the Iberian peninsula, but citations and allusions in his many compositions show him to have had access to a minimum of about 200 authors and maybe 450 individual works – an order of magnitude broadly confirmed by what he tells us about his library, which consisted of 14–16 bookcases each containing 30 volumes. This was a hugely expensive collection, one which had potentially benefited from the contents of old Roman public libraries that sometimes seem to have passed into the hands of nearby cathedrals (although Seville was not famous as a centre of literary culture in the late Roman period). That the compositional outputs of a handful of individual bishops stands out so strongly from the early medieval norm (and Isidore's library seems much larger than that available to Caesarius or Gregory) itself suggests that they were exceptional in the emphasis they put on the more intensive forms of education required to prepare individuals for different types of active, compositional literacy.[21]

Nor, in general structural terms, was sixth- and seventh-century monasticism particularly well suited to ensuring the future of high-end Christian learning. There were numerous monasteries in the early medieval west, and numbers continued to grow. By the seventh century, it has been estimated, Gaul was home to about 220, Italy to around 100, and Spain to a surprisingly precise 86.[22] But many of these were too small to provide secure homes for large libraries. One sixth-century Italian monastery consisted of ten monks, two oxen and two slaves; it could never have afforded more than a handful of books. These figures also include substantial numbers of aristocratic foundations – the continental counterparts to Bede's 'false' monasteries – since Frankish landowning elites also saw founding monasteries as a useful new form of investment strategy. As was the case north of the Channel, these foundations are unlikely to have been great centres of Christian learning, even if it is better to think of them as 'unsatisfactory' or 'limited' rather than false.[23] Still others lacked permanent landed endowments, including, it seems, even Cassiodorus' Vivarium. Despite its fame, the Vivarium disappears completely from view after Cassiodorus' death, presumably because it lacked a property endowment to provide the income that would have kept it in business. To maintain as expensive an item as a large Christian library, a substantial, permanent landed endowment was an absolute prerequisite.[24]

Presumably, all these monasteries – of whatever size and however aristocratic in origin – possessed some Bibles, commentaries, liturgical texts and perhaps also some Latin grammars, with the capacity to make further copies. Bede's Monkwearmouth–Jarrow had its continental European counterparts with more substantial libraries than anything available north of the Channel. As we've seen, Bede's works suggest that he had access to a library of between 200 and 250 volumes (about half the size of Isidore's), the equivalent to something like 1,000 papyrus scrolls. This was certainly the largest library of its day in Anglo-Saxon England, but some continental monastic libraries, especially when drawing on the library of an aristocratic founder (or an old Roman public collection), were many times larger. The library of Pope Agapetus, which eventually came into the hands of Pope Gregory the Great (this was one of the collections raided for texts by Monkwearmouth–Jarrow's founder, Benedict Biscop), weighed in at ten thousand papyrus scrolls, ten times the size of Bede's library. This collection was surely one of the largest still in existence by the sixth century, and, despite various sacks and fires, there surely were more books available still in the city of Rome (thanks to its cultural heritage of imperial and aristocratic libraries) than elsewhere.[25] There were also extensive book collections elsewhere in the west (in places such as Bordeaux, Arles, Lyons and Trier), and some of the foundations of the Irish monk Columbanus, such as Luxeuil and Bobbio, developed into major centres of Christian learning in the seventh and eighth centuries (although this probably wasn't so much a part of the founder's original design as used to be thought). But Christian monasticism has meant many different things in different eras (witness the eternal pilgrim dynamic characteristic of so much early medieval Irish asceticism), and monastic ideologies of the immediate post-Roman era did not generally place enormous emphasis on the importance of high-level Latin learning.

No single model of monastic rule prevailed in the immediate post-Roman west, but there were norms, and these usually made some provision for study within the standard monastic day. Characteristic sixth-century monastic rules like the original Italian *Rule of St Benedict* (closely modelled on the equally Italian *Rule of the Master*) allocated one portion of the monastic day to study, with the other two given over to manual labour – monks were meant to grow their own food – and to prayer. This general pattern for the monastic day is echoed in many other early medieval rules (in this era, monasteries each tended to have their own precise regulations) from Gaul and Spain. But working in the fields and the daily round of services took up most of a monk's day, and no surviving sixth- or seventh-century rule puts any great emphasis on the importance of building up extensive libraries of Christian knowledge or on training monks for complex composition. The *Life* of the seventh-century Hispanic monastic founder Ildefonsus, for instance, dismisses Isidore of Seville as less of a Christian than Fructuosus, Braulio's student who was so worried about the fate of Noah's grandfather, because Fructuosus' ascetic credentials were stronger. In some Church circles in seventh-century Spain, therefore, classical learning was considered a less important Christian virtue than ascetic rigour. This was no isolated perspective. From the same century, we have two surviving texts offering a series of brief biographies of distinguished Christian leaders of the Visigothic kingdom (*De Viris Illustribus*, a Christian adaptation of an old classical literary genre). One was composed by Ildefonsus himself; the other by the ascetic enthusiast and monastic founder Valerius of Bierzo. Like the *Life* of Ildefonsus, both these texts place no emphasis on the importance of high-level Christian learning. The overarching concern of much of early medieval monasticism, rather, was to provide a path to salvation through moderate, communal monastic discipline, with more than a nod to curbing the problems of solitary asceticism (p. 58). High-end Christian learning was not at this point central to the monastic mission statement.[26]

The failure of Christian institutions to compensate for the disappearance of grammarians and centres of high-level studies was in part a result of ideological choice, as with those monastic traditions that deliberately rejected the importance of a classical literary education. But, in part too, it was a question of resources in a world where public and aristocratic libraries had dispersed, and where elite status and career opportunity were no longer dependent on advanced literary studies. In effect, the post-Roman decoupling of complex literacy and elite career patterns removed a hidden subsidy that had supported advanced Christian learning throughout the late Roman period. Christian institutions had not had to devote resources to schools and more advanced training in this period because the practical functioning of elite secular society already provided most of what was necessary. The unravelling of the imperial system, and the career ladders it supported, constituted a major structural change in cultural terms. Overall, a much smaller percentage of GDP was being spent by post-Roman Europe's secular elites – compared to their late Roman predecessors – on education and book production. And Church institutions were not geared up to fill the gap. This erosion of educational infrastructure had a series of important effects on the development of the western Church in the post-Roman period.

While Latin literacy in a more simple form – a capacity to read Bibles, commentaries and service books – remained widespread among both secular and ecclesiastical elites, more intense forms of education – the foundation of active compositional literacy – were confined to relatively few institutions. It's hard to put a number on these centres, or the size of their libraries, because of the systematic destruction of earlier manuscripts that followed the adoption of new script forms in the mid-eighth century. What can be gleaned of the original provenance of those manuscripts that did survive, together with the less direct evidence provided by the intellectual formation of the smaller number of Christian scholars who engaged in active compositional literacy in the period, suggests that in the early Middle Ages no more than a few dozen continental Christian institutions had anything like the level of library provision set out by Cassiodorus in his *Institutiones* as necessary to produce a fully trained student of the Bible. Seville in the later sixth and seventh centuries must have come close (indeed, Isidore's library went far beyond Cassiodorus' prescriptions), and there were far more books available in the city of Rome and some other continental centres of learning, whose holdings are now not so clearly visible to us.[27] Even so, most of the larger ecclesiastical institutions – cathedrals or monasteries – seem to have had access to only limited portions of the late Roman Christian educational tradition, or, if their libraries did contain more books, no one was reading them.

Most cathedrals and monasteries had little more than a few Bibles and service books, supplemented by some saints' *Lives* and biblical commentaries, with the odd grammatical volume thrown in. As a result, the late Roman Christian intellectual and literary heritage found itself divided between a number of (usually) small educational centres, most of which possessed only limited portions of the whole. Jonas of Bobbio, for instance, was a well-trained seventh-century Christian intellectual who wrote an important *Life* of the Irish monk-missionary Columbanus, the founder of the monastery in which Jonas himself was trained before he later moved on to missionary work in his own right. Established in 614, in what is now the northern Italian province of Emilia-Romagna, the monastery of Bobbio quickly became a major intellectual centre of the seventh-century west. But even Jonas wrote in a non-classical form of Latin: 's' and 'x' were pretty much interchangeable for him, and his writing also contains non-standard verb conjugations, case and gender endings, as well as some significant changes of declension. Nor does the intellectual formation on display in his writings suggest any large-scale exposure to classical literature.[28] The point is not that Jonas's Latin was 'bad' or 'wrong', but that its non-standard nature reflects the fact that his education – like that of the Merovingian courtiers encountered by Venantius in the previous century – had not involved intensive study of the grammarians' manuals that had made the written language of the old Roman elite so uniform. It is a safe conclusion, therefore, that Bobbio's library did not contain all the necessary grammatical works to have instilled in Jonas a detailed grasp of classically correct Latin, one consequence, in all likelihood, of monasteries of the early seventh century not privileging that particular form of education.

Everything suggests that this situation prevailed across most of the post-Roman Latin west. The bulk of the surviving manuscripts copied between the sixth and earlier eighth centuries are marked by non-classical Latin linguistic forms, which became increasingly prevalent over time. This affected both new compositions of the period, and any older classical texts that were being recopied. It even applied to the existing centres of Christian learning in the city of Rome itself. Not only did Bishop Braulio need to point out in the mid-seventh century that Pope Honorius couldn't tell his Isaiah from his Ezekiel, but a series of important ecclesiastical texts that Rome supplied to Frankish Churchmen in the later eighth century likewise contained many deviations from the standards of 'correct' classical Latin.[29] Educated Churchmen, and members of the secular elite alike, could understand one another's spoken Latin perfectly well, but in copying and composing written texts, they were increasingly using their own individual versions of non-classical Latin. This, in all probability, was not because they had no grammars available, but because no one had put in the kind of work that was being undertaken by Irish and Anglo-Saxon scholars to supplement the main grammatical teaching texts available (Donatus' *Ars Minor* and *Ars Maior*) with more basic primers containing the detailed knowledge that his manuals presupposed (above, p. 292). When coupled with the fragmentation in higher-level ecclesiastical authority structures, which prevented any coherent overall response to the erosion of the educational infrastructure on which it was so dependent, this fragmentation in the operative language of the inherited tradition had major knock-on effects for the development of post-Roman Latin Christianity.

The disappearance of any real equivalent to the highest level of the Roman educational structure removed much of the advanced training and intellectual context, particularly in terms of philosophical studies, which might have fuelled further theological development. Many key doctrines, especially those involving the Trinity (Father, Son and Holy Ghost), had arrived at a relatively full level of exposition in the late Roman period, but other important intellectual stages of theological development would still be required to complete the work of turning

Christianity into a fully coherent religious system, not least, for instance, in relating fully worked-out understandings of sin and salvation to more developed concepts of the Christian afterlife, initially, and then in turn coupling these to paradigms of detailed everyday piety.

Not, of course, that Christians of the period ceased to think about such important matters, nor to continue to inform their thinking by consulting existing Christian tradition. In the 590s, Bishop Gregory of Tours had a lengthy conversation with one of his priests who thought – more after the patterns of pre-Constantinian Christianity (p. 48) – that Heaven was a place reserved for only a handful of out-and-out saints. In the 680s, likewise, Bishop Julian of Toledo pulled together a compendium of material from earlier writers on what happened to Christian souls after death, for an elderly colleague whose time was drawing nigh. The post-Roman period also saw some important new ideas get an initial airing – not least a new emphasis on almsgiving as a significant element in the kinds of regimes of tariffed penance which had originally emerged as a remedy for sin in an Irish context.[30]

In their different ways, however, all these moments and developments reflect the various structural limitations of the post-Roman Latinate Church. It is striking, for instance, that, more or less two centuries later, the kind of broadened vision of the scale of salvation that is so striking a feature of the thought-world of Augustine and other Christian thinkers of *c.* 400 (p. 52) had still not won general acceptance, even among Christian priests. Julian of Toledo's library had some substantial gaps in its holdings, seemingly lacking anything by Tertullian, who had important things to say about the afterlife. Julian also didn't seem to realize (or didn't feel the need to explain his thought processes, if he did) that his compilation created a false unity of perspective among writers who substantially disagreed with one another. Likewise, no single model of tariffed penance emerged in this period to explain what level of action was required to deal with particular intensities of sinning, and the evidence suggests that such tariffs were limited to a small number of largely Gallic monastic contexts, and won no widespread acceptance across the broader horizons of western Christendom in this period.

Christians clearly continued to read and think, but there was no extensive canon of shared reading, and much less in the way of training, too, in logical disputation. There was also no longer any unified authority structure across the Latin Church through which good ideas might come into general usage. Compared to what we will witness in later chapters of the situation that began to prevail in the aftermath of the educational and institutional restructuring of the ninth century and beyond (which brought a renewed emphasis on the kind of intensive education that had always formed the backbone of active compositional literacy, and the emergence once again of more unified authority structures), it is hardly surprising that the post-Roman centuries are marked by relatively little theological systematization.[31] In this earlier period, the response of even such a comparatively well-trained bishop as Caesarius of Arles, as we have seen, was to retreat from the potential complexities of predestination, for example (p. 321), while even the effective defeat of Homoean Christianity had been more the result of diplomatic pressure and military victory than superior theological argumentation.

The simplification and fragmentation of inherited Christian tradition also created conditions in which local variants of religious practice could flourish. Basic résumés of the conclusions from the major theological debates of the fourth and fifth centuries were available in Creed form, particularly in the succinct statements of the Apostles' Creed, which formed the centrepiece of the reduced baptismal instruction given to Christianity's new peasant consumers, and which maintained some basic outline doctrinal unity across western Europe, all the way from Rome itself to Britain and Ireland. But within this framework, local diversity flourished.

Take, for instance, the Bible text itself, whose evolution can be explored thanks to the survival of a substantial number of pre-ninth-century manuscripts. The late Roman intellectuals of the Latin west had never managed to define a standard, agreed, Latin translation of the Greek Old and New Testaments (despite the project of the fourth-century Jerome to go back to the original Hebrew as the foundation for his new Vulgate translation, p. 79). In the fifth century and beyond, four different basic Latin versions of Christianity's core Greek texts remained in circulation in different parts of the Roman west and, as the dominance of the grammarians' standardized Latin broke up, the amount of variation increased exponentially. Bibles were copied and recopied by scribes who mixed and matched their own choices of readings from the four different translations, and they introduced their own variations in a world where they were not trained to use one standardized form of written language. As Braulio's letter to Fructuosus makes clear, uneven post-Roman access to existing learning made it still more difficult to control the spread of variations. The problem of Mathusale's age at the time of the Flood had been 'resolved' (i.e., edited into non-existence) by Jerome in the fourth century – but Fructuosus did not have access to Jerome's *Hebrew Questions* and the interpretative wheel had to be reinvented.[32]

So much of the Church's liturgy made substantial use of the Bible (for daily readings during Mass and other prayers) that increasing variation in the inherited biblical tradition also had a substantial effect upon Church services. The bar of unity had not been set especially high by late Roman Christianity, which – reflecting the religion's pre-Constantinian roots in relatively loosely affiliated regional faith groups – continued to tolerate a great deal of disparate local practice, even in something as fundamental as baptismal ritual. The Spanish Church, for instance, zealously protected its particular rite of triple immersion.[33] But poor training and the loss of control over the Bible text generated still greater and sometimes problematic liturgical variation in the early Middle Ages. An extreme example was reported by the Anglo-Saxon missionary Boniface, who found a Bavarian priest baptizing people *in nomine Patria et filia* ('In the name of the Fatherland and the daughter') instead of *in nomine patris et filii* ('In the name of the Father and the Son'), confusing not just case and gender but pretty much everything else besides. It's an indication of exactly how much linguistic chaos was out there and being generally accepted, moreover, that, on asking the pope for a ruling, Boniface was told – to his surprise – that the priest's baptisms were nonetheless valid.[34]

The overall fragmentation in tradition caused by the ruptures in inherited educational structures spilled over into actual teachings, especially in missionary contexts. We have already encountered Boniface's bête noire, Clemens, an Irish missionary to the Continent, who adopted an alternative, non-canonical view of the Harrowing of Hell which went down much better with potential warrior converts than the traditional exposition of the doctrine, which confined their much-revered ancestors to Hell for all eternity (p. 270). The Irish clergy back at home who sanctioned marriage customs that did not conform to early medieval continental norms – including levirate marriage practices (allowing a 'replacement' in-law to be substituted into a marriage after the early death of one of the original partners) and the broad approval of the effective polygamy practised by Irish kings – knew their Bibles perfectly well. Both levirate marriages and polygamy are well attested in the Old Testament, which formed a central part of the canon of sacred texts to which a Christian might naturally turn for guidance. While established Christian tradition in the Roman period had ruled these practices illegitimate, not least in biblical commentaries on the relevant passages which explained why these Old Testament marriage practices should not now be followed, a more literal reading of select passages of the Old Testament could potentially license them.

The operations of early medieval western Christianity were not entirely chaotic. For the most part, the textual variations within the Bible generated only relatively minor differences in the wordings of services, and major deviations from established tradition (such as uncanonical marriage practices) are likely to have been found mostly in missionary contexts. But the proliferation of variant views was certainly made much easier by the absence of a developed, coherent educational regime for passing on agreed teachings to Christian scholars and priests, based on a common interpretative framework to the key biblical texts which stood at the heart of the religion – and this problem was not remotely confined to missionary contexts. Many of the new churches of the post-Roman countryside were constructed, as we have seen, by landowners – not bishops – and staffed by one of the landowners' peasants, whose capacity to teach and run services according to established Christian tradition is likely to have been limited, even within the heartlands of Latin Christianity. Equally important, not only was the training of higher-level clergy generally limited by the new educational structures of post-Roman Europe, but the practical interaction of Church and state in the era of the successor states further undermined knowledge of established Christian tradition at the highest levels of the clergy, and left the Latin Church open to the widespread intrusion of decidedly non-Christian values.

CHURCH AND STATE

In terms of underlying principles, not a lot changed in Church-state relations with the unravelling of the Roman imperial system. Western successor-state kings, like their Roman imperial predecessors, considered themselves appointed by God, and continued to take ultimate responsibility for high-level religious decision-making, both directly and through the calling of quasi-ecumenical councils of the bishops of their kingdoms. As a result, we see early medieval kings deeply involved in doctrinal decisions, in making senior Church appointments, and promulgating laws that affected ecclesiastical operations.

Royal religious authority was also the fundamental reason why the Christian Empire of the Roman period had to give way in the west to an early medieval Christian commonwealth composed of kingdom-sized units – and this, in practice, proved a further source of substantial religious transformation. On the broad spectrum of pre-modern state organizations, the Roman Empire must be placed towards the end of 'large state' structures, with its ability to raise substantial taxation from the limited surplus wealth produced by its overwhelmingly agricultural economy to support relatively large professional military forces. The complex process of extracting and redistributing all this value in turn required the extensive bureaucratic machinery and complex training in advanced forms of literacy which, as we've seen, defined the characteristic patterns of elite life in the late Roman period. Although most of the western successor states initially inherited some of the tax-raising structures of the Empire they replaced, they quickly gravitated towards the 'small state' end of the spectrum. By the later sixth century, these states were fast shedding their tax-raising powers, and their bureaucratic structures had simplified accordingly. Because successor state kings did not support large professional armed forces – instead getting their military capacity from mobilizing now militarized landowning elites – most of the structures of the Roman state had become redundant. And since it was no longer essential to the state-level process of waging war, successor-state kings progressively eroded their own tax base by giving grants of tax exemption to deserving supporters as an easy form of patronage.

Not only did this transformation undercut elite demand for advanced forms of classical education, but the militarization of elite life also meant that the same kind of syncretic cultural adaptation we observed north of the Channel took hold on the Continent as well: Christianity retooled itself to become a religion for warriors, against all the recorded commands of its founder in the Gospels. The Christian elites of the Frankish and Visigoth kingdoms (whatever their older ethnic origins) – not to mention their Burgundian, Vandal and Suevic counterparts for as long as these survived as independent entities – were just as focused on war-making as their Anglo-Saxon and Irish peers, and early medieval Christianity catered for their needs in straightforward ways. This is pithily summed up by the hilt of a Frankish sword, found in Sweden, inscribed with a telling verse from Psalm 144: 'Blessed be the Lord my strength, which teacheth my hand to war, and my fingers to fight.'

While there were probably late Roman equivalents which haven't directly survived, the first known Christian liturgies giving thanks for victory in battle are Merovingian Frankish in origin.[35] Many of the law codes produced in the successor states were also predicated on an acceptance of the same kind of honour systems that operated north of the Channel and which, as we've seen, might periodically require members of a social kin group to kill in support of one of their fellows.[36] Both north and south of the Channel, the militarization of elite life forced Christianity to license new value systems.

The new smaller state structure that generally prevailed across the post-Roman west also exercised more limited central authority than its imperial predecessor, meaning that relations between ruler and constituent landowning elites now operated on a fundamentally different basis. The Roman Empire and its western successors differed markedly in both the range and the strength of the levers of power that their respective central authorities could deploy to maintain the loyalties of local elites. Without the same tax-raising powers, successor-state kings lacked the same capacity to generate large amounts of annually renewable wealth, which could be used in various ways to keep the loyalties of local elites focused on the centre. With successor states relying on much simpler bureaucratic structures, with a smaller number of functionaries performing a wider range of tasks, their rulers also had far fewer jobs in their gift to distribute as rewards for loyal service. The fact that successor-state kings were now dealing with militarized landed elites, rather than civilian landowners, likewise made it much less straightforward for them to coerce dissident local communities back into line than in the Roman period, when emperors could – if push came to shove – simply unleash their military on unarmed local communities.[37]

In this transformed context, Christianity's continued close dependence on the authority of the ruler generated important further transformations in ecclesiastical operations in the post-Roman period. As the landed endowments of dioceses built up over time, one temptation for kings – who now lacked many of the reward systems that had been available to Roman emperors – was to use their well-established rights to appoint bishops as a means of rewarding loyal supporters. The quarter share of a see's income due to the bishop in Gaul (or third in Spain) made such posts a lucrative retirement bonus for loyal servants, and from the sixth century, as Gregory of Tours chronicles, Church positions were regularly used for this purpose. The widespread entrenchment of this practice across the seventh- and early eighth-century west is suggested by complaints in both Visigothic conciliar proceedings and the letters of Boniface that leading Churchmen had been purchasing their offices. It was, after all, only a short step from rewarding a trusted henchman with a well-endowed see to receiving a payment of some kind in return, especially in court circles where gift-giving was the cultural norm. Late Roman emperors had also sometimes effectively appointed their leading Churchmen, particularly at the level of the patriarchates, but their chosen loyalists had at least always been clergy, since, by the year 400, Roman rulers also had thousands of bureaucratic positions available for rewarding loyal service.[38]

One significant religious outcome of this sea-change in state organization, therefore, saw members of the 'ordinary' secular aristocratic elite of western Europe regularly hold episcopal office. The precise consequences of such appointments varied, but, at the very least, it meant that early medieval senior Church hierarchies often contained individuals who had not graduated from one of the limited number of available centres of Christian educational excellence. At worst, such appointments produced prelates of the calibre of the brothers Bishop Sagittarius of Gap and Bishop Salonius of Embrun in later sixth-century Gaul. Their colourful careers feature strongly in the pages of Gregory of Tours' *Histories*, and for men such as these becoming bishop involved no substantial change at all in the normal patterns of secular aristocratic behaviour, even down to fighting in person on the battlefield. Personal participation in combat was beyond the pale for the Christian establishment, and led to their eventual deposition at the council of Lyons in 567 – though it is wonderful testimony to the chaotic impact of entirely random papal intervention in this period that a supportive king (the same Guntram who otherwise played a major role in kick-starting the Church reform process of the 580s, p. 311) called in a favour from Rome to get them temporarily reinstated afterwards. But even if most early medieval secular aristocrats-turned-bishops were not generally so worldly as this, their appointment allowed aristocratic values to penetrate the functioning of Church institutions. And whether such appointees had any real interest in the pressing issues of early medieval Christianity – such as developing an effective religious infrastructure to reach the peasantry, or in spending large amounts of their retirement bonus on new books for their cathedral libraries – is unclear.

The broader impact of such developments can be seen in many instances Gregory of Tours gives us of the later sixth-century Frankish Church in action, one of the most vivid being an account of the difficult problem which unfolded on his watch at the nunnery of the Holy Cross in Poitiers, originally founded by Venantius' patron, Queen Radegund. After the queen's death, her chosen abbess found herself in notional charge of two Merovingian princesses who had been installed there (perhaps because celibacy was seen as a good way – as in Anglo-Saxon England – to control the number of potential heirs of the royal blood that might appear in the next generation). The two princesses, however, did not like taking orders from the abbess (their social inferior), the plain clothing they were supposed to wear, or having shared bathrooms. In the end, they revolted against the abbess's authority, organizing the dependents who were with them as servants (these clearly included men as well as women) to riot and expel her, reducing this grand and well-endowed institution to utter chaos in the process. When the bishops intervened to restore order, the reigning king rescued the princesses from the consequences of their actions, setting them up instead with a lucrative royal estate.

All this unfolded in exactly the same era that Merovingian bishops were building up the active and innovative conciliar legislative tradition that eventually led, as we've seen, to the creation of a brand-new code of canon law for the Frankish kingdom: the *Vetus Gallica*. And, in one sense, the Holy Cross riot, and several of the other incidents recorded in Gregory's works, do in fact show the power of an increasingly well-organized Frankish episcopate in action. The first response to the princesses was organized by Gregory, using his metropolitan authority (as archbishop of Tours with responsibility for Poitiers) to gather around himself a posse of bishops who then attempted to settle the matter according to the dictates of canon law. On this and several other occasions, Gregory shows us high-level Frankish clerics with a strong vision of themselves as an independent interest group, armed with a clear set of regulations, pushing Frankish kings towards particular modes of appropriate religious behaviour.[39]

At the same time, however, both Gregory's writings and the broader history of the Frankish Church in this era capture some of the underlying problems inherent in such a high degree of dependence upon the kings of relatively unstable political structures. In the end, even in the Holy Cross incident, the written regulations of the Church were not properly applied: royal intervention prevented any appropriate punishment being visited upon the rebellious princesses. It was another royal intervention which likewise hampered the collected bishops' capacity to deal with the problematic warrior-bishops Salonius and Sagittarius. When King Chilperic put Gregory himself on trial, likewise, at a Church council, the bishop was eventually forced to 'prove' his innocence by undertaking a symbolic ritual – saying Mass at four altars placed at each point of the compass – which he knew to be completely contrary to all Church practice and tradition.[40] The overall power of the king, however, left him with no choice, underlining the degree of authority which early medieval monarchs regularly exercised over the internal operations of the Church. Sometimes, when it suited their broader interests, these monarchs supported their Church communities in operating according to clearly established written rules, calling the councils that allowed Churchmen to get on with their further elaboration. When it didn't suit, however, rulers had no hesitation in acting otherwise, and Churchmen put up little opposition – not least because several of their number in each generation were probably also directly appointed former royal servants. Sometimes, lines got so crossed that kings even used Church law to get their own way. In 577, when other avenues were closed to him, King Chilperic was able to trick Bishop Praetextatus of Rheims into condemning himself at a council which the king had called. The king suspected the bishop of treasonable behaviour, which Praetextatus initially denied, but then, on being assured that the king would forgive him if he told all, effectively changed his plea. At that point, the king's clerical supporters pulled out a little-known conciliar decree that a bishop convicted of lying should be stripped of his position. Praetextatus found himself duly condemned, and there was nothing the assembled bishops could do about it.[41]

Gregory's writings vividly illustrate the impact of the political and cultural transformations of the post-Roman period on the underlying character and modes of operation of the Latin Church in the Frankish kingdom. But the basic transformations themselves – militarized aristocracies, weaker central authority structures, simpler elite and specifically ecclesiastical educational structures – were common to the post-Roman west in general and generated broadly similar effects right across it. In every kingdom, secular values and even secular aristocrats regularly infiltrated the episcopate so that, in each generation, only limited numbers of Church leaders were trained in existing Christian traditions and compositionally literate enough to see where they might need further development.

Though imperial Nicene orthodoxy successfully faced down the initial challenge posed to its continued dominance by the Homoean alternative, thanks mainly to the influence of Constantinople both on Clovis's religious choices and via Justinian's wars of expansion in the western Mediterranean, the unravelling of the Roman imperial system nonetheless unleashed a second period of revolutionary transformation in the prevailing structures and patterns of the Latin Church. The Islamic conquests of the seventh century separated Christian western Europe from established lines of contact with what had been, up to that point, the beating heart and brain of the developing Christian tradition. All the dominant intellectual centres of late Roman Christianity (including North Africa from the old western Empire) were swallowed up into the new Islamic world of the Caliphates, leaving the Latin west – where Christian traditions and structures outside the city of Rome were neither so old nor so well established – to develop under their own steam.

Thanks to the disappearance of the top-level religious decision-making structures dependent upon the existence of Roman emperors – imperial legislation and the ecumenical councils – these traditions and structures were forced to develop in regional, kingdom-sized units. These, because of the newly militarized character of elite life, struggled to replace the old Roman educational structures, and hence both to preserve inherited Christian traditions (all transmitted in book form), and to prevent the intrusion of previously alien values (and underqualified individuals) into the Church's operating structures. To this must be added the syncretic processes of religious adaptation, which the act of reaching out to new congregations of warriors and peasants necessarily forced upon Christianity.

Considered in the round, therefore, the fall of the Christian Roman Empire, in both east and west, generated a set of transformations in the structures and operating practices of Christianity that were every bit as revolutionary as those unleashed in the fourth and fifth centuries by Constantine's 'conversion'. Early medieval Christianity was neither 'better' nor 'worse' than its late Roman predecessor. Dependent as it was upon regional kings and warrior aristocracies, struggling to reach out to peasants and warriors, and transmitting its core traditions via a much more limited educational infrastructure, early medieval Christianity was, however, profoundly different in character.

That Roman imperial Nicene orthodoxy managed to survive the unravelling of the west Roman imperial system therefore gives a misleading sense of continuity to the real religious history of the period – one in which Christian structures, which had been firmly anchored to that imperial system, were forced to reinvent themselves in an entirely new set of socio-political contexts. This is, in other words, another moment – like the conversion to Christianity of the late Roman elite – when a very direct linkage between political and cultural history comes to the fore. The cultural evolution of developing Christianity was not left untouched by the disappearance of the Roman imperial system (in either east or west) because this was no 'surface disturbance' – as the great *Annales* historian Fernand Braudel famously labelled some kinds of political events – but a fundamental transformation in the prevailing institutional structures that define the nature of state systems. The 'large' pre-modern state structures of the Roman world gave way to the much 'smaller' (non-taxing) structures of the early medieval west. In Braudel's terms, this is a change of system, and, as such, bound to be a driver of significant historical change on every level.[42] As a result, the fall of the Roman Empire forced Christianity to evolve in new ways, not only incorporating new congregations with new cultural values, but developing new institutional patterns as well.

Dependent as it was on the power of relatively weak monarchs, this in effect hard-wired into early medieval Latin Christianity a structural problem of enormous potential significance. Anything that weakened the power of any of these monarchies would automatically impact upon the capacity of the relevant regional Church community to continue to operate as an effective collective body. By the middle of the eighth century, the inherent weakness of this new form of state structure had thrown – for different reasons – virtually all the regional communities of the Latin Christian commonwealth into chaos. The longer-term response to this intense period of general crisis in Church and state would, in turn, kick-start the third systemic revolution in the practices and structures of Latin Christianity that underlay the eventual emergence of a fully fledged medieval European Christendom.

PART THREE

Christian Empire Renewed

9
Christian Expansion in a Second Age of Empire

By the later seventh century, the new Christian order brought into being by the collapse of the Roman imperial system had reached apparent equilibrium. After defeating its Homoean rival, Nicene Christianity had proceeded to establish itself energetically across much of the former Roman west, reaching out to new congregations of peasants and warriors. As effective imperial religious authority collapsed, it had also reorganized itself into kingdom-sized Church communities, whose episcopal councils were now firmly in charge of their own religious development in a Latin-dominated cultural world cut off from the old Near Eastern heartlands of Christianity by the rise of Islam. All in all, the omens looked good for post-Roman Christianity. The last of England's pagan Anglo-Saxon ruling lines – that of the Isle of Wight – was extinguished in 681 and, further east, the first rush of Muslim conquest had been halted. There, in 681 again, Constantinople's political and ecclesiastical establishment abandoned the Monothelite heresy that had been its initial response to the advance of Islam (Chapter 5). So great was the renewal of confidence that the eastern emperor Justinian II tried to win back some of his lost provinces. The result was catastrophic. His defeat restarted Islamic expansion, costing Constantinople control of its North African prefecture centred on the city of Carthage, and prompted extreme instability at the imperial core. The Byzantine Empire survived – but only just, and at enormous cost, measured not only in more lost provinces, but also in a further bout of ideological turmoil when the regime of Leo III adopted iconoclasm in the later 720s to assuage God's evident wrath.[1]

The renewal of Islamic expansion also destabilized – directly and indirectly – large parts of the post-Roman west. After a few exploratory raids, in 711 a larger Muslim invasion force crossed the straits of Gibraltar to the Iberian peninsula. The Visigoth king Roderic headed south to the River Guadalete with everyone he could muster. There, in the resulting Hispanic battle of Hastings, Roderic and so many of the leading men of the Visigoth kingdom were killed that Muslim rule spread, within a decade, over the entire peninsula, bar a small Christian enclave in the far north-west. With the destruction of the monarchy on which it relied, the sequence of kingdom-wide Church councils that had become such a defining feature of the Visigothic Christian microcosm in the seventh century came to an abrupt halt. Over the next century and a half, elite Visigoth culture acquired new trajectories, towards the Arabic language and, eventually, Muslim conversion (above, p. 231).

Renewed Islamic expansion had profound, albeit indirect, impacts elsewhere. In Italy, a desperate Emperor Leo ratcheted up tax demands, generating huge resentment among the militarized landowning networks of all Constantinople's remaining Italian provinces. The landowners of the administrative area around Rome, the *ducate*, announced a collective refusal to pay, using Pope Gregory II (715–31) as their spokesman, and, under papal leadership, went into open revolt against their imperial masters. The Empire's response was predictable: in 725, the exarch of Ravenna, the chief imperial representative in the entire Italian peninsula, advanced on Rome with all the troops he could muster, but he was forced to retreat at the Milvian Bridge when he found that Gregory had rallied superior forces in his own defence, both from among Roman landowners of the *ducate* and from the neighbouring Lombard duchies of Spoleto and Benevento.

At this moment, the independent Republic of St Peter was born. It took a few more years for everyone to realize that something momentous had occurred because there had been lengthy periods of de facto Roman independence before, especially during the Monothelite schism in the mid-seventh century, and some factions within the city still wanted to bring Rome back under imperial control in the early 730s. Once these were defeated, however, Rome's political split with Constantinople quickly became irrevocable, and an independent Papal State emerged into the light of history.

Leo III's decree in favour of iconoclasm in the late 720s had also offered Pope Gregory the chance to assert his religious authority. Promptly excommunicating the emperor, Gregory lectured him – by letter – on how secular rulers had no right to interfere in theological issues. The emperor, unimpressed, responded by confiscating all the papal estates in those parts of southern Italy, Sicily and Illyricum (which stretched along the eastern coast of the Adriatic Sea) that were still under imperial control, at an annual cost to the papacy of 350 pounds of gold, something close to half its overall income. By the mid-730s, therefore, the local, militarized landowners of the old imperial *ducate* of Rome were part of something new: an independent, if somewhat impoverished, Roman Republic under the overall leadership of the papacy, whose elections they controlled.[2]

This was only the opening salvo, however, in a progressive destabilization of eighth-century Italy. The imperial tax crisis of the 720s generated a wave of local revolts not just in Rome but right across those parts of the Italian peninsula that remained under Byzantine control. In Ravenna, the capital of Byzantine Italy and home to the exarch, the already strained ties between local landowning networks and Constantinople were put under further pressure. Neighbouring Lombard rulers exploited the situation by progressively carving off pieces of the remaining imperial holdings around the city, until the capital itself was taken and the entire exarchate finally extinguished in 751. Some parts of the south remained under Constantinople's control, but, as Lombard power increased, the situation facing the newly formed Papal State grew increasingly perilous. Now minus imperial protection, a modest-sized Roman Republic stood alone, its immediate neighbours the slightly larger independent Lombard duchies of Spoleto and Benevento, and the much larger Lombard kingdom to the north (Map 5). All these rulers had predatory intentions towards parcels of lands at the fringes of St Peter's new republic. From the moment of the republic's birth, therefore, popes spent much of their time worrying about armies, finance and diplomatic relations.[3]

These were decades of crisis, in fact, right across the former Roman west. In north-western Europe, the kingdom of the Franks fell into sustained political turmoil, if not, this time, primarily because of renewed Islamic expansion (though Muslim raiding did also spread north of the Pyrenees). Much of our information about what was going on comes – well after the event – from partisans of a new dynastic line, which definitively replaced Clovis's Merovingian descendants in the mid-eighth century. These sources justified regime change by presenting the last Merovingians as morally unfit to rule, as manifested in a sustained lack of royal authority. This supposed lack of moral worth is nonsense, but later members of the Merovingian dynasty did lose control of the reins of effective power. By the 690s, real power in the kingdom's five main constituent regions – Austrasia (covering much of what is now France north-east of Paris, with parts of Belgium and north-western Germany), Neustria (Normandy and other areas north-west of Paris), Aquitaine, Burgundy, and, to a lesser extent, Septimania in the south-west (Map 5) – was passing into the hands of a series of semi-independent regional aristocratic networks, who controlled more of the key revenue sources, and hence could command more loyalty, in their home regions than did the central monarchy. Initially, the leaders of these different networks continued to pursue factional gains at the royal court. These manoeuvres were regularly punctuated by bouts of open civil war with one another, however, and, in the second decade of the eighth century, what was already a fragile balance broke down still further. Each regional network effectively declared itself independent of Merovingian control, and competed more openly with its rivals for overall supremacy over as much territory as possible. The resulting disintegration of the political superstructure of the Frankish kingdom had inevitable consequences for the ecclesiastical structures whose fortunes had become so tightly bound to it.[4]

As Francia's newly independent regions jostled with each other for supremacy, and the struggle for power became overtly military, ecclesiastical resources were increasingly deployed to secular ends. Land that notionally belonged to larger ecclesiastical institutions was re-purposed by competing regional factions to buy the warrior support that was now at a premium. Frankish landowners, like their Anglo-Saxon counterparts, had often 'given' land to the Church as part of an investment strategy, which allowed them to continue to use much of what they had donated to advance family interests (above, p. 276). Now, as interregional competition intensified, the contenders interfered in these arrangements, transferring control of important assets to their own supporters. Important bishoprics and abbacies also provided attractive rewards that could again be used to buy the support of key powerbrokers.

The erosion of monarchical authority also undermined much of what remained of the growing sense of episcopal solidarity that had been evident in the late sixth century. Where close to fifty Frankish regional Church councils were held between 511 and 614, the bulk of them after 580, less than half that number are known from the next century and a half. Without a strong monarchy to support it, as the Church communities of Visigoth Spain and Anglo-Saxon England demonstrated in their different ways, sustaining a kingdom-wide corporate Church identity was impossible. In Francia, the decline in Merovingian royal power only accelerated the well-established tendency for secular, aristocratic values to intrude into ecclesiastical circles, and the breakdown in the Frankish conciliar tradition contributed to a marked further decline in ecclesiastical discipline among Frankish Church leaders in the first half of the eighth century. Archbishop Milo of Trier was another bête noire of the Anglo-Saxon missionary Boniface. A strong supporter of Charles Martel (688–741), undisputed leader of Austrasia from the late 710s, Milo succeeded his father as bishop (no episcopal celibacy there) and held Trier simultaneously with the bishopric of Rheims – another practice that was, in theory, forbidden. According to local sources, Milo also robbed the churches under his care blind, as well as being prone (at least according to Boniface) to adulterous liaisons and fighting in battle alongside Charles Martel. Not every Frankish bishop was as worldly as Milo, but the problem was clear. Engaged in a winner-take-all struggle with rival regional aristocratic factions, Martel had need of powerful, loyal supporters like Milo, and was not about to remove him from office for lack of ecclesiastical discipline. Martel himself was likewise remembered among Churchmen for 'stealing' Church land, which usually meant taking over the assets of one set of local landowners to reward his own supporters.[5]

By the early decades of the eighth century, the regionally based institutional Church structures of the bulk of the Latin west – from Italy and Spain to Francia – were in substantial disarray. It would take something truly extraordinary to set the Latin Church on a path to greater, and more independent, institutional stability. The first step came on Christmas Day 800, with the restoration of political power on a truly imperial scale.

CHRISTMAS DAY 800

The roots of this remarkable imperial restoration can be traced back to the north-eastern corner of the Frankish kingdom: Austrasia. There in the mid-seventh century a marriage alliance was forged between Ansegesil the son of Arnulf of Metz and Begga the daughter of Pippin of Landen. It created a new aristocratic network, one that proved powerful enough first to dominate Austrasia, and then to spread its control over the entire realm. Later that century, their son Pippin of Herstal (635–714) extended the family's control and influence over neighbouring Neustria by victory at the battle of Tertry on the Somme in 687. In the next generation, Pippin's son Charles Martel, the 'Hammer', won a series of further military victories which extended the line's power – for the first time – over the rest of the old Merovingian Frankish heartlands (Burgundy, Aquitaine and Septimania). Martel also scored a famous victory over an Islamic force at Poitiers in 732 (though this was much more the defeat of a force raiding north from Spain than the battle of annihilation that, as imagined by Edward Gibbon, prevented the whole of Europe from falling under Muslim rule).

By the late 730s, Charles's hegemony over Francia was unchallenged, but he nonetheless stepped back from having himself crowned king, happy instead to keep compliant Merovingians in place as a puppet monarchy. It was Charles's son, Pippin the Short, who secured both the emerging dynasty's complete domination of Francia, and, dispatching the Merovingian incumbent, Childeric III, to a monastery, the throne. Crowned king of the Franks in 751, Pippin the Short became the first of a new dynasty: the Carolingians.[6] Under his son Charles the Great – Charlemagne – the Carolingian line accelerated from royal to imperial power through a series of victorious wars of conquest, both of territories that had previously moved in and out of Frankish hegemony under Merovingian rule (Alamannia, Bavaria, Thuringia), and of completely new lands: the Lombard kingdom and duchies of Italy in the 770s, followed by Frisia, Saxony and the Avar

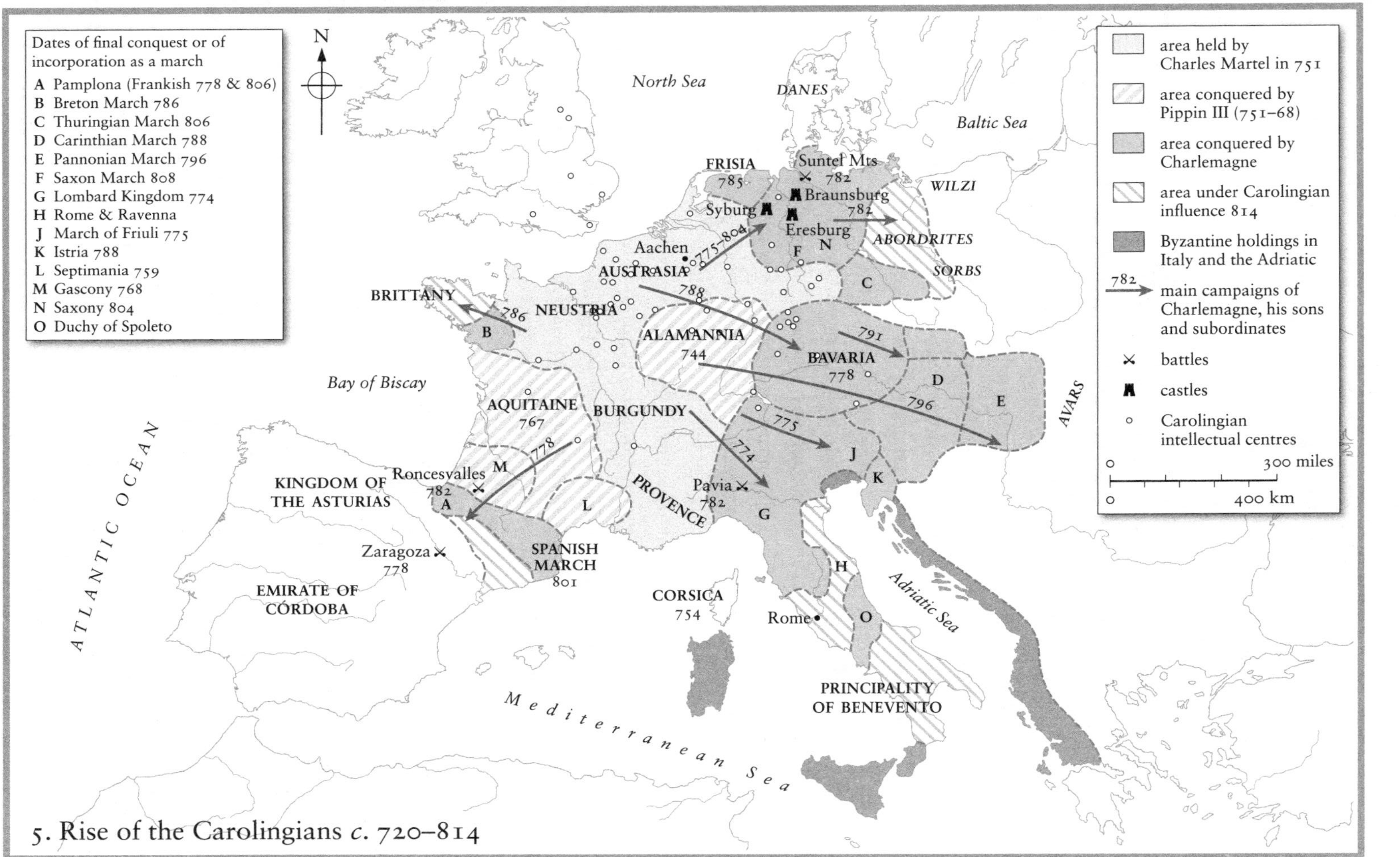

5. Rise of the Carolingians *c.* 720–814

Empire of the Middle Danubian region (Map 5). By the end of the century, Charlemagne had constructed an empire which, even if its epicentre was now north of the Alps, rivalled that of his west Roman predecessors.[7] The second age of Christian Empire in the west had begun. Its official inauguration came on 25 December 800 at St Peter's Cathedral in the city of Rome. There Charlemagne, king of the Franks and Lombards, was crowned emperor of the Romans by Pope Leo III.

The coronation is shrouded in myths, several of which have sometimes been swallowed whole by historians who ought to know better. Perhaps the most misleading is the claim that Charlemagne was an unwilling recipient of the imperial crown. This is reported by Einhard, a Carolingian partisan who knew Charlemagne personally and wrote the first life of the emperor shortly after his death, who said that Charlemagne would not have entered St Peter's had he known that he was about to be crowned emperor, the implication being that it was a spontaneous ceremony that took him by surprise.[8] Einhard's story is simply a version of the old Roman trope that anyone who sought imperial power could not by definition be worthy of the office. Only God chose emperors, meaning that a proper candidate for the position (or any high office: the trope was quickly extended in the early Middle Ages to the post of bishop) was expected to show appropriate modest hesitation before being overcome by the inevitability of the Divine Will. Charlemagne's reported reluctance was simply a nod to this convention. Other evidence makes it clear that he had had designs on the imperial title for at least a decade before he was crowned.

The concept of empire was being discussed explicitly in the 790s, in the writings of some of the intellectuals at Charlemagne's court. The concept had two key components. First, 'empire' clearly signified a level of political power that went beyond that of an ordinary king – which applied well enough to Charlemagne, given that he had been running more than one kingdom since his conquest of Lombard Italy in the 770s. Second, and by extension, an emperor was understood as standing in a uniquely close relationship to God, since without the Divinity's direct intervention no individual could possibly have achieved an imperial level of political success. There was nothing new about either of these ideas. Deriving originally from Hellenistic concepts of kingship, they were exactly what had empowered late Roman emperors from Constantine onwards to exercise overarching religious authority in a rapidly expanding Christian Roman world; Byzantine emperors, despite their many losses to advancing Islam, had continued to draw upon them to justify their control of the eastern Church. On a lesser scale, the emergence of kingdom-based regional Church communities in the post-Roman west had been based on the assumption that the successor-state kings clearly enjoyed a special (if not an imperially special) relationship with the Christian God. Now, for the first time since the fifth century, a western ruler had emerged with a level of political authority that went far beyond that of an ordinary king.

Not only were Charlemagne and his court intellectuals discussing the restoration of Empire and the imperial title, but at the same time they went out of their way to criticize the rival imperial pretentions of the rulers of Constantinople. At the Church council of Frankfurt in 794, Charlemagne's court orchestrated a response to the end of the first period of Byzantine iconoclasm. This explicitly and deliberately damned the eastern vision of the imperial office, which claimed that an emperor actually 'ruled with God'. Charlemagne's Churchmen didn't doubt that the relationship between divinity and emperor was a special one – but claiming so much equality, they argued, was presumptuous in the extreme. Three years later, when the eastern throne was seized by a woman, the empress Irene (who blinded her son to seize personal control), the Carolingian court weighed in again, with the further thought that only a male could legitimately exercise imperial power. Charlemagne's actual coronation, therefore, was preceded by at least a decade's worth of periodic discussion at his court about both the significance and properly legitimate forms of imperial office-holding, something that makes it crystal clear he had set his sights on a grander title than the royal one he had inherited from his father – possibly as early as the 770s, following his conquest of Lombardy.

Another myth accepted wholesale by earlier historians was that Charlemagne's imperial coronation established the ideological pre-eminence of the papacy within the Latin west – because it showed that only popes could crown an emperor. In the later Middle Ages, popes would claim an authority which ranked higher than that of any of Europe's secular rulers, and it has sometimes been thought that this was already the case in the time of Charlemagne. In the previous generation, for instance, Charlemagne's father, Pippin, had sought papal endorsement when seizing the Frankish crown, and Einhard's fake news implicitly gives some further support to such lines of thought, suggesting that the imperial coronation ceremony was organized by the pope, not the king-emperor elect. They are apparently supported, too, by the papal response to Charlemagne's rampant success. Pope Leo's own version of the significance of the imperial title – encapsulated in a glittering mosaic that he commissioned – explicitly claimed that he, and not Charlemagne, was in charge of the proceedings. The original mosaic is long gone, but a facsimile can still be seen; in it, Leo and Charlemagne kneel side by side beneath the figure of St Peter (Plate 23). The point here is that, in the pope's vision of what was going on, the imperial office was not the gift of God but of the Prince of the Apostles: St Peter. Charlemagne's new status, in other words, did not have its roots in any intimate personal connection to the Divine Will. Rather, the Divine Will manifested itself via an intermediary, St Peter – whose direct successor (surprise, surprise – not) was of course Pope Leo.

The containment strategy encapsulated in the mosaic – cutting Charlemagne down to size by portraying his imperial title as the gift not of God but of St Peter – was no improvised ideological manoeuvre on Leo's part. Rather, it reflects an ongoing papal response to Charlemagne's extraordinary career of conquest. In a series of letters to the then king of the Franks, Leo's predecessor, Pope Hadrian I (772–95), consistently attributed Charlemagne's victories not to God, but to the intercession of St Peter. One of Hadrian's letters also includes the first explicit mention of what would become the cornerstone of the papal claim to ultimate authority over the west: that when in the early 320s Emperor Constantine had left Rome for Constantinople to reunite the entire empire under his sole control, he had granted authority over the west to the then pope, Sylvester, and his heirs in perpetuity. This claim soon took formal written shape in a forgery called *The Donation of Constantine*, which presented itself as a copy of Constantine's original grant. On closer inspection, however, the related arguments that – at the moment of its first appearance in the late eighth century – the *Donation*'s ideas had already gained widespread acceptance, and that both Pippin the Short and Charlemagne required formal papal approval to take their respective royal and imperial titles, are deeply unconvincing.[9]

In the eighth century there was still a wide gulf between papal ideological self-presentation and actual reality. The real relationship between the papacy and the emerging Carolingian imperial dynasty was almost the exact reverse of that outlined by Pope Hadrian and the *Donation of Constantine*. Charlemagne's father, Pippin, was proclaimed king in 751 by an assembly of the Franks, two years before he bothered to approach the pope for his blessing – the latter, clearly, being extra icing on the royal cake rather than a central plank in Pippin's strategy for self-promotion. In fact, the papacy generally occupied the junior, suppliant position in the developing relationship between the nascent Papal Republic and the emerging Carolingian Frankish monarchy – something of which popes were uncomfortably aware. In the middle decades of the century, a sequence of popes – notably Zacharias (741–52) Stephen II (752–7) and Stephen III (768–72) – all sought Frankish assistance against the ambitious designs of the Lombard kings of northern Italy, who had their eyes on the now papally controlled territories of the old Byzantine Roman *ducate*: a particularly troubling problem in an era when Rome had already had so many of its previous revenues confiscated by the Byzantine emperor. These papal requests prompted several Frankish interventions south of the Alps, including Charlemagne's decisive campaign of 773/4. After the destruction of Lombard independence, the papal requests changed in nature, but they remained requests, not directives. What Pope Hadrian now wanted was for Charlemagne to increase Rome's revenues by granting him a substantial share of the spoils of victory.[10]

Equally important, as far as Charlemagne and his court advisors were concerned, his victories were not a gift of St Peter. They came straight from God, with whom the king had a direct and personal relationship: neither God nor Charlemagne required any papal intercession. And with great power came great responsibility, as Charlemagne set out in his first letter to the newly appointed Pope Leo III in 796:

> It is our function – to the extent that divine goodness aids us – externally to defend Christ's holy church on every side by force of arms against the incursions of the pagans and the devastations of the infidels, internally to strengthen it in knowledge of the Catholic faith. It is yours, most holy father, to aid our struggle with hands raised to God, like Moses, to the

> end that, with you interceding and God guiding and granting, the Christian people should at all times and in all places enjoy victory over the enemies of its holy name and the name of our Lord Jesus Christ be glorified throughout the whole world.[11]

For Charlemagne, in other words, the pope was in charge of exactly nothing. The personal job description of the king (and soon to be emperor) – as outlined by himself – involved both smiting unbelievers and taking care of the proper observance and spread of the Christian faith; the pope was there merely to pray for his success. This is exactly how Charlemagne acted in practice. Even before taking the imperial title, he paid little heed to papal pretentions even to theological and spiritual authority. When news reached the west that the Byzantine ecclesiastical and political establishment had abandoned its support for iconoclasm in 787, Pope Hadrian had held a celebratory council in Rome to offer Constantinople entirely uncritical congratulations on its return to orthodoxy. In direct contrast, Charlemagne's council of Frankish Church leaders at Frankfurt – summoned independently of the pope – took an independent line. While duly thankful that iconoclasm had been abandoned, Charlemagne's council directly rejected Byzantine teachings – reiterated in the messages that came west – that icons should be treated as intrinsically holy images which captured something of the essence of the portrayed saints' spiritual virtues. That Pope Hadrian had taken a different approach did not bother those assembled at Frankfurt in the slightest. Not only did Charlemagne have all the money and all the big battalions in western Europe, where popes had very little of either; he was minded both in theory and practice to continue the patterns of claimed and enacted supreme religious authority that had developed under Rome's Christian emperors.

Neither Charlemagne nor any of the Churchmen around him had the slightest doubt that he had been hand-picked by God to rule, and the broader evidence makes it entirely evident that Charlemagne – all misinterpretation of Einhard's modesty trope aside – had been aspiring to the imperial title for at least a decade. Such a title represented ultimate recognition of the unique, divinely approved origin of his astounding range of conquests, and hence of his authority to rule on all matters, including those pertaining to the Christian religion.[12]

Given the fundamentally religious significance attached to the imperial title, and the fact that the papacy was already worried enough to try to downplay the religious significance of Charlemagne's conquests in the 780s (by attributing them to St Peter rather than directly to God), you might think that Pope Leo would actually not have been best pleased to find himself presiding over an imperial coronation that would only add extra lustre to the Frankish ruler's already intimidating authority, both secular and religious. All of which is fully confirmed by the detailed sequence of events leading up to the actual moment of coronation.

It began on 25 April 799, when Pope Leo was kidnapped by some of his opponents within the Roman nobility and accused of perjury, simony (the buying or selling of Church offices) and sexual impropriety. Control of the papal office was so significant to the Roman landowning elites, because of the various forms of patronage that a pope had the power to distribute, that it regularly generated intense factional competition among them. Leo's captors then reportedly attempted to gouge out his eyes and cut off his tongue, but rather mysteriously somehow failed to do the job properly. Perhaps these indignities were only threatened, but Charlemagne reportedly inspected some (healed) wounds later in the year. Either way, Leo eventually escaped his captors, one of his servants helping him over the wall of the Roman monastery in which he'd been imprisoned, to find sanctuary with Charlemagne's duke of Spoleto, who'd rushed to the city (a distance of about 90 miles (150 km)) when he heard of the pope's overthrow and detention. The pope then travelled north, under Frankish protection, to meet the king at Paderborn later the same summer.

We will never know the exact details of the ensuing discussions, but their circumstances and overall outcome speak volumes: Leo had lost control of the city of Rome, condemned as a disgrace to the papal office, and – at least – threatened with personal mutilation. He had then trekked 900 miles (1,500 km) north to the Frankish kingdom, which was itself remarkable given that most medieval popes rarely ventured beyond the suburbs of Rome. This first encounter between pope and king then set in motion a series of further moves which culminated eighteen months later in Charlemagne's imperial coronation, some of which had clearly taken months to put in place. (As part of the ceremony, for instance, a delegation from its patriarch presented the new emperor with the ceremonial keys to the holy city of Jerusalem.)

Immediately after the meeting, Charlemagne ordered Leo to be returned to Rome with a Frankish escort and restored to his papal throne. This was eventually reinforced by the intimidating arrival of the king himself in Rome, at the end of November 800. Charlemagne had met the pope at Paderborn in 799 because he was already committed to a major Saxon campaign (to be run jointly with his son Charles) in that year, for which Paderborn was his base, but then headed off to Italy for the campaigning season of 800, even though the Avars had been causing considerable trouble in the Middle Danube (including killing the king's commander in Bavaria). Once in Rome, Charlemagne convened an initial council, at the beginning of December, which declared that no one had the authority to pass judgement on the pope because he was heir to St Peter. This was followed on 23 December (just before the coronation, notice) by a solemn ceremony in which, supposedly of his own volition, Leo swore an oath confirming his complete innocence of all charges. To my mind, this extended sequence allows only one reasonable line of interpretation. Leo's fall from grace in 799 gave Charlemagne the opening he'd been looking for since at least the early 790s, and perhaps longer: sufficient leverage to 'encourage' a pope to conduct the imperial coronation that would confirm the king-emperor's unique authority – including over religious matters – but which it would not have been seemly for an aspiring emperor (who had to be seen as God's unambiguous choice) to organize for himself.

Far from being a reluctant emperor who didn't know what was about to happen, Charlemagne had been manoeuvering towards the title for at least a decade before Leo's problems in Rome presented him with a pope who had to say yes, however reluctant the papacy generally was to add further lustre to the king's intimidating profile. And once the deed had been done, the new emperor of the Latin west happily dispensed with any further papal approval. Though he could not be seen to nominate himself for the title, once Charlemagne had been crowned, there was nothing unseemly in an emperor designating his successor. On the contrary, the closeness of his relationship to the Divinity meant that it was entirely right that he should do so. Who could be better qualified to make such a choice? Hence, when it came to the next generation, Charlemagne had no qualms about personally crowning his own son, Louis the Pious, as emperor, with no papal participation in the process – a move which confirms the entirely subsidiary future role his mind had allotted to the papacy once the inaugural imperial coronation was complete.[13]

TRANSLATIO IMPERII

For two long generations, Europe's new imperial dynasty stood at the head of a further connected set of transformations that were to change the face of Christianity in the remaining centuries of the first millennium. The first two Carolingian emperors – Charlemagne himself (ruling from 768 to 814) and his son Louis the Pious (814–40) – were so long-lived that their combined reigns amounted to the best part of three-quarters of a century: a period in which all the impetus for further religious transformation in the Latin west originated at, or around, Christendom's new imperial court.

But for all its immediate grandeur, the Empire over which the Carolingians presided remained a geographically enlarged version of the same kind of small-state structure which had replaced Roman modes of government in the fifth and sixth centuries. Carolingian rulers did not systematically tax the agricultural production that constituted over 90 per cent of economic activity within their realm; neither did they develop any large-scale bureaucratic machinery either to undertake actual administrative action or to function as a patronage distribution system for its landowning elites. Nor, as a result, did the Empire maintain large-scale, professional armed forces. While rulers had core bodies of more or less professional soldiers, the bulk of their military manpower continued to be provided by contingents of landholders and their trusted henchmen, obliged to give military service in return for the lands they held. In practice, this meant that the enthusiasm with which this military obligation was met varied substantially according to the quality of the relationship then in operation between ruler and ruled. That in turn depended on two related factors: the degree to which a ruler could instil dread in his subjects; and the range of attractive rewards he had to offer – a classic mix of stick and carrot.

The key to both was usually military expansion. Successful wars of conquest both built a ruler's reputation and provided him with a ready source of rewards that could be distributed in return for loyal service, without a king having to dip his hands into his own existing pockets – the royal fisc containing not only actual land, but a series of valuable rights and concessions (such as to appoint to various positions, to hold courts, or markets, or extract renders of different kinds), which combined to generate the bulk of a ruler's income.

In the years of its ascent, the Carolingian dynasty had ridden an expansionary bandwagon with huge success. Charles Martel and Pippin the Short both not only brought some non-Frankish territories under their control but extended their control over ever-wider tracts of the old Merovingian Frankish heartlands. Both processes provided them with plenty of valuable new rewards to distribute, as well as expanding their own royal fiscs. Charlemagne was blessed with still greater success, confirming the dynasty's complete control over stubbornly independent regions in Francia, and bringing Italy, Saxony and a whole range of other territories under his rule (see Map 5).

Expansionary campaigning could not go on forever, however. To be successful, it had to satisfy its own straightforward cost-benefit equations. Not only did you have to win the necessary victories, but the gains achieved by those victories had to be worth the effort and financial outlay, not to mention the deaths involved, otherwise political resistance among the militarized landowners who were doing most of the actual fighting would grow. None of which was a problem when Charlemagne was ransacking Lombard Italy to offer his supporters tranches of Mediterranean real estate, or looting the nomadic Avar Empire of the Great Hungarian Plain to the tune of seventeen wagonloads of treasure. By the early decades of the ninth century, however, the low-hanging fruit had been picked. The problem of maintaining political loyalty without bankrupting the Frankish crown began to gather momentum under Louis the Pious from the 820s, when the sources already report elite resistance to further campaigning in Muslim Spain (which was rich enough to be worth fighting for but controlled by a well-organized enemy, which made victory difficult and costly).

The problem became acute when, in the third imperial generation, long-standing dynastic succession patterns took a new turn. During the Carolingian rise to imperial grandeur, the dynasty was blessed with a series of relatively straightforward successions. Charles Martel was succeeded by two sons, Pippin and Carloman (the latter retiring – voluntarily or otherwise – to Italian monastic seclusion). Pippin in turn was succeeded by two sons, Charlemagne and another Carloman, but the latter (conveniently) died after only three years, leaving Charlemagne in charge of the entire realm. As late as 807, Charlemagne planned to divide the Empire between three of his sons, but Louis the Pious's two older brothers predeceased their father, so Louis again inherited the whole. Hence for pretty much the entire century after Charles Martel first secured his position in Austrasia, Carolingian dynastic succession was straightforward, with little in the way of internal dispute – helped, along the way, by male relatives 'disappearing' in mysterious circumstances, or being eliminated in failed revolts.

In 840, however, Louis the Pious died leaving three adult sons. Three years later, the Empire was eventually partitioned between them by the Treaty of Verdun. Lothar, the oldest, inherited the imperial title together with northern Italy and a long stretch of territory from the Alps to the North Sea (comprising much of what is now Lorraine, Alsace, Burgundy, and Provence); Louis the German took control of East Francia; and Charles the Bald, West Francia. Not only was the Empire now divided, but the succession process had been anything but smooth. With territorial expansion effectively ceasing in the 820s, Louis struggled to maintain elite loyalties – and this became all too visible in the later years of his reign. Charles the Bald, the youngest of Louis' male heirs, was the offspring of Louis' second marriage, and the king's other sons had to be deprived of some of the lands they'd previously been promised to provide their half-brother with a realm. This sparked three separate civil wars in the 830s between Louis and various combinations of his sons, as they manoeuvred to secure their futures. The three-year gap between Louis' death and the Treaty of Verdun was punctuated by more civil wars, prompted not least by Lothar's attempt to seize the entire Empire for himself. Significantly, the quarrelling sons were able to secure enough elite support to maintain serious rebellions, even when fighting their father in the 830s: a clear sign that the stick-and-carrot combination was already losing its potency before Louis the Pious's death. And support, of course, was not given for nothing; every time the brothers (or Louis himself) mobilized supporters they expected rewards – which, in the absence of imperial expansion, had to come out of the Carolingian rulers' existing stocks of fiscal assets. These rewards came in the form both of grants of actual pieces of land or of valuable revenue-generating rights (over economic activities or Church appointments, for instance), and handing them over to someone else necessarily reduced the wealth, and hence eventually the power, of the ruler.

There's no need to follow the subsequent history of the dynasty in minute detail, but an outline understanding of the Carolingian succession helps explain the particular characteristics of the second age of Christian Empire in Latin Europe. Even after the partition of Verdun, quarrels between Louis' sons continued, and regularly spiralled into outright warfare. There was no renewal of imperial expansion, and, with civil war never far from the surface, dependable military manpower became ever more desirable – meaning that the price of loyalty tended to go up. Further complexity came with the next generation of Carolingians (Louis the Pious's grandsons), who displayed a marked willingness to plot with their uncles against their fathers, which again required loyal military supporters. From the mid-ninth century, therefore, a reverse political dynamic set in. Competing Carolingian dynasts now had to expend more of their no-longer-expanding resources to buy the necessary support to fight off their rivals' ill-willed attentions.[14] Over time, this naturally generated a substantial transfer of assets from the various Carolingian fiscs – the building blocks of political power – to the hands of those from whom they sought support. This extended process of internal dynastic competition generated different outcomes in different parts of the Empire.

The middle kingdom of Emperor Lothar quickly fragmented. He divided it still further, between his three sons, but the youngest (Charles) died so early that his two older brothers took over the lands he'd been allocated in Provence and Burgundy. Of these, the middle brother, Lothar II, died without a legitimate male heir in 869, and the eldest, Louis II, who'd originally inherited Italy and the imperial title, died without sons in 875. In West Francia (from which the medieval French kingdom would eventually emerge), Charles the Bald's line managed to hold on to royal power (bar a brief interregnum) until the last West Frankish Carolingian, Louis V, died without an heir in 987.

Real power in West Francia, however, had long since started to devolve to a series of local magnates, most of whom had started life as Carolingian loyalists, rewarded for their support by royal gifts of land and other valuable rights. As a result, they eventually came to exercise, within their own more limited domains, the kind of authority previously enjoyed by the early Carolingian rulers across the entirety of their domains – including the control of religious institutions and senior ecclesiastical appointments. By the middle decades of the tenth century, therefore, effective Carolingian rule in West Francia had narrowed to a small area around Paris in the north. In Italy, too, the longer-term political fall-out from the extinction of the male line descended from Lothar I generated a similar pattern of sustained political devolution, with local and regional magnates again seizing the reins of effective power from the indirect heirs of Carolingian rule in the later ninth and early tenth centuries.

In the middle of the tenth century, however, northern and central Italy became the focus of renewed expansionist ambitions from a new political force that had been gathering strength east of the Rhine, in neighbouring East Francia. There, too, the Carolingian line died out relatively quickly. Louis the German had three sons, but the two oldest died without male heirs, passing on their lands to the third, Charles the Fat, but he too died without a legitimate male heir in 888. Power at that point passed to a collateral Carolingian line, but its last representative, Louis the Child, died childless in 911, at the age of eighteen. During this period, again, a class of powerful magnates established themselves at the heads of regional dukedoms – Bavaria, Swabia, Franconia, Saxony and Lotharingia – their rise fuelled by the royal assets bestowed on them or which they had leeched away from successive East Francian kings.

Unlike in West Francia or Italy, where political fragmentation was in full flood, in East Francia the emergence of these dukedoms coexisted with a stronger commitment to the idea of a governing royal line. In the years of political manoeuvring that followed the death of Louis the Child, Duke Henry of Saxony emerged as predominant: eventually, on 24 May 919, he was acclaimed king of East Francia by his ducal peers. In the following decades the house of Saxony's hold on power tightened, due in large part to two factors unique to the lands east of the

Rhine. The first was the emergence of a major external threat to the East Frankish realm as a whole. This came in the form of pagan Magyars, who arrived in force on the great plains of Pannonia (stretching from modern-day Poland across Hungary, Slovakia and Serbia) at the turn of the tenth century. By inflicting a series of heavy defeats on individual regional armies, these nomadic horse archers provided the dukes of East Francia with a serious reason for continued mutual cooperation. The second was that the rulers of Saxony had their own considerable sources of renewable wealth, in the form of newly opened silver mines in the Harz Mountains, and the fruits of an expansionary process of colonization into Slavic territories east of the River Elbe.

Both these factors allowed the non-Carolingian former dukes of Saxony to maintain a much stronger level of central political authority east of the Rhine in the first half of the tenth century than their Carolingian peers could sustain to the west. Then, in 955, Henry's son and successor, Otto I, inflicted a crushing defeat on the still-pagan Magyars at the battle of the River Lech. Henry had already enforced one punitive treaty on them in the 930s, and the Magyars were making a last-ditch attempt to regain their previous military ascendancy. To no avail: Otto's glorious victory (and especially because the Magyars were still pagan) gave him the chance to claim that same aura of ultimate Divine validation which both Constantine back in the fourth century, and Charlemagne much more recently, had enjoyed. It also opened the way for him to conquer most of northern and central Italy – and, with these conquests, to renew the idea of Empire. After the death of the last Carolingian emperor in direct line of succession from Charlemagne and Louis the Pious – Emperor Louis II in 875 – a number of others had attempted to take the imperial title, not least Charles the Fat, who for a brief period reunited most of the old Empire in the mid-880s. But none of them held power for a lengthy period, or handed it on to a directly designated successor, until, in 924 with the death of Berengar I, the line of pretenders ran out. The credentials of Otto I, however, were too impressive to be denied, and in 962, following in Charlemagne's footsteps, he was crowned emperor in Rome by Pope John XII. What would become known as the Holy Roman Empire had been born through the union, under the imperial title, of the crowns of East Francia and Italy.

The new Emperor Otto's direct dynastic line – the Ottonians – lasted a further two generations until the death of his still unmarried grandson, Otto III, in 1002. At this point, the imperial title passed to a cousin, Henry II, descended from Otto the Great's brother Henry (I of Bavaria). But Henry also died childless in 1024. At that point, the great magnates of East Francia gathered at Kamba on the east bank of the Rhine and elected a new ruler from among themselves, the Franconian aristocrat Conrad the Elder. Descended from a daughter of Otto I, he was a distant cousin of the Ottonian line, and his elevation inaugurated the third imperial line of the second age of Christian Empire: the Salians. Crowned emperor in Rome three years later, Conrad founded a dynasty that presided over the Holy Roman Empire for a century and more.[15]

The second age of Christian Empire in the Latin west spanned over three centuries, from the mid-eighth to the mid-eleventh. Unlike the first Christian imperial age, inaugurated by Constantine's adoption of Christianity in the fourth century, these later imperial dynasties – Carolingian, Ottonian and Salian – all stood at the head of an inherently weaker type of small-state structure. Generally, they needed additional resources – whether from external expansion or by opening important new revenue flows like silver mines – beyond the holdings of their own fiscs to maintain central authority at a continuously high level. As a result, the second age of Christian Empire is more a series of imperial moments, when unitary leadership was being exercised by the courts of western Europe's new emperors, rather than the period of continuous authority exercised by their late Roman predecessors. But all three dynasties shared the same conception that the imperial title carried an inherent and irreducible component of religious authority conferred upon it through the unmistakable sign of divine favour that had been shown to its holder. Indeed, the Ottonians and Salians understood themselves as holding exactly the same imperial title – notwithstanding the odd chronological interruption – and exercising the same imperial functions as had Charlemagne.

In order to cement this claim, Ottonian propagandists effectively invented the concept of *translatio imperii* – the transfer of imperial power from one dynasty to another at God's direct command – as part of the justification for Otto I's revival of the imperial title, and it was acted out in practice in the year 1000, when his grandson Otto III made a state visit to Aachen to view the tomb of Charlemagne, and removed some of its relics. Despite an often-intermittent authority, different emperors from these three dynasties exercised enough periodic religious authority to drive forward two further processes of transformation central to the emergence of medieval European Christendom.

THE CROSS GOES EAST[16]

In 772, Charlemagne set out to subdue the Franks' Saxon neighbours, whose territories lay largely between the Rivers Weser and Elbe in what is now northern Germany. The determinedly pagan Saxons had never adopted Christianity to any significant extent, despite having to recognize periodic Frankish hegemony. Three decades previously, the Anglo-Saxon missionary Boniface was forced to give up plans for a projected Saxon mission because even Charles Martel could not guarantee the safety of its personnel; up to that point, indeed, Christianity had still barely spread beyond the old Roman frontiers broadly marked by the Rivers Rhine and Danube. Charlemagne, however, emphasized the religious dimension of his campaign at its outset, by destroying one of the Saxons' chief religious shrines: the Irminsul, or great pillar, located perhaps at Priesterberg (in the modern municipality of Marsberg). After five long years of campaigning, he compelled the Saxon nobility to appear before him at his newly built castle of Paderborn in 777, after which he thought it safe to declare victory. This proved wildly optimistic. Under the leader Widukind, who had sought refuge with the Danes of Jutland rather than surrender along with the rest of his Saxon peers, before returning to stir up rebellion, conflict was renewed.

The violence that followed was sustained and brutal. Saxon society was organized around a series of fortified hilltops, which Charlemagne's armies systematically destroyed over three decades of warfare. Forced baptism and mass deportation were stock tactics; on one infamous occasion, Charlemagne even ordered the mass execution of four and a half thousand Saxon prisoners: apostates who had returned to pagan worship after baptism had been forced upon them. The inherent violence of the process is clear in a set of laws passed in or around 782,

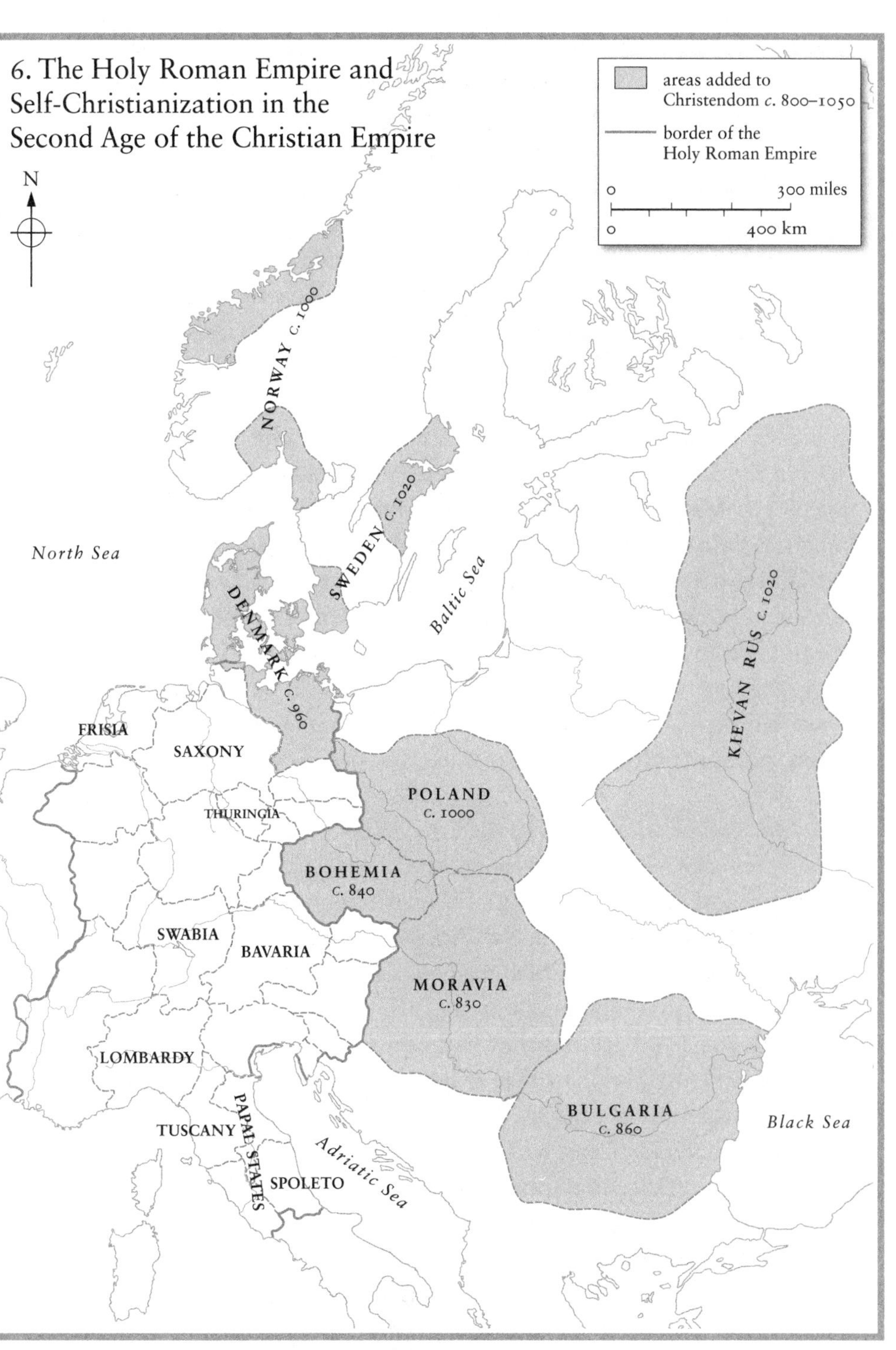
6. The Holy Roman Empire and Self-Christianization in the Second Age of the Christian Empire
areas added to Christendom c. 800–1050
border of the Holy Roman Empire
0 300 miles
0 400 km
N
NORWAY c. 1000
SWEDEN c. 1020
DENMARK c. 960
North Sea
Baltic Sea
KIEVAN RUS c. 1020
FRISIA
SAXONY
THURINGIA
POLAND c. 1000
BOHEMIA c. 840
SWABIA
BAVARIA
MORAVIA c. 830
LOMBARDY
BULGARIA c. 860
Black Sea
TUSCANY
PAPAL STATES
SPOLETO
Adriatic Sea

which aimed to guarantee the integrity of Christian observance within the partly subdued Saxon lands. These identified a series of non- or anti-Christian acts – attacking Church buildings or clergy, refusing to pay tithes, belief in witchcraft, eating meat during prescribed fasts, avoiding baptism, making sacrifices – for which they stipulated an appropriate punishment. In each case, the punishment was death. There was a get-out clause: you could avoid execution by confessing to a priest and duly repenting for any of the forbidden practices. In other words, the conquered Saxons had two options: accept Christianity, or die. These laws probably licensed the infamous mass execution.

After decades of attritional conflict, Charlemagne's 'conversion by conquest' policy eventually managed to spread the word of God among the conquered Saxons. Half a century on from its final subjugation, Saxony was a fully integrated element within the East Frankish kingdom inherited by Louis the German in 843. Twin processes of colonization and continued conversion turned it into a new bastion of Christianity, and lives of new Saxon saints were soon being written, biographies which claimed that being conquered by Charlemagne gave their territory a special, sanctified status. In the hands of the tenth-century Ottonian court historian Widukind of Corvey, this claim morphed into the idea that this was one of the many features that made the Ottonians worthy imperial heirs of Charlemagne: *translatio imperii* at sword point.[17]

Charlemagne's forced conversion of Saxony was only phase one in a vast expansion in Christianity's European boundaries that unfolded in the second age of the western Christian Empire. In the later eighth and ninth centuries, the faith spread as far east as the River Elbe and the Middle Danube regions of the Great Hungarian Plain, as well as regaining some old ground that had been lost when former Roman territory in the Balkans had been taken over by pagan Slavic groups in the sixth and seventh centuries. Saxony, Bulgaria and several Middle Danubian successor states to the Avar Empire – notably the increasingly prominent Moravian polity based on modern Slovakia – were all won over to a Christian allegiance in the Carolingian period alone.

The gains that followed under the Ottonians and Salians were even more spectacular. Christian missionaries spread the word north through much of Scandinavia (Denmark officially became Christian in the mid-tenth century and Norway a generation or so later); as far east as the River Vistula in northern Europe, when an emergent Polish kingdom accepted Christianity in the second half of the tenth century; and up through the waterways of Ukraine and western Russia, as the Kievan Rus became Christian in 987 (Map 6). After its decisive defeat at the battle of the Lech in 955, the Magyar kingdom (which had destroyed Christian Moravia in the early tenth century) also eventually converted in the reign of Grand Prince Geza, baptized as Stephen I (972–97). While large tracts of the north-eastern Baltic hinterland remained predominantly non-Christian, the old Roman imperial religion had now spread so far beyond the old boundaries of the western Roman Empire that, around the year 1000, it becomes reasonable to think for the first time of a predominantly Christian Europe. As this process unfolded, its missionaries had become increasingly aware that they were stepping far beyond what they considered the civilized pale, and mentally readied themselves for anything. Preparations for a mission to Scandinavia in the ninth century involved earnest discussions about whether the famous dog-headed men – *cynocephali* – of Graeco-Roman geographical anthropology, whom they were sure they were about to meet, would turn out to have souls.[18]

Most of this expansion of Christian Europe, however, did not follow Charlemagne's conversion-by-conquest model. Though it had eventually worked in Saxony, the approach presented too many problems to be more generally applicable. Even for the subservient clergy of warrior Christian rulers, the amount of violence required sat uncomfortably alongside the prescripts of the Gospel concerning love and peace (Æthelberht of Kent at the end of the sixth century had understood that he shouldn't just force people to follow him into baptism: see p. 245). One of Charlemagne's closest clerical advisors, the Anglo-Saxon scholar Alcuin of York, even went as far as to criticize the Saxon conversion strategy in public, in a series of letters to Archbishop Arn of Salzburg in the mid-790s. With Carolingian dominance now starting to embrace the pagan Avars and Slavs of the Middle Danube region, Alcuin didn't want the Saxon mistakes – as he saw them – repeated. Alcuin wasn't against force per se, but he did want baptism and preaching to be given a chance to work first, before formal structures of clerical organization (church buildings and priests) and the financial exactions to support them (tithes) were imposed on conquered populations. In Alcuin's view, it was overhasty tax demands, rather than conversion to Christianity itself, which had provoked the ferocious Saxon resistance.[19]

Alcuin was more correct than he realized, perhaps, because imposing Christianity by force had a distinct tendency to provoke more intense religious as well as political resistance. As well as eighth-century Saxony, this was also true for the Elbe Slavs, who, by the last quarter of the tenth century, were conquered subjects of the Ottonian imperial dynasty. Ottonian expansion beyond the Elbe took the form of a series of fortified colonial settlements called burgwards, which were local military commands and newly established bishoprics, with dependent parish-church networks, all supported by tithes extracted from the local conquered populations. When Emperor Otto II suffered a major defeat at the hands of Muslim forces in southern Italy in 983, this provided the opportunity for pent-up Slavic resentment at this oppressive colonial regime to explode into widespread revolt. What happened in the burgward of Brandenburg was typical. The bishop and military commander barely escaped with their lives, anyone captured was slaughtered, the tomb of the previous bishop was desecrated and the church itself plundered.[20]

The revolts also spawned a new political confederation among the Elbe Slavs of the southern shores of the Baltic. Known as the Liutizi (perhaps from their word for 'fierce' or 'wild'), this confederation was driven both by a political determination not to fall back under Ottonian domination, and by a new-found pagan religious militancy. Its most important cult site was the darkly imposing Radgosc, probably somewhere in what is now Mecklenburg:

> It is surrounded everywhere by a great forest which the inhabitants hold to be inviolable and holy ... In the fort, there is nothing other than a skilfully made wooden shrine supported on a foundation composed of the horns of different types of animals. Marvellous sculpted images of gods and goddesses adorn its outer walls ... Inside, stand gods made by human hands, each with a name inscribed and frightfully clothed with helmets and armour. Among them, [the god] Swarozyc occupies the first place and all the heathens honour and worship him

> above the others. Their banners may never be removed from this place except in time of war and then only by warriors on foot.[21]

This temple and its gods, which had their own full-time priests, represents the clearest, longest-lived case where existing religious cults, faced with the arrival of Christianity, managed to resist its advance for a prolonged period via an aggressive pagan religious rebooting. The fourth-century Gothic Tervingi, who began to persecute the Christian community among whom Ulfilas originated, provide an early example, and something similar seems to have happened in ninth-century Scandinavia as well, as we shall see later in the chapter. But the Elbe Slavs of the southern shores of the Baltic provide the clearest, most sustained example. There, native cults survived their first contact with organized, aggressive Christianity to become the focus for resistance to Christian imperialism – in this case, for centuries. While Radgosc was destroyed by the forces of Bishop Burchard of Halberstadt in 1068 (after another revolt that had begun with the decapitation at the temple of the captured Bishop Johann of Mecklenburg, whose head was stuck on a spear), it seems to have been rebuilt subsequently. Even after its terminal destruction, the Slavic pagan priests of other temple sites – notably, that of Arkona on a peninsula on the Baltic island of Rügen – continued to articulate religious resistance to the aggressively intrusive Christianity of the Slavs' colonial oppressors.[22]

Whether or not Christendom's new emperors realized that Charlemagne's conversion-by-conquest model risked transforming existing pagan cults into much tougher forms of religious opposition altogether, they were certainly aware of the costs of extensive campaigning in the economically relatively undeveloped landscapes of central and eastern Europe. Charlemagne's thirty-year-long campaign of conquest in Saxony had required a huge military and financial investment. Such was the king-emperor's political authority and wealth, after the conquest of Lombardy in the early 770s, that he had sufficient clout – and sufficient rewards – to persuade his militarized landowners to fight over this prolonged period. Few of his Carolingian, Ottonian, or Salian successors, however, enjoyed anything like the same leverage over their warrior elites. The Carolingian Empire's lack of further expansion in the generations after

Charlemagne was in large measure due to its landed warriors gradually withdrawing their consent from continued campaigning, the decreasing rewards failing to compensate them for their efforts and losses.[23] As a result, the massive extension of Christianity's borders during the second age of Christian Empire was largely the result of an ostensibly different process: a positive choice on the part of a whole sequence of regional dynasties in previously non-Christian Europe to Christianize themselves – and to invite missionaries to work among their populations. Most of Europe's new Christian converts were products, in other words, of a larger-scale version of the kind of process that had unfolded in much of the British Isles between the fifth and eighth centuries.[24]

All the same, missionary work could still be hair-raisingly dangerous, and not every invitation proved that secure. In the early 960s Adalbert, future archbishop of Magdeburg, was dispatched to Russia at the request of Princess Olga, who had come to power over the Kievan Rus state after the death of her husband Igor, ruling as regent for her son Sviatoslav. On Adalbert's arrival, and perhaps in direct response to it, the resolutely pagan Sviatoslav seized the reins of power: several of Adalbert's companions were killed and he himself barely escaped the Rus state with his life. In the following generation, another Adalbert – one-time bishop of Prague and originally the Bohemian prince Vojtěch (renamed for his archiepiscopal namesake and teacher following a decade of study at Magdeburg) – led his own mission to Baltic Prussia in 997. Before they got there, two of his companions, awaiting papal letters of commission in Prague, were murdered, apparently for the ten pounds of silver they were believed to be carrying. On arriving in Prussia, the remainder were roughed up and imprisoned. Adalbert himself was executed shortly afterwards, his dismembered body eventually ransomed by a recently converted king of Poland. Adalbert's biographer, Bruno of Querfurt, recorded the intense and clearly well-founded anxiety of his subject on the eve of his journey to Prussia (recalling the hesitation felt by Augustine before his arrival in Kent four centuries before). Bruno's own death followed shortly after. Also educated in Magdeburg, he too headed for Prussia in the autumn of 1008 with eighteen companions. The following March, he was beheaded and most of his companions hanged (one, Wibert, had his eyes torn out but survived). And all this in a region where the already-Christian rulers of Poland and Russia could provide some measure of introduction.[25]

To understand why, amid the sacrifices of the missionaries in the furthest reaches of the north, the self-Christianization model proved so popular across the bulk of the European landmass in the second age of Christian Empire, we need to recognize that this mass expansion in elite-level Christian allegiance coincided with a second process of equal moment: a decisive revolution in patterns of broader socio-political development, which was unfolding simultaneously across eastern and northern Europe. At the start of the first millennium AD, population densities even between the Rhine and the Vistula in north-central Europe had been thin, and the characteristic size of primary political units correspondingly small (the area covering present-day Germany, Poland and the Czech Republic was home to more than fifty distinct Germanic-speaking 'tribes'). East of the River Vistula, there were still more trees, fewer people, and no sign in either the archaeological or historical evidence of non-local political structures of any scale or substance whatsoever. Between AD 800 and 1000, however, major new dynastic networks grew up in both east-central and eastern Europe proper, spawning the first known state-like structures ever to appear across much of this vast expanse of territory.

The first of these structures to appear in our historical sources was so-called Great Moravia, whose impressive archaeological remains have been identified in the territory of modern Slovakia. The most important of the successor states to the Avar Empire, which Charlemagne had destroyed in the 790s, its ruling line was already a central focus of the foreign policy of the East Frankish kingdom by the middle of the ninth century, being regarded at different moments with either suspicious hostility or tolerated approval according to the degree of independence and ambition shown by its individual members. To the north-east, centred on Bohemia, a second powerful central European duchy, dominated by the Prĕmyslid dynasty, came to prominence shortly after the year 900; at roughly the same time, the Rurikid dynasty began to stretch out its power from the trading entrepôt of Kiev, north and east along the Dnieper and Volga river systems (Map 6). Further north-west, by the middle decades of the tenth century, a third dynasty, the Piasts, was consolidating its hold over the heartland territories of the first Polish kingdom. Scandinavia, too, saw dramatic change in the second era of Christian Empire. While a larger political entity had previously emerged in southern Denmark before the time of Charlemagne, this collapsed in the first half of the ninth century. It was not until a century later that the dynasty of Harald Bluetooth was able to re-establish the foundations of a new and lasting Danish kingdom. In Norway, supra-regional power is documented for the first time around the year 1000; royal power took a little longer still to emerge in what is now Sweden. It was these same newly emergent dynastic lines – all the way from Bohemia to Russia by way of Scandinavia – who made the key decisions to invite in Christian missionaries. Adopting Christianity was intimately connected, on a whole series of levels, to the political revolution that was simultaneously establishing these families in power.[26]

KINGS AND CHRISTIANITY IN THE SHADOW OF EMPIRE

Genuine religious conviction played its part in the adoption of Christianity by these political elites. Later stories associated conversion to Christianity with appropriately miraculous events in the life stories of the first members of each dynasty to convert. The Piast ruler Miesco I suddenly recovered his sight aged seven, we are told, a development which the chronicler links to the spiritual effects of his future baptism, while the new religion prompted in 'Good King' Wenceslas of Bohemia a profoundly Christian change of lifestyle, in terms of both fasting and liturgical observance. In the end, he was assassinated for showing, in the opinion of his magnates, far too much piety, which manifested especially in his disapproval of the slave trade from which the Bohemian elites derived much of their wealth (Prague being the main market for slaves being moved west and south overland out of central Europe). Wenceslas's successor, his brother Boleslas I (935–67/72), enjoyed a long, successful reign. Boleslas, while also Christian, was smart enough, unlike his brother, not to let religion get in the way of what it took to be an effective ruler of the emerging Bohemian polity.[27] As in seventh- and eighth-century England, adopting Christianity – and, in particular, establishing the kinds of relationship with powerful neighbouring Christian states that conversion made possible – did not generally challenge prevailing cultural values so much as facilitate an unfolding political revolution.

For the aspirational rulers of these emergent central and eastern European states, the whole apparatus of government associated with their impressively imperial Christian neighbours – more effective administration (especially the ever-popular exaction of tax revenues: ecclesiastical and secular), law codes and justice, and the ideological self-promotion that came from being regarded as God's anointed, all of which was dependent upon literate Churchmen – must have provided an attractive model of what rulership *could* be. But Christianity's revolutionary effects upon the ideologies and mechanics of government, while real enough, tended to unfold over the longer term, and the business of politics is always much more immediate. East of the Elbe – as north of the Channel in seventh-century Anglo-Saxon England – Christianity had to work for rulers and their leading supporters as they dealt with the issues of the moment. To understand why elites converted en masse to Christianity in this period, we need to set these decisions against a detailed understanding of how the new dynastic realms were created.

In the second half of the twentieth century, with Poland under Communist rule, the emergence of Piast Poland in the early Middle Ages was presented in textbooks as a kind of Marxist ideal-type, even a fairy tale, with increasing differentiation of labour and growing inequalities of wealth leading slowly but inevitably from the supposed general equality of early Slavic society to the rise of a 'feudal' state by the year 1000. Both aspects of this narrative fall wide of the mark. Early Slavic society of the sixth and seventh centuries may have been simple in its material culture, but it nonetheless contained sharp distinctions in social status. Dramatic advances in archaeological analysis have also forced a complete rethink about the final emergence of Piast rule. There was, it turns out, nothing gradual about it. Thanks to dendrochronology – tree rings reveal exactly which year a tree was felled – it has become clear that the domains of the Piast dynasty were carved out by sudden, violent conquest in the second quarter of the tenth century. Within a generation, all the old, larger hillforts that had functioned across Greater Poland for centuries, acting as the socio-political centres of local population groupings (tribes for want of a better word), were destroyed and replaced by smaller garrison forts under direct Piast control. This had been thought a gradual process, but the tree-ring evidence shows that all the new forts were built within a decade or two of each other.

The Piasts – perhaps a leading clan of the Polani who previously occupied a relatively restricted area of what is now central Poland – were one of the prime beneficiaries of the major slave trade that grew up in the ninth and tenth centuries, supplying men and (especially) women from east-central Europe overland to the west and south via the slave markets of Prague, and also to the rich Near Eastern heartlands of the Islamic world via the river systems of western Russia, where Scandinavian Vikings were often the middlemen. The dynasty used the hard cash this generated to build up powerful, professional armed forces, equipped with the latest in military hardware – above all coats of mail. Perhaps initially created to expand their trade in slaves, these forces were eventually deployed to spread Piast control across the broader Polish landscape (which, up to this point, had been divided between half a dozen or more named Slavic groupings). During this process, which politically unified large parts of the territory for the first time, the Piasts destroyed the hillfort social and political centres of the old groupings, and then built their new-style garrison forts to control the territories they had just conquered. It is not possible to date the entire process very precisely, but the new forts were constructed in the 930s and 940s, and the first mention of a substantial Polish kingdom in Ottonian sources dates to the 960s. All the same, however you date it, the first Polish kingdom was not the result of long-term, organic processes of social evolution, but of a military-political revolution sparked by the competitive control of large new inflows of wealth, the product of intensive trade contacts with more developed neighbours.[28]

A broadly similar political process seems to have underwritten all the new dynasties of northern and eastern Europe, from the Přemyslids and Rurikids to their peers in Scandinavia. All these emergent dynastic lines used access to new wealth, acquired via more intensive relations with imperial neighbours, to build up sufficient military strength to spread their hegemony through a mixture of negotiation, intimidation and outright conquest. It's not possible to reconstruct anything close to a complete historical narrative of the emergence of the new Scandinavian and Kievan Rus kingdoms in the mid- and later tenth century, but enough of the significant moments and underlying processes are securely enough documented to confirm the point, as they are for Moravia and Bohemia.

In Bohemia, everything culminated in one breathtaking moment of violence on 28 September 995. At that point, the multiple competing local leadership lines of ninth-century Bohemia had been whittled down to just two contenders: the Přemyslids and the Slavniks. Libiče – about 30 miles (50 km) east of Prague – was the Slavnik headquarters, and on that early autumn day the Přemyslids were ready to eliminate their rivals once and for all. By nightfall, the Přemyslid assault had reduced the Slavnik compound to a burnt-out ruin; most of its inhabitants, including every Slavnik male, lay dead. The missionary bishop Adalbert of Prague was a Slavnik: his decision to seek martyrdom in the wilds of Prussia shortly afterwards (see above) was surely related to the effective extermination of the rest of his family.[29] The final shoot-out between the Přemyslids and Slavniks of Bohemia is particularly well documented, but the political process behind the formation of Christendom's other dynastic states was similarly violent. Adopting Christianity brought a whole series of highly material – political and economic – advantages for emergent dynasts caught up in these Darwinian struggles for dominance, advantages that were predicated upon the existence of powerful Christian neighbours.

Conversion was sometimes informed by a negative political motive. Adopting Christianity could allow a smaller entity to use an accompanying political alliance with a greater Christian power to fend off the undesired attentions of a potentially predatory dynastic neighbour. In the later eighth century Boruth, ruler of the Slavs of Carinthia, turned to Charlemagne's deputies in neighbouring Bavaria to help him fend off oppressive Avar dominion, converting to Christianity in return for military aid. (Boruth's grandson was eventually trained in Bavaria as a Christian priest.) In the mid-ninth century, in slightly different circumstances, the pattern repeated itself. A later Carinthian leader, Priwina, agreed to strengthen the position of the archbishopric of Salzburg in his territory (Salzburg being responsible for the Christian mission in the Middle Danubian region), in return for the support of Louis the German, king of East Francia, against the Moravian ruler Mojmir. Like Bohemia, Carinthia was located on the fringes of a Moravian polity that was rapidly developing into the most powerful of the Slavic-dominated successor states which had emerged from the wreck of the Avar Empire. A similar motivation was probably also in play when in 845 fourteen ruling Bohemian dukes accepted baptism at the court, again, of Louis the German. Much the same pattern has also been noted among smaller Slavic entities of the Balkans, who orchestrated relationships with the Byzantine Empire to fend off the unwanted attentions of larger Slavic neighbours.[30]

For the most part, however, conversion was overwhelmingly a means for the winners in these power struggles to consolidate their positions. Not least, it helped emerging states establish good relations with Christian neighbours who, at least to start with, were the prime source of both the new wealth flows and the new military hardware that were driving forward the political revolutions. Charlemagne, for instance, was already attempting to limit the export of coats of mail across the Elbe into Slavic lands by formal imperial command in 805, but this obviously met with little long-term success since creating armoured warrior troops was one of the key developments behind the emergence of the new dynasties. Most of the wealth for purchasing these new and expensive military toys also came from the same sources. In this context, anything that helped smooth relations with such important neighbours was likely to move up the political agenda. The question of religion was close to the top because the Christian identity of the nearest of these neighbours – the kings and emperors of East Francia – was integral to their own ideological understanding of themselves as uniquely legitimate, divinely appointed rulers. This gave the emergent dynasts of northern and eastern Europe reason enough to make some kind of accommodation with their imperial neighbour's defining Christian ideology: both positively, to help create the kind of alliance which might facilitate valuable economic and political connections; or negatively, to fend off potentially damaging imperial interventions. Or indeed both.[31]

In the year 1000, Emperor Otto III made a state visit to the Piast kingdom. The visit was to inaugurate a new Church province there, establishing an archbishopric at the Piast dynastic centre of Gniezno, Poland's first capital. There, Otto wept over the tomb of the missionary Adalbert, recently martyred in Prussia, and created three other bishoprics, following which the Piast ruler Boleslaw honoured Otto with rich presents and promised to send him three hundred warriors whenever they might be required for the emperor's subsequent campaigns. Boleslaw and an illustrious entourage then escorted Otto back to imperial territory at Magdeburg, where they celebrated Palm Sunday together with great festivities.[32]

Faced with Christian imperial neighbours who considered themselves directly appointed by the Almighty, conversion had an obvious political dimension, for even if a neighbouring Christian king or emperor was not minded to make the necessary investment to conquer you outright, their hostility was deeply undesirable – as became evident in Poland in the next generation. After Otto III's death, the imperial crown passed to his cousin, Henry II, who was not so persuaded of the virtues of this inherited Polish alliance. Henry proceeded to use every means available (including alliances with the pagan Liutizi) to undermine the stability of the still-emergent Piast kingdom.[33]

Conversion also brought its own momentum. Once dynasts had come to the faith, they started to deploy Christian ideologies of rulership within their own developing political networks. As a result, the faith spread not just directly from Christian king or emperor to aspirant dynast, but also from one emergent dynasty to another. The Bohemian Prĕmyslids seem to have been baptized through the influence of their powerful Christian Moravian overlords at the end of the ninth century (when the still pagan Borivoj of Bohemia attended the Moravian court, he was told that, unfit to sit alongside his Christian peers, he should eat his dinner off the floor with the dogs). A century later, the conversion of the Piast ruler Miesco I was strongly influenced by his Christian Prĕmyslid wife, Dobrawa.

As these new dynasties expanded their control, Christianity also helped them cement their authority over recently conquered populations. The evidence suggests that each of the previously independent Slavic groupings (the denizens of the destroyed older hillfort systems) brought under centralizing dynastic control in the late first millennium – whether in Poland, Bohemia, or Russia – probably had its own specific cults, rather than subscribing to one common Slavic pantheon. In this context, adopting Christianity, with its associated imperative to suppress such cults, had the obvious advantage of licensing the eradication of these traditions of local difference. Nor were such processes limited to areas of Slavic conversion. In the year 1000, the Icelandic Althing – the great island-wide meeting of freemen (which took place in the valley of Thingvellir, where the European and North American tectonic plates meet, and where the summer flies will eat you alive) – agreed to accept Christianity to fend off any greater assertion of power over the island on the part of the ambitious Norwegian king Olaf Tryggvason.[34]

The story of Christian expansion in the second age of Empire cannot be reduced solely to political motivations. The zeal of missionaries and the personal devotion of individual converts played key roles; so too – as in the British Isles in earlier centuries – did the material magnificence of Christian culture. One vignette (from a thirteenth-century source, but referring to the conversion process of the later tenth century) records the impact of witnessing Mass in Justinian's magnificent Church of Holy Wisdom in Constantinople on some visiting Kievan Rus: 'The Greeks [Byzantines] . . . led us to the edifices where they worship their God, and we knew not whether we were in heaven or on earth. For on earth there is no such splendour or such beauty. We only know that God dwells there among men . . . For we cannot forget that beauty.'[35] Nonetheless, the cultural, economic and political connections which generated the individual decisions to embrace Christianity in the final centuries of the first millennium are inconceivable without the existence of powerful, and reasonably proximate, Christian rulers – as two final examples of religious transformation from this same period help to confirm.

The Volga Bulgars, who controlled the key riverine trade route by which slaves and furs from northern and eastern Europe were shipped to the Islamic caliphate (Scandinavian middlemen often sold their wares on to Muslim traders in the markets of the Bulgars), also decided on religious conversion in the early tenth century, but they converted to Islam. They were part of the same extended networks of economic and political connection as the European dynasts who chose Christianity but lived much closer to the Islamic world of the Near East, and, for them, it was the attractions of better relations with the nearby Muslim Empire that drove their choice. The move also prompted an embassy to the region led by one of the most famous travellers and diplomats of the Abbasid world, Ahmad ibn Fadlan (d. *c.* 960), whose surviving account provides hugely important insight into the functioning of these trade connections, and of their transformative cultural, political and military effects upon the different societies he encountered.[36] The Volga Bulgars clearly felt the same kind of pull towards the culture of a neighbouring metropole as the societies of Europe beyond the Elbe – but in their case, the imperial power was Islamic. The second example involves the cultural history of a northern European society that suddenly decided its imperial Christian neighbours weren't so impressive after all.

At the start of the ninth century, Christianity was beginning to spread into the northern fringes of the Carolingian Empire, through the self-Christianizing of local elites. As he manouevred to regain power, one exiled regional ruler from southern Denmark – Harald Klak – developed such close relations with the court of Charlemagne's son Louis the Pious that he eventually accepted baptism in 826. Throughout this time, Louis had also been interfering more generally in Danish politics, to such effect that even Harald's prime political opponent, the ruling Danish king Horik I, felt the need to allow missionaries – in the person of St Anskar, whose *Life* allows us to reconstruct this story – to start working in his realm, and even to build a church at the important trading centre of Ribe in south-west Jutland. Three years later, an invitation came to Louis' court from a Swedish king called Bern, who controlled an important trading entrepôt on the island of Birka, to send a mission there: again, Anskar answered the call.[37] So far, so good: events in Scandinavia in the first half of the ninth century were following the established script. The reality of Carolingian imperial power was combining with self-interested dynastic calculation and an admiration of the evident superiorities of Christian civilization to prompt a variety of Scandinavian regional dynasts to explore the exciting political possibilities opened up by accepting the emperor's religion.

In the next decade, however, something went wrong. In 845, the Swedes expelled the missionary Gautzbert from Birka and attempts to restart the Swedish connection failed. In the same year, the archbishopric of Hamburg-Bremen, established in 831 to co-ordinate the Scandinavian mission, with Anskar as its first incumbent, came under violent attack. The church itself was destroyed, along with all its treasures and books, by Scandinavian Vikings. And when Anskar, now archbishop of Hamburg, made a second visit to Denmark in 854, he found that Horik and all his chief counsellors had been eliminated. Not only had Christian missionary work to Scandinavia come to a grinding halt, but the broader evidence suggests that, in these years, it even went into reverse. Scandinavian burials of the mid- to later ninth century reveal, for the first time, the widespread use of Thor's hammer and other aggressively non-Christian religious symbols. From the 860s onwards, likewise, the great Viking armies' progressive conquests in England – much of the manpower being Danish in origin – involved the systematic destruction of Christian religious institutions and occasional acts of possibly anti-Christian ritual execution. The evidence for a systematic and violently negative reaction to the attempted missions of the first decades of the ninth century, in other words, is widespread and persuasive. It was to be another century before Christianization in Scandinavia regained momentum, with the conversion of Harald Bluetooth of Denmark in the 960s.[38]

Why did the missionary work that had begun so promisingly in the early ninth century fail so spectacularly? Its failure coincided with two brute facts: the collapse of the Carolingian Empire into civil war in the 840s, as the sons of Louis the Pious fought over his inheritance; and the more or less simultaneous rise of large-scale overseas predation on the part of Scandinavian warlords. Although Viking raiding began in the 790s, it acquired much greater momentum from the 830s onwards, when higher-status Scandinavians started to lead larger expeditions overseas, first into British waters and then, with increasing intensity as the 840s unfolded, towards continental Francia too. These two processes were probably directly connected. When the façade of Carolingian imperialism began to crack, the overall attractiveness of Christianity for Scandinavian warlords, recently drawn into the imperial orbit, started to decline. As conditions changed, rivals hostile to the first generation among self-Christianizing Scandinavian elites clearly felt empowered not only to halt evangelism in its tracks, but also to eliminate its supporters and even to sack the missionary centre of Hamburg, while simultaneously making aggressive moves against their imperial Christian neighbours under the banner of an increasingly hostile, anti-Christian religious ideology.[39] It can be no accident, likewise, that Christianity only began to look more attractive again to would-be Scandinavian dynasts in the mid-tenth century, when the increasingly powerful Christian Ottonians were closing in on the imperial title. In these centuries, the astonishing geographical spread of Christian allegiance was clearly predicated upon the existence and power of Christendom's new imperial dynasties.

All these cases of self-Christianization, from the eighth to the early eleventh centuries, took fundamentally the same form: top-down processes initiated by the decisions of local and regional warrior elites. The religious outcomes generated on the ground in central and eastern Europe did not look very different, therefore, from what we've already encountered in the British Isles between *c.* 500 and 750. There were some highly intense individual experiences of conversion. Adalbert of Magdeburg left behind him thirty devoted Christian converts among the Pecheneg steppe nomads when he was expelled from Russia; while the *Life of Anskar* preserves moving anecdotes of individual Christians abandoned by the collapse of the first Scandinavian missions there in the mid-ninth century.[40] But if numerous 'ordinary' Christian believers found the faith in northern and eastern Europe in these centuries, most of our evidence, as with Anglo-Saxon England in the earlier era, relates to members of the social elite, and doesn't tell us much about the spread of Christianity among those further down the social scale. Scandinavian runestones from the tenth and eleventh centuries provide one measure of Christianity's dissemination, but these were expensive items put up by the wealthy. The same is true of other obvious measures of expanding religious allegiance, such as Church foundations or individual stories recorded in contemporary chronicles, including that of Ørlygr Hrappson who left the Hebrides for Iceland in the tenth century, complete with all the timbers needed to build a new church, and consecrated earth to place under each of its corners. (Clearly the Scandinavian propensity for convenient, pre-prepared, flatpack wooden structures did not begin with IKEA.) But, even if his church was not so big, shipping the necessary timbers was an undertaking requiring both money and commitment.[41] And, again, like Anglo-Saxon England in the aftermath of initial conversion, Christendom's new territories of the late first millennium were systemically short of both churches and priests. Even the extensive list of Church foundations detailed in legal documents drawn up around 870 by the archbishopric of Salzburg records only a few tens of churches and priests within the kingdom of Moravia, rather than the thousands that would eventually prove necessary to provide a regime of regular pastoral care for the entire population of a region the size of Slovakia in the high Middle Ages.[42]

The missionary strategies employed to win over these local military elites again allowed a considerable degree of accommodation with existing cultural practice. At the Althing of the year 1000, Icelanders agreed to accept Christianity only if they could continue to eat horse-flesh, abandon any unwanted children (either to die, or to be taken in by others who might want them) and sacrifice to the old gods in private. The text recording these caveats is not contemporary, being written in 1122/3, but is likely to be an accurate enough description of actual religious practice subsequent to the formal act of conversion.[43] As we have seen in previous chapters, many missionaries were clearly willing to cut such liberal deals with new converts throughout the early Middle Ages. There is nothing remotely unbelievable in the idea that Icelandic-style conversion came with many significant strings attached, or, more generally, that the warrior-elite conversions of the late first millennium produced substantially syncretic religious outcomes, comprising local combinations of new Christian and existing traditional cultural components.

Examples abound. The first 'Christian' king of the Magyars, Geza, continued to sacrifice to his existing gods as well as – occasionally – going to church. One of King Wenceslas's good Christian characteristics was his avoidance of non-Christian cultic celebrations. This suggests that the latter were still alive and kicking in the 920s, even though Wenceslas was born three generations after those fourteen Bohemian magnates presented themselves to Louis the German for baptism in 845. The missionary bishop Otto of Bamberg likewise found that, even in the twelfth century, baptized Christians in northern Poland (modern Pomerania) were still sacrificing to the old gods as well as the new. Nor was syncretism limited to religious practice but also extended into actual belief structures, as the *Life of Anskar* illustrates in two fascinating episodes. After the eviction of Gautzbert from Birka, one of his holy books was looted by a non-believer, whose wife and children quickly died. A local diviner told the looter that this was God's revenge and he acted appropriately, but the story assumes that a non-Christian diviner would have sufficient wisdom to perceive the power of a Christian object. In similar vein, Anskar himself told a force of Swedes who, despite appealing to all their gods, were failing in their efforts to attack an eastern Baltic coastal settlement, to try his God instead. They did so: success followed. On one level, the story is designed to illustrate the overwhelming power of the Christian God. But, at the same time, Anskar – and his God – are portrayed as happy enough to show their authority by helping a group of warriors wreak death and destruction. As earlier in Anglo-Saxon England, the type of conversion unfolding in late first-millennium northern and eastern Europe saw two related adaptations. Not only did Christianity itself change – because, to succeed, it had to accommodate itself to at least some of the value structures operative in the new context; but also, for many, the new faith was as much an addition to as a replacement for existing religious practice.[44]

The second age of Christian Empire in the west nonetheless played the central role in a vast expansion of the borders of European Christendom in a three-hundred-year period from about AD 750. Throughout these centuries, Christian emperors spent their time smiting pagans and exhorting pagan Europe's new rulers to convert to Christianity – all of which was in tune with the job description Charlemagne had set out for himself in his first letter to Pope Leo III in 795. The same letter also defined it as an imperial duty to care for the internal development of the Christian Church and to uphold true religion – and you don't have to look very hard in the sources to find that emperors of the Carolingian, Ottonian and Salian dynasties also played a central role in the major internal transformations of Latin Christendom which unfolded during this second age of Christian Empire.

10

Charlemagne's City of God

In 774, as he began to contemplate an imperial future, Charlemagne asked Pope Hadrian for a copy of the *Dionysio-Hadriana*, an updated version of the monk Dionysius Exiguus' compilation of decisions from Christian councils of the late Roman period, and papal decretals. Charlemagne's clerics then incorporated it wholesale into the would-be emperor's comprehensive manifesto of necessary Christian reforms, the *Admonitio Generalis* or 'General Correction' of 23 March 789. The *Dionysio-Hadriana* was just one of many texts Charlemagne sought and received from Rome, including copies of the pope's best Latin Bible texts and of the city's current service books (along with singing masters from the city to teach Gallic Churchmen how to perform the Mass 'properly', that is, as it was done in Rome). All of which has sometimes led the unwary to conclude that the papacy played a central role in the internal reforms to Latin western Christendom that unfolded in the Carolingian imperial era. The reverse was true.

As we have seen in the coronations of both Charlemagne himself and his father, Pippin, Frankish rulers, rather than following any lead from Rome, manipulated the papacy to play a useful role in advancing their own political ambitions – ambitions that were not dependent on Roman approval or initiative. In the case of Charlemagne's imperial coronation, there's every reason to think that Pope Leo had to be pretty much dragged to the altar. The full run of available evidence also demonstrates that in both theory and practice it was Charlemagne, not the popes, who took full responsibility for reforms to the internal functioning of the Church at the start of the second age of Christian Empire.

Charlemagne's claim to be blessed with a unique relationship to the

Almighty – which underpinned his claim to the imperial crown – was already implicit in the *Admonitio Generalis*, which set out a long list of religious targets – standards of moral behaviour – that the entirety of the population, and important office holders in particular – secular and religious – of Charlemagne's realm were expected to hit. This claim to a unique relationship with the Christian God also appears in the works of the king-emperor's chief ecclesiastical advisors, such as Alcuin of York, and figures, too, in a partially preserved court poem, entitled *Charles the Great and Leo the Pope*. This gave the Carolingian view of the great summit meeting at Paderborn in the summer of 799, which prepared the ground for the king's imperial coronation a year and a half later.

In the poem, Pope Leo is treated with the greatest sympathy and respect. The horrified poet recalls the appalling behaviour of the citizens of Rome towards 'the greatest pastor in the world' and pays homage to the pope's miraculous recovery from those mysterious attempts to cut out his tongue and blind him. But it is Charlemagne who is depicted as the dominant figure, physically towering over the pope, and linked by his own spiritual hotline to the Will of the Almighty. According to the poet, Charlemagne knew all about Leo's problems long before any messenger came from Rome, because God sent him news of it in a dream. (As we saw in the case of Constantine, dreams were a highly convenient, biblically validated, mode of Divine communication.) The poem also carefully sets out a slightly extended version of the same religious job description found in that initial letter to Pope Leo:

> [Charlemagne] admonishes [the unjust] to learn justice by godly deeds,
> Bowing the heads of the impious, shackling them with stiff chains,
> And teaching them to fulfill the commands of God enthroned on high . . .
> Those who, barbarian-like, have long refused to be pious
> Are compelled from impiety to piety by a righteous fear.

And the reason Charlemagne is able to do this?

> He alone has deserved to take possession of all approaches to learning,
> To penetrate its hidden paths and understand all its mysteries,
> For to him God reveals the universe's development from its beginnings.

Where popes Hadrian and Leo tried to counter such views by presenting St Peter, and not God, as the source of Charlemagne's success, the clergy of the Carolingian realm, including many in northern Italy, were having none of it. Long before his imperial coronation on Christmas Day 800, Charlemagne and his Churchmen were taking an independent religious line when it suited them to do so. Where Pope Hadrian greeted the end of the first period of Byzantine iconoclasm in 787 with enthusiastic approval, Charlemagne and his Churchmen, gathered at the council of Frankfurt seven years later, declared that the eastern Church was still in the wrong – a move implicitly critical of the papacy too of course – because icons should not be viewed as holy relics (p. 378). It was Charlemagne's Frankish Churchmen, likewise, who championed a significant change to the old Creeds of Nicaea and of Constantinople, both of which stated that the Holy Spirit proceeds from God the Father. On the basis of New Testament evidence – Christ says that he will get the Father to send the Holy Spirit to help his followers at various points – many Christians had long believed that the Spirit came also from the Son, a view that had been formalized by the addition of the Latin *filioque* – 'and from the Son' – clause to the standard Creed of Constantinople in some western contexts as early as the sixth century. For instance, in 589 the Visigothic third council of Toledo adopted it when formally declaring its new allegiance to Nicene Christianity. From the late 780s, however, Charlemagne and his Churchmen formally sanctioned the clause for use right across the Empire – not least because it was another useful stick with which to beat the Greek east at a time when Charlemagne wanted to bolster his own claims to the imperial title by discrediting Constantinople's use of it. At the same time, Charlemagne started to pressure a highly resistant papacy, which wanted to avoid picking a further religious fight with Constantinople, into accepting the change.[1]

So, while the pope might enjoy unique prestige as the *apostolicus*, the heir of St Peter and 'the greatest pastor in the world', Charlemagne considered it his responsibility to run the Church, and no effective contemporary opposition to this proposition came from Rome – or anywhere else, for that matter. All the king-emperor was doing, in reality, was asserting the old status quo, firmly established in the post-Constantinian Roman Empire and dutifully preserved at the regional level in the western successor states: that it was correct for kings and emperors to have responsibility for religion, because God had put them in charge of everything for precisely that purpose. In the case of Charlemagne, following his astonishing run of military success, the point seemed more than usually clear. When you add in all the newly acquired wealth, as well as effective military muscle that these successes put at his disposal, it is not remotely surprising to find that his court, rather than the Lateran Palace in Rome, became the epicentre of practical religious reform at the beginning of the second age of Christian Empire.

CORRECTIO

A Carolingian dynastic commitment to religious reform had already shown itself in the previous generation. Both Charlemagne's uncle Carloman and his father Pippin individually launched their own ecclesiastical reforming councils in the mid-740s, under the joint auspices of the Anglo-Saxon missionary-bishop Boniface and one of the leading Frankish proponents of Church reform in this era: Bishop Chrodegang of Metz. These included a council at the French city of Soissons in 744, at which Boniface finally managed to have Milo, the adulterous, warlike and pluralist bishop of Trier and Rheims, removed from office. (Presumably, with Carolingian power now secure, and his protector Charles Martel gone to a better place, Milo was no longer untouchable: true to aristocratic form, he was eventually killed about a decade later in a hunting accident.) These initial conciliar efforts focused on themes that would be highlighted again under Charlemagne, from discipline within the clerical hierarchy to issues of individual morality, such as incest and adultery.[2] But reforming agendas were pursued with unprecedented intensity during the reigns of Charlemagne and Louis the Pious: five decades in which these two rulers could deploy the united resources of most of western Europe to achieve their religious goals. Undoubtedly, this involved a strong element of regal image-making. As God's appointees, legitimate rulers were expected to show due care for His religion: it is no accident that Carloman and Pippin had made determined efforts to tick the religious box in the 740s, just as they sought to establish the legitimacy of their rule in place of the Merovingians whom they were in the process of finally displacing.

At first sight, the declared aims of Charlemagne's religious reforms also have a distinctly box-ticking quality. The Carolingian task, as set out in the Preface to the *Admonitio Generalis*, was to build a properly Christian society on earth. Maintained consistently throughout his reign, this vision recurred in a general description of Charlemagne's religious aims drawn up in 812 by one of the leading ecclesiastical intellectuals of his court:

> For this is always dear to [Charlemagne]: to exercise bishops in the search of the Holy Scriptures and prudent and sound doctrine, every cleric in discipline, philosophers in knowledge of things divine and human, monks in religion, all generally in sanctity, primates in counsel, judges in justice, soldiers in practice of aim, prelates in humility, subjects in obedience, all generally in prudence, justice, fortitude, temperance and concord.

Judges delivering justice, soldiers training, and bishops studying the Scriptures: all could be talked of in the same breath because the Carolingian programme recognized no fundamental distinction in kind between these ostensibly different fields of action. Everything had to be according to God's will in the Empire that God had brought into existence. Einhard, the poet, servant and biographer of Charlemagne, tells us that Augustine's *City of God* was the emperor's favourite book. If so, the emperor seems to have misunderstood its central message. Augustine argued that a perfected Christian society could only come into being after the Last Judgement at the end of time; it could never exist beforehand here on earth. But maybe Charlemagne did not so much misunderstand Augustine's ideas, as take them as a challenge. Either way, building heaven on earth was the dream outlined by the emperor's court intellectuals – including Alcuin, whose Latin was much too good for us to suppose that he hadn't grasped Augustine's drift.[3] Much more importantly, the sheer weight of resources available to Charlemagne and his son meant that what might sound like pious platitudes could in fact be translated into a practical series of actions: actions which, in this case, were to transform Latin Christendom forever.

First, in order both of chronology and practical importance,

Charlemagne's wealth allowed him to assemble an extraordinary body of Christian scholarly expertise at his court: the best he could find from every corner of western Europe. This process began in the 770s, when the conquest of the Lombard kingdom gave him access to the leading Christian intellectuals of the Italian peninsula. These included the prominent historian of the Lombards and man of letters Paul the Deacon, and Peter of Pisa, who had already built up a considerable reputation as a classical Latinist at the court of the last Lombard king, Desiderius (whom Charlemagne had steamrollered to defeat), and who reportedly became Charlemagne's personal Latin tutor. Several other Italian clerics were also drawn into the king's orbit, such as Fardulfus and Paulinus who ended up, respectively, as abbot of St Denis on the outskirts of Paris and archbishop of Aquileia, on the north-eastern edge of the Venetian lagoon. In the 780s, reinforcements arrived from further afield: the Anglo-Saxon Alcuin from York (which had one of the best libraries in Anglo-Saxon England), and Theodulf from Spain, together with multiple scholars of Irish origins. The result was a fluid assembly of a few tens of scholars from across Latin Christendom (individuals came and went from court over time, either losing favour, or leaving to tend the bishoprics or abbacies with which they were rewarded): a unique gathering of intellectual talent that only a ruler with Charlemagne's reach could possibly have assembled. It was this group, in consultation with their ruler, which utilized the Empire's abundant economic resources to address what they identified as a series of weaknesses in contemporary Latin Christianity – or, as the process came to be labelled, *correctio*.[4]

The basic intellectual premise of *correctio* was set out in *De litteris colendis* (*On the Study of Letters*), a letter from Charlemagne to Abbot Baugulf of the influential monastery of Fulda, founded in 744 by one of Boniface's disciples. Written close in time to the *Admonitio* of 789, it focused attention on one issue in particular: failings in Latin literacy among monastic clergy. Having received 'numerous letters . . . from various monasteries' detailing all the brothers' prayers on the king's behalf, Charlemagne was pleased to find in the vast majority of these letters what he called 'correct sentiments'. He was, however, deeply troubled about the prevalence of 'incorrect language', which was evidently the direct product of 'neglect of learning'. Hence, he was now concerned that where 'skill in writing was deficient, so also wisdom for understanding the Holy Scriptures might be much less than it ought properly to be'.

As we have already explored in Chapter 8, the disappearance of the classical Latin grammarian had created a major structural issue for early medieval Christendom. Leaving aside the particular problems of translation issues north of the Channel, a text-based religion was being transmitted in a wide variety of non-standardized forms of the Latin language, with predictable results. Existing discrepancies between the various Latin Bible traditions were multiplied, and all the supporting but equally vital texts that made Christianity work – everything from biblical commentaries to service books – were dispersed in random combinations across a number of, for the most part, small libraries where they were subject to substantial linguistic variation, depending upon the particular grammatical proclivities of individual scribes and authors. By the early eighth century, this was fast becoming an accepted state of affairs. In the 740s, as we've seen, Pope Zachariah had told Boniface that even substantial linguistic variations didn't matter; baptism in the name of the 'Fatherland and daughter' was perfectly valid (p. 354). But two generations later, Charlemagne and his scholars were ready to back Boniface. Linguistic infelicity, in their view, not only muddled the texts of Bibles and service books; it risked adversely affecting the efficacy of Christian prayers.[5]

If 'correct' Latin – whose importance is also stressed in the *Admonitio* – was to be imposed on the clergy, clerics needed more intensive, standardized training in Latin language and linguistics. To achieve this, Charlemagne mandated a new linguistic curriculum, under the influence particularly of Peter of Pisa (also a teacher of Latin grammar) and Alcuin. This curriculum focused on the old teaching texts of the professional Latin teachers of the late Roman period, supplementing them with a range of new materials. The particular expertise that Alcuin brought to the table stemmed from the fact that the Anglo-Saxons, and the Irish who basically taught them, had been learning Latin as a completely foreign language for centuries (while many continental Churchmen saw no difference between 'Latin' and their own emerging versions of proto-Romance: p. 340). As a result, the Irish had developed a range of additional teaching materials – no less than five surviving Irish grammatical teaching texts were composed before AD 700 – to supplement the basic teaching texts available; usually the *Ars Minor* and/or *Ars Maior* of the later Roman grammarian Donatus. These additions provided a lot more of the basic instruction, and many more of the illustrative examples, that Donatus' texts already presupposed. To these existing resources Alcuin contributed his own influential work on pronunciation, while Peter of Pisa added further late Roman teaching texts, particularly the important works of Priscian and several different commentaries on Donatus, into the textual mix. This fuller range of late Roman teaching materials was then rounded out by the next generation of Carolingian scholars, who produced their own highly influential works (particularly the commentary on Donatus by the monk Smaragdus), to create an effective curriculum in Latin language and linguistics that could turn out competent users of fully standardized, classicizing Latin. The first practical contribution of Charlemagne's galaxy of intellectual talent, then, was to generate a canon of grammatical teaching manuals, which between them defined 'correct' Latin and allowed it to be taught in a newly stabilized form.[6]

The same project led Carolingian scholars to copy and circulate substantial quantities of classical Roman literary texts in a wide variety of genres: everything from ancient astronomy to the love poetry of Catullus. With remarkably few exceptions, the pattern of textual transmission for classical Latin texts is straightforward: anything that did not get copied by Carolingian scribes in the later eighth and ninth centuries has not survived. But the 'Renaissance' label, which was borrowed from the fourteenth-century original for the Carolingian era, in some ways fails to capture the particular characteristics of what was going on in the earlier period. The Renaissance proper marked a rebirth of interest in Greek and Latin classics for their own sake, where anything classical – from literature to the visual arts – acquired an overwhelming cultural cachet. The Carolingian Renaissance was substantially different. Not only was Greek little known among them, but Charlemagne's scholars were also interested in Latin texts for different reasons. Most straightforwardly, knowledge of classical literature reinforced understanding of 'correct' Latin, including its more arcane poetic forms and grammatical oddities. These texts also contained useful knowledge that any educated Christian might need to know – everything from geography to history (which charted the unfolding of God's plan for human salvation) to mathematics and astronomy (crucial for working out the date of Easter). Some scholars trained in the newly restored classicizing Latin soon started to enjoy composing in its various genres for their own sake, generating a range of sophisticated poetical composition at Charlemagne's court (including the account of Charlemagne's celebrated meeting with Pope Leo, *Charles the Great and Leo the Pope*). In other words, *correctio* was a cultural programme in which classical letters were explicitly subjugated to Christian purposes: something which directly suited the purposes of Charlemagne and his successors, whose imperial title required them to show full and proper care for the faith.[7]

Where had all the newly rediscovered Latin literature been hiding? As we've seen, a limited amount of Latin literature had always featured in cathedral and monastic libraries of the third quarter of the first millennium, but it's unclear where texts of the much larger body of work that eventually came to be copied and read in the Carolingian period had been preserved since the end of the western Roman Empire in the fifth century. Some of this material surely came from the old Roman public libraries, but whether it had been in private hands in the meantime or gathering dust in various ecclesiastical institutions – such as the monastery of St Andrew founded by Gregory the Great on the Caelian Hill in Rome, where the collection of Pope Agapetus eventually ended up – is unknown. Neither do we know whether the Carolingian scribes copied absolutely everything that was still available by the ninth century, or whether they exercised a hidden censorial function, choosing not to copy certain texts that had come back to light.[8]

Whatever the case, the new range of texts was quickly mobilized to redefine the overall shape of the educational curriculum. Extending some lines of thought that he found in the works of Augustine, Alcuin conceptualized and popularized – through his own treatises, especially *De vera philosophia* ('On True Love of Wisdom') – a vision of knowledge divided into the seven Liberal Arts: an introductory *trivium* (from which we get 'trivial') of grammar, logic and rhetoric; and the more advanced subjects of the *quadrivium* – arithmetic, geometry, music and astronomy. Where Augustine had thought of these things as accidentally useful for the key task of studying and interpreting the Bible, Alcuin asserted that they were of Divine inspiration: instruments which God had made available to human beings to advance them in spiritual wisdom. (In a sense he was reasserting, within a different religious system, the status which pre-Christian grammarians had ascribed to their labours: p. 72.) Alcuin was also responsible for reasserting the importance of logic within the developing Christian curriculum, in the process misidentifying a Latin translation of Aristotle's *Categories* as an original work of Augustine, and thereby giving this line of study a much higher status. In time, this reconceptualization of the overall shape of Christian education would become standard, right across Latin Christendom, and for the rest of the Middle Ages.[9]

Education, however, was only the means to an end, not an end in itself. As the newly standardized form of written Latin spread, it was harnessed to provide Latin Europe with improved copies of its essential religious texts. The reform councils of 813, summoned at Charlemagne's command late in his reign, defined the minimum set of necessary texts for a well-equipped Christian library as the Gospels and Acts from the New Testament (because of the size of medieval manuscripts, complete Bibles – *pandects* – with every book bound under one cover were extremely rare), liturgical books (defined in the *Admonitio* as Gospel books, psalters and missals: Mass books), the writings of the Church Fathers, the *Rule of Benedict* for monks, the *Cura Pastoralis* ('Pastoral Care') of Pope Gregory the Great for bishops and priests, canon law, and secular law codes for royal officials.[10] Implicit in this list, too, was the basic linguistic toolkit of grammatical primers without which it was impossible to learn 'correct' Latin (for which works of Latin literature were of course useful, but it is striking that no Latin literature was considered essential in itself).

From the 780s onwards, Charlemagne's scholarly collective had been working to ensure that his realm was provided with the best possible versions of all these categories of key texts. Although Pope Hadrian had supplied the emperor with that major source for the *Admonitio Generalis*, the *Dionysio-Hadriana*, this was very much the exception: Frankish Churchmen found other materials that came from Rome insufficient for their purposes. For one thing, the Latin in use in papal circles was not fully 'classical', meaning that texts from Rome required careful editing according to the new standards of linguistic correctness. More problematically, the contents of Pope Hadrian's missal, his own personal Mass book which he sent to Charlemagne at the latter's request, wouldn't work in the Frankish context. Hadrian's missal contained prayers for the great festival Masses that the pope himself celebrated in the churches of Rome, but it lacked appropriate prayers for some of the other occasions of the ordinary Christian year (Sundays after Christmas, Epiphany, Easter and Pentecost), as well as rites for baptisms, weddings, funerals and votive Masses as they were generally celebrated in the Frankish world. It was also arranged differently from the Epistle and Gospel lectionaries currently in use in Charlemagne's realm. As a result, although a fictive Roman label was retained to give it added spiritual status, the new 'corrected' Mass book that gradually came into general use across the Carolingian Empire in subsequent years had, in fact, been thoroughly rewritten.

It used to be thought that the adaptations were the work of Alcuin, but he declared emphatically that he didn't want the task. More recent scholarship has identified the new missal of Charlemagne's Empire as the work of Benedict of Aniane: a Church leader and monastic reformer originally educated at the court of Charlemagne's father. Benedict not only corrected what Hadrian had sent, but supplemented its text with a large quantity of additional material taken from the so-called 'mixed Gelasian text' of the mid-eighth century (its name based on a false ascription of the original materials to the fifth-century Pope Gelasius I), an earlier attempt to produce a better Mass book for the Frankish kingdom produced in the time of Charlemagne's father, which combined some Roman liturgical material again with older Frankish texts.[11] Where older scholarship took the Roman label of Benedict's revised missal at face value, and consequently overvalued papal influence on the process of Carolingian reform, the more detailed evidence demonstrates that home-grown Carolingian intellectuals were at the heart of the process of reform, and never shrank from 'correcting' anything that they obtained from Rome.

Alcuin, meanwhile, was busy on another project, one critically important for liturgical purposes: a revised biblical text. The result of his efforts was not a completely new version of the Latin Bible, but one founded on the biblical text traditions that were already familiar to him from his own education in Anglo-Saxon Northumbria, and particularly the well-equipped library of York Cathedral. Basing his edition on the late Roman Vulgate created by Jerome and a team of other anonymous translators (p. 79), Alcuin undertook a substantial linguistic revision of its grammar, punctuation and orthography, in the process removing many of the linguistic peculiarities of the late Roman original. This new 'corrected' version of the Bible was reputedly presented to Charlemagne by Alcuin's pupil Fridugisus on the day of his imperial coronation, which only emphasizes the new Bible text's importance to the projection of his imperial status.[12]

If Alcuin and Benedict of Aniane's new Bible and missal texts were largely produced by re-editing existing texts, greater creativity was sometimes involved. One already widely known collection, Pope Gregory the Great's *Forty Homilies on the Gospels*, was corrected anew, then copied and circulated – straightforward editing once more. But new collections were also compiled. Paul the Deacon worked his way through existing sermons from the great Church Fathers to create a second, new collection of sermons for the religious instruction of the laity. In *c.* 784 Charlemagne duly celebrated the end result, noting that Paul:

> has read through the treatises and sermons of the various catholic fathers, culled all the best things and offered us two volumes of readings, suitable for each separate festival throughout the whole course of the year, and free from errors. Having examined the text of all these with our perceptive judgment, we confirm the said volumes by our authority and deliver them . . . to be read in Christ's Churches.

Towards the end of his reign, another large sermon collection was put together by the monk Hrabanus Maurus, later archbishop of Mainz. These different examples provide characteristic snapshots of Carolingian *correctio* in action: define a 'correct' version of important religious texts in the newly standardized written form of the Latin language, and get the king-emperor to endorse the outcome.[13]

Serious and industrious Christian intellectuals as many of them were, Charlemagne's scholars were just a few dozen individuals. Had *correctio* remained solely their project, its impact could only have been limited: no more than a handful of manuscripts now survive that can be linked directly to Charlemagne's court.[14] Much more important than the scholars' reworking of particular religious texts, arguably, was the massive, simultaneous reinforcement of the educational infrastructure of Latin Europe, which was ultimately responsible for what proved to be an astonishing volume of overall output. All told, some nine thousand manuscripts, many containing several individual works, survive from the Carolingian ninth century, all beautifully written out in newly standardized Latin. It was this renewed infrastructure which made possible a much wider distribution of the individual fruits of the scholars' labours, and institutionalized the overall imprint of their work upon prevailing patterns of religious practice across Latin Christendom.

One of the necessary components for revamping the educational infrastructure of Latin Christianity already existed before Charlemagne came to the throne. It was a new type of script, the Carolingian minuscule, variants of which had been coming into use since about AD 650. Smaller and more cursive than older uncial hands (which used unjoined, large and often capital letters) characteristic of the late Roman world and employed across most of the post-Roman west, it could be written faster, and you could put much more text on a page. (The Romans employed cursive scripts for business and legal purposes, but all their religious texts were written in uncial hands, a distinction that had broken down in the early medieval west.) In a world where manuscripts were hugely expensive, this was a major advance. True to form, Carolingian *correctio* identified one particular cursive minuscule as the best of all possible forms, and this script duly won out over all comers.[15]

The second tool, straightforwardly, was money: under Charlemagne, religious institutions had more of it to spend. The wealth that the emperor liberated from his conquests provided some of the funds. While he didn't found any new monasteries, Charlemagne made many donations to existing foundations, as he did to many of the cathedrals of his Empire, all the metropolitan, archiepiscopal sees of his Empire receiving particularly generous bequests in his will. Another source of extra funds was tithing, which in the Carolingian era became firmly established practice. The reform councils of his father and uncle had insisted upon the payment of this ecclesiastical tax; now, Charlemagne threw his imperial weight behind that demand. As a result, 10 per cent of imperial GDP (nearly as much as most developed nations now spend on healthcare) was being directed towards religious spending. Obviously overall output and the size of any surplus production in the Carolingian era were tiny in modern terms, but it is worth taking full stock of what percentage of the empire's overall wealth was at least notionally now devoted to the Christian religion. In practice, tithes belonged to individual religious institutions (churches and monasteries) rather than to the Church as a whole, and members of the landowning class – normally those who had founded these institutions and their descendants – continued to exercise rights over them, including a cut of church dues. Nonetheless, imperial income from tithes increased substantially, and additional measures ensured that a significant portion of this extra money was spent on creating institutions that prioritized the teaching of 'correct' Latin, and the building up of working libraries containing the texts which Charlemagne's scholars had identified as critical to the performance of 'correct' Christianity.[16]

From the publication of the *Admonitio* in 789 onwards, great weight was put on the importance of cathedrals and monasteries having their own schools: a standard royal command, frequently repeated. Charlemagne and Louis the Pious also pushed through more specific reforms to the regulations governing cathedral and monastic communities, which again increased the emphasis on education. Under Charlemagne, individual cathedral and monastic communities sometimes received specific financial aid, while leading reformers were appointed to oversee the development of new standards of Christian learning in particular institutions, such as Alcuin's appointment from 796 as abbot of Tours. But progress was uneven. Many ecclesiastical, particularly monastic institutions were either not blessed with sufficient resources to engage with the more complex patterns of Christian literacy now being championed at the court, or remained positively hostile towards them, still considering that the monastic vocation should be more directed towards lifestyles of ascetic piety.

In the reign of Louis the Pious, the push for reform received more systematic impetus. At two major synods held at court in Aachen in August 816 and July 817, Louis threw his imperial weight behind the strict observance of defined constitutional models to standardize life in the cathedral and monastic communities of his Empire – the written

Rules, respectively, of Bishop Chrodegang of Metz and of St Benedict. As mentioned above, Chrodegang was a Church leader and reformer from the generation of Charlemagne's father, while the original St Benedict was an Italian monastic pioneer of the sixth century. In the case of the monasteries, Louis' model was not the original, sixth-century *Rule of Benedict*, but a revised version produced by Benedict of Aniane which incorporated several important modifications to the original. Up to this point Latin monasticism had largely operated according to generally recognized norms, and there had never been any expectation that everyone would conform to one precise rule. After the reforming synods at Aachen, however, absolute, literal obedience to Benedict of Aniane's revision of the *Rule of Benedict* was held up as the only 'correct' way to do 'proper' monasticism.

The underlying ideological vision of this revised Benedictine rule was that, in the monasteries they inhabited, monks were creating a small piece of heaven on earth. The rest of human society, even that of fellow Christians, was so dangerous for the soul that it had to be avoided. Even in architectural design, therefore, reformed monasteries walled the monks off in a physically separate compound of their own, as pictured in the famous ninth-century *Plan of St Gall* (Plate 25). The revisions changed the monks' daily routine in ways that reflected this new ideology. Back in the sixth century, the original St Benedict had divided a monk's day into three equal parts: prayer, physical work (growing the monastery's food) and study. The revised version promoted a two-part day divided between prayer and study. The number of holy offices, or daily services, was substantially increased, again reflecting the desire to create heaven on earth: heaven being marked, as reported in the Book of Revelation, by eternal, unceasing praise of God. Over time, physical labour increasingly became the preserve of lay brethren, who were not fully part of the community, rather than of the monks themselves.

But *correctio* also dictated that all these extra prayers should be performed 'properly', as *De litteris colendis* – Charlemagne's letter to the abbot of Fulda – had commanded back in the 780s. A much greater emphasis on Christian learning thus also lay at the heart of the revised monastic ideal, so that, as the number of reformed monasteries increased, they all acquired new or expanded libraries, stocked with up-to-date versions of the key religious texts – as defined by Charlemagne's scholars and their successors – and with the Latin schoolbooks that were required to ensure the new traditions of Christian learning could be passed on to subsequent generations.[17]

The *Rule of Chrodegang*, as revised by Benedict of Aniane, did a similar job for cathedral canons, the groups of clergy who lived alongside a bishop, both to be trained as priests and to assist him generally in his pastoral work. Here, too, the emphasis of the new rule was not primarily educational, but devotional. Benedict's edition of Chrodegang's *Rule* increased the number of daily offices that cathedral priests should be singing, while emphasizing the importance of celibacy and communal poverty – thus extending a quasi-monastic umbrella over communities of pastorally engaged priests, whose lifestyles had not previously been so different from the norms of secular society, particularly in terms of marriage and private property. But, like reformed Benedictine monasteries, the cathedral communities living under Chrodegang's *Rule* were also required to adhere in their liturgical practices to the new correct standards, and to establish or strengthen their own schools and libraries accordingly.[18]

The two Aachen synods did not spawn any sudden revolution. Libraries and schools containing and transmitting the new standards of Christian learning did not spring up overnight across the Carolingian world. Louis the Pious's own efforts to encourage Benedictine-style monastic reform in the aftermath of the Aachen meetings seem to have borne more fruit east of the Rhine, in the new territories added to European Christendom in this era, than in the old Frankish heartlands further west where many long-established houses saw no reason to come into line. After Louis' death in 840, however, much of the imperial impetus behind further reform began to ebb away, as the influence of the dynasty declined in the time of Charlemagne's grandsons. All the same, over the final two centuries of the first millennium, under the general oversight of and with the periodic direct encouragement of the three imperial dynasties in turn, an increasingly dense network of cathedral and monastic communities grew up across Latin Christendom which all adhered to the new educational standards. This network shared the essence of the new libraries and teaching traditions, both in the new territories added to European

Christendom at this time (a broad tranche of territory including much of Scandinavia and central and eastern Europe up to the River Vistula: Map 5), and in its older heartlands.

Moreover, the new standards set out in the second Benedict's revised *Rule* emerged triumphantly in the later ninth and (particularly) tenth centuries, with Ottonian and Salian emperors continuing to uphold its standards in the new religious foundations they established. It was also in this era, crucially, that revised Benedictine monasticism finally began to take firm hold west of the Rhine as well as east of it, spreading like wildfire there in the tenth century thanks to its acceptance as 'correct' by a whole series of non-royal, more-local noble monastic patrons, both secular and ecclesiastical. A classic case in point is the great abbey of Cluny, founded by gift of Duke William III of Aquitaine in 909, which went on to head a vast interlinked family of Benedictine houses, each reformed in turn by a succession of Cluny's abbots. At more or less the same time, the count of Flanders used Gérard of Brogne, a local aristocrat turned monastic reformer, to bring a series of important monastic foundations within his territories (including the famous old houses of St Bertin, St Amand and St Omer) into line with the new standards; a generation later, the bishop of Metz prompted John of Gorze to begin a similar reform process in the Rhineland. From the 970s onwards, England, too, started to follow the new reform ideals. A new generation of Anglo-Saxon Church leaders (particularly Dunstan, Æthelwold and Oswald), heavily influenced by continental developments, persuaded King Edgar to champion the new standards despite considerable resistance.[19] The revised *Rule of Chrodegang*, meanwhile, had become the undisputed benchmark for cathedral communities. The overall effect of these initiatives – if not necessarily their prime intention – was to resolve the weakness in educational infrastructure that had been left at the heart of early medieval western Christianity by the unravelling of the cultural infrastructure of the Roman imperial system, in particular the disappearance of the Latin grammarian and the old centres of high-level studies. Christian education had never disappeared in the intervening centuries, but it had increasingly depended upon local cathedral and monastic initiatives, which generally did not devote such high levels of their resources to the task (p. 334).

The Carolingians and their scholars set in motion a long-term transformation that redefined a standard for written Latin, in which all the key texts of Christianity could now be consistently coded. They identified a critical body of knowledge and interpretive traditions necessary for any educated Christian, and, above all, created a broad-based Christian educational infrastructure to transmit this shared body of knowledge across time and space via an increasingly dense network of cathedral and monastic schools. By the end of this process, around the year 1000, the crucial, well-defined minimum knowledge base of Latin Christianity was shared across several hundred institutions (Map 5), all of which maintained schools equipped with sufficient libraries to transmit that knowledge safely on from generation to generation. As a direct result, opportunities for the kinds of breaches of accepted tradition – which had, for instance, allowed sixth- and seventh-century Irish clerics to use the Old Testament conveniently to license royal polygamy, and to offer alternative interpretations of the Harrowing of Hell (see p. 270) – were drastically curtailed.[20]

The educational rebooting of Latin Europe cannot be attributed just to Charlemagne and Louis the Pious. Without the continued contributions of non-imperial and non-Carolingian ecclesiastical reformers and their patrons in the later ninth and tenth centuries, the new emphasis on education, and a newly defined Christian curriculum, would never have spread. Modern scholarship, likewise, has downgraded the emperors' personal contributions to the creation of new editions of a handful of 'correct' liturgical and other texts. Where Charlemagne and Louis used to be portrayed as intensively involved in textual production, closer consideration yields a different picture. While the emperors' overall enthusiasm for *correctio* is beyond doubt, the new texts were generated by individual and sometimes overlapping scholarly initiatives. In an age of scribal reproduction of manuscripts, it was simply not possible for any new text suddenly to be imposed right across the Empire, even if it did gain imperial approval. Alcuin's version of the Latin Bible was only one of several attempts to provide a corrected biblical text in the Carolingian period. Slowly, over the course of the ninth century, it established itself as the new standard version, as the monastic and cathedral libraries of Charlemagne's Empire increasingly adopted both its text and its physical layout.

Rather than a reflection of the imperial will, its success was mostly due to the growing prestige of the scriptorium of the abbey of Tours after Alcuin's death.[21] Not only did the new libraries of 'corrected' texts spread slowly, but they also generated a substantially mixed set of cultural outcomes.

By the time the reform process reached maturity at the end of the first millennium, all participating cathedrals and monastic institutions shared in the fruits of the Carolingian Renaissance, to the extent that their libraries stocked at least the minimum collection of books defined as 'necessary' by the reform councils of 813. Their schools were also capable of teaching 'correct' Latin. Some grander cathedrals and monasteries quickly built up much more extensive libraries, allowing them not only to teach Latin and perform Divine services according to the new standards, but to provide brighter students with a wide-ranging education in Latin literary and philosophical traditions.

Library catalogues from the mid-ninth century onwards survive from a small number of the larger religious houses, including Lorsch, Bobbio and St Gall. These boasted libraries that went far beyond the minimum, each encompassing around five hundred volumes by a wide range of authors, and each going far beyond the standard minimum in their range of subject matters too – collections bigger than anything that Isidore had drawn upon, and much larger than anything available north of the Channel. Equally important, these institutions had dedicated librarians to look after their collections (including physical maintenance), who also functioned as senior schoolmasters. As well as ideological energy, these religious houses were provided with budgets to keep expanding the collection. While none of these ninth-century institutions (and there were other cathedral and monastic libraries that were similar in scale) were anywhere near as large as the old Roman public libraries, which had subsidized the existence of the centres of higher-level studies, they were more than large enough to inspire more ambitious forms of compositional literacy.[22]

First and foremost, western Christendom's new educational infrastructure was geared to producing accurate copies, in newly standardized Latin, of the key texts required by clerics. That many cathedrals and monasteries could perform this function with competence is illustrated by the material evidence of the nine thousand and more surviving manuscripts produced in the ninth century alone, all in the new standard Latin defined by Charlemagne's scholars. Compared to the late Roman period, however, the evidence for active, compositional literacy – where scholars felt empowered to produce new works of their own, within or across established literary genres – is more limited.

There is some. Just as the larger libraries contained every piece of classical literature that could be found, as well as the more basic Christian culture kit, there was also a steady trickle of eminent scholars engaging in more ambitious composition. In the mid-ninth century, the dominant figure was Hrabanus Maurus (*c.* 780–856). A monk of the abbey of Fulda, we have already met him as the editor of a new collection of sermons which received Charlemagne's imperial approval. The climax of his public career was the archbishopric of Mainz, which he held from 847 until his death; today, he is known to historians for his authorship of a stream of hymns, biblical commentaries, sermons, and a series of treatises on doctrinal and practical matters. He also taught a series of impressive pupils – Walafrid Strabo, Lupus of Ferrières and Otfrid of Weissenburg – whose own collected compositional works are highlights of the next generation of scholars.[23] Similar patterns persisted into the tenth century as well; there were many institutions now with decent teaching libraries and solid educational traditions, capable of faithful copying of important books in accurate Latin. More creative, complex compositional literacy, however, was limited to a smaller number of prominent, individual scholars, though their number certainly increased with each passing generation.

For all its limitations, it is important not to underestimate the long-term significance of this Carolingian cultural revolution, nor the importance of the particular contributions of Charlemagne and his son. During the final two centuries of the first millennium, the fully fledged version of this shared Latin Christian culture came to be maintained and nurtured in the better-endowed of the 180 cathedrals, and dozens of the greater monasteries, of his Empire, while the minimum requirement of texts could be found in several hundred humbler institutions. Whereas much of this cultural proliferation was post-Carolingian, the original energy, validation and allocation of resources that made the whole process possible can be traced back to the religious commitment of Charlemagne and Louis the Pious.

In the two key areas outlined in Charlemagne's letter to Pope Leo III – smiting pagans and care for the internal functioning of the Church – Carolingian reality closely followed the ideological script. When it came both to eliminating paganism – either by waging war against its proponents or bringing them to the faith – and to promoting initiatives in ecclesiastical culture, western Christendom's new emperors set the pace. What, however, of *correctio*'s broader ambitions? For Charlemagne, smiting the pagans and restocking the libraries were, as the grand vision set out in the *Admonitio Generalis* and a host of other programmatic statements makes clear, only the first steps towards building the City of God on earth, and his vision was fully shared by his son and successor.[24] How far did the second age of Christian Empire manage to realize this altogether more ambitious aim?

MASS RELIGION

Religious agendas in the Carolingian imperial era initially focused on the clergy, for excellent reasons. If clerics did not respond to *correctio*, there was no chance of it having any effect on the wider population. One of the earliest formal texts to survive from Charlemagne's reign – a programmatic capitulary (a set of resolutions laying out a coherent agenda of related necessary changes) generated at the council of Herstal in 779 – emphasized that broader religious reforms were to be imposed from the top down, from archbishops to bishops, and from bishops to their parish clergy, a message that was reiterated at regular intervals. The powers of metropolitan archbishops to supervise the work of the ordinary bishops under their control, and to supervise the latter's appointments, had been defined at Nicaea back in 325. However, these powers had often been exercised more in theory than practice. This was especially the case in times of relative political disorganization, when the limited resources available to early medieval kings tended to make bishoprics a valuable reward, and individual bishops too important as political supporters to subject them to much in the way of hierarchical discipline from the archbishops who were their notional superiors. Under Charlemagne, this changed. His archbishops – and they were increasingly 'his', chosen by the king-emperor for their support of his religious policies – became the principal agents of reform: episcopal subordinates (well over thirty of them) who did not respond with sufficient enthusiasm were promptly dismissed from office. The grand programmatic statements of early intent, such as Herstal and the *Admonitio Generalis* (789), were followed up by periodic enquiries into their implementation and, towards the end of Charlemagne's reign, by a special series of reform councils. The happenstance of surviving records means that we know councils were certainly held in 813 at Arles, Chalons, Mainz, Rheims and Tours (all but Chalons were archiepiscopal sees), and there were probably many more for which no records survive.

Bishops in turn were tasked with ensuring compliance among subordinate clergy, and at this level, too, serious energy was periodically expended. During Charlemagne's time, episcopal statutes made their first appearance. These were instructions drawn up by bishops for priests of their dioceses regarding the general religious observance to be followed by their congregations, a custom that would endure for centuries. The first five surviving examples, all created before the reforming councils of 813, offer wide variations in religious intensity. At Liège, in the north-east of Francia, Bishop Gerbold emphasized only the most basic of Christian duties: baptizing children and paying tithes. Further south-west at Orléans, where Christianity had older, deeper roots going back to the late Roman period, Bishop Theodulf set out a more ambitious programme, including full lay participation in the fasts and vigils of the liturgical year. That there should be so much variety in their contents strongly suggests that these statutes were substantially practical texts, responding to the realities of existing local religiosity.[25]

Carolingian religious reform also focused on the intimately related issues of tithing, or religious taxation, and church-building. With bishops lacking the financial resources to mount their own building programmes, conciliar decrees regularly exhorted landowners to build more churches for their dependent peasants. This sat alongside equally regular demands that the Empire's Christian population should be handing over 10 per cent of its annual income for religious purposes. In itself, tithing was no Carolingian innovation: its deepest roots lay in Old Testament requirements that the Children of Israel support the Temple in Jerusalem, while similar demands surface periodically in Christian contexts from the late Roman period onwards. Under the Carolingians, however, a series of conciliar pronouncements – beginning in the generation of Charlemagne's father and uncle – gave the demand unprecedented legal teeth, and the surviving evidence indicates much more effective levels of enforcement from the later eighth century onwards.[26] Tithes, moreover, were paid not to the Church in general, but to specific local ecclesiastical institutions with recognized legal rights to levy them. In practice, this meant that landowners could be incentivized to build religious foundations by the prospect of acquiring heritable control of the valuable annual revenue flows which might be attached to new ecclesiastical structures.[27]

Charlemagne and his Churchmen were equally concerned with the nature and quality of the worship taking place inside both existing and newly constructed churches. A specific demand, frequently repeated in conciliar decrees, was that priests should preach regularly, instructing their parishioners in 'true religion'. Charlemagne's scholars devoted serious effort to providing useable sermon collections, as well as initiating a drive towards much greater liturgical uniformity, targeting the wide variation in services (and even basic ritual) which so characterized post-Roman Christianity in western Europe. The basic toolkit here was the range of new service books, where innovation often lay concealed beneath a façade of tradition: Alcuin's revised version of the Bible; a new missal setting out the readings to be used for every day of the Church year; lectionaries doing the same job for other services; supporting materials such as new psalters (again based on Alcuin's version of the Psalms); and new sermon collections.

Still more ambitiously, Carolingian Churchmen attempted to disseminate new, spiritually more intense understandings of the significance of the revised orders of service, particularly for the Mass, among both parish priests and the laity. Probably in the reign of Louis the Pious, Amalarius of Metz (*c.* 775–850) – a pupil of Alcuin, and at different times archbishop of both Trier and Lyons – produced the first great medieval reflection on the deeper meaning of Christian liturgical practice, his *Liber Officialis*, or Book of Holy Offices. In it, Amalarius interpreted the unfolding sequence of prayers in the Mass as an allegorical re-enactment of the different stages of the life of Christ: an understanding that has been broadly standard in the Latin Church ever since. In a move that proved much more contentious, it was also in the Carolingian period that the doctrine of the Real Presence – the idea that the elements of bread and wine are transformed in the Mass into the literal body and blood of Christ – was first fully articulated by a monk of the abbey of Corbie in north-eastern Francia named Paschasius Radbertus, in his treatise *On the Body and Blood of the Lord*, composed in the early 830s as part of a scholarly quarrel with a fellow monk named Ratramnus.

These ideological developments had significant practical consequences. If what was unfolding in the Mass was indeed an allegorical re-enactment of the life of Christ, whose crowning moment was – as Paschasius maintained – the actual presence of His physical Self, the whole event needed to be surrounded with an appropriate level of ceremonial dignity. In his episcopal statute, for instance, Bishop Theodulf of Orleans insisted that Mass should only be celebrated inside a dedicated church (an order which also provided a further stimulus to new church-building). It also became normal for the clergy to provide the bread and wine, to ensure their purity. (Previously, these had often been offerings from the congregation.) These new doctrinal ideas also stimulated new requirements for an appropriate level of ritual 'purity', among both those celebrating the Mass and those partaking of Christ's Body and Blood: for the first time, the laity began to face consistent demands that they should only come to Mass after making confession of, and doing penance for, their sins.[28]

From texts of the Carolingian imperial era, a clear picture emerges of a broadly coherent programme for transforming religious practice across Latin Christendom. Not all of it originated with Charlemagne, nor was there a single moment of genius behind a monolithic cunning plan. Rather, the texts illustrate, as you might expect, numerous individual Churchmen alternately lobbying and quarrelling with a succession of Carolingian monarchs over religious matters, as well as squabbling, sometimes viciously, among themselves (as Paschasius and Ratramnus did over the Real Presence). All the same, consensus developed around a related set of concerns, which between them defined a revolutionary agenda for the religious practice of Latin Christendom: build more churches, distribute among them copies of the same 'correct' religious texts, and improve the understanding and behaviour of both clergy and laity, until, for the first time in Christian history, every congregation would be, more or less literally, singing from the same hymn sheet.

All these various reforms are described in loving detail in the writings of contemporary clergy, and generally senior clergy at that. This is usually true of almost everything in early medieval Europe because advanced compositional literacy was limited to so few individuals. This poses a particular issue in this instance, however, because, especially when writing about the laity, senior Churchmen of the period rarely engaged in simple, factual reportage. Most of these texts were written with particular axes to grind: to celebrate the author's own (or some other religious hero's) exemplary achievements; to upbraid the spiritually lax; or to lay down normative models of what ought to be happening. One late Carolingian text, a brief handbook on Church practice produced in *c.* 906 by Regino, a monk at the abbey of Prüm, envisages, for instance, diocesan bishops making regular visitations – tours of inspection – of the local churches under their control, and goes on to list no fewer than ninety-six questions for bishops to ask each of their parish priests, and another eighty-nine for their lay parishioners. In Regino's view, this questioning provided the opportunity, among other things, to verify that the season of Lent had begun – as he was sure that it should do – with a great penitential moment: a general confession of sins on the part of the laity in preparation for celebrating the death and resurrection of Christ at Eastertide. But what should we make of this text? No written visitation records survive for another three hundred years, so what had actually been happening in the intervening centuries before records began to be kept? Were visitations happening regularly, conducted orally? Did they never happen? Or did they happen sometimes in some places? Getting past the smokescreens laid by the surviving barrage of normative clerical writing to the actual impact the Carolingian religious programme may have had on the ground, among real local communities, is far from straightforward.[29]

Whatever else happened, *correctio* didn't create the City of God on earth. The Carolingian Empire remained a flawed, human construction. On his accession, Louis the Pious declared his father's palace 'full of whores', while Archbishop Hincmar of Rheims later condemned the court of Louis' grandson Lothar II as the haunt of witches and soothsayers.[30] There is no evidence, likewise, that under the Carolingians judges judged more justly, or that any of the other pious hopes of Charlemagne's *Admonitio Generalis* came to fruition. What was more, from the middle of the ninth century Charlemagne's edifice fell apart in a political process that, as we have seen, was every bit as violent and treacherous as the one from which it had emerged. Nonetheless, Carolingian reforms initiated some important changes in the religious practices of Latin Christendom, which proved to have enough traction to survive even the collapse of the imperial structure in which they had originated.

Even as the Carolingian political empire fell apart, the rate of new church-building accelerated, ushering in a revolutionary phase of construction that lasted two centuries and more. Rates of construction varied from region to region through Christendom, partly according to need. In the north Italian diocese of Verona, the number of churches doubled in the century and a half after AD 1000. In the Limousin, in what is now central France, the process had begun earlier. This region already had a thousand churches by the turn of the first millennium – a density of one for every 2–2½ sq. miles (5–6 sq. km) – which is probably the main reason why only two hundred new churches were constructed in the following two centuries. In the Ardèche, by contrast, there were only twenty churches in the ninth century, with another eighty-three built in the tenth and eleventh centuries; in England, an astonishing six to seven thousand churches were constructed between 900 and 1200. Obviously, church-building north of the Channel can't be directly attributed to the Carolingians and their imperial successors, but the Anglo-Saxon monarchs who united England for the first time in the tenth century closely followed continental paradigms of good Christian kingship, while copies of the Carolingian legislation on tithes and church-building were well known both to them and their clerical advisors; the influence, if indirect, was nonetheless profound.

In the geographical areas added to Christendom during the second age of Christian Empire, likewise, the pattern was remarkably similar. Poland and Scandinavia were starting from a much lower base, and the acceleration took a little longer to get up to speed, but in the twelfth and thirteenth centuries these areas saw a substantial increase in local church construction equal to that witnessed elsewhere in Latin Christendom a century or two before. All this was set in motion by the same Church laws and administrative structures that the Carolingian imperial era had set down as a basic blueprint. The process clearly began in the ninth century, and the whole phenomenon – pushed forward overwhelmingly by local lords – was catalysed by the new tithe-related incentives set out in Carolingian legislation.[31] This was a process not an event, but the provision of a much fuller network of local churches was a striking religious achievement of the second age of Christian Empire.

It is much more difficult to know what kinds of services were being provided in all these new churches, and the degree of piety they might have instilled in their congregations. The main evidence available to us takes the form of surviving dated manuscripts of Alcuin's Bible, and the new service books created under Carolingian rule. From these, we can tell that the old patterns of service were not swept away in any sudden revolution. Alcuin's Bible was not – could not be – imposed by imperial fiat, but slowly came to predominate in the two to three generations after its creation, along with the new missals, lectionaries and sermon collections, which survive in relatively numerous ninth- and tenth-century manuscript copies. This pattern repeats itself with the penitential texts, which laid out appropriate penances for different kinds of sin. Most were pre-Carolingian in composition, and Carolingian Church councils periodically condemned them for their variety, uncertain origins and dubious authority. Paradoxically, however, the manuscript evidence for their use is all Carolingian and beyond: over three hundred penitential manuscripts survive that date between 800 and 1000, showing that, however dimly the councils thought of them, these texts enjoyed considerable popularity, and seemingly well beyond the monastic circles in which they were first employed. Some of the marginal annotations suggest that the penalties were being applied to laymen as well as to monks, although discussion continues over whether they were mainly being used by bishops for dealing with major sins, or whether they enjoyed a broader circulation.[32]

While impressive in relative terms, the quantity of surviving liturgical manuscripts from the last two centuries of the first millennium is completely dwarfed by the several tens of thousands of new churches constructed after 800. As the process which secured the eventual pre-eminence of Alcuin's Bible reminds us, the technology did not exist suddenly to flood the Empire with enough copies of all the key texts for each of its churches. There are other excellent reasons for thinking that any large-scale transformation of ritual and practice was bound, like the construction of churches, to have been a slow-moving process of longer-term change. Only a minority of the priests serving these foundations would have had sufficient Latin to use the new service books, or sufficient training to implement the new ritual practices appropriate for Masses that were now understood to reach their climax with the Real Presence of the Living Christ.

Some of the new churches were under the control of the growing number of reformed Benedictine monasteries, which took responsibility for the services being conducted within them. Ordained monks from these reformed houses, trained in well-equipped libraries, were surely capable of employing the new liturgical texts, which were quickly adopted in the chapels of reformed monasteries in which they lived. The same was probably true of any of the new churches served by canons and other cathedral clergy, whose schools and libraries again quickly came to possess copies of the new texts. But reformed canons and monks represented only a small minority of the clergy conducting Christian services across Latin Christendom in the second age of Christian empire. The vast majority of priests serving the tens of thousands of new churches were local men, often chosen by a founding landowner, with rarely any training at a large religious institution. With limited or non-existent Latin literacy, such priests would hardly have been able to use the new liturgical texts – even if they had had access to them.

This is a point picked up by another important Carolingian text of the ninth century, the *Admonitio Synodalis*. Laying out what bishops might reasonably expect of most of their diocesan clergy, it places a striking emphasis on priests having to learn much of their craft by heart.

> Let him *understand* well the prayers of the Mass and the canon, and, if not, at least let him be able to *quote them from memory* clearly. Let him be able to read the epistle and gospel well, and *would that he could explain its meaning*, at least its literal meaning. Let him know how to

> *pronounce* the words of the psalms regularly by heart, along with usual chants. *Let him know by heart* . . . the sermon of Bishop Athanasius about the creed of the Trinity. He must be able to *utter distinctly* the exorcisms and prayers for making catechumens . . . Likewise, he must at least know how to *say well* the order of baptism for helping the sick . . . [emphasis added]

And so the list goes on. In some ways, this *Admonitio* suggests that a local Carolingian priest might know a great deal of liturgy, and probably have some capacity to read the Epistles and Gospels aloud in Latin – though as we have seen, a capacity to read Latin out loud (*lectio* in the jargon of the grammarians) – need not have been accompanied by any real understanding of the language (p. 341). In overall terms, the general drift of the *Admonitio*'s demands strongly indicates that its author expected much of a priest's liturgical task to be tackled by rote learning in what was still essentially an oral cultural context. With many local priesthoods being hereditary positions, we can imagine father-to-son instruction in the priestly trade, with occasional interventions from a keen diocesan bishop to add the odd new prayer or liturgical form.

The circumstances of the original composition of the *Admonitio Synodalis* and the name of its author are unknown, but it proved popular, surviving in over a hundred manuscript copies from the tenth century and beyond (sometimes with local additions), which confirms how generally applicable its contents were to Church leaders of the period. This suggests that the fundamental situation it envisages did not change at all quickly. Indeed, even in the later Middle Ages, when the picture becomes much fuller, most 'ordinary' parish priests did not have the capacity to preach sermons as we would understand them; i.e., to take a passage of the Bible and improvise their own exposition of its contents and their relevance to the lives of the assembled congregation. The Carolingian order to 'preach' may often have been fulfilled by no more than careful, repetitive exposition of the meaning of the two basic mantras that all baptized Christians knew by heart: the Lord's Prayer and the Apostles' Creed, perhaps supplemented, as the *Admonitio* suggests, by an ability to recite what was known as Athanasius' Creed – the so-called *quicumque vult*, 'whoever wishes [to be saved]' – which wasn't by Athanasius (the fourth-century patriarch of Alexandria, famous for defending Nicene orthodoxy against Arian heresy), and weighs in at about 660 words in the standard English translation.[33]

In sum, therefore, the impact of the new liturgical standards defined in the Carolingian era was probably gradual and uneven. In all likelihood, they spread only slowly outwards from the cathedrals and the larger, reformed monastic houses equipped with the necessary books to train their clergy in line with the new liturgical texts and understandings which emerged in the period.[34] Services in many of the tens of thousands of new churches built at this time will have been much more rudimentary and were clearly fundamentally performed orally by rote. And all this of course is really dealing only with the externals of religious practice. None of the materials relating to church-building and the spread of new liturgies and practices – a few marginal notations in some penitential manuscripts aside – tell us anything much about the extent to which these changes generated more intense forms of Christian piety among the mass of the laity. Serious top-down efforts were made to move prevailing patterns of Christian spirituality on beyond the improvised, highly syncretic local belief-systems that characterized most of the post-Roman countryside in the sixth and seventh centuries, but no body of evidence survives from the last two centuries of the first millennium which would allow us systematically to explore their effectiveness.

Clear evidence does, however, survive from the eleventh century that at least some of the wider population – as opposed to the monks and cathedral clergy who pioneered them – were beginning to internalize the deeper belief-systems underlying the new liturgical forms. These indications of a more intense lay engagement with Christian piety are incidentally preserved within a large cache of material, generated in the course of a complete restructuring in the patterns of top-level ecclesiastical authority in the same era. It is to this fundamental sea-change in the internal workings of Latin Christianity, which saw supreme religious authority in the Latin west move from emperors to popes, that we must now turn, and to the revolution in practical Christian piety that followed in its wake.

11

Popes and Emperors

Early in 1077 Emperor Henry IV, his wife, Bertha of Saxony, and their son Conrad risked their lives to cross the Alps in the depths of winter, to attend a summit meeting with Pope Gregory VII. On 25 January, they arrived at the northern Italian castle of Canossa, where the pope awaited them. The castle was owned by the Margravine Matilda, a distant cousin of Henry's and the current head of the most important territorial lordship in the southern part of his Empire, a lordship which stretched from the banks of the River Po to the northern borders of the Papal Republic of St Peter. Matilda herself had close ties to the Roman see and strong interests in Church reform, so she was acting as honest broker in an ongoing conflict between emperor and pope. The previous year, Gregory had excommunicated Henry in response to the emperor's decree requiring him to abdicate; both parties believed that the other had acted outrageously. But now, facing rebellion at home, Henry came to beg forgiveness. Gregory initially refused him entrance, keeping the emperor waiting outside the castle gates on his knees in the snow – for three days, so the story went – before agreeing to lift the sentence of excommunication. Such a scenario could not have been more different from Charlemagne's imperial coronation back in December 800, crowned by a grateful Leo III in return for Charlemagne having restored him to his papal throne. Emperor Henry's abject penitence at Canossa almost three centuries later encapsulates a striking transformation in the balance of religious authority within Latin Christendom, one that was both consequence and cause of the Carolingian-inspired processes of religious reform.

POPES AND MISSIONARIES

Back in the late eighth century, the papacy benefited magnificently from the fruits of Charlemagne's Italian conquests. Hadrian I had lobbied the emperor for financial benefits incessantly following his conquest of the Lombard kingdom, presenting these requests as a restoration of ownership. This was partly true, since successive Lombard kings had been eroding some of the fringe territories of the original Papal Republic since the 730s – but Hadrian also leant heavily on the myth of the *Donation of Constantine* – the argument, based on forged documents, that back in the fourth century the Roman emperor Constantine had granted control of the western Empire to Pope Sylvester. The end result was a series of gifts from Charlemagne to the pope, conveyed in two formal grants dated 781 and 787. These added substantial new holdings to the papal patrimony, together with a series of valuable additional rights, such as the control of markets and tolls, across a much wider area. These new revenues paid for a spectacular revamping of the city's secular and religious amenities. Hadrian spent one hundred pounds (in weight) of gold on renovating Rome's defences, put three ancient aqueducts – the Sabbatina, Virgo and Claudian – back into working order, and commissioned a major restoration of the river bank and porticos in front of St Peter's. His successor, Leo III, disbursed gifts totalling over a thousand pounds in weight of precious metals, distributed among the various religious institutions of the city.[1]

But neither the greater wealth, nor the short-term increase in profile generated by the pope's role in Charlemagne's imperial coronation generated any discernible increase in the papacy's overall religious authority. In practice, the emperors continued to run western Christendom. The papacy's role in the whole process of *correctio* was marginal: the organizing energy, the necessary funding, and even the legal incentivization behind the eventual expansion of local church-building, all had their origins at a sequence of Carolingian imperial courts. The main missionary initiatives of the first half of the ninth century – in different forms in Saxony, the old Avar realms of the Middle Danube, and towards Scandinavia – were likewise primarily driven forward by

Carolingian emperors and their ecclesiastical advisors. In all this, the papacy played a walk-on role: it was a generally accepted principle, for example, that Rome should license, where required, the creation of brand-new bishoprics, such as that of Hamburg-Bremen from which the Scandinavian mission was directed.

In the second half of the ninth century, however, a sequence of popes began to feature more prominently in the self-conversion process gathering momentum beyond the boundaries of European Christendom. All the different dynasts who opted for Christianity in the ninth and tenth centuries, as we have seen, were fundamentally led towards this choice because their own increasing profiles at home were dependent upon effective working relationships with their powerful Christian neighbours. At the same time, they wanted to negotiate an acceptance of the Christian faith on terms advantageous to themselves. In many cases, this prompted a complex series of diplomatic manoeuvres in which the papacy played an increasingly conspicuous role.

Emerging from the wreck of the Avar Empire in the first half of the ninth century, its heartlands lying in what is now Slovakia, the new state of Moravia provides an excellent initial case study. Its ruling dynasty quickly built a polity which became the most important eastern neighbour of the East Frankish kingdom. In the mid-ninth century, King Mojmir I (d. 846) was expanding his powerbase within an umbrella of accepted East Frankish hegemony. This led him to accept Christian conversion at the hands of Frankish clergy, following which mass baptisms took place within the kingdom in 831. After Mojmir's death in 846, relations with the Franks worsened, however, and by 855 Mojmir's nephew, Rastislav I, was at war with Charlemagne's grandson, the East Frankish king Louis the German, who had become suspicious of growing Moravian power. In the early 860s, attempting to distance himself from Frankish ideological hegemony, the self-assertive Rastislav approached both Pope Nicholas I and the Byzantine emperor Michael III to send non-Frankish missionaries. This eventually resulted in the arrival in Moravia of two Byzantine Churchmen, the brothers Cyril and Methodius.

Cyril and Methodius had already undertaken one major missionary expedition, to Byzantium's Khazar neighbours at the eastern end of the

Black Sea, and they were talented linguists. Slavic counterparts to Ulfilas among the Goths (Chapter 4), as part of their work in Moravia, the brothers created the first written version of a Slavic language, translating the Bible and key liturgical materials. This aroused the hostility of East Frankish Churchmen – particularly the archbishop of Salzburg and the bishop of Passau – who had previously exercised overall control over the Moravian mission. The papacy became involved because, in the middle of this growing rivalry, Pope Nicholas I (858–67) invited the brothers to visit Rome, following which his successor, Hadrian II, revived an old (and long redundant) Roman ecclesiastical title – the archbishopric of Sirmium – and in 869 named Methodius as its first holder (Cyril by this time having died). As we saw in Charlemagne's coronation, popes didn't particularly relish the untrammelled religious authority of Latin Europe's new imperial dynasty and were keen to assert their rights, which were well established in the field of mission, the tradition stretching back, of course, through Boniface to Augustine of Canterbury. The new archbishopric gave Methodius complete independence from the East Frankish Church hierarchy. The results were predictable: ousted East Frankish clergy were livid, as was their king, and an opportunity for revenge was not long in coming. In 870, Rastislav's nephew Svatopluk, with whom he was already sharing power, entered into negotiations with the sons of Louis the German to oust his uncle and seize control of the entire realm. The coup was successful, and, in return for the Franks' support, Svatopluk handed Methodius over to them. Charged with usurping the ecclesiastical rights of the archbishopric of Salzburg and bishopric of Passau, Methodius was dragged through a show trial and imprisoned for over two years in an East Frankish monastery, until papal intervention secured his release. At that point, Methodius returned to Moravia, where he continued to work until his death in 885.[2]

Similar patterns recur at intervals throughout the conversion stories of the ninth and tenth centuries. The Bulgars, who ran a substantial Empire in the northern Balkans, and periodically fought Constantinople for control of larger parts of the peninsula, converted to Christianity under Khan Boris-Michael (852–89). He eventually accepted baptism from Constantinople, but not before he had played the Christian field, inviting Frankish Churchmen into his realm and sending a further diplomatic mission to Rome in 866 to Pope Nicholas I. In the next century, before Boleslaw of Poland hosted Otto III's state visit (p. 401), his father Duke Miesco had signed up in the 990s to an extraordinary document, the so-called *Dagome Iudex*, which placed his whole realm under papal protection (the document survives in a later papal copy of *c.* 1080, with Miesco's name corrupted in its first line). Likewise, the conversion of the Rus: Vladimir I, son of the resolutely pagan Sviatoslav, eventually turned to Christianity in 988. However, after a brief flirtation with Latin missionaries from the Ottonian Church, which is why Adalbert of Magdeburg had found himself in the wilds of Russia in the early 960s (p. 394), Vladimir eventually accepted baptism, Churchmen, and the basis of Church organization from Constantinople. (He indirectly benefited from the work of Methodius, as the texts all came ready-translated into Slavic.)

At stake in all this religious manoeuvring was the degree of independence to be enjoyed by the new regional Church communities being brought into existence. The question, in each case, was whether the new Church province would be entirely independent, under a new archbishop, or whether it would be under the control of an archbishopric that already existed on the territory of an immediate, and often imperial, Christian neighbour. One bone of contention here was ideological. The whole point of an imperial title, whether held by a western or Byzantine ruler, was the unique relationship it implied to the Christian God, with its inherent claim to overarching religious authority. This raised potential conflicts of interest for Christians within the emerging dynastic states, should their rulers fall out at any point with a neighbouring emperor – which was something they were always likely to do. Such conflicts could be acute if the new Church community in question was hierarchically subordinate to one of the imperial archbishoprics responsible for missionary work in the different regions: Magdeburg for Elbe Slavic regions, Hamburg-Bremen for Scandinavia, Salzburg for the Middle Danube. As emerges from the documentation generated for Methodius' trial, such subordination meant not only that many of the leading clerics of the new Church communities were foreign appointees under the control of an imperial prelate, but also – as Church buildings and supporting property endowments grew – that imperially controlled Churchmen exercised rights over important chunks of real estate within the domains of the dynast in question. For a ruler emerging from a violent political process in which the support or hostility of a neighbouring emperor was often involved, and where support could change easily with every new imperial regime, it is easy to see why a system of hierarchical subordination looked problematic.[3] As a result, converting dynasts consistently preferred to establish their own independent branch of the Christian Church, under an independent metropolitan archbishop of their own choosing. Their manoeuvres to that end offered a series of popes useful opportunities to advance the profile of the Roman see.

Turning to an alternative, more distant source of Christian authority – the pope (for all our different dynasts) or the non-neighbouring imperial power (East Franks or Constantinople for the Rus and Moravians respectively) – was an attempt to avoid subjugation to a near Christian neighbour. In practice, it never quite worked. Because an imperial neighbour was such an overwhelming source of immediate political support or threat, some broad accommodation always had to be reached with the authority it represented. The process certainly gave popes additional opportunities to participate in the unfolding process of Christian expansion, but, even in Moravia where papal influence was at its greatest, it still proved secondary to that of East Frankish rulers. As the examples of Svatopluk and Rastislav illustrate so clearly, if one member of a dynasty wanted and was able to mobilize papal assistance to fend off a neighbouring imperial power in the short term, its web of attractions would always be difficult to ignore. The case of Moravia, in fact, never reached its natural conclusion. While East Frankish religious hegemony was restored on Methodius' death, and all his clergy were expelled from the kingdom, that wasn't the end of the story. One of the last glimpses we have of the Moravian kingdom is Pope John IX sending a new archbishop (another John) and two suffragans, Benedict and Daniel, there in the late 890s, just before this new Church province disappeared completely, submerged in a wave of conquest by the pagan Magyars, who would eventually create their own new Christian structures in the region in the late tenth century (p. 391).[4]

In many other cases, however, the new Christian rulers of northern and eastern Europe were able to achieve an acceptable outcome. While the near imperial neighbour always exercised pre-eminent influence, determined diplomatic manoeuvring – often with the periodic assistance of various popes – could result in the creation of a new, autonomous province of the Church (which required papal authorization in the west), geographically coincident with the dynast's domains, and under the overall control of an archbishop whom the dynasts could appoint. This was the deal enacted in Emperor Otto III's state visit to Gniezno in the year 1000. Broadly similar deals had already been negotiated by both Bulgaria (its archbishopric recognized by Constantinople in around 870), and Russia, where the first known metropolitan of Kiev and all the Russias was Bishop Michael I (988–92). (Bohemia, on the other hand, was too small and too close to the Frankish border ever to negotiate its own archbishopric.[5]) Often, these deals preserved a veneer of imperial sovereignty, at least in the moment of their granting: Otto III's state visit to Poland emphasized his imperial dignity, and Bulgaria's archbishopric had to be negotiated by ambassadors sent to a council in Constantinople, whose patriarch remained its theoretical superior. Once the grant had been made, however, the new Church provinces operated in practice for the most part in cheerful independence, with their ruling dynasties happily in control of property endowments and top appointments.

Although papal participation in this overall process was largely limited to intermittent and generally reactive interventions prompted by the diplomatic initiatives of one converting dynast or another, it nonetheless helped raise Rome's leadership profile and reinforce its general standing as a centre of religious authority, from the mid-ninth century onwards. In the same era, this increasing prominence in the missionary sphere was matched by some equally high-profile moments of papal self-assertion in the internal affairs of the Latin Christian world.

On Christmas Eve 862, Pope Nicholas I intervened dramatically in a quarrel between Archbishop Hincmar of Rheims and his suffragan bishop of Soissons, Rothad. Nicholas demanded, out of the blue, that the case should be brought to Rome on appeal for his final judgement. This was a revolutionary move: never before had a pope made such a pre-emptory claim to ultimate authority in the cases of ecclesiastical dispute. Quarrels between clergy north of the Alps had found their way to Rome in the past, but never regularly, and only when it suited a king for them to do so (as when Guntram, back in the sixth century, sent the case of the disreputable episcopal brothers, Salonius and Sagittarius, to Rome to overturn – temporarily – their deposition by a council of their Frankish peers, p. 359). During the remainder of his papacy, Nicholas showed a taste for interfering in the quarrels of the Carolingian world, including an even bolder intervention when he prevented the Lotharingian king Lothar II's attempt to divorce his childless wife, Teutberga.[6] Nicholas's successor, Hadrian II, was just as assertive, demanding Methodius' release following his condemnation by the kangaroo court of Regensburg in 871.

The increase in papal self-assertion on display in these incidents is striking. On closer inspection, however, its underlying cause emphasizes just how dependent, in practice, any real assertion of papal authority remained upon the Carolingian structures of Empire in this era, even if it does also bring into the foreground one of the key pieces of the jigsaw that would finally shift the tectonic plates of religious authority within the Latin west in the direction of Rome.

THE FORGING OF PAPAL AUTHORITY

From late antiquity, the papacy had periodically resorted to forgery to shore up key elements of its claim to unequalled prestige within the Christian world, based on its unique ties to St Peter, the Prince of the Apostles. In the late fourth century, the forged *Clementine Recognitions*, presented as an authentic letter of the first-century Pope Clement, 'documented' two points: that St Peter had been the first bishop of Rome, and that he had passed on his unique status as Prince of the Apostles to all subsequent bishops of Rome. In the late Roman period, this papal claim to unique status within the Christian world – though pushed hard on occasion – was not widely acknowledged across the Mediterranean; rather, Rome was reckoned one of five equal patriarchates (three of the others also founded by one or more of the Apostles). It is also vital to make a clear distinction between prestige and authority. While all the patriarchs enjoyed huge prestige in the emerging Christian world, their actual authority (to control bishops, priests and laity) was limited to their own specific regions (central and southern Italy and Sicily in the case of Rome, Egypt in the case of Alexandria, and so on). The only figure of supra-regional religious authority was the emperor. In this context, the *Recognitions* was not designed to challenge overarching imperial religious authority. It did, however, explicitly claim that the bishop of Rome should rank higher than his fellow patriarchs. This claim was also pushed by other means: specifically, the argument that Rome was also superior because, unlike the other patriarchal sees, it had in fact been founded by two apostles, Peter and Paul.

In the mid-ninth century, another bout of forgery, this time of legal materials contained within a broader collection of canon (Church) law, attempted further not only to enhance the status of the papal see, but also to revise existing understandings of the limits of its actual, effective religious authority. There may have been an intention to pass it off as the authentic work of the great Christian scholar Isidore of Seville, as the forgery came to be known as *Pseudo* (= false) *Isidore*.[7] The *Pseudo-Isidore* collection came in three parts: recent Carolingian imperial legislation on ecclesiastical matters; Church council rulings down to the seventh century; and a large number of official papal decretals. Taken together, the collection pulled together the main materials that contemporary Latin Churchmen would have looked towards to help them settle legal disputes, and all three parts contained at least some largely genuine texts that would have been broadly familiar to the same audience. The collected decretals from the fourth century to the time of Gregory II (715–31), and the Church conciliar material, for instance, both drew heavily on the earlier works of Dionysius Exiguus. But alongside the genuine texts, multiple individual forgeries were folded in, the most important being a set of brilliantly forged 'earlier' papal decretals dating from Pope Clement I (who died around AD 100) to Pope Miltiades (d. 314).[8] These decretals included the so-called *Donation of Constantine*, a fully worked up fabrication of what purported to be an official imperial edict of the first Christian emperor. This declared that, as he was about to depart for Constantinople, Constantine granted full authority over the west to Pope Sylvester, in his place.

Constantine's fabricated grant to Sylvester is mentioned explicitly for the first time in a letter of Pope Hadrian to Charlemagne dated to 778, where the pope cited it to bolster his argument that Charlemagne should 'restore' lands lost to the Lombards to Rome's control. Although the earliest extant text of the *Donation* appears in a manuscript copied at St Denis in Paris under Abbot Fardulf (792–806), the chances are that the *Donation* was a later eighth-century forgery of the papal curia.[9] In the *Pseudo-Isidore* collection proper, the implicit statement of principle set out in the *Donation* – that the pope should exercise overarching religious authority over the western church – was reinforced by a barrage of material – especially that contained in the forged early decretals – which apparently showed practical papal authority in action in the Roman period. Yet, for all its emphasis on papal religious authority and the likely Roman origin of the specific text of the *Donation*, the *Pseudo-Isidore* collection as a whole was actually forged by a small group of well-connected Frankish Churchmen, probably in the 830s and 840s, working somewhere in the dioceses of Rheims or Trier.[10]

In the ecclesiastical reform process instituted by Charlemagne and Louis the Pious, ordinary bishops had often found themselves in the first line of fire, regularly sacked when they failed to live up to expectations. *Pseudo-Isidore* was written to reverse this trend, the fundamental drift of all its forged materials being to strengthen the position of individual bishops. It asserted the principle (as an ancient Christian tradition) that, without a confession of wrong-doing, seventy-two independent witnesses were required before legal proceedings could even begin against a sitting bishop. Once a trial was underway, the *Pseudo-Isidore* also claimed, an accused bishop was allowed to reject locally appointed judges – including his own archbishop – and appeal at any point to the authority of the Roman papacy. None of these procedures had ever happened in practice – and the principles themselves were a complete fabrication.

By dint of outrageous forgery, *Pseudo-Isidore* conjured into existence a late antiquity in which papal authority had dominated a unified and independent Church hierarchy, within which the key players were not overbearing emperors and archbishops, but papal representatives and diocesan bishops operating with much greater security of tenure.[11]

In their original context, then, the central purpose of these forgeries was not to increase papal authority at all. Its heightened vision of the papacy's importance was largely incidental to the forgers' central concern: to reinforce local episcopal independence. Because Rome was so far away and the papacy lacked any effective levers of power north of the Alps, you could trundle out a vision of ancient Roman ecclesiastical authority, safe in the knowledge that the popes had no practical enforcement mechanisms which would allow them to put any of this supposed authority into practice in mid-ninth-century Gaul. But asserting papal supremacy as a principle, and locating that principle in a raft of apparently unimpeachable legal texts, could play an extremely useful role within an ongoing campaign to curb the all-too-imminent authority of emperors and archbishops, which had led to so many episcopal redundancies.

Pseudo-Isidore doesn't therefore signify a grandiose expansion in papal ambitions in the early Carolingian period. The *Donation of Constantine* was forged in Rome as part of Hadrian's attempt to get Charlemagne to hand over a significant chunk of his recently conquered Italian assets, but the collection as a whole was produced by Frankish Churchmen, who were manipulating the idea of papal religious authority for their own ends.

More generally, *Pseudo-Isidore* is an excellent starting point from which better to understand the apparently grander profile of some of the later ninth-century popes. Some individual holders of the office did engage in striking moments of self-assertion, both in the field of Christian mission and otherwise, but most of the time their ability to project authority depended on what was happening in the broader Carolingian imperial world. They were heavily reliant either on imperial support, or upon opportunities presented to them by imperial Churchmen.

When in 860/1 Nicholas I curtailed the independence of the archbishop of Ravenna – a long-standing papal aim going back to the sixth century – he was able to do so because the then emperor Louis II (for his own reasons) refused any longer to support the archbishop's independence.[12] More generally, most of the papacy's developing levers of influence – everything from its larger income to the arsenal of fake legal precedent provided by *Pseudo-Isidore* – were provided by the

Frankish Empire, which individual popes exploited, within limits, for their own purposes. The arrival in Rome of the deposed bishop of Soissons, armed with his own copy of *Pseudo-Isidore*, is what changed Nicholas I's attitude to Rothad's attempt to appeal his case to the pope. Nicholas's initial response had been to refer Rothad's case back to the jurisdiction of his archbishop, Hincmar of Rheims, with whom he was currently in dispute, according to long-established ecclesiastical precedent. After reading *Pseudo-Isidore*, however, Nicholas decided to hear the appeal himself.[13]

We do see a more active papacy in the second half of the ninth century, in part basing itself on the forgeries of *Pseudo-Isidore*, but one whose ability to assert its religious authority remained largely dependent, like the text itself, on the machinations of Frankish Churchmen. The evolving political context played its part. Nicholas could exercise much greater influence than his immediate predecessors not because the papacy was suddenly inherently much more powerful than it had been in the first half of the century, but because Charlemagne's Empire was now divided between competitive descendants, who could be played off against one another. The self-interested desires of Charles the Bald and Louis the German, their eyes set firmly on inheriting their nephew's lands, did far more to prevent the divorce of Lothar II (which would have allowed him to marry his mistress and legitimize their offspring) than did Nicholas's noisy intervention. If there had still only been a single Carolingian ruler who needed a divorce to safeguard the succession, he would certainly have obtained it, whatever the pope or any other Churchmen thought.[14]

In structural terms, the dependence of papal authority on the lingering edifice of Carolingian imperialism ran deeper still. The gifts of Charlemagne and Louis the Pious to the papal see had many short-term benefits, not least in allowing a sequence of popes to refurbish the city. But they also had one serious drawback. Because the papal office now commanded a much larger income, the struggle for its control – which had never lacked in ferocity – quickly spiralled into venal and murderous violence. It was violent rebellion against Leo III that had given Charlemagne the leverage he needed to bring the pope to the altar on Christmas Day 800, and Leo survived a second rebellion towards the end of his reign. To hold on to power, Pope Paschal I (817–24) had respectively to blind and decapitate two of his most senior officials, the *primicerius* (chief bureaucrat) Theodore and the *nomenclator* (chief secretary) Leo, respectively, who were plotting against him. Paschal's successor, Eugenius II (824–7), was a compromise candidate imposed by Lothar I in the face of multiple, clashing contenders for the throne; Sergius II (844–7), meanwhile, only achieved power by crushing a large group of opponents in a running battle through the streets of Rome which left many dead.[15] But so long as Carolingian rulers remained strong enough to intervene, a degree of order prevailed. Charlemagne's rescue of Leo III was reprised on several subsequent occasions in the ninth century, while the investigation of Lothar I, Louis the Pious's eldest son and emperor-designate, into the lethal activities of Paschal I generated the *Constitutio Romana* of 824. This document set out agreed procedures for electing a pope – including a cooling-off period while the emperor's approval was sought – which were all designed to minimize election violence.[16] But, as Carolingian imperial power dwindled in the final decades of the ninth century, this important check on the violent internal divisions within the aristocratic networks of the city of Rome and its immediate surroundings disappeared, with cataclysmic results for the internal stability and external dignity of the papal see.

In January 897, Pope Stephen VI put the mouldering corpse of his predecessor Formosus on trial in the Lateran Palace.[17] This was the latest in a bizarre sequence of scandals, including the demise of Pope Hadrian II (867–72) who was bludgeoned to death by his own retinue when they got fed up waiting for the poison they'd already given him to work. Formosus' 'trial' stands in the middle of a run of nine papacies in the same number of years (896–904), in which violent, contested succession was the norm. Between 872 and 1012, an astonishing 33 per cent of all popes died in suspicious circumstances, besides those who met their ends in well-documented assassinations. This latter group included Stephen VI, killed by strangulation in August 897; John X (914–28), who was suffocated; and the Greek anti-Pope John XVI (997–8), who somehow survived the removal of his eyes, nose, lips, tongue and hands to die a few years later in the German monastery of Fulda.

Despite an initial period of chaos following the disappearance of its Carolingian backstop, however, Rome did not collapse into complete anarchy. In the first decade of the tenth century, the outlines of a new, post-Carolingian order began to emerge within the city, one which saw the papal office become essentially reabsorbed into the power structures of the local landed nobility of central Italy, from which the Carolingians had partly elevated it. For much of the next 150 years, two aristocratic networks dominated control of the papacy: first, that of Count Theophylact of Tusculum, a great landowner near Rome, whose dynastic line was responsible for the majority of papal appointments between *c.* 910 and 950; and second, in the later tenth century, the Crescentii, whose estates lay in the Sabine hills to the south and east of the city. They exercised a similar dominion over the papal office for half a century, before, in the early eleventh century, a branch of Theophylact's descendants regained control.[18]

Both these family networks essentially used the papacy to control the distribution of the extensive revenues with which Charlemagne had endowed the papal see, though some papal incumbents of this period also paid serious attention to the religious dimensions of their post. Theophylact's grandson, Alberic II of Spoleto, sponsored Pope Leo VII (931–9), and had a long-established friendship with the great monastic reformer Odo of Cluny, which resulted in reformed Benedictinism reaching three ancient Roman monasteries: Sts Paolo, Lorenzo and Agnese. Likewise, the eleventh-century counts of Tusculum produced Pope Benedict VIII (1012–24), who co-operated closely with Emperor Henry II in ecclesiastical reform. But for every 'good' pope appointed in the tenth and early eleventh centuries, there was another with little or no interest in religion at all. As well as Leo VII, Alberic II appointed one of his own sons as John XII (955–64); taking up office at the uncanonical age of eighteen (bishops were supposed to be thirty), the sybaritic John enjoyed the wealth and other perquisites of his position to the utmost, before dying nine years later, reputedly in bed with a married woman. In 1032, Count Alberic III installed one of his sons as Benedict IX (1032–48/56), thereby instituting a papal reign synonymous with sex, assassination and violent opposition.[19] But if the papacy itself lacked the structural capacity during this time consistently to exercise high-level religious leadership, two other important constituencies within Latin Christendom refused to allow it to become a mere service-vehicle for the financial interests of central Italian landowners, even after the collapse of the Carolingian imperial state.

Given Charlemagne's precedent, no aspiring emperor wanted to be crowned by a disreputable pope.[20] After the breakdown of Carolingian imperial order around the year 900, this tradition periodically brought north European potentates and their armies to Rome, their presence rupturing the rotating dominance of the Tusculani and Crescentii. Emperor Otto I broke the first period of Tusculan domination as he manoeuvred towards his imperial coronation in 962; Henry II the hold of the Crescentii as he set up his own in 1014.[21] By the year 1000, such interventions had begun to generate a new mechanism for driving forward religious reform: periodic alliance between God-chosen emperors and reform-minded popes. In this enterprise, Charlemagne's Ottonian and Salian imperial successors initially remained the senior partners. In the 990s, Otto III was so unimpressed by the standard of potential appointees he found in Rome that he installed two northern Churchmen with a passionate commitment to Church reform: first, his cousin Bruno as Pope Gregory V (996–9), and then Gerbert of Aurillac as Sylvester II (999–1003).[22] Emperor Henry II, for his part, was content to work with the Tusculan Benedict VIII, who was himself committed to reform; the pair jointly presided over a reforming synod at Pavia in 1022.

In this era, the question of religious reform – still driven by Carolingian-era demands for 'pure' clergy to preside over the Mass (p. 430) – was coalescing around two central issues: simony and clerical marriage. Named for Simon Magus, who offered cash to the Apostles for the power to confer the Holy Spirit (Acts 8:9–24), simony was the label given to the purchase of ecclesiastical office. Because so many Church institutions (especially smaller, unreformed monasteries and the now geometrically expanding quantity of new local churches) were the private property of the landowners who constructed them, and since founders and their heirs retained financial rights over them, it was often customary for new incumbents to pay the owner some kind of compensation on taking up their valuable religious position. Depending on the nature of the post in question, its income might include not only the annual produce of the landed endowment attached to it but also other rights and privileges (including the taking of tolls from markets, or a percentage of the fines levied at local courts). Outright purchase was already attracting general condemnation by the turn of the eleventh century, but the norms of medieval European society generated a significant grey area involving 'presents'. If the issue of simony was to be tackled, it first had to be defined, and this was no easy task.

Like many other societies before and since, medieval Europeans lubricated their social relationships by reciprocal (but not equal) processes of gift-giving. If a religious appointee presented an owner with a thank-you present, did this constitute simony? More radical reformers among the clergy thought so, and they extended the definition of simony still further to demand that no layman should have any say whatsoever over ecclesiastical appointments. But then again, who was a layman? Kings and emperors, who still controlled high Church appointments within their jurisdictions, did not believe they fell into that category – though alternative views were soon being aired, particularly among some of the more radical products of the monastic reform movements of the ninth and tenth centuries. In these circles, it became axiomatic that lay interests, particularly in monastic wealth, were the main hindrance preventing monasteries from signing up to the new standards of behaviour, learning and liturgy encapsulated in the revised Benedictine Rule, which, since Louis the Pious's reform synods of the 810s, had become the canonical benchmark for 'real' monasticism.[23]

The uproar against clerical marriage, meanwhile, generated the expectation that clergy attached to cathedrals (canons) – like their counterparts in monasteries – ought to live communal, sex-free lives, and give up private property rights. This was the overall vision of the revised *Rule* of Chrodegang of Metz – again brought to prominence in the time of Louis the Pious, and to which increasing numbers of such communities subscribed. This developed into the more general argument that no cleric of any kind could properly administer the sacraments if they were married or kept a concubine. This new way of thinking represented a radical break with established tradition, inherited from late antiquity, which held that, once promoted, only the highest clergy – bishops – should be unmarried, or at least give up having sex with their wives. While some had always believed that lesser clergy – priests and deacons – should also be celibate, this had never been a formal rule. In both Latin west and Greek east, therefore, it remained entirely normal for priests and deacons to be married, and indeed for the priesthood itself to be a hereditary position in some (perhaps many) of the small local churches built by landowners in substantial numbers since the year 900. (Even the sons of bishops could inherit their fathers' positions, so long as they had been born before their father attained his crook and mitre.) But during the tenth and eleventh centuries, this all started to change, with reform-minded clerics making increasingly vocal demands that not just monks, but all priests who might administer the Mass needed to be 'pure': i.e., fully celibate. As Peter Damian, one leading eleventh-century voice in favour of clerical celibacy, put it, 'if you commit incest with your spiritual daughter, with what conscience do you dare to handle the mystery of the Lord's body?' (This was, it is worth noting, a purely western phenomenon, a product of the heightened, originally monastic understandings of the Mass which grew up in the west from the ninth century; Orthodox Greek clergy – though not bishops – can still be married.)

During the tenth century, these demands for complete clerical quasi-monastic celibacy, and a closer policing of clerical sexuality in general, gathered momentum. In 927 the council of Trier vigorously promoted sexual continence among the clergy and reiterated older Merovingian legislation against priests having women living in their houses; it also set out procedures for dealing with priests accused repeatedly of adultery. A council of the East Frankish Church at Augsburg in 952 trod the same ground. So too did a more or less contemporary gathering of leading Anglo-Saxon Churchmen, the tenth-century Anglo-Saxon Church being extremely well informed on, and strongly influenced by, mainstream religious developments on the Continent. Legal and penitential texts of the time also addressed the same themes.[24]

The main driver behind these intensifying demands for both celibacy and for an end to simony in the guise of 'gifts' is not difficult to fathom. Increasingly, the leading monasteries and cathedrals of the Latin west subscribed to the principles of reformed Benedictine monasticism and its counterpart for canons, the *Rule of Chrodegang*. Both these highly influential normative texts, drawn up in the time of Charlemagne's son Louis the Pious, established an intimate link between a state of personal religious purity and the importance of celibacy and poverty. These institutions, themselves increasing in number in the later ninth and tenth centuries, began to form an ever more influential constituency within the broader Latin Church as a whole, which at this point basically comprised the entire area of the old Carolingian Empire, even after that Empire itself had ceased to exist. The higher level of education available within these institutions generated larger numbers of articulate, influential clerical voices, who were increasingly promoted to senior positions in the ecclesiastical hierarchies. Not surprisingly, the kings, emperors and other princes of Latin Christendom, who still generally controlled senior Church appointments during these centuries, wanted the brightest and best educated to populate their episcopates, an impulse that helped foreground demands for reform. It also simultaneously created a powerful new clerical constituency, originating beyond the boundaries of Rome itself, with a strong interest in promoting a higher papal profile.[25]

One reason why north European Churchmen showed greater interest in the papacy as the millennium approached was straightforwardly practical. Two hundred years before, the great Charlemagne, after his extraordinary career of conquest, could realistically present himself as the undisputed leader of Latin Christendom; and the ecclesiastical reforms undertaken by Charlemagne himself and Louis the Pious applied – notionally at least – to the entirety of this vast region (give or take a few exceptions, such as a few Byzantine holdings in southern Italy, and the Christian communities of Britain and Ireland). Although they claimed the same titles, and basked in the same reflected Roman ideological glory, Charlemagne's Ottonian and Salian imperial successors of the tenth and eleventh centuries exercised nothing like the same degree of control over the Christian west. Broadly speaking, their dominance extended only over the original core territories of what eventually became the Holy Roman Empire, comprising East Francia (ancestral to modern Germany) and northern and central Italy. In Carolingian terms, West Francia lay beyond their imperial control (divided between Carolingian and then Capetian kings in the north and a host of local potentates); so too, of course, did the Christians of the British Isles. Meanwhile, as the area of Carolingian authority shrank, Latin Christendom – defined as those areas converted by Latin-speaking western Churchmen, rather than their Greek counterparts – was rapidly expanding.

By the early eleventh century, the list of new additions included a significant set of territories prised from Muslim rule in the Iberian peninsula (although much more would follow in the later eleventh and twelfth centuries) and the great tracts of northern and eastern Europe (Bohemia, Poland, the Magyar kingdoms and much of Scandinavia) added to Latin Christendom in the second age of Christian Empire. And although the overall process of Christian expansion in the late first millennium had been substantially dependent upon the overarching influence of Latin Christendom's new emperors, the fact that native dynasts themselves took the decision to convert – often employing papal leverage as they went – meant that a whole new tranche of kings and princes had ended up in day-to-day control of their own new regional branches of the Christian Church, appointing their own bishops and archbishops. And so, not only were the Ottonians and Salians not able to exercise religious authority over the entirety of the old Carolingian Empire, but the overall reach of Latinate Christianity was now much wider, essentially returning western Christendom to more of a post-Roman pattern, where a series of self-governing Christian regional communities had replaced a unified Christian Empire.

At the start of the new millennium, therefore, much of this recently extended western Christendom was administered by Churchmen who owed their allegiance to many different Christian kings and princes, both long-established and newly converted, who would all be likely to resist imperially led initiatives to transform religious practice in their lands. At the same time, thanks to the continued unfolding of the originally Carolingian process of *correctio*, most senior Churchmen were the products of reformed monastic and cathedral communities and, despite answering to different rulers, shared essentially the same ecclesiastical culture.

In this context, the papal see took on a somewhat different role, as a politically neutral ally for both emperors and a cross-section of their senior, monastic-minded clerics keen to promote the values of religious reform. Around the turn of the millennium, a striking new pattern began to emerge. Back in the eighth and ninth centuries, Charlemagne had paid only the merest lip-service to the dignity of the papal see, and otherwise pushed forward issues of Church reform entirely on his own authority and as he saw fit. Two hundred years later simony and clerical marriage, by contrast, were now increasingly being addressed at reforming councils held jointly by his Ottonian and Salian successors and incumbent popes (such as the great meeting at Pavia in 1022 conducted by Henry II and Benedict VIII). This gave later popes a much more prominent role in ongoing processes of religious reform than anything enjoyed by their Carolingian predecessors. In straightforwardly practical terms, the later emperors of the second age of Christian empire did not control enough of Christendom simply to enforce their authority over it in the same ways that Charlemagne had been able to do. Instead, they began to operate jointly with compliant popes, and these partnerships became an excellent mechanism for advancing reform agendas.

Equally important, this same new constituency – the intermediate and higher ecclesiastical leaders distributed between the Holy Roman Empire and the various other kingdoms and principalities of this much-expanded western Christendom – was also predisposed to accept the idea that the papacy *ought* to play a more active overall leadership role than had customarily been the case. One major element of the shared cultural tradition transmitted within the network of cathedral and reformed monastic schools in which these leaders were trained was the fake vision of a papal-run Roman-era Christianity to be found in the *Pseudo-Isidore* collection. There were some sceptical voices. Archbishop Hincmar of Rheims had challenged the authenticity of some of its texts in the ninth century; in the mid-tenth, likewise, Emperor Otto I condemned the *Donation of Constantine* as a forgery. But, over the longer term, such moments of resistance were of little significance compared to the positive general reception that the collection as a whole enjoyed among the cathedrals and reformed monasteries of Latin Christendom. Over one hundred partial or complete manuscripts of *Pseudo-Isidore* survive from before the year 950, within the first hundred years of the collection's existence (a huge number for this era), while thirty complete copies date to before the year 900. And when new handbooks of Church law were produced in the tenth century, such as those by the scholars Regino of Prüm and

Burchard of Worms – they incorporated many of *Pseudo-Isidore*'s fabrications. This expanding text tradition, then, exerted a powerful and growing influence in favour of the idea that papal authority should be – as it was now widely perceived once to have been – central to the running of the Latin Church.[26]

The astonishing success of the *Pseudo-Isidore* collection is a combined tribute to its authors' skill in forgery and the accident of perfect timing. By the mid-ninth century, with *correctio* in full swing, educated Churchmen were clear both that their practices ought to be governed by established Church law, and on what the main sources of that law actually were. Aside from Scripture and the writings of authoritative Church Fathers, it had been hammered into them – from Charlemagne's *Admonitio Generalis* of 789 onwards – that correct Christian practice was to be defined by consulting the past rulings of the Church, particularly ecumenical councils, relevant rulings of Roman emperors, and papal decretals – updated, where appropriate, by the new imperial law of the Carolingian capitularies. In this context, *Pseudo-Isidore* filled a glaring gap. For in the time of Charlemagne and Louis the Pious, the new educational patterns had spread to only a handful of institutions, and even important recent texts, such as the rulings of Charlemagne and his son, were not yet being systematically collected. This only began to happen in the 850s under Charles the Bald, when, for the first time, royal councils began to issue official texts of their decisions, and to make new decisions with explicit reference to existing written laws as Carolingian government developed a stronger element of bureaucratic sophistication. It's a telling sign of the preceding state of legal chaos that, as late as the 830s and 840s, the *Pseudo-Isidore* forgers were able to fabricate with impunity no less than a third of the various rulings of Charlemagne and Louis the Pious that they included in their collection.[27]

Against this cultural backdrop, the *Pseudo-Isidore* collection had enormous attractions for senior clerics and their educated assistants, apparently gathering together most legally significant material for the running of the Church then in existence (except for Scripture and the writings of Church Fathers, which were always transmitted separately) into one convenient collection, in excellent classicizing Latin; any differences in detail between its readings and older versions of apparently the same law could easily be ascribed to scribal error. *Pseudo-Isidore*, in other words, appeared at a moment when Carolingian Churchmen had become familiar with the canon of legal materials that they believed should form the basis of best ecclesiastical practice, but had as yet insufficient detailed knowledge of those materials to see through the collection's plausible forgeries.

One of the most important consequences of the *Pseudo-Isidore*'s all-too-convenient farrago of invention was to establish the idea that the papacy had once exercised great practical religious authority across the Latin west. At a time when monastic reform ideologies were extending older definitions of simony into a more general emphasis on the importance of freeing Church institutions from lay control, it was – especially with the *Pseudo-Isidore*'s help – no great leap, therefore, to start thinking that it was high time for the papacy to regain its long-lost power. Apart from the new pattern of joint reform councils, this greater focus on the practical potential of papal religious authority is also reflected in two other innovations of the tenth and early eleventh centuries.

From around the year 900 various reformed monastic houses started to put themselves under papal protection, obtaining (or forging) written charters to express the new relationship. Although popes could have been able to do little to help in practice – post-Carolingian Rome was then at its chaotic worst – monastic foundations were always looking to maximize the amount of religious sanction available to protect the landed holdings that provided them with an income. It is a sign of Rome's greater profile that papal protection suddenly began to be seen as a worthwhile additional line of defence against the claims of annoying neighbours – particularly if those neighbours were well connected within local aristocratic power networks, or if a donor's relatives weren't happy about losing part of their inheritance. The first monastery to do this was Cluny, which obtained a papal charter in 909 and went on to obtain further confirmations of this original document throughout the century, before attaching the name of Pope Gregory V to a major inventory of its landed holdings put together in 998. Given that popes exercised no effective leverage in tenth-century Burgundy, these papal charters had little practical legal or political value – but clearly their symbolic value was well worth having. The fact that monastic houses began to claim papal authorization for their landholdings is striking testimony to how far the papal profile had increased in the minds of western Churchmen. Over the next century and a half, a variety of religious institutions across western Christendom drew up 630 papal charters – the majority written by the institutions themselves – in support of their claimed rights and privileges. About a quarter of them, like the *Pseudo-Isidore* itself, are forged. Presumably, these institutions didn't want to go to the expense of sending representatives (and paying the necessary backhanders) to obtain genuine documents from Rome.

Then, in the last decade of the tenth century, came a second new development: the cathedral community of Augsburg turned to Rome to validate its proposed sanctification of Bishop Ulrich, a major voice in favour of reform within the Ottonian Church establishment. On 31 January 993, Pope John XV was happy to confirm his sanctity, the decision announced in a formal papal pronouncement or 'bull'. This was quickly followed by the papal canonization of five of the new martyrs, including Adalbert of Prague, who had just been executed in Prussia on their ill-fated mission to the Baltic (p. 394). This papal endorsement of proposed saints (outside the city of Rome at least) was unprecedented. Previously, local Christian communities had simply declared the sanctity of their own holy dead and sought to convince their neighbours of the fact, with no reference to a higher ecclesiastical authority. Soon, however, this new, centralized method for making saints was adopted right across western Europe, an indication both of the prestige that papal endorsement conferred upon sainthood, and the potential for practical religious leadership that many leading Churchmen now found in the papal see.[28] The overall effect was, once again, to increase the importance of the papacy across western Christendom.

All the same, by the early decades of the eleventh century, in both ideological and practical terms, papal authority remained both patchy and limited. The papal see had not yet been liberated from its structural ties to the elite landowning networks of central-southern Italy, and only a minority of Church leaders, those educated in reformed cathedrals and monasteries, had even begun to formulate the notion in principle that practical papal religious authority ought to rival – or even surpass – that of the princes of Latin Europe, who continued in practice to control many of the operations and most senior clerical appointments within their realms.

In the first two centuries of the new millennium these problems would be solved. The papal office would be redefined in such a way as to exercise practical overarching religious authority right across western Christendom: setting standards of appropriate behaviour for both clergy and laity, defining correct doctrines, and exercising some kind of quality control over senior Church appointments. Given that the reinvigorated papacy of the ninth and tenth centuries had largely been created by northern European potentates and Churchmen imposing their own agendas and needs upon the papal see, rather than by any initiative hatched in Rome, it should come as no great surprise that it was another burst of reforming zeal on the part of the religious leaders of northern Europe which finally set western Christendom on a definitive path towards a new, central authority structure, with Rome firmly at its apex.

THE ROAD TO CANOSSA

In 1039, Henry III inherited the kingdom of Germany from the first Salian emperor, his father Conrad II. By the mid-1040s, Henry was ready to add the imperial title to his collection, by the now customary route of papal coronation in Rome. Arriving there, Henry faced the unedifying prospect of choosing between no fewer than three popes, none of whom made a remotely attractive coronation partner. The most unpleasant of the trio was Benedict IX who, having used his papal office for over a decade to fund a life of dissolute pleasure, and having been evicted from and returned to office, then sold off the title to his godfather, John Gratian, in 1045 for a thousand pounds of silver. Regretting his decision, Benedict attempted another comeback two years later, and set up a three-way contest for recognition as pope between himself, his godfather, and Sylvester III, who had also briefly held the post in 1045. Henry III's solution was simple. He swept all three from office, instead appointing as pope one of his own clerics, Bishop Suidger of Bamberg. As Pope Clement II, Suidger crowned

Henry emperor on Christmas Day 1046. When Clement died a year later, Henry replaced him with Damasus II (another German cleric) and, on Damasus' death, appointed yet another pope.[29] It was Henry's third-choice appointee, elected in 1049, whose astonishing energy set in motion a chain of events that eventually culminated in a new type of Roman Empire altogether.

A cousin of the emperor, this third pope, Leo IX, was born Bruno of Egisheim-Dagsburg into an aristocratic family of the Lorraine. Bruno was educated in the cathedral school at Toul in what is now north-eastern France; there, he showed a particular devotion to the shrines of the Holy See, making regular pilgrimages to Rome. Appointed bishop of Toul in his mid-twenties in 1026, he proved himself an ardent supporter of the reforming campaigns against simony and clerical marriage, and of the Cluniac version of reformed Benedictine monasticism, with its emphasis on ritual, learning and creating a monastic heaven on earth. None of which was exceptional for an aristocratic German bishop of his age. What really marked him out, however, was the energy and imagination he showed in refashioning the practical operating methods of the papacy so that it could begin to exercise effective religious leadership over the western Church.

Once elected pope, Leo's first move was to flood Rome with like-minded Churchmen. These included the celebrated monastic intellectual Humbert, imported from the Benedictine house of Moyenmoutier in Leo's home diocese, and other northern cathedral clergy such as Frederic, brother of Godfrey duke of Lorraine, from the cathedral chapter of Liège; and an Italian cleric named Hildebrand (on whom much more in a moment). These recruits were promoted to senior positions within the Roman clerical establishment, breaking up the long-standing ties between its leadership and the aristocratic networks of central Italy that still controlled many of its operations, particularly its distribution of patronage. Leo's strategy resembled Charlemagne's assembling of Europe-wide intellectual talent, but he also maintained close contacts with a wide range of other Church leaders interested in the project of reform, such as the prominent northern Italian hermit Peter Damian. This strategy enabled Leo to refocus the energies of the papacy, as an institution, away from the allocation of its Italian estates and other financial assets, and onto the project of religious reform.

Immediately after his enthronement, Leo held a synod in the Lateran Palace, condemning simony and clerical marriage. Going further than the previous papal condemnation of these practices in 1022, he now declared that all clergy at the level of subdeacon and above should be celibate, drawing the line further down the clerical ladder than ever before. He also pursued simony with unprecedented directness, so intimidating the bishop of Sutri (a local see about 30 miles (50 km) from Rome) with a face-to-face accusation that the unfortunate bishop dropped dead on the spot. Neither did Leo confine his activities to Rome and Italy; he held a dozen or so reforming synods across France and Germany during his brief five-year reign. This too was a radical departure from established papal custom. Previous popes barely left the vicinity of Rome: if they travelled north of the Alps they did so only in great need, or at imperial invitation. Leo's proactive projection of Roman authority north of the Alps broke with all existing precedent. On his travels, he summoned regional clergy to synods where the reform agenda was emphasized, and reputed offenders confronted. In another dramatic incident, Leo turned the translation (the ceremonial reburial in a grander tomb) of the remains of St Remigius at Rheims in 1049 into a great reform council, at which he asked twenty French bishops – point-blank – whether they were guilty of simony. When the bishop of Langres refused to answer, Leo excommunicated him; the archbishop of Besançon was struck dumb trying to defend his colleague. In the heat of the moment, five more bishops confessed, were forgiven and reappointed. Only the bishop of Nantes, who had succeeded his father, was deemed too far beyond the pale and so was deposed.[30]

After this initial drama, Leo's reign petered out in confrontation with the colonizing Normans who had taken over much of Sicily and southern Italy in the first half of the eleventh century. Having defeated the limited forces the pope could scrape together at the battle of Civitate in 1053, they took Leo himself hostage. (Emperor Henry III was too preoccupied with wars against the Magyars and the Poles to provide any real assistance.) While the Normans treated the pope with deference, he was nonetheless held in captivity for the best part of a year, and died soon after his release, in April 1054. Leo was succeeded by two further northerners, Victor II (1055–7, the former bishop of Eichstatt) and Stephen IX (1057–8, the Frederic of Lorraine brought to Rome by Leo IX). After Stephen's death, and with Henry III also having died in 1056, the Tusculani clan saw an opportunity to return Rome to business as usual. They imposed their own choices of pope in Benedict X, and, following him in 1061, Honorius II. But Leo had put strong reforming foundations in place within the Roman ecclesiastical establishment, enabling his much-enhanced vision for the papacy to outlast what proved to be only a brief interruption to its continued development. In the second half of the eleventh century, a self-confident body of leading Churchmen at the heart of the papacy determinedly carried the revolution forward. A direct reforming line from Leo continued after Stephen's death, in the pontificates of Nicholas II (1059–61, another imported northerner, born Gerard of Bourgogne near Arles) and Alexander II (1061–73, previously the reforming Bishop Anselm of Lucca).[31]

All these clerics and their many allies, both within Rome and across many of the leading ecclesiastical circles of the Latin west, shared Leo's fundamental vision – that the papacy could and should exercise overall religious authority over the entire Church. This included not just the Latin west, but also the Greek east as well: an unprecedentedly atavistic pretention which went far beyond even the bounds 'licensed' by the *Donation of Constantine*. As one of their number, Peter Damian, put it:

> Now the Roman Church, the see of the apostles, should imitate the ancient court of the Romans. Just as of old the earthly Senate strove to subdue the whole multitude of the peoples to the Roman Empire, so now the ministers of the apostolic see, the spiritual senators of the Church Universal, should make it their sole business by their laws to subdue the human race to God, the true emperor.[32]

This sweeping claim translated into a series of more specific demands. Inserted into the formal register of papal letters under the year 1075 is a single manuscript sheet known as *Dictatus Papae*, 'the dictation of the pope', which set out the understanding of desirable practical papal religious authority current among the reformers, in twenty-seven succinct statements. These included the following assertions of apostolic supremacy:

2. That the Roman pontiff alone can with right be called universal.
9. That of the pope alone all princes shall kiss the feet.
12. That it may be permitted to him to depose emperors.
16. That no synod shall be called a general one without his order.
17. That no chapter and no book shall be considered canonical without his authority.
20. That no one shall dare to condemn one who appeals to the apostolic chair.
25. That he may depose and reinstate bishops without assembling a synod.
27. That he may absolve subjects from their fealty to wicked men.

These claims – and the list in full – constituted an extraordinary statement, one loaded with political as well as religious significance. In sum, they amounted to a complete appropriation from emperor to pope of all those key rights and powers that had defined headship of the Christian Church from the time of Constantine onwards: overall responsibility for defining doctrine, especially by calling ecumenical (general) councils; the power to make senior ecclesiastical appointments; and the right to act as the highest court of appeal in trials under Church law. This ambitious vision was set out in the *Dictatus Papae* in clear and concrete terms. None the less, it was still very far from achieved reality. It had not even been accepted by the majority of Latin clerics yet, let alone the emperors, kings and other princes who appointed them. It would take a fundamental reordering of the operating structures of the Latin Church to bring it even partially to fruition.[33]

Most immediately, the new-style papacy needed to secure its effective legal and financial independence, from both the distant imperial authority and the all-too-present Italian aristocrats who had been central to its functioning since the founding of the Papal Republic back in the early eighth century. At Easter 1059, Pope Nicholas II gathered 113 bishops to a council in Rome, where they voted through a profound change in papal election procedure. Henceforth, elections were to be conducted by the so-called cardinal clergy alone. These consisted of the seven cardinal bishops (of the seven old suburbicarian sees, immediately subordinate to the pope's metropolitan authority: Ostia, Velletri-Segni, Porto–Santa Rufina, Frascati, Palestrina, Albano, Sabina); the twenty-eight cardinal priests in charge of the city's major churches; and the eighteen cardinal deacons who ran what had originally been the papacy's centres of charitable distribution. No longer were popes to be chosen via back-door deals conducted among local Italian aristocrats. Emperors, too, were completely excluded from the process: in this, Nicholas's new arrangement broke formally and completely with the terms of the old Carolingian *Constitutio Romanum*, which required the results of papal elections to be referred to a sitting emperor for his approval. This dramatic rupture was matched by an equally dramatic, and entirely necessary, political switch. In 1059, Nicholas concluded a peace deal with the aggressive Normans, which gave them papal recognition for their south Italian conquests in return for their direct and much-needed military and political support. Without this pact, Nicholas and his immediate successors would have stood no chance of maintaining their newly asserted independence against the two powers that had long since swapped control of the papal see: the Empire, on the one hand, and central Italian aristocratic networks like the Tusculani on the other.

This revolution continued under Nicholas's successor Alexander II, who oversaw a significant transformation in the papacy's administrative machinery. Echoing imperial practice, the papal chancery began – or recommenced – registering pontifical letters: making a second copy of every significant missive to ensure that there was a formal, centrally preserved record of all the papacy's important decisions. A partial copy of the register of one much earlier pope – Gregory the Great in the 590s – has come down to us, so this had been done before, in the distant past. But there is no trace of papal bureaucrats keeping a register again until the eleventh century, and it seems most likely (although this has been contested) that the habit was lost somewhere in between. The renewal of more careful record-keeping marks the re-emergence of the papacy as a self-confident bureaucratic authority – or at least an institution with the ambition to become one – with parallels in the evolution of more centralized governments in both the late Roman and Carolingian worlds. Once a central authority keeps formal copies of its own decisions, it has started to regard itself as a permanent and influential force in the world around it.[34] Late Roman archival practice had developed this habit, along with its more extensive bureaucracy, in the course of the fourth century; the western third of the Carolingian Empire did the same in the time of Charlemagne's grandson Charles the Bald.

Pope Alexander also now initiated a significant reorganization of the papal financial bureaucracy (this would be a running theme throughout the twelfth century, too) to win back control over some of the landed endowments that provided much of the see's revenue flows: both those that had survived from late antiquity and those deriving from the huge re-endowments of the Carolingian era. (Under the Tusculani and Crescentii, many papal estates and other types of financial asset had been leased out on generous terms to favoured Italian nobles; bringing these back under direct papal control was a key priority.) Outside Rome, popes Nicholas and Alexander followed Leo IX's proactive example, sending out papally appointed judges – legates – to assert, wherever possible, an active Roman voice in the affairs of Latin Christendom. Nicholas sent Peter Damian to force the archbishop of Milan – one of the more unwilling attendees at Nicholas's synod of 1059 – to accept papal authority. Under Pope Alexander, Peter also convened a major council at Chalon-sur-Saône, again raising the institution's profile in a ruling which broke with long-standing practice that the monastery of Cluny should be completely independent of any jurisdiction of the local bishop of Mâcon.[35]

Twenty years on from the appointment of Leo IX, the ecclesiastical world of Latin Christendom had begun to turn. After initial resistance, the new emperor, Henry IV, had eventually agreed to recognize the new papal election procedure and, along with it, the papacy's right to independence from secular authority. Having succeeded his father, Henry III, as king of Germany while still a child of only six in 1056, Henry IV faced a much more complicated political situation back in Germany, making him considerably less able to intervene in Italian affairs (which is why he didn't succeed to the imperial title for nearly thirty years, until 1084). Moreover, the king-emperor was surrounded by Churchmen who all subscribed to the general principle that ecclesiastical institutions should be independent of lay control, and who were willing to extend that principle to the see of Rome itself. It was, in other words, an idea whose time had come. The revamped institution now even had a name. Clement II had coined the term *papatus*, creating a new abstract noun from the old honorific term 'pope' – meaning 'father' – which the bishops of Rome had originally shared with all the other patriarchs of the late Roman period.

Notwithstanding these significant steps, the reformers' vision of a papal religious authority exercised across the Christian world was only partly shared even by other western Church leaders. In practice, too, Rome's ability to intervene in the wider affairs of the western Church was still largely restricted to moments when its participation was invited, or to geographical regions that lacked strong supra-regional government. Where sovereign rulers were powerful (as were many Holy Roman emperors, together with the kings of France and kings of England), popes were often unable to interfere at all in Church affairs; besides which, these rulers still saw themselves – as their predecessors had done for over half a millennium – as directly appointed by God. Hence, for all its fire and fury, Leo IX's great reforming synod at Rheims had been attended by just twenty bishops; over a hundred more stayed away, because the king of France forbade them to attend. Further changes in both the degree of recognition being afforded the claims of the new papacy, and in its practical reach, were still required to complete the transformation of its ancient prestige into a practical capacity to provide centralized religious leadership for the entirety of western Christendom.

Fresh impetus for change came in summer 1073, in the form of Alexander II's successor, Pope Gregory VII – Hildebrand of Sovana. For the first eighteen months of his rule, Gregory trod a path of conciliation and co-operation, trying to persuade the ruling powers of the Latin west to act decisively against simony. When this proved fruitless he shifted tack, his new approach marked by directness, confrontation and unilateral action. In January 1075, in a blistering letter widely distributed among the courts and major ecclesiastical institutions of western Europe, he put on record his scorn for much of

Christendom's clergy, and the secular rulers who were failing to uphold God's word:

> I scarcely find bishops who are lawful in respect of their succession or life and who rule the Christian people from love of Christ and not from secular ambition. And amongst all the secular princes, I do not know any who place God's honour before their own and righteousness before lucre ... And ... seeing that there is no prince who cares for such things, [we must] protect the lives of religious men.[36]

Gregory's final barb was aimed at Emperor Henry IV, whose reform-minded father had kick-started the transformation of the papacy back in the 1040s, and Gregory chose to carry his spiritual fight directly into imperial territory. His target was the see of Milan, the great imperial city in the Italian north, where simony and clerical marriage remained common. Gregory called on the city's population to boycott all church services offered by simoniac and married clergy. In this one revolutionary proclamation, he attempted to undercut both imperial and the archbishop of Milan's metropolitan religious authority.[37]

Faced with rebellions at home, the emperor had at first had to tolerate what he regarded as Gregory's entirely presumptuous intervention in the affairs of an imperial Church province. But, having dealt with the first of the German rebels, Henry sent officers to suppress the rebels in Milan (the so-called Patarenes who had responded to Gregory's boycott with violence towards some of the city's clergy) and called his own Church council at Worms, which formally condemned Gregory's message of January 1075 and deposed him from office on 24 January 1076. The pope responded by excommunicating the king-emperor on 22 February. As the year progressed, Henry's enemies in Germany used his excommunication as a pretext for further rebellion – which is why he ended up at Canossa in the depths of the following winter, seeking papal absolution. But though Gregory had won this battle, the pope's choice of direct confrontation proved disastrous in the longer term.

After Canossa, Gregory seemed to believe he had a free hand. He set his sights on preventing laymen – in which category he included aristocracy, kings and emperors – from having any say at all in the appointment of bishops and other clergy, a practice they had dominated for centuries, unleashing what came to be known as the Investiture Controversy. Lasting for decades, this quarrel dragged into the early twelfth century and involved a succession of popes and emperors. It focused on the ceremony by which bishops were promoted, in the course of which they were 'invested' with a ring and staff as symbols of the religious dimensions of their office. In imperial territory, it was customary for these symbols to be presented by the emperor himself – but Gregory declared the practice simoniac. Though no cash changed hands, the ceremony was a sign, as far as he was concerned, of lay influence over the Church, which could no longer be tolerated. By early 1080, emperor and pope were at loggerheads again. In March of that year, Gregory excommunicated Henry a second time, declaring the leader of a major rebellion of German regional aristocrats against Salian rule, Rudolf of Swabia, king of Germany in his place.

Gregory, however, had overplayed his hand. Even if they had wanted to do so (which was moot), it was not practically possible for Henry IV – or any of his fellow rulers – to surrender complete control over leading ecclesiastical appointments. The bishoprics and major monasteries of medieval Europe were all funded by large portfolios of landed estates, amounting to between a quarter and a third of the entire landed wealth of western Christendom. No ruler could allow so much of his domain's resources to be controlled by what was in effect a foreign power, or for the individuals controlling such wealth to be completely independent of his control. In practice, leading abbots and bishops were often entrusted, too, with oversight of large administrative sub-units of kingdoms. The landed holdings of their bishoprics and monasteries were also always subject to knight service, which entailed setting aside a portion of their actual land or its income to maintain a designated number of soldiers, whom the ruler had the right to mobilize when he needed an army. In post-Conquest Norman England, where eleventh-century records are fullest, bishoprics and major monasteries provided about a third of the kingdom's forces, a proportion which will not have been much different elsewhere. Because bishops, and often major abbots, were personally appointed by rulers, their military contingents were often politically more reliable than those provided by hereditary landed aristocrats.[38]

Far too much was at stake, then, for the ruling powers of the Latin west voluntarily to surrender to papal demands for an ecclesiastical hierarchy that was completely independent of their control – and Gregory lacked the means to force them to do so. In the end, the rebellion of the German princes did not prove strong enough either to win outright, or to force Henry IV into major concessions in response to Gregory's demands. And, as Henry's position strengthened, the extent of Gregory's miscalculation became clear. In 1080, Henry felt confident enough officially to depose his opponent and to appoint his own pope in his place, Clement III. In 1084, he then took Rome itself and was finally crowned emperor by his chosen antipope. The deposed Gregory negotiated enough Norman assistance to force Henry's withdrawal from the city, but his allies' behaviour in sacking the city so incensed its population that they drove Gregory out of his own city. He died in exile the following year in the castle of Salerno, under Norman protection. Gregory's chosen path of direct confrontation ended up inflicting serious damage on the reputation of the emergent papacy, not least within the city of Rome itself. Given that Henry IV had already accepted the principle of papal independence, and was far from hostile to the general cause of ecclesiastical reform, it was in many ways an unnecessary confrontation, pushed forward in the cause of an unattainable level of ideological purity.

The mess created by Gregory's miscalculated ambition took the best part of forty years to clear up, the subsequent twists and turns of the Investiture Controversy being marked by multiple blind alleys and half-victories. So much bitter recrimination was aired on both sides – each damning the other for heresy and breaking with established tradition – that it was not until 23 September 1122 that the final resolution of the conflict was signed in the German city of Worms: the so-called Concordat of Worms, which finally sealed a compromise. In this document, with the bitter enemies Henry IV and Pope Gregory long-since dead, Emperor Henry V and Pope Callixtus II agreed that kings and emperors could still take part in the ceremonial installation of bishops, though only to invest them with a lance as the symbol of their secular responsibilities, and no longer with the ring and staff of their spiritual office. But these new regulations covered simply the public ceremony of installing a bishop, not the much more private business of selecting the individual to be invested. In this, kings and emperors continued by and large to get their way – as political considerations dictated they must – even though from this point on they increasingly referred their choices to Rome for rubber-stamping.[39]

Both sides had saved face and the emperor managed to keep overall control of the ecclesiastical magnates in charge of such important assets. Not everyone quickly learned the lesson that head-on confrontation damaged both parties, so occasional collisions continued between Church and state across Christendom (among the most significant being the clash involving Henry II of England which ended in the death of Thomas Becket). For its part, the papacy had secured at least a symbolic victory in extracting recognition that kings and emperors should no longer bestow the ring and staff of spiritual authority. To celebrate this 'success', Pope Callixtus called a new type of council in March 1123. For centuries, popes had been holding councils of local Church leaders from within their patriarchal jurisdiction in the Lateran Palace in Rome. This latest Lateran council, however, was different in character and significance. Enacting clause 16 of the *Dictatus Papae*, Callixtus declared himself now to be holding a general – ecumenical – council of the entire Church. This was a huge breach with past precedent since, from Constantine onwards, only emperors had had the authority to call ecumenical councils. Still more important, Pope Callixtus' assertion won considerable support, as reflected in a conciliar attendance list of three hundred bishops and six hundred abbots from across western Christendom.[40] This was not yet anything like a full roll call, but the reformed papacy had managed to emerge from all the dramatic ups and downs of the highly confrontational Investiture Controversy with a substantial increase in the degree to which its authority was being recognized. Beneath the surface of quarrelling emperors and popes, however, two entirely different, and much less confrontational, processes were simultaneously elevating the pope's religious authority to a level that no subsequent emperor could even begin to challenge.

12
'God Wills It'

In summer 1099 a force of armed men from western Europe stormed into the holy city of Jerusalem, killing and looting as they went. The First Crusade had arrived at its self-appointed goal, and a story which had begun the best part of four years previously reached its tumultuous climax. In many ways, the whole enterprise had been a fiasco. It started in March 1095 with a request from the Byzantine emperor Alexius I to Pope Urban II, presented to him at the council of Piacenza, for a limited mercenary force of western knights to come to Constantinople's aid against continued incursions by the Muslim Seljuk Turks into what remained of the Byzantine Empire. After their demolition in 1071 of the main Byzantine field army at Manzikert, in what is now eastern Turkey, the Seljuks had steadily advanced into Byzantine territory. The major cities of Antioch and Smyrna (modern Izmir) had both fallen by 1084, and by the early 1090s the Seljuks had conquered all of Byzantine Syria and everything in Asia Minor, bar a thin coastal strip in the north. Backed into a corner, Emperor Alexius had opened negotiations with the papacy to end the current religious schism between Rome and Constantinople – which had been largely generated by the papal reformers' claims that Rome should have primacy over the entire Christian Church – with a view to using ecclesiastical reconciliation as a means for securing practical military assistance. By March 1095, the negotiations had gone nowhere, and Alexius was desperate. In response to his pleas for military aid, however, not only the requested knights but a ragbag mass of western European peasants set off for the east in two main groups, in the spring and summer of 1096. Their espoused aim was to liberate Jerusalem from Muslim control – which, again, was not what Alexius had requested. The crusaders also lacked proper leadership, realistic planning, and, in many cases, even basic supplies.

The result, from the outset, was chaotic. Murderous, anti-Jewish pogroms were launched in the towns of the Rhineland before the expedition got properly underway. Extensive looting marked its overland progress along the long trails through central Europe to Constantinople, and then across Asia Minor to Antioch and the fringes of the Holy Land itself, which the surviving crusaders eventually reached in October 1097. By this point, all their horses were long since dead, along with the majority of the crusaders themselves. Of a total (including non-combatants) of around a hundred thousand who set off, tens of thousands from the first contingent to reach Constantinople (the so-called Peasants' Crusade, which did comprise large numbers of peasants but also included some lords and their military retinues) had been slaughtered, or taken as slaves, in a series of running battles with Seljuk armies in the autumn of 1096. Most of the survivors then attached themselves to the slightly better-organized second contingent, which arrived after the slaughter. However, the increasingly hungry remnants who fought their way as far as Antioch by autumn 1097 then found themselves locked into a punishing eight-month siege of the well-defended city. This looked set to turn into the crusaders' own last stand when, in June 1098, a Turkish relief force arrived, trapping the crusaders between the proverbial rock and hard place.

At that moment of despair, the miracles suddenly began. Following a vision experienced by Peter Bartholomew (a monk travelling with the expedition), the trapped crusaders were led to a nearby cave, where they found the Holy Lance that had pierced the side of Christ on the Cross. Buoyed by this discovery, the crusaders gambled everything on a last desperate foot charge, on 28 June 1098. Astonishingly, they routed the Seljuk relief force, a success that prompted the fall of Antioch itself a few days later. After rest, recuperation and plenty of squabbling over the division of the spoils, most of the remaining crusaders advanced south into the Holy Land proper in January 1099. Arriving at Jerusalem itself in early June, they stormed its defences on 15 July 1099. Against all the odds, and despite all the incompetence, disorganization and death, the battered survivors achieved their goal. Inside the walls, they massacred all the city's Muslim and Jewish inhabitants, along with the garrison (Christians had been expelled before the siege began). Jerusalem returned to Christian political control for the first time since it had been conquered by Muslim Arab armies in the late 630s.[1]

This is not the place for an in-depth exploration of the extraordinary and in many ways appalling phenomenon of medieval crusading: a subject with its own rich and rapidly developing historiography. But the crusading phenomenon played a crucial role in the final emergence of medieval European Latin Christendom. Not least, crusading was both a reflection and a projection of increasing papal religious authority in the later eleventh century and well beyond.

THE FOREIGN POLICY OF THE PAPACY?

The whole crusading enterprise began as an initiative of Pope Gregory VII's successor but one, Urban II, who, in response to Alexius' request for military assistance, went on a preaching tour in the summer of 1095 to drum up support. It was aimed primarily at the regions of central and southern France, where Urban already had a web of well-established connections from his time as grand prior of Cluny. The tour culminated in a great set piece on 27 November, with the pope preaching to a vast crowd that had gathered around a Church council being held at Clermont Ferrand: a response to all the excitement Urban had stirred up over the previous months. He took as his text Matthew 16:24: 'Then Jesus said to his disciples, if anyone wants to follow me, let him deny himself and take up his cross and follow me.' At the moment of revivalist climax, when Urban called out for crusaders, Bishop Adhemar of Le Puy shouted *Deus le veult* – 'God wills it' – and led the initial surge to sign up.

This climactic moment was clearly prearranged: Adhemar would be Urban's legate or personal representative on the crusade, playing a major role in co-ordinating its strategy. The overall impact of Urban's preaching, however, still beggars belief. One hundred thousand individuals – including several tens of thousands of warriors of various ranks – responded to Urban's preaching. Nothing could better

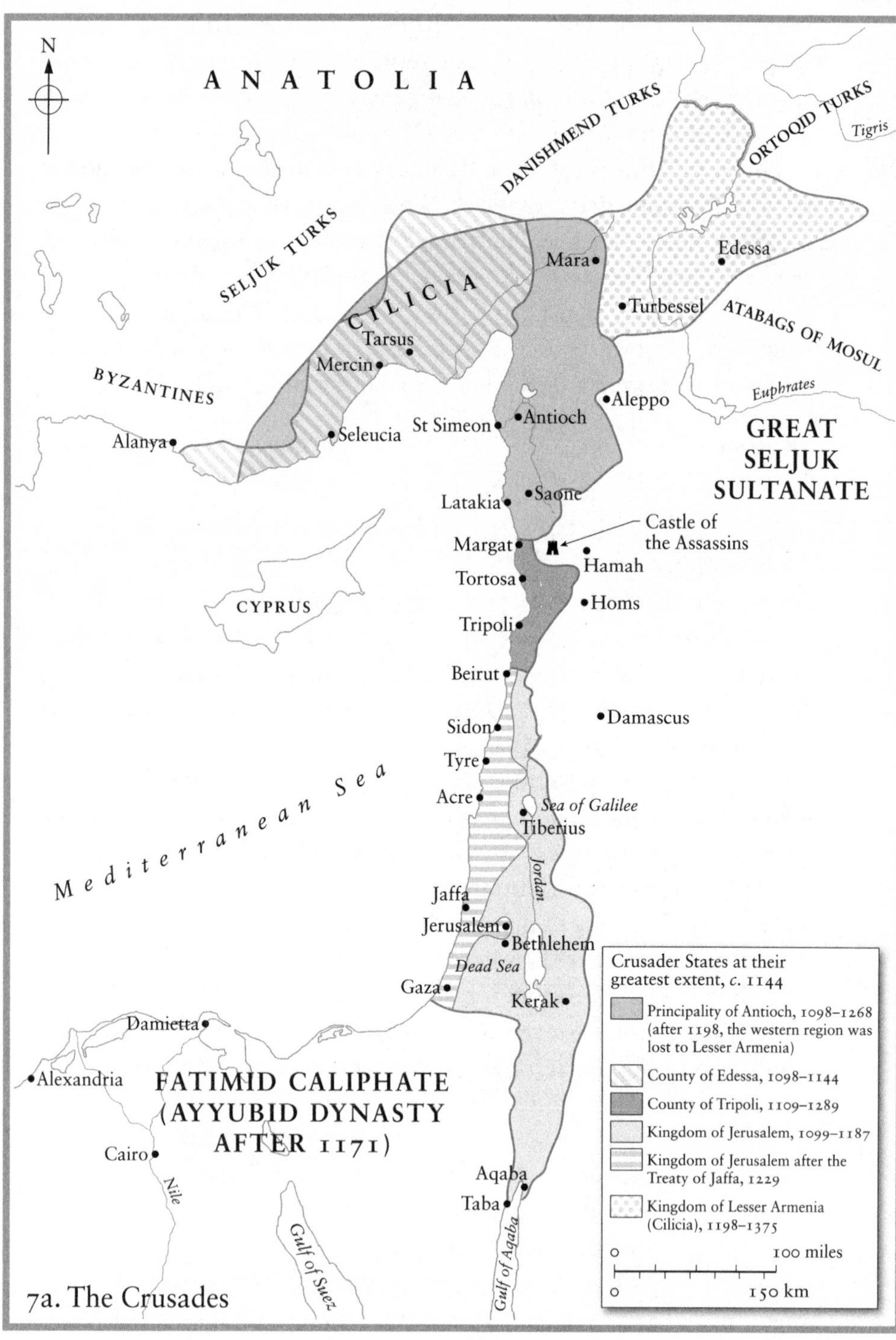

7a. The Crusades

illustrate the new level of traction that the reformed papacy had already generated within parts at least of western Christendom – influence now stretching far beyond a group of reform-minded clerics. And, of course, the campaign was carefully designed to extend that influence still further, at a moment when the Investiture Controversy between pope and emperor was still in full flood. The idea of a pope reaching out beyond the immediate environs of Rome to prompt warrior groups in western Europe into a life-changing course of action, completely bypassing the influence of kings and emperors, would have been completely inconceivable in the Carolingian era, when the emperor was in firm control of any campaigning against Christianity's external enemies.[2] Like the calling of ecumenical councils, this traditional role of the emperor as head of Christendom was passing over into papal hands.

The great military explosion which headed to the Holy Land was a product of the relationship which reform-era popes had been building with some warrior groups in western Europe over the previous half century. Leo IX began the process, offering remissions of penance to the warriors he needed for his – ultimately unsuccessful – attempts to fend off the intrusive Norman presence in southern Italy. After his successors threw in their lot with the Normans, Norman warriors were then equipped with fully blessed papal banners – among them Duke William, when he invaded England in 1066. Early reform-era popes were all too happy to bless the actions of warriors they deemed to be fighting in God's cause – which, in practice, meant fighting in papal interests. The fuller contours of this new relationship became more discernible over time. Pope Gregory VII supposedly urged on his soldiers with Jeremiah 48:10, 'Cursed be he that keepeth back his sword from blood', while papal blessing was also granted to the Christian kings of northern Iberia, whose campaigns against the Muslim south started to gather momentum in the last decades of the eleventh century, in particular with Alphonso VI of Castile's capture of Toledo in 1085. Developing papal ideology, and – sometimes desperate – efforts to ensure its political independence from the Holy Roman Empire, had already brought the papacy most of the way to the concept of crusade by 1095, while its establishment of new ties to some of the landed warrior networks of western Europe – particularly those of Spain, south-western France and, of course, the Normans of southern Italy from whom it sought protection – made those networks all the more receptive to the crusading call, when it came.[3]

The perceived success of the First Crusade – 'successful' in that, despite all the chaos, death and destruction, Jerusalem was eventually 'liberated' – enabled the whole concept of crusade itself to become a further building block of papal religious authority. In retrospect, all the setbacks and hardships en route only added to the overall lustre of the First Crusade's eventual success. It had nearly ended in disaster on multiple occasions; in fact, it had no right to have succeeded at all. Entirely by chance, the crusaders – at least the better-organized second contingent – managed to arrive in the Near East at a moment of maximum Muslim fragmentation. The Byzantine losses which generated Emperor Alexius' original request for military aid had been inflicted by the two great early rulers of the Seljuk Turkish Empire: Alp Arslan (1063–72) and Malik-Shah I (1072–92). After the latter's death, however, the Empire quickly shattered into a series of local dominions. Competing successor states of real power emerged only in the twelfth century, not least in direct response to the Christian challenge laid down by the events of 1097–9: their emergence being one of the main reasons why the larger, better-organized subsequent expeditions which followed the First Crusade to the Holy Land never achieved the same level of success. Had the First Crusade arrived at any other point in the history of the Islamic Near East, the chances are that it would have ended in ignominious defeat.[4] But succeed it did, against all the odds – and that it did so was clearly the work of God. 'God wills it', as Bishop Adhemar declared, or, as another contemporary labelled it, 'the Greatest Miracle since the Resurrection'.[5] By its very success, therefore, the First Crusade added enormous lustre to papal prestige – the same kind of proof positive of Divine support that Constantine and Charlemagne had both previously drawn from victorious warfare.

Urban's successors were quick to exploit this ideological windfall by ensuring that the papacy remained the prime mover of the broader western European crusading enterprise. For over two centuries, from the initial capture of Jerusalem down to the early fourteenth century, a whole era of crusading both extended papal authority and unleashed a series of further dramatic changes that profoundly shaped some key

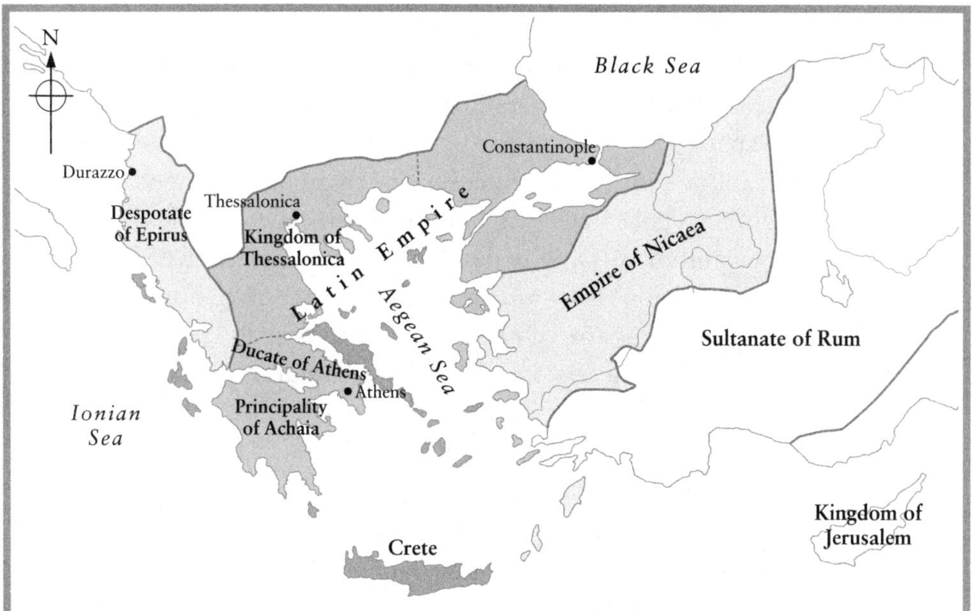

N
Black Sea
Constantinople
Durazzo
Thessalonica
Despotate of Epirus
Kingdom of Thessalonica
Latin Empire
Aegean Sea
Empire of Nicaea
Sultanate of Rum
Ducate of Athens
Athens
Ionian Sea
Principality of Achaia
Kingdom of Jerusalem
Crete

7b. The Aftermath of the Fourth Crusade (1204)

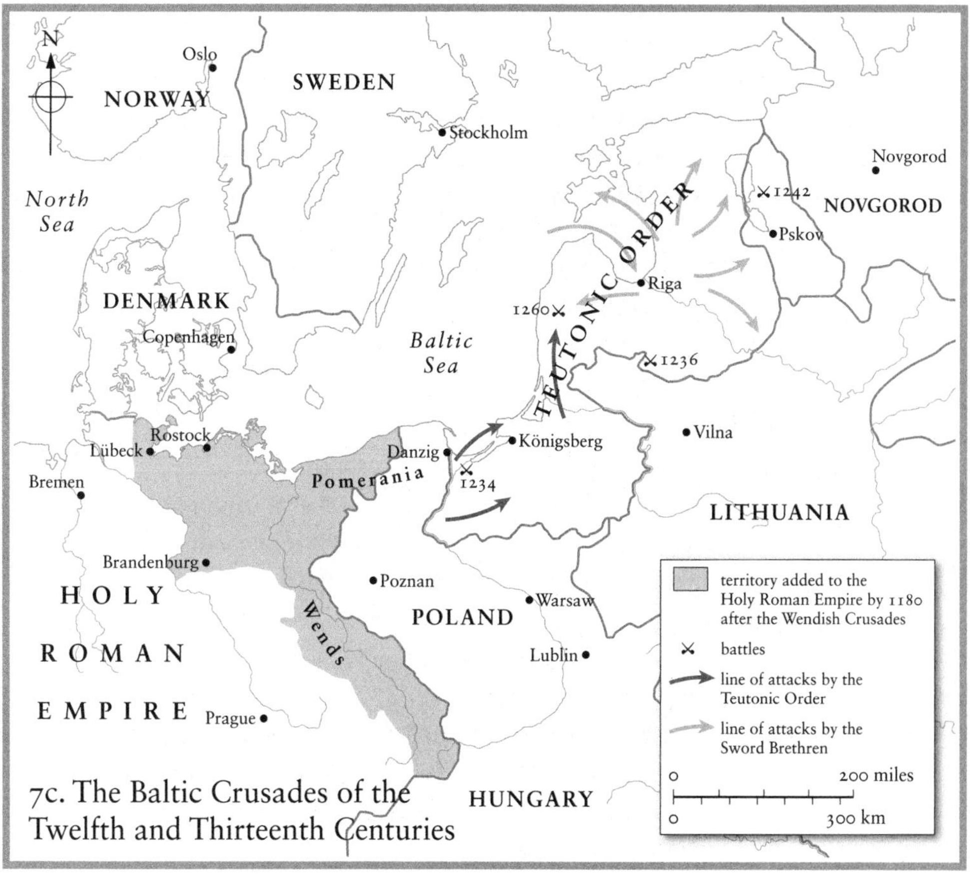

N
Oslo
NORWAY
SWEDEN
Stockholm
North Sea
Novgorod
1242
NOVGOROD
Pskov
TEUTONIC ORDER
Riga
DENMARK
1260
Copenhagen
Baltic Sea
1236
Vilna
Rostock
Lübeck
Königsberg
Danzig
Bremen
Pomerania
1234
LITHUANIA
Brandenburg
Poznan
HOLY ROMAN EMPIRE
Warsaw
POLAND
Wends
Lublin
Prague
HUNGARY

territory added to the Holy Roman Empire by 1180 after the Wendish Crusades
battles
line of attacks by the Teutonic Order
line of attacks by the Sword Brethren
0 200 miles
0 300 km

7c. The Baltic Crusades of the Twelfth and Thirteenth Centuries

contours of medieval Latin Christendom as a whole.[6] As one famous judgement put it, the crusades were in a very real sense 'the foreign policy of the Papacy'.[7]

During the twelfth and thirteenth centuries, crusading developed as a tool for enforcing papal agendas and emphasizing the reality of Rome's religious authority. Only popes could call crusades, or define any particular expedition as a crusade, thereby conferring upon its activities a sacred status; over time, warriors engaged in crusading enterprises in ever larger numbers. For the First Crusade, Urban II had deliberately targeted warrior networks that fell outside the control of the major monarchies of the day, not wanting or daring to tread on the toes of powerful kings of France – and particularly not the Salian emperors, with the Investiture Controversy still raging. One unintended consequence of this approach was that the expedition lacked clear leadership. This was obviously true of the utterly chaotic Peasants' Crusade, but it was equally true – for different reasons – of the more organized second contingent, which arrived at the gates of Constantinople in the late summer and autumn of 1096. This consisted of six major components, each with its own leaders. The papal legate Adhemar spent an enormous amount of time trying to minimize the fractious quarrelling between the contingent's grander participants, such as Raymond of Toulouse, Godfrey of Bouillon (from the Lorraine), and the Normans Bohemond of Taranto and Robert Curthose (son of William the Conqueror). By the Third Crusade (1189–92), however, the umbrella of developing papal influence had extended to include sovereign rulers: the kings of both France and England participated. By this date, too, the concept of crusade had expanded beyond Jerusalem and the Holy Land to include 'just' Christian wars being waged against Muslims in Spain and pagans in the Baltic.

The papacy also took the lead in dealing with the many problems of finance and logistics involved in waging 'holy' war over vast distances. Crusading was hugely expensive as well as dangerous, something which subsequent papal initiatives attempted to address. Whereas the First Crusade relied on the personal financial resources of its participants, by the time of Innocent III (1198–1216) a century later, campaign finance had been put on a much firmer footing. Drawing royalty into expeditions was a major advance, since kings could be licensed to institute kingdom-wide taxation to fund major crusading expeditions. The fourth Lateran council of 1215 also authorized Innocent to dedicate one-twentieth of Church income throughout the Latin west for three years while he developed plans for what is generally known as the Fifth Crusade: another ruinously fruitless attempt to reconquer the Holy Land (much of which had been lost in 1181). At the level of the individual crusader, too, the papacy enacted practical measures to encourage participation. By Innocent III's time, an attractive protection package was on offer. Anyone who had publicly taken a crusading vow was not to be charged interest on their debts, and creditors were not allowed to pursue them; crusaders were also immune from pending lawsuits for the duration.[8]

Through this raft of measures, the crusading enterprise exposed a larger proportion of Europe's warrior elites to emergent papal authority. The warriors' papally authorized activities in turn had significant religious consequences, especially in expanding the boundaries of Latin Christendom. In the Iberian peninsula, the structures and ideologies of crusade were deemed transferable to wars already being fought against the Muslim lords of Al-Andalus from the 1090s onwards, a move formalized by the first Lateran council of 1123 (which also formally brought the Investiture Controversy to a close: p. 472). More crusading against the 'Moors' of Spain was authorized at the time of the Second Crusade to the Holy Land in 1147 (an expedition designed to reconquer the city of Edessa, which had just been lost to Muslim counter-attack), with other papally approved expeditions following on at regular intervals thereafter. Draping the banners of religious warfare over these expeditions naturally prompted a powerful Muslim reaction (not least when the Almohad Caliphate intervened from its North African base in the later twelfth century), but, over the long term, the developing concept of the crusade played a central role in returning the bulk of the Iberian peninsula to Christian rule. Even if the final expulsion of the Moors did not occur until 1492, for the previous two centuries Muslim rule had been confined essentially just to Granada in the south.[9]

Crusading played a similar role much further north, where Christian expansion in the second age of Empire had bypassed a vast tract of territory south of the Baltic Sea and east of the River Elbe. In 1147, at the time of the Second Crusade to the Holy Land, Pope Eugenius III formally declared the first Wendish Crusade: a military offensive against those Elbe Slavic groups (the 'Wends') who some 150 years before had united around a revamped version of their traditional paganism to throw off Ottonian control (p. 392). A mixed body of Christian warriors – mostly from German, Scandinavian and Polish lands – descended on the region. The campaign that followed was bloody and politically messy, punctuated by many changes of allegiance and the usual quarrels between rival Christian leaders over dividing the spoils. In terms of its violent imposition of Christianity on another significant chunk of the European landscape, however, the crusade was – on its own terms – broadly successful. By the 1180s, no pagan dynast controlled any land west of the River Oder, and, across much of the region, landed estates were being distributed to the Christian knights who had led the charge.

The violence in northern Europe only intensified when the prince archbishop of Bremen appointed Albert of Buxhoeveden, a canon of his city's cathedral, as the first bishop for Livonia, territories east of the Oder, in 1199. It was a post that as yet existed only on paper. Albert's task was to make it reality – no easy one given that Livonia covered most of modern-day Estonia and Latvia, and was still at this point resolutely non-Christian in belief (Map 7c). Six years earlier, Pope Celestine III had issued a crusading bull for the Baltic region; Albert – who led his army in person – was authorized to implement its provisions. After a preaching tour of Germany to drum up recruits, he landed at the mouth of the Daugava River a year later with twenty-three ships and five hundred soldiers. This was enough to establish an initial Christian enclave and encourage more Christian warriors to flock to his standard. By the time Albert – now bishop of Riga (which he reputedly founded and where his statue still stands in imposing magnificence in its own niche on the cathedral exterior: Plate 30) – died thirty years later, much of Livonia had been subdued too.

Further east and north, the Lithuanians, Finns and Prussians proved tougher nuts to crack, and the swamps of the Baltic hinterland more than slightly problematic for heavily armoured Christian knights. One of Albert's innovations had been to found his own crusading order, the Sword Brothers of Livonia, who carried on the work of

Christianizing the eastern Baltic after their founder's death. They scored great successes until lured into a swamp at the battle of Saule (probably near the modern town of Vecsaule in southern Latvia) on 22 September 1236, where their master, Volkwin, and three-quarters of his knights came to grief. At this point, the surviving Sword Brothers were formally transferred to the Teutonic Order, who continued the wars. Swamps remained an issue: a similar disaster at the battle of Durbe in July 1260 (near the modern Latvian town of that name) cost the now united crusading order another 150 out of the 190 knights committed to the field. Every defeat for the crusaders prompted more pagan uprisings, but the military pressure was continuous and, with the Swedish crown weighing in further north, both the Prussians and Finns had been brought to heel by the 1290s. Lithuania managed to resist for another three generations, until its ducal family fended off the inevitable by adopting its own version of the self-Christianization model that had played such a role in the expansion of western Christendom in the Carolingian and Ottonian eras, officially converting to Catholic Christianity in 1387.[10]

At this point, Christianity finally had become the defining faith of at least the political elite of pretty much the entirety of the European landmass, and, across much of it, of the entire population. The process was not quite complete: Muslim rulers would control some southern reaches of the Iberian peninsula for another century following Lithuania's religious capitulation. Everywhere else, Europe had Christian rulers, and the continent's population as a whole was now set definitively on a path to the Christian religious identity that has since been one of its centrally defining cultural characteristics. Papal-sponsored crusades played a major role in the final stages of the process, which had seen a small Jewish sect become the dominant religion of the European continent in four broad eras. In the later Roman Empire, Christianity's absorption into the Roman imperial system ensured that it gained a strong hold on the provincial landowning elites of western Europe. In the post-Roman era, the faith had spread a little further than its old Roman boundaries in the north. It then made massive gains to the east as a whole range of new European dynasts adopted Christianity under the influence of the three imperial dynasties of the second age of Christian empire. The overall process then came to completion in the crusading era, with the expansion of Christian rule in Iberia and, particularly, into the north-eastern Baltic. That this final stage of Christian expansion occurred under a papally sanctioned crusading umbrella also underlines the extent to which, from early in the twelfth century, papal religious authority had grown to take over the kinds of roles previously filled by Christian emperors.

CRUSADE AND THE LIMITS OF CHRISTENDOM

However, if the concept of crusade might have been deliberately created and developed to expand both papal prestige and the physical boundaries of the papacy's authority, the Roman see did not exercise complete control over the phenomenon. Different interest groups were invested in the idea of crusade, adapting Rome's emergent religious authority for their own purposes. (In much the same way, papal interests had previously been advanced, incidentally and accidentally, by Frankish would-be emperors seeking coronation, Frankish bishops wanting to escape the unwelcome attentions of their archbishops, and northern Churchmen looking for a suitable vehicle through which to enact a unified religious reform agenda.) Often, therefore, a declaration of crusade did little more than cast a thin veil of papal respectability over bloody processes of acquisitive expansion.

Many crusaders were clearly on the lookout for financial gain. As one fascinating strand in recent scholarship on crusading has underlined, although most of its participants either died en route or eventually returned home showing not the slightest sign of wanting to make material gains, this was even true of the First Crusade, to some extent. This expedition resulted in the creation of the four so-called Crusader States in the conquered territories of the Holy Land: the counties of Edessa and Tripoli; the principality of Antioch; and the kingdom of Jerusalem (Map 7a). Some of the crusade's leaders had always had this aim in view, such as the Bohemond of Taranto who, having become prince of Antioch, didn't even march on to Jerusalem. When Jerusalem fell to the crusaders, each of these four new states acquired a western ruler, following which landed patrimonies within them were distributed between a mix of crusaders, who settled in what came to be known as Outremer ('over the sea'), and newcomers who came east in the aftermath of the crusade's success.

The acquisitive element is even more strongly marked in other crusading regions, where expansionary land-grabbing exercises would probably have gathered momentum with or without the emerging concept of crusade (in contrast to the Holy Land, which was too far distant to make it a likely target). Much of the action on the southern shores of the Baltic – the so-called Northern Crusades – was carried forward by Christian German knights and Christian Scandinavian princes on the make, and it is hard to think that they would not have eventually turned their predatory attentions to the Slavic- and Baltic-speaking populations to their north and east at some point, whether or not the First Crusade had succeeded.

This was still more true of the *Reconquista* movement: the steady expansion of Christian rule over former Muslim territories of the Iberian peninsula. There, as the peninsula's unifying Umayyad caliphal structure began to fragment from the later tenth century onwards, smaller Christian states in the north started to extend their territories, drawing in warriors from north of the Pyrenees in search of their fortunes well before the crusade label had emerged to rebrand rampant self-interest. Such was the case with Rodrigo of Vivar, a Castilian knight and warlord of the later eleventh century, better known as El Cid (*c.* 1043–99). An epic verse account of his life of the mid-twelfth century (the text on which the great Charlton Heston film was based), portrays him as the archetypical Christian hero of the *Reconquista*, freeing large tracts of the Spanish countryside from Muslim domination. But, as the more contemporary first *Life* of Rodrigo makes clear, El Cid is much better understood as a mercenary adventurer, building up a personal fortune and landed patrimony in the course of his life: in the years prior to the First Crusade, he was happy to serve Muslim and Christian masters alike.

Rodrigo's activities reflect a much broader, well-documented eleventh- and twelfth-century phenomenon which was partly set in motion by changing inheritance customs among northern Europe's elite families. As Europe's economy became increasingly monetarized, where younger sons used to receive a life interest in a portion of their families' landed holdings, they were instead increasingly granted a cash payment, the land being reserved entirely for their eldest brother – a system known as primogeniture. This process sent many younger sons of western Europe's landed elite off into the world with – or as part of – a warband for hire, with the aim of carving out new landed patrimonies of their own: acquiring land remained, as ever, the ultimate goal. The collapse of centralized control of Spain's Umayyad Caliphate in the first half of the eleventh century had provided promising opportunities for warriors on the make, of which El Cid was only one (if one of the most successful). Different parts of Europe offered other opportunities. Norman expansion into Sicily and southern Italy from the 1040s onwards – which the reforming popes eventually looked to harness as a vehicle for cementing their political independence – never attracted the crusade label, although Sicily was taken from Muslim Arab control; nonetheless, it falls into this category, as, arguably, does the whole Baltic crusade movement. In many contexts, therefore, crusading was just a nasty quid pro quo, which allowed warrior groups to validate their bloody and self-gratifying wars of acquisition.

In the worst cases, the lust for profit, despite any putative crusading label, passed so far beyond papal control as to work against the Roman see's direct interests. The ultimate example, perhaps, is the Fourth Crusade of 1204, which Pope Innocent III took the lead in organizing and funding. Having succeeded to the papal throne in February 1198, he began preaching the crusade the following August and, as originally designed, the aim was to open up the ports of Egypt as a potentially easier point of access to the Holy Land. After a long and convoluted preparation (which in January 1203 saw Innocent excommunicate some of the participating contingents), the actual campaign culminated in – from the crusaders' point of view – a highly lucrative sack of the Byzantine imperial capital of Constantinople in April 1204. This sacking was totally contrary to Innocent's design. In its aftermath, the Byzantine Empire was reduced to three autonomous principalities, centred on Nicaea, Trebizond and Epirus, while the rest of its territories, including Constantinople itself, acquired new Latin overlords (Map 7b).[11]

At this point, despite the frustration of Innocent's original plans, it looked briefly as though the whole of the European landmass – together with its new colonial extension into Outremer – might unite under papal religious leadership. However, many of the territories newly brought under Latin control could not be held in the longer term. In the Holy Land, the four new Christian principalities established in the aftermath of the First Crusade – Jerusalem, Tripoli, Antioch and Edessa – all eventually fell to Muslim counter-attack, despite repeated attempts to mount relief expeditions. Edessa fell in 1144 (prompting the Second Crusade of 1147–50), then Jerusalem itself in 1187 (triggering the Third). Christian rule over the Holy City was restored by diplomatic negotiation in the 1220s, but Jerusalem was lost again to Muslim control (definitively this time) in 1291, the final act in a process which had seen Antioch taken in 1268 and Tripoli in 1289. Throughout the twelfth and thirteenth centuries, the papacy had done its best to keep Outremer afloat, but the task proved beyond its capacities to organize sufficient western resources.

In many of the former Byzantine territories, likewise, Latin colonial rule could not be long maintained. Operating from his original base around Nicaea, the Byzantine emperor Michael VIII Palaeologos returned Constantinople to Greek rule in 1261, and quickly eliminated Latin rule over most of the other principalities that the victorious crusaders had established in the Balkans in the aftermath of 1204. In the same era, counter-attacks such as Alexander Nevsky's famous victory over the northern crusaders at the battle on the ice on Lake Peipus in 1242 halted any further eastward extension of Latin Christian hegemony into territories that already belonged to the Orthodox communion.

On reflection, the loss of Outremer was only to be expected. Its creation had involved so much luck that its maintenance in the long term was a forlorn hope. Once the Muslim power blocks of the Near East had started to reconstruct themselves, it was wildly unlikely that western Europe would find sufficient resources to keep the Crusader States in being. The conflicts between crusaders and fellow Christians – Byzantine Greeks in the Balkans and Russian Orthodox in the north-east – were of greater consequence, therefore, in defining the limits of medieval Latin Christendom because, by cementing in place an unbridgeable divide between it and fellow European Christians, the crusades defined its ultimate geographical limits.

Tensions between Greek east and Latin west had a long history. In the late Roman period, bishops of Rome had claimed that their prestige ought to rate higher than any of the other four apostolic patriarchates, both because of the unique status of St Peter and because their city also guarded the remains of St Paul. They were generally ignored by their eastern counterparts. There were also, as we've seen, periodic breaks in communion between the bishops of Rome and Constantinople in the post-Roman era, usually generated by various imperial religious initiatives that different popes considered heretical. The Acacian schism, prompted by Emperor Zeno's *Henotikon*, which attempted to bring peace to a divided eastern Church by downgrading the ecumenical status of the council of Chalcedon in the 490s, was the first. It was to be followed by longer-lasting disputes over the Monothelite and iconoclast heresies as the Constantinopolitan political and ecclesiastical establishments struggled to find an appropriate ideological response to the devastating defeats they suffered at the hands of the Muslim Arabs in the seventh and eighth centuries (see pp. 213 and 215).

These earlier breaches between west and east had eventually been healed. In the later eleventh century, however, the reformed papacy was responsible for an entirely different order of dispute with the patriarchate of Constantinople and the Byzantine imperial structure with which it remained so intimately entwined. Buoyed up by the heightened visions of its own antique authority, as enshrined in the *Pseudo-Isidore* collection of forgeries, the reign of Pope Leo IX saw a new break in communion with Constantinople over two main issues – one doctrinal, the second more practical. Doctrinally, the reformed papacy demanded that the *filioque* clause ('and the Son') should be added to the Nicene Creed, on the basis of its own assumed overarching authority. As we have seen, the claim that the Holy Spirit came from both God the Father and God the Son had older roots in the west, but in the 790s the *filioque* clause was championed as a general addition to the Creed by Charlemagne and his Churchmen as a further ideological stick with which to attack the Byzantine establishment's ecclesiastical credentials, at a time when Charlemagne himself was seeking to justify his own claims to an imperial title. The Greek Church firmly resisted any change to the Creed – as, in the late eighth and ninth centuries, had the papacy itself. But Charlemagne's support had been sufficient to establish the general use of the additional clause across his Empire and, once the reformers took control of the papacy, they reopened the issue with Constantinople.

Leo IX took an equally aggressive approach to the long-standing dispute concerning who had jurisdiction over the lucrative sees of Sicily and southern Italy. Back in the eighth century, when the Papal Republic had declared its independence from Byzantine control, the eastern emperor Leo III had confiscated control of both regions; now the pope wanted it back. His claim was marked by the first explicit, official papal citation of the forged *Donation of Constantine*, which he used to assert that Constantine had granted popes dominion over the entire territory of the western Empire. When the Byzantines refused to hand back control of the bishoprics, Leo excommunicated the patriarch of Constantinople in 1054, once again initiating schism between the Orthodox and Latin churches.[12]

In isolation, these disputes might well have found eventual resolution. The phenomenon of crusading, however, added another dimension to the conflict between east and west. In 1054, and for many years afterwards, in accord with long-established precedent, the patriarchs of Constantinople were still being chosen by Byzantine emperors, and the eastern Church remained closely aligned with the structures of the Byzantine imperial state. With the late-Roman model of the confessional imperial state still very much alive and kicking in the east, any dispute between crusaders and eastern emperors was always likely to acquire a religious dimension. Tension between the emperor and western crusaders had surfaced as early as 1096, when Emperor Alexius found not the specialist force of warriors he had asked for outside his capital city, but a vast ragbag army short of supplies and determined to conquer Jerusalem. The fact that the First Crusade also ended up establishing a series of principalities independent of Constantinopolitan control, when Alexius thought all the crusade's conquests (not just those in Asia Minor) should be returned to his jurisdiction, only made matters worse. Each round of subsequent crusading only added to the developing mutual resentment between east and west, until matters came to a head in 1204 when the Fourth Crusade captured and looted Constantinople itself, setting up colonial Latin rule in the city, and in many of the Empire's former possessions in the Balkans and western Asia Minor.

By the time Emperor Michael VIII returned Constantinople to Byzantine imperial rule in 1261, much additional resentment had been piled on top of the issues of 1054, and Rome's aggressive self-assertion prompted a determined Constantinopolitan response. While his city was still under Latin rule, in 1232 Patriarch Germanus II responded to papal pretentions to complete religious supremacy by carefully listing, in a letter to the cardinals of the Roman curia, the many churches that owed their allegiance to the Orthodox communion of which he was the head. The list ranged from the Ethiopians and 'all the Syrians' to the Georgians and other peoples of the Caucasus, 'the victorious realm of the Bulgars' and 'the numberless people of the Rus' (who included the soon-to-be victorious Alexander Nevsky).[13] The eastern patriarch's authority over this broader territory was largely imaginary, but Germanus' determination to counter Roman pretentions was marked. His list marked a new assertiveness among the patriarchs of Constantinople, who from this point on consistently presented themselves as the head of a wide communion of allied churches. More structural responses to Rome's assertions of spiritual authority soon followed. From 1315, patriarchs of Constantinople, echoing Roman practice, started for the first time to register their letters, looking to transform themselves into the same kind of legally normative body that the Roman Church had become under its reformed popes.

As Islamic – in particular, Ottoman Turkish – pressure built up around the beleaguered Byzantine state, some of Constantinople's later emperors made further efforts to end the schism as part of increasingly desperate negotiations for much-needed military assistance from the Latin west. Conversations around the theological problems of the *filioque* clause had begun in the first half of the thirteenth century, during the period of Latin rule in Constantinople, and had even identified a potential compromise. The writings of influential Greek Church Fathers of the late Roman period had talked about the Holy Spirit proceeding 'through the Son', and this, it was suggested, represented exactly the same theological point as the *filioque* addition to the Creed. At three different moments – in 1276, 1323 and 1439 – 'union' (the ending of the schism) was proclaimed, but in each case the eastern emperor who had negotiated it with papal representatives, even when backed by his patriarch, failed to sell it to the broader Orthodox clerical establishment. The underlying reason in each case was not so much disagreement about the *filioque* compromise itself, but the simmering resentment generated among the broader leadership of the Greek Church by the period of colonial Latin rule in Constantinople, and the overweening – in the Greek view, illegitimate – claims to supreme spiritual authority being made by the papacy. In each case, the terms of the proposed 'unions' involved Greek recognition of papal primacy as well as the full legitimacy of the *filioque* clause: in the end, neither proved acceptable to the broader Greek clerical establishment. Thanks to additional conflicts of the crusading era, therefore, the schism of 1054 was never healed, and eventually earned its sobriquet 'the Great Schism'.[14] (Rome and the Orthodox communion are still formally to be reconciled today, though both sides got as far as rescinding their mutual decrees of anathema at the Second Vatican Council in 1965.)

The extra fillip that papal authority derived from the crusading era was down to luck. Had the First Crusade not succeeded, and it had no right to, there would probably have never been a second, nor any subsequent extension of the crusading concept to Iberia and the Baltic. But because the crusaders did 'succeed' (in their own terms at least), the phenomenon of crusade greatly strengthened papal prestige at a difficult moment. As the crusaders fought their way into Jerusalem, the papacy was still locked in the punishing Investiture Controversy with a succession of Holy Roman emperors. Not only that, crusading also provided the papacy with an entirely new mechanism for expanding its authority among the socially and economically powerful landowning elites of Latin Europe, which, at the very least, meant that their processes of acquisitive expansion acquired a religious component, each materially extending the geographical boundaries of Latin Christendom, and hence of the broader region that acknowledged the papacy as the functioning head of its faith. Compared to the amount of European territory added to Latin Christendom in the second age of Christian Empire, the new gains were relatively small, but it was crusading which finally defined the European limits of papal authority.

Latin Christendom now spanned an extraordinary physical space. Stretching from Iceland to the Balkans on one diagonal, and from the Atlantic coast of Spain to the north-eastern shores of the Baltic on the other, its extent – defined as those Christian territories that had come to accept papal religious authority by the thirteenth century – was enormous by any measure (Map 8). When you factor in how slowly people travelled in the Middle Ages – no more than 25 miles (40 km) a day overland – its lived reality was still more enormous. The real measure of distance is how long it takes a human being to cover the ground, and in the thirteenth century people moved maybe only one-twentieth of the kinds of distance that can be achieved nowadays. Hence, it took over a month to travel from England to Rome – if the journey went smoothly. What this means, of course, is that this new papal Empire was in practical terms twenty times larger even than it initially seems to be to the modern eye. Nor, in fact, was its choice of capital at all convenient. Set in central-southern Italy, the city of Rome was a very long way from much of western Christendom – as it had been from much of its conquered territory in the first Roman imperial period. Which is why, in the Roman era, actual imperial power had quickly moved outwards from the city of Rome itself. In the words of a fourth-century imperial spokesman, Rome was 'a sacred precinct far from the highway'.[15] As the twelfth and thirteenth centuries unfolded, and ever more territory came to acknowledge papal religious authority, the same problem of distance came to be solved in a different way, which fundamentally changed both the mechanisms and, by so doing, the practical geographical reach of papal religious authority – cementing it so firmly in place as an unshakeable pillar of Latin Christendom that it was proof now even against the ultimate failure of the crusading enterprise with which the Roman see was so closely identified.

A HARMONY OF CANONS

The Investiture Controversy of the late eleventh and early twelfth centuries stimulated a renewed interest in canon law, as both the imperial and papal camps sought to bolster their positions. Pope Gregory VII and his supporters encouraged the production of new collections of

Church law to justify Rome's claims to overarching religious authority.[16] Thanks to *Pseudo-Isidore* and the subsequent collections it influenced, pro-papal lawyers naturally found it straightforward to use canon law to support their positions. At the same time, all this new legal work reinforced everyone's dawning realization of a more general point: that in its current state, western canon law was unwieldy to the point of being more or less unusable. It encompassed such a vast range of potentially authoritative sources – Scripture, the writings of major Church Fathers, the decisions of ecumenical and regional councils, imperial decrees, papal pronouncements – that it was impossible for Church lawyers to be sure that they had covered every potentially relevant ruling, conciliar decision, or scriptural passage. Still worse, on most contentious or intellectually tricky issues, the range of relevant passages of Scripture – not to mention various pertinent conciliar decisions and decrees of emperors and popes – gave a wide variety of possible answers. By the late eleventh century, therefore, complicated differences in detail made it often impossible to cite authoritative chapter and verse on 'correct' Church practice – even without the kinds of deliberate fabrication that *Pseudo-Isidore* had brought to the table.

Over the centuries, an equivalent problem of what constituted 'correct' belief had been slowly addressed through the generation of a large body of scriptural exegesis that explained how to read ostensibly conflicting passages of Scripture in a way that ironed out the difficulties (p. 78). But, when it came to correct practice, canon lawyers of the late first and early second millennia, in more of a hurry and facing many pressing issues apart from the papal reform disputes, could not wait centuries. The *Pseudo-Isidore* forgeries represented one kind of attempt to resolve the problem, and others followed. In 906, the late-Carolingian scholar Regino of Prüm produced (without explaining his choices) a selection of the legal materials he considered most useful. It's a sign of how problematic canon law was at this point that although his selection was both extremely concise and originally designed for use only within two archbishoprics, those of Trier and Mainz, the manuscript evidence shows that other Church leaders quickly employed it.

A more ambitious and, it turned out, influential response to the problem was produced in the late eleventh century by Ivo, bishop of Chartres from 1090 until his death in 1115. Ivo was said to have trained in Paris and then at the Norman abbey of Bec, which prepared him well to make two passes at the tangled mess of canon law, prompted not least by the Investiture dispute then raging (Ivo was a strong supporter of the drive against simony). His first legal compendium, the *Decretum*, weighed in at an enormous seventeen books. More popular – in a more manageable eight volumes – was his second effort, the *Panormia*. Well aware of the fundamental problem of inconsistency between different legal authorities, Ivo offered some general thoughts on how matters might be resolved in principle in his prefatory remarks, which may have started life as a separate treatise on the problems of canon law and how to resolve them. The central thrust of his project was to bring intellectual coherence and conceptual clarity to the resolution of any particular problem of inconsistency encountered by his readers, by both urging on them the overall aims of Church law (achieving a balance between mercy and discipline to achieve maximum spiritual benefit) and reminding them to distinguish carefully between absolute rules and general advice, and limited exceptions which might apply only to a small number of cases. The selection of rulings that followed in the main text were presumably based on these same principles, though Ivo did not set out the reasoning behind his choices.

The first tentative effort to lay out both some choices between competing rulings and the reasoning behind those choices in writing – although clerics must have long been doing something similar orally in court – was offered around the year 1100 by Alger of Liège, then a canon of the city's cathedral and personal secretary of its bishop. As such, he had a professional interest in the practicalities of canon law which his bishop was supposed to apply. But his small treatise – *On Mercy and Justice* – could deal with only a few of the many problems lawyers were encountering in the tangled mass of Church legal materials.[17]

The final unravelling of the mess that was canon law found its inspiration in an intellectual enterprise directed towards another problem entirely. It also irrevocably cemented in place the legal authority of the Roman see. As both sides in the Investiture Controversy were trying to establish their respective legal positions, a monumental sixth-century collection of Roman law – much of it originally excerpted from a vast body of older legal sources – was rediscovered in the southern Italian city of Amalfi, around the year 1000. The text in question was Justinian's *Digest of Roman Law*, a prestige political project of the emperor dating from the 530s. It summarized a thousand years and more of evolving Roman legal tradition, aiming to excise redundant rulings and remove any contradictions to generate one coherent text of impeccable legal authority. Our detailed knowledge of the project entirely depends upon one sixth-century Italian manuscript copy, perhaps originally produced for the city where it was discovered. Early in the second millennium, the manuscript was taken to Pisa, where its contents were subjected to the closest scrutiny. This process triggered two related legal revolutions, which were to remake the history of medieval (and modern) Europe.

The manuscript's rediscovery drove the emergence of medieval western Christendom's first centre of high-level studies since the disappearance of their late Roman equivalents in the fifth and sixth centuries – what would eventually become the university of Bologna. While the university received its first formal charter in 1158, the city's schools were already developing a reputation as centres of advanced learning in the final decades of the previous century, based on the range of teachers now offering courses in all the Liberal Arts of the *trivium* and *quadrivium* there. But as the twelfth century progressed, what brought students flocking to the city from all over Europe were the specialist legal studies on offer, based on intensive analysis of the rediscovered text of the *Digest*. The legal scholars working at Bologna didn't just read the text and teach its contents. Justinian's introductory remarks to the *Digest* claimed that, if you scrutinized the text hard enough, any seeming contradictions would in fact disappear (though, in practice, the contradictions were many and varied, reflecting the fact that the *Digest* was as much a political as a legal project in origin and had been rushed to completion). The Bologna law school took Justinian's claims at face value and, over the course of the twelfth century, several generations of scholars – many tens of individuals – set about resolving the text's problems through reasoned, principled argumentation.

Some of the problems could be resolved through detailed grammatical or rhetorical analysis. More generally, the scholars also considered each problematic passage alongside every other potentially relevant ruling contained within the text, allowing the kind of detailed comparative analysis which itself generated important lines of potential explanation. Hence, in many cases, seeming contradictions could be resolved by categorizing one or more of the apparently contradictory rulings as 'exceptions', to be allowed only in precisely defined circumstances (a move that Ivo of Chartres had also proposed in response to the problems of Church law in the late eleventh century): the distinction between 'general' and 'particular' laws proving a particularly fruitful avenue of approach. The scholars' proposed resolutions to specific problems – and it is important to understand that, particularly in the early years, different scholars were offering competing resolutions of the same identified problem – quickly came to be set down in writing in a specialized written form: the gloss. A gloss consisted of all the passages from the *Digest* under discussion, then, in an accompanying commentary, a full explanation of their significance and the justification behind the preferred resolution of any apparent contradictions between them. Over the course of the twelfth century, so many detailed glosses were produced by scholars on so many different passages of the *Digest* – especially once later scholars began modifying the resolutions of their predecessors – that the whole enterprise began to spiral out of control. Order was restored by the Roman jurist Accursius. A lawyer from Florence, he became a professor at Bologna where, between 1220 and 1240, he collated over a hundred years' worth of legal argument – consisting of tens of thousands of individual contributions – into a two-million-word text. This phenomenal work, the *Glossa Ordinaria*, soon became the standard commentary upon the Justinian legal corpus: the basic tool of all trainee and practising Roman lawyers.[18] The development of the Roman law school of Bologna played a major role in the final emergence of western Christendom, because its techniques and methods offered the Church's canon lawyers an appropriate set of mechanisms to allow them to cut their own legal Gordian knots.

There was from the outset some overlap between Roman law and canon (Church) law, because late Roman emperors, as the self-proclaimed and fully recognized heads of the Church, had been accustomed to legislate on ecclesiastical matters. In the last decade of the eleventh century, Ivo of Chartres had seen the potential for some of the emerging techniques of Roman legal analysis to be applied in the field of canon law. Towards the end of his preface to the *Panormia*, for instance, he commented on the potential of the Roman legal category of a personal law – applying a benefit or penalty to a particular named individual – to help resolve some knotty issues in canon law, since such laws could never be employed as any kind of general legal precedent. Building on Ivo's general comments, the great breakthrough in the field of canon law came two generations later, with the publication in around 1140 of the first edition of the pioneering *Concordantia disconcordantium canonum* or *Harmony of Discordant Canons* (often just called the *Decretum*) of the canon legal jurist Gratian. Almost nothing is known of Gratian's life, except that he wasn't himself a Roman lawyer, but he worked at Bologna alongside the now flourishing school of Roman law and applied its practical principles for reconciling apparent legal disagreements to the much thornier difficulties presented by Church legal materials. The first edition of the *Decretum* was followed about a decade later by a much-enlarged second edition, which may or may not have been by the same man, but more than doubled the 1,860 rulings considered by its predecessor to 3,800.

The working principles for resolving disagreements between older authorities that Gratian followed in his *Decretum* closely echoed those of the Roman lawyers, though he faced a far from easy initial problem which they had not. Justinian's *Digest* came with a coherent order of subjects and associated sub-headings: the work of Roman lawyers of the imperial period. Canon law, in comparison, was a massive jumble. Gratian's first job, therefore, was to create a coherent structure of thematic main and sub-headings under which to pull together all the relevant passages from the different potential sources of canon law.[19] Having begun to establish a framework of headings, Gratian then set about resolving identifiable contradictions between the relevant texts he had assembled under each one, applying the principles of Roman legal analysis to the problems of Church law. As with Roman law, language was always carefully analysed, with particular laws interrogated as to whether they should always apply, or only in particular cases. Like his Roman counterparts, Gratian also generally worked on the principle that the most recent ruling was going to be the most authoritative, but with one crucial exception. Faced with a contradiction that could not be resolved by other means, you should always – so both Ivo and Gratian agreed – follow the legal source of highest authority. Here, the influence of *Pseudo-Isidore* was profound, for, following its many statements to this effect, both Ivo and Gratian ranked papal decretals highest of all. As Gratian put it: 'The holy Roman Church imparts right and authority to the sacred canons, but is not bound by them. For it has the right of establishing canons, since it is the head and hinge of all churches, from whose ruling no one may dissent.'[20] In terms of their inherent legal authority, Gratian's *Decretum* thus put papal decretals above even the rulings of ecumenical councils and emperors. (Local, provincial synods came last in the pecking order.) Scripture and the writings of the Church Fathers were always relevant sources, but existing traditions of exegesis made it possible to read most of them in too wide a variety of ways for them to be likely to override a papal ruling. Gratian also borrowed the crucial innovation pioneered on a very small scale in the case of canon law, as we've seen, by Alger of Liège, whereby the principle behind each individual legal resolution offered in the *Decretum* was carefully explained in an accompanying commentary (or *dicta*).

Gratian's *Decretum* was so obviously superior to any previous canon law collection that, without ever being formally authorized, its second, expanded edition quickly became the starting point for all serious canon legal training. One hundred and sixty manuscripts of the second edition of the *Decretum* have survived dating from the final few decades of the twelfth century alone, their provenance showing the collection's rapid dissemination through Italy, northern Spain, northern and southern France, the Anglo-Norman territories (including western France), and even Scandinavia. Its conclusions quickly became the focus of canon legal dispute (as, for instance, in the Becket dispute in England between 1163 and 1170). By the third quarter of the twelfth century, a good knowledge of Gratian's text – and of contemporary Bolognese canon legal scholarship – was fast becoming essential for senior Churchmen, who were responsible for enforcing the precepts of canon law both informally (in terms of ensuring proper clerical discipline in different contexts) and formally, in settling legal cases that came before the Church courts over which they presided. They had to ensure, therefore, either that they gained sufficient knowledge themselves (Thomas Becket, among others, spent a year at Bologna), or employed specialist clerics who had done so.[21]

Inevitably, however, even the expanded second edition of the *Decretum* left many topics unresolved, and the study of western canon law continued to develop broadly in parallel with the Bologna school's approach to Roman law. In both systems, the gloss was the way in which these further problems were dealt with, and another *Glossa Ordinaria* – this one devoted to canon rather than Roman law – was the result. In the case of canon law, 90 per cent of the work of collecting the post-Gratianic canon legal glosses of individual scholars into one coherent text was done in the 1210s by Johannes Teutonicus, a German Dominican friar who was later the fourth master of his order, with a supplement produced by Bartholomaeus Brixiensis in the 1240s. As the new texts of the *Decretum* with its glosses began to be employed in practice, it quickly became apparent that, in the case of canon law (unlike its Roman secular counterpart), a continued process of clarification by gloss would still not be sufficient to turn the mass of inherited materials into a fully coherent legal system: different popes had given equally authoritative but contradictory rulings on certain subjects, for instance, and there were many other pressing matters which lacked any means of final resolution.[22]

What the developing canon legal tradition needed, therefore, was a set of targeted new rulings to fill in the gaps where even the most learned and ingenious of glossers could not deliver an authoritative answer. From *Pseudo-Isidore* onwards, the developing western canon law tradition acknowledged that papal rulings carried greatest legal authority. Given this, there really could only be one possible source for these necessary legal additions: Rome itself. It was with this acknowledgement that we get to the heart of the process which made it possible for practical papal religious authority, at the everyday level, to be exercised across the vast physical space of Latin Christendom. Where the legal tradition could not provide an answer, the pope, as Christendom's supreme spiritual authority, was coopted to fill in the gap.

The issuing of necessary additional papal legal rulings, in the form of new decretals, rapidly gathered momentum in the second half of the twelfth century. Whereas Pope Eugenius III (1145–53) issued just twelve in the eight years of his pontificate, and Hadrian IV (1154–9) eight in five, Alexander III (1159–81) issued over seven hundred in twenty-two. We can see, then, that it took about twenty years for the full implications of Gratian's *Decretum* to percolate properly through the ecclesiastical world of western Christendom – but, once they did, new business came the papacy's way thick and fast. Few of the new rulings dealt with really contentious issues; many consisted of automatic grants of favour, whereby the pope simply parroted back the language of the original request. A good case in point concerns one particularly tricky corner of marriage law. In tackling the issue of the validity of unfree marriages in the *Decretum*, for instance, Gratian had cited – with no further comment – a ruling from the Carolingian Church council of Chalons (813), which said that the marriages of serfs could not be dissolved 'where there was a lawful union, especially with the lord's consent'. But what did that mean? Was a lord's consent necessary to a lawful marriage between serfs, or not? Bishop Eberhard of Salzburg (1147–64) eventually solicited from Hadrian IV the papal ruling *Dignum est* to clarify the situation by asserting the absolute right of serfs to marry, whether or not their lord gave permission.[23] The overall effect of this flow of requests, and the answering barrage of decretals, was to place the papacy at the heart of the practical operations of Latin Christendom. It also quickly became necessary to collect the answers that popes were giving, since some of them – even if only a minority – were decisively changing existing practice.

The first decretal collections seem to have been do-it-yourself initiatives on the part of practising Church lawyers, often on the staffs of serving bishops who needed to keep up to date as they resolved practical disputes. As early as 1181, the clergy of Worcester Cathedral in England assembled a collection of 274 recent decretals, showing how important it was becoming to follow canon legal developments, and that different cathedral staffs were sharing between themselves knowledge of new rulings (about half of the forty-nine rulings in book I of the Worcester collection had originally been given to Church institutions outside England). Indeed, by this date there was a network of papal judges operating across western Christendom, a formalization of the sending out of legates which had been such a hallmark of the early years of the reformed papacy (p. 463), and they and their staffs were co-operating with cathedral clergy in framing the wording of further questions that required resolution. With the teachers of Bologna also assembling their own working collections of recent decretals, it was only a matter of time before something more official appeared. In 1234, Pope Gregory IX authorized the publication of the *Liber Extra*, so-called because it contained material not in Gratian's *Decretum*: a set of 1,971 important decretal rulings organized into five books. A second supplement to Gratian followed in 1298, when Boniface VIII authorized the publication of *Sixtus*, so-called because it was a sixth book of decretal legislation to go with the other five contained in the *Liber Extra*. Gratian's *Decretum* and its glosses, together with the six supplementary decretal volumes, were now so legally comprehensive and effective that they remained the standard collection of western canon law for six centuries, down to 1918.[24]

Resolving the inherited confusions of ancient canon law completed the transformation of the papacy into the fully functioning executive head of western Christendom in both principle and practice. By the time of the prolific Pope Alexander III, it was widely accepted there was only one point of authority for resolving questionable religious issues, and that point was Rome. Papal rulings had long been one possible mechanism for resolving an ecclesiastical dispute of any kind, but in the late Roman period (and for long afterwards) decretals had been overwhelmed numerically by imperial and conciliar rulings, and outgunned in terms of authority by the decisions of ecumenical councils. These earlier patterns of Christian legal authority had changed out of all recognition in the course of the twelfth century. First, the papacy had taken over the mantle of calling ecumenical councils (first in 1123) and, thanks to Gratian and the school of canon legal studies his work generated, it quickly became established among western Churchmen that new papal rulings ranked highest in authority, so that papal decretals consequently became the weapon of choice for resolving all new problems. Even here, however, much of the initiative remained outside Rome, since it was how the academic lawyers excerpted and commented upon the initial papal decisions which determined their ultimate significance. More than 150 of Alexander III's rulings, for instance, tackled tricky problems of marriage, but for the most part on an individual and ad hoc basis. It used to be argued that a clear line of evolution in his thought on the subject could be traced, but closer scrutiny has shown this to be illusory. Alexander's individual decisions in particular were often inconsistent with one another, and any greater coherence was actually the work of the academic commentators and judges who applied the rulings in practice.[25] All the same, this unfolding revolution in western canon law not only made the system usable, but also resolved the very real problem of distance, which would otherwise have continued to hinder the exercise of root-and-branch papal influence over the functioning of the dispersed local Church communities that in principle owed it allegiance.

The emergence of a coherent and universally recognized body of papally authorized canon law, and especially the developing practice of referring new or otherwise unresolvable legal issues to Rome and collating the results in written legal collections, eventually circumvented the logistical problems which had up to that point hamstrung Rome's capacity to dictate local religious practice in any detail. By the middle of the thirteenth century, Roman authority was available in a comprehensive set of law books, which could be transported even to the most far-flung locality. To know what a pope thought in late antiquity or in the early Middle Ages, you had to travel to Rome or send him a letter and wait for a reply. From 1234 onwards, with the publication of the *Liber Extra*, papal opinion on most matters was now available in books that papally licensed judges could use to settle cases in every part of the Latin Christian world. For the first time, western Christendom, and all its many, diverse local congregations, could now reasonably be expected to define accepted Christian practice according to the one unified, basic pattern set out in this collection of texts.

Accepting the utility and authority of the emerging body of papal-focused canon law also resolved any remaining ideological deficit. During the Investiture Controversy, papal decisions had been regularly disputed – by other Church leaders as well as by the emperor, and not just within the lands of the Holy Roman Empire, but across much of western Christendom. By the early thirteenth century, it was no longer possible to do so, because the clerical leadership of every realm and territorial lordship had accepted the authority of the new legal texts. The new canon law meant that in both theory and practice, the rhythms of religious life across broad tracts of Europe were now, and for the first time, being dictated from Rome.

The emergence of this alternative religious Roman Empire of the central Middle Ages was the result of a long, and often counter-intuitive process. The prestige of the congregation of the city of Rome was an established fact of the Christian world from its earliest beginnings. But such prestige did not (and in fact could not) translate into any recognized authority to exercise regular practical leadership, even in the Latin west, before the year 1000. The kinds of powers exercised by later popes had, in both theory and fact, been exercised between the early fourth century and the end of the millennium by a sequence of Roman, Byzantine, Carolingian and other emperors. In that era, popes exercised considerable rights within their established patriarchal domains in central and southern Italy (and Sicily, before papal control was lost in the period of iconoclasm), but widely recognized papal religious authority was the product of gradual processes of religious and legal transformation that unfolded only slowly over a period of about three hundred years from the mid-ninth century. Not only did practical papal authority emerge much later than has often been supposed, but the process which cemented it in place depended more upon the initiatives of leading Churchmen in northern Europe than any master plan hatched in Rome itself.

It was Carolingian and post-Carolingian Churchmen north of the Alps who first began to imagine a world of overarching papal religious authority, a vision based in no small measure on the imaginary patterns of *Pseudo-Isidore*, which some of their peers had conjured into existence through masterful forgery. And it was again primarily a sequence of northern Churchmen who, when opportunity presented itself in the mid-eleventh century, set in motion the practical reforms required to rescue the papal see from the hands of competing Italian aristocratic networks and turn it into a self-conscious centre of general religious authority, equipped with the necessary institutions and procedures to project that authority across the Roman west. By this stage, the logic of a much-enlarged Latin Christendom – encompassing far too many separate polities for a single ruler, even a Holy Roman emperor, to dominate – probably meant that papal authority was going to win out in some way and at some time, for there was no other available authority structure with sufficient breadth to offer unified leadership to a Latin Christian community. A community, moreover, which, thanks to the reform processes set in motion under the Carolingian emperors, now understood itself as forming one, closely united Church. But contingency still had a part to play: in the form of both the First Crusade (whose miraculous success, against all the odds, greatly advanced the ideological authority of the papacy) and the sudden impact of analytical techniques imported from Roman law, which inspired generations of canonists to turn the inchoate mass of potential sources for Church regulations that existed in around 1100 into a functioning, coherent system of papal canon law over the course of about a century.

In the later twelfth century, and perhaps from the reign of Pope Alexander III when the decretal revolution really exploded, it starts to make sense – for the first time – to talk about the Latin Church as a singular corporate entity. Up to this point, the Christian Church of western Europe had in reality consisted of largely autonomous local Christian communities, with generally devolved, polymorphous authority structures. The impact of more centralized decision-making was only periodic and limited, in the area primarily of doctrine under late Roman emperors, and of practice under their early Carolingian successors. Even under the latter, the impact was more theoretical than practical, something evident in debates over the great reforming bugbears of simony and, especially, clerical marriage. Despite all the huffing and puffing from the ninth century onwards, clerical marriage was still widespread at all levels in the Latin west long into the twelfth century. Archbishop Thurstan of York (1114–40) and his brother, Bishop Audoen of Évreux (1113–39), both originally followed their father, Ansgar, into clerical orders as canons of St Paul's. Examples both north and south of the Channel could easily be multiplied; the same applied further down the scale as well, where local priesthoods (not well represented in surviving sources) may often have been hereditary positions in practice, as with the benefice of Eye in Hertfordshire, which is known still to have passed through several generations of one clerical family in the century after 1150.

Gratian's *Decretum* and the new decretal legislation it inspired massively reinforced the pious declarations of all the earlier reforming synods of the tenth and eleventh centuries and, in the later twelfth and thirteenth centuries, serious, centrally driven change finally set in. Clerical marriage was declared legally invalid, and clerical keeping of concubines became an increasingly punished offence. While familial patronage, the dynastic passing on of ecclesiastical office, did not disappear, it began to take the form of uncles preferring nephews, rather than fathers their sons. One well-documented life story which illustrates this sea-change is that of Ælred of Rievaulx, who came from a long family line of priests from the north-east of England. His great-grandfather had cared for the incorrupted body of St Cuthbert, cutting the saint's hair and nails; his grandfather and father had both cared for the saints of Hexham. But in 1138 Eilaf, Ælred's father, fell ill. He decided, with the world changing around him, to give up all claims to the hereditary family property and end his days as a monk at Durham. Ælred himself thought much the same: he had already joined the Cistercians.[26]

What was true of Ælred gradually became true for many local clerical families across the Latin west: an unstoppable tide of Church law, working in combination with the ideological expectations that underlay it, was pushing them all in the same direction – and with increasing momentum – as the twelfth century unwound. By the mid-thirteenth century, the western Church's leadership had not only declared emphatically that priests should be celibate, breaking with ancient Christian tradition, but had generally managed to enforce that decision as well. In effect, clergy were now subject to the same rules on celibacy as monks, collapsing the long-standing older tripartite Christian conception of humanity – monks, clergy, laity – into just a two-fold distinction between clergy and laity.

The besetting sin of clerical marriage – first raised in monastic circles back in the ninth century as part of a heightened vision of the significance of the Mass (p. 430) – had finally been resolved. Over the same time frame, the associated problem of simony also found some resolution. The new rhetoric demonizing the lay domination of ecclesiastical institutions, which had also begun in reformed monastic contexts in the Carolingian period, found practical expression in new attitudes towards the local parish churches that landowners had been erecting in such vast numbers since the ninth century. Between 1028 and 1126, the monastery of Monte Cassino was gifted the ownership of no less than 193 local churches, of which 186 were handed over by former lay owners. At Angers in the Loire valley, 44 transfers of churches from lay ownership are recorded for the period 1050 to 1100, and another 102 in the subsequent half century.[27] Myriad similar transfers were taking place all over Christendom: the previous owners, it seems, ready to respond to the new clarion call that to work properly ecclesiastical institutions needed to be freed from secular control. The overall pattern is clear. By the end of the twelfth century, not only had the new canon law helped create a much more unified priesthood right across Latin Europe, but different ecclesiastical authorities at the regional level were exercising much more unified control over tens of thousands of local churches as well, their lay owners having responded to demands that they should surrender control. In effect, several originally separate strands of revolutionary transformation – church-building, a massive expansion in ecclesiastical education, and the emergence of effective papal authority over a Church structure that had been partly separated from lay control – had now come together to create, for the first time, a unified religious institutional structure with the potential capacity to deliver a singular vision of lay religiosity to every local congregation across the Latin west. A weapon with so much potential would not lie idle for long.

13
The Economy of Salvation

The largest council of Christian leaders the world had ever seen opened in Rome on 11 November 1215. Four hundred bishops and eight hundred abbots made the journey to the city that was now indisputably the practical as well as the symbolic capital of western Christendom. Bishops unable to attend sent representatives; also in attendance was a team of observers sent by the eastern patriarchs. Nothing could better illustrate the complete transfer from emperors to popes of overall religious authority over the Latin Church. The fourth of the new-style ecumenical councils to be held in the Lateran Palace, headquarters of the popes for some nine hundred years, its sessions took place in the palace's Great Hall and were presided over by the man who had convoked the council in the first place: Pope Innocent III. Not only did the pope call the council, but – usurping a second long-standing imperial prerogative – he was also responsible for setting its highly ambitious agenda. As he put it in his invitation to the leading clergy of the French province of Vienne, the council's aim was 'to root out vices and plant virtues, to correct excesses and reform morals, to eliminate heresies and strengthen faith, to silence discords and establish peace'.[1]

Not surprisingly, given all the background noise about simony and clerical marriage, one prevailing theme of the council was clerical corruption. The council accordingly outlawed various practices that had come to be associated with these greatest of evils (in the eyes of reformers) – including the appointing of underage relatives to Church positions, the selling of clerical offices, and open unchastity – and backed up the usual condemnations with practical enforcement measures, decreeing that any formal complaint against a cleric had to be fully investigated, not swept under the carpet. Monks also came in for close scrutiny, with each archiepiscopal province mandated to establish a supervisory body or 'chapter' to ensure that monastic discipline was being properly maintained within its boundaries (generalizing precedents set in Denmark in 1205, and Rome itself in 1210). Here, the council was pushing at an open door. In the two generations before the fourth Lateran council, growing acceptance of the authority of the new-style, papally dominated canon law had already seen the consolidation of official new standards of behaviour with regard to clerical sexuality and modes of appointment. These were written into both Gratian's *Decretum* and the subsequent, supportive papal decretals. At the start of the thirteenth century, therefore, Pope Innocent found himself in charge not only of a much more geographically extensive organization of priests and churches, thanks to the many thousands of new church buildings constructed in the previous few centuries, but also of a much more united institutional entity, brought together by its newly codified legal system. Lateran IV set out to put this brand-new religious delivery-system to work, by defining a comprehensive programme of required religious practice for all the laity of Latin Christendom.

While much of its agenda for the laity would have been perfectly recognizable to Charlemagne and his Churchmen, the council broke new ground by anchoring its requirements within a fully articulated doctrine of seven sacraments, rituals which were henceforth to accompany good Christians from cradle to grave, giving defined religious shape to their lives. These were baptism, confirmation (a rite where the individual confirmed the promises to be faithful made on their behalf at baptism), ordination, marriage, confession, Eucharist (Holy Communion), and extreme unction (anointing with holy oil those about to die) (Plate 32). All seven were not available to everyone, marriage and ordination now defined alternative life paths for laity and clergy; the other five, however, were shared in by all the faithful. Of these five, baptism and communion were long-established Christian rituals, but Lateran IV placed equal emphasis on all the other sacraments, some of which, such as confession and extreme unction, had previously been largely confined to the more intense patterns of monastic piety. A striking development was the sacramentalization of marriage. This marked the culmination of a revolutionary change that had gradually taken Christian practice and ideology light years away from its early suspicions about marriage as an act that focused the individual's attention on the things of the physical world, rather than of the spiritual (p. 50). As the council made clear, these sacraments were much more than symbols of God's love, and of the individual's willingness to respond to it. They were acts of spiritual power: grace-imparting processes which advanced the individual on the path to salvation.

Ambitious to instil a pattern of lay religious observance based on these sacraments, the council's directives emphasized two things: first, lay people's responsibility to orient their religious devotions around this potent set of salvific acts; and, second, the responsibility of the clergy to enable them to do so. Perhaps the most significant of the council's directives, Canon 21, decreed that all lay men and women should make confession at least once a year, duly perform any penance they were set, and take Holy Communion at Easter. (Sin could take an infinite variety of forms, though a commonly employed (alliterative in the Latin) formula of interrogation to be used by priests in the ritual of confession – 'when, where, how, with whom, and how often' – inescapably brings to mind sexual transgression.)[2] Taken together, all of the sacraments, above all the emphasis on extreme unction (since death might come unexpectedly), required that priests be constantly on hand to perform their part in these vital rituals. As such, the sacramental definition of piety set out at the fourth Lateran council dictated the required rhythm of religious life in all the local parish churches of Latin Europe – and, by extension, increased central control over the spiritual lives of its flock throughout Christendom. This new sacramental focus on lay piety was made possible by the intense building activity of the previous few centuries, which had effectively put a church and a priest in every local community; without them, its implementation would have been simply impossible.

Further rulings addressed some broader religious agendas. Canon 10 concerned itself with preaching, the crucial mechanism by which the largely illiterate laity had always been taught about its religion. Here, the council was particularly worried about arrangements in large dioceses where the bishop (responsible for preaching within Christianity since antiquity) might struggle to ensure overall provision. Canon 11 was concerned with the quality of religious education, demanding that each metropolitan archbishop teach the Holy Scriptures to priests and all other members of clerical orders who had any responsibility for lay congregations. Canons 19 and 20 turned their attention to church buildings, requiring that pre-consecrated bread and wine (so-called 'reserved sacrament') be kept in sanctified conditions within the church, and that churches themselves should be treated as sacred places, reserved only for religious services (marking the moment when villages started to build communal halls separate from their churches).[3]

Overall, then, the decrees of the fourth Lateran council present us not only with a papacy that had effectively taken over from emperors the reins of overarching religious authority in the Latin west, but with a broad definition of the religious duties of both local clergy and their lay parishioners that has continued in the Catholic world down to the present day. The thirteenth and fourteenth centuries would see some further elaboration of these duties, but the council set out a basic pattern of required practice and belief that would prevail right across Latin Christendom up until the Reformation – and, in many parts of it, far beyond. But while aspects of this coherent, monolithic vision of 'correct' Christianity can be traced directly back to the Carolingian period – for instance, the heightened emphasis on the importance of the Mass, and hence on the purity of its clerical celebrants and on the necessity of ensuring that churches were appropriately holy places – the evidence that these emphases had had much effect on actual practice in the Carolingian era is slight. Carolingian piety also lacked any clearly defined doctrine of seven sacraments.

Where, then, had the new sacramental definition of appropriate religious piety come from, and how was it able to command such comprehensive adherence? To answer these questions, we need to go back more than a century, to the era of the First Crusade, to explore both the precise nature of the more intense – more directly penitential – patterns of lay piety that underlay the act of crusading, and an accompanying revolution in educational culture at the highest levels of the Latinate Church, which eventually redirected that greater intensity along the theological path towards sacramental piety.

'ONLY THE PENITENT SHALL PASS'

Possibly the single most significant point about the whole crusading era – aside from the monumental degree of luck involved in the capture of Jerusalem, which allowed the crusading phenomenon to gather momentum – is the fact that the first expedition set out at all. Without the willing participation of significant elements of the militarized landowning class of the Latin west, neither this initial campaign nor any of its successors could have happened.[4] That they were willing to do so tells us something very important about how patterns of lay piety had evolved since the Carolingian era.

Some crusaders, as we've seen, were in it for the potential gains, and others perhaps didn't have much choice in the matter. Generally speaking, the very early crusaders tended to sign up as part of hierarchical local groupings: if your immediate lord decided to go, you often went too. That said, as an important thread in recent crusading historiography has emphasized, and as many of the documents prepared by the crusaders themselves declare, Christian piety was clearly a powerful strand in crusading motivations.[5]

This coheres with a broader tranche of evidence showing that, alongside many of the leading cathedral and reformed monastic clergy, substantial numbers of western Europe's warrior elite were also buying into the values of the Carolingian and post-Carolingian projects of religious reform in the final centuries of the first millennium. Even by the eleventh century, compositional literary competence was generally still the preserve of the better-educated cathedral and monastic clergy, so there is not a huge amount of direct manuscript evidence. But there is some. The will of Eberhard of Friuli (dated 867), a high-level Carolingian imperial magnate, confirms that Eberhard possessed his own personal prayer books, while examples of the prayer books themselves survive from the time of Emperor Otto III (980–1002). The manual that the Carolingian aristocrat Lady Dhuoda wrote for her son William, as she sent him off to the court of Charles the Bald as a hostage for her husband's loyalty, likewise, not only urged on him a fairly standard range of Christian virtues but stressed the value of praying during the day at the seven canonical hours (while admitting that she had herself sometimes been lax in this regard). Her final advice was for her son to establish a regular routine of praying for the spiritual salvation of the dead on both sides of his family. By the tenth and eleventh centuries, when the manuscript evidence becomes more plentiful, individual members of the warrior elite both owned their own prayer books and used them as part of personal or household regimes of regular piety. In one of many examples, one late Anglo-Saxon lady commanded her trusted servant Ælfwaru – originally the unfree daughter of a huntsman – to say four psalters (each of the 150 psalms recited out loud) every week for the good of her mistress's soul for the first month after the latter's death, and similar examples are easy to find.[6]

Though increasingly numerous as we reach the eleventh century and the era of crusade, such books give us no more than a series of snapshots of upper-class lay piety in action. A second body of material confirms that such piety was generally becoming more intense on the eve of the crusading era: the construction across the Latin west of thousands of local churches, the majority of them built on the initiative of local militarized landowners. Financial interests were certainly in play here – the desire to corner at least a portion of tithe and other ecclesiastical revenues – but piety, alongside financial gain, surely played a significant role. Human action usually involves mixed motives, and many of the founders' descendants proved ready to hand over control of their churches, with their attendant revenues, to ecclesiastical institutions in the eleventh and twelfth centuries (p. 506).

In the same era, too, the really rich landowners among Europe's warrior elite were busy founding or revamping reformed Benedictine monastic houses across much of the Latin west. In England and Wales, the number of nunneries increased from seventy at the end of the first millennium to more than four hundred over the next century and a half. Expressing piety by an act of religious foundation could also now take an increasing variety of forms. Thirty-two new canonries (local priests living according to the revised *Rule* of Chrodegang of Metz: p. 423) were created in the province of Rouen alone between 1119 and 1200. Unlike the builders of parish churches, many of these monastic founders recorded their gifts in writing, providing explicit accounts of their motives. The central, expressed concern of all these grand founders and sponsors – not to mention of the many lesser gift-givers, often from the founders' social networks, who followed in their wake (the abbey of Cluny received more than four thousand donations, many of them small, in the first century of its existence) – was the welfare of their souls. The central claim of revised Benedictine monasticism was that it had created a new, and more powerful form of Christian holiness: a piece of heaven on earth (p. 422). Accepting this claim, in the context of the developing emphasis on penance, landowners great and small, lay and ecclesiastical, were ready to ally themselves to its representatives, so that the monks' prayers could help raise their souls to heaven. As Duke William of Aquitaine put it in 910, in his foundation charter for Cluny, 'This is my trust, this is my hope . . . that although I myself am unable to despise all things, nevertheless by receiving those who do despise the world, whom I believe to be righteous, I may receive the reward of the righteous.' As ever, mixed motives applied. William was asserting his social status by being seen to be rich enough to make such a pious gift, and claiming, too, of course, that he was capable of acting on God's behalf. But a genuine concern for the state of his soul was also part of the package: monastic foundations were animated, as much as anything else, by spiritual concerns.[7]

This was clearly the case, for instance, with the monastery of Vilich, at the junction of the Rhine and Sieg Rivers, founded by Count Megengoz and his wife Gerberga after their only son, Godefrid, was killed on campaign against the Elbe Slavs in 977. Godefrid's body was brought back and buried in the monastery's church, as, in due course, were those of his parents and three sisters. Family tragedy had prompted an intense turn to the spiritual, with the parents also vowing to abstain from sexual intercourse and to devote themselves entirely to study and reflection. While not every new foundation had a religious backstory of such emotional intensity, the basic exchange between donors and reformed Benedictine monasticism was explicitly choreographed in such terms. In return for a financial gift, the occupants of these small patches of heaven on earth would engage in regular prayer to help get a donor's soul into paradise. *Books of Life – Libri Vitae* – and necrologies were the characteristic tools by which revised Benedictine houses organized their relations with participating lay donors. *Books of Life* were undifferentiated lists of all an institution's donors, to be left on the high altar and prayed for in general terms during services. Necrologies recorded specific gifts by date and size, so that commemorations of individual donors could be made on the anniversary of their gifts. In both cases, the nature of the exchange could not be clearer.[8]

These expressions of upper-class lay piety – everything from familial prayer circles to small gifts to large-scale foundations – all share the same striking concern for the state of the human soul, and the necessity of looking after it, even following the death of the body. Such concerns were not in themselves new. Penance for sin, whether paid for by prayer or in almsgiving, periodically features in some of the western pastoral literature written by Churchmen in the immediate post-Roman period, as we have seen.[9] What was new in this period, however, was much more evidence for a general and growing concern among the secular elite with the necessary penance due for sin. Whereas post-Roman Christianity's first engagement with warrior culture seems to have been largely unproblematic – Churchmen of the early medieval west generally mobilizing the Old Testament to make a Christian allegiance a straightforward proposition for an elite for whom violent military action was structurally central to basic life patterns – by the end of the first millennium this was changing. Even legitimate, public warfare to defend the peace on the orders of a prince was now classed as sinful. For such military activity the early eleventh-century legal collection of Bishop Burchard of Worms (which enjoyed widespread circulation before being eclipsed by Gratian's *Decretum*) prescribed three annual forty-day fasts. The recommended penance rose to forty days of fasting for seven consecutive years, for any fighting that was not in defence of the peace.

Monastic saints' *Lives* of the same era, correspondingly, championed the view that it was impossible to live the life of a normal member of the lay elite and find salvation. One such life, of St Gerald – Gerald of Aurillac, a French aristocrat from the Auvergne – apparently offers us an exception but, so his *Life* claims, he had been able to approach sanctity only by rejecting the normal values of his class. Gerald had himself tonsured in clerical style (though he wore a small hat to cover it up); when he was robbed, he deliberately failed to resist, refusing to shed blood. He also refused to marry, carefully safeguarding his chastity:

such was Gerald's sexual modesty, the *Life* reports, that even after death, his hands wouldn't stay on his chest but kept moving to cover his private parts. Even if not everyone shared the pessimism of the *Life of Gerald* about the possibility of elite lay salvation (it was composed by an abbot of Cluny who was heavily invested in the monastic reform agenda), the standards of required, post-*correctio* Christian piety had become much more demanding than in the early Middle Ages, with heaven an infinitely more distant prospect.[10] Against this backdrop, it is hardly surprising that the manuscript evidence for penitential texts begins to proliferate in the same era. Carolingian-era piety brought a new stress on sin and penance, and the evidence strongly suggests that large swathes of the landowning military class increasingly bought into this new vision of Christian piety in the tenth and eleventh centuries. Leading clerics, in response, busied themselves inventing new means by which necessary penance might be performed.

Alongside sexual abstinence, and well-trodden fasting regimes of bread and water, pilgrimage began to be articulated as an explicitly penitential act, in spite of its inherent challenges – or, rather, because of them. Not only was pilgrimage expensive and disruptive of normal life, but long-distance travel could be dangerous. In both 921 and 923, large parties of Anglo-Saxon pilgrims on their way to Rome were killed in the Alps by Saracen raiders, who periodically ranged far and wide up the Rhône valley and into Piedmont from their fortress of Fraxinet in Provence (their *pièce de résistance*, some fifty years later, was to kidnap Abbot Maiolus of Cluny for ransom; on his release he organized the military campaign which finally exterminated them). While Rome was the original destination of choice for the pilgrims of Latin Europe, the tenth and eleventh centuries saw the number of potential sacred targets increase, with Compostela, Mont St Michel, Monte Gargano and, above all, Jerusalem becoming increasingly popular. By the eleventh century, Holy Land pilgrimage was increasingly common, and the rigours and expense of such distant travel universally understood as constituting an act of penance – as, when it came, was the act of crusading itself.

On his great preaching tour in 1094 to drum up support for what became the First Crusade, Pope Urban II couched his call for crusade in terms of penance. Participants could, he said, have some, or all, of the ill-effects of their accumulated sinfulness washed away by joining up for the long march to Jerusalem. Alongside all the evidence for personal regimes of piety, and large-scale ecclesiastical foundation, the willingness of Latin Europe's warriors to participate in large numbers in the arduous, financially demanding enterprise of crusade is direct confirmation that, by the later eleventh century, many had already bought into the new post-*correctio* theology of personal penitential piety.[11]

Given the overwhelmingly military character of western Europe's landowning elite, this might seem unlikely. But, as a group, these landowners had been exposed to a century and more of the ideologies of Christian Empire under Carolingian rule: an ideological package which had continued undisturbed under their imperial successors the Ottonians. The repetition of Christian religious idea-sets, which made the military patterns of their lives so problematic, was a constant of court and public life in this era; so too the greater emphasis on penance as the basic remedy for the state of the soul. With the structures of ecclesiastical and secular power still so intimately intertwined, moreover, many of the clergy pushing forward the new religious ideologies and their accompanying reform agendas belonged to the same social class and familial networks as the warrior aristocracy and gentry. Indeed, high-ranking clergy from important families often continued to participate in some of the characteristic activities of their class: episcopal sees and major monasteries still all owed knight service to the rulers of the territories in which they were situated, and responsibility for the organization and leadership of these military contingents fell squarely on the Churchmen themselves. This was considered normal even by the most reform-minded among them – including by the pope himself. In his younger days, the future pope Leo IX was a senior ecclesiastical administrator to the then aged and ill bishop of Toul, his duties involving the command and organization 'of the forces of knights from Toul', recruited to serve in the imperial army. His *Life* was happy to present Leo as a natural military commander, a 'wise and circumspect' campaigner who personally 'chose the site for his men's camp; he organized their posts . . . he took charge of expenditure and wages . . . he distributed to each . . . his rations in reasonable quantity.'[12]

Leo IX's experience was not remotely exceptional among western Europe's ecclesiastical leadership. With senior clerics (whether they hailed from a monastic or a cathedral background) often related to their secular counterparts – Pope Leo, for instance, was cousin to the Salian emperors – and with most higher-level ecclesiastical appointments coming about through connection and preferment, there was a huge degree of familial overlap between the secular and ecclesiastical leaderships of the central Middle Ages. All of which explains why there should be such a demonstrable overlap, too, in the broad cultural values shared by the two groups, despite the obvious differences between the lives they led.

Another important phenomenon of the period helps confirm the point. In the final quarter of the tenth century, southern France – Burgundy and Aquitaine in particular – witnessed a whole series of locally organized councils (attended by both important clergy and laymen), whose central purpose was to establish ecclesiastical protection for certain non-combatant categories of individual and institution: particularly churches, monasteries and their attendant clergy, but also women and children. The earliest reported 'Peace of God' initiative (so-called after the documents these councils produced) occurred at the town of Le Puy in 975, with some half-a-dozen more examples following in the intervening generation, including an exceptionally well-documented gathering at Poitiers in the 1010s. In the early eleventh century, such meetings and their attendant declarations spread across northern France and into the Rhineland. They were succeeded by a second sequence of councils, focusing this time on the 'Truce of God' – mandating particular times of year when warfare was banned. These included the great Church festivals of the religious year, and also local saints' celebrations. The first truce council was held at Toulouse in 1027, the last closing at Narbonne in 1054.

The Peace and Truce of God movements used to be understood as responses to a general breakdown of law and order, enacted by desperate local clergy as the last vestiges of Carolingian imperial authority disappeared, giving way to local anarchy and the oppressive assertion of tighter forms of local lordship. Every aspect of this story, however, has now been rewritten. The disappearance of Carolingian monarchic power in western Francia did entrench the power of local lordships – but this was no sudden revolution. Nor was the general political character of the times particularly anarchic.

Although under ecclesiastical leadership, still more to the point, the Peace and Truce councils were not a manifestation of Churchmen desperately trying to preserve lives and order. The first meeting at Le Puy was a joint initiative of the bishop acting alongside, and with the unstinting co-operation of, two secular lords to whom he was related: the counts of Brioude and Géronde. Viewed close up, the Peace and Truce of God movements turn out to be a further articulation of shared Christian values among elite networks that included both ecclesiastical and secular leaders, acting to reinforce each other's authority in a changing political context.[13]

This spread of shared, more intensive forms of penitential piety among the religious and secular elites of post-Carolingian Europe provides one key backstory to the new religious ideology institutionalized at the fourth Lateran council. But the precise sacramental articulation espoused at Lateran IV in 1215 was still notably lacking. This extra precision was the product of a cultural revolution that unfolded across the Latin west in the two generations after the First Crusade.

SCHOOL AND UNIVERSITY

In around 1079, a minor Breton nobleman called Berengar celebrated the safe arrival of his firstborn son, Peter Abelard. Originally named Pierre le Pallet, after the village of his birth, Abelard is chiefly known today for his love affair with his pupil, the future nun Héloïse, which ended in his castration at the hands of her outraged uncle. Abelard, who would write up this story in his autobiographical letter of the early 1130s, the *Historia Calamitatum* (*History of My Calamities*), was one of the great philosopher-theologians of the age. Later in life, Abelard was embroiled in two major theological dogfights, both of which focused on his use of classical learning to explore important matters of Christian doctrine. In the first, his account of the Trinity, *Theologia*, was condemned as heretical by a provincial synod held at Soissons in 1121, as a result of which Peter was forced to burn the offending work himself. Twenty years later, he found himself on the wrong side of, among others, the formidable Benedictine Cistercian theologian Bernard of Clairvaux. This culminated in a further condemnation of Abelard's thinking at a major council held in the French city of Sens in June 1141. The sentence was confirmed by a papal bull issued in the following month, which excommunicated Abelard, commanding now that all his works should be burned, and decreed that he himself should be confined in perpetual, silent monastic detention.[14] Why Abelard took the intellectual path he did takes us to the heart of the twelfth-century revolution in Latin educational culture that was directly responsible for the new sacramental definitions of piety enshrined at the fourth Lateran council.

This revolution began with new learning – or, rather, a return to some much older learning – in the late eleventh and early twelfth centuries. At its higher levels, the Carolingian Christian educational programme made some use of classical learning. This was derived from the extensive and primarily Greek philosophical and scientific traditions of the ancient world – but it was only available in the summary Latin translations Boethius had made, back in the early sixth century under Ostrogothic rule, of a limited quantity of introductory material. In the middle of the eleventh century, this narrow intellectual framework was blown open by Latin Christendom's increasing contacts with Constantinople, and, above all, with the world of Islam, where over the centuries Arab-language scholarship had both translated and continued to innovate within many ancient Greek mathematical, scientific and philosophical traditions.

These new contacts took many forms, not least trade, and they were not always peaceful: both *reconquista* within the Iberian peninsula and crusading in the Near East played significant roles in their intensification. In cultural terms, however, western European scholars searched out and translated into Latin a whole series of more advanced Greek texts, works that had not been available in the west for over half a millennium. These included, among many others, Aristotle's works on science, logic and ethics, Euclid's mathematical treatises, Ptolemy's *Astronomy*, and the medical textbooks of Hippocrates and Galen (in many cases supplemented by Latin translations of key Arabic texts, which had expanded on the ancient traditions in important ways). A nice example of the scholarly activity characteristic of the age is provided by the Englishman Daniel of Morley, who in the first half of the twelfth century travelled from his native Norfolk to Toledo in Muslim Spain. There, he attended advanced lectures on all the scientific subjects (mathematics, geometry and astronomy) in which Arab learning had continued the old Greek traditions, and brought back home with him a priceless collection of new texts.[15]

As these new texts became available more widely, their reception redefined the educational curriculum for aspiring high-level Latin Christian intellectuals. The philosophical logic taught entirely through Boethius' introductory translations soon came to be known as 'old logic'. It was demoted to the role of primer for the more complex 'new logic', which could now be studied more or less at first hand through new Latin translations of Aristotle's *Prior* and *Posterior Analytics*. In the hands of Bernard of Chartres (d. *c.* 1124), head of the cathedral school in that city, the new texts became the basis of a more developed version of the Seven Liberal Arts' curriculum – the *trivium* (grammar, rhetoric and logic), then the *quadrivium* (mathematics, geometry, astronomy and music) – first defined in the Carolingian period (p. 416), but now taught through a much wider range of texts. Proving highly influential, Bernard's curriculum – with more of the newly recovered texts added in as they became available – quickly spread to all the major intellectual centres of the contemporary Latin world, both north across the English Channel, and south of the Alps and the Pyrenees.[16]

Abelard was part of an initial intellectual generation that became intoxicated with this new learning, standing in awe of its intellectual authority. Bernard of Chartres himself famously declared that he and his contemporaries were 'dwarfs standing on the shoulders of giants'. Peter of Blois (*c.* 1130–1211) gushed, still more enthusiastically, 'One does not go from the darkness of ignorance to the light of knowledge without rereading with ever more ardent love the works of the Ancients.'[17]

But this was not about knowledge for its own sake. As convinced Christians, Abelard and his contemporaries brought to bear the analytical techniques newly recovered from these great classical authorities to shed new light on the theological problems central to Christian tradition: problems which, since the time of Charlemagne, they had chiefly been studying through the Scriptures and the writings of the old Church Fathers. The result was an explosion of theological enquiry on a scale not seen since the late Roman period. A characteristic, if ultimately unsuccessful, experiment in what is usually known as the Twelfth-century Renaissance saw the philosopher Thierry of Chartres (d. *c.* 1150) make no fewer than four sustained attempts to use Greek mathematics to explain the interrelationships of the three persons of the Christian Godhead.

Abelard likewise mobilized the 'new learning' to pursue the most profound of the Christian mysteries, applying the rigour of Greek logic to the scriptural evidence for Trinitarian relationships. But others were offended by the application of what they saw as pagan logic to the deep mysteries of the Christian faith. In 1121, pupils of Anselm of Laon, formerly a teacher of Abelard, condemned his *Theologia* for using pagan Greek logic to explore these Trinitarian relationships, arguing that following its dictates had led him into heresy. Abelard's later quarrel with Bernard of Clairvaux was similar in character. Trained in the more restricted, Carolingian Benedictine monastic curriculum, Bernard accused Abelard of being led by his intellectual presumption into heretical positions. It was on this basis that Abelard was sentenced to permanent monastic incarceration without the matter being put to formal trial.

All of this was hugely distressing for Abelard, of course, but his cause célèbre can give a misleading impression of the overall reception of the new learning in twelfth-century Latin Christendom. Many of the problems Abelard faced were generated by his own overbearing intellectual arrogance, which alienated many scholars (not to mention former teachers) who were engaged in broadly similar intellectual pursuits. And while argument over details never ceased, the intellectual rigour generated by reintroducing Greek philosophical and scientific traditions into the high-level educational curricula of the Latin west was so obviously superior to what preceded it, that ambitious students were attracted to teachers of the new learning in ever-increasing numbers. And not just students of Christian theology. The new learning produced not only theologians but highly competent bureaucratic administrators, able to handle both complex argumentation and complex written instruments: individuals who were in increasing demand in the twelfth century, a time in which ecclesiastical and royal governmental structures – both focusing more on taxation and legal administration – were undergoing radical expansion. As a result, the new pattern of higher education, as well as being intellectually exciting, quickly became the route to preferment and high office, and the initial furore over using 'pagan' learning to train Christian thinkers and theologians subsided.

Abelard's intellectual calamities belong to a relatively brief period in the first half of the twelfth century, when the rediscovered learning's growing influence still faced serious resistance. It is striking testimony, in fact, to how close its ultimate victory already was that, after his condemnation in 1141, Abelard did not live out the rest of his life in monastic confinement, as his sentence dictated. Rather, he found a warm welcome at the reformed Benedictine house of Cluny whose then abbot, Peter the Venerable, had himself translated some of the important newly discovered classical texts. It puts Bernard of Clairvaux's view firmly into perspective to find that, by the 1140s, the new learning was finding acceptance even within some of the oldest established monastic circles of the Latin west, and an accompanying teaching infrastructure was soon generated.[18]

At the start of the twelfth century, as the newly rediscovered texts began to make an impact, intellectual expertise remained highly fragmented between the different monastic and cathedral schools of the Latin west. This reflected both the haphazard process by which individual scholars such as Daniel of Morley originally collected the new texts, and the random way in which the discoveries then circulated. When Abelard first arrived in Paris as a young man at the end of the eleventh century, he had found only one teacher giving lectures on philosophy at the cathedral school of Notre Dame: William of Champeaux (another of the teachers with whom he later quarrelled). Different areas of expertise could be studied at the hands of different scholars – but they held posts at different schools. This meant that the bright student's natural progression was peripatetic, moving between different masters and schools (as reputations rose and fell) to acquire different skills. Which is why, having mastered Greek logic in Paris, Abelard moved on to the school of Laon in northern France, then enjoying a brief prominence under the direction of the brothers Ralph and Anselm, whose curriculum for biblical studies was highly innovative for its time.

Within Abelard's lifetime, the geographical distribution of scholarly excellence changed out of all recognition. When the English scholar John of Salisbury came in turn to study in Paris in 1136, he found a whole range of expert masters giving lectures not just on the individual subjects of the *trivium* and *quadrivium*, but in the more advanced subjects too: canon and Roman law, medicine, and theology. These teachers included Abelard himself, who, in between disputes, taught logic there. The gathering of scholarly expertise to be found in mid-twelfth-century Paris was unrivalled in Latin Europe – and it meant that there was no longer any need for students to travel between institutions.

Initially, the process of change was organic. Most high-level teachers made their livings by charging fees to students who wanted to attend their lectures. Teachers naturally clustered where student demand was strongest, and students congregated at known centres of intellectual excellence whose reputations would smooth their paths to preferment and higher office within both ecclesiastical and royal administrative structures. (John of Salisbury, among many others, took the latter path.) It didn't take long, however, for this organic clustering of expertise to take on the more structured forms that helped guarantee such centres' continued existence as permanent institutions, as the gathered teachers sought to strengthen their own positions and to protect the quality of the brand with which they were associated. In 1174, for instance, teachers at Paris were exempted from rules banning the levying of fees in other Christian educational contexts, removing one possible barrier to the teachers' capacity to make a living. Then, equally important, the third Lateran council of 1179 gave the existing Paris faculty the right to license (or not) new teachers who wanted to work alongside them. This development essentially created a permanent, self-governing body – known as teaching masters – who could directly control the development of the institution within which they worked.

Similar processes of development were underway at a handful of other centres of higher education across the Latin west, turning gatherings of self-employed teachers into self-regulating educational institutions. The legal schools of Bologna in northern Italy were already following a similar trajectory to Paris in the mid-twelfth century, as did another clustering of intellectual expertise in the English city of Oxford, whose rise to prominence was kick-started by its convenient geographical location. Situated in the centre of the country, it was also the first place above London you could ford the River Thames, making it a natural location for papal judge-delegates to hear cases brought under the emerging system of papal-dominated canon law.[19] The full institutionalization of western Christendom's emerging centres of higher learning came with formal charters of incorporation in the early thirteenth century. In these documents, the concept of the *studium generale* became fully articulated. These centres were given a new name – university – at which every different known subject could be studied. The first university charter was granted by Pope Innocent III's representatives to Oxford in 1214, with Paris following suit a year later, and Bologna in 1219. In the decades that followed, a dozen or more centres of educational excellence across Latin Europe were granted full papal recognition.[20]

In this context of the nascent medieval Christian university, and Paris in particular, post-Carolingian penitential piety was transformed into the fully formed sacramental piety of the fourth Lateran council. A prominent role in this important process was played by a certain Peter Lombard, a teaching master of the Paris schools in the middle years of the twelfth century. Nothing sure is known of him before 1142, by which time he had already acquired a reputation as a teacher and writer there. In 1145, he became a recognized master of the cathedral school of Notre Dame, following which he was inducted into its clergy. He then rose through the ranks until, on 28 July 1159, he became the city's bishop, before dying just a year later (on either 21 or 22 July 1160). What's significant for us about Peter Lombard, however, is not his ecclesiastical career, but the teaching and writing which preceded it. Not only did his work make its own important contribution to the development of sacramental piety, but it gives us access to the teachings of the two previous generations of Parisian masters, all versed in the new learning, who had already laid many of the key foundations of the patterns of sacramental piety enshrined at Lateran IV.[21]

By the time Lombard arrived on the scene sometime in the 1130s, the new learning had already generated an explosion in surviving manuscript evidence for high-level teaching at the Paris schools, reflecting both the new intensity of study and the actual methods employed. In the first decades of the twelfth century, many new insights were developed but teaching methods clearly continued to follow Carolingian and older precedent. In their theological lectures, these early teaching masters worked through parts (or all, in the case of the brothers of Laon) of the Bible, verse by verse, commenting on any points of broader theological significance, as well as the usual linguistic and logical issues that individual passages presented. The textual counterpart to this method was the interlinear or marginal gloss, incorporating the lecturer's thoughts in written form next to the particular passage being discussed. Up to around 1130, this teaching method is reflected in manuscript form in collections of 'Sentences': individual teachers' comments on specific passages, not arranged by theme but following the verse or paragraph order of the biblical or patristic text under discussion.[22] Which is where Peter Lombard comes in. The title of his most important work, *Sentences*, echoes the older teaching traditions and is full of scriptural quotations: more than a thousand of them from nearly every book of the New Testament, and most of the Old besides. But the title is completely misleading. Reflecting his own, innovative teaching methods, Peter completely rearranged his quotations and their accompanying explanatory discussions around a new, coherently organized, logical structure of exposition.

The *Sentences* of Peter Lombard is the first systematic work of Christian theology ever produced. It is arranged in four books: Book I deals with the Trinity; Book II with Creation; Book III with Christ as Saviour of Fallen Creation; and Book IV with the Sacraments. In a strong sense, Lombard's *Sentences* did for Latin Christian theology exactly what Gratian's *Decretum* was currently doing for its legal traditions. In both cases, an inchoate mass of material was rearranged into a logical order by subject matter, while accompanying analytical discussion ironed out the various problems of coherence posed by relevant source texts from different potential authorities. And, like Gratian's *Decretum*, the *Sentences* became the starting point for all the further work of elaboration and reconciliation that the developing tradition of Latin theological teaching still required. By the later twelfth century, students wanting to progress from the *trivium* and *quadrivium* to the higher study of theology had to pass two qualifying tests. At the lower level, they had to compose a thesis on a particular passage of the Bible; at the higher, which qualified them as a *baccalaurus sententiarus*, they had to write a commentary on a section from Lombard's *Sentences*, which remained the standard teaching textbook of Latin Christian theology until the sixteenth century. Highly innovative in form, Lombard's masterwork incorporated the three crucial contributions of the Paris school of theology, which transformed post-Carolingian penitential piety into a fully developed, sacramental path to Salvation.[23]

Sacramental language had a long history within the Christian Latin tradition, stretching back to before Augustine (who had himself emphasized the power and significance of baptism and communion in particular). But before the twelfth century, there was no precise definition of what a sacrament was, other than some kind of symbol of divine grace or power – and certainly no agreement on how many there might be. Indeed, more or less anything could be identified in a general way as a symbol of divine grace, given the kind of non-literal approaches that had long characterized Christian exegesis both of texts and events.

The increased focus on sacramental definition was initiated by Lombard's older contemporary, and likely teacher, Hugh of St Victor, who taught theology in Paris from about the year 1120. His teaching divided the history of Creation into three different eras based on the extent to which God's message was known to humankind: before Moses (the era of natural law); between Moses and Christ (the era of written law); and from the time of Christ onwards (the – current – era of 'grace'). Each of these eras, Hugh argued, had its own appropriate sacraments. In Lombard's hands, Hugh's definition of sacrament found further systematization, as follows:

> It is proper to name a sacrament that which is a sign of God's grace; in the form of his invisible grace, so that it bears the image of that grace, *and is also its cause* [emphasis added]. Therefore, the sacraments were instituted not only for the sake of signifying, but of sanctifying as well.[24]

For Lombard, then, a sacrament was (no longer) just a symbol of grace, but an act which positively conferred it: that is, which carried within itself an active charge of divine power. This extra twist made it possible for him (again probably following Hugh) to limit the number of sacraments precisely to seven, a process encouraged by the long-standing association of that number with perfection and completion (both good and bad: the same era saw the enumeration of both the seven gifts of the Holy Spirit, and the definition of seven deadly sins). The clarity and logic of the new sacramental system (reflecting in a general way the rigours of Greek logic) made it attractive to both students and fellow Christian theologians, from where it spread into the hierarchies of the Church's leadership. One of the largest additions to the definitive second edition of Gratian's *Decretum*, published in *c.* 1160, was a lengthy new section devoted to the seven sacraments as expounded in Lombard's *Sentences*.

Second, the same Parisian school was responsible for articulating a new doctrine of Purgatory, which radically revised – and again clarified – prevailing Christian mental maps of the afterlife. As reflected in the New Testament letters of Paul, dating back to the first century, the issue of what happened to the individual after death had come to a head early in the history of the developing Christian community, when the faithful started to die off before Christ's – then imminently anticipated – Second Coming. The longer the delay, the greater the problem, since Christian tradition quickly embraced old Jewish Apocalyptic ideas of a Final Judgement, which meant that the dead had to be somewhere else 'now', awaiting the End of Time. By the time of Augustine, four centuries later, via important contributions from Tertullian among others, this had evolved into a generally (but not universally) held four-fold view of the afterlife. Apart from Heaven and Hell, to which a very limited number of out-and-out saints and utter sinners were respectively despatched immediately after death, it was widely understood that there were two extremely large waiting rooms for everyone else: 'near Heaven' and 'near Hell'. According to their deserts, the vast majority of human souls ended up in the appropriate waiting room, probably conscious of their eventual fate, but waiting for Final Judgement to be pronounced at the End of Days.

Despite the overriding importance of judgement and the afterlife in Christian world-views, however, there was a striking lack of overall clarity. This muddiness extended into some of the visionary literature, where particular saints were taken on tours of the afterlife (a striking feature of eighth- and ninth-century hagiography in particular). Read closely, it is not actually clear where the saints thought they had been taken – to Hell to see the punishment of the damned, or to one of the waiting rooms where, in some conceptions of the afterlife, the souls of redeemable sinners might undergo necessary purgation to prepare them for a happy outcome on Judgement Day. To this opacity, the Paris theologians brought clarity and system: inspired by the demanding standards of Aristotelian logic, they generated the coherent vision of Purgatory that is to be found in Peter's *Sentences*. The old four-fold vision was collapsed into three. Heaven and Hell remained as before, but now there was only the one intermediate zone. Here again, the new teachings caught on. Not immediately, but over the few decades either side of the year 1200, this new vision of post-mortem cosmic geography became pre-eminent across Latin Europe.[25]

Third, Lombard's *Sentences* also marked an important step forward in developing conceptions of what could be done to mediate the effects of sin on the fate of an individual soul, and by whom. The long-standing Christian interest in the geography of the afterlife had never just been idle curiosity, or even a purely selfish concern for one's own likely fate. Christians had long wondered whether propitiatory acts like almsgiving or praying for the dead, and especially for their own dearly departed, could have a positive effect on the latter's cosmological destiny. Back in the fifth century, Augustine thought that, while saints obviously didn't need anyone's help, and the utterly damned were beyond assistance, the prayers of the faithful could help those stuck in one of the waiting rooms; a view bolstered by the trickle of recorded stories in early medieval Latin vision literature, where revenants appear to the living, particularly in dreams, to ask for help in ameliorating their current and future fate. (This became a powerful enough tradition within post-Carolingian Christianity for the reformed monastery of Cluny to institute, probably around the year 1030, the entirely new festival of All Souls' Day on 2 November – commemorated immediately after the much older All Saints' Day of the 1st – dedicated to prayers for the departed.) The Paris teachers of theology again tied all these different strands together – sacramental theology, Purgatory, care for the departed, and the penitential tradition – into a single, coherent account of the immediate effects on the health of the soul of any particular sin, and what could be done about it – both by the sinner themselves in the here and now, and, after their death, by anyone else who cared for them.

Despite the clarifying work of Lombard and his contemporaries, debate over details, and even over some matters of profound importance, continued long into the thirteenth century. The *Sentences*, for instance, already emphasized one crucial distinction between 'mortal sins' – which, if unmitigated, would consign the unfortunate individual to Hell – and their 'venial' counterparts, whose consequences might still be seriously unpleasant, but which could be worked through by a period of Purgatorial penitence. The distinction was based on a passage from John's first letter (I John 5:16–17):

> If a man sees his brother committing a sin which is not a deadly sin, he should pray to God for him, and he will grant him life: that is, when men are not guilty of deadly sin. There is such a thing as deadly sin, and I do not suggest he should pray about that; but although all wrongdoing is sin, not all sin is deadly sin.

But doubts remained over the distinction's full significance. Pope Innocent IV (1243–54) declared in writing that only the effects of venial sins could be worked off in Purgatory, so that unconfessed – and hence unforgiven – mortal sins carried beyond the grave necessarily took you to Hell. Gregory X, by contrast, took a rosier view in 1274: thanks to God's mercy all kinds of remissions were possible. In the interim, a comprehensive and highly influential set of equivalences had been worked out by the Gloucestershire-born Alexander of Hales (*c.* 1185–1246): a Paris teacher of theology from around 1220. His major commentary on Lombard's *Sentences* set out the exact consequences of every possible kind of sin, and by what penances the due punishment might be mitigated, whether by the sinners themselves while alive, or by loved ones after they had died. The sacrament of confession was central to Alexander's system, as was extreme unction, but so too was the Mass: paying for Masses, especially for the departed, became a regular form of palliative penance. Overall, Alexander established a coherent economy of salvation: the scale of offences (venial, mortal), their corresponding punishments at different points (penitential, here on earth, and in the hereafter: whether in Purgatory or Hell) and how each type of penitential remedy might be converted into the other: 'each punishment is commuted into the punishment corresponding to it'.[26]

By the time the fourth Lateran council came round in 1215, therefore, the application of Greek philosophical logic to the texts, traditions and existing exegetical trajectories of Latin Christianity had effected a powerful transformation in the basic theological framework within which lay piety was now conceived. Some of the building blocks were long-standing ideas within the Christian tradition, but that doesn't make the new doctrinal ideas any less revolutionary, because never before had they been knitted together into a complete system. On the one hand, Purgatory dealt a fatal blow to older notions that most individuals could satisfactorily pay off any debt of punishment owed for their sins before their own deaths. That was the bad news. More positively, if sacramental piety offered a much-expanded vision of sin and its lethal consequences, it also offered much more clearly defined hope for its eventual remission, and a much wider range of mechanisms by which both the living and the dead might achieve eventual salvation. The new tariffs set out exactly how large the remaining debts were likely to be for any deceased individual – but also by whom they could be paid, and under what conditions. The seven sacraments, then, provided both a necessary guide to the path of salvation, and a set of mechanisms for meeting many of the debts of sin. The emergence of this newly systematized model of salvation coincided chronologically with the emergence, as we have seen, of a much more expansive and coherent religious delivery mechanism: tens of thousands of new parish churches staffed by clergy, who, thanks to twelfth-century canon law, were now much more firmly part of one unified corporate Church body. All of which meant that, at the fourth Lateran council, the leaders of Latin Christianity assembled by Pope Innocent III could give their imprimatur to a highly developed theological theory of how and why the individual might be saved, and, simultaneously, pass a series of practical regulations for the operations of a parish delivery system of unprecedented reach, through which it might all be put into practice.

As the council came together, however, the words 'in theory' still hung heavily over these last two observations. For all this conciliar ambition, the new theology of sacramental piety was the product of a few university intellectuals, and the wider clergy were only beginning to come into line with the unified corporate standards and operating procedures demanded of them by the new canon law of the later twelfth century and sanctified in the council's canons. To understand why the papacy adopted sacramental piety with such enthusiasm, and how precisely this theological vision made it out of the schoolroom to transform actual religious practice across the vast geographical space of Latin Christian Europe, we must explore one final, striking dimension of western Christianity in the early centuries of the second millennium.

THE POOR MEN OF LYONS

Sometime in the 1160s, a rich cloth merchant from the French city of Lyons, Peter Waldo, underwent a radical change of life. Deep and ongoing reflection on certain passages of the New Testament combined with the sudden death of a friend at dinner to generate an existential spiritual crisis. Following the example of Jesus' disciples given in the Bible, Waldo gave up his wealth to embrace the *Vita Apostolica*: a life of complete poverty, with his days dedicated to preaching the Gospel. Early in the 1170s he persuaded a local priest to produce a vernacular translation of the New Testament. Armed with this text, he founded a self-appointed preaching order dedicated to poverty and preaching: the self-styled Poor Men of Lyons. Around the same time, a similar movement was gathering momentum among cloth workers in the towns of northern Italy, particularly Milan. The *Humiliati* (of *Name of the Rose* fame) likewise dedicated themselves to the full demands of the *Vita Apostolica*. Both movements were large enough to attract attention, and they grew fast. Waldo's old mercantile network had extended to the Low Countries, which produced much of the cloth he had sold in his former life; his new religious followers trod similar paths, spreading their message far and wide. Moreover, the Waldenses (as the Poor Men were also known) and the *Humiliati* are only the most striking examples of a wave of revivalist popular religious enthusiasm, which periodically convulsed the Latin west in the eleventh and twelfth centuries.[27]

A smattering of individual examples and small groups feature in sources from the first half of the eleventh century. One of the earliest was the French peasant Leutard, from the diocese of Châlons-sur-Marne, who received a vision in the form of a swarm of bees entering his body. This experience led him to start preaching on his own authority and he gathered around him a large number of followers. There is then a fifty-year lull until the early twelfth century, when revivalist preachers start to figure again in the sources, this time with more frequency.

One of the most prominent figures in this new wave was Arnold of Brescia, who left his monastery to turn radical popular preacher in about the year 1115, again dedicating himself to the demands of the *Vita Apostolica*. After a career spanning several decades, he eventually found himself on the side of an aristocratic faction in Rome that briefly expelled Pope Eugenius III to take control of the city (1146–8). The faction was interested in power, but Arnold was critical of Church wealth, as contrary to New Testament example. More typical is the shorter-lived Henry of Le Mans, who rose to brief prominence in northern France also around 1115, and then disappeared again almost immediately. He also espoused poverty and self-authorized preaching, with a strong dose of anti-clericalism, having been originally inspired to follow the *Vita Apostolica* by the scandalous behaviour of much of his local clergy. Peter de Bruis (fl. 1119–39) likewise was originally a village priest in south-eastern France before he turned to poverty and preaching. His particular message emphasized a literal response to the New Testament (combined with a positive rejection of the Old), and a certain hostility to elements of contemporary piety – offerings for the dead, veneration of the Cross, and the central focus on the Eucharist. There were many others, from the apparently more coherent thinkers to the ostensibly much less so (such as Éon de l'Étoile, the younger son of a Breton nobleman who declared himself 'Son of God' – though it's important to add that, often, our only accounts of such individuals are to be found in the writings of their clerical opponents).[28]

Why, in the eleventh and (especially) the twelfth centuries – a time when the new learning emerged and sacramental piety was being fully defined – was the religious history of the Latin west suddenly littered with self-authorized, revivalist preachers? Although it might seem counter-intuitive given the marked anti-clerical tone to much of the preaching, there is a strong sense in which these new preachers and movements reflect the relative success of late- and post-Carolingian clergy in selling their general message that good Christians needed to adopt a more intense form of penitential piety. The patchy geographical distribution of actual churches between the ninth and eleventh centuries, when the great wave of new construction had only just begun, and the rather random nature of clerical education in the same era meant that, in practice, the penitential message must have been distributed with varying degrees of intensity across different parts of the Latin west. But evidence survives of clergy determined to bring more intense regimes of lay piety to the masses in England, the Rhineland, Lotharingia, and northern and central Italy, often through extensive preaching. Close study of the sermon cycles produced by the Anglo-Saxon ecclesiastical reformer Ælfric (*c.* 955–1010) shows that, while most of his sermons were aimed at clerical audiences, he clearly expected laity to be present at the greater Church festivals and geared his messages for these occasions accordingly. Unsurprisingly, the penitential message gained serious traction among at least some elements of the lower social ranks.[29]

Alterations in the physical form of churches during this time also reflect the spread of more intense forms of lay piety. In the eleventh century, newly constructed local churches in northern Europe were for the first time regularly equipped with fonts. This demonstrates that baptism, originally the preserve of often distant bishops, was now expected to take place immediately a child was born: a clear sign that at least one of the soon-to-be-seven sacraments was playing a central role in everyday lay piety. In the same era, too, local churches began to acquire bell towers. This is also significant of changing patterns of lay piety because, echoing the by now well-established patterns of monastic ritual, the area beneath the tower, its bells continually tolling, was associated with more-developed Christian rituals for the dead, before the corpse of the deceased was committed to the earth.[30]

Also in the mid-eleventh century, religious institutions in need of funds for building work in particular started to take their most important relics on tour – a means of raising cash from those who asked spiritual favours in return. The first recorded example involved the Flemish monastic community of Lobbes parading the corpse of its founder, St Ursmer. The lay response to this initiative was powerful enough for it to be repeated by other religious houses. Altogether, some eighteen 'miracle tours' are recorded in later eleventh- and twelfth-century sources. A related phenomenon from the same era is the so-called 'cult of the carts', the laity rallying round to provide the physical labour required for church construction and repair, bringing their carts to transport the necessary materials.[31]

Relic tours and cart cults were both clerical initiatives, but their effectiveness relied on the willingness of the laity to respond with enthusiasm. And in other contexts, ordinary lay men and women were taking their own religious initiatives. Pilgrimage, because it now encompassed a wider diversity of religious destinations, now attracted a much wider social range. The point is confirmed by that penitential pilgrimage to end all others: the First Crusade. Urban II's call may have been originally directed at Europe's warriors, but it was taken up by self-appointed preachers, above all Peter the Hermit, a priest from Amiens (who went on to play a starring role in much of the action all the way to Jerusalem). The response to these preachers, from all walks of medieval society, was electric. The overwhelming majority of the many tens of thousands of participants who set out for the Holy Land in the first wave of the spring and early summer of 1096 consisted of peasants, of all ages and both sexes. (The arrival of this so-called Peasants' Crusade outside Constantinople terrified the Byzantine emperor Alexius, who quickly shipped them over the Bosporus: once there, most perished at the hands of the Turks, in a series of massacres through the autumn of 1096: p. 474.) The preachers could never have generated such an astonishing popular response had not a revivalist, penitential message already gained significant traction among large sections of the Latin European laity.[32]

Another, more specific, unifying theme in the profiles of many of these self-authorized preachers – uniting everyone from Leutard at the beginning of the eleventh century to the more conspicuous phenomena of the *Humiliati* and Waldenses in the later twelfth – is a striking degree of self-confident literacy, manifesting itself in a determination to read and follow the Gospels at first hand. This literacy was sometimes vernacular rather than Latin, but most of the preachers showed not the slightest hesitation in using the New Testament, especially its accounts of Christ's instructions to the Apostles, both to license their own activities and sometimes to criticize the behavioural standards of regular clergy. Although self-appointed preachers can be found periodically throughout Christian history (Gregory of Tours records a few excellent sixth-century examples), their increased frequency in the first two centuries of the new millennium certainly reflected a broader socio-economic transformation unfolding across Latin western Europe.

This was an age of explosive economic development in the Latin West, founded on agricultural progress. New farming regimes on larger, more integrated estates in grain-producing regions, such as southern England and northern France, brought about an increase in crop yields from an average of around 2:1 in the early Middle Ages (where each pound of seed grain sown would generally yield two pounds of crop, one of which had to be reserved as seed for the following year) to a much more productive 3:1 in the years after 1000, which amounted to a colossal increase in the available food supply. This in turn powered both massive demographic growth (according to some estimates, western Europe's population trebled in the first three centuries of the second millennium) and a striking degree of economic diversification. For the first time since the Roman period, Europe's economy saw the growth of a significant non-agricultural, urban sector, especially in northern Italy and the Low Countries. Bologna's new twelfth-century walls enclosed an area of 38 sq. miles (100 sq. km), four times the size of the fifth-century city; an expansion matched by Arras in the north, which in the same century expanded from a small footprint of around 4 sq. miles (11 sq. km) to around 40 sq. miles. In these boom towns of high medieval Europe, recently urbanized populations made their livings in a wide variety of ways linked to manufacture and to trade, creating new groups of people detached from primary agricultural production: craft workers of different kinds (particularly in the cloth trades) towards the poorer end of the spectrum; merchants, manufacturers, guildsmen and bankers among the more prosperous.[33]

This socio-economic transformation intersected with revivalist preaching in three key ways. First, economic developments intensified patterns of literacy: primarily in the vernacular and in more pragmatic forms, with merchants, bankers and craftsmen developing the skills they needed to control their businesses – rather than complex compositional literacy. The determination shown by an ex-merchant like Peter Waldo to read the words of the New Testament for himself, unmediated by the exegetical traditions of the Church, reflects an important trend of the period. Second, the rise of new entrepreneurial classes, and of the more sophisticated monetary economy which supported them, underscored the new emphasis on the link between poverty and true Christian virtue, as exemplified in the *Vita Apostolica*. Rejection of wealth figures strongly in the story of Waldo and many other preachers of the age. More generally, numerous Church commentators both noted the rise of the new moneyed classes – labelled the 'tertiary' professions; fighting and farming being numbers one and two – and lamented the moral consequences. From Gregory the Great to Peter Lombard, basic Christian source texts, such as 'the love of money is the root of all evil' (I Timothy 6:10), powered an outlook which saw it as particularly difficult for merchants to make their way safely to Heaven. And with agricultural produce becoming increasingly monetized, allowing some of the larger agricultural surpluses now available to be sold for cash, these same socio-economic transformations underlay the concern with simony, the buying and selling of Church privileges. Since benefices could now potentially produce incomes in cash rather than agricultural produce, they became more financially attractive, and the price for obtaining them seems to have gone up – together with the eagerness with which they were sought. This monetization of agriculture highlighted a disconnect between contemporary clerical behaviour, which often had one eye on distinctly temporal profits, and the Gospel's precepts on apostolic poverty. In turn, this generated a critique of cash wealth that struck a powerful chord with a significant body of increasingly literate Christian opinion.[34]

Third, and more generally, such an intense process of socio-economic development was bound to prompt transformations in prevailing patterns of Christian devotion for another, much simpler reason: Christianity's ongoing ability to adapt to incorporate new groups of religious consumers. The rise of medieval urbanism generated another new group of Christians, whose emergence again stretched and challenged the existing teachings and pastoral structures of the Church. (One self-appointed preacher, Tanchelm of Antwerp (active 1112/15), was able to win over his followers because this rapidly expanding town was then served by only one priest, who also happened to be living in sin with his niece.[35])

The history of Peter Waldo, then, needs to be seen in the context of a much broader phenomenon of religious revivalism, which, even if each individual preacher was producing their own specific message, had important common themes and causes. Economic development, intersecting with the growing impact of penitential pastoral agendas in the post-Carolingian west, had generated a new body of religious consumers with a stronger sense of their own agency and a greater ability to respond to and reinterpret the New Testament, independent of the traditional clerical establishment.

The first phase of papal reform, the era of Leo IX and Gregory VII in the mid- and later eleventh century, then added further fuel to the fire. Much of the reformers' initial rhetoric could not help but arouse more general expectations among an increasingly committed lay audience that a moralizing crusade was about to be unleashed against lax moral standards among the clergy charged with serving their pastoral needs.

Under Pope Gregory VII (of Emperor Henry IV's humiliation at Canossa fame), the recently reformed papacy lent its support to radical, direct lay action against clerical corruption. At this point in its history, the clerical reform party was looking to justify its ongoing seizure of the reins of overarching religious authority from the Salian emperors by taking direct, and radical, control of the anti-simony agenda. The same Easter synod in 1059 which approved the new rules to guarantee papal elections that were independent of any imperial interference (p. 465), also questioned the validity of sacraments delivered by morally deficient priests. This was backed up with practical support for the so-called Pataria lay movement's direct, violent protests against the simoniac higher clergy of the imperial city of Milan. Between 1057 and 1075, the same kind of violent protests spread across northern Italy to Brescia, Piacenza and Cremona, and, at this stage in its history, the reformed papacy provided staunch support. In 1075, Gregory VII even publicly honoured as a martyr one of the Pataria's leaders, Erlembald, who had been killed in a recent bout of street fighting. In the later eleventh century, therefore, the newly reformed papacy was overtly encouraging the kind of fiercely anti-clerical sentiments directed against morally deficient clergy that would become characteristic of many of the popular preachers who made names for themselves in the early twelfth century: the likes of Arnold of Brescia, Henry of Le Mans and Tanchelm of Antwerp most obviously. But no such preachers figure in sources from the second half of the eleventh century, when the anti-simony crusade of Gregory VII was at its height, and this is surely no coincidence.[36]

By the time of Peter Lombard, in the mid-twelfth century, however, a new, modified 'official' papal position on anti-clericalism had begun to crystallize. The earlier doubts expressed about the religious efficacy of morally deficient priests (at the synod of 1059 for instance) had been abandoned, largely because of the new doctrines of sacramental piety produced by the new learning in western Europe's emerging universities and eventually sanctified at the fourth Lateran council of 1215. Because sacraments directly transmitted God's grace and power, the moral standing of the priestly celebrant was neither here nor there. Now, as far as the twelfth- and early thirteenth-century papacy was concerned, a particular priest's moral standing (or lack of it) provided no justification whatsoever for general anti-clericalism, or any broader resistance to the necessity of living life according to the new sacramental prescription. Any such stance, the papacy ruled, was invalid.

In context, this was an entirely logical shift of position. Previously, the papacy had supported violent anti-corruption movements (such as the Patarenes) as a way of establishing its own ideological legitimacy and seizing the moral high ground. Once that overarching religious authority had been secured, however, anti-clericalism became not an asset to the papacy but a menace, attacks on the ecclesiastical establishment threatening the Church's whole legitimacy. This was obviously counterproductive for a papacy which now controlled it. In any case, Church wealth was necessary for a whole series of religious reasons: not least to support the buildings, personnel, educational establishments and all the expensive books that were required to make Christianity function. Now that Purgatory, penance and sacramental piety – as codified by the Paris theologians – was a fully worked-out system, there was no need to attempt to revolutionize all-too-human behaviour and operating practices among the existing clergy.

Though this transformation in papal policy was both sensible and necessary, it did nothing to address the strong existing strand of anti-clericalism fuelled by direct comparisons between the medieval Church and the ideals laid out in the New Testament, which Gregory VII's support of the Pataria had encouraged. It is hardly surprising, therefore, that the twelfth century – when the papacy turned away from its original anti-clerical stand – saw a striking further revival in the popularity of self-appointed preachers embracing the *Vita Apostolica*. The linkage also explains why these preachers often also expressed an open hostility to elements at least of the papacy's sacramental piety agenda, precisely because it was a means of sweeping under the carpet, rather than tackling more directly, the Church's venality and the aberrant behaviour of its priests. Many of the known preachers, indeed, had begun their careers within the auspices of the Church, before becoming fierce critics of it – Arnold of Brescia as the head of a community of canons, Peter de Bruis as a village priest – so they understood perfectly well what was going on.[37] In the eleventh century, tithes and prayers for the dead had been singled out by preachers for particular condemnation – tithes being a symbol of clerical greed, prayers for the dead a pastoral innovation that some found difficult to accept – while explicit resistance to some of the new sacraments and other innovative elements of contemporary religious practice became more marked in the twelfth, when the use of the crucifix (a cross with the figure of Christ superimposed on it, as opposed to a simple cross), infant baptism, and greater emphasis on the humanity of Christ all attracted the ire – in different combinations – of various of the preachers who found such a ready audience among the massed faithful of western Europe.[38]

The new sacramental theology and associated patterns of lay piety, which the fourth Lateran council enshrined as a universal model, were therefore in part a way of heading off the kinds of anti-clerical sentiments that the reformed papacy had itself previously sponsored, and which remained popular down to the time of Peter Waldo in the later twelfth century. Given that the new sacramental piety actually frustrated some of the earlier expectations of widespread Church reform, it was never going to be straightforward to sell it to the mass of Latin Europe's religious consumers. Further dimensions of Waldo's tortuous relationship with the institutional Church, however, provide an excellent pathway into the extended process, after 1215, by which the ecclesiastical hierarchy eventually overcame initial resistance to win much more widespread acceptance of the new patterns of sacramental piety and the theological concepts which underlay it.

CO-OPTION AND CREATIVITY

Waldo's determination to become a self-authorized preacher of the Gospel, and his commissioning of a vernacular French New Testament translation, both posed a threat to the established order of ecclesiastical authority, bypassing the clerical monopoly over biblical interpretation. In 1179, the papacy offered Waldo a deal: his adoption of a lifestyle of poverty was fine – but there was to be no preaching. For Waldo, this was an unacceptable limitation on his divine calling and he refused. The resulting confrontation eventually led to his formal excommunication in November 1184 by the then pope, Lucius III. This ruling also meted out the same punishment to the Italian *Humiliati*, whose relationship with the Church hierarchies had resulted in a similar confrontation.

But the groundswell of lay support behind the kinds of ideas espoused by the Waldenses and *Humiliati* was formidable, and, at this stage in its development, the Church had few mechanisms available for enforcing its rulings. Acknowledging this, the university-trained Pope Innocent III, elected in 1198, took a more imaginative approach to the problem than simple condemnation. He succeeded – in part – where his predecessors had failed, negotiating a partial reconciliation with Waldo in 1208, and eventually with the *Humiliati* too. The resulting compromise ruled that, while the groups were forbidden to preach to the general populace, they were at liberty to constitute themselves formally as religious orders and otherwise run their internal affairs autonomously.

Innocent's greater flexibility towards the Waldenses and *Humiliati* as new expressions of lay religious enthusiasm, independent of the Church establishment, illustrates one central dimension of the Church hierarchy's approach to selling sacramental parish piety to the mass of Europe's laity.[39] Since it was impossible closely to police all grassroots religious activity, Innocent in particular, but also many of his successors, were willing to compromise with groups that showed some willingness to co-operate, bringing them inside the institutional umbrella of the Church. Eventually, this led to official approval for a whole series of popular religious initiatives. Particularly illuminating is the ecclesiastical response to the particular place of women within the rapidly developing patterns of Christian piety.

In the early years of Christianity, St Paul had famously declared the religion equally open to all, irrespective of gender, in his letter to the Galatians (3:28): 'There is neither Jew nor Gentile, neither slave nor free, nor is there male and female, for you are all one in Christ Jesus.' Paul was writing at a time when the early Church willingly recognized female religious figures of independent power and authority; the second-century *Life of Thecla*, for instance, portrays a woman who was called by God after the example of St Paul himself to a life of independent religious action. Late Roman Christianity and that of the early Middle Ages had in turn thrown up similarly powerful female figures, who used their secular standing and resources to carve out significant religious profiles as monastic founders, such as St Radegund, and abbesses, including the seventh-century Anglo-Saxon St Hilda, who hosted the synod of Whitby in 664 (Chapter 7). Over the long term, however, deeply entrenched patriarchal attitudes generally won out in the ideologies and practices of western Christianity. Women came generally to be seen as profoundly 'weaker vessels': second-class humans much more prone to sin than their male counterparts.

This misogyny stemmed in part from the prevailing cultural attitudes of the Graeco-Roman world in which Christianity first became a mass religion. In Graeco-Roman understandings of humanity, the rational mind was always at war with the irrational body to control the human will; and prevailing attitudes perceived women, for whom much of life revolved around child-bearing and child-rearing, as much more open to domination by the physical than the rational. Within Christian tradition, this outlook was reinforced by the standard interpretation of the Book of Genesis's account of the Fall, in which, having herself succumbed to the wiles of the serpent, Eve helps persuade Adam to take the fatal bite from the apple of knowledge. Combining classical and developing Christian traditions, medieval Christianity came to be dominated by men, the general place of women being carefully demarcated to reflect separation and subordination.

Hence, despite earlier examples of female religious authority, the Carolingian era and its immediate aftermath provide few instances of powerful religious women. The priesthood remained a male-only profession, and even female saints in the Carolingian era found themselves relegated to the private sphere (at least, as described by the male authors of their *Lives*), performing miracles of feeding, rather than fulfilling any more public religious roles after the fashion of earlier saints like Radegund and Hilda. In the same era, new doctrines on clerical celibacy heightened the sense that any kind of sexual contact with women would also generate ritual impurity. And not just for clergy: such attitudes spilled over into the laity, with the new canon law promulgating the idea that sex before Holy Communion, or during periods of penitential fasting, was deeply sinful. Sex was necessary for procreation, obviously, but women and sexual intercourse were seen by the established Church as potentially dangerous to the health of the soul: plenty of intellectual hairs were split defining when it was legitimate even for married persons to have sex. Against this background, the generally suspicious approach of medieval Christian piety to women makes perfect sense. Women and men were physically segregated in church, while childbirth required an act of purification (the churching of women) on the new mother's part before she was readmitted to Communion.[40]

Nonetheless, the intensification of theological reflection in the twelfth century and beyond found justification for a wider range of legitimate female religious action. Much of this still required licensing by men, not least in the context of university theology where new interpretations of some well-known Christian texts – pioneered by male scholars – redefined the significance of female religiosity. These centred on Jesus' mother, Mary. While Mary's four principal feasts – Candlemas, the Annunciation, the Assumption and the Nativity of the Virgin – had been observed in east and west for centuries, the new penitential focus on Christ's humanity directed new attention towards the role of his mother. Fresh consideration of the mystery of the Incarnation – the mixing of Divine essence with human flesh – could not but bring Mary to the fore: what was it, male scholars pondered, about this particular woman, out of all the daughters of Eve, which made her God's choice? Reflection on the likely answer to this question – that there was something uniquely virtuous (i.e., sinless) about her – was reinforced by interpretation of two key passages in Luke's Gospel: Gabriel's greeting to Mary (the *Ave Maria*, 1:28); and Mary's song (the *Magnificat*, 1:46–55). Interpretation of these passages now turned Mary – 'full of Grace' according to Gabriel – who willingly accepted God's role for her whatever the cost to herself, into a figure who was qualified to act as the chief intercessor with God for her infinitely more sinful fellow humans: a figure who could quite literally tip the scales of judgement in favour of the poor human sinner. As a result, the eleventh century onwards saw a massive increase both in Mary's presence within the Christian liturgy and in the ecclesiastical fabric: most newly erected parish churches after this time acquired Lady chapels, Lady altars, or at least a statue in Mary's honour. As Martin Luther later pointed out, this visibility partly undercut her Son's previous monopoly on the distribution of saving grace.[41]

Another line of thought emphasized the constancy shown by two biblical Marys (Mary, the mother of Jesus, again, and Mary Magdalene, one of Jesus' followers), who stood at Christ's side throughout the crucifixion, and who discovered his empty tomb on Easter Sunday: their faithfulness standing in sharp contrast with Peter's triple denial of Jesus on the night of his arrest. Another New Testament passage to acquire new significance was the moment when Jesus, on the Cross, addressed his mother and his disciple John: 'Woman, here is your son', he told Mary; and, to the disciple, 'Here is your mother.' Peter Abelard interpreted this passage to mean that female religious figures, as brides of Christ, enjoyed a particular intimacy with God that their male counterparts could never match. Another scholar, Abelard's contemporary Robert of Arbrissel, combined the new and traditional interpretations of women's roles in the Divine Plan. He argued that, because of both their prevailing weakness and their special relationship with God, there could be no higher calling for men than to devote themselves to the religious service of women as priests and spiritual counsellors. This led Arbrissel to revive an old Christian model, the double-monastery for both men and women, when he and his followers established their own community at Fontevraud in 1101.[42]

Despite Christianity's overwhelming patriarchy, this lively ideological context licensed a wider range of practical female religious activity than anything seen in the preceding centuries. The life and career of Hildegard of Bingen (1098–1179) illustrates some of the new possibilities. Born into a Rhineland gentry family, she was, as a younger – possibly the youngest – daughter, enclosed in a Benedictine nunnery from an early age, where the first part of her life conformed to established Carolingian patterns of private female sacrality. But from her youth, the often-sickly Hildegard experienced intense spiritual visions, which in the 1140s she was eventually persuaded to commit to writing. She was prompted to take this radical step not only by her male confessor, but also – and significantly – by divine visionary authorization. Eventually, Pope Eugenius III, attending a synod in nearby Trier in February 1148, heard about her visions. When he declared them authentic, Hildegard began to write them down, and was also empowered to face down the immediate male authority that had so far constrained the course of her life, asserting the right to create her own new religious foundations: the abbeys of Rupertsberg (in 1150) and Eibingen in 1165. Her visions circulated widely, together with further writings on the medical properties of precious stones (which – so her visions told her, after the Book of Revelation – were fragments of Heaven descended to earth, from which New Jerusalem would be constructed at the end of time) and a body of musical composition for her nuns. The role of the male ecclesiastical hierarchy remains obvious here: Hildegard had to win its official recognition that her visions were genuinely from God. At the same time, this hierarchy was now willing to recognize, as it had not been in the Carolingian era, a much more active female sacrality. Once bestowed, Hildegard could mobilize this recognition to achieve a considerable degree of practical (if not threatening) religious autonomy. As well as founding her own monastic houses, she also initiated some idiosyncratic practices. On the great Christian festivals, she and her nuns (she only recruited upper-class women) abandoned their traditional monastic habits for the finest dresses, decorated with all the jewels (normally used for medicinal purposes) the foundations possessed. Her exegetical justification, of course, was that the jewels were pieces of heaven, but part of me likes to think that Hildegard just liked a good party.[43]

Though Hildegard's career was exceptional, there were other female visionaries in her own era and well beyond. And while most female religiosity was constrained within rather tighter limits, the range of religious possibility for women was expanding. At the opposite end of the socio-economic spectrum to Hildegard's gathering of the very grand was a quite different female religious movement. The Beguines were associated with the new towns which grew up around the developing cloth industry in the Low Countries. Cloth-working had always been a female preserve. Its proto-industrialization in Flanders during the eleventh century made it possible for many women in the region to earn their own livings for the first time, beyond the confines of family farms. The immigration patterns which brought these new towns into existence, therefore, featured significant numbers of single women. Responding to the penitential piety of the times, some of these immigrants began to live in semi-monastic communities, taking vows of celibacy and mutual support for as long as they remained part of the community (such vows did not prevent them from leaving to marry in due course). From these highly informal beginnings, the Beguine movement (the origins of the name are obscure) began to grow. While its earliest formal rules date to the early thirteenth century, Beguine communities existed from about 1175 onwards. Again, male sponsorship helped win the movement wider approval, in that attendant priests wrote the *Lives* of the Beguines' early leaders, but it is notable that, despite initial suspicion and hostility, the Church hierarchy was eventually willing to recognize the validity of a novel, self-generated form of female piety.[44]

If Hildegard's upper-class Benedictine monasticism and the organically evolving regimes of the cloth-working Beguines mark two extremes of female religious possibility, the centre ground was also populated. The twelfth and thirteenth centuries saw a massive expansion not only in the number of monastic orders founded across the Latin west, but also in their forms and prevailing ideologies, for both men and women. A key moment was the emergence of the Cistercians – called after the Latin name of the Burgundian town, Cîteaux, in which they were founded – at the end of the eleventh century. A branch of the Benedictine order, they were dedicated to a much stricter observance of something more akin to the original *Rule of St Benedict*, rather than the revised version of Benedict of Aniane that had prevailed since the Carolingian period. This meant a return to monks (rather than lay brothers) doing their own manual labour, and a greater physical separation from the world of the laity (which is why many Cistercian foundations were established in what were then relatively remote locations such as the North York moors). In the same era, the communal monastic form, as defined by the *Rule* of Benedict, was blown open by a raft of new religious orders, encompassing quite different visions of piety and associated religious lifestyles. These ranged from solitary, enclosed orders to much more socially engaged movements, most of which (including the Cistercians) experimented (if sometimes briefly) with versions of their own specific monastic ideologies for women.[45]

These diverse orders – with their male and female variants – were all responses to, and reflections of, the heightened religious enthusiasm across Latin Europe for a wider range of individuals to engage in some form of more-intensive Christian piety. In licensing this religious variety as legitimate, a sequence of twelfth- and thirteenth-century popes showed considerable flexibility and positivity when responding to bottom-up religious enthusiasm – as long, of course, as such enthusiasm could be legitimated and absorbed within the Church establishment. At the same time, popes took more direct action to integrate the new sacramental patterns of piety sanctioned at the fourth Lateran council of 1215 into the everyday rhythms of parish life. This process again involved a defining dimension of creative co-option – right across western Christendom – to entrench the necessary idea-sets into the world-views and everyday lives of every parishioner.

'LESSER BRETHREN'

Winning wholesale acceptance for the new patterns of sacramental piety, among both clergy and laity, required a massive effort. This was not just because such piety stood in some tension to popular anti-clerical sentiments, but also because, at least in its fully fledged form, it was a considerable departure from existing and long-entrenched

Christian custom. These were not ideas that could be spread from Spain to Scandinavia overnight. Widespread acceptance of the new ideas and the pattern of behaviours they required was originally an uneven process, as could only be the case given existing technologies of manuscript production, limited communications, and an innate conservatism among the clergy. Even around Paris, the theological package brought together by Peter Lombard started to find its way out of the textbook and into parochial practice only from around 1175; elsewhere the time lag was considerably longer.

Towards the end of the twelfth century, the bishop of Lincoln, Hugh of Avalon (1186–1200), interpreted a reported case of haunting within his diocese with recourse to the new theology of Purgatory. For the bishop, the soul in question was visiting its loved ones to ask for help in overturning the extremely unpleasant post-mortem effects of an unpurged sentence of excommunication. But Hugh had to force this interpretation through, in the face of opposition from the other senior clergy of his own cathedral – then one of England's main religious centres – who as yet had no functioning concept of Purgatory and the possibilities of post-mortem remission of sins. In their view, the haunting was the work of a condemned and evil spirit, and peace would only be restored to the diocese by digging up the corpse and burning it. Even senior and comparatively well-educated clergy of a major English cathedral, in other words, had not by this time accepted the new economy of salvation – which makes perfect sense when you look at the cathedral library at that point. At the time of the haunting, it did possess a copy of Peter Lombard's *Sentences* – but not yet the raft of supporting materials which helped turn theological theory into pastoral parochial practice. The limited reception of the new ideas in even such a major cathedral community as Lincoln, and the documented hostility of popular late twelfth-century preachers to the sacramental focus of the new teaching, underlines the point that, when Innocent III enshrined these ideas at Lateran IV, the council's formal approval was an early stage in the process of winning broad acceptance for their validity in the many thousands of parish churches of Latin Europe.[46]

Part of the subsequent effort to entrench the new teaching focused on educating existing parish clergy. To judge by the diocese of Lincoln, higher cathedral clergy are likely to have become fully exposed to the new ideas in the generations either side of the year 1200, a time when universities also began to proliferate across Latin Europe. As the number of university-educated senior clerics increased, so too did the acceptance of the new ideas among the senior diocesan clergy, long responsible for most of the preaching and more advanced pastoral care within their bishops' domains (p. 323). After winning their allegiance, it was then necessary to spread the new ideas among the front-line priests in charge of individual parishes, who were charged with hearing confessions and administering penance. All this took time. Surviving records of a Worcester diocesan synod from the 1260s show that, half a century after the fourth Lateran council, its basic messages still had to be reiterated to the parish clergy. The synod accordingly worked its way through the fourth Lateran programme, instructing the assembled diocesan clergy (and through them, the laity) in their new responsibilities. Churches were to be separate sacred spaces, and priests were to be celibate and available at all hours of the day – because you could never tell when key sacramental actions, especially baptism (which *in extremis* could now be administered by the laity themselves) or extreme unction (which could not), might be needed.[47] In time, this patient attention to detail proved conclusive. On the eve of the Reformation, in the late fifteenth century, parish priests and members of the laity had fully internalized the teachings and practices of the new piety; both, too, were taking their own initiatives to ensure that they were followed in local parish communities. Back in the thirteenth century, however, the process of winning widespread allegiance to the Lateran IV's new theology of salvation also directly depended on another of Pope Innocent III's imaginative responses to lay religious enthusiasm.

In 1181 or 1182, around the time of Peter Waldo's initial condemnation by Pope Lucius, a prosperous silk merchant of the southern Italian town of Assisi celebrated the birth of a son, who was baptized Francesco: Francis. After an indulged, boisterous youth, and a series of military adventures, Francis, like Waldo, experienced his own call to the *Vita Apostolica* in 1205. At first, he became a dirt-poor, solitary hermit. His defining religious epiphany, however, came in February 1208, when he heard a Mass that included a passage from the Gospel of Matthew (10:1–4):

> Then he called his twelve disciples to him and gave them authority to cast out unclean spirits and to cure every kind of ailment and disease . . . 'Go . . . to the lost sheep of the house of Israel. And as you go proclaim the message: "The Kingdom of Heaven is upon you."'

Francis understood these words as a direct personal instruction from the Almighty to follow a different vocation from his current life as a solitary hermit: a calling to preach the Gospel to the mass of Europe's laity. In this, he again resembled his older contemporary Peter Waldo – but Francis's vocational ideology involved one critical difference. In contrast to Waldo's conviction that God had authorized him to do everything in his power to spread the Gospel, even if it meant opposing the official Church, Francis espoused a greater and conspicuous humility. Labelling his followers *Fratres Minores*, the Lesser Brethren, he carefully limited the extent of his (and their) calling by vowing complete obedience to the pope and the formal hierarchies of the institutional Church.[48]

Francis explicitly stated this principle in his surviving letters, and above all in his carefully crafted *Testament*. It also manifested itself in several important behavioural characteristics. First, Francis refused to found an actual monastic order without official sanction. He eventually presented his original rule – which summarized the rationale and operating practices of himself and his followers in a collection of a few passages from the Gospels – to Pope Innocent III, who, according to tradition, authorized it on 16 April 1210. (The surviving, revised and much more detailed *Rule* – still on display in Assisi – dates to 1223, when it was inscribed in a formal papal letter of Honorius III (1216–27): hence its Latin name, *Regula Bullata*.) Second, he taught his followers never to criticize an ordained parish priest. In this, Francis consciously echoed papal sacramental teaching, with its implicit clampdown on anti-clericalism. Whatever their apparent personal failings, Francis stressed, priests were ordained servants of God who could administer the sacraments and therefore deserved absolute respect. Third, though called to preach a revivalist Gospel message, his followers were never to operate in any locality without first receiving permission from its bishop (thereby respecting the ancient Christian tradition that bishops controlled all preaching within their dioceses). Given that Francis was creating his order at the exact moment Pope Innocent was attempting to reach a degree of compromise with both Waldo and the *Humiliati* (p. 540), it is extremely unlikely that these key differences were accidental. Where earlier self-authorized movements embraced the anti-clerical themes that had united many of the individual revivalist preachers of the twelfth century, Francis conspicuously rejected them. He deliberately presented his movement as ideologically subordinate to the official Church.

Francis, in other words, offered Innocent III a non-threatening version of the kind of revivalist preaching movement that was currently striking such a chord with the laity of the Latin west. Quickly seeing the potential of Francis's movement to spread sacramental ideas, Innocent licensed the order. This papal espousal of the so-called Franciscans continued under Innocent's successors, a sequence of university-educated popes, who fostered Francis's movement and, after his death in 1226, his associated cult. Acknowledging Francis's exceptional spirituality, not to mention his exceptional usefulness to the Church, Pope Gregory IX declared Francis a saint and commissioned one of Francis's oldest followers, Thomas of Celano, to write a first *Life* of the saint in 1228/9. Further papally commissioned *Lives* followed, together with an evolving sequence of *Rules*, which combined to give the Franciscan friars a central role in selling sacramental piety to the laity of Latin Europe.

Not everything ran smoothly. While the Lesser Brethren already had several thousand members by the time of Francis's death, they did not all agree on what was supposed to happen next. The argument focused on the degree to which Francis's original vision of absolute apostolic poverty should bind the movement he had created. Taken literally, this would have meant its members living hand-to-mouth on alms received on any particular day, the order never possessing any buildings or building up permanent endowments. But this was hardly practical, given the broader role that they were beginning to play in the development of Christian Europe. In the 1230s, a deputation of Franciscans won permission from Pope Gregory to abandon the rigours of absolute poverty, which allowed the order to build up some permanent income streams and maintain a range of houses (called convents). The world-view of so-called 'Conventual Franciscans' – one that placed its overall ideological emphasis more on the founder's other key watchwords, obedience and preaching, rather than absolute poverty – duly became the dominant strand within the movement. A competing strand of opinion – eventually labelled 'Spiritual Franciscans' or *fratelli* – continued to declare all wealth an outrage and, in the most extreme interpretations, as an absolute barrier to proper Christian virtue, which the well-endowed Church establishment found impossible to accept. Some radical *fratelli* pushed this argument so forcefully that they were condemned for heresy by Pope Boniface VIII in 1296 (an episode that forms the backdrop to Umberto Eco's *The Name of the Rose*).[49]

Arguments over wealth also spilled over into the Franciscans' partner order for women, set up by Clare of Assisi, who had come under Francis's influence around 1212. Moved by his preaching, she rejected her wealthy family to embrace monastic seclusion, Francis helping her found her own enclosed order for women dedicated to manual labour and poverty. Clare received as much papal backing as Francis himself, her canonization being rushed through in just six days after her death by another Pope Innocent (the fourth), who had happened to be at hand to perform her requiem Mass; his successor, Alexander IV (1254–61), commissioned the *Legends of St Clare*. As with Francis, there were disputes over how to provide for her order in perpetuity. Clare herself had won the right for her two personal foundations to exist – endowmentless – on the basis of absolute apostolic poverty. But conventually minded Franciscans were concerned that they might find themselves financially responsible for countless houses of poverty-stricken women. As a result, most new houses of Poor Clares were only licensed where there was sufficient endowment income to support their existence.[50]

Amid these ideological wranglings, the Franciscan order went from strength to strength, playing a key role in selling the pastoral package of Lateran IV to the wider public of Latin Europe. Pope Innocent III had realized, shrewdly, that Francis's commitment to absolute obedience to ecclesiastical authority meant that his order's emphasis on preaching could be mobilized safely to spread the key elements of the new papal-endorsed sacramental piety. Nor were the Franciscans the only new order of this kind in his sights. Shortly after Francis had approached Innocent to authorize his activities, a Spanish contemporary, Dominic de Guzmán, asked the pope to license another order dedicated to poverty, obedience and preaching. After some hesitation, Innocent's successor Honorius III duly recognized Dominic and his followers – the Dominicans – in the winter of 1216–17, consciously creating a second 'Order of Preachers' (*Ordo Praedicatorum*).

Dominic himself had been trained in the Liberal Arts and theology in the schools of Palencia in the 1180s, shortly before they gained formal recognition as a university. When famine hit Spain in 1191, he experienced a vision of his new calling, abandoning his studies to found a preaching order – but he never lost his belief in the importance of advanced Christian learning. Both Franciscans and Dominicans shared the same basic conviction that effective preaching needed to be not just theologically accurate, but rhetorically persuasive. From the 1210s onwards, both orders quickly set up university-based training houses: the Dominicans had opened a teaching house in Oxford by 1221, and Franciscans followed three years later. Both orders stipulated that no brother would be licensed to preach unless he had been trained at a university, or at the hands of a brother who had himself been trained in one.[51]

All of which meant that Franciscan and Dominican preachers were fully versed in the new sacramental piety of the Lateran programme, and were kept fully up to date with subsequent doctrinal developments. Both orders also attracted established university teaching masters, with the result that several of the most important theologians of the thirteenth century came from their ranks: Alexander of Hales (who played a crucial role in systematizing the tariffs of Purgatory) eventually became a Franciscan; the two greatest theologians of the thirteenth century, Albertus Magnus (1200–1280) and Thomas Aquinas (1225–74), were Dominicans. The emphasis on Latin grammar and rhetoric at the entry level of the university curriculum – the *trivium* – also played a vital role in preparing preachers for the job of selling the theological package to massed parish laity. As one contemporary memorably put it, 'first the bow is bent in study, then the arrow is loosed in preaching.'[52]

These two new mendicant preaching orders were not the first Christian groups to tackle the problem of selling complicated theological messages to a mass public. Back in the sixth century, the miracle collections of Gregory of Tours had much the same purpose, while in the eleventh, the *Miracles of St Foy* and *Deeds of the Bishops of Cambrai* were composed to reinforce elements of contemporary clerical agendas, such as greater emphasis on the sanctity of church buildings, and on both the taking of Communion at Easter and of receiving the last rites on the eve of death.[53] What was fundamentally different about the Franciscans and Dominicans to anything that had gone before, however, was the sheer professional intensity of their preparatory training, and the fact that it was rolled out on an industrial scale.

Endorsed by the papacy, the two mendicant orders worked to fulfil the papal brief: to put thousands of trained preachers to work spreading the unified vision of the fourth Lateran council across Latin Europe, and among the tens of thousands of parish communities that constituted it. Both orders provided their members with practical preaching manuals, which still survive in their thousands. The standard reference collection of surviving Latin sermons from the period 1150–1350 runs to nine volumes of a thousand pages each (with two volumes of indices); each listing consists of no more than the sermon's opening paragraph, and a note of where to find it (in manuscript or printed edition). In scale, this material utterly dwarfs all previous types of edificatory Christian literature. The new sermon genre continued to develop throughout the fourteenth and fifteenth centuries. From about 1350, manuals were produced in the vernacular languages of Christendom; and, from 1450, in printed editions. Equally important, the grammar and rhetoric mastered in the initial stages of university training taught the preachers to use their manuals creatively: not as collections of sample sermons simply to be read out, but as exempla to provide the basis for ad hoc extemporization in the vernacular, even when the manuals themselves were in Latin. The preachers were trained to adapt their messages to the particular audience they faced on any given day (urban, rural, richer, poorer, whatever the case might be) and to use the manuals to find the most effective, illustrative stories appropriate to the audience in question.[54]

The need for this kind of educational programme was appreciated throughout the Church hierarchies of Christendom. In 1281 Archbishop Peckham of Canterbury disseminated his own, much simpler teaching manual to the parish priests of his diocese, to remind them – in memorably enumerated form – of the key doctrinal elements on which they should focus: the twelve articles of faith, the ten commandments, the six acts of mercy, seven each of virtues and vices, and, last but not least, the seven sacraments. As the thirteenth century unfolded, some parish priests attended the new universities, even if they could not afford to stay long enough to acquire a formal bachelor's qualification.[55] But the two preaching orders of Franciscans and Dominicans provided the necessary ideological shock troops of the fourth Lateran council, bringing a unified, coherent vision of the new forms of required lay piety to the parishes of Latin Europe through a combination of rhetorical skill and theological sophistication. Never before in Christian history had such a complex religious message been communicated to such a large and disparate population with such thoroughness, or on so industrial a scale. As a result, thirteenth- and fourteenth-century Latin European Christians were exposed to the most intensive religious education programme that Christendom had ever seen.

Over the long term, Innocent III's imaginative punt on the followers of Francis and Dominic had hugely significant consequences – though how much he had envisaged of what would follow is impossible to say. By the fifteenth century, parish priests and congregations alike had internalized the theology of sacramental piety, becoming active participants in the new rhythms of parish life it dictated; and both had developed them further on their own initiative. The rhythm of parish piety instituted by Lateran IV was not, in its daily functioning, one monolithic set of beliefs and practices but a developing tradition, albeit one given unity by a belief in Purgatory and the spiritual efficacy of sacramental action. New feasts and practices were regularly introduced into the mix, often starting as spontaneous initiatives in one locality that, winning hierarchical sanction, became widely adopted. The greatest feast of the late medieval Church, Corpus Christi, began life that way, in 1264 – it was made a prescribed festival just over fifty years later – as did so many other features of an evidently vigorous late medieval religiosity. These traditions continued to develop down to the Reformation, with the accretions of mystery plays, confraternities of myriad kinds, new saints, and new devotional practices, which were many and varied enough to cater for both clergy and laity, and rich and poor alike.[56]

The role of the preaching orders in generating the richly varied but fundamentally unified religious landscape of post-Lateran Christian Europe can hardly be overstated; nor, for that matter, the willingness on the part of the Church hierarchy to embrace and channel the abundant lay and clerical religious enthusiasm that came to the fore at the start of the second millennium. But it was not just the imaginative co-opting and directing of pre-existing religious enthusiasm that enabled this remarkably unified Christian religious system to attain such an overwhelmingly dominant hold over pre-Reformation Latin Europe. There was also a much darker side to this history.

14
Christendom and Coercion

The widespread adoption of the specific definition of Christian piety enshrined at the fourth Lateran council ultimately brought medieval western Christendom into existence. Not all Europe's Christians subscribed to it: in particular, the Orthodox congregations of the continent's eastern and southern reaches did not. But these were relatively limited exceptions compared to the geographical areas and populations who eventually accepted Lateran IV's understanding of 'proper' Christianity. A huge swathe of territory – stretching from Spain to Scandinavia, Iceland to Poland – was brought to a striking and utterly unprecedented degree of religious uniformity under the authority of the Roman papacy. All of which was the result of the two profound and intertwined journeys of cultural transformation explored in this book. The first brought the population of Europe from an original position of enormous religious diversity to Lateran uniformity, while the second transformed – in multiple ways in three great eras of revolution – the Christian religion itself.

In the fourth and fifth centuries, first of all, the pre-Constantinian Christian Church (which was itself already substantially different from the 'Jesus Movement' of first-century Palestine) was fundamentally reconfigured by the adoption of a Christian allegiance by the Roman imperial state and – consequently – large numbers of its constituent landowning elites. This not only created the first Christian confessional state but set what was still a small sect of committed devotees, at the time of Constantine's conversion, on its journey towards mass religious movement by acquiring new, more centralized authority structures – based on the administrative patterns of the imperial state and the religious authority of the imperial office – operating practices, and doctrinal articulation.

Such was the intensity of the practical and ideological intertwining of the Christian religion and the Roman imperial state that the latter's unravelling could not but generate a second period of revolutionary transformation. The unmistakable defeat of a Christian confessional Empire necessarily prompted an ideological crisis in both the western and eastern halves of the Roman world. In the west, imperial Nicene orthodoxy survived, but by a narrower margin than is usually imagined, while in the east the Christian Roman Empire's loss of ideological legitimacy and actual power eventually generated large-scale conversion to Islam (again especially among elites in the first instance, who faced the most immediate effects of the emergence of an alternative Muslim confessional state). And even where Christian dominance survived, the accompanying practical consequences of the unravelling of the Roman imperial system were profound enough to push Christianity into a further bout of revolutionary transformation. Christianity's newly unified authority structure collapsed. This combined with the disappearance of the large-scale educational infrastructure that the imperial state had supported to generate a series of structural limitations within post-Roman western Christianity, which hampered both its own internal unity and the religion's overall continuity of development. When new congregations of peasants and pagan warriors then came to be integrated into the faith in the same era, the result was another set of dramatic transformations in prevailing religious ideologies and standards of lay piety.

A third phase of revolutionary development was ushered in by a sequence of new imperial dynasties, who provided unified religious leadership to most of the Latin west again across the last quarter of the first millennium. Ultimately responsible for a massive geographical extension in Christian allegiance, they also oversaw an enormous increase in the educational and structural underpinnings of the religion. In the end, however, their authority did not reach far enough, and reform-minded Churchmen – many from outside Italy – transformed the Roman papacy into a new institution, capable, for the first time in its history, of providing overarching religious leadership for the majority of Europe's

8. European Christendom in 1400

ORWAY
SWEDEN
ENMARK
Baltic Sea
Lübeck
RUSSIA
POLAND
Krakow
RMANY
idelberg
Prague
Vienna
HUNGARY
Vicenza
Padua
Ferrara
Bologna
ITALY
Rome
Naples
Adriatic Sea
SERBIA
BULGARIA
Black Sea
BYZANTINE EMPIRE
KINGDOM OF
THE TWO SICILIES
Mediterranean Sea

Christians. This revamping of Latin Christianity's authority structures was always closely tied to a desire to enact still more far-reaching changes to general Church practice and operating standards, and it was these desires – with important inputs from the new universities of the Christian west – which eventually came to fruition in the religious programme given unanimous approval at the fourth Lateran council of 1215. In part, as we've just explored, the successful implementation of this programme depended on directing and shaping the energies of spontaneous Christian religious enthusiasm in some very particular directions. But it relied on something else, too. At the same time as the new Franciscan and Dominican preaching orders were winning hearts and minds in the parishes of Catholic Europe, the ecclesiastical establishment also began to exercise much tighter corrective discipline against identified heretics, thought to pose a serious threat to the salvation of their own souls – and to those of any to whom they transmitted their beliefs.

ACCUSATIO AND *INQUISITIO*

The formal exclusion of individuals from Church services and the broader Christian community had a long history. The first documented individual rite of excommunication to survive was performed on 6 July 900, by twelve bishops in the cathedral of Rheims condemning the murderers of its former archbishop: 'we condemn them', the text ran, 'with the anathema of a perpetual curse so that their recovery cannot ever be effected by man nor [may they have] any conversation with Christians.'

Formulas of this type – which not only damned those affected in the next world, but also, at least theoretically, made it impossible for them to live among Christians in this world too – proliferate through the following centuries, along with specific records of individual condemnations. By the 1100s, excommunication had become the main weapon in the episcopal armoury for dealing with religious transgression, and it was deployed against some of the revivalist preachers. These spiritual penalties ranged from condemnation, sometimes with a monastic prison sentence (used against Abelard, Henry of Le Mans,

Peter Waldo and the *Humiliati*) to the incitement or indulgence of 'spontaneous' lynchings, inflicted on the likes of Tanchelm and Peter de Bruis. Arnold of Brescia received the full range of punishments. Initially condemned at the second Lateran council of 1139, he was then condemned again by a council of bishops at Sens in 1141, excommunicated in 1148, and finally executed in 1155 by the secular authorities, since canon law did not allow clerics to shed blood.[1]

Yet limits to the effectiveness of ecclesiastical discipline remained. Even in the more vigilant twelfth century, you still had to do a lot of transgressing to get yourself executed. Arnold of Brescia acted as religious front man for a rebellion which drove Pope Eugenius III out of Rome in 1146, but he was not executed for the best part of another decade. (Neither did his excommunication overly discourage his followers; even afterwards he continued to command a large public following in Rome.) In a world where a bishop's jurisdiction was confined to his own diocese, the practical consequences of excommunication – or any other spiritual sanction – at this point were pretty easy to avoid. In 1167, a priest named Jonas quarrelled with the abbot of the Flemish monastery of Jette over an ecclesiastical living, and the case was eventually referred to the bishop of Cambrai. As it was investigated, letters from the archbishops of Trier and Cologne and two successive bishops of Liège came to light, showing that Jonas had previously been tried and condemned for heresy in Liège as early as 1152. He had simply moved on.[2]

For a while, at least, Jonas had found it relatively straightforward to circumvent ecclesiastical sanction. But things were changing. If the emerging unity of canon law in the century after the publication of the second edition of Gratian's *Decretum* in 1160 helped create a unified Church hierarchy, it also revolutionized the range of weaponry that could be deployed against religious dissidence.

A first dramatic innovation in the pursuit of heresy came in 1208, when Innocent III adapted the existing concept of crusade for use not against external enemies of Christendom, but internal dissidents in the Languedoc, the large and fiercely independent province in what is now south-western France. When Innocent's legate in southern France, Pierre de Castelnau, was murdered, officials blamed his killing on Cathar heretics. The Cathars, like the late Roman Manichaeans who had attracted St Augustine in his younger days, were dualists. They believed, contrary to the Book of Genesis, that there were two Divine principles at work in the cosmos: one good, the other evil. The physical world, they held, was a creation of the latter, which undermined fundamental Christian conceptions of Divine omnipotence. Traditionally, the Cathars of the Languedoc have been viewed as a well-organized alternative Church, with their own bishops and dioceses, and strong connections to parallel networks of fellow believers in other parts of the west and beyond – particularly northern Italy and the Balkans (where another dualist heretical group, known as the Bogomils, seems to have flourished from the late tenth century onwards). While there are reasons to doubt some of this, there was no doubt at all about the ferocity of Innocent's response to the murder of his legate at the hands of dangerous heretics.

In declaring a crusade against the Cathars, Innocent appealed to the militarized landowning classes of northern France to intervene. Led by the zealous Cistercian abbot of Cîteaux, Arnaud Amaury, and a nobleman-adventurer by the name of Simon de Montfort – father of the Simon who later directed the Baronial Revolt against Henry III of England – campaigning started the same year. The so-called Albigensian Crusade (*Albigenses* was an alternative name for the Cathars, derived from the name of Albi, the town particularly associated with the heretics) would last fully twenty years and include episodes of extreme savagery. For the first seven years or so, up to 1215, the crusaders scored a series of military successes against their local peers, including de Montfort's victory over King Peter II of Aragon in 1213, who had intervened from south of the Pyrenees. As ever, issues of power and wealth were wrapped up in the religious conflict. Most crusaders went to the Languedoc to take advantage of Innocent having declared open season on the region's landowning establishment, who were generally opposed to the idea of having the French crown as overlord: Peter of Aragon became involved in the conflict to protect his own regional interests. Whether Peter and other local landowners were also acting to protect Cathar heretics is much less clear than the crusaders' propaganda claimed.

The crusaders' initial successes were brutal: their sack of the city of Béziers in July 1209 alone saw twenty thousand people killed.

From mid-1215 the run of victories then stalled, especially following de Montfort's death in 1218, until King Louis VIII of France intervened in person in the mid-1220s, which finally stamped out the flames of resistance. In 1229, the king's victory was confirmed by the Treaty of Paris, by which the local overlord, Count Raymond of Toulouse, confirmed his effective submission to the French crown. But while the crusade had successfully extended the power of the French crown, which was why the king of France had become involved, it proved much less effective against heresy, which, Church officials reported, was still rife in the region in the 1230s. Overall, crusade proved a rather blunt, if certainly bloody, instrument for suppressing internal religious dissent, one which would be used only very occasionally over the subsequent centuries (against, for instance, the Hussites of Bohemia in the fifteenth century).[3] In the war against entrenched religious dissidence, a second, legal innovation proved much more effective.

Before the thirteenth century, charges of heresy could be brought only under the old Roman legal action of *accusatio*. Classical Roman law functioned by defining a series of legal pathways, each with its own specific process. Under *accusatio*, plaintiffs had to make accusations in public – and the burden of proof fell on the accusers themselves, rather than on a court or public official. You could only call adult witnesses of good legal standing to testify. If your accusation failed and the defendant were found innocent, you faced serious personal jeopardy, for the accuser faced the same punishment that would have been meted out to the defendant in the case of a guilty verdict. Since the punishment for heresy could be being burnt alive, *accusatio* was never a very popular route into the problem.

In the later twelfth and early thirteenth centuries, the investigation of heresy was revolutionized by the development of an entirely new form of legal action: *inquisitio*. *Inquisitio* operated under different rules. It did not have to be triggered by a public accusation: anonymous denunciations were perfectly sufficient. And under the terms of this legal process, investigation and burden of proof fell not on the initiator (whose identity might never be known), but on the ecclesiastical officials who chose to take up the case. The range of allowable witnesses included children and convicted criminals – and no appeals were allowed against guilty verdicts.

The new legal process of inquisition was not originally developed to deal with heretics. Defined in the later twelfth century in the legal schools of Bologna, and sanctioned in 1215 at the fourth Lateran council, it was designed for use against simoniac priests and other clerical transgressors. Only in the following generation was *inquisitio* turned against heretics. The catalyst for its redeployment was the continued existence in south-western France of Cathar heresy, which Pope Innocent III's bloody and prolonged crusade had failed to extinguish. In 1231 – after lobbying by the founder of the Dominican order Dominic de Guzmán – Pope Gregory IX codified the regulations on *inquisitio* in 1231, repurposing the entire legal package for the prosecution of heresy.

Trying it out on the ground in south-western France led to a number of further innovations, which were duly sanctioned in the 1240s by local Church councils such as Tarragona, Narbonne and Béziers. It also resulted in papal rulings such as 1252's *Ad extirpanda*, in which Innocent IV authorized the use of torture against heretics; and further legal treatises, such as those by the thirteenth-century Spanish canon lawyer and Dominican inquisitor Raymond de Peñafort, who was also responsible for the decretal collection of Pope Gregory IX. By the early fourteenth century, this interaction of theory and practice had matured into a tried-and-tested regime of investigation and punishment, as set out in the Dominican inquisitor Bernard Gui's classic instruction manual for trainee inquisitors: the *Practica Inquisitionis* of the mid-1320s. (Bernard, who makes a significant appearance in Umberto Eco's *The Name of the Rose*, finished his career as bishop of Lodève in south-western France.) Alongside torture in the list of acceptable inquisitorial techniques, Bernard added indefinite imprisonment: both as a form of punishment and as a mechanism for securing confession. Its forms could be correspondingly punitive: solitary confinement, the systematic deprivation of food and water, and the loading of prisoners with chains were all recommended and papal-endorsed practices. It was also no longer sufficient for an accused just to confess their own guilt. To be legally admissible, a confession also had to denounce everyone in the prisoner's circle who shared the same heretical beliefs.[4]

Inquisitio, then, was specifically developed as a practical tool for enforcing compliance with the required set of religious beliefs and practices – the new Latin Christian orthodoxy – set out at the fourth Lateran council. Its immediate impact was dramatic. In the early days, it could also be chaotic. In the same year that Gregory IX redirected *inquisitio* against heretics, a local chronicler described the arrival of two would-be inquisitors in the Rhineland city of Worms, within the archdiocese of Mainz. 'There came a certain friar', the chronicler wrote, 'called Conrad Dors, and he was completely illiterate and of the Order of Preachers, and he brought with him a certain secular man named John, who was one-eyed and maimed, and in truth utterly vile.' The pair started denouncing heretics, 'firstly among the poor . . . and they began to burn them . . . '[5] This ghastly episode illustrated typical inquisitorial practice, with Dominicans (the Order of Preachers referred to here) often taking the lead in running inquisitorial tribunals, as, too, did Franciscans and, occasionally, groups of bishops.

For the most part, however, thirteenth-century inquisition was not nearly so grimly ramshackle as the proceedings in Worms. More representative of the developing process was the minutely organized repression of Cathar activity in the Languedoc. Enough of the inquisitors' records survive (though many more have been lost) to illustrate what a massive and intimidating process inquisition quickly became in the region. In the century after 1231, at least eight thousand individuals – and potentially up to five times that number – were subject to intensive interrogation under the terms of the process of *inquisitio*. Many were subsequently punished. These estimates of scale are based on occasional, surviving flashes of light. In 1245–6, the Dominican inquisitor Bernard de Caux, operating in the vicinity of Toulouse, carried out collective inquisition and punishment on a massive scale, arresting 5,471 people from two neighbouring archdeaconries, 420 of them from just one Languedoc village, Le-Mas-Saintes-Puelles. In 1308, in an episode brilliantly documented by the French historian Emmanuel Le Roy Ladurie, Geoffroy d'Albis likewise arrested the entire population of the village of Montaillou. The people were held for initial sorting at a local castle, with large numbers then being sent on to the city of Carcassonne for further questioning, detention and torture.

In pursuit of their truth, inquisitors were licensed to keep individuals under lock and key for years. One Guillem Salvaret, of the city of Albi, was held for over nineteen years before he was finally sentenced. As recommended by Bernard Gui's instruction manual, the inquisitors kept meticulous written records, usually arranged by place, which allowed them to cross-check testimonies carefully, especially when they interrogated individuals on more than one occasion. In 1325, an inquisitor named Jacques Fournier used written interrogation records to catch out one of his prisoners, exposing what he described as a blatant lie (the unfortunate prisoner may well have simply been disoriented by mental and physical privation, and punishment); many similar examples abound. There is no doubting the scale on which these records were kept. In the early eighteenth century, when the archives of the inquisitorial commission of Carcassonne (one of several operating simultaneously in the Languedoc) were moved to Montpellier, an inventory was made. At that point, the records consisted of nineteen registers, fifty-six books, nineteen rolls, and various other documents, with seventy-nine out of the total of one hundred and fifteen items dating to the century after 1231.[6]

With the emergence of inquisition, the official hierarchies of the Church had developed a legal enforcement mechanism of unprecedented power, brutality and reach. Never before had licensed operatives of the official Church had the power to arrest at will, and – on nothing more than unsubstantiated suspicion – to imprison and torture their victims, and even to hand them over to the secular authorities for the ultimate punishment for heresy, burning alive. What unfolded in the Languedoc, in the century after Gregory IX's rebooting of *inquisitio* in 1231, was extraordinarily horrifying in its scale and effect.

It is important, however, not to exaggerate its overall direct impact. Outside the inquisitorial epicentre of the Languedoc, commissions of *inquisitio* tended to operate for much more limited periods and affect the lives of much smaller numbers of people. When English bishops deployed it against the late fourteenth- and early fifteenth-century Lollards – who shared with other radical groups a desire to read the Bible in the vernacular and interpret it for themselves – only a few hundred people were caught up in its sporadic operations. Inquisitors could also face serious and sometimes effective resistance.

The inquisitors' progress in the Languedoc was held up from time to time by well-conceived plots to murder inquisitors, or to burn the interrogation records that were the root of much of their power. However, because there was secure secular support for the inquisitors in south-western France (at least in the aftermath of the Albigensian Crusade), Cathar resistance there usually provoked brutal military reprisals.

As so often in persecutions throughout history, the poor and disenfranchised were also disproportionately affected, as illustrated in the early *inquisitio* at Worms. Conrad and the one-eyed John were eventually joined by a second Conrad – of Marburg – who had developed a reputation as a harsh confessor (of Elizabeth of Hungary: 1217–31). When the three switched from burning the poor with impunity to bringing charges against some of the local nobility, resistance to their activities suddenly stiffened. The elites, as became clear, had power and influence of their own. When the regional archbishop of Mainz wrote to the pope to complain about the activities of the inquisitors, a Church council promptly dismissed the charges. A few days later, all three inquisitors were found murdered. The three had massively overplayed their hand, and, lacking support among or any strong ties to local elites, they made themselves easy targets.

Even where support for the inquisition was strong, inquisitors did not always resort to the most extreme measures. Bernard Gui's *Book of Sentences*, compiled when he headed the inquisition at Toulouse between 1308 and 1323, records that, over a fifteen-year period, he condemned 930 individuals for heretical beliefs: 42 of them were burnt at the stake, 307 imprisoned for varying periods, 143 had to wear crosses sewn onto their clothing for life, 9 were sent on various pilgrimages, 69 corpses were exhumed and cremated (the punishment meted out on supposed heretics who were already dead), and 22 houses were demolished. The rest received more minor sentences.[7] However, even if Bernard was not burning hundreds of people, the list of the punishments inflicted in the name of a supposedly loving God is horrific. It also played a role in creating a more general climate of repression and fear across western Christendom, without which the blanket implementation of the fourth Lateran council's programmatic piety would have been impossible.

THE GREAT LEPER SCARE

On 5 July 1322, one of the most notorious of the Languedoc inquisitors, Jacques Fournier (the future Pope Benedict XII), sentenced Guillaume Agasse, leader of the leper colony in the Languedoc commune of Pamiers, to indefinite detention. As far as we know, he died in gaol. Agasse's imprisonment drew a line under one of the most bizarre episodes of medieval European history. Under torture – he was tried by *inquisitio* – Agasse had confessed that in May 1320 a secret council of the leaders of forty leper colonies from across southern France had met in Toulouse. They agreed, on being paid (as Guillaume also confessed) by the Jews, to poison all the wells of the region, to kill all of their good Christian neighbours or turn them into lepers as well. The whole story was a nasty fantasy: neither Jews nor lepers had been plotting against anybody. While its origins are unclear, the scare was fostered by King Philip V of France, who used it as a pretext to shut down leper colonies and confiscate their charitable endowments. Nor was this an isolated moment of Christian religious paranoia. Barely a decade before, the council of Vienne (1311–12) had issued the bull *Ad nostrum*. This identified and anathematized the so-called Free Spirit heresy, condemning a minutely enumerated set of heretical religious practices and beliefs. But the heresy never existed.[8] Like the Great Leper Scare, it was a by-product of the paranoid mindsets and methods of university-trained medieval inquisitors.

These methods are worth careful consideration. Besides the potential combination of torture, solitary confinement, starvation, and open-ended imprisonment that they used to extract confessions and punish confirmed heretics, the inquisitors' training manuals carefully described the particular characteristics of each individual heresy, and detailed the lines of questioning needed to make a correct identification and elicit the appropriate confession. It was recommended practice to keep asking the same questions repeatedly, on different occasions, and to compare each set of answers to those a prisoner had previously given by consulting the interrogation records. (Some surviving records still contain marginal annotations commenting on discrepancies between earlier and later answers.) In addition to this record, the fourteenth-century Spanish inquisitor Nicholas Eymerich recommended keeping a small notebook per diocese, containing a briefer aide-mémoire of identified heretics for easier cross-reference.[9] Similar interrogation regimes are still regularly employed against supposed 'terrorists' in some parts of the world, attracting strong criticism from human rights' groups. And not just because the methods are self-evidently abusive. Another, deeper problem with these kinds of interrogation methods is their inherent tendency to generate false confessions. Held in psychologically distressing circumstances, threatened with physical pain of the most intense kind, half-starved, and badgered to death with repeated questioning, the general tendency for all but the strongest is to make it all stop by telling the interrogators exactly what they want to hear and already seem to know. (While many convictions can be obtained this way, they will not all be safe ones, as the UK police were eventually forced to admit, at considerable reputational cost, in relation to suspected IRA bombers in the 1970s.) The medieval interrogators' records are full of confessions, in other words, which would never stand up in a modern court of law. The campaigns against the lepers and Free Spirit heretics fall into this category, so too the inquisitorial pursuit of the order of Knights Templar, who were set upon by Philip IV of France in 1307. Under torture, they duly confessed to all kinds of heresy – thereby giving the king ample justification for confiscating the order's fabulous wealth.[10]

This makes it essentially impossible to use the inquisitors' records to assess the scale or even the nature of heresy in thirteenth- and fourteenth-century Europe. The occasional instances of lying individuals caught out by the inquisitors' methods might tempt us to conclude (as the inquisitors themselves thought) that they were possessed of effective techniques for uncovering the 'truth'. But what they had really developed was a set of techniques which, in the overwhelming majority of cases, would conclude with the inquisitors being told exactly what they wanted to hear. Isolated examples – the lepers, Free Spirit heretics, or Templars – aside, the two great heretical groupings consistently highlighted as posing an existential threat to Latin Christendom in the manuals of the inquisitors, and who feature most strongly in the surviving inquisitorial records, are the Cathars and the Waldenses (who, after Peter Waldo's own reconciliation to the Church, carried on preaching as well as living in poverty and hence attracted the ire of the authorities). In both cases, our understanding of the scale of the threat they posed has changed dramatically over time.

The traditional view of the Cathars of the Languedoc – as a large and well-organized alternative Church, with bishops, dioceses and strong international connections to parallel networks of fellow dualist believers – was directly constructed from the inquisitors' records (few written records survive from the heretics themselves). Some instances of dualist belief are recorded in the early eleventh-century west, but these were small and very localized. This is why the traditional account of the Cathar heresy contended that the greater contact with Constantinople and beyond occasioned by the First Crusade provided a conduit for direct Bogomil dualist influence to work its way westwards. This in turn generated the much larger and better organized Cathar movement in the Languedoc, where it took such a strong and socially broad-based hold that, even after the Albigensian Crusade destroyed its elite protectors, a century of inquisition was required to extinguish it.[11]

No one would deny that some strands of dualist belief existed in south-western France in the twelfth and thirteenth centuries. But many passages of the Bible can easily be read to imply some kind of dualism, portraying the Devil as more of a co-eternal cosmic enemy to Goodness than the relatively minor irritant to the Divine Plan that is the official Christian position.[12] Equally important was the fact that inquisitors always drew heavily on existing accounts of heresy for their instruction manuals when describing the most important religious deviations. In the confessions extracted by interrogation, and in the formal descriptions of the inquisitors' instruction manuals, the Cathars strikingly resemble the dualist Manichaeans of the late Roman period – who are particularly well known because St Augustine was attracted to them for a period before his conversion (p. 61). The Cathars, like the Manichaeans, rejected the Old Testament, because they understood the world to have been created by a second, evil Divine principle; like them, too, they comprised an inner elite, who lived highly ascetic, vegetarian lives, alongside a broader group of 'hearers'.

While traditional accounts of the Cathars generally feature a direct line of heretical descent from the late Roman Manichaeans, to the early medieval Paulicians (from Asia Minor) to the Balkan Bogomils, and then on to the western Cathars, it is perfectly possible that the whole Cathar phenomenon had totally different roots. Having read their Augustine, the thirteenth-century inquisitors had convinced themselves that all suspected dualists were really Manichaeans in disguise – and deployed their intimidatory, interrogative weaponry to extract the necessary confessions proving that this was indeed the case. The dualist beliefs detected among the ordinary inhabitants of the Languedoc could potentially represent no more than garbled, misconstrued variants of 'normal' Christianity, placing just a bit too much emphasis on the Devil, rather than any real adherence to some alternative, fully formed dualist world-view and its institutionalized Church.[13] Like the Great Leper Scare or Free Spirit heresy, in other words, it is conceivable that the Cathar Church was little more than a creation of the inquisitors' paranoid fantasies. The dualists to be found in the Languedoc may simply have consisted of a series of isolated local groups with little sense of cohesion – unless or until the attentions of the inquisitors imposed it on them. Similar revisionist salvos have also been fired in the direction of the Waldenses.[14] In other words, both heresies were self-fulfilling prophesies of a Catholic Church that needed them as an excuse to implement the measures of the fourth Lateran council, and to tighten its spiritual hold over Latin Christendom.

The revisionist lines of argument haven't gone unchallenged, however, and the Waldenses probably did have a continuous existence as a small underground mendicant order: a loose network of unofficial preachers working unobtrusively in small corners of Latin Europe from the twelfth to the fifteenth centuries. (There exist trial records mentioning the Waldenses from locations as disparate as Quercy, Piedmont and Prussia.) Their adherents often went under the radar, attending normal parish churches, and only occasionally attracting the attention of the ecclesiastical authorities. A handful of the Waldenses' own writings survive to bolster this view, along with a collection of late-fourteenth-century interrogations from the Polish city of Stettin. These yield a portrait of a papal inquisitor, Peter Zwicker, who took a more nuanced approach than the likes of Bernard Gui. Rejecting literary stereotypes (such as heretics sleeping with the Devil), Zwicker asked a variety of different questions, and listened to the actual responses, rather than persisting with his questions until he got the answers he wanted. What emerges from his notes is a much more plausible picture of visiting itinerant preachers being welcomed by Stettin citizens with varying degrees of enthusiasm. The aptly named Mechtyld ('Mighty Hilda') listened with rapt attention to the travelling preachers whenever she could; Heyne Melkaw, who had also been brought up as a Waldensian, distanced himself from the movement at the age of sixteen, however, much preferring a beer to religious meetings.[15] But if there is evidence to suggest that the Waldenses were a genuinely organized heretical order, the Cathar question remains more elusive.

For a start, it is something of a stretch to believe that such a powerful, alternative Church structure – as portrayed in the surviving inquisition records from the Languedoc – could really have existed in a world in which its official, papal counterpart was only just coming into being in the twelfth and early thirteenth centuries. The key piece of evidence in favour of a direct Bogomil connection with Catharism, likewise, is shaky in the extreme. It consists of a note describing the journey of a certain Bogomil Bishop Nicetas from the Balkans to south-western France in 1167, where he convened a council of local Cathar leaders. However, this note survives only as an appendix to a seventeenth-century regional history; it does not exist in any official inquisition record and could easily be a fabrication or a forgery. On the other hand, the local Church authorities in south-western France clearly perceived a level of dualist threat in the region unlike anything reported elsewhere in Christendom.[16] To my mind, the scale and degree of organization of the dualist networks of south-western France have to remain open questions – although I have no doubt that the interrogators' methods have at the very least substantially exaggerated both. What is undoubtedly the case, however, is that not only did the new regimes of repressive enforcement have an unprecedented power to coerce, but they also possessed an inherent capacity to invent enemies for the official Church's machinery of power to destroy – whether those enemies really existed or not.

The list of invented enemies was not limited to deviant Christians. The inquisitors' manuals also identified two other great threats to Christian order: Muslims and Jews. For the most part, Muslim and

Christian populations came into contact only beyond the boundaries of Europe (Spain became an exception as the *reconquista* gathered momentum). Jewish communities, however, were fairly widespread – but, during the later Middle Ages, Christian attitudes towards them underwent a sea-change. In the late Roman and early medieval periods, Jewish populations under Christian rule had faced discriminatory regimes of a limited kind (Jews were not, for instance, allowed to own Christian slaves). But outright persecutions and attempts at forced conversion were rare. One Jewish community in the Balearic Islands was subject to something close to it in the early fifth century, but, otherwise, only the Iberian Visigoth kingdom of the later seventh, as recorded in its Church conciliar legislation, ever made forced conversion an official policy. (Because the source material here consists of normative legal texts, there's no way to know how many people were actually affected: some Jewish communities certainly continued to exist in the Iberian peninsula after the Islamic conquest.)[17] Across the first millennium, this outright Visigothic persecution was generally at odds with more mainstream Latin Christian attitudes towards their Jewish neighbours. These were defined ideologically by a combination of the teachings of St Augustine and Pope Gregory I, both of whom highlighted the crucial role assigned to the Jewish people in the Divine Plan for humanity's salvation, being the first group of humanity to recognize the One True God. On that basis, both concluded, conversion should only be by persuasion, and Jews were entitled to legal protection of their basic rights to exist and worship.[18]

Towards the end of the first millennium, this started to change. Greater Christian theological emphasis on the death and suffering of Christ led to a substantial hardening of attitudes among many thinkers, which found expression in charges of 'deicide'. The Jewish people, ran this toxic accusation, were responsible for killing the loving God in the person of Christ – and, moreover, had been in league with the Devil to do so from the beginning of time. No longer were they the people whose faith and example had helped bring true religion to the rest of humanity. The economic expansion of the central Middle Ages, which spawned the new emphasis on living in accordance with apostolic poverty, also fed these anti-Semitic attitudes. By this point, Jewish communities were now spread more widely across the European landscape and, prevented from following many of the more everyday occupations by increasingly hostile Christian legislation, they found themselves pushed towards the unpopular 'tertiary' occupations: including, most notoriously, money-lending.

By the late eleventh century, anti-Semitism had become entrenched. The departure of the First Crusade for the east was punctuated by large-scale pogroms, particularly in the Rhineland (despite the unavailing efforts of the horrified bishops of Mainz, Worms and Speyer to offer refuge to the Jewish communities of their cities within their episcopal palaces). Anti-Semitism continued to intensify in the twelfth century. On 22 March 1144, the body of a young Christian apprentice tanner called William was discovered in a wood outside the English city of Norwich. The cause of death was unclear – but, with William's profession having brought him into regular contact with the town's Jewish community, accusations were instantly directed at the Jews. Within a generation, the legend had grown up (and was formally committed to writing) that William had been ritually murdered: tortured, crucified, and his blood drained so that participating Jews could drink it. This is the first known example of a specific kind of blood libel that was to recur at irregular intervals in different parts of medieval Europe. Having enjoyed inflicting pain and death on the innocent person of Christ, the accusation ran, Jews were now out to repeat the act on unsuspecting Christians.[19]

The increasingly widespread hatred and suspicion of Jews was institutionalized by the fourth Lateran council in 1215. Canon 68 played to the popular gallery. Demanding that Jews dress differently from their Christian neighbours, in particular to prevent any accidental sexual contact, it also forbade Jews from appearing in public for three days before Easter Sunday, and encouraged secular authorities to punish any Jewish disparagement of Christ's name. This combined ideological and legal assault had periodically horrible consequences. Mass pogroms became a marked (if irregular) feature of subsequent centuries; so too did the cynical manipulation of anti-Jewish feeling by Christian rulers in search of cash. This resulted in a cycle of expulsions from European cities and kingdoms, in which entire Jewish communities were forced to abandon their homes amid a wave of arrests and executions, leaving behind all their goods (and wealth) for the authorities to mop up. In 1182, Philip Augustus of France expelled the Jews from Paris, an edict which in the thirteenth century was expanded to the entire French kingdom. Edward I of England, among others, followed suit, expelling all Jews from the kingdom in 1290.[20]

The spread of the more intense regimes of Christian piety set out at Lateran IV, then, was accompanied by equally fervid ideological campaigns to identify and act against the Church's perceived internal and external enemies. These ideologies fostered accompanying legal innovations, which became the bases of brutal campaigns of official repression aimed at enemies of the Christian order, themselves creating an ideological context which led periodically to frenzied anti-Jewish pogroms and the lynching of identified heretics. One influential group of historians has characterized this overall change in atmosphere as the institutionalization of a 'persecuting society'. An alliance of educated clergy and emergent state bureaucracies combined to identify dissident minorities (whether or not they really presented a danger to the Church, or were even particularly deviant) in order to provide a supposed threat against which everyone else could unite ('othering', as this process has come to be known), and both to legitimize and encourage the most extreme forms of punishment against them.

The violence that accompanied this unfolding process is undeniable; so too, the toxic effects of the resulting fear and suspicion. Relations between Europe's Jewish and Christian populations were poisoned for centuries, while the arrival of inquisitors in any locality not only brought fear in its wake but turned local populations against one another. Placed in a situation in which confession and absolution under *inquisitio* meant naming fellow heretics – and faced with inquisitors who were unlikely to accept claims of innocence – individuals unsurprisingly reacted by using the denunciation process to settle old scores. To get yourself off the hook, you now had to implicate somebody else: it was only natural to cast suspicion on your enemies to protect your loved ones.[21]

If creative, co-optive and educational encouragements to more intense lay participation were one hallmark of the post-Lateran sacramental enforcement process, we also need to add a series of much more disturbing processes to the equation. These included intimidatory violence, periodically unleashed against minorities on an industrial scale, and cases of serial othering: stirring up hatred against identified outsiders (above all Jews, but also heretics, Muslims and lepers) to foster a stronger sense of identity among the good Christian majority.

Due emphasis must be given, however, to the word 'periodically'. *Inquisitio* was unfurled in the medieval period on a large scale only in the Languedoc of the thirteenth and early fourteenth centuries (and perhaps parts of northern Italy in the same era). It's also the case that no one sat down in 1215 to construct a master plan for enforcing Lateran IV. Church intellectuals and canon lawyers may have created a prevailing set of conditions, but local initiatives triggered each individual outbreak of violent repression (even in the Languedoc) and, taken as a whole, crusade, inquisition and other forms of outright persecution remained periodic events. One recent overview has suggested that the most you can really say is that high medieval Europe was an 'occasionally' persecuting society, although it is arguable that there was enough periodic persecution to generate a more prevalent climate of fear.[22] Alongside these different kinds of outright persecution, moreover, the Lateran programme was also inculcated across Christendom by some more subtle, but more powerfully coercive, dimensions of everyday life in the medieval parish.

THE VISITATIONS OF RICHARD DE CLYVE

The parish communities of late fifteenth-century Europe were not, as used to be argued, full of proto-Protestants, disgusted with the excesses of medieval Catholicism and waiting for the Reformation to happen. Two and a half centuries after the fourth Lateran council, the patterns of lay religiosity it laid down had been thoroughly internalized. Parish churches blossomed with artistic and ritual expressions of popular adherence to its basic patterns, while new initiatives – products of both clerical and lay enthusiasm – continued to elaborate its practical functioning.[23] But the rhythms of everyday post-Lateran parish life were based, too, on some elements of constraint. The Church authorities were unrelenting in their collection of revenues. Tithing provided much ecclesiastical income, and the fourth Lateran council had taken direct steps to close loopholes of avoidance. Canon 54 insisted that tithes had precedence over any other forms of taxation that parishioners might be obliged to pay, while canon 53 attempted to stop people from renting out land to individuals (such as Jews) who were not subject to tithing. Further legislation demanded that should people die owing tithes, the Church should have first claim on their estate. And although religious services were notionally free of charge, many additional fees and 'gifts' were both an expected part of parish life and the source of periodic resentment among the laity.[24] Peasants were especially resentful, and understandably so. Subsisting close to the poverty line, they were constrained to hand over a substantial part of their hard-earned, often meagre harvests to the Church.

Another mechanism of constraint underpinned the widespread adoption of Lateran-style parish piety: the parish visitation. In the early tenth century, the reformed Benedictine abbot Regino of Prüm considered that parish visitations – where the bishop went round to each of the dependent parishes of his diocese in turn – should be a normal feature of a bishop's job description, particularly at the onset of Lent. There is no way of telling how regularly such visitations occurred at that point, nor for several centuries afterwards: no records survive, because the largely informal process didn't generate any. Surviving anecdotal glimpses consistently portray visitations around the turn of the millennium as focusing only on the state of church buildings and the lives of the clergy, with offending clerics apparently facing little more than exhortations to reform: after a few encouraging words, the bishop said some prayers, collected his fees, and moved on. Life in the parish comes much more firmly into focus from the thirteenth century onwards, however, when detailed written visitation reports start to survive. In the aftermath of Lateran IV, as these records show, the whole process of visitation underwent root-and-branch transformation. One detailed illustration from the end of the thirteenth century not only shows us the new-style visitation process in action but takes us to the heart of the enforcement of the Lateran programme at local level.[25]

Between 1292 and 1294, the see of Canterbury was vacant. With no archbishop in post, the job of visitations accordingly fell to the prior of the chapter of Canterbury Cathedral, Richard de Clyve, who worked his way round twenty-five local church parishes in the poor and remote Romney Marsh region of Kent, checking religious practice in these communities against the model of parish piety laid down at the fourth Lateran council some eighty years previously. Clyve carefully surveyed the state of church buildings, along with the availability of books and church plate necessary for properly conducted services, the conditions in which pre-consecrated ('reserved') sacrament was being kept, and the religious lives of both clerics and their lay parishioners. What survives is overwhelmingly a list of breaches, set down parish by parish: Clyve clearly felt there was no point in detailing what was in order.[26]

In no previous era of Christian history would such a clear and comprehensive set of standards, established by a council held in the city of Rome, have even been conceived of applying to such a backwater; nor had there been any similar mechanism checking actual practice so systematically against the theory. Some of the snippets of information Clyve included confirm that the guidelines set out by the council were being absorbed into parish life in late thirteenth-century Kent. One parish priest was absent at university, picking up the kind of education which would enable him to give much better sermons; in other cases, the parishioners themselves wanted Clyve to resolve deficiencies (judged by Lateran standards) in the religious services they were being offered.

At the same time, Clyve found plenty to dismay him in the depths of Romney Marsh. Of the twenty-five parish communities he surveyed, twelve were found to have faulty buildings (mostly a mix of missing locks, leaky roofs and bad fencing), while eight churches had problems with chalices or other items of service equipment, and four lacked a proper complement of service books. This dimension of Clyve's survey bore comparison with traditional visitations, but forms only a relatively small component of the record. The remainder, however, was rather different in feel. Clyve didn't simply survey the material fabric of the buildings and their interiors. He also intensely examined the behaviour of the clerics attached to them and punished any deviations accordingly.

First, Clyve subjected the celibacy (or otherwise) of the clergy to close scrutiny. In doing so, he uncovered seventeen cases in which the rules were definitely, or potentially, being breached, or in which some unaccounted-for female was living in the priest's house. Some of these cases involved minor clerics who did not celebrate Mass – but the fact that they served the altar in other ways was now enough to require them to be celibate. Clyve was equally severe on cases in which improvised local arrangements meant that the sacraments were not properly provided to parishioners. Altogether, he excommunicated twenty-two clergy of different kinds during his visitation: gone were the days of cheerful exhortations to do better.[27]

Clyve's scrutiny was not just limited to the clergy. With marriage now numbered among the seven sacraments of salvation, sexual impropriety, which breached the Church's vision of God's Holy order, fell within the inspectors' remit. There was, unsurprisingly, plenty of it about. In Woodbridge, the first village Clyve visited, he recorded the following cases:

> Robert le Ster is noted for adultery committed with a certain Carter. He doth not appear. Wherefore we suspend him from entering the Church.
>
> Juliana de Hornyngbroke is noted for adultery with Ralph de Pysinghe. The woman cited, does not appear, therefore suspended.
>
> John the Chaplain who was [previously] at Woodchurch in a former year is noted in connection with Joan the wife of William le Hert. The woman cited, does not appear, therefore suspended, subsequently cited again does not appear, therefore excommunicated.
>
> The same John is accused concerning the widow of le Spyle . . .

And so Clyve's lists go on, parish by parish, cataloguing the many – if not so varied – human failings of the Christian inhabitants of Romney Marsh.

Not only did visitations like Clyve's put personal morality under the microscope, but they applied force to bring it into line with the dictates of the fourth Lateran council. The next entry from Woodbridge reads how William, son of William Lucas, got 'Juliana Bructyn with child. The man appears and confesses and renounces his sin and is whipped three times round the Church.' Juliana was excused 'because she lies in childbed'.

This does mean what it seems to. Sexual transgression could and did result in beatings. William was literally whipped as he moved ritually around the church, although the terse visitation record gives no sense of how hard the lash was being wielded. In some cases, as Clyve noted, whipping round the church was combined with a second level of sanction. In the parish of Snave, Adam Cook and Lymna, daughter of John de la Bregge, confessed to living in adultery. They were duly 'whipped five times through Romney market place and five times through Warehome market place, and each five times round the Church'.

Here, and in four other cases Clyve recorded, wider public humiliation at a local market and more public whipping was added to locally inflicted punishment in front of the accused's fellow parishioners. While the fourth Lateran council's package of required piety may have become internalized by the fifteenth century, much of it seems to have been set in place by means of corporal punishment. If, that was, you belonged to the poorer classes. The same offences committed by a member of the elite generated financial penalties, physical punishment not being deemed seemly for those of higher status.[28]

Another significant feature of Clyve's visitation process also deserves a bit more thought. The inspection of the Romney Marsh parishes was carried out by a senior diocesan cleric, with no personal knowledge of the communities in question. Deficiencies in church buildings or service books and equipment were easy enough for him to recognize – but how could he know the details of villagers' transgressive sexual activity, except in cases, like that of William, son of William Lucas, where the accused actually confessed? For the most part the document doesn't say. However, information on the many sexual peccadilloes of the village populations can only have been provided by other members of the same communities: a mixture, perhaps, of angry, wronged partners, you might think, curtain-twitching busybodies, and people using the opportunity to settle scores. We can at least be more specific about the busybodies. In some visitation documents, a small group of key local witnesses who accompanied the visitor on his tour are named. Sometimes, surviving local documentation allows these witnesses to be identified. Wherever that can be done, they have turned out to be the richer free peasantry of their village communities.[29] In practice, then, the new visitation mechanism depended on the dovetailing of two processes: the more aggressive intrusion of central ecclesiastical authority into parish communities; and the co-operative provision of information from inside the communities themselves.

Romney Marsh is entirely representative of the new-style visitation process that emerged in England between 1250 and 1300, and which set a pattern for the rest of the Middle Ages. According to canon law, visitations were meant to happen every three years, an expectation which seems to have been broadly met.[30] Never before had the lives of the clergy and their provision of services been subject to such intense and regular scrutiny and punishment; nor had earlier visitations regularly searched out and punished offences against the Christian order committed by members of the laity. There remain questions over the extent to which such a visitation model was being followed across the rest of Latin Europe, since some details of the English process closely echoed particular contemporary developments in the operations of English government. But systemic pressure to conduct more intensive local questioning, homing in on clerical celibacy and the provision of the sacraments, and with a simultaneous focus on lay morality, was explicitly central to the Lateran programme. Contemporary canon law – not confined to English conditions – devoted much attention to many of the issues raised by the new-style process: how much testimony constituted valid suspicion of immorality; and whose testimony, in general terms, could be trusted (canon law agreeing with English practice in its conclusion that wealthier peasants were the most reliable witnesses). While there might well have been some significant regional variations, therefore, a similar transformation of the traditional episcopal visitation process was clearly underway right across thirteenth-century Latin Christendom.[31]

Exploring how the Lateran agenda played out at parish level allows us to understand how its innovative programme of piety managed to take such a firm hold on the population of medieval Western Europe. Part of the story, as we've seen, was a substantial dose of religious excitement: the enthusiastic adoption, on the part of laity and clergy alike, of its coherent idea-sets, persuasively championed by the newly formed, papal-backed preaching orders. The new theology of salvation developed in the twelfth-century universities carried an ultimately optimistic message: while humanity is deeply sinful, and all sins must be paid for, redemption can be achieved. And even if Purgatory will be a horrible experience, Heaven awaits. Visitation documents like Clyve's focus on resistance to this theological process, more or less consciously articulated, by individuals whose lives were breaching the new standards in one way or another, and who were accordingly named and shamed. Implicit within the record, but an essential part of the overall story, is the much greater percentage of the population whom the inspectors found no reason to censure.

Equally persuasive as the preaching of the friars, and drawing on the same bodies of zealous, disciplined manpower, was the utterly unprecedented level of repression that the newly unified ecclesiastical establishment was prepared to unleash against religious dissidence. Unlimited imprisonment in brutal conditions, physical torture, burning at the stake – there was no limit to the violence that the Church was willing to deploy to eliminate perceived resistance. Meanwhile, as Clyve's report vividly shows, lower-level coercion, more pervasively distributed, was central to the new sacramental rhythm of the medieval parish.

Alongside these direct applications of different levels of force, the new order rested upon a series of indirect but arguably still more effective pressures to conform. The evident fear and anxiety generated by the activities of the inquisitors and the 'othering' of invented enemies, from Jewish communities to perceived heretics, were also evident at parish level, albeit at lower volumes. Here, the regime of visitation and informing was more than enough to enforce at least outward compliance with the new order over the long term. Highly instructive, I think, is the fate of the one group of dualist heretics recorded to have made it across the Channel to England in the twelfth century. They were neither arrested nor executed; rather, during the winter after their arrival, they perished from a combination of starvation and exposure. Sufficient discipline had been built into the operation of parish Christianity in England to cut them off from any community-level protection or support.[32]

The full range of enforcement methods in play after 1215 has, to my mind, a peculiarly familiar ring to it. The general dissemination of an ultimately positive ideology was backed up by periodic witch-hunts of breath-taking brutality, justified by a process of paranoid fantastical othering. This invented enemies for the new Christian order, in the same way that the inquisitors' methods might turn pretty much any individual into a transgressive heretic. At the local level, the process of generating behavioural and ideological conformity was reinforced by regular tours of inspection, which both encouraged and depended upon a culture of informing. This has strong resonances of the mechanisms that allowed the security apparatuses of the old Soviet bloc countries to work so effectively before the Berlin Wall came down in 1989. Only afterwards, when the East German Stasi files were ripped open, did it become so apparent how much of the population – in the hope of gaining advantage for themselves or those they loved, or simply to stave off hostile official attention – had been willing to inform on their neighbours.

As the Lateran enforcement process gathered pace throughout the late Middle Ages, western Christendom increasingly resembled a one-party state. Its universalizing, monolithic ideology was used to generate a clear profile of model behaviour. Those unwilling to conform were then forced into line by a whole series of positive and negative enforcement mechanisms, ranging from a cycle of enjoyable festivals to ruthless violence, enacted against a backdrop of manufactured fear and ongoing pressures to conform – not least by recruiting neighbour to inform on neighbour.

Medieval Latin Christendom was, however, an arthritic and deeply inefficient form of one-party state. The power of the Church hierarchy had always to co-exist with that of secular rulers, who could occasionally be constrained but mostly had to be negotiated with – and whose co-operation, particularly in carrying out the most extreme punishments, remained absolutely necessary.[33] The geographical distances involved also meant that, while Rome may have set the rules from the late twelfth century onwards, it was often not in close control of what actually happened on the ground. Small-scale dissident movements such as the Waldenses could also operate between the cracks of the structure, even if its preachers and their hearers did periodically fall foul of inquisitors. All the same, the overall picture is striking. Positive ideological enthusiasm and pervasive threat of punishment for any deviation were inseparable components of a powerful, two-pronged strategy of enforcement that, over the long term, brought much of Europe into line with patterns of religiosity sanctified by Innocent III's great council of 1215. This overarching conclusion prompts two final lines of thought.

First, it adds a significant gloss to current understandings of pre-Reformation religiosity. The pattern of parish piety set out at Lateran IV may have been internalized and still vigorous in the late fifteenth century, but this was to a substantial extent an imposed set of cultural norms. One-party cultural contexts, by their very nature, massively complicate the identification of properly voluntary behaviour. If you turn the spotlight on any particular conforming individual, their actions will tend to appear voluntary. Since some individuals always did (and do) dissent from imposed cultural–political systems, this means that it is theoretically possible that any individual *might* do. And the existence of that possibility, however theoretical, makes any conformist behaviour look voluntary. But if you think about the overall situation, the pressures to conform are so many and so varied that in fact most individuals will always choose to conform, to the extent that the system allows them to. Once proper account is taken of the constraining pressures, therefore, what might look like purely voluntary behaviour actually isn't. People conform because, faced with this much pressure, nearly everyone does. Take away that force, and behaviour will change.

This has resonance for our understanding of the partial unravelling of Lateran piety that unfolded in the Reformation of the sixteenth century. Given the degree of force that was required to hold Lateran piety in place, the fact that, once people understood that deviation – as licensed by Protestant critiques of the late medieval Church – had now become permissible, substantial elements of the population of western Christendom began to move in different religious directions becomes more explicable. In sixteenth-century England, for instance, large swathes of the population remained devoted to the old order. But that devotion did ultimately rest (all the same) on the application of a large amount of coercion, and when that coercion was removed it is no surprise to find that disenchantment began to emerge.

Second, the degree of coercion involved at the climax of European Christianization prompts some final reflection on the overall process which created this monolithic cultural edifice. 'Conversion' – when applied to this long-term process of religious transformation – has turned out to be a deeply misleading singular noun. In practice, it encompassed a wide variety of phenomena. At one extreme, Christian conversion could be the result of life-changing personal spiritual experience, after the classic model of St Paul on the road to Damascus. Such experience was a recurring feature in the spread of Christianity in every phase of its history, whether it was conversion in the sense of a total change of allegiance from a different religion, or in the sense of a new understanding of how 'proper' Christianity required you to behave. There is of course nothing unique to Christianity in generating intense spiritual experience.

Nonetheless, as we have seen, intense personal conversion stories represent only one strand within the many shifts in religious allegiance that brought European Christendom into existence. Many other conversion stories were completely involuntary. The Saxons were battered into religious submission by Charlemagne; the Elbe Slavs were brought to Christianity by the combined sword power of the Holy Roman Empire and a recently converted Polish kingdom; the Northern Crusades spread the faith to the north-eastern Baltic at sword point. Then there were the many individuals who found themselves the recipients of top-down processes of religious change instituted by ruling elites, who had accepted Christianity along with its inherent obligation to spread the faith. No doubt a significant proportion of the peasantry of early medieval Europe voluntarily embraced the resulting processes of religious change in the sixth century and beyond. But there is substantial evidence of passive and active peasant resistance, and we need to take seriously the willingness of Gregory the Great and other Church leaders to tax and beat their peasants into at least an outward show of Christian submission.[34] Similarly coercive processes, if not so fully documented, also played a central role in the mass peasant conversions – again top-down in nature – which followed the many cases of elite self-conversion recorded north of the Channel in the early medieval period, and east of the Elbe in the second age of Christian Empire.

In between documented cases of intense personal conversion and the many instances of larger groups being forced to adopt Christianity stands the fascinating phenomenon of ostensibly voluntary elite self-conversion. Encompassing everything from the adoption of Christianity by landowning Roman elites in the fourth century to the subsequent self-Christianization of a host of northern and central/eastern European warlords, these conversions played a fundamental role in the emergence of European Christendom. The Christian elites of early medieval western Europe – and, subsequently, northern and eastern Europe – eventually built the churches and monasteries, became higher-level church officials, and also constrained their subordinate peasantries into accepting their new religion. In terms of simple geographical extent, it was this kind of conversion process that initially brought Christianity to the majority of the European landmass, and to most of its population.

Some of this was certainly the result of spiritual conviction. The intensity of St Augustine's experience in the garden was clearly shared by a number of his peers. But highly spiritual Christian biographies survive disproportionately in the source material because medieval monks were responsible for preserving ancient texts. For every Augustine, there were unrecorded numbers of others who, faced with Christian emperors and the Christianization of the public life of the late Roman Empire, concluded that they needed to conform, at least outwardly, to protect their local standing. It remained possible to dissent entirely, and some did so, but the Roman imperial system had always demanded ideological conformity from its elites, operating as its own one-party state, and the penalties faced for not coming into line after its cultural structures had decisively shifted in a Christian direction in the final decades of the fourth century, directly threatened the individual's continued elite status. Despite the many elite saints of the late Roman period, therefore, many contemporary elite conversions were the product of calculation rather than conviction, a point confirmed by the fact that many of their descendants would later convert again, to Islam, for very similar reasons.

A less direct but equally profound element of constraint also underlay the elite self-conversion processes that unfolded north of the Channel in the sixth and seventh centuries, and east of the Elbe in the ninth and beyond. Here the converting elites were responding to the preferences of powerful, neighbouring Christian rulers, and attempting to recruit those neighbours' support. Again, there were varying degrees of religious enthusiasm on display, but some of the most enthusiastic – like 'Good King' Wenceslas – came to a bad end, and careful calculation was again a prominent theme. So it was, too, with the ebb and flow of the Christian missions to Scandinavia in the Viking period, which initially flourished – then failed – in direct relationship to the perceived power of the Carolingian and Ottonian dynasties.

In the end, the fully fledged Christian one-party state of high medieval Europe has to be seen as the culmination, therefore, of a long history of more and less directly forced conversion. Many processes of transformation came together to generate the unified religious mix of ideology and practice that constituted the programmatic piety of the fourth Lateran council, but from the time of Constantine onwards, the Christianization of Europe was closely linked to the exercise of power at every level: imperial, royal, ecclesiastical and, even, in the late medieval parish, of one peasant over another. Which, on reflection, is perhaps not such a surprising conclusion. Many people have religious beliefs and intense spiritual experiences, not least because the course of all human life, above all the inescapable interplay of love and death, has always generated existential reflection. But spirituality does not usually express itself within the defined norms of a monolithic cultural edifice. There's still plenty of religion in the modern world, despite the combined impacts of science, rationalism and materialism – and plenty of Christianity too. Only in the unique circumstances of the first few centuries of the second millennium, however, was a unique level of social and institutional force assembled to sanctify one particular, detailed interpretation of the biblical texts as 'correct' Christianity, and to enforce an almost monolithic level of individual compliance with its required norms of religious belief and ritual practice.

Notes

INTRODUCTION

1. You will find no sense that Christianity might not have won in the otherwise wonderful later nineteenth-century studies of Harnack (1924, cf. Harnack (1908)) or in the twentieth-century overview of Pelikan (1971–89). 2. Just for purposes of illustration, and there are of course many more monographs I could have chosen: Brown (2013) strays only a little outside the period 300–800, for instance, where the central focus of Smith (2005) is 500–1000, while Hamilton (2013) covers primarily *c.* 900–1200. Fletcher's account of the conversion of Europe (1998) does cover the entire period but has relatively little to say about the internal development of Christian institutions, beliefs and disciplinary practice. The point is reinforced by the wonderfully rich volumes of the *New Cambridge History of Christianity*, which sustain much of the argument which follows, but which have the overall effect of subdividing the field into a series of distinct chronological tranches (up to Constantine, Constantine to AD 600, 600–1100, and 1100–1500).

1. 'BY THIS CONQUER . . .'

1. Eusebius *Life of Constantine* 1.28–9, trans. Cameron and Hall (1999). On the surrounding events, among many possibilities, see Lenski (2006); Barnes (2011), chs. 3–4; Bardill (2012), ch. 1. 2. For more detail on the politics, see e.g., Barnes (2011), ch. 5. 3. Lactantius *On the Deaths of the Persecutors* 44.5. 4. *Pan. lat.* 6 [7].21.3–4. 5. *Pan. lat.* 4 [10]. 14–15. 6. I am very much in agreement here with the argument of Flower (2012); cf. Weiss (1993) and in English (2003), whose argument that the solar halo vision was progressive reinterpretation has won considerable support; Lenski (2016), 69–70 for refs, including notably Barnes (2011), 30ff.; and Girardet (2010), 44–52, (2012), who considers that the vision had been reinterpreted in Christian terms as early as 311, before the victory over Maxentius. At p. 288 n. 5 Flower acutely observes in response to all the rather desperate attempts to cite solar halos: 'While rings and "crosses" have been documented [during solar halos], meteorologists and astronomers have so far not recorded any sightings of the words "By this conquer" in either Latin or Greek – at least as far as I am aware . . .' 7. Most recently Lenski (2016), 29–31 who emphasizes the extent to which the portraiture of Constantine from this era conformed to Tetrarchic norms. Liebeschuetz (1979) remains an excellent introduction to Tetrarchic-era pagan cult. 8. Lenski (2016), 32–4 on the broader change in Constantine's presentation from loyal Tetrarch to slayer of tyrants. 9. The letters (which relate to the Donatist dispute: see p. 130): Eusebius *Ecclesiastical History* 10.15.8; Optatus *Against the Donatists* App. 3, 5 with (e.g.) Lenski (2016), 70–72. Chi-Rho

milestones: *L'Année épigraphique* 2000: 1799, 1801; cf. Lenski (2016), 8–9. As Lenski rightly emphasizes, these early uses of the Chi-Rho and on a portrayal of a helmeted Constantine on a silver medallion of 315 undermine the argument of Bardill (2012), 160–78 that the Chi-Rho was a significantly later Christianized reinterpretation of the vision. **10.** Arch of Constantine: Elsner (2006), 258–60. Sunday law: *CJ* 3.12.2 with Girardet (2007). Highest God: *Pan. Lat.* 12; Nixon and Rogers (1994), 292–3. **11.** See esp. Eusebius *Life of Constantine* 2.55.1–2 for Constantine's triumphantly Christian Letter to the Provincials after his victory over Licinius; cf. (among many possibilities and with full refs.) Lee (2006), 170–77; Lenski (2016), ch. 3. On the council of Nicaea, see below pp. 27–35. **12.** Zosimus 2.29–30, deriving from the anti-Christian fourth-century historian Eunapius of Sardis. **13.** See e.g., with discussion of many other alternatives, Drake (2000), ch. 5; Drake (2006), 113–16; Girardet (2007); Barnes (2011), 74ff.; Bardill (2012), chs. 7–8. **14.** On imperial ideology in general, see Dvornik (1966), with McCormick (1986) on the specific importance of victory. For a sustained exploration of the intersection between victory and politics in the imperial system, see Heather (2018) *passim* but esp. ch. 2. **15.** Corcoran (1996), 179–86. **16.** *Pan. lat.* 6 [7]; cf. among many possibilities Barnes (1981), 35–7 for further comment on the politics. **17.** Refs. as n. 9. **18.** Julian *Ep.* 111 of 362 records that he had then been a non-Christian believer for eleven years, dating his conversion to *c.* 351. Ammianus 21.2.4 reports his deliberately misleading attendance at the Epiphany service of 361: Matthews (1989), 122–3. **19.** Helena: Edwards (2006a), 144–5, though the idea that she discovered there the True Cross was a late-fourth-century addition. Constantius Chlorus: Eusebius *Life of Constantine* 1.28–9. The indications of long-standing familial Christian allegiance have been discussed before (e.g. Elliott (1987), cf. *id.* (1996)), but not been set against the political significance of the precise dates of Constantine's progressive revelation of a Christian religious allegiance. **20.** Corcoran (1996), 179–86. **21.** I am not the first to follow this argumentative path: Barnes (2002), (2011), chs. 2–3. There are exceptions, but the average age of death for emperors was around 50 and Diocletian and Maximian were both there or thereabouts by the early 300s, so the political focus would have been firmly on succession, as it almost always was: Heather (2018), 148–9, 163–4, 315–16, 328–9. **22.** Elliott (1987), with below p. 44 on the subsequent toxicity in Christian circles of any accusation of having avoided persecution. **23.** Burckhardt (1949). **24.** 'Go therefore and make disciples of all nations, baptizing them in the name of the Father and of the Son and of the Holy Spirit, teaching them to observe all that I have commanded you.' Matthew 28:19–20. **25.** Origen *Contra Celsum* 3.45. On the Catholic Francophone tradition, see Moderan (2004) citing e.g. Daniélou and Marrou (1963). The sociological study is Stark (1996). **26.** Notably MacMullen (1984), 32; Hopkins (1998), cf. *id.* (1999), 84–6; Frend (2006); Barnes (2011). But Edwards (2006a), 137ff., Cameron (2006) and Trombley (2006), for instance, are more sceptical. Among the older literature, Gibbon guessed 5 per cent, but Harnack (1908) and Jones (1964), ch. 22, refused to commit themselves. **27.** Trombley (2006) is a very useful general survey of the evidence for actual Christian conversion. No. of bishoprics *c.* 300: Moderan (2004) with refs. Later fourth-century Antioch: Sandwell (2007). **28.** On the Dura Church, see now Peppard (2016). The evidence for the developing pre-Constantinian community in Rome is surveyed by Trombley (2006). **29.** Eumeneia: Mitchell (1993), vol. 2, 37–42 (cf. 58–64). On the problems of Gregory of Nyssa's *Life* of Gregory Thaumaturgus, see Mitchell (1993), 53–7. Cirta: Lepelley, vol. 2 (1981), 383–9. **30.** Stark (1996) additionally proposes that Christianity's emphases on love and charity mean that it is likely to have cared more intensely for its members, giving them a slightly higher likely survival rate compared to their pagan neighbours, whose numbers were also limited by a habit of exposing unwanted children. Possibly, but all of these suggestions are questionable, and, as we shall see in more detail in a moment, any numerical advantage on these fronts was probably balanced by early Christianity's distinct ambivalence towards marriage, sex and procreation (which he doesn't mention). Edwards (2006a), offers some additional well-judged criticism, focusing on the evidence for higher conversion rates in the early years, which then tailed off, and the negative effects of persecution. 31. The text with English translation of the Nicene canons and Creed: Tanner (1990), 1–19, with more detailed discussion of the Creed below p. 31. The main source for Nicaea itself is Eusebius *Life of Constantine* 3.4–24, with commentary in the relevant notes to Cameron and Hall (1999). On the myth of 318 participants, and for general introductions to the council, see e.g., Edwards (2006); Barnes (2011), ch. 6. Examples of the comprehensive formality of later conciliar proceedings and their recording are the materials from Carthage (411) and Ephesus (432): see respectively Lancel (1972–5) and Schwartz (1922–30). 32. The best general guide to the Arian dispute in English remains Hanson (1988) but see also – among many possibilities – Edwards (2006); Williams (2001); Anatolius (2007); Uthemann (2007) with full refs., supplemented by the useful essays in Berndt and Steinacher (2014). 33. Vincent of Lerins *Commonitory* 2.6. 34. On the journeys of Abercius of Hierapolis, see Mitchell (2006), 295–6 with further refs. 35. For a good introduction to Marcion, emphasizing the link between textual preference and system of belief: Gamble (2006); Brakke (2006) with refs. There remains considerable debate over whether Gnostic dualism was 'simply' a Christian heresy or had deeper pre-Christian origins. 36. The bibliography on, first, the emergence of a broader Christian literature and then of its narrowing down to an approved canon is enormous, but Metzger (1997) is fundamental. For introductions in English see e.g., the essays of Evans, Grant and Birdsall in Ackroyd and Evans (1970); Wiles (1967); Mitchell (2006); Elliott (2013); Verheyden (2013) with full refs. Marcion: refs. as n. 35. The Revelation of St Peter was still being read at Easter in Palestine a century after Eusebius condemned it: Herrin (1987), ch. 3, but it unfortunately doesn't survive. The Nag Hammadi texts can be read in translation (Robinson (1996)): their survival in such late copies suggests, again, that while an official canon had been more or less defined by *c.* 200, there remained enormous variation in the range of venerated texts on the ground for at least another century and a half. For an introduction to the evidence for continued editing of even the canonical books of the NT, see Parker (2013) with refs. 37. Good introductions to Monarchian theologies, and Paul of Samosata in particular, can be found in Young (2006); Hall (2006) with full refs. 38. Kelly (1952), chs. 1–5, provides a basic history to the prehistory of Creeds, with ch. 6 comparing Nicaea. 39. Kelly (1952), chs. 10–11. 40. Excellent general guides in English to the period between Nicaea and Constantinople: Kopecek (1979); Hanson (1988); Ayres (2004); Gwynn (2007). For a recent restatement of the 'court party' hypothesis, see Parvis (2014). Further comment, below pp. 127–30. 41. Early controversies over the dating of Easter have a huge scholarly bibliography going back to the fundamental work of Krusch (1880), built upon by Strobel (1977). For an accessible introduction in English, see Talley (1986), 5–33. Even after Nicaea, the outcome was not unform: in the 5th century Easter was still being calculated on different bases in east and west: Herrin (1987), 111–13. 42. A classic expression of more traditional views on developing Christian–Jewish relations is Harnack (1908), vol. 1, 80–83. For an excellent introduction with full primary refs. and extensive secondary bibliography to more recent discussion, see Marcus (2006); Lieu (2006); Trevett (2006), 319ff.; cf. Dunn (1991); Lieu (2004). On the development of post-Rabbinic Judaism after the destruction of the Temple, see e.g., Goodman (1998); Barclay (2004); Neusner (2006). On the early spread of Christianity through diasporic Jewish communities, see Rajak (2006); cf. Pearson (2006) and Roberts (1979), ch. 1, on the early Christian papyri from Egypt. 43. For an introduction to pre-Constantinian patterns of religious authority, see generally Bradshaw (2002); Vinzent (2016); with more particular studies of Meeks (2006), 153–5 (on episcopal origins: note especially that bishops were primarily elected by their communities); Vinzent (2006) (Rome); Pearson (2006) (Alexandria); Hall (2006); Rapp (2005), chs.1–2, all with full refs. New Prophecy movement: sources collected in de Labriolle (1913) with commentary in Strobel (1980); cf. Trevett (2006), 320–25. **44.** Medieval ecclesiology would later insist that Nicaea was actually the *second* world or ecumenical council, with every Christian community represented: the first being a meeting of the twelve disciples in Jerusalem recorded in Acts. This was pious wishful thinking. **45.** For an introduction to the more limited pre-Nicene tradition of holding regional councils, see Hall (2006), 428–33. Papal confusion between Nicaea and Serdica: Jasper and Fuhrmann (2001), ch. 2. **46.** The relevant bibliography is enormous, but for good introductions to the institutional development of the Church in the 4th/5th centuries and its consequences, see e.g., Rapp (2005); Brown (1992); Herrin (1987), chs. 1–3, Jones (1964), ch. 22 with full refs. On the rowing back in the authority of episcopal courts, see Harries (1999), ch. 10; Humfress (2007), ch. 7. **47.** A selection from the huge bibliography on Ambrose and the Cappadocians: McLynn (1994); Rousseau (1994); Van Dam (2003); Elm (2012); cf. Brown (2012), esp. ch. 2 on the Constantinian Church. On independent Christian intellectuals of the late 4th century, see e.g., Rebenich (2002); Stancliffe (1983). **48.** For further discussion of the Melitian schism, see Barnes (1993), ch. 17; Williams (2001) with full refs. Most of the non-Athanasian texts are collected in Bell (1924), 38–99. Much more is known of the development of the long-lived Donatist dispute: see most recently Whitehouse (2016) with full refs. **49.** Tertullian *Apology* 40.2. **50.** Musurillo (1972) collects the 'authentic' early martyr *Acta*, including that of Perpetua: for recent discussion of which see Cooper (2013), ch. 5. The History of the Martyrs in Palestine can be most easily read in the reissued old English translation of Cureton (2016). The general literature on early Christian martyrdom is again enormous, but good general introductions are provided by Castelli (2004); Hall (2006a); and the collected essays in Gemeinhardt and Leemans (2012). **51.** Samarin (1972), 293. **52.** *Didascalia* in English: see Connolly (1929). *Didache*, and the *Dream of the Shepherd of Hermas* can be found in translation in Stevenson (1957). **53.** See esp. Young (1997) *passim* on *paranesis*. **54.** Good general introductions to the strict demands of early Christian practice, with full refs. to the broader literature and a good sense of regional variation, can be found in Meeks (2006); Osiek (2006); Tilly (2006); Hall (2006). The general intensity of early baptismal preparation emerges from *The Catechetical Lectures of Cyril of Jerusalem*; cf. Cramer (1993), chs. 1–2. Tertullian *De Spectaculis* can be read in the English trans. of Glover (1931). **55.** Quoted from Matthew 19:21–24; the story is also told in Mark 10:21–25. **56.** Baptism (among many possibilities): Cramer (1993), chs. 3–4; Hall (2006); Casiday (2007), with below p. 324. Sex and marriage: good introductions are Brown (1998) and Hunter (2007), both with full refs. Wealth: Brown (2012), but the compromise was not reached without great soul-searching. See esp. pp. 291–300 on Melania the Younger. **57.** Good introductions to the evolution of penitence: Hall (2006); Casiday (2007); Greer (2007); the essays in Firey (2008); Hillner (2015), but it should be noted that pre-Constantinian public penance is known more in theory than from actual examples. The 6th-century Gallic bishop was Contumeliosus: *Epp. Arelat.* 35, 37; cf. Hillner (2015), 301–2. **58.** Good introductions to the process of change here are provided by Rébillard (1994); Hall (2006a); Casiday (2007). But see especially now the important study of Brown (2015) and esp. chs. 1–3 contrasting the pre-Constantinian Church with the changed world of St Augustine. **59.** The potential bibliography is immense, but for good introductions see Elsner (1998); Jensen (2006); Brenk (2007) with full refs. and the essays in Jefferson and Jensen (2015). **60.** The typology of 'world rejecting' vs 'world accepting' religions goes back to Max Weber: see Weber (1925), 225–356; Weber (1947); with the English trans. of an important summary essay at Weber (1948). Dunn (2009), ch. 1, usefully surveys some of the major strands in the socio-anthropological analysis of religion. **61.** On Cyril, see now Drijvers (2004). **62.** The *Life of Antony* played a crucial role in the conversion experience of St Augustine, who also records its electric effect earlier upon two would-be imperial civil servants: below p. 62. Peter Brown (1971a) kick-started modern, more positive discussion of Holy Men (previously seen largely as a sign of growing superstition) and returned to the topic in Brown (1997). On the increasing importance of the example of martyrs to the ascetic tradition, see (among a host of possibilities) Brown (1981); Elm (1994); Leyser (2000). On Jerome: see, among many possibilities, Kelly (1977); Rebenich (2002). **63.** See Elm (1994) on Eustathius' influence nonetheless on the Cappadocians. Pelagius and Augustine: Brown (1967), ch. 29; Rees (1988). Priscillian: Burrus (1995). **64.** Trans. Ward (1981). **65.** A good general introduction to this evolution (found in 6th-century monasticism in general, not just the Rule of Benedict) is Lawrence (1984). **66.** My whole discussion in this section is profoundly shaped by the late, very great Robert Markus's wonderful book, *The End of Ancient Christianity*: Markus (1990).

2. CONVERSION IN A CHRISTIAN EMPIRE

1. The calling of the disciples is told in various versions: Matthew 4:18–22; Mark 1:16–20; Luke 5:1–11. Paul on the road to Damascus: Acts 9. Augustine's *Confessions* is available in many convenient translations, but none better than Chadwick (1991). Brown (1967) is an indispensible companion to its reading, with more detail in O'Donnell (1992). **2.** On the background to its composition: Brown (1967), ch. 16. On the garden scene in particular, see now the convincing treatment of Turner (2012), 138–45, with full discussion of previous scholarship. **3.** Julian *Ep.* 19 with Lamberton (1986), chs. 2–5, on the theological significance of the *Odyssey* and *Iliad*. **4.** Augustine at Cassiacum: Brown (1967), chs. 10–11. Ausonius: Green (1991) with Matthews (1975), ch. 3, on his hugely successful political career. Synesius: Bregman (1982). But contrast Paulinus of Nola: Trout (1999). **5.** Among many good introductions: Stewart (1994); Leopold (2004); Maroney (2006), all with refs. to further reading. Particularly in the context of Christian missionary work, syncretism can be a dirty word, but most human practice – outside polarized contexts at least – turns out to be wonderfully complex. I was fascinated to come across, in the account of an early 19th-century traveller to Crete, converted Cretan Muslims regularly acting as godparents for the children of their Christian neighbours: Pashley (2012), 10. **6.** Bowes (2008), ch. 3, reinforcing existing accounts such as Fletcher (1998), ch. 2; Brown (2013), ch. 6. This fundamental gap in Christian coverage is the prime reason why some of the more optimistic accounts of Christian conversion in the late Roman period cannot be correct: p. 20. **7.** Curse tablet: Tomlin (1988). Antioch: Sandwell (2007). Egypt: Fluck *et al.* (2015), pt 5. **8.** Egypt: Bagnall (1982), (1988); Dijkstra (2008) on evidence for Christianization, with the further thoughts of Frankfurter (1998), (2007), whose account profoundly shapes my discussion. On Asia Minor, see Trombley (2007) with the *Council of Laodicaea*, esp. canons 29, 34, 36, 37, 38, 39. Antioch: Sandwell (2007). **9.** Further discussion of the spread of Christianity among the senatorial elites of Rome, with refs., see Salzman (2002), (2007), with Salzman (1990) on the Calendar of 354; Cameron (2011). **10.** For further discussion, see Kaster (1988); Marrou (1982) with above p. 12 for the broader ties of this educational rationale to imperial ideology. Some teachers were expert in both Latin and Greek, many in just the one language. For an introduction to the nature and importance of public libraries, see the helpful essay collection of König *et al.* (2013), especially those of Bowie, Johnson, Tucci and Huston on the libraries of the Roman world. **11.** Augustine: compare Brown (1967), chs. 3, 11, 23. His evolving position is explored in more detail in the essays collected in Pollmann and Vessey (2007). Basil: e.g. Wilson (1975). Marius Victorinus: see n. 12 below. Note, too, Jerome's famous dream where he was accused of being a Ciceronian rather than a Christian: Kelly (1977); Rebenich (2002). Brown (1992), esp. chs. 1–2, explores some deeper background and consequences of this debate. **12.** Marius

Victorinus: Augustine *Confessions* 8.2.3–5 with Hadot (1971), 7–76. *Senatus matronum*: Bowes (2008), 99–103; cf. Kelly (1977); Rebenich (2002) on Jerome's Roman career. My broader discussion here depends on Bowes (2008), ch. 1 and 63–103, with Hillner (2006) on the *Tituli*. **13.** Bowes (2008), 103–23; On Chrysostom more generally, see Holum (1982); Liebeschuetz (1990); Barry (2019). **14.** Vessey (1988), and with his collected essays in Vessey (2005), is an excellent guide to the longer-term development of a Christianized version of classical literature in Late Antiquity, with below p. 79 for Augustine. **15.** One of Origen's works that hasn't survived was his *hexapla*, which laid out side by side the variant texts of no fewer than six different versions of parts of the Old Testament, four of them alternative translations into Greek. The complex tedium of this entirely necessarily philological masterpiece probably explains why it wasn't copied enough after his death to survive. **16.** On the basic analytical methods of the grammarians, see Vessey (2004), 22ff.; cf. Lamberton (1986), ch. 4, on the use of allegorical interpretation within the pre-Christian classical tradition. On the history of biblical translation and interpretation to establish norms of both behaviour and belief, see among many possibilities Lampe (1969); Sutcliffe (1969); Hanson (1970); Wiles (1970); Sparks (1970); Allison (2013); Graumann (2013). More interpretive treatments: Wiles (1975); Markus (1996); Young (1997); Dawson (2002) with further refs. **17.** The clearest account of the overall process I have found is Hanson (1970), 440–47, but see also Barnes and Williams (1993) for an important collection of supplementary essays. The supposed 'proof texts' were also subject to the same kinds of interpretation, with much immediately post-Nicene debate centring on Proverbs 8:22, 'The Lord brought me forth as the first of his works'. Opponents of Nicaea consistently interpreted this text as referring to the Son, a position which its supporters had to refute. Hanson (1970), 448, comments on the overall 'inefficiency' of these mechanisms of reading, since they could effectively support both the Nicene point of view and that of its various opponents. Someone less invested in the subject might substitute the word 'arbitrary', since you can more or less use the grammarians' techniques to reach any preferred intellectual position. As we shall see in the next chapter, the techniques of argumentation and reading were also insufficient by themselves to bring the dispute to an end: p. 127. **18.** According to one classic statement of the *Annales* vision of history, events are no more than 'surface disturbances', which often distract our gaze from more profound developments at work beneath the visible surface: Braudel (1973) preface. There are now many introductory guides to the Cultural Turn in historical studies and to the *Annales* school in particular (within which Braudel represents only one strand): e.g., the relevant essays in Bentley (1999); Iggers (2005); Gunn (2006). **19.** Most recently and influentially Brown (2013), esp. intro. and chs. 2–3 with full refs. More generally, Brown (2013), 10ff. (the introduction to the 2nd edn of 2002) picks out Braudel's influence upon his own work, which also shows up clearly in the way in which politics and states have always played a secondary role in his work compared to long-term cultural change, e.g., the highly influential Brown (1971), which deliberately subordinated political history to processes of cultural transformation. The broader historiographical project to identify a unified long Late Antiquity – AD 200–800 – in place of old notions of Decline and Fall also reflect, similar historiographical leanings, manifest for instance in the wonderful edited guide to Late Antiquity, one of whose central intellectual tendencies is to downplay the possibility that really important historical consequences might have followed from the end of particularly the western half of the Roman Empire: Bowersock, Brown and Grabar (1999). We will return to these important issues in Part Two of the book. **20.** Eusebius *Life of Constantine* 2.56. **21.** Administrators of Maxentius and Licinius: Dillon (2012), 119–21. Delphi: Lenski (2016), 216–17. Sopater: Eunapius, *Lives of the Sophists* 6.2–3; cf. *PLRE* 1, 846. Termessos and Sagalassos: Lenski (2016), 212–13. **22.** Themistius *Or.* 5.68d–69a. **23.** Jovian's religious policies are explored in Heather and Moncur (2001), 154–8. Death: Ammianus 25.7.9–11;

cf. John Chrysostom *Homilies* 15 for the suggestion that he was poisoned. **24.** *Life of Constantine* 3.55–8; cf. Cameron and Hall (1999), 301ff. *Life of Constantine* 3.54 does, however, make more general claims about the emperor stripping pagan temples of their wealth, treasures and roofs. **25.** Physical archives and quantity of business: Connolly (2010), 36–40; cf. Kelly (1994); Millar (1992), esp. chs. 3, 6. From the 390s in the east and 410s in the west, the legal evidence suggests that different departments of the palace bureaucracy started to keep more systematic archives of relevant legal decisions: Honoré (1998), 137–41. **26.** Bradbury (1994); Heather and Moncur (2001), chs. 1–2. **27.** I follow here the convincing arguments of Lenski (2016), ch. 4 (with full refs. to an extensive literature) against other treatments – e.g., Van Dam (2007a), 150–219) – which have argued that there was no religious dimension to the story. **28.** Lenski (2016), ch. 5, again with full refs., who is once more utterly convincing on the significance of the crucial phrases (contra e.g., Van Dam (2007a), 23–129). There was also a flat road between the two towns, but there's never been a law against making your case as rhetorically persuasive as possible . . . The inscriptions also put great emphasis on securing divine aid to protect the Constantinian dynasty: a key additional imperial concern. **29.** Libanius *Ep.* 66.2, trans. Norman (1992) as *Ep.* 52. **30.** See in more detail Heather and Moncur (2001), esp. chs. 1–2. The Neo-Platonic tradition of hostility towards Christianity is explored below, p. 142, but Themistius' self-image is a direct inversion of its archetype as set out in the various lives of its adepts: Fowden (1982). **31.** For introductions to the imperial cult and its wide-reaching effects, see Mitchell (1993), vol. 1, esp. ch. 8; Price (1984), chs. 7–8; de Blois *et al.* (2006), esp. pt 4; Ando (2008), esp. chs. 4–6. On the more general process of Romanization of which it formed a central part, see, e.g., the Gallic case study of Woolf (1998), with Gonzalez (1986) for the full text of the standard municipal constitution, and the more general account of Ando (2000). **32.** Tacitus *Annals* 14.31; cf. Mitchell (1993), vol. 1, 107. **33.** Dvornik (1966) remains an excellent introduction to the full ramifications of the classical ideology of rationality. **34.** Woolf (1998); Mitchell (1993), vol. 1, 109–17; Ando (2000). **35.** Persia: p. 69. Egyptian temple revenues were confiscated at the same moment: n. 8. **36.** City finance: Jones (1964), ch. 19, remains the essential introduction, with overviews such as Lewitt (1991); Ward-Perkins (2000) for the now overwhelming archaeological evidence (with refs.), which confirms the abundant literary evidence for the survival and prosperity of Roman provincial landowning elites. Dossey (2010) is an excellent North African case study. **37.** For introductions to the general evolution of the Roman legal system, see Jones (1964), ch. 14, though more recent treatments have tended to be less pessimistic: Liebs (1993), (2002); Harries (1999), ch. 1; Humfress (2007), pt 1. **38.** Symmachus *Relatio* xx: the case came to him as urban prefect because both parties were of senatorial rank. Heather (1994a) provides some examples of attempting to fix cases, but these could easily be multiplied. **39.** Basil *Ep.* 299; with Jones (1964), chs. 13, 20 on the system; Heather (1994a) again provides several specific examples. **40.** Skocpol *et al.* (1985). **41.** Mid-3rd century: Pflaum (1950), ch. 2. For a general account of bureaucratic expansion, Jones (1964), chs. 12, 15, 16, remains basic, supplemented now by a series of individual studies of specific bureaux: Delmaire (1989), (1995); Teitler (1985); Vogler (1979). **42.** Older views: e.g. Reid (1911); Vinogradoff (1911); Rostovtzeff (1926); Ennsslin (1939), (1939a). Politics of recruitment and interaction: Heather (1994a). **43.** Honorary grants: Jones (1964), 528–9. This has sometimes been seen as a way of ducking out of the imperial system, but that is to ignore the mechanisms by which honorary grants had to be secured. **44.** Amnesties: *C.Th.* 12.1.13, 22, 31, 38, with Heather (1994a), which also contains further discussion of the phenomenon of the *principales*: landowners who chose to remain in the cities. Examples of bureaucratic fortunes in action can be found in Banaji (2001), esp. ch. 5 (although Banaji to my mind underestimates the extent to which the new landowners probably came from the old curial classes) and Hickey (2012): the latter a case study in the success of the Apion family. **45.** Wilkinson (2009) for the redating of Palladas to the era of Constantine. **46.** Von Haeling (1978); Barnes (1989), (1995); cf. Heather and Moncur (2001), 58f. **47.** Themistius *Or.* 5; Symmachus *Relatio* 3 with below p. 146 on Hecebolius: clearly a notorious turncoat. **48.** This process is examined in more detail in Chapter 5 below. **49.** Tudors: helpful introductions to the operations of compliance at elite level are Rex (1993), (1996); Bernard (2005). A similar pattern also worked on the Continent, of course, where the individual preferences of German princes largely dictated which Lände remained Catholic, and which turned Protestant.

3. THE ALTAR OF VICTORY

1. *C.Th.* 16.10.7–20; cf. Fowden (1978). **2.** Symmachus *Relatio* 3; answered by Ambrose *Epp.* 72 and 73. An excellent introduction to the dispute can be found in McLynn (1994), ch. 3, with refs. to the older literature. The relevant documents are conveniently translated together in Croke and Harries (1982). **3.** *C.Th.* 16.10.11 for Theodosius' ban on sacrifice; cf. Sozomen *H.E.* 7.25.9 for the events at Thessalonica; cf. traditional accounts such as Palanque (1933), 245–50. On the impact on the Portian Basilica dispute of the finding of the relics of Gervasius and Protasius: Brown (1981); McLynn (1994), 209ff. **4.** See respectively Matthews (1975), ch. 3; McLynn (1994), ch. 4. **5.** McLynn (1994), ch. 3; Ambrose states that he hadn't seen the *relatio* at *Ep.* 72.13. **6.** Theodosian self-presentation: Heather and Moncur (2001), ch. 4; cf. Browning (1952) on the riot of the statues in Antioch. Theodosius and Ambrose: McLynn (1994), 323–30. **7.** On Ambrose's unmatched control of the narrative, see McLynn (1994), 181–96 (Portian Basilica), 298–309 (Callinicum), 315–30 (Thessalonica) with full refs. to previous scholarship taking Ambrose essentially at face value. **8.** Ammianus 22.16; cf. the general discussion of Hahn and Emmel (eds.) (2008). **9.** *C.Th.* 16.10.11. **10.** Fowden (1978), 69–70. **11.** Lib. *Or.* 30.8–9 with commentary in McLynn (2005). Egyptian iconoclasts: Frankfurter (1998), 265–284, (2007), 183–5; Gaza: Fowden (1978), 72–5, but see MacMullen (1984) on the problems posed by the *Life of Porphyry*. The essays in Hahn and Emmel (eds.) (2008) provide a series of excellent, regionally focused case studies. **12.** Shenoute: Michigan ms. 158, quoted in Frankfurter (1998), 265; see further the helpful essay of Emmel (2008). More generally, see Nixey (2017); Frankfurter (1998), 277–84. **13.** McLynn (1994), 330–35. **14.** Libanius and Gaza: refs. as n. 11. Apamea: Fowden (1978) discussing Theodoret *H.E.* 5.21.1, 5–15. **15.** An obvious exception is Athanasius, patriarch of Alexandria: Barnes (1993). **16.** Which is why imperial patronage tended to work, as explored in Chapter 2, by rewarding or punishing cities as a whole for their willingness to come into line (or not) with imperial religious preferences: pp. 88–91. The eventual fate of Marcellus is recorded at Sozomen *H.E.* 7.15.12–14. **17.** Notably Brown (1995); cf. Cameron (2011): a very long and wonderfully illuminating study, but the conclusion lays out his general model, which can then be followed up in more detail in the individual chapters. **18.** *City of God* XIX 17. **19.** *City of God* V 12. **20.** See for instance *City of God* XIX 6 on the limited quality of the justice delivered by the Empire's legal systems. **21.** On the *City of God*, see further Brown (1967), chs. 26–7; Vessey *et al.* (2013). **22.** The canons of the first four ecumenical councils are translated in Bright (1892), and the proceedings of II Constantinople (553) in Price (2009). On classical literary analysis and the evolving interpretation of the biblical canon, see above p. 78. **23.** Constantius II and the Arian crisis: Hanson (1988); Kopecek (1979); Barnes (1993); Gwynn (2007). Justinian: Heather (2018), 78–80, 202–10; Price (2009) with deeper background and much more detail provided by Gray (1979), (2005); Frend (1972). **24.** Constantine at Nicaea: Eusebius *Life of Constantine* 3.4; cf., among many commentators, Drake (2000), 250–55; Edwards (2006); Barnes

(2011), ch. 6 with refs. The central importance of emperors and their officials to the running of ecumenical councils emerges clearly from the fully minuted *Acta* of later councils such as Ephesus, Chalcedon and II Constantinople; cf. Edwards (2007). It is traditional among those with more skin in the game than myself to dismiss those hostile to Nicaea as some kind of 'court party' as opposed to proper, Orthodox Christians: see e.g., Parvis (2014). The reality is that *all* rival Churchmen had to operate as court parties in the late Roman world, or they had not the slightest hope of success: see further n. 29 on enforcement. **25.** Two classic instances are the patriarchs Athanasius and Cyril of Alexandria, on whom see e.g., Barnes (1993) and McGuckin (2004) with refs. Flower (2016) is an excellent collection of ecclesiastical invectives against Constantius II from Churchmen (including Athanasius) opposed to the trajectory of his theological policies, but this did not stop Athanasius from simultaneously lobbying to change the imperial mind: Barnes (1993). **26.** Esp. *C.Th.* 16.5. 6–24: all within the reign of Theodosius I; cf. McLynn (2009), no. 3. **27.** It is hard not to think that Constantine's more measured approach to the Melitian schism, and indeed the whole Arian crisis at Nicaea (p. 32), was one of the more positive fruits of this bitter experience; cf. Barnard (1982); Drake (2000), 251–2. **28.** There was, it seems, a second period of persecution of the Donatists somewhere between 347 and 361, but then nothing more for the next thirty years. On the failures and vacillations of Constantine and his fourth-century successors in dealing with the problem, see most recently: Miles (2016); Lenski (2016a). **29.** On the endgame, see Lenski (2016a), 180–86; cf. Lancel (1972–5) for the council of 411 with the further commentary of McLynn (2016). **30.** This point, it should be stressed, was not accepted by the eastern patriarchs of Alexandria, Antioch, Jerusalem and Constantinople. **31.** Brief introduction to developing Church (canon) law in this period: Brundage (1995), ch. 1; Pennington (2007). Church courts: Jones (1964), ch. 22; Harries (1999), ch. 10; Humfress (2007), ch. 7. For papal decretals of the late Roman period, see Jasper and Fuhrmann (2001), chs. 1–3; d'Avray (2019). **32.** For an introduction to papal elections and their associated violence, see Curran (2000), esp. ch. 4. Introductions to the fall of Chrysostom: Holum (1982); Liebeschuetz (1990); Barry (2019). **33.** Dvornik (1966) for the theory, usefully supplemented by MacCormack (1981) on some of its ceremonial expression. Constantine's burial arrangements: Mango (1985). **34.** For some introduction to the concept of the Confessional State, see Clark (1989); Braddick (2000); Gibson (1995); Morris (2005). It is worth noting that, even with more powerful administrative and legal levers of power, these later counterparts, while sometimes aiming at 'uniformity', never achieved more than a functioning conformity, though, admittedly, across a wider section of the total population than their Roman predecessor was ever aiming at. **35.** On this extraordinary 'summer of blood', see Burgess (2008). **36.** Matthews (1989), chs. 6–8, for a general introduction to Julian and his reign, with Ammianus 25.3 on the circumstances of the emperor's eventual death; cf. Eunapius *Lives of the Sophists* 6–7; cf. *PLRE* 1, 583–4, for Julian's choice of teacher. There are many studies of Julian's theological and philosophical preferences: e.g., Athanassiadi (1992); R. Smith (1995). **37.** On Julian's religious policies, see e.g., Bidez (1930), 236ff.; Jones (1964), 120–24; Matthews (1989), ch. 7; Athanassiadi (1992), chs. 5–6; Lieu (2007). The rationale to cause chaos in Christianity behind recalling all the exiles is set out in *Ep.* 114. **38.** *Ep.* 22 (high priest of Galatia). Moral guidelines: *Letter to a Priest*. Secondary refs. as n. 36. **39.** See in particular *Against the Galileans*. By contrast, and probably as a deliberate spite to Christianity, which was becoming increasingly hostile to Judaism in the post-Constantinian era (see pp. 3–38), he reversed punitive taxes on the Jews and promised to rebuild Jerusalem as a Jewish city: *Fragment of a Letter*; *Ep.* 51. **40.** Mitchell (1993), vol. 2, ch. 16. **41.** General introductions (among many possibilities): North (2000); Ando (2008); Bowes (2008), ch. 1. **42.** Good introductions to Plotinus are provided by Chiaradonna (2009) and the essays in Fowler (2018). On Augustine's familiarity with the general idea-set through Latin translations: Brown (1967), esp. chs. 9–11. **43.** Themistius: Heather and Moncur (2001), ch. 1. For more on 'the highest God' and upper-class Platonizing religion: Mitchell (1993), vol. 2, 43–51; Athanassiadi (1992), intro.; Lane Fox (1986), ch. 4; Dillon (1977); Matthews (1989), ch. 7; Bouffartigue (1992); Trombley (2007). **44.** *C.Th.* 13.3.5 but denuded of its original religious significance, which is set out in Julian *Ep.* 36. Prohaeresius: Eunapius *Lives of the Sophists* xx. Ammianus' condemnation: 22.10.7; 25.4.20. Secondary refs. as n. 37. The law also forced Marius Victorinus to stop teaching in Rome. **45.** Julian *Ep.* 78; cf. Eunapius *Lives of the Sophists* xxii; *PLRE* 1, 202. **46.** Sozomen *H.E.* 5.3–4. **47.** Babylas: Lieu (1986). More generally, see Sandwell (2007); Matthews (1989), ch. 8, on Julian's travails in the city. But also Gleason (1986) for the argument that the *Misopogon* was not the misguided or bad-tempered response to the situation portrayed by later Christian commentators. **48.** Hecebolius: *PLRE* 1, 409. *Misopogon* 375c (Emesa), *Ep.* 58 Beroea and Batnae; cf. Bidez (1930), 228–35, on the broader response to Julian's policies. **49.** With the exception of those few parts of the Empire where there are signs of a burgeoning, increasingly syncretic religion: Egypt above all (where the evidence is best), but probably also parts of Asia Minor and North Africa (p. 23). **50.** On the campaign: Matthews (1989), ch. 8 with now also McLynn (2020), 293–325. **51.** As have more recent treatments, strongly influenced by different dimensions of the Cultural Turn: refs. as above Chapter 2, nn. 18–19. **52.** Jones (1964), ch. 22 (after Gibbon), with Gwynn (2008) on 'idle mouths'.

4. NICAEA AND THE FALL OF THE WEST

1. Victor of Vita *Hist. Pers.* 2.38ff. The best introduction to Victor remains Courtois (1954), supplemented now by the introduction and commentary to Lancel (2002). The best secondary account remains Courtois (1955), pt 2, ch. 2, supplemented by the commentary to the relevant sections of Lancel (2002). **2.** Victor *Hist. Pers.* 3.62. On Huneric's persecution, see generally Courtois (1955), pt 2, ch. 2, supplemented by the commentary to the relevant sections of Lancel (2002). **3.** Dawson (1932) asserts the early importance of the papacy; cf. Ullmann (1970). Among more recent overviews, Brown (2013), 24–5, identifies 550–750 as the critical period of transition (cf. Part Three), while Smith (2005), 220, sees Roman Christianity facing serious challenge only north of the Channel, where imperial political collapse was accompanied by profound socio-economic and cultural restructuring. **4.** See below Chapters 7 and 8. **5.** Only Wales, south-western England and possibly parts of Brittany remained under the primary political control of rulers whose ancestors had been indigenous to the western Empire in the year 400. **6.** Schmidt (1933), (1938–40) is among the best of the older accounts. The warband theory can be found in, for instance, Kulikowski (2002); Drinkwater (2007); partly followed in the broader overview of, e.g., Halsall (2007). **7.** From the social sciences, the most influential text here is Barth (1969). The revolution in the understanding of Germanic groups began with Wenskus (1961) and has worked its way through to the present without generating total consensus: see e.g., Pohl (2000), (2013); Gillett (2002); Halsall (2007), ch. 14. See Brown (2013), xi ff., for the application of these ideas to create a self-destruct model for the unravelling of the west Roman imperial system. **8.** Only Burgundians settled in the Rhône valley were not demonstrably a new confederation, and that may be a mirage since the sources for their early history are minimal: Favrod (1997), ch. 1. My own academic career began with a detailed reconstruction of the emergence of the two new Gothic confederations of the late Roman period: Heather (1991). **9.** Latin poetry from the Vandal court: Moussy and Camus (1985); Moussy (1988); Kay (2006); cf. more general discussions of the Vandal adoption of Roman culture: Merrills and Miles (2010), 97–108, ch. 8; Conant (2012), ch. 3; Steinacher (2016), ch. 5. Heather (1993) surveys similar phenomena around the court of Theoderic the Ostrogoth in Italy, while Hen (2007) looks more generally at all the courts of the post-Roman west. **10.** Heather (2009), ch. 6: the evidence for disruption from north-eastern Gaul is similar in its overall nature. **11.** Goffart (1980) posited the tax reallocation theory. This won considerable immediate support, but see Wickham (1993) and now the broad range of more critical responses in Porena *et al.* (2012), which emphasize that even the best of the new deals involved significant financial loss for provincial Roman elites. Geiseric's extensive confiscation of Roman estates in part of Vandal Africa is recounted by Victor of Vita, *Hist. Pers.* 1.13, and confirmed by the extensive evidence for dispossessed Romans seeking redress: *Nov. Val.* 2.3, 12.34. **12.** Victor, *Hist. Pers.* 1.2. Even two recent revisionist views – Goffart (2006), ch. 5 and Halsall (2007), 206ff. – accept that the Rhine crossing was a very large-scale intrusion. In Victor's account, Geiseric divided his force into 70 pretended units of a thousand to exaggerate the number of his followers. Older estimates worked with a notional ratio of 1:5 of warriors to total population, but thirty years on the road (off and on as the grouping worked its way from the Rhine via Gaul and Spain to North Africa) is likely to have been particularly tough – as in all migrant flows – on the old and the young, so that a total population of more like 50,000 might imply closer to *c.* 15,000 warriors. **13.** Goths of 376: Heather (1991), ch. 4. Radagaisus: Zosimus 5.26.4 and Olympiodorus fr. 9 with fuller discussion in Heather (2009), 174–6. **14.** Goffart (1981) claims that most of the late fourth/early fifth-century intruders were invited onto Roman soil, but this is demonstrably incorrect, and even the admission of the Tervingi in 376 was dictated by necessity: Heather (1991), ch. 4. **15.** Hoffmann (1969), 450–58. Two-thirds of Valens' army wiped out: Ammianus 31.13.18. **16.** Hydatius *Chron.* 59 [67]. **17.** Hydatius *Chron.* 69 [77]; cf. Merills and Miles (2010), 44–7 (I don't believe, as they assert based on no evidence whatsoever, that most of Castinus' defeated army attached itself to the Hasding dynasty at this point); Steinacher (2016), 74–83. The evidence for the scale of west Roman military losses in the period *c.* 395–420 emerges from the under-utilized but authoritative discussion of Jones (1964), 355ff. **18.** Tax reductions: *C.Th.*11.28.7, 12; *Nov. Val.* 13. West Roman army of the 420s: Jones (1964), 355ff. **19.** Those interested in detail will be clear that I'm arguing the case here for a substantially different picture of the unravelling of the west Roman imperial system than appears in the influential Brown (2013), xiff. The latter relies on the conclusions of studies such as Shaw (1999) that Roman civil wars killed more Roman soldiers than conflict with outside intruders to make the case that internal Roman dissent was more central to the process of collapse than any input from outsiders. This probably was so in the mid-fourth century, but ceased to be true from Hadrianople onwards, when the new barbarian coalitions started to destroy Roman field armies such as those of Valens and Castinus (see nn. 15, 17). This new level of Roman–intruder violence, and the effects of lost provincial tax revenues on the capacity of the system to sustain itself, are consistently ignored by proponents of the self-destruct model. **20.** Most of the western senatorial aristocracy had lands typically in southern Italy, southern Spain and North Africa, all of which were threatened or lost as fifth-century events unfolded: Heather (2016). **21.** This vision of west Roman imperial unravelling is argued more fully in Heather (1995), (2005) and (2009). **22.** The two main sources for the life of Ulfilas are *The Letter of Auxentius of Durostorum* and Philostorgius *H.E.* 2.5. What they report broadly agrees but there are some incompatibilities on points of chronological detail which require choices to be made: Heather and Matthews (1991), ch. 5. **23.** Heather and Matthews (1991), ch. 6, for introduction: more detailed treatments of the Gospel and Epistle text in, respectively, Friedrichsen (1926) and (1939). **24.** On the search post-Nicaea for a broadly acceptable definition of the relationship between Father and Son, see above p. 33 with refs. Parvis (2014) tries to establish a direct relationship between Ulfilas and Arius, but the suggestion is tenuous and to my mind unnecessary, given the range of diverse east Christian opinion that clearly found *homoousios* a problematic term: p. 34. On the preservation of *The Letter of Auxentius* and other Homoean materials in Latin, see Gryson (1980). **25.** I remain happy with the reconciliation of the contradictory source materials offered in Heather (1986). The alternative reconstruction of Lenski (1995) suffers from the – to my mind – insuperable objection that it relies on using the late and less detailed account of Socrates to 'correct' the more detailed and contemporary account of Ammianus Marcellinus. **26.** On the imperial origins of the surviving Gothic Church Calendar fragment and Commentary on the Gospel of John – *Skereins* – see Brennecke (2014); cf. Heil (2014). Wolfe (2014) discusses the problems of translating *homoousios*. Given its background as imperial orthodoxy for the best part of half a century, I am unpersuaded that Homoean Christianity was a simpler, entry-level form of Christianity that non-imperial populations found easier to grasp: an old idea recently revived by Dunn (2013), ch. 3 with refs. **27.** On the evolution of these relationships in more detail, see Heather (1991), ch. 6. Kulikowski (2002) attempts to argue that there was no treaty in 382 and no continuity between the Goths of 376 and those who rose in revolt under Alaric in 395. The argument only works by ignoring a large body of contemporary material which indicates precisely the opposite: Heather (2009), ch. 4. **28.** Alaric and Attalus: Sozomen *H.E.* 9.9. Suevi: Hydatius *Chron.* 222 [226], 228 [232]; cf. Garcia Moreno (2006). Schäferdiek (1978), (2007) explores the spread of Christianity more generally among the different Germanic-speaking intruders onto Roman soil. **29.** Date limits: Salvian *De gub. Dei* 7.11/46; Orosius *Hist. Ad Pag.* 7.41.8. Nicene conversion: Hydatius *Chron.* 79 [89]. Huneric's first marriage: Jordanes *Getica* 184. **30.** Victor *Hist. Pers.* 1.4–7, 10; cf. Courtois (1955), 155ff. for the broader circumstances and more detail. Courtois also plausibly argues that had bishops been killed, they would have been remembered as martyrs, and the specific information given by Victor refers only to torture rather than death. As part of this peace deal, Huneric was betrothed to an imperial princess and his previous Visigothic bride was sent back to Gaul, reportedly having suffered mutilation as well as mistreatment. **31.** Victor *Hist. Pers.* 1.9 (cathedral), 1.15–16 (other churches); cf. Courtois (1955), 226. See now on the physical remains of these churches, Ennabli (1992). **32.** Victor *Hist. Pers.* 1.17, 22. Later confiscations of Nicene churches in the time of Huneric explicitly included the portfolios of landed endowments that went with them (*Hist. Pers.* 3.2), and a church without its endowment would have been a white elephant, since the costs of lighting, heating and essential maintenance represented a substantial annual expense. Although Victor is not explicit, it seems highly probable, therefore, that the confiscated churches of Proconsularis also came with property endowments attached. On this point (only), I depart from Courtois (1955), 284ff. On the confiscation of landed estates in Proconsularis, see n. 11. **33.** Victor *Hist. Pers.* 1.22–3 (bishops), 1.15 (Quodvultdeus). If Quodvultdeus did pen the anti-Vandal sermons attributed to him, they may also have been the cause of his exile: Braun (1964), 94–113. On overall episcopal numbers, see Courtois (1955), 135ff. **34.** Victor *Hist. Pers.* 1.29 (but Victor doesn't mention the context, and his comment on the subsequent decline of episcopal numbers in Proconsularis is taking the story down to his own day; i.e., over a quarter of a century later, and after the ravages of Huneric's persecution). **35.** Victor *Hist. Pers.* 1.17–18. **36.** These kinds of shortages are standard features of the early stages of any conversion processes. Compare Chapter 6 on conversion north of the Channel. **37.** On Maximinus, see further Gryson (1980). **38.** On the continuing power of the Empire's religious ideologies, pace Augustine, see above Chapters 2 and 3. **39.** Victor *Hist. Pers.* 1.43ff. **40.** Manton (1988) and Raven (1993) provide accessible introductions in English to the riches of Roman North Africa. **41.** Hence the Roman state prepared and/or mounted three major expeditions to reconquer the lost provinces, in 441/2, 461 and, above all, 468. See in more detail Heather (1995), (2005), 390–407. **42.** Gregory of Tours *Hist.* 2.26, 36; *Life of Caesarius* 1.21ff.; cf. Wood (1977). **43.** Griffith (2018), ch. 2. **44.** *Life of Caesarius*

1.36ff.; cf. Klingshirn (1994), ch. 5; Heather (2016). **45.** Courtois (1955), pt 3, ch. 2. **46.** The figures don't quite add up. The final listing has 88 'perished' versus 378 'endured' for a total of 466 bishops, as compared to 90 out of a total of 461 if you add up from the actual text, but this is clearly just some kind of copying or transmission error. **47.** Moderan (2003); Lancel (2002), 223ff. (the introduction to his edition and French translation of the *Notitia*). **48.** Courtois (as n. 1) thought that Victor's appeal was directed at Constantinople, hoping for religious rescue from the eastern half of the Roman Empire. But Courtois had Justinian's (much) later armed intervention of 532/3 in mind, and this was the product of a highly contingent series of events: Heather (2018), chs. 4–5. There was not the slightest prospect of an east Roman intervention in the circumstances of 484, and there is no need to think that Victor's message had anything other than a North African audience in mind. **49.** Gregory *Hist.* 2.29–31 (conversion), 32–38 (victorious expansionary campaigns). **50.** Avitus *Ep.* 46.1, trans. Shanzer and Wood (2002), 369. My argument generally follows that of Shanzer and Wood, pp. 362–9, with one detailed exception. They date Clovis's baptism to Easter 508, because Easter Sunday was a traditional date for baptism, but so – in this era – was Christmas Day (see Chapter 6 for mass baptisms at Christmas in Kent) and Avitus' text strongly indicates Christmas too in this instance: 'it is fitting that [the king's new Christian light] began to shine on the birthday of our Redeemer'. **51.** See more generally Heather (1996), ch. 8.

5. ISLAM AND THE FALL OF THE EAST

1. A small and at this date Homoean Suevic kingdom dominated north-western Iberia. **2.** Two contemporary descriptions emphasize the element of light: Procopius *Buildings* 1.1. 30–54; cf. Paul the Silentiary when the church was rededicated over the Christmas period in 562/3: Bell (2009), 195ff. **3.** Procopius *Secret History* 9.10–30 (Theodora), cf. the equally but differently damning account of Justinian at 8.22–33. But see now Potter (2015), chs. 2–3. **4.** My understanding of Justinian's rise to power and the evolution of his decision to attack the Vandal kingdom is set out in more detail at Heather (2018), chs. 3–4. **5.** In the *Secret History*, Procopius presents Justinian's wars as a complete disaster for all of mankind. I have tried to construct a less rhetorical balance sheet at Heather (2018), chs. 10–11. **6.** Justinian *Nov.* 37 with the excellent commentary of Merrills and Miles (2010), 249–51. Some of Justinian's soldiers took up with some of the dead/exiled Vandals' women and used this as the basis of a claim to the Vandals' landed estates. Their claims were rejected. **7.** *P. Ital.* 2; cf. Tjader (1972). St Anastasia's writing office may well have produced the *Codex Argenteus* MS of Ufilas's Bible (p. 173). On the survival of Gothic communities in contrast to Vandal genocide: Heather (2018), 251–68. **8.** On the problem of Lombard Arianism in northern Italy, see Fanning (1981). **9.** Wood (2014), chs. 1, 3; cf. Heather (2018), ch. 6, for the Ostrogothic withdrawal from south-eastern Gaul. **10.** Liuvigild also terminated the independence of the kingdom of the Suevi in north-west Iberia. **11.** There are many possible narratives of the 6th-century crisis of the Visigothic kingdom and Liuvigild's (various) responses to it, of which his unificatory religious policy was only one part: Thompson (1969), ch. 3; Collins (1992), ch. 2; Garcia Moreno (1989), ch. 4; Heather (1996), 276ff. **12.** The evidence is set out conveniently in the contradictory arguments of Hillgarth (1966) and Collins (1983). I follow the former in thinking that religion was a significant issue in the revolt. The Acts of III Toledo can be found at Vives (1963), 107–45 (note the Gothic signatories at pp. 122–3). The works cited in the previous note all discuss Reccared and the Visigoths' conversion to Nicene Christianity. **13.** 587/8: *Lives of the Fathers of Merida* 5.10 (a number of Gothic counts including the future King Witteric). 588: John of Biclar *Chron.* 90.6 (a Gothic queen and Udilo, probably the bishop of Toledo). 589: *Lives of the Fathers of Merida* 5.12 (two leading Gothic nobles and the Gothic bishop of Narbonne). 590: John of Biclar *Chron.* 94 (the *dux* Argimund). **14.** There are many good studies of Persian/Roman warfare in the late Roman period: see e.g., Dodgeon and Lieu (1991); Greatrex (1998); Greatrex and Lieu (2002); Whitby (1988); Howard-Johnson (2010). **15.** There are likewise many excellent recent studies of the great era of Muslim conquest: in English see esp. Donner (1981); Kennedy (2007); Hoyland (2015). **16.** For an introduction to the source problems, see esp. Crone and Cook (1977); Crone (1987); Robinson (2003), chs. 1–3. Hoyland (2019) explores non-Islamic materials. **17.** For further reading on the *Qur'an* with full refs., see e.g. Nöldeke (2013); the essays in Al-Sha'ar (2017); Neuwirth (2019). **18.** The point emerges clearly from Sartre (1982); cf. more generally on Arabia in Late Antiquity (with refs.) Donner (2005); Dignas and Winter (2007), ch. 5; Zahran (2009). **19.** See further Heather (2018), ch. 3. **20.** The *Chronicon Paschale*'s account of the siege of Constantinople can be read in the English translation of Whitby and Whitby (1989), 168ff. The sources for the Persian wars of Phocas and Heraclius are brilliantly examined in Howard-Johnston (2010). For more detailed narrative reconstruction, see e.g., Dignas and Winter (2007), 44ff., 115ff., 148ff.; Sarris (2011), 242–57. **21.** Maurice and the Ghassanids: Whitby (1988), ch. 10. **22.** Sardis and Ephesus: Foss (1977), (1996), with Wickham (2005), 626ff. on more recent findings. On Constantinople itself, see e.g., Whittow (1996), 98ff. Ward-Perkins (2000) and Wickham (2005), 609ff., both emphasize the contrasting continued prosperity of old Roman cities in Egypt and the Fertile Crescent that had fallen under Islamic, Umayyad rule. **23.** Ottoman documents: Hendy (1985), 613–69; cf. more generally Haldon (1997), esp. chs. 5 (tax) and 6 (military organization). **24.** For a more detailed introduction to the course of this dispute, see Heather (2018), esp. chs. 2, 7, 11 with full ref. to an extensive scholarly literature, and below ch. 7, p. 297. **25.** Price *et al.* (2014) provides an excellent introduction to the Monothelite controversy as well as a translation of the Lateran Synod of 649, where the doctrine was formally condemned in Rome. A good introduction to the theology of the Monothelite controversy is Hovorun (2008). **26.** Events: Haldon (1997), ch. 2; Whittow (1996), ch. 4; Mango (1977). **27.** The potential bibliography on the iconoclast dispute is vast, but for introductions with full refs. see Whittow (1996), ch. 6; Brubaker and Haldon (2001); Auzépy (2008); Brubaker (2012); Noble (2009), esp. ch. 2. Price (2018) provides not only an excellent modern translation of II Nicaea, but a detailed introduction to the dispute and to the previous council of 754 (see esp. pp. 93–8 for the first session of the council, which dealt with readmitting the now repentant Iconoclast leaders). The ease with which the Empire moved in and out of periods of iconoclasm does not suggest to me that the mass of the population yet had much invested in the dispute. For a contrary view, see Brown (1973). **28.** Haldon (1997), esp. chs. 8–9. **29.** In most of the old Christian heartland, as a result, all that you can see today, as Bulliet (1990) romantically puts it, are 'deserted Cathedrals, abandoned monasteries, and a scattering of Christian villages [in what was] once the center of Christendom'. **30.** Bulliet (1990a); cf. the introduction to McLynn *et al.* (eds.) (2015). Sijpesteijn (2013), 165–7, summarizes early Islamic discussion of whether circumcision was necessary to conversion. **31.** Speed: Morony (1990). Motivations: Bulliet (1990) with full refs. to earlier studies such as Dennett (1950). **32.** Bulliet (1979); cf. Morony (1990): supplemented by particular regional studies such as Anawati (1990); Hadad (1990); Robinson (2000); with below p. 229 on Arabization. What's particularly convincing about the revised picture of Islamic conversion, in my view, are the marked regional variations in the pace of change. **33.** The 7th-century Egyptian pattern is now illuminated in the magisterial work of Sijpesteijn (2013), ch. 2; cf. Levy-Rubin (2011), ch. 1 (surrender treaties); 'Awaḍ (2018), (John of Damascus). Apions: Hickey (2012), 1–2. **34.** Sijpesteijn (2013), ch. 3; cf. Robinson (2005). **35.** Griffith (2008), esp. chs. 3–6; cf. Little (1990) with refs. on later ghettoization. **36.** Levy-Rubin (2011), chs. 2–4. **37.** There are several accessible accounts of the general history of the creation and subsequent development of Muslim Spain: Collins (1994), (2012); cf. Millet-Gérard (1984); Christys (2002) and Aillet (2010) in particular on Christians under Islamic rule. The texts relating to the martyr movement of Córdoba are now available in the translation of Wolf (2019) with introduction and notes drawing on an extensive previous literature. The main recent studies in English are Coope (1995), Wolf (1988) and Colbert (1962). Stroumsa (2018) attacks the general reliability of the texts, and it is certainly the case that Paulus and Eulogius in a sense created the movement by reifying a particular set of Christian actors, but this does not either suggest that the deaths didn't happen or undermine the broader context of cultural interaction, Arabization and Islamic conversion within which they were unfolding: see further Wolf (2019), 51–66, 100ff. **38.** Eulogius *Memorial of the Saints* Pref. 2–5. **39.** Paulus Alvarus *Life of Eulogius* 13ff: it was his involvement with Leocritia which led to Eulogius' own death. **40.** Alvarus *Life of Eulogius* 2, 8–9. **41.** Eulogius *Memorial of the Saints* 2.16.2, 3.1; Wolf (2019), 15–16; the Abbasid Caliph al-Mutawakkil had enforced similar measures across the rest of the Islamic world the year before: Levy-Rubin (2011), 103. **42.** An *exceptor reipublicae*: Eulogius *Memorial of the Saints* 3.2; cf. Wolf (2019), 13–14 for specific instances of Christian officials coming under stress. **43.** Reccafredus is fiercely condemned by Paulus Alvarus *Life of Eulogius* 6–7, 12ff.; cf. Wolf (2019), 13, on problems of identifying him securely; he was previously bishop of Córdoba. Both Paulus and Eulogius, in contrast to many of their fellow Córdoban clergy, moved on from merely recording martyrdoms to actively encouraging them: Wolf (2019), 100ff. **44.** Both situations generated minority instances of diehard resistance, with the martyrs of Córdoba finding their counterpart perhaps not so much in the pagan emperor Julian the Apostate and his allies, who tried to stem the rising tide of Roman imperial Christianity in the 350s and 360s, as the Neo-Platonic philosophers of the fifth and early sixth centuries who continued to resist Christianization. Julian himself, interestingly, came from a similarly hybrid cultural background to that of the 'apostate' martyrs of mid-ninth-century Spain, having been brought up a Christian before reverting to classical pagan beliefs as an adult. **45.** Mocianus: *PLRE* 3, 893; Opilio and Cyprianus: Cassiodorus *Variae* 8.21–22. **46.** Victor of Vita *Hist. Pers.* 2.23 records that the king's first move was to declare that no Nicene could hold an official position in the palace hierarchy.

6. 'NOT ANGELS': CONVERSION IN NORTH-WESTERN EUROPE

1. Gildas can be read in the translation of Winterbottom (1978). The *Tribal Hidage* is translated in Whitelock (1996). Good introductions to early Anglo-Saxon political structures as they emerged from the settlement phase can be found in – among many possibilities – Campbell (1982); Bassett (1989); Yorke (1990); Kirby (1992); Higham (1994); Harrington and Welch (2014). My own views on the Anglo-Saxon takeover of south-eastern Britain are set out at Heather (2009), ch. 6, but note discussion there of the main alternatives in what remains a highly contested subject area. **2.** Bede's *Ecclesiastical History* is edited and translated in Colgrave and Mynors (1991); cf. the commentary of Wallace-Hadrill (1988). There is a vast body of scholarship on conversion and the Anglo-Saxons, but for excellent introductions, see – among many possibilities again – the general accounts of Mayr-Harting (1991); Blair (2005); Yorke (2006); Dunn (2009) augmented by essay collections such as Carver (2003); Carver *et al.* (2011); Flechner and Ní Mhaonaigh (eds.) (2016); Flechner *et al.* (eds.) (2017). **3.** Bede *H.E.* 1.25. **4.** Bertha and her chaplain, Bede notes (*H.E.* 1.26), used a leftover, small Roman-era church near Canterbury for their devotions: see further

n. 8. On saints Alban and Sixtus, see Bede *H.E.* 1.7; cf. Blair (2005), 13, 24 with refs. **5.** Wood (2001), 25; Brown (2013), 414; cf. below p. 391 on the mental preparations of late first-millennium missionaries for what they might encounter in the utterly uncivilized north. Another, or perhaps additional factor, as we'll see in the next chapter, is the degree to which human and financial resources were still required for spreading religion into the (ex-) Roman countryside. **6.** On the Irish, see (among many possibilities) Blair (2005), 43–9; Charles-Edwards (2008). **7.** Nicaea and Easter: see above p. 35. **8.** Blair (2005), 10–34, surveys the available evidence for legacy British Christianity among the intrusive Anglo-Saxons. On the west Midlands, see Bassett (1992). **9.** I'm disagreeing slightly here with Wood (2001), 9–10, 42–5 (cf. Brown (2013), ch. 15), who concludes that Bede has deliberately written a very substantial British element out of the story; cf. Stancliffe (1999). **10.** Excellent general accounts of the process can be found in e.g. Fletcher (1998), chs. 3, 7; Wood (2001), 25ff.; Smith (2005), 227ff.; Dunn (2009); Brown (2013), 230ff., chs. 14–15. **11.** Trans. Whitelock (1996), 391–4; for useful commentary, among many possibilities, see Wormald (2005) and Lambert (2017), esp. ch. 2. **12.** Hewalds: Bede *H.E.* 5.10; Willibrord: Fletcher (1998), ch. 7; Brown (2013), 415–18; cf. Wood (2001), ch. 4. **13.** Bede *H.E.* 1.26; cf. Smith (2005), 227ff. for many parallel examples. Though I don't believe – contra John (1966) – that early Anglo-Saxon kings controlled all of their kingdoms' landed wealth, their powers of patronage were clearly substantial, even if there is reasonable room for debate about the chronology of the emergence of truly royal power: Bassett (1989) (earlier) vs Scull (1999) (later); cf. Blair (2005), 49–51, and the literature cited in n. 1 above. **14.** Gregory *Ep.* 8.29; Bede *H.E.* 2.14. **15.** Edwin: Bede *H.E.* 2.9. Kent and Essex: Bede *H.E.* 2.3, 2.7. Radbod: Wood (2001), 57–8. The important study of Lynch (1986) demonstrated that the godparenting relationship created by sponsoring a baptism was generally considered to create bonds as strong as those of blood ties. **16.** Bede *H.E.* 2.13; cf. among many possibilities Charles-Edwards (2000), ch. 5; Brown (2013), 130–33 on Patrick. **17.** Hope-Taylor (1977); with further interpretation (and full refs.) in Blair (2005), 54–7. **18.** The king was Æthrelred's much more ready son Edmund Ironside: *Anglo-Saxon Chronicle* 1017. The *Life* of St Guthlac is edited and translated in Colgrave (1956). Sigebert: Bede *H.E.* 3.18; cf. Stancliffe (1983); Yorke (2003a). **19.** Frankish warrior (Barontus): Brown (2013), 262; cf. Brown (2013), ch. 14, on Irish Christianity. **20.** Cf. Smith (2005), ch. 1 with refs. **21.** The Christian religion is not alone in changing substantially over time, and there are more than a few indications that intervening, intense contacts with Christianity had prompted religious evolution in the Nordic pantheon by the time Snorri Sturluson wrote it all down. Further reading on this problem: Smith (2005), 231ff.; Blair (2005), 166ff.; Dunn (2009), ch. 4; cf. North (1997) for a deliberately maximum attempt to recover the outlines of Anglo-Saxon paganism. **22.** *Penitential of Theodore* 1.15.2–3; cf. Blair (2005), 167–8. **23.** The two base texts are the Prose Edda and the Poetic Edda; an excellent recent introduction to some of the astonishing inconsistencies they contain is Price (2020), pt 1. **24.** Boniface *Ep.* 23 with above Chapter 2 on the slow formalization of Christian belief structures. Smith (2005), 66–71, rightly emphasizes the imminence of death in early medieval European societies. **25.** Boniface *Ep.* 21; cf. Smith (2005), ch. 1, on pre-Christian literacies. For an introduction to the anthropology of literacy, see Goody (1986), (2000). **26.** Boniface *Ep.* 23. **27.** Gregory's letter: Bede *H.E.* 1.32. Columba: quoted in Brown (2013), 329. **28.** Geake (1997), 107–39; Chadwick Hawkes (1981). **29.** The two predecessors were Edwin, from the Deiran dynasty, who ruled all of Northumbria, and Oswald's brother Eanfrith who ruled Bernicia. Heavenfield remains a wonderfully evocative site, but still very much a cattle field: mind where you put your feet . . . **30.** Bede *H.E.* 3.6 (death), 9–14 (miracles). When the tomb of St Columba at Durham Cathedral was opened in the 19th century, investigators found an extra head, which may possibly be that of Oswald. On Oswald's cult see further Stancliffe (1995a),

(1995b); Yorke (2003a). **31.** *The Battle of Maldon* is edited with translation in Griffiths (1991). **32.** Bede *H.E.* 2.13; cf. Smith (2005), ch. 7, on the impact of the missionaries' revolutionary literate technologies upon heroic culture. **33.** Good introductions, among many possibilities, to the general process: Bassett (1989); Kirby (1992), esp. chs. 5–7; cf. Blair (2005), 49ff., ch. 2. **34.** For an attempt to reconstruct pre-Christian royal ideologies, see Moisl (1981). The last king from Edwin's Deiran dynasty, Oswine, was deposed and killed by Oswiu in 651. **35.** Edwin: Bede *H.E.* 2.16; cf. Wormald (1977) on the ideological significance of early medieval law-making, but also Wormald (1978) on the slow pace of real religious cultural change. **36.** On the general development of kingship structures in Ireland, and the role of developing Church institutions, see Byrne (1973); Charles-Edwards (2000), esp. chs. 11–13. In the case of Ireland, it is arguable that the Vikings were a more important catalyst for political unification than Christianity (as indeed they were in some ways in England, where they destroyed the coherence of the East Anglian, Northumbrian and Mercian kingdoms, allowing the Wessex dynasty to create a first united kingdom of England), but this has been contested, esp. by Ó Cróinín (1995), who places the emphasis more on internal Irish developments. **37.** Bede *H.E.* 1.30; cf. Markus (1970). But note also the (former) Northumbrian pagan high priest's determination to desecrate/destroy that kingdom's pagan shrines: Bede *H.E.* 2.13 with Blair (2005), 183–91, for possible examples of reused pre-Christian sites. **38.** Augustine of Hippo: cf. Flint (1991), ch. 1. **39.** The excavations at Yeavering (see now Semple (2011)) produced some potential archaeological evidence of an Anglo-Saxon pagan temple site, and Aldhelm of Malmesbury reports pagan temples being replaced by churches in a letter to Heahfrith in the 680s (see Blair (1995)). But the evidence is slight and the idea that a Mediterranean-inspired model of paganism has been imposed is strong: refs. as n. 2 with, in addition, Markus (2001); Church (2008). **40.** *The Dream of the Rood* is translated by Bradley (1982); cf. Abrams (2008) on the Anglo-Saxon presentation of Peter and the Apostles. Further comment: Dunn (2009), 135–7; Brown (2013), 377–8. **41.** Trans. Bradley (1982). **42.** For an introduction to the Franks Casket, see Dunn (2009), 64–7, and with further discussion of the competing interpretations of e.g. Becker (1973); Wood (1990); Webster (2012). **43.** An excellent introduction is Crick (2012), (2013); with much other relevant material in the various essays of Gameson and Brown in Gameson (ed.) (2013). **44.** Radbod: *Life of Wulfram of Sens* 8–9; Wood (2001), ch. 4; Brown (2013), 417–18, with Lebecq (1994) on the broader context. Clemens: Brown (2013), 422. **45.** Lizo and Pretorius (1997). As this suggests, I am very much in sympathy with the general approach of Dunn (2009), esp. chs. 2, 4–5, who successfully uses comparative evidence to blow open the parameters of discussion of what religious patterns might have really looked like on the ground in 7th/8th-century Anglo-Saxon England. My own instinct would be to widen still further, however, the range of potential possibility. Many of the contributions to Carver *et al.* (eds.) (2011) are also relevant here. **46.** Rædwald: Bede *H.E.* 2.15. Sons of Sæberht: *H.E.* 2.5. Earconberht: *H.E.* 3.8; cf. Laws of Wihtred and Ine: Whitelock (1996), 396–407; cf. Smith (2005), 122–5. Yorke (2003a), 243–5, suggests that different members of the same dynasty may have espoused Christian and non-Christian beliefs to retain the broadest possible base of support. **47.** See Charles-Edwards (2000), esp. ch. 3 on the Irish material. **48.** *The Battle of Maldon* is translated in Griffiths (1991). Sarti (2013) is a recent study of Frankish military culture in the early Middle Ages, but see now the ground-breaking treatment of O'Connor (2019); cf. Meens (2008) for further comment on the survival of apparently non-Christian values centred on honour, violence and feud. **49.** *The Life of Wilfrid* is edited and translated in Colgrave (1927). On his career, see e.g. Cubitt (1989); Blair (2005), 92–9, with further refs. **50.** As shows up in all the 7th-century English law codes: Whitelock (1996), 391–406; cf. Smith (2005), 94–110; Dunn (2009), 135–7. For an introduction to honour and feud, see Wallace-Hadrill (1962), but note that it applies only to equals, while the death of slaves has to be paid for the

compensation goes to their owners. **51.** Brown (2013), 241–6. **52.** *Penitential of Theodore* 1.4.5; cf. Dunn (2009), 135–6. Alcuin: trans. Whitelock (1996), 863–4; Smith (2005), 107–8. **53.** Bede *H.E.* 3.22; cf. Dunn (2009), 136–7. **54.** The charter discussing the case is translated as no. 68 in Whitelock (1996), 526–7; an excellent general discussion of high-status female monasticism in the Anglo-Saxon context is Yorke (2003). **55.** Bede's *Letter to Egbert* is translated in Whitelock (1996), 799–810. For excellent commentary, Blair (2005), 100–118. **56.** Blair (2005), 84–91, easily envisaged as a response to the kind of process of 7th/8th-century dynastic demotion outlined in e.g. Bassett (1989). **57.** The bibliography on Irish monasticism is enormous but excellent orientation can be found in Charles-Edwards (2000), esp. chs. 7–8, with supplementary material in the collections of Wooding (2010). **58.** Bede *H.E.* 1.27. Boniface: *Epp.* 33 (cf. 26); cf. Smith (2005), 131–3; Dunn (2009), 137ff., on the general problem and Wemple (1985) on marriage types. **59.** Eadbald and Cedd: Bede *H.E.* 2.3, 3.22 respectively. On the continuing problem of extracting nuns from monasteries into the 8th century and general lay interference in monastic operations, see Cubitt (1995), 229–42; Yorke (2003). **60.** Brown (2013), ch. 14 (Ireland), 421–2 (Clemens); cf. Smith (2005), 238–9. **61.** For an introduction to Theodore and his work, see the essays in Lapidge (1995); cf. esp. Cubitt (1995), chs. 1–2, for his episcopal reforms and the conciliar tradition he generated. **62.** The best introduction to Bede's library (from which almost no original manuscripts survive) is Lapidge (2008) with full refs.; cf. Brown (2013), ch. 9, on the institutional infrastructure. **63.** Canterbury: Brooks (1984). York: Godman (1982). Aldhelm's poetry: Lapidge and Rosier (2009). Aldhelm's prose: Lapidge and Herren (2009); cf. more generally Barker and Brooks (eds.) (2010). My overall discussion here follows the general judgement of Lapidge (2008). **64.** I follow here Blair (2005), chs. 2–4, with full refs. to the extensive scholarly literature on the topic. On the massive multiplication of local churches around and after the year 1000, see below p. 433. **65.** Ó Cróinín (1995), ch. 6; Charles-Edwards (2000), ch. 6; Brown (2013), ch. 14: a pattern which the early Anglo-Saxon Church of the west Midlands – above n. 8 – seems to follow. Many of the essays in the collections of Blair and Sharpe (eds.) (1992), Flechner and Ní Mhaonaigh (eds.) (2016) and Flechner *et al.* (eds.) (2017) shed light on the similarities and differences either side of the Irish Sea. **66.** Charles-Edwards (2000), chs. 6–10 with full refs. to what is an extensive debate. **67.** Dunn (2009), ch. 5, 162ff. with full refs. provides an excellent introduction to the burial evidence and the wide range of possibilities it opens up. **68.** Laws of Wihtred and Ine: Whitelock (1996), 396–407. **69.** There have been some archaeological finds of writing styluses in recent years, which do suggest that there was some literacy at local Christian sites in pre-Viking Anglo-Saxon England – cf. Crick (2012) – but the evidence for what needed changing in the education and training of local priests from the 9th and 10th centuries onwards (which we'll explore in Chapter 10) strongly indicates that many of the practitioners will have had only a very limited capacity to lead simple Christian services. **70.** Bede *H.E.* 3.25. Bede makes a great deal of the Easter dating controversy, although, by the mid-7th century many Irish churches on the other side of the Irish Sea were already coming round to the now general western norm: Brown (2013), chs. 15–16; Charles-Edwards (2000), ch. 9. The monastery of Iona – responsible directly and indirectly for much of the original missionary work in Northumbria – held out the longest, not accepting the change until about fifty years later. **71.** Cubitt (1995), chs. 5–7. **72.** Simony is named after Simon Magus (Acts 8:9–24): in much more detail below pp. 452–5. Wine: Bede *H. E.* 4.12. Gift-giving and Clofesho: cf. Cubitt (1995), ch. 4. **73.** The Laws of Wihtred and Ine again: as n. 68. Bede *Letter to Egbert* c. 5 (see n. 55); cf. *Council of Clofesho* 747 canons. 10–12; Blair (2005), 161. **74.**
I believe in God, the Father almighty,
creator of heaven and earth. I believe in Jesus Christ, his only Son, our Lord,
who was conceived by the Holy Spirit
and born of the virgin Mary.

He suffered under Pontius Pilate,
was crucified, died, and was buried;
he descended to hell.
The third day he rose again from the dead.
He ascended to heaven
and is seated at the right hand of God the Father almighty.
From there he will come to judge the living and the dead. I believe in the Holy Spirit,
the holy catholic church,
the communion of saints,
the forgiveness of sins,
the resurrection of the body,
and the life everlasting. Amen.

75. The particular Irish contribution to Latin grammar has been lovingly recovered in the works of Vivien Law: see e.g. Law (1994), (2003), ch. 6. Good introductions to Irish ecclesiastical culture more generally: Ó Cróinín (1995), chs. 7–8; Charles-Edwards (2000), chs. 7, 9; Smith (2005), 25–6, 33–5. At one time it was fashionable to credit Irish monks with saving virtually the entirety of classical Latin literature, supposing Ireland to have been the crucial medium by which all of the surviving texts were transmitted through the so-called Dark Ages. But the majority of texts displaying insular scripts and copying techniques were actually produced in continental monasteries, many of which were influenced by scriptorial innovations from north of the Channel. 76. Flechner (2017); cf. Brown (2013), ch. 9, on the 'powerhouses of prayer'. 77. *Life of Cuthbert* trans. Colgrave (1985). *Letter to Egbert*: see n. 55. 78. Cf. Smith (2005), ch. 2; Brown (2013), ch. 6.

7. LATIN CHRISTIANITY RESTRUCTURED

1. Above p. 126. 2. An excellent introduction to the backdrop is Gray (2005), 215–21. 3. The eastern emperor Anastasius I (491–518) continued to downgrade Chalcedon, though he did try to negotiate some kind of accommodation with Rome; Justin I (518–527) restored Chalcedon and embraced Pope Leo's point of view, but in the process split the eastern Church: see further Heather (2018), 79–82, 86–7. 4. Anastasius I made some attempt to end the Acacian schism in the last years of his reign, but got nowhere. Justin I ended the schism between Rome and Constantinople in 518, but at the cost of splitting the eastern Church. For more detail on these events, see Heather (2018), 80–87. 5. *CJ* 1.1.6–8 with commentary in Gray (2005), 232–3; cf. Heather (2018), 202ff. 6. Markus and Sotinel (2007); with Sotinel (2007) on Vigilius, and Moderan (2007) on the initial North African protests and subsequent coming into line. 7. On the *Clementine Recognitions*, see Ullmann (1970), 13ff. (cf. his fuller discussion in Ullmann (1960)), with a useful supplement in Schatz (1990). 8. A famous letter survives from Pope Clement I – trans. Staniforth (1987) – from AD 96 to the congregation of Corinth, where he interferes in an intra-Corinthian dispute over the rights of priests. A hundred years later, Pope Victor I excommunicated any Quartodeciman Christians who insisted on celebrating Easter on the same date as the Jewish Passover: Eusebius *Ecclesiastical History* 5.24. 9. See further Ullmann (1970), 12ff; Jasper and Fuhrmann (2001), 7–22 with refs; d'Avray (2019). 10. *Nov. Val. III.* 17; cf. Mathisen (1989), esp. chs. 3 and 7 on use of the pallium in Gaul. 11. Gelasius: see, e.g., Ullmann (1970), 31–5; Llewellyn (1971), 38–40; Richards (1979), ch. 4. Somerville and Brasington (1998), ch. 2, provide both an introduction to the

work of Dionysius, and translations of his various Prefaces. **12.** The manuscript evidence also demonstrates that popes at this stage were not collecting their own letters, i.e., they were not acting as a self-conscious legally authoritative body: Jasper and Fuhrmann (2001), 22–8 with refs. See below p. 466 for subsequent change and its significance. **13.** Gregory I: Markus (1997), chs. 7–8 (with 206ff. on the surviving letters); cf. Brown (2013), ch. 8. Leo: above n. 8. **14.** Caesarius: Klingshirn (1994), 117–24; the relevant texts are translated in Klingshirn (1994a). Brunhild: Markus (1997), ch. 11. **15.** Brown (2013), esp. ch. 16 (but note that this is a summary conclusion to part III of the book as a whole), rightly underlines the significance of the emergence of these 'micro-Chistendoms' (I'm following his term). He is not interested, however, in royal religious authority and the new pattern of authoritative kingdom-based councils which replaced the imperially dominated ecumenical councils of the late Roman period. As we saw in the previous chapter, Anglo-Saxon England also tended to operate along the same lines, with a Southhumbrian micro-Christendom coalescing around the hegemony of Mercian kings in the 8th century: above p. 290 with Cubitt (1995). **16.** The *Histories* are translated in Thorpe (1974); various of the miracle collections in Hillgarth (1986); James (1985); Van Dam (1988), (1988a). The secondary bibliography on Gregory is enormous, but excellent orientation can be found in a combination of Heinzelmann (2001); Mitchell and Wood (2002); and Murray (2016); with full refs. **17.** Gregory of Tours' *Histories* 3.2; 4.35; 6.9; 6.15–16; 7.31, for a few examples of royal control of episcopal elections in the Frankish kingdom. Select letters of Sisebut can be found in translation in Martyn (2008). For the Anglo-Saxon situation, see p. 290. **18.** Introduction to the Hispanic tradition: Stocking (2000). The precocious initiatives of Caesarius can be explored in more detail through Klingshirn (1994), 137ff. Developing tradition from the 580s onwards: Turner (1903); Vessey (1993); cf. Mordek (1975) on the *Vetus Gallica*. It was a standard progression in the late Roman and medieval periods to collect new written law initially in chronological order, before moving to a thematic reordering when the volume of material started to become unmanageable. **19.** On all this, see now Griffith (2018). **20.** Braulio's letters are translated in Barlow (1969). **21.** Brown (2013), 158. **22.** Excellent treatments of this hugely important theme include Hillgarth (1980); Klingshirn (1994), ch. 8; Fletcher (1998), ch. 2; Brown (2013), esp. chs. 6 and 9 with full refs. to the detailed studies on which they are based. **23.** The best overall treatment is now Wood (2006), ch. 1; cf. Stancliffe (1983); Hillgarth (1980); Klingshirn (1994), 137ff., on Tours, Braga and Carpentras respectively. **24.** Caesarius: Klingshirn (1994), 137–8; Hillgarth (1980) on Visigothic Spain. **25.** Klingshirn (1994), ch. 6; cf. Hillgarth (1980) for the eventual acceptance of this innovation in Spain. **26.** The *Glory of the Confessors* is translated by Van Dam (1988). The Prefaces to his other works – *Life of the Fathers*, *Glory of the Martyrs*, *Miracles of St Martin* – are similarly (and equally deceptively) self-deprecatory. The studies in Murray (2016) provide helpful guidance on a range of important topics. Goffart (1986), ch. 2, understands Gregory's purpose in the miracle collections in much the same way as I do. On 6th-century sermon collections more generally, see Klingshirn (1994), ch. 6; Bailey (2010); Hillgarth (1980). **27.** Toledan *Homilary*: Hilgarth (1980). This message is very similar to that transmitted in all the parallel Gallic materials: refs. as previous note. **28.** For later patterns of Church provision and preaching, see pp. 433 and 546. **29.** Irish *peregrinatio*: above p. 269. On Columbanus' impact in Gaul, see the essays in Clarke and Brennan (1981); Fox (2014); O'Hara (2018). **30.** In addition to the bibliography cited in the previous note, Wood (2001), chs. 5–6, 8, surveys the general evidence; cf. O'Hara and Wood (2017), esp. introduction on Columbanus and the Irish tradition. **31.** III Toledo 16, cited in Hillgarth (1980), 15. **32.** Markus (1997), esp. ch. 5; cf. Klingshirn (1994), 238–40. **33.** Cf. Smith (2005), ch. 2. **34.** Klingshirn (1994), 224–5; North African Christians were already doing it in the time of Augustine a century earlier. **35.** A good introduction to the expansion of the liturgical year is Talley (1986); on Julian, see now

Puglisi (forthcoming). 36. Klingshirn (1994), 209–26; Brown (2013), 145–54. 37. Brown (1977), (2013), 154–65, specifically on Gregory; cf. more generally Brown (1981). The use of the supernatural to make the universe rational is a central theme of the classic study of Gluckman (1965), ch. 4, drawing on a wide body of anthropological literature on the subject of 'magic'; cf. Bartlett (2008).

8. CULTURE AND SOCIETY IN THE POST-ROMAN WEST

1. Braulio *Ep.* 44 commenting on Genesis 5:25–29. 2. Anthropology of literacy: above p. 254 n. 25. For applications of some of these ideas to the late Roman and post-Roman worlds, see e.g. the essays collected in McKitterick (1989), (1990); Bowman and Woolf (1994); and with important further reflections in Smith (2005), ch. 1. 3. Isidore of Seville *Etymologies* 1.1. History, being all about probable and possible arguments (as it won't have escaped the alert reader), is most definitely an art in Isidore's terms, and was categorized and considered a branch of rhetoric in the classical Graeco-Roman world. 4. The literature on Isidore and Braulio, particularly Isidore, is enormous, but for good introductions, see Henderson (2007); Fontaine (1983); Madrid Medrano (2015); Fear and Wood (2020). 5. See Velázquez Soriano (2000); with Courtois and Albertini (1952) on the *Tablettes Albertini*. 6. A selection of Venantius' work is translated in George (1995); cf. George (1997) and Roberts (2009) on his career and Latinity. On Gregory, see above p. 328, while Wood (1990a) explores the surviving letters of the late 6th-century Gallic elite. 7. For an introduction to Sisebut, including translations, see Martyn (2008). 8. Roman educational patterns: above p. 71. Kaster (1988) surveys the evidence for the disappearance of grammarians. 9. Heather (2000), (2010) for the evidence and further discussion; but note that residual royal revenues were used to support small professional military cores. 10. Heather (1994). 11. Braulio *Ep.* 16; cf. *Epp.* 15, 18, 19–20 (all to women). These new patterns are discussed in more detail in the literature cited at n. 18. 12. Parisse (1999), 146 quoted in Smith (2005), 24–5. 13. Liudger *Vita Gegorii abbatis Traiacensis* 2; Smith (2005), 40. On the more general shift to Romance, see e.g. Wright (1982), (1996). 14. Wood (1990a). 15. Halporn and Vessey (2004), 79ff., provides an excellent survey of the evidence with full refs. to an extensive specialist literature. 16. Cassiodorus' *Institutiones* can be read now in the English translation of Halporn and Vessey (2004). On Cassiodorus' design for Christian education and its relation to the commentary 'project' of the late Roman period, see Halporn and Vessey (2004), esp. 37ff.; cf. Brown (2013), 196–8, both with full refs. to an extensive literature on Cassiodorus and his works. 17. On Boethius, see e.g. the essays in Marenbon (2009) and Gibson (1981); cf. e.g. Marenbon (2003); Chadwick (1981). On other, similar educational initiatives, such as that of Martianus Capella, see the magisterial survey of Riché (1976), esp. pt 1, chs. 1–4. 18. Gregory of Tours: see Chapter 7, n. 17. On Braulio and Spain generally, see Fontaine (1983); cf. Riché (1976), pt 1, ch. 4., 2 and pt 2, ch. 3, 1–2 for a general survey of the available evidence. 19. Smith (2005), 48–9. 20. The definitive study now is Wood (2006): see esp. chs. 1 and 3 on the early evolution of diocesan Church property rights. 21. On Isidore, see the still fundamental work of Fontaine (1983); Lapidge (2008), 21–2 (on Isidore) and 23–5 on the fate of the Roman public libraries, with full refs. to the more detailed palaeographical scholarship on which this, admittedly pretty tentative comment, is based. 22. O'Hara and Wood (2017), 78 for the figures; cf. S. Wood (2006), esp. chs. 4–8, on the early evidence for the scale and legal status of monastic property. 23. As above p. 276. 24. This remained the only available mechanism to provide guaranteed funding for any permanent institution until the industrial

revolution. **25.** On Agapetus' library, see Lapidge (2008), 15–20 (putting it into context against other public libraries of the city). Bede and Benedict Biscop: above p. 283. **26.** On the evolution of learning within the Columbanian tradition, see now O'Hara (2018); O'Hara and Wood (2017); Brown (2013), chs. 10–11, with refs. to the sometimes inflated estimates of earlier discussions. Fructuosus: Barlow (1969); Nock (1946). Ildefonsus: Braegelmann (1942). See also Smith (2005), ch. 1; Lawrence (1984), chs. 2–3; Riché (1976), pt 1, ch. 4, 1, pt 2, ch. 3, 3, for general surveys of specifically monastic education and learning. **27.** The problem posed by the Carolingian-era destruction of older manuscripts is intractable: how big was the Carolingian waste-paper basket? See further below p. 415. The identification of pre-Carolingian centres of learning depends on manuscript clusters such as for Canterbury and York – Brooks (1984); Godman (1982) – or the evidence for the scale of reading of individual authors such as Bede, Isidore, or Braulio: Lapidge (2008); Fontaine (1983). **28.** O'Hara and Wood (2017), 54–61. **29.** Braulio, p. 313. On Carolingian scholars and the papacy, see below p. 417. **30.** All of this is extremely well explored in Brown (2015): introduction (Julian), ch. 5 (Gregory), and epilogue (tariffed penance). **31.** Julian's reading is discussed in Brown (2015), 4ff. On the importance of Tertullian and the extraordinary theological and institutional developments, which later allowed tariffed penance to play a major role in the patterns of piety which came into general use within the whole Latin Church after the Fourth Lateran council, see chapters 9–12 below. **32.** On Jerome and the Latin biblical tradition of the early Middle Ages, see Sutcliffe (1969); Loewe (1969); Sparks (1970). As with determining the age of Noah's grandfather, anybody wanting to identify the likely original wording of a particular Bible passage was – and is – usually reduced to guesswork. The earliest surviving manuscripts of the Bible already contain so many variants, reflecting the existence of originally separate Greek text traditions and multiple Latin translations, which then subsequently influenced one another (with a healthy dose of copying errors thrown in), that the search for the urtext rapidly leads in ever decreasing circles. Friedrichsen (1939), 200, 236f., identifies just two places where Ulfilas's Gothic translation *could* be potentially accused of importing pro-Homoean readings, into Phil. 2:6 and I Corinth. 15:26ff. But if you look at the textual witness of the early biblical MSS it is actually impossible to resolve whether the Gothic reading or the less Homoean alternative is more likely to be correct. In any case, you do not need to interpolate the New Testament canon to arrive at a Homoean Trinity: above pp. 126–8. **33.** A useful explanatory survey of the wide variety in early baptism ritual is Spinks (2006). **34.** Brown (2013), 418–25. **35.** Sword hilt: Brown (2013), 466. Liturgies: Hen (2007), 120–23. **36.** On the requirements of killing for honour, see above p. 273. **37.** See in more detail Heather (2000), (2010) with full refs. **38.** This is one of the major reasons why bishops start to figure so powerfully in post-Roman Gallic society; cf. Heinzelmann (1976). Examples in Gregory of Tours: Sidonius' son Apollinaris; Marachar, count then bishop of Angoulême; Ursicinus, ex-referendarius; Flavius, bishop of Chalons-sur-Saône; Badegesil of Le Mans; Slavius of Albi; Count Nicetius gets written permission to become bishop of Dax; Desiderius; Gundegesil, bishop of Bordeaux; Licerius at Arles; Chararic at Verdu; Bauderius at Tours. Compare Hillgarth (1980) for Spanish councils on simony with Brown (2013), ch. 18, and Reuter (1980), ch. 4, on Boniface's quarrels with Frankish bishops. Much of the honour code behind this mutual exchange of favour that got in the way sometimes of more pure Christian values is beautifully and influentially explored in Mauss (1969). **39.** Salonius and Sagittarius: Gregory *Histories* 4.42; 5.20; 7.38; Holy Cross: Gregory *Histories* 9.39; 10.15. **40.** Gregory *Histories* 5.49. **41.** Trial of Praetextatus: Gregory *Histories* 5.18. **42.** Cf. Braudel (1973), Preface. In arguing this view, I am obviously disagreeing profoundly with the arguments of Peter Brown that the successor states were mini versions of the western Roman Empire, which continued to be run by Roman administrators for 'barbarian' kings. His views are set out in many of his works, but see esp. Brown (2013), preface to the Tenth Anniversary edition, with a succinct restatement at Brown (2015), 142–4.

9. CHRISTIAN EXPANSION IN A SECOND AGE OF EMPIRE

1. Byzantium: Mango (1977); Whittow (1996), ch. 4. 2. Noble (1984), ch. 2, is the best account in English; see Davis (1992) for English translations of the late 7th- and early 8th-century papal lives. 3. On Italian politics of the early to mid-8th century, see Wickham (1981), 28ff.; Gasparri (2012); Azarra (1997). 4. The scholarly literature on the transition from Merovingian to Carolingian Francia is enormous, but an excellent beginning in English is provided in Gerberding (1987), esp. chs. 6–7; Wood (2014), esp. chs. 16–18; Fouracre (2000), all with full refs. 5. On Boniface and Milo, see Reuter (1980), ch. 4; Fouracre (2000), ch. 5; Wallace-Hadrill (1983), 150–60. Fascinatingly, Boniface identified very similar problems among the Anglo-Saxon episcopate: above p. 291. 6. In its earlier generations, the family is usually referred to as the Pippinids; I have kept to Carolingian for the sake of clarity. 7. Again the relevant bibliography is enormous, but among the many treatments in English see esp. Fouracre (2000), esp. ch. 6; the essays in Story (2005); and above all now the magisterial study of Nelson (2019). 8. Einhard *Life of Charlemagne* 28. 9. An argument put most influentially by Ullmann (1960), (1970), though it by no means originated with him; cf. Dawson (1932). 10. On the coronation of Pippin, see esp. Nelson (2005), with e.g., Noble (1984), 71ff., and Heather (2013), ch. 7, on the general pattern of Franco-papal relations in the second half of the 8th century. 11. Probably composed by Alcuin: trans. King (1987), 311–12; cf. Wallach (1968), 272ff., for the attribution. 12. On the highly independent Carolingian response to the end of Byzantine iconoclasm round 1, see e.g., McKitterick (2008), 311ff., and the very full treatment of Noble (2009), ch. 4. On the reflections of Charlemagne's intellectuals on the subject of Empire, see e.g., Godman (1987), ch. 2; Collins (2005); McKitterick (2008), 114–18, Costambeys *et al.* (2011), 160–70. The relative unimportance of the imperial title to Charlemagne has sometimes been asserted from the fact that his behaviour changed little after 800. This is to misunderstand the fact that he had been implicitly and explicitly asserting imperial status – with all its connotations of divine approval – for many years before: Heather (2013), ch. 5. Nelson (2019), 380ff., rightly emphasizes Charlemagne's control over the sequence of rituals that led to Leo's exculpation and the king's imperial coronation. 13. The sequence of events from the attack on Leo to Charlemagne's coronation has to be reconstructed from Carolingian and papal sources equally determined to spin their accounts in ways that best suited their own interests. Good recent approaches are Noble (1984), 291ff.; Collins (2005); McKitterick (2008), 88ff.; Costambeys *et al.* (2011), 160ff. I have set out my reasons for preferring the outline reconstruction set out here in more detail at Heather (2013), ch. 5. Nelson (2019), 372ff., thinks that the final deal was not made at Paderborn. 14. I follow here the convincing basic model set out in Reuter (1985), (1990). 15. These divergent outcomes from the same basic political process can be followed in much more detail in a combination of Hallam (1980); Nelson (1992); MacLean (2003) for West Francia. See likewise on East Francia: Leyser (1979); Reuter (1991); Goldberg (2006). 16. This section title is a homage on my part to the wonderful edited volume of Carver (2003). 17. On Boniface's projected Saxon mission, see Boniface *Epp.* 46, 47 with Wood (2001), ch. 3. Several Carolingian Annal collections provide important insight into Charlemagne's conquest of Saxony, but for the most part the others are supplementary to the basic narrative provided by the *Royal Frankish Annals* (trans. Scholz (1972)). The two Saxon Capitularies are translated by King (1987),

205–8, 230–32. The poetically premature celebration of a victorious conquest is translated in Rabe (1995), 54–9. On the Saxon conquest and subsequent process of integration, see now Rembold (2018), ch. 1. Older scholarship tended to add a caveat to this, in that the Stellinga Revolt, which unfolded in Saxony in the mid-840s, was understood as a covert sign of continued Saxon resistance to both the Carolingians and their religion. But the Stellinga are called pagans only in hostile, West Frankish sources, looking to blacken the name of Charlemagne's grandson Lothar I, who had stirred them up against his brother Louis the German, king of East Francia. Louis suppressed the revolt with particular ferocity, but really, it seems, to discourage any further East Frankish support for his brother, not because the Stellinga represented some kind of pagan Saxon independence movement: Rembold (2018), ch. 2; Nelson (2019), esp. chs. 7, 11–12. **18.** Ratramnus *Ep.* 12 with Wood (2001), 132–4. **19.** Alcuin *Ep.* 110; trans. Loyn and Percival (1975), 120–23; cf. Wood (2008). **20.** Thietmar 3.17. **21.** Thietmar 6.22. **22.** See further Reuter (1991), ch. 6, on the original revolt and its consequences, with Shepherd (2008), esp. 140 with further refs. on evolution of the cult, and Heather (2009), ch. 10, on the political context. **23.** Refs as above n. 14. **24.** I echo here the conclusions of important recent studies such as Wood (2001), *passim*, but esp. ch. 12; Smith (2005), ch. 7. Anglo-Saxons: above Chapter 6. **25.** The story of the first Adalbert's mission is told in *Adalberti continuatio Reginonis* s.a. 962. On the Magdeburg missionary corpus in general, see Wood (2001), chs. 10–11. **26.** On this backdrop in more detail, see Heather (2009), esp. chs. 9–10. **27.** There are three 10th-century Latin accounts of Wenceslas, one of which might be a forgery; cf. Kantor (1990) for Eng. trans. The third is the potential forgery. There is also an undatable Old Slavonic *Life*. For further analysis, see Wood (2001), ch. 9. **28.** Heather (2009), 533–4, drawing in particular on Dulinicz (1994), (1997); Kurnatowska (1997). The recent Oxford 'Dirhams for Slaves' project has shed a bright new light on all the Arab coin evidence. **29.** Fourteen Bohemian *Duces* still existed in 845 when they presented themselves for baptism at the court of Louis the German: *AF* s. a. 845. One Slavnik male – Sobibor, the eldest child – was in Germany at the time of the massacre and retreated to a Polish exile before finding his death trying to exact revenge on the Přemyslids: Thietmar 6.12. On the Bohemian process in general, see Heather (2009), ch. 10 with full refs. **30.** Priwina's grant to Salzburg is recorded in a Deed of 12 October 848: Wolfram (1979), (1995); cf. Wood (2001), ch. 8. Bohemia: see previous note. Byzantine/Slavic parallels: Shepherd (2008). **31.** Capitulary of Thionville (805): trans. King (1987), 248; cf. Heather (2009), 553ff. for further comment. **32.** Thietmar 4.45–6. **33.** Thietmar's *Chronicle* is the basis of our understanding of this process, which, at the moment of its most dramatic collapse, led to a brief Bohemian occupation under Bretislav I of the heartland of the Polish kingdom in 1039. For a detailed narrative in English, see Dvornik (1949). **34.** Slavic dynastic interconnections: Shepherd (2008); cf. Brown (2013), 472ff., on Iceland. **35.** *Russian Primary Chronicle* trans. Cross and Sherbowitz-Wetzor (1953), 111; quoted and discussed in Brown (2013), 467–8. **36.** Ibn Fadlan can be read in the translation of Lunde and Stone (2012). On the Volga Bulgars and Islam, see now the important essay collection of Shepherd and Treadwell (2018). **37.** On all this, and esp. Rimbert's important *Life of Anskar* – ed. Trillmich (1961); trans. Robinson (1921) – see Wood (2001), ch. 6. **38.** *Life of Anskar* 16 (destruction of Hamburg); 17 (Gautzbert); 31–2 (elimination of Horik); cf. Wood (2001), ch. 6. Sanmark (2004) provides an excellent introduction to the chronology of the appearance of Thor's hammers and other expressions of Norse paganism. **39.** Cf. Smyth (1977), which is generally convincing, although there have been some outraged responses. The clear sea-change in Norse attitudes to Christianity provides a more precise reason – beyond the mere passage of time – why medieval patterns of Norse religion cannot simply be backdated to the Anglo-Saxon era. The intense interactions of the Viking era generated considerable religious change in the north. **40.** Pechenegs: Bruno of Querfurt *Epistola ad Heinricum II*, ed. Von Giesebrecht

(1875); Christians in Birka: *Life of Anskar* 18–19. **41.** Runestones: Sanmark (2004) with full refs. Ørlygr Hrappson: *Landnámabók* 15; cf. Smith (2005), 230. **42.** Wolfram (1979); Wood (2001), ch. 8. **43.** *Book of the Icelanders* 7ff.; cf. Jochens (1999); Brown (2013), 473–4. **44.** Geza of Hungary: Thietmar 8.4; cf. Smith (2005), 235f. Wenceslas: cf. Wood (2001), ch. 9. The *Life of Otto of Bamberg* can be read in translation in Robinson (1920); cf. Demm (1970). *Life of Anskar* 18, 30; cf. Brown (2013), 471.

10. CHARLEMAGNE'S CITY OF GOD

1. The text and translation of the poem can be found in Godman (1985), 197–207. The *filioque* was not formally accepted for use in Rome until 1014; Leo III had been pressured into accepting that the doctrine was orthodox, but didn't authorize a formal alteration to the Creed, which he knew could only generate hostility in Constantinople; see further Noble (1995); McKitterick (2008), 311–15. New Testament passages: (e.g.) Matthew 3:11; Luke 3:16; John 14:26; John 15:26. **2.** On Chrodegang, see now esp. Claussen (2004). Boniface and Milo: as above p. 371 with Reuter (1980); Wallace-Hadrill (1983), 152–8. **3.** The *Admonitio Generalis* is translated in King (1987), 209–20. It is followed there by further translations of much of Charlemagne's capitulary legislation. For further discussion of the general principles of reform, see e.g. de Jong (2005); McKitterick (2008), ch. 5; Costambeys *et al.* (2011), ch. 3. On Alcuin's reception of Augustine, see now Moesch (2019), pt 2. **4.** The bibliography on Charlemagne's intellectuals is enormous, but, for a fuller introduction, see e.g. Godman (1987), ch. 2; the highly useful collection of essays in McKitterick (1994), esp. those of Law, Garrison and Rankin; the essays of Bullough and McKitterick in Story (2005). These can be supplemented by studies of individual thinkers, such as Dutton (1998) (Einhard), and Bullough (2003) (Alcuin). It is generally impossible to distinguish Charlemagne's own precise inputs beyond the general provision of resources: see further n. 6. **5.** *De litteris colendis* is translated in King (1987), 232–3. On the late Roman grammarian, see Kaster (1988), and on the subsequent evolution of Latin Wright (1982), (1996); cf. Heather (1994) on the underlying sociological transformations with above pp. 335–41. **6.** See further, among many possibilities, Law (1994), (2003), ch. 7; McKitterick (2005), with refs. The detailed individual studies collected in Bischoff (1994) shed intense, specific light. **7.** On the general cultural significance of the Carolingian period for Latin literature as a whole, see Reynolds and Wilson (1991). Nelson (1977) is particularly good on the ideologically imposed limits of Carolingian intellectual activity. Otherwise, the works cited at n. 4 are all extremely helpful. **8.** Latin literature in libraries *c.* 500–750: above pp. 283 and 346. **9.** A good introduction is Marenbon (1994). The curriculum expanded later on, of course, but by adding in new teaching texts, not by any fundamental change in subject matter: see further p. 520. **10.** The so-called reform councils of 813 were held at Arles, Chalon, Mainz, Rheims and Tours: texts Werminghoff (1906), 245–93. They amplify the programme set out at *Admonitio* c. 72: McKitterick (1977), ch. 1. More generally, the essays collected under thematic headings in McKitterick (1994) provide an excellent introduction to the portfolio of key texts. **11.** McKitterick (1977), ch. 4. **12.** Loewe (1969). **13.** Charlemagne's letter celebrating the work of Paul the Deacon is translated at King (1987), 208. On sermons more generally, see McKitterick (1977), ch. 3. **14.** McKitterick (2008), 345ff., is an excellent survey. **15.** The best introduction to the history of this script is Bischoff (1990), but see also Ganz (1989) and McKitterick (1994a). **16.** Nelson (1987); Wood (2006), chs. 14–15. **17.** On the cathedral schools and learning, see e.g. McKitterick (1994a); Costambeys *et al.* (2011), 142ff.; Lawrence (1984), chs. 2–3, provides a good introduction to Carolingian monastic reform, and Cabaniss (1979) an English translation of Ardo's contemporary *Life* of Benedict of Aniane. **18.** Chrodegang's *Rules* are translated and studied in Bertram (2005); cf. Claussen (2004) for detailed discussion. **19.** Lawrence (1984), chs. 3–4, provides a good overview; cf. more specific studies of individual moments of enthusiasm for monastic reform such as Iogna-Prat (2013) (Cluny); Nightingale (2001) (Gorze); Reuter (1982) (Ottonians). 9th-century Carolingian-style monastic reform – as sponsored by monarchs – eventually made it to England in the later 10th century. Blair (2005), 341–54, provides an excellent introduction with full refs. to an extensive bibliography, out of which I might pick Cubitt (1997) for particular mention. **20.** The centres marked on Map 5 are based on Costambeys *et al.* (2011), fig. 4, p. 150. **21.** McKitterick (1977), ch. 1 and 118ff. with refs., convincingly downgrades the personal contributions of Carolingian monarchs as it tended to be estimated in the older literature. Loewe (1969) explores the process by which Alcuin's biblical text came into general use (and its rivals). **22.** Ganz (2009); cf. Lapidge (2008); Bischoff (1990). **23.** A good introduction to Hrabanus Maurus is provided by the studies in Depreux (2010). Walafrid Strabo, Lupus of Ferrières and Otfrid of Weissenburg have all generated extensive literatures; cf. the general comments of Smith (2005), 47ff. **24.** The chronological narrative treatment of Nelson (2019) rightly emphasizes the king-emperor's consistent interest in religious reform throughout his reign. The best introduction to Louis the Pious is de Jong (2009). **25.** On episcopal statutes, see e.g. McKitterick (1977), ch. 2; Van Rhijn (2007); cf. Hamilton (2013), ch. 3. **26.** Not least, the 'pagan' Saxon and Slavic revolts of the 780s and 980s encountered in Chapter 9 both indicate their effective enforcement: pp. 388, 392. **27.** On the push for church-building and its accompanying financial arrangements, see now Wood (2006), esp. chs. 3, 15–17, 22 with full refs. On the consequences, see below pp. 540ff. **28.** Amalarius has generated an enormous bibliography: see e.g. Steck (2000). The *Liber Officalis* can be read in the translation of Knibbs (2014). For Paschasius on the Mass, see Vaillancourt (2020). On the practical consequences of these new interpretations of the Mass: McKitterick (1977), ch. 4; Palazzo (2008); Hamilton (2013), 226–9. **29.** *Libri duo de Synodalibus*: I (questions for priests), II (questions for laity); cf. Hamilton (2013), ch. 1, on both Regino in particular (p. 14ff.) and the broader range of intellectual problems posed by normative ecclesiastical evidence. When visitation records survive in the 13th century, they shed crucial light on patterns of local Christian religiosity: see further Chapter 14. **30.** On Louis the Pious's aggressive use of piety as a weapon of self-assertion, see e.g., Collins (1990); Nelson (1990); de Jong (2009). For full discussion of the later condemnations of the court of Lothar II, see the works cited in Chapter 11, n.6 below. **31.** For overviews of the evidence, see Wood (2006), esp. ch. 12; Hamilton (2013), 36–40. These are based on detailed studies such as Moretti and Stopani (1972); Toubert (1973); Aubrun (1981); Gorecki (1993). The evidence from England is analysed in Blair (2005), chs. 7–8, with e.g. Campbell (1975); R. Morris (1989), 140–67, on the influence of Carolingian legislation on the 10th-century kings. Much of the available evidence is provided by documentary materials recording when local places of worship acquired the financial and other rights of full parish church state. These will, by their nature, post-date the construction of the local centre of worship, but there is enough archaeological evidence too to confirm the generally late dates of local church construction. **32.** Bible: above p. 418. On the practice of penance, see Hamilton (2001); Meens (2006); Körntgen (2006); cf. Hamilton (2013), ch. 5. **33.** Trans. Reid (1991), 450, after the text established and analysed in Amiet (1964); cf. Hamilton (2013), 73ff. Preaching limitations of later medieval clergy, below pp. 548–55. Hereditary local priesthoods: p. 504. **34.** The new standards also spread north of the Channel into the English Kingdom both before and after the Norman Conquest. Wulfstan and Ælfric around the turn of the millennium were heavily influenced by contemporary continental developments – on whom, among many possibilities, see Gatch (1977); Cross and Hamer (1999); and the collection of Barrow and Brooks (2005). After 1066, Lanfranc of Bec, newly installed as archbishop of Canterbury by the conqueror, reformed insular practice after contemporary continental norms: Cowdrey (2003).

11. POPES AND EMPERORS

1. A good selection of Hadrian's begging-cum-demand letters to Charlemagne after his conquest of Italy is translated by King (1987), 276ff., with the translation of the letter mentioning the donation of Constantine at 286–8. Noble (1984), ch. 5, is an authoritative treatment of the extent of the re-endowments, while the individual gifts of Leo and Hadrian to various institutions in the city are listed in their biographies in the *Liber Pontificalis*, trans. as nos. 97 and 98 in Davis (1992); cf. Krautheimer (1980), ch. 5; Noble (1995) for further discussion. 2. The key texts are the *Life of Constantine* (Cyril) – trans. Kantor (1983) – and the *Conversio Bagoariorum et Carantanorum*: ed. Lošek (1997); cf. Smith (2005), 38–9, and in much more detail Dvornik (1969), (1970); Wolfram (1979). 3. The *Conversio Bagoariorum* was carefully prepared for the trial: Wolfram (1979); Wood (2001), ch. 8. 4. The literature on Great Moravia and its very impressive archaeological remains is extensive and not without its points of contention (not least its precise location). For introduction and orientation, see e.g. Poulik *et al.* (1986); Bowlus (1995); Eggers (1995). 5. See more generally: Prinz (1984); Godja (1988), (1991); Kantor (1990). Bohemia seems to have suffered imperial intrusion in more detailed ways too, as illustrated by the cult of St Wenceslas, original of the Good King of feast of Stephen fame. He was assassinated in 935 by supporters of his brother Boleslas I (dynastic in-fighting being a recurrent feature of the state formation process). Boleslas was supported by the neighbouring dukes of Bavaria, whereas Wenceslas was favoured by the Ottonian line, and the Ottonians seem to have been instrumental in developing his subsequent cult, even though Boleslas and his heirs continued to control the Duchy; cf. Wood (2001), ch. 8. Boleslas II was therefore perhaps sticking two fingers in an imperial direction when he chose to wipe out the Slavniks (above p. 399) on the anniversary of the day his father had slaughtered Wenceslas, but the Bohemians still never got their own archbishop. 6. Rothad: see below n. 14. Nicholas also interfered in a quarrel between Hincmar of Rheims and Bishop Wulfad of Bourges. In the case of the divorce, Nicholas held his own Lateran synod in October 863, which declared the rulings of a previous provincial synod invalid and excommunicated its two presiding archbishops: Airlie (1998); Nelson (1992), 215ff.; Goldberg (2006), 292–5. 7. When someone – presumably – noticed that some of the material dated from after Isidore of Seville's death, the author morphed into the unidentifiable 'Isidore Mercator'. 8. An excellent introduction is Jasper and Fuhrmann (2001), 135ff. with 154–5 and 184–6 on the MS dissemination. 9. Fried (2007), esp. ch. 4, is convincing that the text of the *Donation* was originally meant to refer only to religious authority at the moment of its forging. Its further extension into the realm of secular authority was a later development, as we shall see below. Goodson and Nelson (2010) convincingly argue the case for a Roman origin of the *Donation*, against the view of Fried who argues that the forged text originated in Francia, as the rest of *Pseudo-Isidore* certainly did (see next note). 10. Jasper and Fuhrmann (2001), esp. 173ff.; Fried (2007), esp. 88ff. with the App. A, 115–28 (by Wolfram Brandes). The smart money is now on the collection having grown up in stages, with some of it, at least, putting in a first appearance at the time of the quarrel between Louis the Pious and his sons in the early 830s. 11. On the legal-conceptual vision of the text, see generally Jasper and Fuhrmann (2001); Fried (2007); Reynolds (1995). 12. *Liber Pontificalis* 107.21–35. 13. Jasper and Fuhrmann (2001), 186–95. Jasper and Fuhrmann (2001), 173ff., and Fried (2007), 88ff., provide other examples of its practical impact. 14. So too in the cases of the

suffragan bishops Rothad of Soissons and Wulfad of Bourges: Nicholas was able to face down their archbishop, Hincmar of Rheims, but only with the active consent of Charles the Bald, whose (temporary) quarrels with his leading archbishop provided the opportunity. Fuller discussions of these incidents are available in Davis (1995), 189–202, 249–58 (introductions to the lives of Nicholas and Hadrian). **15.** See the introductions to, and actual biographies of, these popes, with the lines of contention running through them, in Davis (1995). Hadrian II's reign is also infamous for an incident which saw his daughter possibly raped and certainly kidnapped, along with her mother, by a certain Eleutherius, who then went on to have both women killed. Eleutherius was the brother of Anastasius, who had been an imperially supported potential candidate for the papal throne since around the year 850: Davis (1995), 249ff. **16.** Noble (1984), 308–22; Davis (1995), 1–4. **17.** Liutprand *Antapodosis* 1.30; cf. Grabowsky (2021) for full bibliography. **18.** General accounts in English: e.g. Llewellyn (1971), ch. 10; Ullmann (1970), chs. 5–6; C. Morris (1989), 18–33; Duffy (2006), 103–21. Wickham (2015) explores the deeper structures behind the conflicts. **19.** On Benedict IX, see C. Morris (1989), 82–4, drawing esp. on Herrmann (1973). **20.** You needed to be an emperor already – like Charlemagne – to use the alternative do-it-yourself route employed for the crowning of Louis the Pious. But this perhaps never carried so much conviction, and many later Carolingian and subsequent non-Carolingian pretenders to the title – such as Otto I in 962 – did not have a sitting emperor available to perform the ceremony, and hence looked to Rome. **21.** Otto I's intervention was something of a post-imperial afterthought. The excesses of John XII (955–64), son of the Tusculan count Alberic II, were already stirring up glimmers of internal Roman revolt by the early 960s. This made John willing to crown Otto emperor on 2 February 962, in search of some heavyweight political support, even though he knew that the imperial title would give Otto licence to intervene in Roman affairs. Once Otto had left Rome, John tried to minimize the damage by stirring up an alliance of Byzantines and Magyars against the emperor, so Otto returned and replaced him with a new man, Leo VIII, a move which also eventually allowed the Crescentii to take control. For more detailed narratives in English, see above n. 18. **22.** Both were highly educated products of the post-Carolingian Church of northern Europe: Gregory, as Otto's chaplain, was trained in the cathedral schools of East Francia – cf. Reuter (1982); McKitterick (2000) – while Gerbert, as one of the greatest scholars of his day, trained in the famous house of Aurillac in the Haute Auvergne: see further Riché (1987). **23.** Hamilton (2013), 66–9, with full refs., provides an excellent introduction to the developing ecclesiastical discourse concerning simony. **24.** Among many other good introductions to this dimension of the reform agenda in English, see C. Morris (1989), 28–33 and chs. 3–4 (the quotation from Peter Damian is from p. 103); Robinson (2004a), 1–12; Leyser (2009), or, in more detail, Cowdrey (1970); cf. Hamilton (2013), ch. 3. Perisanidi (2018) is particularly illuminating on the Latin west's divergence here from the patterns of late antiquity, which continued to prevail in the Greek eastern Church. **25.** Hamilton (2013), ch. 3, with above pp. 421ff. on the *Rules* of Chrodegang and Benedict. Amazingly, there is no comprehensive treatment of the origins of bishops in the 10th and 11th centuries, but their generally aristocratic origins are clear enough from the kinds of biographies preserved in contemporary texts, such as the *Chronicle* of Thietmar of Merseburg and writings of Fulbert of Chartres (on the latter, see Gowers (2007)). Jaeger (1994) provides a more general introduction to the cathedral schools of this era, but the reviews should be read carefully. I am particularly grateful to Bernard Gowers for his help here. **26.** Ullmann (1970), ch. 7, overstates the situation in labelling it 'The Age of Pseudo-Isidore', since the text seems to have been little used in practice: Jasper and Fuhrmann (2001), 184–6 (with full refs.). But the broad, general reception of the text is extraordinary nonetheless: Jasper and Fuhrmann (2001), 154–9; Winroth (2009). On Burchard and Regino, see Austin (2009), esp. pt 1. **27.** On the collection of Carolingian capitulary texts, see Nelson (1983). **28.** Cluny and the papacy: Rosenwein (1989); cf. McKitterick (2000); Wood (2006) on more general patterns. Canonization procedures: Perron (2009), 27–8 with refs. **29.** Damasus II (previously Bishop Poppo of Brixen, another of Henry's bishops) who lasted from 17 July to 9 August 1048: still only the seventh shortest papacy ever. **30.** There are many excellent accounts of Leo IX, but good introductions in English can be found in C. Morris (1989), 79–89; Cowdrey (2004); Blumenthal (2008); Robinson (2004), 17–36. The latter also includes an English translation of the more or less contemporary *Life* of Leo. Further accounts of Leo can be found in the works cited above in n. 18. **31.** On the Norman expansion into Sicily and southern Italy, see Donald (1992); Brown (2003). **32.** *Ep.* 97, quoted in Cowdrey (2004), 260f. **33.** Opinion is divided as to whether Gregory VII composed the *Dictatus Papae* himself or whether it was inserted into the register at a slightly later date. Its outline description of the specific characteristics of papal authority closely match those illustrated in a key selection of decretals published by one of Gregory's closest allies, Cardinal Deusdedit. **34.** Had this practice been followed consistently in earlier eras, it would have made the forged papal decretals of *Pseudo-Isidore* impossible. **35.** On Nicholas and Alexander in general, see C. Morris (1989), 89–108; Cowdrey (2004); Blumenthal (2008); cf. in much more detail Schmidt (1977). On the return to registration, Cowdrey (2002), xi ff. Alexander sent out further legates besides, not least to England in 1070 at the invitation of William the Conqueror (whose expedition he had blessed in 1066) to help modernize the Anglo-Saxon Church, and north into the Empire to judge in a quarrel between the bishops of Bamberg and Constanz, and eventually to persuade Henry IV not to divorce his wife Bertha. **36.** *Ep.* 2.49; trans. Cowdrey (2002), 139–40. **37.** On Gregory's radical extension of the reform programme, see further C. Morris (1989), ch. 5; Ullmann (1970), ch. 7; Duffy (2006), 120ff.; Robinson (2004a); Blumenthal (2008). Gregory's letters are translated in Cowdrey (2002), and other contemporary materials relating to his pontificate in Robinson (2004), 158ff., which also provides a good introduction to his pontificate and these documents at 36ff. **38.** There is now an excellent general guide to the processes of granting lands and other financial rights to ecclesiastical institutions in the Middle Ages: Wood (2006). For England, the evidence is comprehensive thanks to the Doomsday Book and the *Cartae Baronum* of 1166: Douglas and Greenaway (1952), 903ff. On the situation in Germany: Reuter (1982), and note in particular the *Indiculus Loricatorum* or Index of Armoured Contingents: when Otto II was in trouble after defeat in Italy in 981, it was exclusively to bishoprics and monasteries that he sent for reinforcements. **39.** The available scholarly literature on the Investiture Controversy and its eventual resolution at the council of Worms is enormous, but for orientation, see Miller (2005 in English); Zey (2017). **40.** Perron (2009), 23ff., explores the new phenomenon of Lateran 'ecumenical' councils.

12. 'GOD WILLS IT'

1. I commend to any interested reader the eyewitness account of the *Gesta Francorum* – trans. Hill (1962) – which is utterly compelling. Excellent secondary accounts, among many other possibilities, can be found in Riley-Smith (1986) and Tyerman (2012), which supplement the classic treatments such as Runciman (1954) and the excellent recent overview of Bull (2009). For the other contemporary witnesses, see Peters (1971). **2.** Riley-Smith (1992); Tyerman (2006), chs. 1–2; cf. Bull (1993) and above Chapter 9 on Charlemagne. **3.** Riley-Smith (1986), esp. chs. 1–2; Tyerman (2006), ch. 1; drawing on older studies such as Erdmann (1977). On Gregory VII, see esp. Cowdrey (1982). **4.** For more on the Seljuks, see e.g. Rice (1961); Kafesoglu and Leiser (1988). Excellent accounts of the decline and fall of Outremer can be found in the works cited in n. 1. **5.** Quoted in Tyerman (2005), 19.

6. Including campaigns against enemies internal to Christendom, such as the Hussites, crusades were still being periodically declared well into the 15th century. 7. By Marshall Baldwin in his introduction to Erdmann (1977), p. xvi. 8. On these subsequent developments, see among many possibilities Tyerman (2006), ch. 16; Brundage (1969); Cazel (1989). 9. Again there is a vast potential bibliography, but good introductions include Lomax (1978); Fletcher (1984), (1987). 10. Christiansen (1980) offers an excellent basic account, but see also Tyerman (2006), ch. 21; Urban (1994); Lotter (1989). 11. Fourth Crusade: see the general works cited in n. 1 with, in much more detail, the specific study of Queller (1978). Rodrigo of Vivar: Fletcher (1989). 12. Origins of the *filioque*: above p. 410. On the break of 1054, see further C. Morris (1989), 107–8; Fried (2007), esp. 16ff.; Shepherd (2006) drawing again on an extensive scholarly literature. 13. Quoted in Shepherd (2006), 22. 14. Excellent brief introductions in Shepherd (2006); Angold (2006), drawing on more detailed studies such as Gill (1979). 15. Themistius *Orations* 6.83c–d; which is why the later Roman Empire had ended up being governed not from Rome but from political centres much closer to its key frontiers such as Trier, Constantinople and Antioch: Heather (2005), ch. 1. 16. Anselm the younger of Lucca produced a first reforming collection in 1083, and others soon followed: that of Cardinal Deusdedit in 1087, and the *Anonymous Collection in 74 Titles* from the same decade. These collections were all produced in support of the papal reform agenda. The *Anonymous Collection* has been both edited and translated: Gilchrist (1973), (1980). 17. See further Robinson (1978); Brundage (1995), ch. 2; C. Morris (1989), 126–33, drawing on more detailed studies such as Fuhrmann (1973) and Mordek (1985); cf. Austin (2009) on the deeper background. Ivo's Preface is translated in Somerville and Brasington (1998), 132–58. 18. An excellent introduction to the rediscovery of the *Digest* is Stein (1999), 43–8 with full refs. Clarence Smith (1975) is an extremely helpful prosopographical guide to Roman and canon lawyers of the 12th and 13th centuries. On Justinian's legal projects, see Honoré (1978), with further comments in Heather (2018), esp. ch. 7. 19. The sub-headings (and their order) of Roman legal collections had been set since at least the first century AD: Matthews (2000), esp. ch. 4. 20. Gratian *Decr.* C. IX. Q. 1 dictum post c. 16 (1011). 21. On the dissemination, see Duggan (2012), 366–72; Duggan (2004), 47–56, on the role of this collection in the Becket dispute. 22. Good introductions: e.g. Brundage (1995), ch. 3; Stein (1999), 49ff.; Winroth (2000); cf. Winroth (2009). The first part of Gratian's text is translated in Thompson and Gordley (1993), who also provide an extremely helpful introduction. 23. Duggan (2012), 370–72. 24. There are many possible treatments, but see, e.g., C. Morris (1989), 397–416; Brundage (1995), ch. 3; Stein (1999), 49ff.; Winroth (2009). Duggan (2012), 372–8, explores the Worcester decretal collection and Duggan (1995) the role of papal judge-delegate in developing the law. 25. Duggan (2012), 387–401, with full refs. to previous scholarship. 26. Leyser (2009), 13. This example is something of a cause célèbre, cited in most treatments. 27. C. Morris (1989), 60–62; Wood (2006), chs. 24–6.

13. THE ECONOMY OF SALVATION

1. Quoted in Hamilton (2013), 353. 2. Lateran IV was actually rowing back here on a more ambitious earlier requirement, found, among others, in the legal collection of Regino of Prüm, that the laity should take communion three times a year. 3. The bibliography on Innocent III and Lateran IV is immense, but a good introduction is provided by C. Morris (1989), ch. 17, esp. 447–51; with fuller discussion in e.g. Tillmann (1980), a translation of the German original of 1954. An English version of the conciliar canons can be found in Rothwell (1975), 643–75, and the eight hundredth anniversary generated some important collections of papers: Álvarez de las Asturias (2016); Melville and Helmrath (2017). Rubin

(2009) is an excellent introduction to the seven sacraments; cf. in more detail Holcomb and Johnson (2017); Nutt (2017) with refs. to specific studies of the emergence of the individual sacraments, such as Reynolds (1994) (marriage) and Paxton (1990) (extreme unction). **4.** While there was peasant participation too, particularly in the First Crusade, to which we'll return later in the chapter, the crusading phenomenon fundamentally depended upon Europe's warrior elites. **5.** Bull (1993), Riley-Smith (1997) are representative of what has been a highly fruitful line in recent scholarship; cf. Hamilton (2013), 304ff. **6.** My thoughts here are heavily dependent upon the general survey of Hamilton (2013), ch. 6, with full refs. On Eberhard, see esp. Kershaw (2007). A partial translation of Dhuoda's advice to her son is available in Dutton (2004), 336ff. **7.** The evidence for monastic foundation and the increasing endowment of houses of canons is surveyed in Hamilton (2013); cf. Bernard and Bruel (1876–1903) for the charters of Cluny. **8.** Vilich: Hamilton (2013), 143–5; cf. Böhringer (2004). An excellent general discussion of the *Libri Vitae* is Geuenich (2004). Necrologies: Lauwers (1997). **9.** Brown (2015) with above p. 352. **10.** The *Life of Gerald of Aurillac* is translated in Sitwell (1958); cf. Kuefler (2014) for further comment on Odo's careful presentation of the cult, and Leyser (2009) for more general comment. For contrasting 'good' lay piety required of the western European warrior class in the immediate post-Roman period, see above pp. 248ff., 357ff. **11.** Pilgrimage: Hamilton (2013), ch. 8, offers an excellent survey of its rise in the post-Carolingian period with full refs. to previous scholarship, and esp. Vogel (1964) on the penitential pilgrimage. First crusade: refs. as above Chapter 11, n. 1. **12.** Leo's *Life* 7, trans. Robinson (2004), 107–8. **13.** Hamilton (2013), 268–70, provides an overview; cf. the useful collection of essays in Head and Landes (1992), supplemented by more particular studies, which tend to stress the aristocratic dimension over more popular participation: Bowman (1999); Head (1999), (2006). **14.** *The History of My Calamities* can be read in the translation of Muckle (1964); cf. most recently Luscombe (2019) on the correspondence with Héloïse. The scholarly literature on Abelard as theologian is immense, but good places to start are Clanchy (1997); Hellemans (2014); Marenbon (2013). **15.** Le Goff (1993), 18f. **16.** The classic study in English remains Southern (1995), esp. chs. 2–6, but see also Le Goff (1993) and Moore (2007), ch. 4. **17.** Quoted in Le Goff (1993), 10. **18.** Southern (1995), ch. 6 (2002), chs. 7–8. **19.** Or, as my children used to put it, Oxford is about as far from the seaside as you can possibly be in what is really a very small island. **20.** There are many possible overviews of the process, but in English see still the classic account of Rashdall (1987); Pedersen (1997); Post (2017). Each of the major universities has its own specialist bibliography: see e.g. Zimmermann (1976) (Paris); Lange (1993) (Bologna); Catto (1984) (Oxford). **21.** The potential for the chances of MS survival to give a misleading impression at this crucial moment of change is strong. Hugh of St Victor was a figure of major importance in the evolution of Peter Lombard's thought, but nothing directly survives in his own voice: Southern (2002), ch. 5. **22.** BL MS Arundel 1734 (northern Italy, late 11th century) and Lib. Paris 1130 are two particular examples discussed by Southern (2002), ch. 4. I have also found Smalley (1969) extremely helpful. **23.** Good recent introductions to Peter Lombard: Doyle (2016); Monagle (2013); Rosemann (2004). *The Sentences* can be read in the translation of Silano (2007–10). For subsequent commentary on Peter, see Rosemann (2002–14). **24.** Quoted in Rosemann (2007), 66; cf. Rubin (2009), 222. **25.** Le Goff (1984) and Walls (2011) provide comprehensive accounts of the evolution of Purgatory, from its inchoate roots in older Christian thought, some of which is examined in more detail in Brown (2015). Watkins (2002) and Berenstein (2009) are also extremely helpful; cf. Brown (2013), esp. 258–65, 375–6, for early medieval examples where the adverse effects of sin were overcome post-mortem. **26.** An introduction is Berenstein (2009), with more detail in the essays collected in *Franciscan Studies* (1969). On Alexander of Hales, see most recently Schumacher (2020). **27.** Little (1978), ch. 8, and Moore (2007), chs. 1–2, provide overviews; cf. more particular studies such as Biller (2006) with full refs. (Waldenses); Andrews (1999) (*Humiliati*). **28.** In addition to the overviews cited in the previous note, see also Lambert (2002), chs. 4–5; Biller (2009); Mayne Kienzle (2000), (2009). Wakefield and Evans (1969) and Peters (1980) provide English translations of many of the major sources. **29.** Hamilton (2013), 168–81, surveys the evidence which is usually indirect in form: higher clergy looking to reach the masses via local priests. Cf. the materials cited in nn. 31–2. The Peace and Truce councils also attracted at least an element of more popular participation. **30.** Fonts: Morris (1991); cf. Drake (2001). In Italy, control of baptism remained centralized for longer; cf. Hamilton (2013), 184–6. Bell towers: Hamilton (2013), 196–204 with refs. **31.** Miracle tours and cults of the cart: Hamilton (2013), 270ff., who rightly warns that the monastic record had every interest in, and biblical literary models for, maximizing the numbers of participatory laity supposedly involved in these phenomena. **32.** For a comprehensive treatment of Peter the Hermit, see Flori (1999). For the fate of the masses who participated in the first wave, see Porges (1946), in addition to the works cited in Chapter 12, n. 1. **33.** Little (1978), ch. 2; Moore (2000), ch. 2; Keene (2004) provide good overviews. **34.** Little (1978) is again fundamental, but see also Little and Rosenwein (1974); Abulafia (1992); Mayne Kienzle (2009). **35.** The sources relevant to Tanchelm are translated with some commentary in Wakefield and Evans (1969), 96–101. **36.** This coincidence has long been recognized: Lambert (2002), esp. chs. 3–6, provides an excellent introduction in English to the general 'revival' of heresy in the 11th and 12th centuries, which brings out the overall chronological patterning in accusations of heresy. **37.** Gregory and Pataria: see esp. Cowdrey (1968). Peter de Bruis: Wakefield and Evans (1969), 118–122. Arnold of Brescia: *idem.* 147–50. Henry of Le Mans: *idem.* 107–15. Tanchelm: see n. 35. The individual at the centre of another heresy accusation in Chartres in 1022 was likewise a cleric: *idem.* 76. **38.** Tithes: Leutard (Wakefield and Evans (1969), 72f.) and Tanchelm (*idem.* 96ff.). Penance and prayers for the dead: Arras heretics of 1025 (*idem.* 82 ff.; Henry of Le Mans (*idem.* 107–18, 122–6); Peter de Bruis (*idem.* 118–22). Crucifix and Christ's humanity: Leutard (as above); Peter de Bruis (as above). Real Presence: Orleans heretics of 1022 (*idem.* 76 ff.); Arras heretics of 1025 (as above); Trier heretics (*idem.* 105ff.); Peter de Bruis (as above); Arnold of Brescia (*idem.* 146–50). Infant baptism: Arras heretics of 1025 (as above); Trier heretics (as above). Disputed sacramentalization of marriage: Henry of Le Mans (as above). Refusal to accept that sacraments have their own validity whatever the moral qualities of priests: Ramihrdus of Cambrai (*idem.* 95f.); Tanchelm (as above); Henry of Le Mans (as above); Peter de Bruis (as above); Arnold of Brescia (as above). **39.** On Innocent and the Waldenses and *Humiliati*, see Moore and Bolton (1999). The truce did not last: cf. the literature cited in n. 33 above. **40.** Women were also, as the weaker sex, placed on the south side of the church in northern climes to protect them from the bad weather, and vice versa in the south to protect them from the heat. For basic ideological orientation, see Smith (1999); Coon (2008); McLaughlin (2009), (2010). Smith (1995) explores the relegation of Carolingian female sanctity to the private sphere, while Brundage (1987), chs. 3–4, has fun with the Church's teaching on married sex. **41.** See in more detail Fulton (2009); Rubin (2009), esp. pt 3. **42.** Arbrissel's *Life* is edited and translated in Venarde (1997); cf. Venarde (2003), with Griffiths (2008) for further commentary. **43.** A selection of Hildegard's writings can be read in translation in Ahterton (2001). She has generated an extensive secondary literature, but see esp. Newman (1998); Mayne Kienzle (2014). **44.** Other famous medieval female visionaries include Margery Kempe and Julian of Norwich. The authoritative treatment of the Beguines is Simons (2001). **45.** McGuire (2009) provides an introductory survey, and notes that most of the new orders, at least at the beginning, also offered versions of their Rules catering for female enthusiasts. **46.** Lincoln case study: Watkins (2002); cf. Le Goff (1984); Walls (2011), and esp. Baldwin (1970) on the importance of Peter the Chanter (d. 1197) in integrating the new theology of Purgatory into practical parish piety. Among those recorded resisting any practice of praying for the dead – the pietistic reflex most associated with belief in Purgatory – were the Arras heretics of 1025 (Wakefield and Evans (1969), 82–6) and their Cologne peers of 1143/4 (*idem.* 127ff.). Among the potentially larger heretic networks, Waldenses and Cathars (on whom see below, pp. 568ff.) also denied the efficacy of the practice. **47.** The proceedings of the synod can be read in English trans. in Rothwell (1975), 691–704. **48.** The key sources for St Francis can be read in translation in the excellent collection of Brooke (1975). The relevant literature – not least recently under the stimulus of the appointment of the current pope – is enormous, but an excellent introduction and further guidance can be found in the collection of essays in Robson (2012). **49.** Burr (2003) is an excellent introduction to the Spiritual Franciscans. **50.** Armstrong (2005) translates her writings; cf. Pattenden (2008) on her canonization and Mueller (2010); Mooney (2016) with full refs. for good introductions, among an almost endless range of possibilities. **51.** A recent introduction to the Dominican order is Giraud and Leitmeier (2021); cf. Horst (2006) on Dominican relations with the papacy. D'Avray (1985), esp. chs. 1, 3, is excellent on the more general background. **52.** The quotation is from the Dominican Hugh of St Cher, cited in Smith (2009) – drawing esp. on Boyle (1981); Goering (1992) – which provides an excellent account of the relationship between university training and the friars, in addition to the literature cited in nn. 48 and 51. **53.** Hamilton (2013), 327ff. Similar too are the moralizing stories collected by the Cistercian Caesarius of Heisterbach (1170–1240) in his *Dialogue on Miracles*: Smirnova *et al.* (2015). These collections can have specific additional agendas beyond straightforward moral instruction: see, e.g., Riches (2007) on the importance of the Cambrai collection in re-establishing local episcopal authority. **54.** D'Avray (1985) is a magisterial response to this material, after esp. Schneyer (1969–90). Cf. d'Avray (2001), esp. ch. 1. This probably represents quite a small sample of what once existed since the loss rate is likely to have been high. **55.** Peckham: Powicke and Cheney (1964), 905; cf. Rubin (2009), 231. Priests and Oxford: Dunbabin (1984). **56.** Corpus Christi and the Christian countryside: Rubin (1992); cf. more generally the thriving later medieval Christian culture explored magisterially in Duffy (1992).

14. CHRISTENDOM AND COERCION

1. Excommunication formulae: Hamilton (2013), 322ff. (quotation from p. 322). Waldo: above Chapter 13, together with Henry of Le Mans, Arnold of Brescia, etc. **2.** Hamilton (2013), 342. **3.** The Albigensian Crusade receives coverage in most of the standard crusading literature: see Chapter 12, n. 1, but see also in particular Hamilton (1974); Sumption (1978); with Léglu (2014) on the sources and Fudge (2002) on the Hussites. **4.** An excellent general guide is Prudlo (2019), but see also among many possibilities: Arnold (2009); Moore (2012); Given (1989), (1997); Hamilton (1981). **5.** *Annales Wormatienses* quoted in Arnold (2009), 355. **6.** Given (1989), 348f., is a particularly helpful overview: otherwise consult the literature cited in n. 4 above. Hill (2019) is a monograph devoted to the inquisition manuals of Bernard Gui and Nicholas Eymerich. Many of the original records disappeared in the French Revolutionary era. **7.** Worms: Arnold (2009); Languedoc: Given (1989), (2017). **8.** Leper scare: Given (1989), 351; Free Spirit heresy: Biller (2009), both with refs. to further literature. **9.** Eymerich *Directorium inquisitorium* 413; cf. Given (1989), 348. **10.** The fall of the Templars has its own massive, often fantastical, literature, but a sane introduction is provided by the collected papers in Barber (2012) with full refs. The interrogators' methods under *Inquisitio*, as one of my recent MA students, a trained police interviewer, pointed out in his dissertation, break every rule in the current UK police interrogation manual. These rules were formulated precisely to counter the high-profile false positives, such as the case of the Birmingham Six, generated under the old regime. **11.** Excellent versions of the broadly traditional understanding of the Cathars can be found in e.g. Lansing (1998); Barber (2000), with full refs. to a very broad literature, including esp. Obolenksy (1948) on the broader background of dualist thought from late antiquity onwards, and its posited direct transmission from Manichaeans to Paulicians to Bogomils to Cathars. **12.** That is, the Devil is no more than a fallen angel, whose real enemy is not God – whose omnipotence is utterly overwhelming – but Michael, God's prime but subordinate archangel, who will slay the Devil at the end of time. **13.** In similar vein, as I now look back on the religious phase of my teens with a more theologically informed view, it seems to me that many of the Christians I mixed with then – myself included – could, if exposed to an inquisitor's methods, find themselves classified as Arian dualists: holding that God the Father is obviously superior in some way to God the Son, and that both were pitted against the power of the Devil. **14.** The attack on the classic account of the Cathars was led by Pegg (2001). See now also the broadly revisionist essays by Moore, Pegg and Théry-Astruc in Sennis (2016). Waldensians: classic accounts include Audisio (1999); Cameron (2000); cf. Biller (2006) for discussion of the attempts to discredit the general approach. **15.** Biller (2006), (2009). **16.** Nicetas's visit: Pegg (2001), 187 n. 14. But see, in response to the revisionist position, the essays of Biller, Hamilton, d'Avray and, above all, Feuchter in Sennis (2016). **17.** Balearics: Bradbury (1996). The hostile sequence of Visigothic legislation culminated in 694 at the council of Toledo, which ordered adult Jews who refused to convert to be enslaved and any children aged seven or above to be handed over to the care of Christians. The texts are conveniently collected in Linder (1997); cf. Bat-Sheva (2008). There was certainly still a substantial Jewish population in the early 8th century at the time of the Muslim conquest of Spain, which had survived several 7th-century legal demands for its forcible conversion. **18.** Stroumsa (2007) provides an overview; cf. more specialist studies such as Fredriksen (2008). **19.** On William of Norwich, see most recently Rose (2016). In practice, the cult which developed around William's memory does not seem to have been particularly anti-Semitic, his recorded miracles focusing more on protective actions towards children and the family. **20.** The sorry history of the increasing tide of Christian anti-Semitism in mid- and later-medieval Europe is well-explored: see e.g. Bat-Sheva (2008) and Limor (2009) for basic orientations, supported by many more-detailed studies: Moore (2007), esp. 26–42; Abulafia (1995); Cohen (1999); McMichael and Myers (2004). **21.** Persecuting society: Moore (2007). Behaviour in the face of inquisitors: Given (1989), (1997); Le Roy Ladurie (1990); Arnold (2009). **22.** Arnold (2009) responding to the general case made by Moore (2007). **23.** See e.g. Duffy (1992); Burgess and Duffy (2006). **24.** A good introduction is Reisl (2009). **25.** Fundamental here is the work of Ian Forrest (2013), (2016), (2018). **26.** Trans. Rothwell (1975), no. 146, 705ff. **27.** These were recorded in a separate document. **28.** Noted in the case of an adulterous knight. **29.** Forrest (2013), (2016); explored in much more detail in Forrest (2018). In the Canterbury Visitation, the importance of this group is noted on two specific occasions, but it is impossible to be more specific about them. **30.** Forrest (2016), who notes that visitation records were customarily destroyed after the issues they noted had been resolved. **31.** Forrest (2013). **32.** Wakefield and Evans (1969), 245–7. **33.** As we have seen, the necessity for kings of being able to draw reliably on the resources of ecclesiastical institutions for the defence of their realms in practice required that they be allowed at least a veto over the most senior ecclesiastical appointments within their kingdoms: pp. 471–2. An analogous caveat applied even to the new-model papacy. It's beyond the remit of this study, but when Rome became too closely allied with one of the two great powers of 14th-century Europe, the other started to appoint its own pontiffs: as classically explored, among many possibilities, in Tuchman (1979). **34.** Pp. 325–6.

Bibliography

PRIMARY SOURCES

As per normal conventions, editions of standard classical works are not cited in the bibliography; most are translated in either or both of the Loeb and Penguin Classics series. All Christian authors are available, if sometimes in outdated form, in *Patrologia Latina* or *Patrologia Graeca* editions. More recent (sometimes competing) editions of most of the texts cited in the introductions and notes can be found in *GCS* (*Die Griechischen Christlichen Schriftsteller der ersten Jahrhunderte*), *CSEL* (*Corpus Scriptorum Ecclesiasticorum Latinorum*), *CC* (*Corpus Christianorum*), and *SC* (*Sources Chrétiennes*). Many are translated in the Nicene and Post-Nicene Fathers, and Library of the Fathers collections. Many medieval texts are available in excellent editions in the different strands of the *Monumenta Germaniae Historica* (*MGH*) series. Otherwise, the following editions and English translations have been used:

Abelard, *The History of My Calamities*: trans. Muckle (1964).
Acts of Toledo III: ed. Vives (1963).
Admonitio Generalis: trans. King (1987).
Admonitio synodalis: ed. Amiet (1964); trans. Reid (1991).
Alcuin, *Letters*: trans. Loyn and Percival (1975).
Amalarius, *Liber Officalis*: trans. Knibbs (2014).
Ammianus Marcellinus: ed. and trans. Rolfe (1935–9).
Anglo-Saxon lawcodes (Æthelberht, Wihtred and Ine): trans. Whitelock (1996).
Annals of Fulda (*AF*): trans. Reuter (1992).
Anonymous Collection in 74 Titles: ed. and trans. Gilchrist (1973), (1980).
Ardo, *Life of Benedict* (of Aniane): trans. Cabaniss (1979).
The Letter of Auxentius of Durostorum: trans. Heather and Matthews (1991).
Avitus, *Letters*: trans. Shanzer and Wood (2002).

The Battle of Maldon: trans. Griffiths (1991).
Bede, *Ecclesiastical History*: ed. and trans. Colgrave and Mynors (1991).
Bede, *Letter to Egbert*: trans. Whitelock (1996).
Boniface, *Letters*: trans. Talbot (1981).
Book of the Icelanders: trans. Grønlie (2006).
Braulio of Saragossa, *Letters*: trans. Barlow (1969).
Life of Caesarius: ed. Morin (2010); trans. Klingshirn (1994a).
Canterbury Visitation: trans. Rothwell (1975).
Capitularies of Charlemagne: partial trans. King (1987).
Cartae Baronum of 1166: trans. Douglas and Greenaway (1952).
Cassiodorus, *Institutes*: trans. Halporn and Vessey (2004).
Cassiodorus, *Variae*: trans. Bjornlie (2019), cf. Barnish (1992).
Charlemagne, *De litteris colendis*: trans. King (1987).
Charles the Great and Leo the Pope: trans. Godman (1985).
Chrodegang of Metz, *Rules*: trans. Bertram (2005).
Chronicon Paschale: text Dindorf (1832); trans. Whitby and Whitby (1989).
Codex Carolinus: partial trans. King (1987).
Codex Theodosianus (*CTh*): trans. Pharr (1952).
Life of Columbanus (and associated texts): trans. O'Hara and Wood (2017).
Life of Constantine (Cyril): trans. Kantor (1983).
Corpus Iuris Civilis:

1. *Institutiones* (*Institutes*) and *Digesta* (*Digest*): text Krüger and Mommsen (1928); trans. Birks and McLeod (1987), Watson *et al.* (1998).
2. *Codex Justinianus* (*CJ*): text Krüger (1929); trans. Scott (1932).
3. *Novellae* (*Novels*): text Schöll and Kroll (1928); trans. Scott (1932).

Life of Cuthbert: trans. Colgrave (1985).
Dhuoda: partial trans. Dutton (2004).
Didache: trans. Stevenson (1957).
Didascalia: trans. Gibson (1903).
The Dream of the Rood: trans. Bradley (1982).
Dream of the Shepherd of Hermas: trans. Stevenson (1957).
Einhard, *Life of Charlemagne*: trans. Dutton (1998).
Eulogius, *Memorial of the Saints*: trans. Wolf (2019).
Eunapius of Sardis, *Lives of the Sophists*: ed. and trans. Wright (1922).
Eusebius of Caesarea, *Ecclesiastical History*: trans. McGiffert (1905).
Eusebius of Caesarea, *Life of Constantine*: trans. Cameron and Hall (1999).
Eusebius of Caesarea, *History of the Martyrs in Palestine*: trans. Cureton (2016).

Fructuosus, Monastic Rules: trans. Barlow (1969).
Life of Gerald of Aurillac: trans. Sitwell (1958).
Gesta Francorum: trans. Hill (1962).
Gratian, *Decretum*: partial trans. Thompson and Gordley (1993).
Pope Gregory I, *Letters*: trans. Martyn (2004).
Pope Gregory VII, *Letters*: trans. Cowdrey (2002).
Gregory of Tours, *Glory of the Confessors*: trans. Van Dam (1988).
Gregory of Tours, *Glory of the Martyrs*: trans. Van Dam (1988a).
Gregory of Tours, *Histories*: trans. Thorpe (1974).
Gregory of Tours, *Life of the Fathers*: trans. James (1985).
Life of St Guthlac: trans. Colgrave (1956).
Harrowing of Hell (Anglo-Saxon version): trans. Bradley (1982).
Hydatius, *Chronicle*: trans. Burgess (1993).
Ibn Fadlan: trans. Lunde and Stone (2012).
Ildefonsus: trans. Braegelmann (1942).
Isidore, *Etymologies* book 1: trans. Spevak (2020).
John of Biclar, *Chronicle*: trans. Wolf (1999).
Julian (the Apostate) *Works*: ed. and trans. Wright (1913).
Landnámabók: trans. Pálsson and Edwards (1972).
Lateran IV, canons: trans. Rothwell (1975).
Life of Pope Leo IX : trans. Robinson (2004).
Liber Pontificalis: ed. Duchesne (1876–82); trans. Davis (1992), (1995), (2000).
Nag Hammadi: trans. Robinson (1996).
Novels of Valentinian III : see *Codex Theodosianus*.
Optatus, *Against the Donatists*: ed. and trans. Edwards (1997).
Orosius, *Against the Pagans*: trans. Fear (2010).
Life of Otto of Bamberg: trans. Robinson (1920).
Panegyrici Latini (*Pan. Lat.*): ed. and trans. Nixon and Rogers (1994).
Paul Alvar, *Life of Eulogius*: trans. Wolf (2019).
Penitential of Theodore: trans. McNeil and Gamer (1938).
Peter Lombard, *Sentences*: trans. Silano (2007–10).
Poetic Edda: trans. Larrington (2014).
Procopius, *Works*: ed. and trans. Dewing (1914–40).
Prose Edda: trans. Byock (2005).
Rimbert, *Life of Anskar*: trans. Robinson (1921).
Life of Robert Arbrissel: ed. and trans. Venarde (2003).
Royal Frankish Annals: trans. Scholz (1972).
Russian Primary Chronicle: trans. Cross and Sherbowitz-Wetzor (1953).
Sayings of the Desert Fathers: trans. Ward (1981).
Sisebut: trans. Martyn (2008).

Tertullian, *Apology, De Spectaculis*: trans. Glover *et al.* (1931).
Thietmar of Merseburg, *Chronicle*: trans. Warner (2001).
Valerius of Bierzo: *Life of St Fructuosus*: trans. Nock (1946).
Venantius Fortunatus: partial trans. George (1995).
Vetus Gallica: ed. Mordek (1975).
Victor of Vita, *History of the Persecution in Africa*: trans. Moorhead (1992).
Life of Wenceslas: trans. Kantor (1990).
The Life of Wilfrid: trans. Colgrave (1927).
Worcester Diocesan Synod *c.* 1270: trans. Rothwell (1975).
Zosimus, *History*: ed. Paschoud (1971–81); trans. Ridley (1982).

SECONDARY WORKS

Abrams, L. (2008), 'Germanic Christianities', in Noble and Smith (eds.), 107–29.

Abulafia, A. S. (1992), 'Theology and the commercial revolution: Guibert of Nogent, St Anselm, and the Jews of northern France', in Abulafia *et al.* (eds.), 23–40.

Abulafia, A. S. (1995), *Christians and Jews in the Twelfth-Century Renaissance* (London).

Abulafia, D. *et al.* (eds.) (1992), *Church and City, 1000–1500: Essays in Honour of Christopher Brooke* (Cambridge).

Ackroyd, P. R. and Evans, C. F. (eds.) (1970), *Cambridge History of the Bible vol. 1: From the Beginnings to Jerome* (Cambridge).

Aillet, C. (2010), *Les Mozarabes: christianisme et arabisation en peninsula ibérique (IXe–XIIe siècle)* (Madrid).

Airlie, S. (1998), 'Private bodies and the body politic in the divorce case of Lothar II', *Past & Present* 161, 3–38.

Allison, D. C. (2013), 'The Old Testament in the New Testament', in Paget and Schaper (eds.), 479–502.

Al-Sha'ar, N. (ed.) (2017), *The Qur'an and Adab: The Shaping of Literary Traditions in Classical Islam* (Oxford).

Álvarez de las Asturias, N. (ed.) (2016), *El IV Concilio de Letrán en perspectiva histórico-teológica* (Madrid).

Amiet, R. (1964), 'Une "Admonitio synodalis" de l'époque carolingienne. Étude critique et edition', *Mediaeval Studies* 26, 12–82.

Anatolius, K. (2007), 'Discourse on the Trinity', in Casiday and Norris (eds.), 431–68.

Anawati, G. C. (1990), 'Christian communities in Egypt', in Gervers and Bihkazi (eds.), 235–63.

Ando, C. (2000), *Imperial Ideology and Provincial Loyalty in the Roman Empire* (Berkeley, CA).

Ando, C. (2008), *The Matter of the Gods. Religion and the Roman Empire* (Berkeley, CA).

Andrews, F. (1999), *The Early Humiliati* (Cambridge).

Angold, M. (2006), 'Byzantium and the West, 1204–1453', in Angold (ed.), 53–78.

Angold, M. (ed.) (2006), *The Cambridge History of Christianity vol. 5: Eastern Christianities* (Cambridge).

Armstrong, R. (trans.) (2005), *The Lady: Clare of Assisi: Early Documents* (New York).

Arnold, J. (2009), 'Repression and power', in Rubin and Simons (eds.), 353–71.

Athanassiadi, P. (1992), *Julian: An Intellectual Biography* (London).

Atherton, M. (2001), *Hildegard of Bingen: Selected Writings* (London).

Aubrun, M. (1981), *L'ancien diocèse de Limoges, des origines au milieu du XIe siècle* (Clermont-Ferrand).

Audisio, G. (1999), *The Waldensian Dissent: Persecution and Survival, c. 1170–c. 1570*, trans. C. Davison (Cambridge).

Austin, G. (2009), *Shaping Church Law Around the Year 1000: The Decretum of Burchard of Worms* (Farnham).

Auzépy, M. F. (2008), *L'histoire des iconoclasts* (Paris).

'Awad, N. G. (2018), *Umayyad Christianity: John of Damascus as a Contextual Example of Identity Formation in Early Islam* (Piscataway, NJ).

Ayres, L. (2004), *Nicaea and Its Legacy: An Approach to Fourth-Century Trinitarian Theology* (Oxford).

Azzara, C. (1997), *L'ideologia del potere regio nel papato altomedievale (secoli VI–VIII), Testi studi, strumenti* 12 (Spoleto).

Bagnall, R. S. (1982), 'Religious conversion and onomastic change in early Byzantine Egypt', *Bulletin of the American Society of Papyrologists* 19, 105–24.

Bagnall, R. S. (1988), 'Combat ou vide: Christianisme et paganisme dans l'Égypte romaine tardive', *Ktema* 13, 285–96.

Bailey, L. (2010), *Christianity's Quiet Success: The Eusebius Gallicanus Sermon Collection and the Power of the Church in Late Antique Gaul* (Notre Dame, IN).

Baldwin, J. W. (1970), *Masters, Princes, and Merchants: The Social Views of Peter the Chanter and His Circle* (Princeton, NJ).

Banaji, J. (2001), *Agrarian Change in Late Antiquity: Gold, Labour, and Aristocratic Dominance* (Oxford).

Barber, M. (2000), *The Cathars: Dualist Heretics in Languedoc in the High Middle Ages* (Harlow).

Barber, M. (2012), *Trial of the Templars*, 2nd edn (Cambridge).

Barclay, J. M. G. (ed.) (2004), *Negotiating Diaspora: Jewish Strategies in the Roman Empire* (London).

Bardill, J. (2012), *Constantine: Divine Emperor of the Christian Golden Age* (Cambridge).

Barker, K. and Brooks, N. (eds.) (2010), *Aldhelm and Sherborne: Essays to Celebrate the Founding of the Bishopric* (Oxford).

Barlow, C. W. (1969), *Iberian Fathers*, 2 vols. (Washington, DC).

Barnard, L. W. (1982), 'Church–State relations AD 313–339', *Journal of Church and State* 24, 337–55.

Barnes, M. R. and Williams, D. H. (eds.) (1993), *Arianism After Arius: Essays on the Development of the Fourth-Century Trinitarian Conflicts* (Edinburgh).

Barnes, T. D. (1981), *Constantine and Eusebius* (Cambridge, MA).

Barnes, T. D. (1989), 'Christians and pagans in the reign of Constantius', in A. Dihle (ed.), *L'Eglise et l'empire au IVe siècle: sept exposés suivis de discussions* (Geneva), 301–43.

Barnes, T. D. (1993), *Athanasius and Constantius: Theology and Politics in the Constantinian Empire* (Cambridge, MA).

Barnes, T. D. (1995), 'Statistics and the conversion of the Roman aristocracy', *Journal of Roman Studies* 85, 135–47.

Barnes T. D. (2002), 'From toleration to repression: the evolution of Constantine's religious policies', *Scripta Classica Israelica* 21, 189–207.

Barnes T. D. (2011), *Constantine: Dynasty, Religion and Power in the Later Roman Empire* (Chichester).

Barnish, S. J. B. (1992), *The* Variae *of Magnus Aurelius Cassiodorus*, Translated Texts for Historians (Liverpool).

Barrow, J. and Brooks, N. (eds.) (2005), *St. Wulfstan and His World* (Aldershot).

Barry, J. (2019), *Bishops in Flight* (Oakland, CA).

Barth, F. (ed.) (1969), *Ethnic Groups and Boundaries: The Social Organization of Ethnic Difference* (London).

Bartlett, R. (2008), *The Natural and the Supernatural in the Middle Ages: The Wiles Lectures Given at the Queen's University of Belfast, 2006* (New York).

Bassett, S. (ed.) (1989), *The Origins of Anglo-Saxon Kingdoms* (London).

Bassett, S. (1992), 'Church and diocese in the West Midlands: the transition from British to Anglo-Saxon control', in Blair and Sharpe (eds.), 13–40.

Bat-Sheva, A. (2008), 'Christians and Jews', in Noble and Smith (eds.), 157–77.

Becker, A. (1973), *Franks Casket: Zu den Bildern und Inschriften des Runenkastchens von Auzon* (Regensburg).

Bell, H. I. (ed.) (1924), *Greek Papyri in the British Museum*, vol. 6 (London).

Bell, P. (2009), *Three Political Voices from the Age of Justinian: Agapetus, 'Advice to the emperor'; 'Dialogue on political science'; Paul the Silentiary, 'Description of Hagia Sophia'* (Liverpool).

Bentley, M. (1999), *Modern Historiography: An Introduction* (London).

Berenstein, A. (2009), 'Heaven, hell and purgatory', in Rubin and Simons (eds.), 200–216.

Bernard, A. and Bruel, A. (1876–1903), *Recueil des chartes de l'abbaye de Cluny*, 6 vols. (Paris).

Bernard, G. W. (2005), *The King's Reformation: Henry VIII and the Remaking of the English Church* (New Haven, CT).

Berndt, G. M. and Steinacher, R. (eds.) (2014), *Arianism: Roman Heresy and Barbarian Creed* (Farnham).

Bertram, J. (2005), *The Chrodegang Rules: The Rules for the Common Life of the Secular Clergy from the Eighth and Ninth Centuries: Critical Texts with Translations and Commentary* (Aldershot).

Bidez, J. (1930), *La Vie de l'Empereur Julien* (Paris).

Biller, P. (2006), 'Goodbye to Waldensianism?', *Past & Present* 192, 3–33.

Biller, P. (2009), 'Christians and heretics', in Rubin and Simons (eds.), 170–86.

Biller, P. (2016), 'Goodbye to Catharism?', in Sennis (ed.), 274–304.

Birdsall, J. N. (1970), 'The New Testament text', in Ackroyd and Evans (eds.), 308–77.

Birks, P. and McLeod, G. (trans.) (1987), *Justinian's Institutes* (London).

Bischoff, B. (1990), *Latin Palaeography: Antiquity and the Middle Ages*, trans. D. Ó Cróinín and D. Ganz (Cambridge).

Bischoff, B. (1994), *Manuscripts and Libraries in the Age of Charlemagne* (Cambridge).

Bjornlie, M. S. (2019), *The* Variae*: The Complete Translation* (Berkeley, CA).

Blair, J. (1995), 'Anglo-Saxon pagan shrines and their prototypes', *Anglo-Saxon Studies in Archaeology and History* 8, 1–28.

Blair, J. (2005), *The Church in Anglo-Saxon Society* (Oxford).

Blair, J. and Sharpe, R. (eds.) (1992), *Pastoral Care Before the Parish* (Leicester).

Blumenthal, U.-R. (2008), 'The Papacy 1024–1122', in Luscombe and Riley-Smith (eds.), 8–37.

Böhringer, L. (2004), 'Der Kaiser und die Stiftsdamen. Die Gründung des Frauenstifts Vilich in Spannungsfeld von religiösen Leben und adliger West', *Bonner Geschichtsblätter* 53, 57–77.

Bouffartigue, J. (1992), *L'Empereur Julien et la culture de son temps* (Paris).

Bowersock, G. W., Brown, P. R. L. and Grabar, O. (eds.) (1999), *Late Antiquity: A Guide to the Postclassical World* (Cambridge, MA).

Bowes, K. (2008), *Private Worship, Public Values, and Religious Change in Late Antiquity* (Cambridge).

Bowlus, C. (1995), *Franks, Moravians, and Magyars: The Struggle for the Middle Danube, 788–907* (Philadelphia, PA).

Bowman, A. and Woolf, G. (eds.) (1994), *Literacy and Power in the Ancient World* (Cambridge).

Bowman, J. A. (1999), 'Councils, memory and mills: the early development of the Peace of God in Catalonia', *Early Medieval Europe* 8, 99–129.

Boyle, L. E. (1981), *Pastoral Care, Clerical Education and Canon Law, 1200–1400* (London).

Bradbury, S. (1994), 'Constantine and anti-pagan legislation in the fourth century', *Classical Philology* 89, 120–39.

Bradbury, S. (ed.) (1996), *Severus of Minorca: Letter on the Conversion of the Jews* (Oxford).

Braddick, M. J. (2000), *State Formation in Early Modern England, c. 1550–1700* (Cambridge).

Bradley, S. A. J. (1982), *Anglo-Saxon Poetry: An Anthology of Old English Poems in Prose Translation* (London).

Bradshaw, P. (2002), *The Search for the Origins of Christian Worship; Sources and Methods for the Study of Early Liturgy*, 2nd edn (Oxford).

Braegelmann, A. (1942), *The Life and Writings of Saint Ildefonsus of Toledo* (Washington, DC).

Brakke, D. (2006), 'Self-differentiation among Christian groups: the Gnostics and their opponents', in Mitchell and Young (eds.), 245–60.

Braudel, F. (1973), *The Mediterranean and the Mediterranean World in the Age of Philip II* (London).

Braun, R. (1964), *Quodvultdeus: introduction, texte latin, traduction et notes* (Paris).

Bregman, J. (1982), *Synesius of Cyrene, Philosopher-Bishop* (Berkeley, CA).

Brenk, B. (2007), 'Art and propaganda fide: Christian art and architecture, 300–600', in Casiday and Norris (eds.), 691–725.

Brennecke, H. C. (2014), 'Deconstruction of the so-called Germanic Arianism', in Berndt and Steinacher (eds.), 117–30.

Bright, W. (1892), *The Canons of the First Four General Councils of Nicaea, Constantinople, Ephesus and Chalcedon*, 2nd edn (Oxford).

Brooke, R. (1975), *The Coming of the Friars* (London).

Brooks, N. (1984), *The Early History of the Church of Canterbury* (Leicester).

Brown, G. S. (2003), *The Norman Conquest of Southern Italy and Sicily* (London).

Brown, P. R. L. (1967), *Augustine of Hippo: A Biography* (London).

Brown, P. R. L. (1971), *The World of Late Antiquity: From Marcus Aurelius to Muhammad* (London).

Brown, P. R. L. (1971a), 'The rise and function of the holy man in late antiquity', *Journal of Roman Studies* 61, 80–101.

Brown, P. R. L. (1973), 'A Dark Age crisis: aspects of the Iconoclastic Controversy', *English Historical Review* 88, 1–33.

Brown, P. R. L. (1977), *Relics and Social Status in the Age of Gregory of Tours* (Reading).

Brown, P. R. L. (1981), *The Cult of the Saints: Its Rise and Function in Latin Christianity* (London).

Brown, P. R. L. (1992), *Power and Persuasion in Late Antiquity: Towards a Christian Empire* (Madison, WI).

Brown, P. R. L. (1995), *Authority and the Sacred: Aspects of the Christianisation of the Roman World* (Cambridge).

Brown, P. R. L. (1997), '*The World of Late Antiquity* revisited', *Symbolae Osloenses* 72, 5–90.

Brown, P. R. L. (1998), *The Body and Society: Men, Women, and Sexual Renunciation in Early Christianity* (New York).

Brown, P. R. L. (2012), *Through the Eye of a Needle: Wealth, the Fall of Rome, and the Making of Christianity in the West, 350–550 AD* (Princeton, NJ).

Brown, P. R. L. (2013), *The Rise of Western Christendom: Triumph and Diversity, AD 200–1000*, tenth anniversary rev. edn (Oxford).

Brown, P. R. L. (2015), *The Ransom of the Soul: Afterlife and Wealth in Early Western Christianity* (Cambridge, MA).

Browning, R. (1952), 'The riot of A.D. 387 in Antioch: the role of the theatrical claques in the later empire', *Journal of Roman Studies* 42, 15–20.

Brubaker, L. (2012), *Inventing Byzantine Iconoclasm* (Bristol).

Brubaker, L. and Haldon, J. (2001), *Byzantium in the Iconoclast Era (c. 680–850): The Sources: An Annotated Survey* (Aldershot).

Brundage, J. A. (1969), *Medieval Canon Law and the Crusade* (Madison, WI).

Brundage, J. A. (1987), *Law, Sex and Christian Society in Medieval Europe* (Chicago).

Brundage, J. A. (1995), *Medieval Canon Law* (London).

Bull, M. (1993), *Knightly Piety and the Lay Response to the First Crusade: The Limousin and Gascony, c. 970–c. 1130* (Oxford).

Bull, M. (2009), 'Crusade and conquest', in Rubin and Simons (eds.), 340–52.

Bulliet, R. (1979), *Conversion to Islam in the Medieval Period: An Essay in Quantitative History* (Cambridge, MA).

Bulliet, R. W. (1990), 'Introduction', in Gervers and Bihkazi (eds.), 3–12.

Bulliet, R. W. (1990a), 'Conversion stories in early Islam', in Gervers and Bihkazi (eds.), 123–35.

Bullough, D. (2003), *Alcuin: Achievement and Reputation* (Leiden).

Bullough, D. (2005), 'Charlemagne's "men of God": Alcuin, Hildebald, Arn', in Story (ed.), 136–50.

Burckhardt, J. (1949), *The Age of Constantine the Great*, trans. M. Hadas (New York).

Burgess, C. and Duffy, E. (eds.) (2006), *The Parish in Late Medieval England: Proceedings of the 2002 Harlaxton Symposium* (Donington).

Burgess, R. W. (1993), *The Chronicle of Hydatius and the* Consularia Constantinopolitana*: Two Contemporary Accounts of the Final Years of the Roman Empire* (Oxford).

Burgess, R. W. (2008), 'THE SUMMER OF BLOOD: The "Great Massacre" of 337 and the promotion of the sons of Constantine', *Dumbarton Oaks Papers*, 5–51.

Burr, D. (2003), *The Spiritual Franciscans: From Protest to Persecution* (University Park, PA).

Burrus, V. (1995), *The Making of a Heretic: Gender, Authority, and the Priscillianist Controversy* (Berkeley, CA).

Byock, J. L. (trans.) (2005), *Snorri Sturluson: The Prose Edda* (London).

Byrne, F. J. (1973), *Irish Kings and High-Kings* (London).

Cabaniss, A. (1979), *The Emperor's Monk: Contemporary Life of Benedict of Aniane* (Ilfracombe).

Cameron, A. (2011), *The Last Pagans of Rome* (Oxford).

Cameron, A. M. (2006), 'Constantine and the "peace of the church"', in Mitchell and Young (eds.), 38–51.

Cameron, A. M. and Hall, S. G. (1999), *Eusebius: Life of Constantine* (Oxford).

Cameron, A. M. *et al.* (eds.) (2000), *The Cambridge Ancient History vol. 14: Late Antiquity: Empire and Successors,* AD *425–600*, 2nd edn (Cambridge).

Cameron, E. (2000), *Waldenses: Rejections of Holy Church in Medieval Europe* (Oxford).

Campbell, J. (1975), 'Observations on English government from the tenth to the twelfth centuries', *Transactions of the Royal Historical Society* 25, 39–54, reprinted in Campbell (1986), 171–90.

Campbell, J. (ed.) (1982), *The Anglo-Saxons* (London).

Campbell, J. (1986), *Essays in Anglo-Saxon History* (London).

Campbell, J. (1986a), 'The first century of Christianity in England', in Campbell, 49–68.

Campbell, J. (1986b), 'Observations on the conversion of England', in Campbell, 69–84.

Carver, M. (ed.) (2003), *The Cross Goes North: Processes of Conversion in Northern Europe, AD 300–1300* (York).

Carver, M. *et al.* (eds.) (2011), *Signals of Belief in Early England: Anglo-Saxon Paganism Revisited* (Oxford).

Casiday, A. (2007), 'Sin and salvation: experiences and reflections', in Casiday and Norris (eds.), 501–30.

Casiday, A. and Norris, F. W. (eds.) (2007), *The Cambridge History of Christianity vol. 2: Constantine to c. 600* (Cambridge).

Castelli, E. (2004), *Martyrdom and Memory: Early Christian Culture Making* (New York).

Catto, J. L. (ed.) (1984), *The History of the University of Oxford vol. 1: The Early Oxford Schools* (Oxford).

Cazel, F. A. (1989), 'Financing the Crusades', in K. M. Setton (gen. ed.), *A History of the Crusades*, 6 vols. (London, 1969–89), vol. 6, 116–49.

Chadwick, H. (1981), *Boethius: The Consolations of Music, Logic, Theology and Philosophy* (Oxford).

Chadwick, H. (1991), *St. Augustine: Confessions*, trans. with an introduction and notes (Oxford).

Chadwick Hawkes, S. (1981), 'Recent finds of inlaid iron buckles and belt-plates from seventh-century Kent', *Anglo-Saxon Studies in Archaeology and History* 2, 49–90.

Charles-Edwards, T. M. (2000), *Early Christian Ireland* (Cambridge).

Charles-Edwards, T. M. (2008), 'Beyond empire II: Christianities of the Celtic peoples', in Noble and Smith (eds.), 86–106.

Chazelle, C. and Cubitt, C. (eds.) (2007), *The Crisis of the Oikoumene: The Three Chapters and the Failed Quest for Unity in the Sixth-Century Mediterranean* (Turnhout).

Chiaradonna, R. (2009), *Plotino* (Rome).

Christiansen, E. (1980), *The Northern Crusades: The Baltic and the Catholic Frontier, 1100–1525* (London).

Christys, A. (2002), *Christians in Al-Andalus (711–1000)* (Abingdon).

Church, S. D. (2008), 'Paganism in conversion-age Anglo-Saxon England: the evidence of Bede's Ecclesiastical History reconsidered', *Journal of the Historical Association* 93, 162–80.

Clanchy, M. (1997), *Abelard: A Medieval Life* (Oxford).

Clarence Smith, J. A. (1975), *Medieval Law Teachers and Writers, Civilian and Canonist* (Ottawa).

Clark, J. C. D. (1989), 'England's ancien regime as a Confessional State', *Albion* 21, 450–74.

Clarke, H. B. and Brennan, M. (eds.) (1981), *Columbanus and Merovingian Monasticism* (Oxford).

Claussen, M. (2004), *The Reform of the Frankish Church: Chrodegang of Metz and the* Regula Canonicorum *in the Eighth Century* (Cambridge).

Cohen, J. (1999), *Living Letters of the Law: Ideas of the Jew in Medieval Christianity* (Berkeley, CA).

Colbert, E. P. (1962), *The Martyrs of Cordoba (850–859): A Study of the Sources* (Washington, DC).

Colgrave, B. (1927), *Eddius Stephanus: The Life of Bishop Wilfrid* (Cambridge).

Colgrave, B. (1956), *Felix's Life of Saint Guthlac* (Cambridge).

Colgrave, B. (1985), *Two Lives of Saint Cuthbert* (Cambridge).

Colgrave, B. and Mynors, R. A. B. (1991), *Bede's Ecclesiastical History of the English People* (Oxford).

Collins, R. (1983), *Early Medieval Spain: Unity in Diversity, 400–1000* (Basingstoke).

Collins, R. (1990), 'Pippin I and the kingdom of Aquitaine', in Godman and Collins (eds.), 363–90.

Collins, R. (1992), 'King Leovigild and the conversion of the Visigoths', in *idem*, *Law, Culture and Regionalism in Early Medieval Spain* (Aldershot), 1–12.

Collins, R. (1994), *The Arab Conquest of Spain, 710–797* (Oxford).

Collins, R. (2005), 'Charlemagne's imperial coronation and the Annals of Lorsch', in Story (ed.), 52–70.

Collins, R. (2012), *Caliphs and Kings: Spain 796–1031* (Chichester).

Conant, J. (2012), *Staying Roman: Conquest and Identity in Africa and the Mediterranean, 439–700* (Cambridge).

Connolly, R. H. (1929), Didascalia Apostolorum*: The Syriac Version Translated and Accompanied by the Verona Latin Fragments* (Oxford).

Connolly, S. (2010), *Lives Behind the Laws: The World of the* Codex Hermogenianus (Bloomington, IN).

Cook, S. A. *et al.* (eds.) (1939), *The Cambridge Ancient History vol. 12: The Imperial Crisis A.D. 193–324*, 1st edn (Cambridge).

Coon, L. L. (2008), 'Gender and the body', in Noble and Smith (eds.), 433–52.

Coope, J. (1995), *The Martyrs of Cordoba: Community and Family Conflict in an Age of Mass Conversion* (Lincoln, NE).

Cooper, K. (2013), *Band of Angels: The Forgotten World of Early Christian Women* (New York).

Corcoran. S. (1996), *The Empire of the Tetrarchs* (Oxford).

Costambeys, M. *et al.* (2011), *The Carolingian World* (Cambridge).

Courtois, C. (1954), *Victor de Vita et son œuvre: étude critique* (Algeria).

Courtois, C. (1955), *Les Vandales et l'Afrique* (Paris).

Courtois, C. and Albertini, E. (eds.) (1952), *Tablettes Albertini: actes privés de l'époque vandale, fin du Ve siècle* (Paris).

Cowdrey, H. E. J. (1968), 'The Papacy, the Patarenes and the Church of Milan', *Transactions of the Royal Historical Society* 18, 25–48, reprinted as no. V in Cowdrey (1984).

Cowdrey, H. E. J. (1970), *The Cluniacs and the Gregorian Reform* (Oxford).

Cowdrey, H. E. J. (1982), 'Pope Gregory VII's "crusading" plans of 1074', in B. Z. Kedar *et al.* (eds.), *Outremer: Studies in the History of the Crusading Kingdom of Jerusalem Presented to Joshua Prawer* (Jerusalem), 27–44, reprinted as no. X in Cowdrey (1984).

Cowdrey, H. E. J. (1984), *Popes, Monks and Crusaders* (London).

Cowdrey, H. E. J. (2002), *The Register of Pope Gregory VII 1073–1085: An English Translation* (Oxford).

Cowdrey, H. E. J. (2003), *Lanfranc: Scholar, Monk and Archbishop* (Oxford).

Cowdrey, H. E. J. (2004), 'The structure of the Church 1024–73', in Luscombe and Riley-Smith (eds.) (2004), 229–67.

Cramer, P. (1993), *Baptism and Change in the Early Middle Ages, c. 200–c. 1150* (Cambridge).

Crick, J. (2012), 'The art of writing: scripts and scribal production', in C. Lees (ed.), *Early Medieval English Literature* (Cambridge), 50–72.

Crick, J. (2013), 'English vernacular script', in Gameson (ed.), 174–86.

Croke, B. and Harries, J. (1982), *Religious Conflict in Fourth-Century Rome: A Documentary Study* (Sydney).

Crone, P. (1987), *Meccan Trade and the Rise of Islam* (Oxford).

Crone, P. and Cook, M. (1977), *Hagarism: The Making of the Islamic World* (Cambridge).

Cross, J. E. and Hamer, A. (1999), *Wulfstan's Canon Law Collection* (Cambridge).

Cross, S. H. and Sherbowitz-Wetzor, O. P. (eds.) (1953), *The Russian Primary Chronicle: Laurentian Text* (Cambridge, MA).

Cubitt, C. (1989), 'Wilfrid's "usurping bishops": episcopal elections in Anglo-Saxon England, c. 600–800', *Northern History* 25, 18–38.

Cubitt, C. (1992), 'Pastoral care and conciliar canons: the policies of the 747 council of Clofesho', in Blair and Sharpe (eds.), 193–211.

Cubitt C. (1995), *Anglo-Saxon Church Councils c. 650–850* (London).

Cubitt, C. (1997), 'The tenth-century Benedictine reform in England', *Early Medieval Europe* 6, 77–94.

Cureton, W. (2016), *Eusebius of Caesarea History of the Martyrs in Palestine* (trans.), reprint edn (Piscataway, NJ).

Curran, J. (2000), *Pagan City and Christian Capital: Rome in the Fourth Century* (Oxford).

Daniélou, J. and Marrou, H. I. (1963), *Nouvelle histoire du christianisme*, vol. 1 (Paris).

Davis, R. (1992), *The Lives of the Eighth-Century Popes (*Liber Pontificalis*)*, Translated Texts for Historians (Liverpool).

Davis, R. (1995), *The Lives of the Ninth-Century Popes (*Liber Pontificalis*)*, Translated Texts for Historians (Liverpool).

Davis, R. (2000), *The Book of Pontiffs (*Liber Pontificalis*): The Ancient Biographies of the First Ninety Roman Bishops to AD 715*, Translated Texts for Historians, 2nd edn (Liverpool).

d'Avray, D. L. (1985), *The Preaching of the Friars: Sermons Diffused from Paris before 1300* (Oxford).

d'Avray, D. L. (2001), *Medieval Marriage Sermons: Mass Communication in a Culture without Print* (Oxford).

d'Avray, D. L. (2016), 'The Cathars from non-Catholic sources', in Sennis (ed.), 177–84.

d'Avray, D. L. (2019), *Papal Jurisprudence c. 400: Sources of the Canon Law Tradition* (Cambridge).

Dawson, C. (1932), *The Making of Europe: An Introduction to the History of European Unity* (London).

Dawson, J. D. (2002), *Christian Figural Reading and the Fashioning of Identity* (Berkeley, CA).

de Blois, L. *et al.* (2006), *The Impact of Imperial Rome on Religions, Ritual and Religious Life in the Roman Empire.* Proceedings of the Fifth Workshop of the International Network Impact of Empire (Roman Empire, 200 B.C.–A.D. 476), Münster, 30 June–4 July 2004 (Leiden).

de Jong, M. (2005), 'Charlemagne's Church', in Story (ed.), 103–35.

de Jong, M. (2009), *The Penitential State: Authority and Atonement in the Age of Louis the Pious, 814–840* (Cambridge).

de Labriolle, P. (1913), *Les sources de l'histoire du montanisme: textes grecs, latins, syriaques, pub. avec une introduction critique, une traduction française, des notes et des 'indices'* (Fribourg).

Delmaire, R. (1989), *Largesses sacrées et res privata: L'aerarium impérial et son administation du IVe au VIe siècle* (Rome).

Delmaire, R. (1995), *Les institutions du Bas-Empire romain de Constantin à Justinien vol. 1: Les institutions civiles palatines* (Paris).

Demm, E. (1970), *Reformmönchtum und Slawenmission im 12. Jahrhundert. Wertsoziolog.-geistesgeschichtl. Untersuchungen zu d. Viten Bischof Ottos von Bamberg* (Lübeck and Hamburg).

Dennett, D. C. (1950), *Conversion and the Poll Tax in Early Islam* (Cambridge, MA).

Depreux, P. *et al.* (eds.) (2010), *Raban Maur et son temps* (Turnhout).

Déroche, F. (2014), *Qur'ans of the Umayyads: A First Overview* (Leiden).

Dewing, H. B. (1914–40), *The Works of Procopius* (London).

Dignas, B. and Winter, E. (2007), *Rome and Persia in Late Antiquity: Neighbours and Rivals* (Cambridge).

Dijkstra J. H. F. (2008), *Philae and the End of Ancient Egyptian Religion: A Regional Study of Religious Transformation (298–642 CE)* (Leiden).

Dillon, J. M. (1977), *The Middle Platonists: A Study of Platonism, 80 BC–AD 270* (London).

Dillon, J. N. (2012), *The Justice of Constantine: Law, Communication and Control* (Ann Arbor, MI).

Dindorf, L. A. (1832), *Chronicon Paschale*, 2 vols. (Bonn).

Dodgeon, M. H. and Lieu, S. N. C. (1991), *The Roman Eastern Frontier and the Persian Wars (AD 226–363): A Documentary History* (London).

Donald, M. (1992), *The Norman Kingdom of Sicily* (Cambridge).

Donner, F. M. (1981), *The Early Islamic Conquests* (Princeton, NJ).

Donner, F. M. (2005), 'The background to Islam', in Maas (ed.), 510–34.

Dossey, L. (2010), *Peasant and Empire in Christian North Africa* (Berkeley, CA).

Douglas, D. C. and Greenaway, G. W. (1952), *English Historical Documents, 1042–1189* (London).

Doyle, M. (2016), *Peter Lombard and His Students* (Toronto).

Drake, C. S. (2001), *The Romanesque Fonts of Northern Europe and Scandinavia* (Woodbridge).

Drake, H. (2000), *Constantine and the Bishops: The Politics of Intolerance* (Baltimore, MD).

Drake, H. (2006), 'The impact of Constantine on Christianity', in Lenski (ed.), 111–36.

Drake, H. (2007), 'The church, society and political power', in Casiday and Norris (eds.), 403–28.

Drijvers, J. W. (2004), *Cyril of Jerusalem: Bishop and City* (Leiden).

Drinkwater, J. F. (2007), *The Alamanni and Rome 213–496* (Oxford).

Duchesne, L. (ed.) (1876–82), *Le* Liber Pontificalis*: Texte, introduction et commentaire*, 2 vols. (Paris).

Duffy, E. (1992), *The Stripping of the Altars: Traditional Religion in England 1400–1580* (New Haven, CT).

Duffy, E. (2006), *Saints and Sinners: A History of the Popes*, 3rd edn (London).

Duggan, A. (2004), *Thomas Becket* (London).

Duggan, A. (2012), 'Master of the decretals: a reassessment of Alexander III's contribution to canon law', in Clarke, P. and Duggan, A. (eds.), *Pope Alexander III (1159–81)* (London), 352–404.

Duggan, C. (1995), 'Papal judges delegate and the making of the "new law" in the twelfth century', in C. Duggan and T. Bisson (eds.), *Cultures of Power: Lordship, Status, and Process in Twelfth-Century Europe* (Philadelphia, PA), 172–200.

Dulinicz, M. (1994), 'The problem of dating of the strongholds of the Tornow type and Tornow-Klenica group', *Archeologica Polski* 39, 31–49 (English summary).

Dulinicz, M. (1997), 'The first dendrochronological dating of the strongholds in northern Mazovia', in Urbanczyk (ed.), 137–42.

Dunbabin, J. (1984), 'Careers and vocations', in Catto (ed.), 565–606.

Dunn, J. D. G. (1991), *The Parting of the Ways between Christianity and Judaism and their Significance for the Character of Christianity* (London).

Dunn, M. (2009), *The Christianisation of the Anglo-Saxons c. 597–c. 700* (London).

Dunn, M. (2013), *Belief and Religion in Barbarian Europe c. 350–700* (London).

Dutton, P. (1998), *Charlemagne's Courtier: The Complete Einhard* (Peterborough, Ontario).

Dutton, P. (2004), *Carolingian Civilization: A Reader* (Peterborough, Ontario).

Dvornik, F. (1949), *The Making of Central and Eastern Europe* (London).

Dvornik, F. (1966), *Early Christian and Byzantine Political Philosophy: Origins and Background*, The Dumbarton Oaks Center for Byzantine Studies (Washington, DC).

Dvornik, F. (1969), Les légendes de Constantin et de méthode vues de Byzance, 2nd edn (Hattiesburg, MS*).*

Dvornik, F. (1970), *Byzantine Missions among the Slavs: Saints Constantine-Cyril and Methodius* (New Brunswick, NJ).

Edwards, M. (ed. and trans.) (1997), *Optatus: Against the Donatists* (Liverpool).

Edwards, M. (2006), 'The first council of Nicaea', in Mitchell and Young (eds.), 552–67.

Edwards, M. (2006a), 'The beginnings of Christianization', in Lenski (ed.), 137–58.

Edwards, M. (2007), 'Synods and councils', in Casiday and Norris (eds.), 367–85.

Eggers, M. (1995), *Das 'Grossmährische Reich': Realität oder Fiktion?: eine Neuinterpretation der Quellen zur Geschichte des mittleren Donauraumes im 9. Jahrhundert* (Stuttgart).

Elliott, J. K. (2013), 'The "apocryphal" New Testament', in Paget and Schaper (eds.), 455–78.

Elliott, T. G. (1987), 'Constantine's conversion: do we really need it?', *Phoenix* 41, 420–38.

Elliott, T. G. (1996), *The Christianity of Constantine the Great* (New York).

Elm, S. (1994), *Virgins of God: The Making of Asceticism in Late Antiquity* (Oxford).

Elm, S. (2012), *Sons of Hellenism, Fathers of the Church: Emperor Julian, Gregory of Nazianzus, and the Vision of Rome* (Berkeley, CA).

Elsner, J. (1998), *Imperial Rome and Christian Triumph: The Art of the Roman Empire A.D. 100–450* (Oxford).

Elsner, J. (2006), 'Perspectives in art', in Lenski (ed.), 255–77.

Emmel, S. (2008), 'Shenoute of Atripe and the Christian destruction of temples in Egypt: rhetoric and reality', in Hahn and Emmel (eds.), 161–202.

Ennabli, E. A. (1992), *Pour Sauver Carthage: Exploration et conservation de la cité punique, romaine et Byzantine* (Tunis).

Ennsslin, W. (1939), 'The end of the principate', in Cook *et al.* (eds.), 353–82.

Ennsslin, W. (1939a), 'The reforms of Diocletian', in Cook *et al.* (eds.), 383–407.

Erdmann, C. (1977), *The Origin of the Idea of the Crusade*, trans. M. Baldwin (Princeton, NJ).

Evans, C. F. (1970), 'The New Testament in the making', in Ackroyd and Evans (eds.), 232–84.

Fanning, S. (1981), 'Lombard Arianism reconsidered', *Speculum* 56, 241–58.

Favrod, J. (1997), *Histoire politique du Royaume Burgonde (443–534)* (Lausanne).

Fear, A. (trans.) (2010), *Orosius: Seven Books of History Against the Pagans*, Translated Texts for Historians (Liverpool).

Fear, A. and Wood, J. (eds.) (2020), *A Companion to Isidore of Seville* (Leiden).

Feuchter, J. (2016), 'The *heretici* of Languedoc: local holy men and women or organized religious group? New evidence from inquisitorial, notarial and historiographical sources', in Sennis (ed.), 112–30.

Firey, A. (ed.) (2008), *A New History of Penance* (Leiden).

Flechner, R. (2017), 'Investigating "peasant conversion" in Ireland and Anglo-Saxon England', in Flechner *et al.* (eds.), 427–54.

Flechner, R. and Ní Mhaonaigh, M. (eds.) (2016), *The Introduction of Christianity into the Early Medieval Insular World: Converting the Isles I* (Turnhout).

Flechner, R. *et al.* (eds.) (2017), *Transforming Landscapes of Belief in the Early Medieval Insular World and Beyond: Converting the Isles II* (Turnhout).

Fletcher, R. A. (1984), *Saint James's Catapult: The Life and Times of Diego Gelmirez of Santiago de Compostela* (Oxford).

Fletcher, R. A. (1987), 'Reconquest and crusade in Spain, c.1050–1150', *Transactions of the Royal Historical Society* 37, 31–47.

Fletcher, R. A. (1989), *The Quest for El Cid* (London).

Fletcher, R. A. (1998), *The Barbarian Conversion: From Paganism to Christianity 371–1386* (London).

Flint, V. I. (1991), *The Rise of Magic in Early Medieval Europe* (Oxford).

Flori, J. (1999), *Pierre l'ermite et la première croisade* (Paris).

Flower, R. (2012), 'Visions of Constantine', *Journal of Roman Studies* 102, 287–305.

Flower, R. (2016), *Imperial Invectives against Constantius II: Athanasius of Alexandria, History of the Arians, Hilary of Poitiers, Against Constantius and Lucifer of Cagliari, the Necessity of Dying for the Son of God* (Liverpool).

Fluck, C. *et al.* (eds.) (2015), *Egypt: Faith After the Pharaohs* (London).

Fontaine, J. (1983), *Isidore de Séville et la culture classique dans l'Espagne wisigothique*, 2nd edn (Paris).

Forrest, I. (2013), 'The transformation of visitation in medieval England', *Past & Present* 221, 3–38.

Forrest, I. (2016), 'The thirteenth-century visitation records of the diocese of Hereford', *English Historical Review* 131, 737–62.

Forrest, I. (2018), *Trustworthy Men: How Inequality and Faith Made the Medieval Church* (Princeton, NJ).

Foss, C. (1977), 'Archaeology and the Twenty Cities of Byzantine Asia', *American Journal of Archaeology* 81, 469–86.

Foss, C. (1996), *Cities, Fortresses and Villages of Byzantine Asia Minor* (Aldershot).

Fouracre, P. (2000), *The Age of Charles Martel* (Harlow).

Fowden, G. (1978), 'Bishops and temples in the Eastern Roman Empire', *Journal of Theological Studies* n.s. 29, 53–78.

Fowden, G. (1982), 'The pagan holy man in late antique society', *Journal of Hellenic Studies* 102, 355–9.

Fowler, R. C. (2018), 'Early Christianity and late antique Platonism – Origen to Evagrius', in H. Tarrant *et al.* (eds.), *Brill's Companion to the Reception of Plato in Antiquity* (Leiden), 274–97.

Fox, Y. (2014), *Power and Religion in Merovingian Gaul: Columbanian Monasticism and the Frankish Elites* (Cambridge).

Frankfurter, D. (1998), *Religion in Roman Egypt: Assimilation and Resistance* (Princeton, NJ).

Frankfurter, D. (2007), 'Christianity and paganism, I: Egypt', in Casiday and Norris (eds.), 173–88.

Fredriksen, P. (2008), *Augustine and the Jews: A Christian Defense of Jews and Judaism* (New York).

Frend, W. H. C. (1972), *The Rise of the Monophysite Movement: Chapters in the History of the Church in the Fifth and Sixth Centuries* (Cambridge).

Frend, W. H. C. (2006), 'Persecution: genesis and legacy', in Mitchell and Young (eds.), 503–23.

Fried, J. (2007), *Donation of Constantine and* Constitutum Constantini (Berlin).

Friedrichsen, G. W. S. (1926), *The Gothic Version of the Gospels: A Study of Its Style and Textual History* (Oxford).

Friedrichsen, G. W. S. (1939), *The Gothic Version of the Epistles: A Study of Its Style and Textual History* (Oxford).

Fudge, T. (2002), *The Crusade Against Heretics in Bohemia, 1418–1437: Sources and Documents for the Hussite Crusades* (Aldershot).

Fuhrmann, H. (1973), 'Das Reformpapastum und die Rechtswissenschaft', *Vortrage und Forschungen* 17, 175–203.

Fulton, R. (2009), 'Mary', in Rubin and Simons (eds.), 283–96.

Gamble, H. Y. (2006), 'Marcion and the canon', in Mitchell and Young (eds.), 195–213.

Gameson, R. (ed.) (2013), *The Cambridge History of the Book in Britain, vol. 1, c. 400–1100* (Cambridge).

Ganz, D. (1989), 'The preconditions for Caroline minuscule', *Viator* 19, 23–44.

Ganz, D. (2009), 'Review article: when is a library not a library?', *Early Medieval Europe* 17, 444–53.

Garcia Moreno, L. A. (1989), *Historia de España Visigoda* (Madrid).

Garcia Moreno, L. A. (2006), 'Iglesia y el Cristianismo en la Galecia de época sueva', *Antigüedad y Cristianismo* 23, 39–55.

Garrison, M. (1994), 'The emergence of Carolingian Latin literature and the court of Charlemagne', in McKitterick (ed.), 111–40.

Gasparri, S. (2012), *Italia Longobarda: Il regno, i Franchi, il papato* (Rome).

Gatch, M. McC. (1977), *Preaching and Theology in Anglo-Saxon England: Aelfric and Wulfstan* (Toronto).

Geake, H. (1997), *The Use of Grave-Goods in Conversion-Period England, c. 600–850*, BAR 261 (Oxford).

Gemeinhardt, P. and Leemans, J. (eds.) (2012), *Christian Martyrdom in Late Antiquity: History and Discourse, Tradition and Religious Identity* (Berlin and New York).

George, J. (1995), *Venantius Fortunatus: Personal and Political Poems*, Translated Texts for Historians (Liverpool).

George, J. (1997), *Venantius Fortunatus: A Poet in Merovingian Gaul* (Oxford).

Gerberding, R. (1987), *The Rise of the Carolingians and the* Liber Historiae Francorum (Oxford).

Gervers, M. and Bihkazi, R. J. (eds.) (1990), *Conversion and Continuity: Indigenous Christian Communities in Islamic Lands, Eighth to Eighteenth Centuries* (Toronto).

Geuenich, D. (2004), 'A survey of the early medieval confraternity books from the Continent', in D. Rollason *et al.* (eds.), *The Durham* Liber Vitae *and Its Context* (Woodbridge), 141–8.

Gibson, M. D. (trans.) (1903), *The* Didascalia apostolorum *in English* (London).

Gibson, M. T. (1981), *Boethius: His Life, Thought and Influence* (Oxford).

Gibson, W. (1995), *The Achievement of the Anglican Church, 1689–1800: The Confessional State in Eighteenth-Century England* (New York).

Giesebrecht, W. von (1875), *Geschichte der Deutschen Kaiserzeit*, vol. 2, 4th edn (Leipzig).

Gilchrist, J. (1973), *Diuersorum patrum sententie siue Collectio in LXXIV titulos digesta* (Vatican City).

Gilchrist, J. (1980), *The Collection in Seventy-Four Titles: A Canon Law Manual of the Gregorian Reform* (Toronto).

Gill, J. (1979), *Church Union: Rome and Byzantium, 1204–1453* (London).

Gillet, A. (ed.) (2002), *On Barbarian Identity: Critical Approaches to Ethnicity in the Early Middle Ages* (Turnhout).

Girardet, K. M. (2007), *Die Konstantinische Wende: Voraussetzungen und Geistige Grundlagen der Religionspolitik Konstantins des Grossen*, 2nd edn (Berlin).

Girardet, K. M. (2010), *Der Kaiser und sein Gott: Das Christentum im Denken und in der Religionspolitik Konstantins des Grossen* (Berlin).

Girardet, K. M. (2012), 'Das Jahr 311: Galerius, Konstantin und das Christentum', in G. Bonamente *et al.* (eds.), *Constantine Before and After Constantine* (Bari), 113–32.

Giraud, E. and Leitmeir, C. T. (eds.) (2021), *The Medieval Dominicans: Books, Buildings, Music, and Liturgy* (Turnhout).

Given, J. (1989), 'The inquisitors of Languedoc and the medieval technology of power', *American Historical Review* 94 (2), 336–59.

Given, J. (1997), *Inquisition and Medieval Society: Power, Discipline, and Resistance in Languedoc* (Ithaca, NY).

Given, J. (2017), 'Les inquisiteurs du Languedoc médiéval: les éléments sociétaux favorables et contraignants', in G. Audisio (ed.), *Inquisition et Pouvoir* (Aix-en-Provence).

Gleason, M. (1986), 'Festive satire: Julian's *Misopogon* and the New Year at Antioch', *Journal of Roman Studies* 76, 106–19.

Glover, T. R. *et al.* (trans.) (1931), *Tertullian: Apology;* De Spectaculis (London).

Gluckman, M. (1965), *Politics, Law and Ritual in Tribal Society* (Oxford).

Godja, M. (1988), *The Development of the Settlement Pattern in the Basin of the Lower Vltava (Central Bohemia) 200–1200*, BAR IS 447 (Oxford).

Godja, M. (1991), *The Ancient Slavs: Settlement and Society* (Edinburgh).

Godman, P. (1982), *Alcuin: The Bishops, Kings, and Saints of York* (Oxford).

Godman, P. (1985), *Poetry of the Carolingian Renaissance* (London).

Godman, P. (1987), *Poets and Emperors: Frankish Politics and Carolingian Poetry* (Oxford).

Godman, P. and Collins, R. (eds.) (1990), *Charlemagne's Heir: New Perspectives on the Reign of Louis the Pious* (Oxford).

Goering, J. (1992), *William de Montibus (c. 1140–1213): The Schools and the Literature of Pastoral Care* (Toronto).

Goffart, W. (1980), *Barbarians and Romans* AD *418–584: The Techniques of Accommodation* (Princeton, NJ).

Goffart, W. (1981), 'Rome, Constantinople, and the Barbarians in late antiquity', *American Historical Review* 76, 275–306.

Goffart, W. (1986), *The Narrators of Barbarian History (*AD *550–800): Jordanes, Gregory of Tours, Bede, and Paul the Deacon* (Philadelphia, PA).

Goffart, W. (2006), *Barbarian Tides: The Migration Age and the Later Roman Empire* (Philadelphia, PA).

Goldberg, E. J. (2006), *Struggle for Empire: Kingship and Conflict under Louis the German 817–876* (Ithaca, NY).

Gonzalez, J. (1986), 'The *Lex Irnitana*: a new copy of the Flavian municipal law', *Journal of Roman Studies* 76, 147–243.

Goodman, M. (ed.) (1998), *Jews in a Graeco-Roman World* (Oxford).

Goodson, C. and Nelson, J. (2010), 'The Roman contexts of the Donation of Constantine', *Early Medieval Europe* 18, 446–67.

Goody, J. (1986), *The Logic of Writing and the Organization of Society* (Cambridge).

Goody, J. (2000), *The Power of the Written Tradition* (Washington, DC).

Gorecki, P. (1993), *Parishes, Tithes and Society in Earlier Medieval Poland c. 1100–1250*, Transactions for the American Philosophical Society 83 (Philadelphia, PA).

Gowers, B. (2007), 'Fulbert of Chartres and his Circle: Scholarship and Society in Eleventh-Century France', unpublished D.Phil. thesis, University of Oxford.

Grabowsky, A. (ed.) (2021), *Der Streit um Formosus: Traktate des Auxilius und weitere Schriften* (Wiesbaden).

Grant, R. M. (1970), 'The biblical canon', in Ackroyd and Evans (eds.), 284–308.

Graumann, T. (2013), 'The Bible in doctrinal development and Christian councils', in Paget and Schaper (eds.), 798–821.

Gray, P. (1979), *The Defence of Chalcedon in the East* (Leiden).

Gray, P. (2005), 'The legacy of Chalcedon: Christological problems and their significance', in Maas (ed.), 215–38.

Greatrex, G. (1998), *Rome and Persia at War, 502–532* (Leeds).

Greatrex, G. and Lieu, S. (2002), *The Roman Eastern Frontier and the Persian Wars: A Narrative Sourcebook* (London).

Green, R. P. H. (1991), *The Works of Ausonius* (Oxford).

Greer, R. A. (2007), 'Pastoral care and discipline', in Casiday and Norris (eds.), 501–30.

Griffith, P. (2018), 'Canon Law in Post-Roman Gaul', unpublished D.Phil. thesis, King's College London.

Griffith, S. (2008), *The Church in the Shadow of the Mosque: Christians and Muslims in the World of Islam* (Princeton, NJ).

Griffiths, B. (1991), *The Battle of Maldon: Text and Translation* (Pinner).

Griffiths, F. J. (2008), 'The Cross and the *Cura monialium*: Robert of Arbrissel, John the Evangelist, and the pastoral care of women in the age of reform', *Speculum* 83, 303–30.

Grønlie, S. (trans.) (2006), *Íslendingabók, Kristni Saga: The Book of the Icelanders, The Story of the Conversion* (London).

Gryson, R. (1980), *Litterature Arienne Latine* (Louvain).

Gundlach, W. (ed.) (1902), *Epistolae aevi merowingici collectae*, MGH Epp. III, *Epistolae merowingici et karolini aevi* (Hanover).

Gunn, S. (2006), *History and Cultural Theory* (Harlow).

Gwatkin, H. M. and Whitney, J. P. (eds.) (1911), *The Cambridge Medieval History*, vol. 1, 1st edn (Cambridge).

Gwynn, D. (2007), *The Eusebians: The Polemic of Athanasius and the Construction of the Arian Controversy* (Oxford).

Gwynn, D. (2008), 'Idle mouths and solar haloes: A. H. M. Jones and the conversion of Europe', in *idem* (ed.), *A. H. M. Jones and the Later Roman Empire* (Leiden), 213–30.

Hackett, M. B. (1984), 'The university as a corporate body', in Catto (ed.), 37–96.

Hadad, W. Z. (1990), 'Continuity and change in religious adherence: 9th-century Baghdad', in Gervers and Bihkazi (eds.), 33–53.

Hadot, P. (1971), *Marius Victorinus: recherches sur sa vie et ses oeuvres* (Paris).

Haeling, R. von (1978), *Die Religionszugehörigkeit der hohen Amsträger des Römischen Reiches seit Constantins I. Alleinherrschaft bis zum Ende der Theodosianischen Dynastie* (Bonn).

Hahn, J. and Emmel, S. (eds.) (2008), *From Temple to Church Destruction and Renewal of Local Cultic Topography in Late Antiquity* (Leiden and Boston, MA).

Haldon, J. F. (1997), *Byzantium in the Seventh Century: The Transformation of a Culture,* 2nd rev. edn (Cambridge).

Hall, S. G. (2006), 'Institutions in the pre-Constantinian *ecclesia*', in Mitchell and Young (eds.), 415–33.

Hall, S. G. (2006a), 'Ecclesiology forged in the wake of persecution', in Mitchell and Young (eds.), 470–84.

Hallam, E. (1980), *Capetian France, 987–1328* (London).

Halporn, J. and Vessey, M. (2004), *Cassiodorus: Institutions of Divine and Secular Learning; On the Soul*, Translated Texts for Historians (Liverpool).

Halsall, G. (2007), *Barbarian Migrations and the Roman West 376–568* (Cambridge).

Hamilton, B. (1974), *The Albigensian Crusade* (London).

Hamilton, B. (1981), *The Medieval Inquisition* (London).

Hamilton, B. (2016), 'Cathar links with the Balkans and Byzantium', in Sennis (ed.), 131–50.

Hamilton, S. (2001), *The Practice of Penance, 900–1050* (Woodbridge).

Hamilton, S. (2013), *Church and People in the Medieval West* (Harlow).

Hanson, R. P. C. (1970), 'Biblical exegesis in the early Church', in Ackroyd and Evans (eds.), 412–53.

Hanson, R. P. C. (1988), *The Search for the Christian Doctrine of God* (Edinburgh).

Harnack, A. von (1908), *The Mission and Expansion of Christianity in the First Three Centuries*, trans. J. Moffat from the 2nd German edn, 2 vols. (London).

Harnack, A. von (1924), *Die Mission und Ausbreitung des Christentums in den ersten drei Jahrhunderten*, 2 vols., 4th edn (Leipzig).

Harries, J. (1999), *Law and Empire in Late Antiquity* (Cambridge).

Harrington, S. and Welch, M. (2014), *The Early Anglo-Saxon Kingdoms of Southern Britain,* AD *450–650: Beneath the Tribal Hidage* (Oxford).

Head, T. (1999), 'The development of the Peace of God in Aquitaine (970–1005)', *Speculum* 74, 656–86.

Head, T. (2006), 'Peace and power in France around the year 1000', *Essays in Medieval Studies* 23, 1–17.

Head, T. and Landes, R. (eds.) (1992), *The Peace of God: Social Violence and Religious Response in France around the Year 1000* (Ithaca, NY).

Heather, P. J. (1986), 'The crossing of the Danube and the Gothic conversion', *Greek, Roman and Byzantine Studies* 27, 289–318.

Heather, P. J. (1991), *Goths and Romans 332–489* (Oxford).

Heather, P. J. (1993), 'The historical culture of Ostrogothic Italy', in *Teoderico il grande e i Goti d'Italia*, Atti del XIII Congresso internazionale di studi sull'Alto Medioevo, Spoleto, 1993, 317–53.

Heather, P. J. (1994), 'Literacy and power in the migration period', in Bowman and Woolf (eds.), 177–97.

Heather, P. J. (1994a), 'New men for new Constantines? Creating an imperial elite in the eastern Mediterranean', in P. Magdalino (ed.), *New Constantines: The Rhythm of Imperial Renewal in Byzantium, 4th–13th Centuries* (London), 11–33.

Heather, P. J. (1995), 'The Huns and the end of the Roman Empire in Western Europe', *English Historical Review* 110, 4–41.

Heather, P. J. (1996), *The Goths* (Oxford).

Heather, P. J. (2000), 'State, lordship and community in the West (*c.* A.D. 400–600)', in Cameron *et al.* (eds.), 437–68.

Heather, P. J. (2005), *The Fall of Rome: A New History* (London).

Heather, P. J. (2009), *Empires and Barbarians: Migration, Development, and the Birth of Europe* (London).

Heather, P. J. (2010), 'Elite militarisation and the Post-Roman West', in G. Bonamente and R. Lizzi Testa (eds.), *Istituzioni, Carisimi et Esercizio del Potere (IV–VI secolo d.C.)* (Bari), 245–66.

Heather, P. J. (2013), *The Restoration of Rome: Barbarian Popes and Imperial Pretenders* (London).

Heather, P. J. (2016), 'A tale of two cities: Rome and Ravenna under Gothic rule', in J. Herrin and J. Nelson (eds.), *Ravenna: Its Role in Earlier Medieval Change and Exchange* (London), 15–38.

Heather, P. J. (2018), *Rome Resurgent: War and Empire in the Age of Justinian* (Oxford).

Heather, P. J. and Matthews, J. F. (1991), *The Goths in the Fourth Century*, Translated Texts for Historians (Liverpool).

Heather, P. J. and Moncur, D. (2001), *Politics, Philosophy, and Empire in the Fourth Century: Select Orations of Themistius*, Translated Texts for Historians (Liverpool).

Heil, U. (2014), 'The Homoians', in Berndt and Steinacher (eds.), 85–116.

Heinzelmann, M. (1976), *Bischofsherrschaft in Gallien: zur Kontinuität römischer Führungsschichten vom 4. bis zum 7. Jahrhundert: soziale, prosopographische und bildungsgeschichtliche Aspekte* (Munich).

Heinzelmann, M. (2001), *Gregory of Tours: History and Society in the Sixth Century*, trans. C. Carroll (Cambridge).

Hellemans, B. (ed.) (2014), *Rethinking Abelard: A Collection of Critical Essays* (Boston, MA).

Hen, Y. (2007), *Roman Barbarians* (Basingstoke).

Henderson, J. (2007), *The Medieval World of Isidore Seville: Truth from Words* (Cambridge).

Hendy, M. F. (1985), *Studies in the Byzantine Monetary Economy, c. 300–1450* (Cambridge).

Herrin, J. (1987), *The Formation of Christendom* (Oxford).

Herrmann, K. J. (1973), *Das Tuskulanerpapsttum (1012–1046): Benedikt VIII., Johannes XIX., Benedikt IX.* (Stuttgart).

Hickey, T. (2012), *Wine, Wealth and the State in Late Antique Egypt* (Ann Arbor, MI).

Higham, N. J. (1994), *The English Conquest: Gildas and Britain in the Fifth Century* (Manchester).

Hill, D. (2019), *Inquisition in the Fourteenth Century: The Manuals of Bernard Gui and Nicholas Eymerich* (Cambridge).

Hill, R. (ed. and trans.) (1962), *The Deeds of the Franks and the Other Pilgrims to Jerusalem* (Oxford).

Hillgarth, J. N. (1966), 'Coins and chronicles: propaganda in sixth-century Spain', *Historia* 16, 482–508.

Hillgarth, J. N. (1980), 'Popular religion in Visigothic Spain', in E. James (ed.), *Visigothic Spain: New Approaches* (Oxford), 3–60.

Hillgarth, J. N. (1986), *Christianity and Paganism: The Conversion of Western Europe, 350-750* (Philadelphia, PA).

Hillner, J. (2006), 'Clerics, property and patronage: the case of the Roman titular churches', *Antiquité Tardive* 14, 59–68.

Hillner, J. (2015), *Prison, Punishment and Penance in Late Antiquity* (Cambridge).

Hoffmann, D. (1969), *Das spatromische Bewegungsheer und die* Notitia Dignitatum (Dusseldorf).

Holcomb, J. and Johnson, D. (eds.) (2017), *Christian Theologies of the Sacraments: A Comparative Introduction* (New York).

Holum, K. (1982), *Theodosian Empresses: Women and Imperial Dominion in Late Antiquity* (Berkeley, CA).

Honoré, A. M. (1978), *Tribonian* (London).

Honoré, A. M. (1998), *Law in the Crisis of Empire 379–455 AD: The Theodosian Dynasty and Its Quaestors, with a Palingenesia of Laws of the Dynasty* (Oxford).

Hope-Taylor, B. (1977), *Yeavering: An Anglo-British Centre of Early Northumbria* (London).

Hopkins, K. (1998), 'Christian number and its implications', *Journal of Early Christian Studies* 6, 184–226.

Hopkins, K. (1999), *A World Full of Gods: Pagans, Jews and Christians in the Roman Empire* (London).

Horst, U. (2006), *The Dominicans and the Pope: Papal Teaching Authority in the Medieval and Early Modern Thomist Tradition* (Notre Dame, IN).

Hovorun, C. (2008), *Will, Action and Freedom: Christological Controversies in the Seventh Century* (Leiden).

Howard-Johnston, J. D. (2010), *Witnesses to a World Crisis: Historians and Histories of the Middle East in the Seventh Century* (Oxford).

Hoyland, R. G. (2015), *In God's Path: The Arab Conquests and the Creation of an Islamic Empire* (New York).

Hoyland, R. G. (2019), *Seeing Islam as Others Saw It: A Survey and Evaluation of Christian, Jewish and Zoroastrian Writings on Early Islam* (Piscataway, NJ).

Humfress, C. (2007), *Orthodoxy and the Courts in Late Antiquity* (Oxford).

Hunter, D. G. (2007), 'Sexuality, marriage and the family', in Casiday and Norris (eds.), 585–600.

Iggers, G. (2005), *Historiography in the Twentieth Century: From Scientific Objectivity to the Postmodern Challenge* (Middleton, CT).

Iogna-Prat, D. *et al.* (eds.) (2013), *Cluny: les moines et la société au premier âge féodal* (Rennes).

Jaeger, C. S. (1994), *The Envy of Angels: Cathedral Schools and Social Ideals in Medieval Europe, 950–1200* (Philadelphia, PA).

James, E. (1985), *Gregory of Tours: Life of the Fathers*, Translated Texts for Historians (Liverpool).

Jasper, D. and Fuhrmann, H. (2001), *Papal Letters in the Early Middle Ages* (Washington, DC).

Jefferson, L. M. and Jensen, R. M. (eds.) (2015), *The Art of Empire: Christian Art in Its Imperial Context* (Minneapolis, MN).

Jensen, R. M. (2006), 'Towards a Christian material culture', in Mitchell and Young (eds.), 568–84.

Jochens, J. (1999), 'Late and peaceful: Iceland's conversion through arbitration in 1000', *Speculum* 74, 621–55.

John, E. (1966), *Orbis Britanniae, and Other Studies* (Leicester).

Jones, A. H. M. (1964), *The Later Roman Empire: A Social, Economic and Administrative Survey*, 3 vols. (Oxford).

Kade, R. (ed.) (1888), *Bruno of Querfort: Vita quinque fratrum Poloniae*, MGH, SS 15, vol. 2 (Hannover).

Kafesoglu, I. and Leiser, G. (1988), *A History of the Seljuks: İbrahim Kafesoğlu's Interpretation and the Resulting Controversy* (Carbondale, IL).

Kantor, M. (1983), *Medieval Slavic Lives of Saints and Princes* (Ann Arbor, MI).

Kantor, M. (1990), *The Origins of Christianity in Bohemia* (Evanston, IL).

Kaster, R. A. (1988), *Guardians of Language: The Grammarian and Society in Late Antiquity* (Berkeley, CA).

Kay, N. M. (2006), *Epigrams of the* Anthologia Latina*: Text, Translation and Commentary* (London).

Keene, D. (2004), 'Towns and the growth of trade', in Luscombe and Riley-Smith (eds.), 47–85.

Kelly, C. M. (1994), 'Later Roman bureaucracy: going through the files', in Bowman and Woolf (eds.), 161–76.

Kelly, J. N. D. (1952), *Early Christian Creeds* (London).

Kelly, J. N. D. (1977), *Jerome: His Life, Writings, and Controversies* (London).

Kennedy, H. (2007), *The Great Arab Conquests: How the Spread of Islam Changed the World We Live In* (London).

Kershaw, P. (2007), 'Eberhard of Friuli, a Carolingian lay intellectual', in P. Wormald and J. L. Nelson (eds.), *Lay Intellectuals in the Carolingian World* (Cambridge), 77–105.

King, P. D. (1987), *Charlemagne: Translated Sources* (Kendal).

Kirby, D. P. (1992), *The Earliest English Kings* (London).

Klingshirn, W. (1994), *Caesarius of Arles: The Making of a Christian Community in Late Antique Gaul* (Cambridge).

Klingshirn, W. (1994a), *Caesarius of Arles: Life, Testament, Letters* (Liverpool).

Knibbs, E. (trans.) (2014), *Amalarius of Metz: On the Liturgy* (Cambridge, MA).

König, J. *et al.* (eds.) (2013), *Ancient Libraries* (Cambridge).

Kopecek, T. A. (1979), *A History of Neo-Arianism* (Philadelphia, PA).

Körntgen, L. (2006), 'Canon law and the practice of penance: Burchard of Worms's Penitential', *Early Medieval Europe* 14, 103–17.

Krautheimer, R. (1980), *Rome: Profile of a City, 312–1308* (Princeton, NJ).

Krüger, P. (ed.) (1929), *Codex Iustinianus* (Berlin).

Krüger, P. and Mommsen, T. (eds.) (1928), *Iustinianus: Institutiones, Digesta* (Berlin).

Krusch, J. B. (1880), *Studien zur christlich-mittelalterlichen Chronologie. Der 84jährige Ostercyclus und seine Quellen* (Leipzig).

Kuefler, M. (2014), *The Making and Unmaking of a Saint: Hagiography and Memory in the Cult of Gerald of Aurillac* (Philadelphia, PA).

Kulikowski, M. (2002), 'Nation versus army: a necessary contrast?', in Gillet (ed.), 69–84.

Kurnatowska, Z. (1997), 'Territorial structures in west Poland prior to the founding of the state organization of Miesco I', in Urbanczyk (ed.), 125–36.

Lambert, M. (2002), *Medieval Heresy: Popular Movements from the Gregorian Reform to the Reformation*, 3rd edn (Oxford).

Lambert, T. B. (2017), *Law and Order in Anglo-Saxon England* (Oxford).

Lamberton, R. (1986), *Homer the Theologian: Neoplatonist Allegorical Reading and the Growth of the Epic Tradition* (Berkeley, CA).

Lampe, G. W. H. (ed.) (1969), *The Cambridge History of the Bible, vol. 2: The West from the Fathers to the Reformation* (Cambridge).

Lancel, S. (ed. and trans.) (1972–75), *Actes de la Conférence de Carthage en 411* (Paris).

Lancel, S. (2002), *Victor de Vita: Histoire de la persécution vandale en Afrique* (Paris).

Lane Fox, R. (1986), *Pagans and Christians* (London).

Lange, H. (1993), Die Anfänge der modernen Rechtswissenschaft: Bologna und das frühe Mittelalter (Mainz).

Lansing, C. (1998), *Power and Purity: Cathar Heresy in Medieval Italy* (New York).

Lapidge, M. (ed.) (1995), *Archbishop Theodore* (Cambridge).

Lapidge, M. (2008), *The Anglo-Saxon Library* (Oxford).

Lapidge, M. and Herren, M. (2009), *Aldhelm: The Prose Works* (Woodbridge).

Lapidge, M. and Rosier, J. (2009), *Aldhelm: The Poetic Works* (Woodbridge).

Larrington, C. (trans.) (2014), *The Poetic Edda*, rev. edn (Oxford).

Lauwers, M. (1997), *La mémoire des ancêtres, le souci des morts: Morts, rites et société au moyen âge (diocèse de Liège, XIe–XIIe siècles)* (Paris).

Law, V. (1994), 'The study of grammar', in McKitterick (ed.), 88–110.

Law, V. (2003), *The History of Linguistics in Europe: From Plato to 1600* (Cambridge).

Lawrence, C. H. (1984), *Medieval Monasticism: Forms of Religious Life in Western Europe in the Middle Ages* (London).

Lebecq, S. (1994), 'Le baptême manqué du roi Rabdod', in O. Redon and B. Rosenberger (eds.), *Les assises du pouvoir: temps médiévaux, territoires africains* (Saint-Denis), 141–50.

Lee, A. D. (2006), 'Traditional religions', in Lenski (ed.), 159–81.

Léglu, C. *et al.* (eds.) (2014), *The Cathars and the Albigensian Crusade: A Sourcebook* (London).

Le Goff, J. (1984), *The Birth of Purgatory*, trans. A. Goldhammer (London).

Le Goff, J. (1993), *Intellectuals in the Middle Ages*, trans. T. L. Fagan (Cambridge, MA).

Lenski, N. (1995), 'The Gothic civil war and the date of the Gothic conversion', *Greek, Roman and Byzantine Studies* 36, 51–87.

Lenski, N. (ed.) (2006), *The Cambridge Companion to the Age of Constantine* (Cambridge).

Lenski, N. (2016), *Constantine and the Cities: Imperial Authority and Civic Politics* (Philadelphia, PA).

Lenski, N. (2016a), 'Imperial legislation and the Donatist controversy: from Constantine to Honorius', in Miles (ed.), 166–218.

Leopold, A. M. *et al.* (eds.) (2004), *Syncretism in Religion: A Reader* (London).

Lepelley, C. (1979–81), *Les cités de l'Afrique romaine au Bas-Empire*, 2 vols. (Paris).

Le Roy Ladurie, E. (1990), *Montaillou: Cathars and Catholics in a French Village, 1294–1324* (Harmondsworth).

Levy-Rubin, M. (2011), *Non-Muslims in the Early Islamic Empire: From Surrender to Co-existence* (Cambridge).

Lewitt, T. (1991), *Agricultural Production in the Roman Economy* A.D. *200–400* (Oxford).

Leyser, C. (2000), *Authority and Asceticism from Augustine to Gregory the Great* (Oxford).

Leyser, H. (2009), 'Clerical purity and a re-ordered world', in Rubin and Simons (eds.), 9–21.

Leyser, K. (1979), *Rule and Conflict in an Early Medieval Society: Ottonian Saxony* (London).

Liebeschuetz, J. H. W. G. (1979), *Continuity and Change in Roman Religion* (Oxford).

Liebeschuetz, J. H. W. G. (1990), *Barbarians and Bishops: Army, Church and State in the Age of Arcadius and John Chrysostom* (Oxford).

Liebs, D. (1993), *Römisches Recht: ein Studienbuch* (Göttingen).

Liebs, D. (2002), *Römische Jurisprudenz in Gallien (2. bis 8. Jahrhundert)* (Berlin).

Lieu, J. M. (2004), *Christian Identity in the Jewish and Graeco-Roman World* (Oxford).

Lieu, J. M. (2006), 'Self-definition vis-à-vis the Jewish matrix', in Mitchell and Young (eds.), 214–29.

Lieu, S. N. C. (ed.) (1986), *The Emperor Julian: Panegyric and Polemic* (Liverpool).

Lieu, S. N. C. (2007), 'Christianity and Manichaeism', in Casiday and Norris (eds.), 279–95.

Limor, O. (2009), 'Christians and Jews', in Rubin and Simons (eds.), 133–48.

Linder, A. (1997), *The Jews in the Legal Sources of the Early Middle Ages* (Detroit, MI).

Little, D. P. (1990), 'Coptic converts to Islam during the Bakri Muhalik period', in Gervers and Bihkazi (eds.), 264–88.

Little, L. K. (1978), *Religious Poverty and the Profit Economy in Medieval Europe* (London).

Little, L. K. and Rosenwein, B. (1974), 'Social meaning in the monastic and mendicant spiritualities', *Past & Present* 63 (1974), 4–32.

Lizo, J. and Pretorius, H. (1997), '"A branch springs out": African Initiated Churches', in R. Elphick and R. Davenport (eds.), *Christianity in South Africa: A Political, Social and Cultural History* (Oxford), 211–26.

Llewellyn, P. (1971), *Rome in the Dark Ages* (London).

Loewe, R. (1969), 'The medieval history of the Latin Vulgate', in Lampe (ed.), 102–54.

Lomax, D. W. (1978), *The Spanish Reconquest* (London).

Lošek, F. (ed.) (1997), *Die* Conversio Bagoariorum et Carantanorum *und der Brief des Erzbischofs Theotmar von Salzburg* (Hannover).

Lotter, F. (1989), 'The crusading idea and the conquest of the region east of the Elbe', in R. Bartlett and A. MacKay (eds.), *Medieval Frontier Societies* (Oxford), 268–306.

Loyn, H. R. and Percival, J. (1975), *The Reign of Charlemagne: Documents on Carolingian Government and Administration* (London).

Lunde, P. and Stone, C. (2012), *Ibn Fadlan and the Land of Darkness: Arab Travellers in the Far North* (London).

Luscombe, D. (2019), *Peter Abelard and Heloise: Collected Studies* (Abingdon).

Luscombe, D. and Riley-Smith, J. (eds.) (2004), *The New Cambridge Medieval History vol. 4: c. 1024–c. 1198, part 1* (Cambridge).

Luscombe, D. and Riley-Smith, J. (eds.) (2008), *The New Cambridge Medieval History vol. 4: c. 1024–c. 1198, part 2* (Cambridge).

Lynch, J. H. (1986), *Godparents and Kinship in Early Medieval Europe* (Princeton, NJ).

Maas, M. (ed.) (2005), *The Cambridge Companion to the Age of Justinian* (Cambridge).

MacCormack, S. A. (1981), *Art and Ceremony in Late Antiquity* (Los Angeles and Berkeley, CA).

MacMullen, R. (1984), *Christianising the Roman Empire (AD 100–400)* (New Haven, CT).

McCormick, M. (1986), *Eternal Victory: Triumphal Rulership in Late Antiquity, Byzantium and the Early Medieval West* (Cambridge).

McGiffert, A. C. (trans.) (1905), *Eusebius: Church History, Life of Constantine the Great, and Oration in Praise of Constantine* (New York).

McGuckin, J. A. (2004), *St. Cyril of Alexandria: The Christological Controversy: Its History, Theology, and Texts* (New York).

McGuire, B. (2009), 'Monastic and religious orders, c.1100–c.1350', in Rubin and Simons (eds.), 54–72.

McKenzie, J. S. *et al.* (2004), 'Reconstructing the Serapeum in Alexandria from the archaeological evidence', *Journal of Roman Studies* 94 (2004), 73–121.

McKitterick, R. (1977), *The Frankish Church and the Carolingian Reforms, 789–895* (London).

McKitterick, R. (1989), *The Carolingians and the Written Word* (Cambridge).

McKitterick, R. (ed.) (1990), *The Uses of Literacy in Early Mediaeval Europe* (Cambridge).

McKitterick, R. (ed.) (1994), *Carolingian Culture: Emulation and Innovation* (Cambridge).

McKitterick R. (1994a), 'Script and book production', in McKitterick (ed.), 221–47.

McKitterick, R. (ed.) (1995), *The New Cambridge Medieval History vol. 2: c.700–c.900* (Cambridge).

McKitterick, R. (2000), 'The Church', in Reuter (ed.), 130–63.

McKitterick, R. (2005), 'The Carolingian Renaissance of culture and learning', in Story (ed.), 151–66.

McKitterick, R. (2008), *Charlemagne: The Formation of a European Identity* (Cambridge).

McLaughlin, M. (2009), 'Women and men', in Rubin and Simons (eds.), 187–99.

McLaughlin, M. (2010), *Sex, Gender, and Episcopal Authority in an Age of Reform, 1000–1122* (Oxford).

MacLean, S. (2003), *Kingship and Politics in the Late Ninth Century: Charles the Fat and the End of the Carolingian Empire* (Cambridge).

McLynn, N. (1994), *Ambrose of Milan* (Berkeley, CA).

McLynn, N. (2005), '*Genere Hispanus*: Theodosius, Spain and Nicene orthodoxy', in K. Bowes and M. Kulikowski (eds), *Hispania in Late Antiquity* (Leiden), 177–220. Reprinted in N. McLynn (2009), *Christian Politics and Religious Culture in Late Antiquity*, Variorum Collected Studies No. III (London), 1–43.

McLynn, N. (2016), 'The council of Carthage reconsidered', in Miles (ed.), 220–47.

McLynn, N. (2020), 'The Persian expedition', in S. Rebenich, H.-U. Wiemer, *A Companion to Julian the Apostate* (Leiden).

McLynn, N. *et al.* (eds.) (2015), *Conversion in Late Antiquity: Christianity, Islam, and Beyond* (Farnham).

McMichael, S. and Myers, S. (eds.) (2004), *Friars and Jews in the Middle Ages and Renaissance* (Leiden).

McNeil, J. T. and Gamer, H. (ed. and trans.) (1938), *Medieval Handbooks of Penance* (New York).

Madrid Medrano, S. (2015), *Isidore de Séville et son temps*, Antiquité Tardive 23 (Turnhout).

Mango, C. (1977), 'Historical introduction', in A. Bryer and J. Herrin (eds.), *Iconoclasm* (Birmingham), 1–6.

Mango, C. (1985), *Le Développement urbain de Constantinople (IVe–VIIe siècles)*, Travaux et Mémoires, Monographies 2 (Paris).

Manton, E. L. (1988), *Roman North Africa* (London).

Marcus, J. (2006), 'Jewish Christianity', in Mitchell and Young (eds.), 87–102.

Marenbon, J. (1994), 'Carolingian thought', in McKitterick (ed.), 171–92.

Marenbon, J. (2003), *Boethius* (Oxford).

Marenbon, J. (ed.) (2009), *The Cambridge Companion to Boethius* (Cambridge).

Marenbon, J. (2013), *Abelard in Four Dimensions: A Twelfth-Century Philosopher in His Context and Ours* (Notre Dame, IN).

Markus, R. A. (1970), 'Gregory the Great and a papal missionary strategy', *Studies in Church History* 6, 29–38.

Markus, R. A. (1990), *The End of Ancient Christianity* (Cambridge).

Markus, R. A. (1996), *Signs and Meanings: World and Text in Ancient Christianity* (Liverpool).

Markus, R. A. (1997), *Gregory the Great and His World* (Cambridge).

Markus, R. A. (2001), 'Gregory the Great's pagans' in R. Gameson and H. Leyser (eds.), *Belief and Culture in the Middle Ages: Studies Presented to Henry Mayr-Harting* (Oxford), 23–34.

Markus, R. A. and Sotinel, C. (2007), 'Introduction', in Chazelle and Cubitt (eds.), 1–14.

Maroney, E. (2006), *Religious Syncretism* (London).

Marrou, H. I. (1982), *A History of Education in Antiquity* (trans.) (Madison, WI).

Martyn, J. R. C. (trans.) (2004), *The Letters of Gregory the Great*, 3 vols. (Toronto).

Martyn, J. R. C. (2008), *King Sisebut and the Culture of Visigothic Spain* (Lewiston, NY).

Mathisen, R. (1989), *Ecclesiastical Factionalism and Religious Controversy in Fifth-Century Gaul* (Washington, DC).

Matthews, J. F. (1975), *Western Aristocracies and Imperial Court A.D. 364–425* (Oxford).

Matthews, J. F. (1989), *The Roman Empire of Ammianus* (London).

Matthews, J. F. (2000), *Laying Down the Law: A Study of the Theodosian Code* (New Haven, CT).

Mauss, M. (1969), *The Gift: Forms and Functions of Exchange in Archaic Societies*, trans. I. Cunnison (London).

Mayne Kienzle, B. (2000), *The Sermon* (Turnhout).

Mayne Kienzle, B. (2009), 'Religious poverty and the search for perfection', in Rubin and Simons (eds.), 39–53.

Mayne Kienzle, B. (ed.) (2014), *A Companion to Hildegard of Bingen* (Leiden).

Mayr-Harting, H. (1991), The Coming of Christianity to Anglo-Saxon England, 3rd edn (Philadelphia, PA).

Meeks, W. A. (2006), 'Social and ecclesial life of the earliest Christians', in Mitchell and Young (eds.), 145–73.

Meens, R. (2006), 'Penitentials and the practice of penance in the tenth and eleventh centuries', *Early Medieval Europe* 14, 7–21.

Meens, R. (2008), 'Remedies for sins', in Noble and Smith (eds.), 399–415.

Melville, G. and Helmrath, J. (2017), *The Fourth Lateran Council: Institutional Reform and Spiritual Renewal: Proceedings of the Conference Marking the Eight Hundredth Anniversary of the Council, Organized by the Pontifico Comitato de Scienze storiche* (Rome, 15–17 October 2015) (Affalterbach).

Merrills, A. and Miles, D. (2010), *The Vandals* (Oxford).

Metzger, B. M. (1997), *The Canon of the New Testament: Its Origin, Development, and Significance* (Oxford).

Miles, R. (ed.) (2016), *The Donatist Schism: Controversy and Contexts* (Liverpool).

Millar, F. (1992), *The Emperor in the Roman World*, 2nd edn (London).

Miller, M. C. (2005), *Power and the Holy in the Age of the Investiture Conflict: A Brief History with the Documents* (Boston, MA).

Millet-Gérard, D. (1984), *Chrétiens mozarabes et culture islamique dans l'Espagne des VIIIe–IXe siècles* (Paris).

Mitchell, K. and Wood, I. (eds.) (2002), *The World of Gregory of Tours* (Leiden).

Mitchell, M. M. (2006), 'Gentile Christianity', in Mitchell and Young (eds.), 103–24.

Mitchell, M. M. and Young F. M. (eds.) (2006), *The Cambridge History of Christianity vol. 1: Origins to Constantine* (Cambridge).

Mitchell, S. (1991), 'The cult of Theos Hypsistos between pagans, Jews, and Christians', in P. Athanassiadi and M. Frede (eds.), *Pagan Monotheism in Late Antiquity* (Oxford), 81–148.

Mitchell, S. (1993), *Anatolia: Land, Men, and Gods in Asia Minor*, 2 vols. (Oxford).

Moderan, Y. (2003), 'Une guerre de religion: Les deux Eglises d'Afrique à l'époque vandal', *Antiquité tardive* 11, 21–44.

Moderan, Y. (2004), 'La conversion de Constantin et la christianisation de l'empire romain', http://aphgcaen.free.fr/conferences/moderan.htm.

Moderan, Y. (2007), 'L'Afrique reconquise et les Trois Chapitres', in Chazelle and Cubitt (eds.), 39–83.

Moesch, S. (2019), Augustine and the Art of Ruling in the Carolingian Imperial Period: Political Discourse in Alcuin of York and Hincmar of Rheims (Abingdon).

Moisl, H. (1981), 'Anglo-Saxon royal genealogies and Germanic oral tradition', *Journal of Medieval History* 7, 215–48.

Monagle, C. (2013), Orthodoxy and Controversy in Twelfth-Century Religious Discourse: Peter Lombard's Sentences and the Development of Theology (Turnhout).

Mooney, C. (2016), Clare of Assisi and the Thirteenth-Century Church: Religious Women, Rules, and Resistance (Philadelphia, PA*).*

Moore, J. C. and Bolton, B. (eds.) (1999), *Pope Innocent III and His World* (Aldershot).

Moore, R. I. (2000), *The First European Revolution c. 970–1215* (Oxford).

Moore, R. I. (2007), *The Formation of a Persecuting Society: Authority and Deviance in Western Europe, 950–1250*, 2nd edn (Oxford).

Moore, R. I. (2012), The War on Heresy: Faith and Power in Medieval Europe (Cambridge, MA*).*

Moore, R. I. (2016), 'Principles at stake: the debate of April 2013 in retrospect', in Sennis (ed.), 257–73.

Moorhead, J. (trans.) (1992), *Victor of Vita: History of the Persecution in Africa*, Translated Text for Historians (Liverpool).

Mordek, H. (1975), *Kirchenrecht und Reform im Frankenreich: die collectio vetus Gallica: die älteste systematische Kanonessammlung des fränkischen Gallien: Studien und Edition* (Berlin).

Mordek, H. (1985), 'Kanonistik und gregorianische Reform', in K. Schmid (ed.), *Reich und Kirche vor dem Investiturstreit* (Sigmaringen), 65–82.

Moretti, J. and Stopani, R. (1972), *Chiese Romaniche in Val di Pesa e Val di Greve* (Florence).

Morin, G. (ed. and trans.) (2010), *Vie de Césaire d'Arles*, rev. edn (Paris).

Morony, M. G. (1990), 'The age of conversions: a reassessment', in Gervers and Bihkazi (eds.), 135–50.

Morris, C. (1989), *The Papal Monarchy: The Western Church from 1050 to 1250* (Oxford).

Morris, J. (2005), 'The demise of the confessional state', in *idem, F. D. Maurice and the Crisis of Christian Authority* (Oxford).

Morris, R. (1989), *Churches in the Landscape* (London).

Morris, R. (1991), 'Baptismal places 600–800', in I. Wood and N. Lund (eds.), *People and Places in Northern Europe 500–1600: Essays in Honour of Peter Hayes Sawyer* (Woodbridge), 15–24.

Moussy, C. (1988), *Dracontius Ouevres II* (Paris).

Moussy, C. and Camus, C. (1985), *Dracontius, De Laudibus Dei* (Paris).

Muckle, J. T. (1964), *The Story of Abelard's Adversities: A Translation with Notes of the* Historia calamitatum, rev. edn (Toronto).

Mueller, J. (2010), *A Companion to Clare of Assisi: Life, Writings, and Spirituality* (Leiden).

Murray, A. C. (2016), *A Companion to Gregory of Tours* (Leiden).

Musurillo, H. (1972), *The Acts of the Christian Martyrs* (Oxford).

Nelson, J. (1977), 'On the limits of the Carolingian Renaissance', *Studies in Church History* 14, 51–67, reprinted as no. 2 in Nelson (1986).

Nelson, J. (1983), 'Legislation and consensus in the reign of Charles the Bald', in C. P. Wormald *et al.* (eds.), *Ideal and Reality in Frankish and Anglo-Saxon Society: Studies Presented to J. M. Wallace-Hadrill* (Oxford), 202–27, reprinted as no. 5 in Nelson (1986).

Nelson, J. (1986), *Politics and Ritual in Early Medieval Europe* (London).

Nelson, J. (1987), 'Making ends meet: wealth and poverty in the Carolingian Church', *Studies in Church History* 24, 25–36.

Nelson, J. (1990), 'The last years of Louis the Pious', in Godman and Collins (eds.), 147–60.

Nelson, J. (1992), *Charles the Bald* (London).

Nelson, J. (2005), 'Charlemagne the man', in Story (ed.), 22–37.

Nelson, J. (2019), *King and Emperor: A New Life of Charlemagne* (London).

Neusner, J. (2006), *How Important Was the Destruction of the Second Temple in the Formation of Rabbinic Judaism?* (Oxford).

Neuwirth, A. (2019), *The Qur'an and Late Antiquity: A Shared Heritage* (New York).

Newman, B. (ed.) (1998), *Voice of the Living Light: Hildegard of Bingen and Her World* (Berkeley, CA).

Nightingale, J. (2001), *Monasteries and Their Patrons in the Gorze Reform: Lotharingia c. 850–1000* (Oxford).

Nixey, C. (2017), *The Darkening Age: The Christian Destruction of the Classical World* (London).

Nixon, C. E. V. and Rogers, B. S. (1994), In Praise of Later Roman Emperors: The Panegyrici Latini (Berkeley, CA*).*

Noble, T. F. X. (1984), *The Republic of St. Peter: The Birth of the Papal State, 680–825* (Philadelphia, PA).

Noble, T. F. X. (1995), 'The papacy in the eighth and ninth centuries', in McKitterick (ed.), 563–86.

Noble, T. F. X. (2009), *Images, Iconoclasm, and the Carolingians* (Philadelphia, PA).

Noble, T. F. X. and Smith, J. (eds.) (2008), *The Cambridge History of Christianity vol. 3: Early Medieval Christianities, c. 600–c. 1100* (Cambridge).

Nock, F. C. (1946), *Valerio of Bierzo: The* Vita sancti Fructuosi (Washington, DC).

Nöldeke, T. (2013), *The History of the Qur'ān* (Leiden).

Norman, A. F. (1992), *Libanius: Autobiography and Select Letters*, 2 vols. (Cambridge, MA).

North, J. A. (2000), *Roman Religion* (Oxford).

North, R. (1997), *Heathen Gods in Old English Literature* (Cambridge).

Nutt, R. W. (2017), *General Principles of Sacramental Theology* (Washington, DC).

Obolenksy, D. (1948), *The Bogomils: A Study in Balkan Neo-Manichaeism* (Cambridge).

O'Connor, P. (2019), 'Warrior Culture in the Post-Roman West', unpublished D.Phil. thesis, King's College London.

Ó Cróinín, D. (1995), *Early Medieval Ireland 400–1200* (London).

O'Donnell, J. J. (1992), *Augustine Confessions: A Commentary* (Oxford).

O'Hara, A. (2018), *Jonas of Bobbio and the Legacy of Columbanus: Sanctity and Community in the Seventh Century* (Oxford).

O'Hara, A. and Wood, I. (2017), *Jonas of Bobbio: Life of Columbanus, Life of John of Réomé, and Life of Vedast*, Translated Texts for Historians (Liverpool).

Osiek, C. (2006), 'The self-defining praxis of the developing *ecclesia*', in Mitchell and Young (eds.), 274–91.

Paget, J. C. and Schaper, J. (eds.) (2013), *The New Cambridge History of the Bible vol. 1: From the Beginnings to 600* (Cambridge).

Palanque, J. R. (1933), *Saint Ambroise et l'Empire romain: contribution à l'histoire des rapports de l'église et de l'état à la fin du quatrième siècle* (Paris).

Palazzo, E. (2008), 'Performing the liturgy', in Noble and Smith (eds.), 472–88.

Pálsson, H. and Edwards, P. (trans.) (1972), *The Book of Settlements:* Landnámabók (Winnipeg).

Parisse, M. (ed.) (1999), *La Vie de Jean, abbé de Gorze* (Paris).

Parker, D. C. (2013), 'The New Testament text and versions', in Paget and Schaper (eds.), 412–54.

Parvis, S. (2014), 'Was Ulfila really a Homoian?', in Berndt and Steinacher (eds.), 49–66.

Paschoud, F. (ed. and Fr. trans.) (1971–81), *Zosimus:* Historia Nova (Paris).

Pashley, R. (2012), *Travels in Crete*, 2 vols. (Cambridge; orig. pub. 1837).

Pattenden, M. (2008), 'The canonisation of Clare of Assisi and early Franciscan history', *Journal of Ecclesiastical History* 59 (2), 208–26.

Paxton, F. S. (1990), *Christianizing Death: The Creation of a Ritual Process in Early Medieval Europe* (Ithaca, NY).

Pearson, B. A. (2006), 'Egypt', in Mitchell and Young (eds.), 331–50.

Pedersen, O. (1997), *The First Universities.* Studium generale *and the Origins of University Education in Europe* (Cambridge).

Pegg, M. (2001), 'On Cathars, Albigenses and Good Men of Languedoc', *Journal of Medieval History* 27, 181–97.

Pegg, M. (2016), 'The paradigm of Catharism; or, the historians' illusion', in Sennis (ed.), 21–52.

Pelikan, J. (1971–89), *The Christian Tradition: A History of the Development of Doctrine*, 5 vols. (Chicago, IL).

Pennington, K. (2007), 'The growth of church law', in Casiday and Norris (eds.), 386–402.

Peppard, M. (2016), *The World's Oldest Church* (New Haven, CT).

Perisanidi, M. (2018), *Clerical Continence in Twelfth-Century England and Byzantium: Property, Family, and Purity* (London).

Perron, A. (2009), 'The bishops of Rome, 1100–1300', in Rubin and Simons (eds.), 22–38.

Pertz, G. H. (ed.) (1841), *Bruno of Querfort: Passio sancti Adalberti episcopi et martyris*, MGH, SS 4 (Hannover).

Peters, E. (1971), *The First Crusade: The Chronicle of Fulcher of Chartres and Other Source Material* (Philadelphia, PA).

Peters, E. (1980), *Heresy and Authority in Medieval Europe* (Philadelphia, PA).

Pflaum, H. G. (1950), *Les procurateurs équestres sous le Haut-Empire romain* (Paris).

Pharr, C. (trans.) (1952), *The Theodosian Code and Novels and the Sirmondian Constitutions* (New York).

PLRE – The Prosopography of the Later Roman Empire, ed. A. H. M. Jones *et al.* (1971–92), 3 vols. (Cambridge).

Pohl, W. (2000), *Die Germanen* (Munich).

Pohl, W. *et al.* (eds.) (2013), *Strategies of Identification: Ethnicity and Religion in Early Medieval Europe* (Turnhout).

Pollmann, K. and Vessey, M. (eds.) (2007), *Augustine and the Disciplines from Cassiciacum to Confessions* (Oxford).

Porena, P. *et al.* (eds.) (2012), *Expropriations et confiscations dans les royaumes barbares: une approche régionale* (Rome).

Porges, W. (1946), 'The clergy, the poor, and the non-combatants on the First Crusade', *Speculum* 21, 1–23.

Post, G. (2017), *The Papacy and the Rise of the Universities*, ed. W. Courtenay (Boston, MA).

Potter, D. (2015), *Theodora: Actress, Empress, Saint* (Oxford).

Poulik, J. *et al.* (eds.) (1986), *Grossmähren und die Anfänge der tschechoslowakischen Staatlichkeit* (Prague).

Powicke, F. M. and Cheney, C. R. (1964), *Councils and Synods, With Other Documents Relating to the English Church vol. 2: A.D. 1205–1313* (Oxford).

Price, N. (2020), *The Children of Ash and Elm: A History of the Vikings* (London).

Price, R. (2009), *The Acts of the Council of Constantinople of 553: With Related Texts on the Three Chapters Controversy* (Liverpool).

Price, R. (2018), *The Acts of the Second Council of Nicaea (787)*, Translated Texts for Historians (Liverpool).

Price, R. *et al.* (2014), *The Acts of the Lateran Synod of 649*, Translated Texts for Historians (Liverpool).

Price, S. R. F. (1984), *Rituals and Power: The Roman Imperial Cult in Asia Minor* (Cambridge).

Prinz, F. (1984), *Bohmen im mittelalterlichen Europa* (Munich).

Prudlo, D. (ed.) (2019), *A Companion to Heresy Inquisitions* (Leiden).

Puglisi, N. (forthcoming), *Elected by God? Reinventing Sanctity in Late Antiquity* (unpublished D.Phil. thesis, King's College London).

Queller, D. E. (1978), *The Fourth Crusade: The Conquest of Constantinople 1201–1204* (Leicester).

Rabe, S. A. (1995), *Faith, Art and Politics at Saint-Riquier: The Symbolic Vision of Angilbert* (Philadelphia, PA).

Rajak, T. (2006), 'The Jewish diaspora', in Mitchell and Young (eds.), 53–68.

Rankin, S. (1994), 'Carolingian music', in McKitterick (ed.), 274–316.

Rapp, C. (2005), *Holy Bishops in Late Antiquity: The Nature of Christian Leadership in an Age of Transition* (Berkeley, CA).

Rashdall, H. (1987), *The Universities of Europe in the Middle Ages*, ed. F. M. Powicke and A. B. Emden (Oxford; orig. pub. 1895).

Raven, S. (1993), *Rome in Africa*, 3rd edn (London).

Rebenich, S. (2002), *Jerome* (London).

Rebillard, É. (1994), 'In hora mortis: Évolution de la pastorale de la mort aux IVe et Ve siècles dans l'Occident latin, *Bibliothèque de l'École française d'Athènes et de Rome* 282, 148–67.

Rees, B. R. (1988), *Pelagius: Life and Letters* (Rochester, NY).

Reid, J. S. (1911), 'The reorganisation of the Empire', in Gwatkin and Whitney, 24–54.

Reid, P. L. D. (trans.) (1991), *The Complete Works of Rather of Verona* (Binghamton, NY).

Reisl, B. (2009), 'Material support I: parishes', in Rubin and Simons (eds.), 96–106.

Rembold, I. (2018), *Conquest and Christianization: Saxony and the Carolingian World, 772–888* (Cambridge).

Reuter, T. (1980), 'Saint Boniface and Europe' in *idem* (ed.), *The Greatest Englishman: Essays on St Boniface and the Church at Crediton* (Exeter), 71–94.

Reuter, T. (1982), 'The "Imperial Church System" of the Ottonian and Salian rulers: a reconsideration', *Journal of Ecclesiastical History* 33, 347–74.

Reuter, T. (1985), 'Plunder and tribute in the Carolingian Empire', in *Transactions of the Royal Historical Society* 35, 75–94.

Reuter, T. (1990), 'The end of Carolingian military expansion', in Godman and Collins (eds.), 391–407.

Reuter, T. (1991), *Germany in the Early Middle Ages c. 800–1056* (London).

Reuter, T. (ed. and trans.) (1992), *The Annals of Fulda* (Manchester).

Reuter, T. (ed.) (2000), *The New Cambridge Medieval History vol. 3: c. 900–c.1024* (Cambridge).

Rex, R. (1993), *Henry VIII and the English Reformation* (Basingstoke).

Rex, R. (1996), 'The crisis of obedience: God's word and Henry's Reformation', *Historical Journal* 39, 863–94.

Reynolds, L. D. and Wilson, N. G. (1991), *Scribes and Scholars: A Guide to the Transmission of Greek and Latin Literature*, 3rd edn (Oxford).

Reynolds, P. L. (1994), *Marriage in the Western Church: The Christianization of Marriage during the Patristic and Early Medieval Periods* (Leiden).

Reynolds, R. E. (1995), 'The organisation, law, and liturgy of the Western Church 700–900', in McKitterick (ed.), 587–621.

Rice, T. (1961), *The Seljuks in Asia Minor* (London).

Richards, J. (1979), *The Popes and the Papacy in the Early Middle Ages, 476–752* (London).

Riché, P. (1976), *Education and Culture in the Barbarian West: Sixth through Eighth Centuries* (Columbia, SC).

Riché P. (1987), *Gerbert d'Aurillac: le pape de l'an mil* (Paris).

Riches, T. M. (2007), 'Bishop Gerard I of Cambrai-Arras, the three orders, and the problem of human weakness', in J. S. Ott and A. Trumbore Jones (eds.), *The Bishop Reformed: Studies of Episcopal Power and Culture in the Central Middle Ages* (Aldershot), 122–36.

Ridley, R. T. (1982), *Zosimus: New History* (Canberra).

Riley-Smith, J. (1986), *The First Crusade and the Idea of Crusading* (London).

Riley-Smith, J. (1992), *What Were the Crusades?* 2nd rev. edn (Basingstoke).

Riley-Smith, J. (1997), *The First Crusaders, 1095–1131* (Cambridge).

Roberts, C. H. (1979), *Manuscript, Society and Belief in Early Christian Egypt* (Oxford).

Roberts, M. (2009), *The Humblest Sparrow: The Poetry of Venantius Fortunatus* (Ann Arbor, MI).

Robinson, C. F. (2000), *Empire and Elites after the Muslim Conquest: The Transformation of Northern Mesopotamia* (Cambridge).

Robinson, C. F. (2003), *Islamic Historiography* (Cambridge).

Robinson, C. F. (2005), *ʿAbd al-Malik* (Oxford).

Robinson, C. H. (trans.) (1920), *The Life of Otto, Apostle of Pomerania, 1060–1139* (London).

Robinson, C. H. (trans.) (1921), *Anskar: The Apostle of the North 801–865* (London).

Robinson, I. S. (1978), *Authority and Resistance in the Investiture Contest: The Polemical Literature of the Eleventh Century* (Manchester).

Robinson, I. S. (2004), *The Papal Reform of the Eleventh Century: Lives of Pope Leo IX and Pope Gregory VII* (Manchester).

Robinson, I. S. (2004a), 'Reform and the Church 1073–1122', in Luscombe and Riley-Smith (eds.) (2004), 268–334.

Robinson, J. C. (ed. and trans.) (1996), The Nag Hammadi Library in English, 4th rev. edn (Leiden).

Robson, M. J. P. (ed.) (2012), *The Cambridge Companion to Francis of Assisi* (Cambridge).

Rolfe, J. C., (ed.) (1935–9), *Ammianus Marcellinus* (London).

Rose, E. M. (2016), *The Murder of William of Norwich: The Origins of the Blood Libel in Medieval Europe* (Oxford).

Rosemann, P. W. (2002–14), *Mediaeval Commentaries on the* Sentences *of Peter Lombard*, 3 vols. (Leiden).

Rosemann, P. W. (2004), *Peter Lombard* (Oxford).

Rosemann, P. W. (2007), *The Story of a Great Medieval Book: Peter Lombard's* Sentences (Peterborough, Ontario).

Rosenwein, B. (1989), *To Be the Neighbor of Saint Peter: The Social Meaning of Cluny's Property, 909–1049* (Ithaca, NY).

Rostovtzeff, M. (1926), *The Social and Economic History of the Roman Empire* (Oxford).

Rothwell, H. (1975), *English Historical Documents vol. 4: 1189–1327* (London).

Rousseau, P. (1994), *Basil of Caesarea* (Berkeley, CA).

Rubin, M. (1992), 'Religious culture in town and country, reflections on a great divide', in Abulafia *et al.* (eds), 3–22.

Rubin, M. (2009), 'Sacramental life', in Rubin and Simons (eds.), 217–37.

Rubin, M. and Simons, W. (eds.) (2009), *The Cambridge History of Christianity vol. 4: Christianity in Western Europe, c.1100–c.1500* (Cambridge).

Runciman, S. (1954), *A History of the Crusades* (London).

Salzman, M. R. (1990), *On Roman Time: The Codex-Calendar of 354 and the Rhythms of Urban Life in Late Antiquity* (Berkeley, CA).

Salzman, M. R. (2002), *The Making of a Christian Aristocracy: Social and Religious Change in the Western Roman Empire* (Cambridge, MA).

Salzman, M. R. (2007), 'Christianity and paganism, III: Italy', in Casiday and Norris (eds.), 210–30.

Samarin, W. J. (1972), 'Sociolinguistic vs. neurophysiological explanations for glossolalia: comment on Goodman's paper', *Journal for the Scientific Study of Religion* 11 (3), 293–6.

Sandwell, I. (2007), *Religious Identity in Late Antiquity: Greeks, Jews, and Christians in Antioch* (Cambridge).

Sanmark, A. (2004), *Power and Conversion: A Comparative Study of Christianization in Scandinavia* (Uppsala).

Sarris, P. (2011), *Empires of Faith: The Fall of Rome to the Rise of Islam, 500–700* (Oxford).

Sarti, L. (2013), *Perceiving War and the Military in Early Christian Gaul (ca. 400–700 A.D.)* (Leiden).

Sartre, M. (1982), *Trois études sur l'Arabie romaine et byzantine* (Tournai).

Sawyer, P. H. and Wood, I. N. (eds.) (1977), *Early Medieval Kingship* (Leeds).

Schäferdiek, K. (1978), 'Germanenmission', *Reallexikon für Antike und Christentum* 10, 492–548.

Schäferdiek, K. (2007), 'Germanic and Celtic Christianities', in Casiday and Norris (eds.), 52–69.

Schatz, K. (1990), *Papal Primacy from Its Origins to the Present* (Collegeville, MN).

Schmidt, L. (1933), *Geschichte der deutschen Stämme bis zum Ausgang der Völkerwanderung. Die Ostgermanen*, 2nd edn (Munich).

Schmidt, L. (1938–40), *Geschichte der deutschen Stämme bis zum Ausgang der Völkerwanderung: die Westgermanen*, 2 vols. (Munich).

Schmidt, T. (1977), *Alexander II (1061–1073) und die römische Reformgruppe seiner Zeit* (Stuttgart).

Schneyer, J. B. (1969–90), *Repertorium der lateinischen Sermones des Mittelalters für die Zeit von 1150–1350*, 11 vols. (Münster).

Schöll, R. and Kroll, G. (eds.) (1928), *Iustinianus: Novellae* (Berlin).

Scholz, B. W. (1972), *Carolingian Chronicles: Royal Frankish Annals and Nithard's Histories* (Ann Arbor, MI).

Schumacher, L. (ed.) (2020), *The* Summa Halensis*: Doctrines and Debates* (Berlin).

Schwartz, E. (1922–30), *Acta conciliorum oecumenicorum* (Berlin).

Scott, S. P. (trans.) (1932), *The Civil Law* (Cincinnati, OH).

Scull, C. (1999), 'Social archaeology and Anglo-Saxon kingdom origins', *Anglo-Saxon Studies in Archaeology and History* 10, 17–24.

Semple, S. (2011), 'In the open air', in Carver *et al.* (eds), 21–48.

Sennis, A. (ed.) (2016), *Cathars in Question* (Woodbridge).

Shanzer, D. and Wood, I. N. (trans.) (2002), *Avitus of Vienne: Letters and Selected Prose* (Liverpool).

Sharpe, R. (1992), 'Churches and communities in early medieval Ireland: towards a pastoral model', in Blair and Sharpe (eds.), 81–109.

Shaw, B. (1999), 'War and violence', in Bowersock *et al.* (eds.), 130–66.

Shepherd, J. (2006), 'The Byzantine Commonwealth, 1000–1550', in Angold (ed.), 1–52.

Shepherd, J. (2008), 'Slav Christianities 800–1100', in Noble and Smith (eds.), 130–56.

Shepherd, J. and Treadwell, L. (eds.) (2018), *Muslims on the Volga in the Viking Age: Diplomacy and Islam in the World of Ibn Fadlan* (London).

Sijpesteijn, P. M. (2013), *Shaping a Muslim State: The World of a Mid-Eighth-Century Egyptian Official* (Oxford).

Silano, G. (trans.) (2007–10), *Peter Lombard: The* Sentences, 4 vols. (Toronto).

Simons, W. (2001), *Cities of Ladies: Beguine Communities in the Medieval Low Countries, 1200–1565* (Philadelphia, PA).

Sitwell, G. (ed. and trans.) (1958), *St. Odo of Cluny: Being the Life of St. Odo of Cluny by John of Salerno, and the Life of St. Gerald of Aurillac by St. Odo* (London).

Skocpol, T. *et al.* (eds.) (1985), *Bringing the State Back In: Strategies of Analysis in Current Research* (Cambridge).

Smalley, B. (1969), 'The exposition and exegesis of scripture 3: the Bible in the medieval schools', in Lampe (ed.), 197–230.

Smirnova, V. *et al.* (2015), *The Art of Cistercian Persuasion in the Middle Ages and Beyond: Caesarius of Heisterbach's Dialogue on Miracles and Its Reception* (Leiden).

Smith, J. M. H. (1995), 'The problem of female sanctity in Carolingian Europe, c. 780–c. 920', *Past & Present* 146, 3–37.

Smith, J. M. H. (1999), 'Gender and ideology in the early Middle Ages', *Studies in Church History* 35, 51–73.

Smith, J. M. H. (2005), *Europe After Rome: A New Cultural History 500–1000* (Oxford).

Smith, L. (2009), 'The theological framework', in Rubin and Simons (eds.), 73–88.

Smith, R. (1995), *Julian's Gods: Religion and Philosophy in the Thought and Action of Julian the Apostate* (London).

Smyth, A. P. (1977), *Scandinavian Kings in the British Isles, 850–880* (Oxford).

Somerville, R. and Brasington, B. C. (1998), *Prefaces to Canon Law Books in Latin Christianity: Selected Translations, 500–1245* (New Haven, CT).

Sotinel, C. (2007), 'The Three Chapters and the transformations of Italy', in Chazelle and Cubitt (eds.), 85–119.

Southern, R. W. (1984), 'From schools to university', in Catto (ed.), 1–36.

Southern, R. W. (1995), *Scholastic Humanism and the Unification of Europe vol. 1: Foundations* (Oxford).

Southern, R. W. (2002), *Scholastic Humanism and the Unification of Europe vol. 2: The Heroic Age* (Oxford).

Sparks, H. D. F. (1970), 'Jerome as biblical scholar', in Ackroyd and Evans (eds.), 510–41.

Spevak, O. (ed. and trans.) (2020), *Etymologies. Livre I, La grammaire* (Paris).

Spinks, B. D. (2006), *Early and Medieval Rituals and Theologies of Baptism: From the New Testament to the Council of Trent* (Aldershot).

Stancliffe, C. (1983), *St. Martin and His Hagiographer: History and Miracle in Sulpicius Severus* (Oxford).

Stancliffe, C. (1995a), 'Oswald, "most holy and most victorious king of the Northumbrians"', in Stancliffe and Cambridge (eds.), 33–83.

Stancliffe, C. (1995b), 'Where was Oswald killed?', in Stancliffe and Cambridge (eds.), 84–96.

Stancliffe, C. (1999), 'The British Church and the mission of Augustine', in R. Gameson (ed.), *St. Augustine and the Conversion of England* (Stroud), 107–51.

Stancliffe, C. and Cambridge, E. (eds.) (1995), *Oswald: Northumbrian King to European Saint* (Stanford, CA).

Staniforth, M. (1987), *Early Christian Writings: The Apostolic Fathers*, rev. A. Louth (London).

Stark, R. (1996), *The Rise of Christianity: A Sociologist Reconsiders History* (Princeton, NJ).

Steck, W. (2000), *Der Liturgiker Amalarius: eine quellenkritische Untersuchung zu Leben und Werk eines Theologen der Karolingerzeit* (Munich).

Stein, P. (1999), *Roman Law in European History* (Cambridge).

Steinacher, R. (2016), *Die Vandalen: Aufstieg und Fall eines Barbarenreichs* (Stuttgart).

Stevenson, J. (1957), *A New Eusebius: Documents Illustrative of the History of the Church to A.D. 337* (London).

Stewart, C. *et al.* (eds.) (1994), *Syncretism/Anti-syncretism: The Politics of Religious Synthesis* (London).

Stocking, R. (2000), *Bishops, Councils, and Consensus in the Visigothic Kingdom, 589–633* (Ann Arbor, MI).

Story, J. (ed.) (2005), *Charlemagne: Empire and Society* (Manchester).

Strobel, A. (1977), *Ursprung und Geschichte des frühchristlichen Osterkalenders* (Berlin).

Strobel, A. (1980), *Das heilige Land der Montanisten: eine religionsgeographische Untersuchung* (Berlin).

Stroumsa, G. (2007), 'Religious dynamics between Christians and Jews in late antiquity (312–640)', in Casiday and Norris (eds.), 151–72.

Stroumsa, S. (2018), 'Single-source records in the intercommunal life of al-Andalus: the cases of Ibn Nagrila and the Cordoban martyrs', *Intellectual History of the Islamicate World* 6, 217–41.

Sumption, J. (1978), *The Albigensian Crusade* (London).

Sutcliffe, E. F. (1969), 'Jerome', in Lampe (ed.), 80–101.

Talbot, C. H. (1981), *The Anglo-Saxon Missionaries in Germany: Being the Lives of SS. Willibrord, Boniface, Sturm, Leoba, and Lebuin, together with the* Hodoeporicon *of St. Willibald and a selection from the correspondence of St. Boniface* (London).

Talley, T. J. (1986), *The Origins of the Liturgical Year* (New York).

Tanner, N. (1990), *Decrees of the Ecumenical Councils* (London).

Teitler, H. C. (1985), *Notarii and Exceptores* (Amsterdam).

Théry-Astruc, J. (2016), 'The heretical dissidence of the "Good Men" in the Albigeois (1276–1329): localism and resistance to Roman Clericalism', in Sennis (ed.), 79–111.

Thompson, A. and Gordley, J. (trans.) (1993), *The Treatise on Laws (Decretum DD. 1–20) with the Ordinary Gloss* (Washington, DC).

Thompson, E. A. (1969), *The Goths in Spain* (Oxford).

Thorpe, L. (trans.) (1974), *Gregory the Great: History of the Franks* (London).

Tillmann, H. (1980), *Pope Innocent III*, trans. W. Sax (Amsterdam).

Tilly, M. A. (2006), 'North Africa', in Mitchell and Young (eds.), 381–96.

Tjader, J.-O. (1955), *Die nichtliterarischen lateinischen Papyri Italiens aus der Zeit 445–700* (Lund).

Tjader, J.-O. (1972), 'Der Codex argenteus in Uppsala und der Buchmeister Viliaric in Ravenna', in U. E. Hagberg (ed.), *Studia Gotica* (Stockholm), 144–64.

Tomlin, R. S. O. (1988), *Tabellae Sulis: Roman Inscribed Tablets of Tin and Lead from the Sacred Spring at Bath* (Oxford).

Toubert, P. (1973), *Les structures du Latium médiéval: le Latium méridional et la Sabine du IXe siècle à la fin du XIIe siècle*, 2 vols. (Rome).

Trevett, S. (2006), 'Asia Minor and Achaea', in Mitchell and Young (eds.), 314–30.

Trillmich, W. (ed.) (1961), *Quellen des 9. und 11. Jahrhunderts zur Geschichte der Hamburgischen Kirche und des Reiches* (Darmstadt).

Trombley, F. (2006), 'Overview: the geographical spread of Christianity', in Mitchell and Young (eds.), 302–13.

Trombley, F. (2007), 'Christianity and paganism, II: Asia Minor', in Casiday and Norris (eds.), 189–409.

Trout, D. E. (1999), *Paulinus of Nola: Life, Letters, and Poems* (Berkeley, CA).

Tuchman, B. (1979), *A Distant Mirror: The Calamitous 14th Century* (New York).

Turner, C. H. (1903), 'Chapters in the history of Latin MSS III: The Lyon-Petersburg MS of councils', *Journal of Theological Studies* 4, 426–34.

Turner, P. (2012), *Truthfulness, Realism, Historicity: A Study in Late Antique Spiritual Literature* (Farnham).

Tyerman, C. (2005), *Crusades: A Very Short Introduction* (Oxford).

Tyerman, C. (2006), *God's War: A New History of the Crusades* (London).

Tyerman, C. (ed.) (2012), *Chronicles of the First Crusade 1096–1099* (London).

Ullmann, W. (1960), *The Medieval Papacy: St. Thomas and Beyond* (London).

Ullmann, W. (1970), *Growth of Papal Government*, 3rd edn (London).

Urban, W. L. (1994), *The Baltic Crusade*, 2nd rev. edn (Chicago, IL).

Urbanczyk, P. (ed.) (1997), *Origins of Central Europe* (Warsaw).

Uthemann, K.-H. (2007), 'History of Christology to the seventh century', in Casiday and Norris (eds.), 460–500.

Vaillancourt, M. G. (trans.) (2020), *Paschasius Radbertus: On the Body and Blood of the Lord: with the Letter to Fredugard* (Turnhout).

Van Dam, R. (1988), *Gregory of Tours: Glory of the Confessors*, Translated Texts for Historians (Liverpool).

Van Dam, R. (1988a), *Gregory of Tours: Glory of the Martyrs*, Translated Texts for Historians (Liverpool).

Van Dam, R. (2003), *Becoming Christian: The Conversion of Roman Cappadocia* (Philadelphia, PA).

Van Dam, R. (2007), 'Bishops and society', in Casiday and Norris (eds.), 343–66.

Van Dam, R. (2007a), *The Roman Revolution of Constantine* (New York).

Van Rhijn, C. (2007), *Shepherds of the Lord: Priests and Episcopal Statutes in the Carolingian Period* (Turnhout).

Velázquez Soriano, I. (2000), *Documentos de época visigoda escritos en pizarra (siglos VI–VIII)*, 2 vols. (Turnhout).

Venarde, B. (1997), *Women's Monasticism and Medieval Society: Nunneries in France and England, 890–1215* (Ithaca, NY).

Venarde, B. (2003), *Robert of Arbrissel: A Medieval Religious Life* (Washington, DC).

Verheyden, J. (2013), 'The New Testament canon', in Paget and Schaper (eds.), 389–411.

Vessey, M. (1988), 'Ideas of Christian writing in late Roman Gaul', unpublished D.Phil. thesis, University of Oxford.

Vessey, M. (1993), 'The origins of the Collectio Sirmondiana', in I. N. Wood and J. Harries (eds.), *The Theodosian Code* (London), 178–99.

Vessey, M. (2004), 'Introduction', in J. Halporn, *Cassiodorus: Institutions of Divine and Secular Learning* (Liverpool).

Vessey, M. (2005), *Latin Christian Writers in Late Antiquity and Their Texts* (Aldershot).

Vessey, M. *et al.* (eds.) (2013), *A Companion to Augustine* (Chichester).

Vinogradoff, P. (1911), 'Social and economic conditions of the Roman Empire in the fourth century', in Gwatkin and Whitney (eds.), 542–67.

Vinzent, M. (2006), 'Rome', in Mitchell and Young (eds.), 397–411.

Vinzent, M. (2016), 'Embodied early and medieval Christianity: challenging its "canonical and 'institutional' origins"', *Religions in the Roman Empire* 2, 103–24.

Vives, J. (1963), *Concilios visigóticos e hispano-romanos* (Barcelona).

Vogel, C. (1964), 'Le pèlerinage penitential', *Revue des sciences religieuses* 38, 113–52, reprinted as no. 7 in C. Vogel, (1994) *En Rémission des péchés: recherches sur les systèmes pénitentiels dans l'église latine*, ed. A. Faivre (Aldershot).

Vogler, C. (1979), *Constance II et l'administration imperiale* (Strasbourg).

Wakefield, W. L. and Evans, A. P. (1969), *Heresies of the High Middle Ages: Selected Sources* (New York).

Wallace-Hadrill, J. M. (1962), 'The bloodfeud of the Franks', in *idem*, *The Long-haired Kings: And Other Studies in Frankish History* (London).

Wallace-Hadrill, J. M. (1983), *The Frankish Church* (Oxford).

Wallace-Hadrill, J. M. (1988), *Bede's Ecclesiastical History of the English People: A Historical Commentary* (Oxford).

Wallach, L. (1968), *Alcuin and Charlemagne: Studies in Carolingian History and Literature* (Ithaca, NY).

Walls, J. L. (2011), *Purgatory: The Logic of Total Transformation* (Oxford).

Ward, B. (1981), *The Sayings of the Desert Fathers: The Alphabetical Collection* (London).

Ward-Perkins, B. (2000), 'Land, labour and settlement', in Cameron *et al.* (eds.), 315–45.

Warner, D. A. (2001), *Ottonian Germany: The* Chronicon *of Thietmar of Merseburg* (Manchester).

Watkins, C. S. (2002), 'Sin, penance and purgatory in the Anglo–Norman realm: the evidence of visions and ghost stories', *Past & Present* 175, 3–33.

Watson, A. *et al.* (trans.) (1998), *The Digest of Justinian*, 4 vols., rev. edn (Philadelphia, PA).

Weber, M. (1925), *Wirtschaft und Gesellschaft* (Tübingen).

Weber, M. (1947), 'Zwischenbetrachtung', in Gesammelte Aufsätze zur Religionssoziologie, vol. 1 (Tübingen), 436–73.

Weber, M. (1948). 'Religious rejections of the world and their directions', in H. H. Gerth and C. Wright (eds. and trans.), *From Max Weber: Essays in Sociology* (London), 323–59.

Webster, L. (2012), *The Franks Casket* (London).

Weiss, P. (1993), 'Die Vision Constantins', in J. Bleicken (ed.), *Colloquium aus Anlass des 80: Geburtstages von Alfred Heuss* (Kallmünz), 143–69.

Weiss, P. (2003), 'The vision of Constantine', trans. A. Birley, *Journal of Roman Archaeology* 16, 237–59.

Wemple, S. (1985), *Women in Frankish Society: Marriage and the Cloister, 500 to 900* (Philadelphia, PA).

Wenskus, R. (1961), *Stammesbildung und Verfassung: Das Werden der fruhmittelalterlichen gentes* (Cologne).

Werminghoff, A. (ed.) (1906), *MGH Leges III. Concilia II: Concilia Aevi Karolini* (Hannover).

Whitby, L. M. (1988), *The Emperor Maurice and His Historian: Theophylact Simocatta on Persian and Balkan Warfare* (Oxford).

Whitby, L. M. and Whitby, J. M. (trans.) (1989), *The Chronicon Paschale*, Translated Texts for Historians (Liverpool).

Whitehouse, J. (2016), 'The course of the Donatist schism in late Roman North Africa', in Miles (ed.), 13–33.

Whitelock, D. (1996), *English Historical Documents vol. 1: c. 500–1042*, 2nd edn (London).

Whittow, M. (1996), *The Making of Orthodox Byzantium, 600–1025* (London).

Wickham, C. (1981), *Early Medieval Italy: Central Power and Local Society, 400–1000* (London).

Wickham, C. (1993), 'La chute de Rome n'aura pas lieu. A propos d'un livre recent', *Le Moyen Age* 99, 107–26.

Wickham, C. (2005), *Framing the Early Middle Ages: Europe and the Mediterranean 400–800* (Oxford).

Wickham, C. (2015), *Medieval Rome: Stability and Crisis of a City, 900–1150* (Oxford).

Wiles, M. F. (1967), *The Making of Christian Doctrine* (London).

Wiles, M. F. (1970), 'Theodore of Mopsuestia as representative of the Antiochene schools', in Ackroyd and Evans (eds.), 489–510.

Wiles, M. F. (1975), *The Making of Christian Doctrine: A Study in the Principles of Early Doctrinal Development* (Cambridge).

Wilkinson, K. W. (2009), 'Palladas and the Age of Constantine', *Journal of Roman Studies* 99, 36–60.

Williams, R. (2001), *Arius: Heresy and Tradition*, rev. edn (London).

Wilson, N. G. (1975), *St. Basil on the Value of Greek Literature* (London).

Winroth, A. (2000), *The Making of Gratian's* Decretum (Cambridge).

Winroth, A. (2009), 'The legal underpinnings', in Rubin and Simons (eds.), 89–98.

Winterbottom, M. (1978), *Gildas: The Ruin of Britain, and Other Works* (London).

Wolf, K. B. (1988), *Christian Martyrs in Muslim Spain* (Cambridge).

Wolf, K. B. (trans.) (1999), *Conquerors and Chroniclers of Medieval Spain*, Translated Texts for Historians (Liverpool).

Wolf, K. B. (trans.) (2019), *The Eulogius Corpus*, Translated Texts for Historians (Liverpool).

Wolfe, B. (2014), 'Germanic language and Germanic Homoianism', in Berndt and Steinacher (eds.), 193–200.

Wolfram, H. (1979), *Conversio Bagoariorum et Carantanorum: das Weissbuch der Salzburger Kirche über die erfolgreiche Mission in Karantanien und Pannonien* (Vienna).

Wolfram, H. (1995), *Salzburg, Bayern, Österreich: die Conversio Bagoariorum et Carantanorum und die Quellen ihrer Zeit* (Vienna).

Wood, I. N. (1977), 'Kingdoms and consent', in Sawyer and Wood (eds.), 6–29.

Wood, I. N. (1990), 'Ripon, Francia and the Franks Casket in the early Middle Ages', *Northern History* 26, 1–19.

Wood, I. N. (1990a), 'Administration, law and culture in Merovingian Gaul', in McKitterick (ed.), 63–81.

Wood, I. N. (2001), *The Missionary Life: Saints and the Evangelisation of Europe 400–1050* (London).

Wood, I. N. (2008), 'The northern frontier: Christianity face to face with Paganism', in Noble and Smith (eds.), 230–46.

Wood, I. N. (2014), *The Merovingian Kingdoms, 450–751* (Oxford).

Wood, S. (2006), *The Proprietary Church in the Medieval West* (Oxford).

Wooding, J. *et al.* (eds.) (2010), *Adomnán of Iona: Theologian, Lawmaker, Peacemaker* (Dublin).

Woolf, G. (1998), *Becoming Roman: The Origins of Provincial Civilization in Gaul* (Cambridge).

Wormald, C. P. (1977), '*Lex Scripta* and *Verbum Regis*: legislation and Germanic kingships, from Euric to Cnut', in Sawyer and Wood, 105–38.

Wormald, C. P. (1978), 'Bede, *Beowulf* and the conversion of the Anglo-Saxon aristocracy', in R. T. Farrell (ed.), *Bede and Anglo-Saxon England*, BAR BS 46 (Oxford), 32–90.

Wormald, C. P. (2005), *The First Code of English Law* (Canterbury).

Wright, R. (1982), *Late Latin and Early Romance in Spain and Carolingian France* (Liverpool).

Wright, R. (1996), *Latin and the Romance Languages in the Early Middle Ages* (Philadelphia, PA).

Wright, W. C. (ed. and trans.) (1913), *The Works of the Emperor Julian* (London).

Wright, W. C. (ed. and trans.) (1922), *Philostratus and Eunapius: Lives of the Sophists* (London).

Yorke, B. (1990), *Kings and Kingdoms of Early Anglo-Saxon England* (London).

Yorke, B. (2003), *Nunneries and the Anglo-Saxon Royal Houses* (London).

Yorke, B. (2003a), 'The adaptation of the Anglo-Saxon royal courts to Christianity', in Carver (ed.), 243–58.

Yorke, B. (2006), *The Conversion of Britain 600–800* (Harlow).

Young, D. (1993), *Coptic Manuscripts from the White Monastery: Works of Shenute* (Vienna).

Young, F. M. (1997), *Biblical Exegesis and the Formation of Christian Culture* (Cambridge).

Young, F. M. (2006), 'Towards a Christian paideia', in Mitchell and Young (eds.), 485–99.

Zahran, Y. (2009), *The Lakhmids of Hira: Sons of the Water of Heaven* (London).

Zey, C. (2017), *Der Investiturstreit* (Munich).

Zimmermann, A. (ed.) (1976), *Die Auseinandersetzungen an der Pariser Universität im XIII. Jahrhundert* (Berlin).

Acknowledgements

It's completely impossible to thank everyone who deserves a specific mention. This book has been too long in the making, and I owe too much to too many people. A few brief thoughts will have to stand in place, therefore, of a properly comprehensive listing.

A huge thank you, first of all, to everyone at Penguin who has worked so hard to refine my original drafts. Tom Penn has laboured tirelessly, as has Eva Hodgkin, and I can't thank them enough. Thank you too to my wonderful picture researcher, Cecilia Mackay, and to Richard Duguid and the small army of copy-editors and proofreaders who have helped bring the text to completion.

My stellar academic colleagues at King's College – past and present – have been a constant source of intellectual inspiration and, often too, of very specific help. As indeed, have the several generations of masters and undergraduate students who have taken successive versions of the courses I adapted to help drive this project forward. They've contributed far more than they know, and there's nothing like trying to explain your thinking to a class of appropriately sceptical students to make you work out what you're really trying to say. In reality, though, this book is the result of all the direct and indirect intellectual stimulus that I have been lucky enough to receive since I was first introduced to the early history of Christianity as an undergraduate. This period now stretches over four decades and more, and I'm only too aware of the collective debt I owe to many.

Last, but certainly not least, I need to apologize to the friends and family who've 'volunteered' to read large parts of the text, or listen to various of its component ideas more or less ad nauseam, or even – I am so sorry – to help with editing and indexing. I'm aware, too, that

I always start big projects with more or less boundless enthusiasm before becoming progressively irritable and hard to live with, as they slowly wind their way to completion. I cannot promise that this will necessarily change in the future, but I am so very grateful for the forbearance of my nearest and dearest, and I will try to do better.

My very final word is for Felicity Bryan. She is sadly late and much missed; not just by me. It was Felicity who suggested that Penguin would provide the right home for this project. As usual, she was entirely correct.

Index

A Note About the Author

PETER HEATHER is chair of Medieval History at King's College, London. His many books include *The Fall of the Roman Empire; Empires and Barbarians: Migration, Development and the Birth of Europe; The Restoration of Rome* and, most recently, *Rome Resurgent*. He lives in London.